TRAVELS WITH TOOY

TRAVELS WITH TOOY

History, Memory, and the African American Imagination

⋆ RICHARD PRICE ⋆

THE UNIVERSITY OF CHICAGO PRESS *Chicago & London*

RICHARD PRICE divides his time between rural Martinique and the College of William and Mary, where he is the Duane A. and Virginia S. Dittman Professor of American Studies, Anthropology, and History. His many books include *First-Time: The Historical Vision of an African American People* (1983; 2nd ed., University of Chicago Press, 2002), *Alabi's World* (1990), *The Convict and the Colonel* (1998; 2nd ed., 2006), and, with Sally Price, *Romare Bearden: The Caribbean Dimension* (2006).

The University of Chicago Press, Chicago 60637
The University of Chicago Press, Ltd., London
© 2008 by Richard Price
All rights reserved. Published 2008
Printed in the United States of America

17 16 15 14 13 12 11 10 09 08   1 2 3 4 5

ISBN-13: 978-0-226-68058-3 (cloth)
ISBN-13: 978-0-226-68059-0 (paper)
ISBN-10: 0-226-68058-4 (cloth)
ISBN-10: 0-226-68059-2 (paper)

Library of Congress Cataloging-in-Publication Data

Price, Richard, 1941–
    Travels with Tooy : history, memory, and the African American imagination /
Richard Price.
        p.   cm.
    Includes bibliographical references and index.
    ISBN-13: 978-0-226-68058-3 (hardcover : alk. paper)
    ISBN-10: 0-226-68058-4 (hardcover : alk. paper)
    ISBN-13: 978-0-226-68059-0 (pbk. : alk. paper)
    ISBN-10: 0-226-68059-2 (pbk. : alk. paper)
    1. Alexander, Tooy.   2. Saramacca (Surinamese people)—Biography.   3. Saramacca
(Surinamese people)—Rites and ceremonies.   4. Saramacca (Surinamese people)—
Relocation—French Guiana—Cayenne Region.   5. Shamanism—French Guiana—
Cayenne Region.   6. Cayenne Region (French Guiana)—Religious life and customs.
7. Cayenne Region (French Guiana)—Social life and customs. I. Title.
    F2431.S7.A547   2008
    988.3'0049141—dc22
    [B]   2007011573

⊗ The paper used in this publication meets the minimum requirements of the American
National Standard for Information Sciences—Permanence of Paper for Printed Library
Materials, ANSI z 39.48-1992.

THE UNIVERSITY OF CHICAGO PRESS

REVIEW COPY

Travels with Tooy

History, Memory, and the African American Imagination
By Richard Price

Domestic Publication Date: December 15, 2007
Foreign Publication Date: January 14, 2008
448 p., 62 halftones, 1 map, 2 figures

Cloth $60.00 £31.00 ISBN 0-226-68058-4
Paper $24.00 £12.50 ISBN 0-226-68059-2

For more information, please contact Robert Hunt by phone at (773)702-0279, by fax at (773)702-9756, or by e-mail at rhunt@press.uchicago.edu

Please send two copies of your published review to:

Publicity Director, THE UNIVERSITY OF CHICAGO PRESS

1427 E. 60th Street, Chicago, Illinois 60637, U.S.A.   Telephone 773-702-7740

ORDERING INFORMATION

Orders from the U.S.A. and Canada:

The University of Chicago Press
Order Department
11030 South Langley Avenue
Chicago, Illinois 60628
U.S.A.
Telephone: 1-800-621-2736 (U.S.A. only);
(773) 568-1550
Facsimile: 1-800-621-8476 (U.S.A. only);
(773) 660-2235
Pubnet @ 202-5280
WWW: http://www.press.uchicago.edu

Orders from the United Kingdom and Europe:

The University of Chicago Press
c/o John Wiley & Sons Ltd.
Distribution Centre
1 Oldlands Way
Bognor Regis, West Sussex PO22 9SA
UNITED KINGDOM
Telephone: (0) 1243 779777
Facsimile: (0) 1243 820250
Internet: cs-books@wiley.co.uk
WWW:
http://www.wiley.com/WorldWide/Europe.html

Orders from Japan:

Booksellers' orders should be
placed with our agent:
United Publishers' Services, Ltd.
Kenkyu-sha Building
9, Kanda Surugadai 2-chome
Chiyoda-ku, Tokyo
JAPAN
Telephone: (03) 3291-4541
Facsimile: (03) 3293-3484
Libraries and individuals should place their
orders with local booksellers.

Orders from Australia, New Zealand, South Pacific, Africa, the Middle East, China (P.R.C.), Southeast Asia, India, Mexico, Central and South America:

The University of Chicago Press
International Sales Manager
1427 E. 60th Street
Chicago, Illinois 60637
U.S.A.
Telephone: (773) 702-7740
Facsimile: (773) 702-9756
Internet: dblobaum@press.uchicago.edu

Orders from Korea, Hong Kong, and Taiwan, R.O.C.:

The American University Press Group
3-21-18-206 Higashi Shinagawa
Shinagawa-ku, Tokyo, 140
JAPAN
Telephone: (03) 3450-2857
Facsimile: (03) 3472-9706
Internet: andishig@po.iijnet.or.jp

CONTENTS

PRELUDE

Clifford Geertz has called anthropologists "merchants of astonishment."[1]
But for me, it's Tooy who plays that role. Some thirty-five years into my
research with Saramakas I met him, and it wasn't long before he took
me through the looking glass and down the rabbit hole. He has shared with
me hidden worlds that, for him, make life worth living and, for me, continue to amaze and fascinate. This book, in unbridgeably different ways, is
his as much as mine—his gift to me, my gift to him.

At first glance, the rough shantytowns that ring Cayenne, where Haitian, Brazilian, Guyanese, and Suriname migrants live cheek by jowl, might
seem the least likely of places to meet a fellow intellectual. And yet . . . The
poverty that threatens to crush the spirit of both the hardworking and the
unemployed can leave largely untouched the richness of the imagination.
Amidst the mud and stench and random violence, Tooy—captain of the
Saramakas of Cayenne—runs a household in which spiritual and rhetori-
cal gifts abound. I've felt privileged to play a part in it during the past seven
years.

Tooy belongs to a long and distinctive tradition of emigration by Saramaka men to French Guiana (or "Guyane"—not to be confused with the former British colony of Guyana). For a century and a half, the migrants have
clustered in sites spread across Guyane. Though often working for outsiders
to earn money, they spend the great bulk of their social lives with other Saramakas. Meanwhile, their *imaginaire*—their thoughts, their dreams, their
hopes—is forever grounded in their homeland in the neighboring country
of Suriname. In Guyane, even if they've come there voluntarily, they're always in exile. Their central point of reference is their home village and its
spiritual possessions, the stretch of river and forest that surrounds it, the
places where they've hunted and gardened, the world that their heroic ancestors first carved out in the Suriname rainforest more than three hundred
years ago.

Saramakas—today some fifty-five thousand people—are one of six Maroon peoples whose African ancestors were brought to the Dutch colony of Suriname as slaves.[2] Individually, in small groups, and sometimes in great collective rebellions, they escaped plantations into the rainforest, where they created a new society and culture, drawing on their diverse African heritages. For nearly one hundred years they fought a war against the colonists and, in 1762, were granted their freedom, a full century before general emancipation in the colony. During the French Guiana gold rush of the 1860s, Saramaka men crossed the border and soon became the mainstays of that colony's river transport, using their extraordinary skills in building canoes and maneuvering them through the fierce rapids to carry merchandise and men upriver and gold back down. During Suriname's recent civil war (1986-92), thousands of new Saramaka migrants joined those who had long been in Guyane, so that today nearly one-third of Saramakas live in this little piece of France in South America, the majority illegally (that is, without French papers).

Beginning with our initial visit to Suriname in 1966, Sally Price and I have spent much of our lives living with Saramakas and writing about their history and culture. Like so many of these people, we have shifted our focus to French Guiana since the Suriname civil war. References to our publications about Saramakas and other Maroons can be found at http://www.richandsally.net.

Many times as I worked on these pages, I've asked myself whom I was writing them for (besides of course myself). I imagine at least three kinds of readers. First, historians, anthropologists, and Afro-Americanists with attitude, who will grasp to what extent this book constitutes a demonstration of the remarkable processes of creolization[3] that occurred in the formative years of Saramaka society and the stunning continuation of similar processes into the present—a testimony to African American, and humankind's, imagination in highest gear. Then, general readers, who are prepared to accompany me—and Tooy—on a fabulous journey. And finally, Saramakas, to the extent that my displaying even a small portion of their collective wisdom may serve as example to the world, and be a source of pride and dignity for themselves in that wider world.[4]

· THE ISSUE OF AUTHORSHIP. A colleague in France, hearing that I was writing a book based on work with a Saramaka "best friend," asked whether I would share with him the "signature" (credit for authorship). She pointed out that a colleague of hers had recently published a book "in two voices" with a homeless man who was his friend, and that their two names appeared as coauthors. A little reflection should make clear that, from the outset, I must take sole responsibility for authorship in this case. Though Tooy's knowledge and imagination and personality animate the text, the act of writing a book, and all it entails, would be as foreign to him as organizing and conducting an *óbia* ceremony would be to me. Tooy humors me and tries to please me by telling me things I can use in my book—though his real dream, he sometimes tells me, is that I'll move down to Cayenne and join him in his *óbia* practice, combining my skills and knowledge with his. We respect each other's expertise, to the extent we find appropriate we share each other's knowledge and passions, and we do our best to make each other's life a bit more worth living. But in the end, I'm the American writer and he's the Saramaka *óbia*-man.[5]

· CAVEAT. Tooy is a wise, spirited Saramaka—but there are a number of other men of his age who share these traits. In a real sense, I present our friendship, and something of his gifts, not because they're unique or because they're typical but because they're exemplary. His personal interests—his own Lángu clan's interests—differ from those of a man of his age belonging to a different clan, and the stories he cherishes and the knowledge he possesses differ as well. But not like night and day. Rather, like different contributing elements of the marvelous world that Saramakas have collectively built in the Americas over the past three and a half centuries.

· ABOUT PERSONAL NAMES. In a very few cases, I have altered names and other identifying markers to protect people's privacy. To assist readers with keeping track of unfamiliar names, I provide a list labeled Dramatis Personae on pp. 391–94.

· ABOUT ORTHOGRAPHY. Following long-standing conventions in the literature, I call the people Saramakas, their language Saramaccan (in Saramaccan, *Saamáka* and *Saamáka-tôngò*, respectively). In Saramaccan, vowels have Italian values, except è = the vowel in English *met*, ò = the vowel in English *all*; vowel extension in speech is indicated by vowel repetition in writing; a nasalized vowel is indicated by V*m* before labial consonants and by V*n* before nonlabial consonants; single prenasalized consonants are indicated by *mb*, *nd*, *ndj*, and *ny*. Both *kp* (= *kw*) and *gb* (= *gw*) are single consonants. High tones are indicated by an acute accent; low tones are unmarked. The texts of songs and other esoteric language materials mentioned in the narrative are spelled out and explained more fully in the Coda.

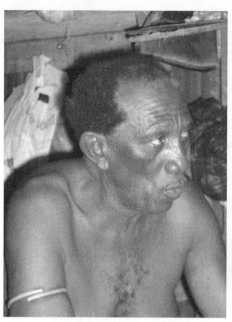

· ABOUT QUOTATIONS. Throughout this book, the passages within quotation marks (or set off as extracts) are translations of verbatim transcriptions from a recording device that I had at hand during the great bulk of my encounters with Tooy—at first a tape recorder, later a digital sound recorder. From 2003 onward, the latter was rarely out of my hand as I spoke with Tooy, who encouraged me to use this "crutch" for my learning. With few exceptions, all paraphrases of Tooy's speech were also written on the basis of these recordings, rather than simply from memory or notes.[6]

· WARNING: Captain Tooy is an inveterate time traveler—so fasten your seatbelts. Like other Saramaka men, he spends a great deal of time thinking about his distant ancestors, some of whose lives he knows intimately, as well as other normally invisible beings. Neither nostalgia nor intellectual exercise, these voyages help him understand who he is—his forebears' specific powers, wrapped up in their individual histories, give him much of the energy he has to confront the world. Tooy has spent a lifetime putting together his knowledge of them as he participated in countless rites, political gatherings, and family councils. Over the years that I've known him, he has generously shared fragments of what he knows of them with me, in part in the hope of learning more from my own stock of stories, built up over years as an ethnographer of the Saramaka past.

Tooy loves crossing boundaries, between centuries and continents, between the worlds of the living and the dead, between the visible and the invisible, between villages on land and under the sea. Whoosh! We're in the eighteenth century, surrounded by African arrivants who are as familiar as our friends and neighbors. Whoosh! We're talking about migrant Saramakas who built a new world in French Guiana at the end of the nineteenth century. Whoosh! We're speaking with the sea gods who control the world's money supply. I'm tempted to let Tooy take us on a quick tour of some of his favorite stopping places: the sister sites of Loango and Dahomey, whence his three best-known African forebears—Gweyúnga, his wife Béti, and her brother Wíi—boarded the ship called Sanfómaíndi for the Middle Passage; Society Plantation on the coast of Suriname, where they landed during a war and where Béti gave birth to Gweyúnga's son Antamá; Wet Eye Creek, where after thirty years as runaways deep in the forest, Gweyúnga unleashed the powers of his rain god against the invading soldiers; Victoria Plantation, where Antamá's younger brother was killed in fierce battle with the whites; Malobí, where Gweyúnga welcomed the double agent Kwasímukámba, who cuckolded him; Bundjitapá, Tooy's natal village where, during the whole second half of the eighteenth century, Antamá held sway as political chief but also as priest of the rains, having inherited these powers from his father, and as priest of all-powerful Flibánti-óbia, which he learned from his father's nemesis, Kwasímukámba; the underwater palace where a bevy of young girls waits on the lucky visitor. And many other places that Tooy likes to visit in his mind and with his ever-flowing words. But, we'll postpone these visits for later, as each ties in to the larger story. (There will be other border crossings as well—between Saramaka pantheism and Christianity, between the Saramaka and French legal systems, and between numerous languages.)

* * *

Derek Walcott, in *Another Life*, asks,

> for what else is there
> but books, books and the sea,
> verandahs and the pages of the sea.[7]

It's a question I, too, ponder, gazing out from our verandah—how much colonial (and anthropological) history that word evokes!—across the breadth of the Caribbean, realm of the marvelous Wénti sea gods.

Anse Chaudière, Martinique
January 14, 2007

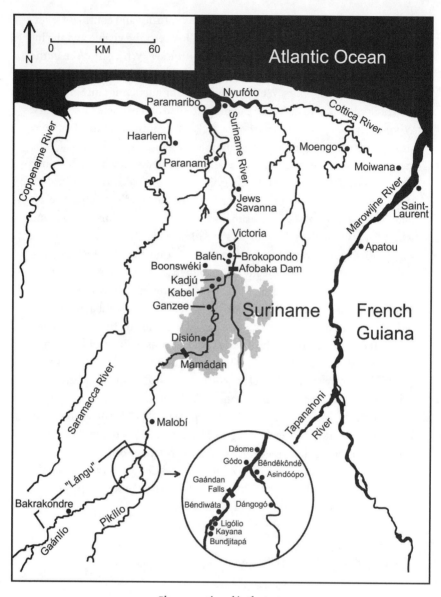

Places mentioned in the text.

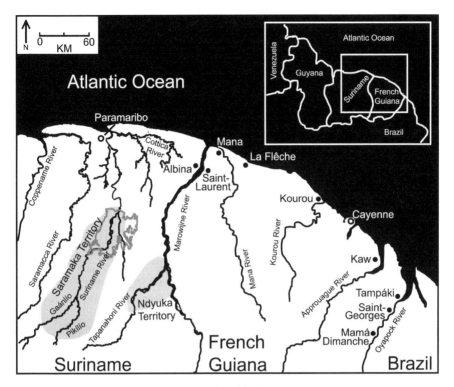

Places mentioned in the text.

MARTINIQUE

When I stop by to deliver New Year's greetings at the local rum shop, Patrick, the proprietor, pulls me aside to deliver a message: his cousin, Roland Legros, has a delicate problem that he thinks I might be able to solve but is hesitant to approach me directly. It has to do with his business but—Patrick reassures me—he's not trying to borrow money. Might I be willing to speak to him about it?

From Patrick's tone, I suspect it's about magic. Curiosity piqued, I say yes.

Roland is an island big man—owner of the largest lumberyard and building supply company on the Atlantic coast, a breeder of champion fighting cocks, and in the process of building a large second house up on the mountain that dominates the southeast of Martinique. I know him only slightly, but within days he phones and comes by for a chat. Over whiskey in our living room (Scotch replaced rum some years ago as the preferred drink of taxi drivers, businessmen, and politicians), Roland pours out a litany of problems to Sally and me, hardly taking a breath for a half hour.

Last year, the henchmen of his biggest cock-fighting rival traveled to Grenada, where they had a coolie priest (a Hindu) sacrifice a goat to assure his dominance—they may even have done it again near his own cages behind the house at night while he slept—"some kind of voodoo," he says, adding that he's been told that a Haitian specialist was called in for the local ceremony. And when he arrives at the lumberyard each morning, he feels something settling upon him which stays until he leaves at night. What's more, the new house he's building on the mountain isn't making progress—for the past two years his workmen have refused to show up.

A while back, there were some break-ins at the lumberyard and he changed the locks. After the employees had left for the day, he climbed up a ladder with the old ones to store them on a platform in a corner, in a magical bath a specialist had prepared for him. There on the platform, he discovered a piece of wood carved in the shape of a goat's head, tied all around with string. Showing his bravery, he grabbed it with his bare hand and started down the fifteen-foot ladder, which promptly collapsed. He saw stars, awoke on the floor, tested his limbs to see that nothing was broken, and as he was leaving, slammed his head against the steel-curtain door, which had been only partially rolled up.

Not long after, he had an accident on the autoroute which shattered his windshield—he found slivers of glass in his socks. And then there are the dreams. In one, he walks into the cock pit all alone and sees a plate containing some sort of offering exactly in the center of the sandy floor. In another, an Amerindian woman ("a real red Carib!") guides him into the entrance to a cave, offers him a glass of champagne, and tells him to go no further. But he keeps going, until he comes upon a black man trembling in trance. He wakes up covered with goose bumps.

Roland insists to me that he is "very Catholic" and "very spiritual"—he absolutely draws the line at sacrifice, any shedding of blood. He's already sought out specialists, including priests who have performed exorcisms at the lumberyard—an abbot from France and a Jesuit from Burkina Faso (where his brother lives). Each time, it helped for a couple of months but the troubles then returned. He's convinced the cause is something in the ground, something that happened during slavery times in the cane fields that once stood where his father built the lumberyard. There must have been tortures, killings, who knows exactly what, but it keeps coming back and won't leave him in peace. Sometimes he dreams about what must have happened there.

And finally he comes to the point.

Might I, through my Saramaka connections, be able to suggest an appropriate specialist to rid the place of its demon, once and for all?

∗   ∗   ∗

What a tangle! How to reconcile personal and professional ethics while trying to bridge the various worlds we inhabit. How to suspend certain kinds of disbelief while holding on to others, never forgetting the inextricable links that bind modernity to magic in our present world. We are plunged into the middle of a very Caribbean imbroglio, with tentacles stretching from Haiti to Trinidad—and now to the descendants of escaped slaves in the tropical forest of Suriname, whose fame as conjurers radiates all the way to Martinique and beyond.[1] On balance, it seems like too good a story—and too good a way of tying together the strands of our own lives—not to see how it will play out. I take the bait and promise Roland to make some phone calls and find an appropriate specialist.

* * *

April 7, 2000. After numerous calls and messages, everything is in place (imagine trying to communicate Air France record locator numbers to non-literate Saramakas over the phone). A man named Tooy Alexander, Saramaka priest of Dúnguláli-Óbia, a power that maintains the separation between the living and the dead, will be arriving that night accompanied by our old friend Kalusé, who will serve as his assistant and traveling companion. They will live in our house for the week of work so that Roland's neighbors and employees won't suspect that he's involved.

Roland picks me up in his powerful sedan for the trip to the airport. Having shelled out for their tickets, he wonders whether they'll really show. The plane is a couple of hours late, giving him time to invite me for a leisurely dinner of braised kidneys (Roland's choice) and fine Bordeaux at the upscale airport restaurant—remember, we're in France. Later, waiting for the passengers to deplane, I worry aloud about the forest leaves and roots and vines the Saramakas will certainly bring, how in the world to get them through customs. Roland disappears to speak to an inspector he knows and tells me he's taken care of it. And soon, Tooy and Kalusé emerge through the glass doors, dragging sacks of vegetable matter plus a couple of sports bags, Tooy, in his seventies, wearing an ill-fitting brown safari suit and matching beret, with shiny shoes that look like they pinch; the younger Kalusé, more worldly, in tee shirt, jeans, and Nikes. Embraces. Greetings. And we're off for a midnight visit to the haunted lumberyard.

* * *

Stepping out of the air-conditioned car, the sweet smell of burnt ready-to-harvest sugarcane overwhelms us. Roland goes to roll up the giant steel door as Tooy calls Kalusé and me over to examine the only tree in the vicinity, announcing it's such-and-such, to which Kalusé says maybe, but Tooy insists and picks two leaves, breaks and smells them, and shows them to Kalusé and me with a smile of triumph. Roland calls us inside and quickly rolls the door shut behind. A row of large, yellow, portable cement mixers greets us on the showroom floor. "I've had them two months and not a single sale! I'm totally blocked!" He ushers us into his inner office, flips on the air-conditioning, offers chairs, and slips into the big one behind his desk. (I feel like we're applying for a car loan.) After asking if Tooy understands Creole (he says maybe half of it), Roland launches into his life history, with me translating—his entrance into the lumber business, his passion for raising cocks, how they worked him over in Grenada (he mimes the slitting of the goat's throat), the dreams about the plate in the exact center of the arena—he says that Nicolas, who used to work for the owner of the cock pit but now works for him, has told him that his main rival personally instructed Nicolas to put that plate in the exact center of the pit—and the Carib woman who offered him champagne at the mouth of the cave, and on and on.

Tooy fixes him with a stare and asks if he has a copy machine, rummaging in his shoulder bag for a sheet of paper and asking for exactly four copies. (I'm excited that he needs a translator, since that means I'm going to be an integral part of the operation, from beginning to end.) Roland takes the paper into the next room while Tooy tells me that what they can do here is merely preliminary, that they'll have to take Roland, and me, to Cayenne, to Tooy's shrine for Dúngulali-Óbia, where he'll get the full treatment—what Tooy refers to as "knocking the stone." Roland calls out that the machine has jammed after making just one copy, then, carrying the papers to me, jokes nervously about how tough his case is turning out to be. Tooy says no problem, we'll make the others tomorrow, and hands me the original for safekeeping. "You see that picture on the wall?" he asks Roland, pointing at a framed photo of Roland's father and some workmen posing in front of a large stack of lumber. "Take it down." And he explains that Roland should take the photocopy, turn it upside down, place it so it will be facing outward toward the room, and tape it against the back of the picture. Roland gets a roll of tape and awkwardly follows the orders, finally returning his father to his place on the wall. The next day, Tooy tells me, he'll give Roland a second copy of the paper to fold up and wear next to his heart.

Tooy tells me to explain the two taboos related to this charm, things Roland will need to hold dear: first, if you have that paper pinned inside your shirt and someone strikes you, he'll die—so, no fighting allowed. Second, if you're wearing it and make love to a woman, it will be your last time—your cock, he winks at me, will never crow again. Roland asks me, hesitantly, if it's OK for him to pose a question to Tooy, who nods. What if he is wearing the paper and makes love because he forgot? Tooy hesitates and answers evasively, saying maybe if you forget just once . . . but certainly not twice. It's very strong! Tooy leans over to me. "It's really to protect you in war," he confides. "A man named Kuset wore it in a war for fifty-five years and lived to tell the tale!" Tooy unbuttons his shirt and shows me that he has a flat red square of cloth containing this very same paper, which he wears over his heart, suspended from a string around his neck. Like other Saramakas of his generation, Tooy has never been to school and cannot read.

Before Roland drives us home, Tooy announces the program: the next night, after closing time, we'll do a "smoking" of the lumberyard (which I translate to Roland as a *parfumage*, the Martiniquan equivalent) and the following night a special bath in the sea to ask the Mother of Waters to help with the problem. Roland is to show up at our house after dark with one bottle of rum, another of sugarcane syrup, another of molasses, six bottles of beer, and three eggs. (Roland asks if supermarket eggs are OK, and Tooy shrugs yes.)

Once Roland drops us off at the house, hugs for Sally, libations for the gods, joy at being together. Tooy speculates about Roland's case—he thinks it could be a woman . . . but concludes with a proverb: "It takes patience to find out what's in the belly of an ant." Suddenly, he spots a toad in the grass and tells Kalusé to catch it. I bring a plastic bag and they suspend it from a beam. Tooy says we'll need it at the lumberyard the next night.

THE SOLDIER'S CHARM

⋆ 0000800 ⋆

Let's back up just a bit. In 1962, while spending the summer in that same fishing village in Martinique (on an undergraduate research project), I visited almost daily with a famous *quimboiseur,* a sorcerer who cured people and canoes from all over the island. Many of the spells he prescribed (along with *parfumages,* aromatic baths, and other potions) came from *grimoires,* medieval books of magic still widely used today by Caribbean sorcerers. These little books were originally printed in Latin (hence *grimoire,* from *grammaire,* alluding to Latin grammar, which was unintelligible to the uninitiated), but they have been reprinted throughout recent centuries in French (and, by the Chicago-based De Laurence company, in English, largely for the British West Indian trade).

The day after Roland affixed Tooy's sheet of paper to the back of the picture of his father in the lumberyard, I searched for its sources in my collection of occult French books, which the sorcerer had helped me build up decades before. *Le Dragon Rouge* (1521), nothing. *Le grimoire du Pape Honorius* (1670), no. *Le livre des conjurations du Pape Honorius* (1670), no matches. And then, bingo!—the *Enchiridion du Pape Léon* (1660), dedicated to the "Serenissimo imperatori Carolo Magno," which had all of the texts and images, spread amongst others, between pages 90 and 102. The edition from which Tooy's page had been constructed is clearly different from the one I own—the type is set in smaller columns but the words and images are identical. Someone had painstakingly cut up the spells and pictures from this seventeenth-century edition of a work that was originally composed (so goes the story) shortly after AD 800, and pasted them together to form the magic page worn around the neck by the soldier, and now by Tooy himself.[1]

First, there's a prayer against arrows, on the page of the *grimoire* following one noting, "It is said that Charlemagne used this in battle and, thereby, remained invincible" ("N." is your own name, to be inserted in the appropriate space):

I implore you, Arrows, by the charity, flagellation, and coagulation of our Lord Jesus Christ, O Arrow, to remain without effect. . . . Do no harm, O Arrow, I implore you by the terrible and frightening Day of Universal Judgment, by the Virginity of the adorable body of our Lord Jesus Christ and that of the glorious Virgin Mary His mother . . . to do no harm, by the Holy Trinity, by the head of Saint John the Baptist, by the Twelve Apostles, by the Four Evangelists, by the Martyrs, Confessors, Virgins, and Widows of God, by the Angels and Archangels. O Arrow . . . I forbid you to wound me or harm me, N., who is the servant of God, and by the ineffable memory of N. + 2 + 1. +q.g. 222. L. M. + 1 + S. J. C. Alpha + and Omega + Emmanuel that no sword can pierce me. . . . Take up your arms! Brandish your shield! Rise up and come to my aid and assistance. . . . Let Him break into a thousand pieces the steel that fights against me. O Arrow, I command you by the aforementioned broken spear, to have no effect upon me and to assure that all my enemy's arms, visible as well as invisible, do not touch me.

Detail of the magic page Tooy gave Roland to protect his lumberyard, which was worn by the Saramaka soldier in World War II, and is now worn around his neck by Tooy himself.

The next invocation on Tooy's page is prefaced, in the book, by the reassurance that "the person who wears this prayer around his neck has nothing to fear from arrows, swords, or other arms, which can do him no harm. Nor can the Devil (unless he has made a pact with him), nor the Magicians, nor other persons do unto him any harm."

> Barnasa + Leutias + Bucella + Agla + Agla + Tetragrammaton + Adonay + our Lord. . . . Help N. your servant, and deliver me from all danger, from the death of my soul and my body, from the attacks of my enemies, visible as well as invisible.

The next protects against "every kind of arm," and the following one quotes the spell that Pope Leo is said to have sent to Charlemagne, king of France, whom he himself had earlier crowned Emperor of the Occident, and which assures protection against fire and water as long as it is worn on the body.

And finally and most miraculously, Tooy's sheet of paper contains, according to the *grimoire* from which it was copied, "the very words spoken by Adam, when he was in Hell or in Limbo, by the banks of the Charon—If a person wears them on his body during war, he cannot be killed by anyone":

> + Valeam da Zazac + Adonay N. + + + + + + . . . Matthew + John + Mark + Luke + + +.

SEA GODS

* 00000000 *

First light, the morning after Tooy and Kalusé arrive in Martinique. Sally and I awake to the sound of Tooy in full voice, sitting on a plastic chair facing the blue-green Caribbean, gesticulating with his arms, happily singing his greetings to the sea gods.[1]

We've had a special relationship with these divinities for forty years, Sally and I, ever since Naai, the nonagenarian sister of Paramount Chief Agbagó, who was our immediate neighbor in the Saramaka village of Dángogó, announced matter-of-factly one day that it was a Wénti-Gádu—a sea god—who brought us to Saramaka. (Saramaka sea gods are known to have particular affinities with whitefolks.) During that time, I have seen and spoken with Wénti-Gádus a number of times, when I happened to be present when they possessed someone, and I have bathed with them in the sea near Cayenne and in the Oyapock River as recently as last year. These particular Wéntis varied from boys who spoke Sranan-tongo, the language of coastal Suriname, with a strong East Indian accent, to voluptuous women who spoke and sang seductively in Saramaccan and enticed men into the deeps of the rivers. Despite considerable individual differences from one Wénti to the next—on the same order as the differences among humans—Wéntis (like humans) do have certain things in common. Pretty much everything that Saramakas know about Wéntis has been learned from people in possession, through whom the gods recount aspects of their normally invisible lives. Let me tell you a little of what I've learned about these marvelous creatures over the years.

Wéntis are much like people, except that they live underwater. Their home territory is the sea, where they have numerous towns and cities (including Gaánlolo, Olóni, Akínawebí, Kínazaan, Sináibo, Laibení, Gongongondóme, Luwézaan, and Loonza[2]), often at the base of mountains that rise steeply from the waters. But they also travel up rivers and sometimes live for a time at the foot of a rapids. When they feel like it, they come ashore and mingle with people, unnoticed, which they very much enjoy. Most important, Wéntis bring humans good things—in particular, money, whitefolks' goods, and babies.

The first Wéntis were discovered by Saramakas working on the coast of Suriname in the late nineteenth century—gods such as Wánanzái, who possessed Kódji (who later became the first Saramaka captain on the Oyapock); Tatá Yembuámba, from the undersea city of Olóni, who possessed Pobôsi of Ligólio and was the first Wénti to show himself in Saramaka territory; and Tulí, who possessed Djamelêti of Gódo and ritually prepared hundreds of early twentieth-century Saramaka men to go to the coast to earn money. I've met men who saw Tulí in their youth and describe him diving into the river and coming up hours later wearing a beautiful necklace and holding a perfectly dry flower in his hand, asking a bystander to take two bottles to the river and to fill them up, and when they tasted them back in the village one was filled with rum and the other with sugarcane syrup.

When Saramakas first came to the Oyapock as canoemen in the gold rush, around 1900, they realized they had truly arrived in the heart of Wénti country. Kódji's god Wánanzái would dive into the river in the morning and come back in the evening with remarkable tales of the underwater world, and he brought back other Wéntis who, in turn, possessed other residents—Kositán got the Wénti called Zaime, Agbagó got Todjê, and one Wénti named Asantéa even came and possessed Antuáni, a Creole woman[3] who was married to a Saramaka. The folks at Tampáki, the village Saramaka men founded along the river, learned from Wánanzái and the other Wéntis he brought back, for example, that at Gaamá Lajan (which might be translated as "The Mother of All Money")—a rock formation several kilometers below Tampáki on the French side of the river—under the water was what might best be described as the Central Bank of the World. There, Wénti maidens—not at all unlike Wagner's Rhine Maidens (Woglinde, Wellgunde, and Flosshilde)—stand watch over barrels and barrels of golden coins, which they sometimes roll out into the sun to dry, singing beautiful songs all the while. They learned that Wénti villages are "almost like a school, there are so many children running around," and that if asked appropriately, Wéntis delight in placing a baby into a human woman's womb. They learned that Wéntis have strong affinities with whitefolks. And they also learned that Wéntis abhor death and blood, nor do they like rum or other strong drink, nor do they like sun or heat, nor do they mix with evil. Rather, they love white, bright, shiny, clean things, sugary, bubbly things, and all things cool from the sea.[4]

At about the same time that Kódji was discovering a host of new Wéntis on the Oyapock, back home in Suriname two girls from one of the northernmost Saramaka villages drowned when their canoe sank in a rapids. Some time later (some people say seventeen days, others three months, others a year), one of them—now called Wentía—appeared on a river rock at Mamádan, the great rapids that marked the effective border between "real Saramaka" and the outside world.[5] When she had been ritually "cured" and could speak once again, she told of having been taken to a beautiful underwater Wénti palace, where she was waited on by a bevy of young girls. She eventually returned, she said, because she missed salt (which Wéntis do not eat) and begged them to bring her up to the surface. Older men have told me how, throughout the first half of the twentieth century when on their way to the Oyapock to work, they would stop at the Wénti shrine at Mamádan and pour an offering of white kaolin-water, and then, on their way back with their canoes laden with whitefolks' goods, they would pour offerings of sugarcane syrup.

Todjê, the Wénti who possessed the future Gaamá (Paramount Chief) Agbagó Abóikóni, was often credited by Saramakas with instigating the program of gradual rapprochement with the world outside tribal territory that took place during the second half of the twentieth century. And Todjê provides one of the links between the early twentieth-century Oyapock and Sally and me, for it was this god who is said to have "brought"

Mamádan Wénti shrine.

us—renowned as "the first outsiders ever to have slept in the village of Dángogó"—into the world of the Saramakas.

This part of the story begins around 1905, when the aged Asimadjó—one the first Saramakas to go to French Guiana—brought his sister's sons Gasitón, Kositán, Gidé, and Agbagó from Mana, where they'd been working for several years, to the recently founded village of Tampáki. There Agbagó married a Brazilian woman named Laguai and had a daughter with her. He also—apparently via relations he had developed with a Brazilian coffee planter across the river—traveled to Belém, where he then shipped out for three years on a freighter that plied the Caribbean, visiting among other places Martinique, Guadeloupe, St. Lucia, and Trinidad. When he was in his eighties, the Paramount Chief used to tell me how he and his fellow sailors, on shore leave once in Fort-de-France, were arrested and spent a brief time in jail in the wake of a political assassination—which dates the incident to 1908, when Mayor Antoine Siger was shot on election day. The chief also enjoyed telling and retelling me about the size of that ship, and imitating the sounds of its powerful, chugging engines.

Steamships, which Saramakas experienced close-up for the first time during this period, exercised a powerful pull on their imagination and play an important role in Wénti lore. In Saint-Georges-de-l'Oyapock, the main town in the region, I recently spoke with Creole women in their sixties, the daughters of Saramaka men, who remember as children standing with the nighttime crowd at Tampáki watching great Wénti ships, ablaze with lights, steam up the far bank of the Oyapock and dock at the mouth of a creek there. They also told me that just below the mouth of this creek, across the river and a bit upstream from Tampáki, was a large underwater Wénti village called Tósuósu. According to men I've spoken with, whenever Saramakas riding downstream in a canoe make an offering of beer in the river near that shore, a hand reaches up to accept the bottle—which they say they have seen many times. I myself saw such an offering being made last year, but I missed seeing the hand.

Agbagó was one of the young Saramakas who was possessed by a Wénti, brought by Kódji's Wánanzái, in the early days of Tampáki. Thereafter this god, Todjê, shaped his life in many ways, bringing him into especially close relations with whitefolks, assuring his success in a broad range of economic and political endeavors, and even bringing him two children with a wife who "could no longer have children."[6] Todjê's full sisters and brothers also possessed Saramakas and played (and continue to play, even today) an important role both in Tampáki and back in Saramaka territory—Tatá Yembuámba (mentioned above, who led his "master," Pobôsi, to become official guide for the ill-fated early twentieth-century Eilerts de Haan expedition into the Suriname interior), and three beautiful Wénti women, Korantína, Amentína, and Yowentína (who is currently married to a god who recently told me, through the mouth of Tooy's elderly, blind brother Sensiló, in Cayenne, that he is "at least nineteen hundred years old" and who, with this same husband, had a Wénti son called Bási Yontíni, who is in the head of one of Tooy's wives and with whom Sally and I swam at dawn recently on a deserted beach on the edge of the city—the very large, middle-aged woman, once possessed, frolicked in the surf like a young mermaid). The parents of this sibling set, Dígbeónsu of Olóni ("a name to be very careful with—she is the sea," says Tooy) and her husband Adjéunsu, are also active today: each has a clay vessel for offerings in Tooy's Wénti shrine. And Sally and I have spent a good deal of time lately at an elaborate shrine to a Wénti called Djéunsu-Etéunsu along the Cayenne/Saint-Laurent-du-Maroni highway, maintained by a classificatory great-grandson of Kódji, whose name is forever associated with the Wéntis of the Oyapock.

★   ★   ★

In any case, here was Tooy, sitting on our verandah in Martinique, singing to the sea gods, feeling what Derek Walcott calls that "sense of elation you get in the morning in the Caribbean . . . the width of the ocean."[7] The clarity of the green-blue water, through which you can see the rocks on the bottom of the sea; the warm, sensual trade winds; the luscious air; the hills behind hills behind hills on three sides; the black snow drifting down and depositing a fine layer of ash from cane fields burning on the other side of the island over the mountains—all this is a joyful discovery for him. His own firmly continental world, whether the rivers and forests of Suriname, where he grew up, or the squalid shacks of Cayenne, where he's lived for decades, are equatorial, damp, hot, and largely still—no hurricane ever touches there, not to mention trade winds. And the sea, as he's known it at the mouth of the Suriname, the Oyapock, or near Cayenne, washes a muddy coast, stretching all the way to the mouth of the Amazon—mangroves, mudflats, the detritus from the great rivers that flow northeast from the Orinoco to the Amazon, leaving the seaside brown and ugly, a place of murk and miasma.

Late afternoon, Tooy summons Kalusé and me for a formal palaver in the living room. How much should Roland be asked to pay for this cure? Kalusé listens with only one ear, watching Real Madrid vs. Barcelona on the TV until Tooy reprimands him. Tooy says he once cured a person in Guadeloupe and received fifty thousand francs ($8,000), and that's what they should ask for

From our verandah.

now. The follow-up Cayenne ceremony—"knocking the stone"—will cost less, he says, though they will have to buy a goat (since the original damage was done, in part, with a goat). We agree to discuss it with Roland later on.

Tooy tells us to select the proper leaves from the sacks and lay them out on the terrace before the sun goes down so that they'll dry out sufficiently. Tonight, he says, we'll first bathe Roland, then "smoke" the lumberyard, then bring some leaves home to do a "smoking" here, since the things we chase away at the lumberyard will try to follow us back home.

DÚNGULÁLI-ÓBIA

✳ 00000000 ✳

We've been sitting on the verandah, Tooy, Kalusé, Sally, and I, watching the sun descend into the Caribbean as Tooy regales us with First-Time stories—tales and songs about his eighteenth-century ancestors. I'm beginning to suspect that I haven't met a Saramaka with his range of historical and ritual knowledge since I worked with the great historian Tebíni near the end of his life, twenty-five years earlier.[1]

Do you know the god called Sáa? he asks, testing me. I say I do and have even seen the raffia skirt she wears when she comes to visit in the village of the *gaamá*—but he retells the story anyway.[2] Then he breaks into a series of beautiful *óbia* songs, many in the esoteric language of Komantí warrior spirits, which as a *bakáa* ("outsider") I've hardly ever been permitted to hear. Kalusé chimes in on the choruses, whenever he knows them, which is much of the time. Tooy's baritone is resonant and throaty, colored by the quantities of tobacco juice he's ingested over the years. Ever the teacher, he explains each song as he goes along. "Woodpecker," he says of the first, "whose name is Gweduánka in Komantí language, says: 'My wings are strong, my beak is strong, my feet are strong—but my tail is the strongest of all!'" Then he sings a Komantí prayer: "The wonderful things you have in your house, bring some to me, too!" Then a lighter Komantí song, "You those crude people, those bullshitting people, today we're calling everyone," calling out to all kinds of people, indiscriminately, to come join the "play."[3] ("When folks get together," explains Tooy, "there will undoubtedly be liars among them and thieves among them, but whoever they are, let's all work together—this song summons them all! . . . That's what Komantí says!" Tooy assures me.) And finally, *Gingéé-o, gingéuwawa!* ("When you go hunting and get deep into the forest and can't figure out which way to go, this is the song you sing to ask the Komantís to help you—we're still praying here!" he says.)

Tooy follows with a couple of songs in the powerful ritual language of Papá, normally reserved for funerals, where they're sung with drums.

(Papá is even more secret and dangerous than Komantí—in all my years in Saramaka, I'd never been able to discuss its songs in any detail.) The first is particularly sweet, *Kónu gó na walá, walá mi yéi, wala mandekú tjénámewa.* "That's how Papá-men from the Matjáu clan sing it," he explains. "Now, here's how the specialists from the Abaísa clan do it: *A kónu misi waná, a kónu misi waná-o, wana mandekú mánde-o, a kónu misi waná, djáemade wána, wana mandekú mánde-o.*"⁴ "This song," he says, "is what Macaque sings to the Awara palm [which has long thorns all up and down its trunk, protecting its orange fruit], after which it simply drops its thorns so the monkey can climb up. It's a prayer you can use whenever things are really rough." And, he adds, really getting into it, "In Apúku [forest spirit] language you sing it this way: *Línga línga kólu, kólu tei, mangánu ta línga kólu-ee, kólu tei* [repeat]." I am reminded how many times I've heard Saramakas say that no one knows Apúkus like the specialists of Tooy's Lángu clan.⁵

Then, as we look out to sea and discuss the shifting patterns traced by the currents on the surface,⁶ he sings a few of his favorite Wénti songs, boasting that he could go on all night and all day without repeating a single one. (I'd heard only a handful of Wénti songs, mainly from Tebíni, in my years in Saramaka.) *Tuun tuun, tuun tuun,* which the Wénti named Mêtolan once sang to stop a "war" between Papágádu (Boa Constrictor) and Akamí (Trumpeter Bird), who ever since have kept their distance from one another. Then, the song of the Wénti maidens who guard the money: *Tuusé, tuusé, a lólo muádji-oo, e-e-e* [sound of hard work] . . . *sobénu zogamê* . . . *tuusé, tuusé.* (*Tuusé,* Tooy explains, "is the Wénti word for 'money.' As the women are rolling the money barrels [*muádji*] into the sun to warm them up, this is what they sing! *Sobénu zogamê* means 'roll them into the sun.'") And then he offers another song about rolling out the barrels: *Panyá mi akí* . . . [normal Saramaccan for "grab me here"]. But not all Wénti songs are celebratory. He next sings a haunting, immensely sad one, *Aladjímèèdji-e, aladjímèèdji-o, téé na Alónugbe.* ("The plant called Waterlily," he explains, "has no paddle, the whole paddy of leaves is powerless to direct where it will go, it's completely adrift, at someone else's mercy. This song is its lament, the way it asks Mother Dígbeónsu to protect it. You can sing it when you've left one place and arrived in a new one and are asking the new one to receive you well, to give you a firm anchorage.")⁷ And then, three Wénti sailor songs: *Den dóu-ye, den dóu-ya. Ya ya di bóto kó* ["They've arrived, they've arrived. Yes, yes, the ship's arrived"] ("In those days," explains Tooy, "the incoming ship would have to wait at the river mouth for the tide to turn and carry it into the river. This is the song of rejoicing sung by the people waiting onshore"), *Naosí, Naosí. Naosí-e, mbéi máu* ("The Wénti ship," says Tooy, "is loaded and ready to depart, awaiting the outgoing tide. With this song, the captain is calling the people on shore to come back on board.") And finally, a song of Wénti sailors in distress at sea: *Gòònsè-e, Gòònsè, yedoo . . .* ("Your ship is sinking, you're going under, this is the way you call on Ma Dígbeónsu to help you").

I wonder again whether anything could be more Wagnerian: the songful maidens guarding their gold under the river, the sailors singing their greetings and departures. The Ring, The Flying Dutchman, Tristan . . . and yet it's another world—or is it? Might there have been ex-Wagnerians among the late nineteenth-century Moravian missionaries who visited Saramaka from Germany? Might Rhine maidens and Rheingelt have influenced the Wénti maidens and their barrels of money at Gaamá Lajan?[8] Or, as I suspect, are we dealing with parallel cases of *la pensée sauvage*?

I ask if Sally can accompany us tonight, and Tooy says sure. So, before Roland arrives, he calls us into the bedroom, where he pours a few drops of foul-smelling stuff from a clay Dúngul(li-Óbia bottle into our cupped hands, with instructions to wash our faces, the bottoms of our feet, and our forearms with the liquid. "We're going to work tonight," he chuckles. "Dúnguláli work!"

*   *   *

Like Wéntis, Dúngulóli-Óbia has long been part of our lives, ever since a particularly traumatic personal experience in the 1960s, when a four-year-old boy who often stayed with us in Dángogó while his mother worked in her rice field was attacked on the head by a flock of hornets and, within a minute or two, died of cardiorespiratory shock in Sally's arms. During the subsequent days, we were treated by the powerful Saramaka *gaán-óbia* ("great spiritual power") called Dúngulóli, in order to ritually "separate" us from the dead child we had been so close to and to prevent him from taking us with him to the land of the dead. Dúngulóli specializes in keeping the living separate from the dead, removing harmful ghosts from the lived environment. Hence its relevance to Roland's lumberyard, where an unspeakable act during slavery was apparently still working its effects.

For Saramakas, the extraordinary powers known as *gaán-óbias*—the magical forces to which they credit their eighteenth-century military victories over whitefolks and their ability to survive in a hostile environment—remain each clan's most valuable possessions, and many are believed to have been brought by specific ancestors from Africa. Dúngulóli is different.

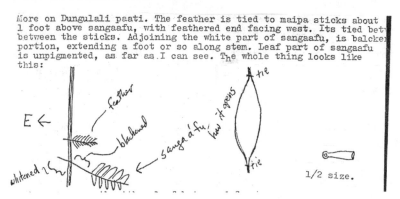

```
More on Dungulali paati. The feather is tied to maipa sticks about
1 foot above sangaafu, with feathered end facing west. Its tied bet
between the sticks. Adjoining the white part of sangaafu, is balcke
portion, extending a foot or so along stem. Leaf part of sangaafu
is unpigmented, as far as.I can see. The whole thing looks like
this:
```

1/2 size.

Excerpt from my 1968 field notes, describing some of the apparatus used to "separate" us from the dead child: the climax involved our being led through the opening in a 9-foot-tall *maipá*-palm frond, planted in the earth in front of the Dúnguláli shrine, with a vulture feather and a piece of *sangaáfu* plant (east side whitened with *keéti*, west side blackened with soot) stuck through it.[9] Three times we circled and passed through, holding the "good" end of the *sangaáfu* that had been lopped off with a machete, and with which we returned to our house, which was then "smoked" by Dúnguláli, and where we were shut in for the rest of the day. The wooden ornament at right is made by men to sew onto their Dúnguláli biceps rings, along with a cowrie shell.

Tooy tells it by means of a parable. "There were three brothers: Bofaángu, the eldest [the *gaán-óbia* owned by the Abaísa clan and said to have been brought from Africa], Madánfo, the middle one [owned by the Awaná clan and said to have been brought from Africa], and Dúnguláli, the youngest." Like so many Wéntis, who are such an important part of present-day Saramaka life, Dúnguláli—despite being a major *gaán-óbia*—was in fact "discovered" for the first time on the Oyapock, only at the very beginning of the twentieth century. The man called Kódji once again played a central role in the story.

Kódji had several gods in his head besides his famous Wénti Wánanzái, including a ghost-spirit known as a Nêngèkôndè-Nêngè (roughly, "an African person"), a class of ghost-spirits conceptualized as ritually powerful African men who can possess Saramakas and teach them *óbias* and other ritual lore. Kódji's ghost-spirit was Akoomí, who worked closely with a Komantí spirit called Afeemaónsu. In an oft-told story, a Saramaka paddling down the Oyapock would see a small, white-haired old man with a short paddle standing on the bank calling out, "Take me across, please! My canoe got loose and drifted downstream." And after the paddler did as requested and continued to the Saramaka village of Tampáki, he would see Akoomí at the landing place, speaking through Kódji, accosting him and joking with him, "Man, that place you left me on the other side of the river—that was no place to leave me, I almost got killed there!" So the miracle of Akoomí's omnipotence would again be confirmed. (Tooy confided to me once that Akoomí's mother was Ma Niní and his father Wangóso—both from Komantí land.)

It was Akoomí (perhaps in the guise of Afeemaónsu, who often spoke through him, becoming almost synonymous with him) who taught the secrets of Dúnguláli-Óbia to Kódji, but Akoomí himself had learned them from his father-in-law in the land of the dead. Here, very much in brief, is how Tooy says it happened. (This, again, is the sort of story that no Saramaka before had felt was appropriate to share with me.)[10] In the land of the dead a powerful man named Pupú, the owner of Dúnguláli-Óbia, had a beautiful daughter called Djesu-akóbita. One day she crossed paths with Akoomí, who was on one of his frequent visits from the Oyapock to the land of the dead—Nêngèkôndè-Nêngès are so ritually powerful that they move effortlessly between the worlds of the living and the dead—and she decided to sleep with him, the dead with the living (as Saramakas say). But other dead people intervened and bound him up preparatory to killing him, so she ran off to tell her father. Pupú prepared himself ritually, throwing his sack of Dúnguláli leaves and roots over his shoulder, grabbing his calabash rattle, putting his pipe in his mouth and lighting the Dúnguláli tobacco, and setting out on the path, very displeased. Eventually, his sack "barked" to warn him he was arriving, and he chased off the aggressors, found his son-in-law, untied him with Dúnguláli-Óbia, taught him the ins and outs of its rituals, and then sent both Djesu-akóbita and Akoomí off to the land of the living, where they lived for a time in a place a day's journey upstream from Saint-Georges-de-l'Oyapock called Dadíafê (a.k.a. Kokosókosóampê), where Saramakas still proffer offerings whenever they pass on the river.[11]

Over a period of years, during the treatment of many cases of illness and misfortune, Kódji learned the leaves, roots, and vines, the taboos, the songs, the drums, the sacrifices, and the other esoterica of the Dúnguláli cult, which has always specialized in separating the living from the dead—helping free living people from the machinations of the dead. In fact, the young Agbagó (the future *gaamá*) was cured by Kódji's Dúnguláli at Tampáki after he had accidentally caused the death of his own brother in a tree-felling accident on the Approuague River, and eventually, he and another brother, Gasitón, learned the *óbia* and, around 1920, brought it back to Dángogó in central Suriname, where Gasitón established the shrine and cult that, in

1968, ritually separated Sally and me from the ghost of the boy who had died in Sally's arms.[12]

* * *

Two hours after dark, Roland shows up at our house. Tooy tells Kalusé to catch and bag another toad—the one from last night died from the midday heat. At the lumberyard, the great steel door rolls up and we file into the showroom, with its lineup of unsold cement mixers and row upon row of hardware, hand tools, and other building supplies. Off to one side, outside Roland's office, are plastic chairs, fake flowers on a table, and magazines on a rack for clients to read. And a large reproduction of the Last Supper on the wall. The rice sacks full of leaves are hauled in and the door lowered and locked. Roland shows us around the place expansively—the modern hardware supermarket plus a couple of large hangars, filled with tall stacks of lumber from different parts of the world, sacks of cement on pallets, and great conical piles of sand and gravel.

Out behind the largest hangar, which is lined with stacks of South American hardwood, there's an empty lot filled with weeds and refuse. Looks like workmen throw the remains of their packaged lunches out here, along with empty soda cans. A few meters outside the door, Tooy tells Kalusé to start digging the hole. Roland brings out a crowbar for Kalusé as well as a shovel, which he uses to dig out the loosened earth. Twenty minutes later, there's a hole a half meter deep and a half meter across. We're in semidarkness, with a single bare lightbulb outside the hangar door. Tooy moves us around, saying we must avoid casting our shadows in the hole. We bring out the bags of supplies and line them up. Kalusé begins to pour a libation of water into the hole from an unmarked calabash as Tooy prays—to various ancestors but mainly to the god-who-has-the-earth. Kalusé gets his turn to pray. Then it's mine. And finally, Roland is told to stand over the hole and slowly pour water as he prays for protection, that the evil—whatever it may be—leave him. Tooy asks me to tell him to say that the evil must become as cold as the water he's pouring.

Tooy next does divination with the bottle cap of a Heineken—it always reminds me of Evans-Pritchard's descriptions of the Azande poison oracle.[13] Tooy says, if such-and-such be true, then flips off the cap, observing whether it falls open-side up (good) or down. From this point on, throughout the evening, he periodically shakes the bottle cap (like a die) in his hands, asks his question, and drops it, getting his instant answer. His first startling finding: Roland, since he's inherited the lumberyard from his father, has never once spoken with the god-who-has-the-earth there, the true owner of the place. (So, when bad things happened, when someone tried to harm Roland, the god of course did nothing, just let it happen. But from now on, the god will stand firm for Roland.) Tooy prays some more, pouring beer into the hole. "We're giving you beer here, we're giving you cane syrup, we're giving you rum, we don't know if you like rum or cane syrup or molasses, so we're giving you all of them. Take them and help the man!" Half a bottle of cane syrup, half a bottle of molasses, half a bottle of rum, and a bottle of beer are poured into the calabash and it's dribbled into the hole as prayers are said. We all drink a bit as the calabash is passed around, with Tooy joking that Kalusé has downed too much, not leaving him enough. Then Tooy directs the filling of the three empty beer bottles, one with the left-over cane syrup, the second with molasses, the third with rum. Kalusé is instructed how to place them in the hole, the first to the west, the next to the east, the third to the north.

Following orders, Roland brings out the carton of six supermarket eggs, and Tooy asks him to select three. Then, Tooy puts them in Kalusé's hand, turns his back, and asks Roland, then Sally, then me to tell which egg we like the best. Turning, he asks Kalusé which one each of us picked. Roland and Sally chose the same one, so, he says, that's the one we'll use. Kalusé places it, on Tooy's instructions, in the very center of the three bottles in the hole. Then two green leaves are pulled out of the sack, and Roland is told to place first one, then the other in the middle of the hole, on top of the other things. He starts to put them in together and Tooy says no, first one and only afterward the other. (Roland has to kneel in the mud, soiling his trousers, to do this.) Tooy continues his bottle-cap divination mixed with prayer and occasionally tells Roland to say such things as "Protect me from my enemies." Tooy asks for the toad and tells Roland, who's beginning to look frightened, to hold it over the hole and feed it the remains of the calabash of beer we've been drinking. He tries to pour it down the toad's throat as the animal wriggles its legs wildly. Then, on Tooy's instructions, he places it in the hole, and Kalusé and Roland, with their hands, quickly pile the earth back in. The toad tries to escape, but they bury it before it jumps out. The earth is smoothed over and packed down, and all is left as if nothing had taken place there at all.

Tooy takes Sally and me inside, telling Kalusé to take care of Roland. Through the doorway, I see Kalusé adding water from a hose to a plastic bucket containing the leaves, roots, and vines they've brought. He then bathes the naked Roland out back in the moonlight, farther from the building, amidst the strewn garbage. Tooy tells us he can't get over that Roland had never even thought to communicate with the god-who-has-the-earth.

When we're all back in the waiting room outside Roland's office, Tooy instructs Kalusé on how to use some special vegetable tinder he's brought to start a fire under a few pieces of charcoal in an old cooking pot—using kerosene as a starter is taboo in Dúnguláli-Óbia. Once the coals are glowing, a dozen varieties of Dúnguláli leaves are placed on top for the smoking. Kalusé is instructed to carry the coal pot to each corner of every room of the establishment, spreading the smoke around with his hand as he intones the sacred chant, *Dúnguláli-éé, Pási-paatí! Dúnguláli-é! Awíi kándikándi, awíi kándikándi!* Tooy lounges in a waiting-room chair. For him, it's just a procedure to be carried out correctly. He's the priest, his acolyte does the work. Roland urges Kalusé, "Do it in there" (indicating where the money is kept), and Kalusé makes sure the broken copy machine gets a full dose as well. When he's done, Tooy has him place the coal pot on the floor in the center of the waiting room.

I try to explain to Tooy that he should do some singing, some fancy explanation in Saramaccan for me to translate, as a kind of show, to make sure that his client, Roland, gets some sense of the gravitas of all this. But neither Tooy nor Kalusé seems interested in persuading Roland of anything. It's as if they're so confident of their procedures that they don't need public relations.

After Roland drives us home around midnight, Tooy tells him to go to the lumberyard at the crack of dawn and throw the remaining cinders from the coal pot to the wind, but to be sure to do it in the front of the building. And he asks me to tell him to bring three things tomorrow: a bottle of Crésyl (a disinfectant for cattle, used by local *quimboiseurs,* too)—it must be the kind that comes in a bottle, not in a can, he specifies—a bottle of kerosene, and a bottle of rum.

THE BEACH AT COCK'S CROW

From his plastic chair, Tooy greets the sunrise and sea gods as usual, se-
ducing them with song. Later in the morning, he decides to prepare a
Dúnguláli bath for Sally and me to use over the coming days. He asks for
a bottle of rum, and he and Kalusé rip up various Dúnguláli leaves and
vines in a plastic basin, sprinkling some ashes from the wild papaya tree
(which Dúnguláli likes to work with, instead of kaolin) on top. I cut three
green sticks as "payment," since no *óbia* can be made without recompense,
and we go through the standard ritual exchange between *óbia*-man and
client: "*Madjómina!*" "*Ká!*" "*Madjómina!*" "*Ká!*" "Payment on the ground"
(I put down the first stick and say, "A jug of rum!") "*Madjómina!*" "*Ká!*"
"*Madjómina!*" "*Ká!*" (I put down the second stick and say, "Thirty lengths
of cloth!") "*Madjómina!*" "*Ká!*" (I put down the final stick, saying, "Twenty-
four bottles of beer!").[1] Tooy then pours a libation of rum to the Dúnguláli
ancestors, from Pupú and Akoomí to those who have served as its priests,
and tells me to put water in the basin and let the mixture soak for a while
under the coconut palm.

Roland arrives to report he's scattered the ashes. Tooy sits us down to
discuss money—how he wants 50,000 francs, how Roland says he can only
pay 3,500 now but will come up with the balance in good time—lots of
back and forth, some of it testy. Eventually, Tooy instructs Roland to buy a
1-meter length of white cotton cloth, a box of eggs, a bottle of cane syrup,
and a bottle of rum for tonight's ceremony. And he should write out on a
sheet of paper all of his problems and all his desires. We'll also need a not-
yet-ripe calabash, which Sally can pick from one of her trees, a bucket, and
some camphor, which Roland will also need to buy. He rushes off before
the stores close in the city—you can't buy cloth for miles around.

Tooy goes into his bedroom and rummages in his carry-on sports bag
that he's shown me holds, among other things, the impressive-looking bottle belonging to Yontíni (his wife's Wénti), heavily swathed in cloths and
surrounded by *óbia* arm rings, along with a complex Komantí whisk, whose

handle is covered with colored cloth and a good bit of kaolin. Standing upright together in the bottom of the bag, they look much like what Europeans of another era called a fetish. He reaches in and brings out an óbia fan, a two-foot-long basketry device folded in two and covered in kaolin. Along the edges are sewn cowrie shells and jingle bells. Tooy sits on a stool and interrogates the fan quietly as it opens and closes according to his questions. Have there been money problems between Roland and an employee? Problems with another woman? Tooy satisfies himself and puts the fan away.

You see that yellow flower? he asks Sally, pointing out toward the yard. It's called komantí sangaáfu. On Tooy's instruction, Kalusé puts a few of its leaves in rum, and we each knock down a swig after carefully crossing our ankles, holding the liquid for a while in our mouths, and covering our ears with our hands as we swallow. (We continue to do this over the next couple of days, whenever Tooy gives the word.) You're supposed to hear "the sounds of the universe" when you swallow the mixture in this fashion.

Tooy spends much of the morning telling First-Time stories and singing sweet óbia songs—in Komantí, Papá, Luángu, and Wénti language. (Oh, for the time—and energy—to record and annotate them all!)

"You see that plant?" he asks me, pointing toward the front gate. "If you wash with seven of its seeds, you won't have pimples for seven years. If you swallow its seeds, snakes won't bite you." He also asks about our palipú palm (native neither to Martinique nor Suriname), which I tell him we brought as a seedling from Guyane. We'd gotten to know its delicious orange fruits, which need to be boiled for an hour before they're ready to eat, in Dángogó, where it had been brought in the early twentieth century by Saramaka canoemen returning from Tampáki, the same ones who brought back Dúnguláli-Óbia.

I take Tooy and Kalusé for a drive in our pickup truck, sightseeing. Tooy whoops it up each time we go over a mountain, like a kid on a roller coaster. (Guyane and Suriname are flat, while Martinique is notoriously hilly.) He teaches whenever the spirit moves him. We see a dead opossum. "You can't eat roadkill if you're with Dúnguláli," he tells us, adding that there's a new taboo for Dúnguláli adepts: if you go hunting and shoot an animal, wounding it but not killing it, and then find it dead the next day, you can't eat it. So-and-so did that and he died. Divination said that's what killed him. This leads Kalusé to ask whether you can eat a chicken that's been used in a ritual. Tooy explains that if it has been used as a sacrificial offering, you can't or you'll die, and gives an example of someone who did. But if it's just been used in divination, you can eat it like a normal fowl.

We drive through the neighboring fishing village of Diamant, where a 1925 election-day massacre marked the height of colonial oppression and where, today, with the boom of tourism, the fruits of globalization flower—there's a new French-owned *boulangerie et patisserie* whose window touts Häagen-Dazs, the Bronx-born ice cream with a name invented to sound "Old World."

Driving through the silent Sunday streets of Martinique's capital, Fort-de-France, Tooy enthuses that it's bigger than New York City—though he's never been beyond Guadeloupe. Tooy has us in stitches for much of the way home, entertaining us with stories, for instance, of how he hoodwinked some gendarmes who'd stopped him for running a red light in Cayenne and discovered he had no driver's license, no insurance, and no registration. (Tooy drives an ancient Toyota that a grateful client gave him as a gift—he drives slowly, seemingly by instinct.) At the police station where they hauled him in, each time they would ask him a question he'd grin broadly and shout "Oui!" (He mimics the gendarme perfectly, asking questions, interrogating him.) No matter what the gendarme asked, he'd say *oui!* In the end, immensely frustrated by the old man, they simply let him go, saying (and Tooy again mimics the French gendarme), "See that in future you drive correctly. Proper conduct on the road is the duty of each citizen of the Republic."

A couple of hours past dark, Roland shows up with his equipment, and after we've settled down on the verandah, he proffers his page of desires. Tooy, who is not literate, asks him to read it out loud. When Roland gets to the part about "regaining his physical, moral, and financial health," he asks if he shouldn't add "and spiritual," and Tooy says why not. Does he need to rewrite the whole? he asks solemnly. They say no, just add the word. We get a pen, and he does. He'd also left out the word *workmen*, which he now adds. Tooy then asks for the paper and examines it. "Where's your signature?" he asks incredulously. Roland seems confused. Tooy presses, "How in the world will they know who sent this, who it's about?" We all laugh—Sally and I thinking of students who forget to put their name on an exam paper. Roland pens his name on the paper and passes it back to Tooy. We agree to set our alarms for a 3:45 a.m. rendezvous on the road in front of our house. Tooy tells Roland to be sure to bring a five-franc coin.

Tooy asks me to make a photocopy of Roland's page for him to take back to Cayenne. On the porch, we set things out to prepare the *óbia* for the cock's-crow ceremony. Kalusé tears a piece of the white cloth into strips for tying with. The remaining rectangle is laid out with the wish list in the center.

On top is placed a small bottle of cane syrup, one of beer, and another empty beer bottle filled with rum. An egg is set in the center of the bottles. (Tooy gives the instructions, Kalusé and I carry them out.) Kalusé folds up the whole packet and ties it tightly, winding a strip of white cloth around the bottles, creating a white bundle with the heads of the bottles on top. Tooy spends the rest of the evening singing.

★   ★   ★

The awkward handwriting on Roland's statement lists his problems and desires (I retain his faulty grammar and spelling):

LEGROS ROLAND
—entreprise bloqué [business fucked]
Argent - n'entrè pas - [money won't come in]
Le materiel - ne se vend pas - [the goods won't sell]
maison sur le morne bloqué [house on the mountain fucked]
—élevage coqs bloqué [cock breeding fucked]
maison du bourg bloqué [house in town fucked]
assiette au pitt [plate in the cock pit]

je demande que mon argent entré [I ask that my money flow in]
que les clients me donne mon argent [that my customers pay me what
    they owe]
que je vends beaucoup de materiels [that I sell lots of merchandise]
que je finisse mon entreprise [that I finish building my lumberyard]
que tous les obstacles soient Rayés [that all obstacles be Removed]
que mes poules retrouvent leur fécondité [that my hens regain their
    fecundity]
que mes coqs deviennent fort et gagnent leurs combats [that my cocks
    grow strong and win their matches]
que je trouve une santé physique [that I get my physical health . . .]
spirituelle morale et financiere. qu'on annule [. . . my spiritual health my
    moral health and my financial health]
tous les travaux diaboliques qui ont été [that they stop all the diabolical
    work that has been . . .]
faits contre moi que je finisse ma [. . . done against me and that I finish
    my]
maison du bourg et sur le morne que [house in town and on the mountain
    that]

tous mes ouvriers retrouve leur dynamisme au travail [all my workmen
find their dynamism once again]

⋆   ⋆   ⋆

The ceremony lasts less than an hour. Roland, who has picked us up in
front of our house, pulls his sedan in under the almond trees at the west
end of the beach, where the surf is highest. Pitch black. I've brought two
flashlights and hand one to Kalusé. The tide is up. Tooy is dressed formally
and keeps on his shoes and socks. Kalusé strips to his underpants. Roland is
told to undress fully and hangs his clothes on a sea-grape branch. He looks
so vulnerable, covering his nakedness with his hand, which he eventually
just drops and stands there, facing Diamond Rock, shivering and miserable.
Roland had given me the five-franc piece they'd asked for earlier; I pass it to
Tooy, who hands it to Kalusé, who now, at water's edge, unwraps the whole
bundle, places the coin right in the middle on top of the egg, and rewraps
everything. (Tooy tells me the money, which he'd forgotten earlier, is to pay
the Mother of the Sea.) Then Tooy instructs Kalusé how to do the bath: first
he pours rum over Roland's head, telling him to rub it all over his body. Then
the same with a bottle of beer. The bottle cap falls open-side up, and we all
nod in approval.

　　Roland is told to pray as he is being washed, and as he rubs the stuff all
over himself he prays his heart out. Kalusé then prays to the sea gods and
Tooy prays to the ancestors, the god-who-has-the-earth at Roland's lumberyard, and to the Mother of the Sea herself. Tooy tells Kalusé to take the
plastic basin with leaves and, using the calabash we'd brought, fill it with
seawater. At the edge of the sea, Kalusé, Tooy, and I each wash ourselves from
the basin and then Kalusé pours what's left over Roland's head, Tooy praying
and singing all the while.

　　Suddenly the sea surges, soaking us all before swishing away in a spray of
foam. Tooy shouts with delight. The god is taking the evil away! For the final
washing, Tooy tells Kalusé to take Roland in up to his waist. They wade out
into the surf, where Roland is told to break an egg over his head and wash
in it but to hold on to the shell. Finally, Tooy tells Kalusé to tell Roland to
throw the eggshell as far as he can, which he does baseball fashion. (Again,
it suddenly looks comical to me, seeing Roland naked and shivering, trying
to fling an eggshell into the wind in the direction of Diamond Rock.) Then
Kalusé goes ashore and returns with the bundle, and Tooy tells Roland to
hold it underwater and let the undertow pull it out to sea. We beat a hasty
retreat, Roland slips on his clothes, and we pile into the car. A few hundred

meters down the road, Roland realizes he's forgotten his baseball cap. Tooy decides we have to go back, and Roland finds it on the sand. Back in the car again, he hesitantly asks if he can go jogging on the beach at 7:00 a.m.—on the other (Atlantic) side of the island near his home—as is his Sunday habit. Tooy says no problem.

★ ★ ★

Tooy's final days in Martinique are filled with song, *óbia*-making, and story-telling. He fabricates various *óbias* as gifts for Sally and me, teaching us much about the sea gods and other invisibles who live all around us, and exchanging the kinds of First-Time lore that creates such a strong bond between us. Libations at every turn, and, of course, intermittent swigs of the mixture that lets you hear the sounds of the universe.

One morning, Roland shows up with his 3,500 francs. Tooy displays his unhappiness with the paltry sum, but Roland assures him he's good for the rest, as soon as his cash flow improves. Tooy lays out the next step: we'll arrive in Cayenne on a Friday, do a washing before noon, do the heart of the matter ("knocking the stone") at his Dúngulálí shrine Saturday night into Sunday morning, and by Monday, Roland can fly home. They'll need three live chickens—the kind raised at home, not "by machines."[2] And, of course, the goat. We agree on a date a couple of months hence.

At the airport, Roland presents the visitors with a jar of candied local plums. As Tooy opens his hand-carry sack to stick it in, Roland, wide-eyed, spots the "fetish." Looking mortified, he asks me how in hell's name they're going to get *that* through the X-ray machine. I say it's stronger than any machine. And so it proves to be.

NIGHT OF THE CATS

★ 06212000 ★

The tiger is the fetish of Dahomey.
ARCHIBALD DALZEL, *History of Dahomey* (1793)[1]

It is one of those sultry June nights at Tooy's when the air stands still and sweat runs in rivers off your face and chest. Mosquitoes "the size," says Kalusé, "of blackbirds" slowly circle, choosing their moment to alight on arms, shoulders, ankles, and backs, our conversations punctuated by the sound of palms slapping skin. The shed behind the house forms a hermetic world, yellowed by the bare lightbulb, surrounded by a deafening wall of insect sound. Beyond the corrugated metal door, the absolute darkness extends, unimpeded by houses or humanity as far as any of us can tell, out through the high trees all the way to Brasília, fifteen hundred miles away.

The last of the day's clients are finishing their business when Sally and I arrive around seven: a Brazilian who'd parked his Yamaha cycle out in the mud, a man Saramakas would call "Syrian," and an Afro-Guyanais married to one of Tooy's relatives who had accompanied him with three of their kids to the consultation. Four of Tooy's acolytes—his sister's son Frank, another twenty-year-old named Lowell, and two others—are chopping vines and bark, pulping roots, and mashing leaves in the side room he uses as pharmacy and bathing place. Kalusé, finished with his construction job for the day, drops by to chat. Before long, the Brazilian, then the Syrian, and finally the Creole/Saramaka family, after having stripped down to their underwear and been bathed by Tooy, pull on their clothes, say their goodbyes, and leave carrying plastic basins of vegetable matter with instructions on how to bathe in them. When the Creole asks if there are any taboos he needs to keep during the week he'll be using the leaves, Tooy jokes, "Only one—you can't play with your wife's titties during that whole time, only I can!"

Whenever the rusty door squeaks open, another tiny pussycat slips in. Tooy reaches down with resignation, curses the beast which he calls only "animal," and tosses it out in the direction of the creek. Kalusé tells us that Tooy already drowned a whole litter last week, and they seem to be coming back now. (The Komantí spirits that Tooy deals with can't tolerate these miniature versions of their tiger-selves, nor can he hear their true name.) As the evening wears on, more and more kittens squeeze under the door, three at a time, four at a time, only to be cursed out and thrown back toward the creek—each time, one or another of the young men teasingly pleads for their lives with Tooy: "Please don't drown them, please don't drown them."

Tooy brings out a six-pack of warm Heinekens, which fizz over when opened, and launches into a hunting story. There's nothing he likes better than to *dá óto*, what we'd call "shooting the breeze." Kalusé and the young men listen raptly.

There was an epic battle with a "spotted beast," a tiger (or, more correctly, a jaguar), at the creek head called Tamanúa ("Giant Anteater") in the north of Saramaka territory. There, turning a corner around a tree, Tooy came face to face with the animal. With one swipe of his paw, the tiger knocked away his shotgun. Tooy stared him down for what seemed like an hour as he ever so slowly inched the gun back toward him by means of the strap that was lying not far from where he stood. Then, a boxer's right hand to the tiger's shoulder, the scratch across his face that the tiger gave him, how he commanded the beast to lie down and how it did. And how he told it he had come to the forest to hunt, not to do battle, and then how "something" took possession of him and the next thing he knew he was waking up in the village, where they'd brought him after finding him stretched out on the forest floor.

Meanwhile, three of the kittens return, slinkily, only to be thrown out the door with a look of disgust from Tooy. The night grows late, and as one of the acolytes leaves with the bucket of leaves Tooy has prepared for him "to give him strength," Tooy hoarsely whispers instructions: "Wash in them as often as you have patience for, keep the bucket at the head of where you sleep."

Kalusé picks up the pace again, following with a story about his father, Tandó, a friend of ours in the 1960s who had a famously powerful Komantí spirit. Once, he ran into a whole band of spotted beasts, and in the ensuing battle managed to shoot four. Kalusé says he saw them dead on the ground with his own eyes. At one point in the pitched encounter, Tandó became a vulture and circled high over the battleground—people later saw the ripped vines in the trees above the scene which couldn't have been broken unless he'd flown right through them.

The tale is interrupted by more kittens and more ejections. Suddenly, Tooy breaks into a Komantí song that warns, "You can play with Jaguar's whiskers, but don't even think about playing with Pussycat's whiskers!" "Because," he explains in a rush of interrelated, abbreviated, stories, "Pussycat's whiskers are the fighting *óbia* of Jaguar!"

Jaguar once went to Pussycat to ask him for Náki-Kíi-óbia ["knock-kill óbia," the power that lets you kill an animal with one swipe of your paw]. Pussycat agreed to teach him. First, Pussycat cut off Jaguar's whiskers, roasted them in a fire, and told him to put a bit of the ashes in a glass before he drank it. After Pussycat left, Jaguar gave some of it to another spotted beast to see what would happen. Two hours later the animal rolled over dead. Next time he visited, Pussycat said he'd teach Jaguar another óbia. He cut his own whiskers, roasted them, and left the ashes with Jaguar. When Jaguar tested it on another spotted beast, in only an hour and a half the animal was dead. So Jaguar knew which was stronger. One day Pussycat came by and left his five children with Jaguar to baby-sit. When he returned a week later, one was missing. Together, they went to divination, which pointed to Jaguar, saying he'd eaten it. Pussycat said he wouldn't take back his óbia, but that thenceforth, if Jaguar used his left paw to knock an animal, he couldn't eat it or he'd die. Jaguar went hunting without success. He'd been hunting for twelve days and twelve nights before he met up with some peccaries. He was so hungry he knocked the first one with his left paw! Realizing what he'd done, he called his older brother, Vulture, who was able to remove the taboo for him so he could eat the animal without dying.

And then Tooy tells us, excitedly, that when you're in the middle of a Komantí "play"—Tooy's a master Komantí drummer and singer—and you hear this song, it makes you think of all these stories.[2]

Komantís, who walk in tiger cats and vultures, are the greatest of Saramaka curing gods and warrior gods—they're also the quintessential meaning of the word óbia. Tooy knows them like the palm of his hand.

END OF THE ROAD

★ 06202000 ★

My house may be small, but it's filled with conversation.
TOOY

When we arrive at the Cayenne airport from Martinique, Tooy, Kalusé, and Tooy's sister's son Frank, who's driving for them, are there to greet us. We rent a car and follow the old Toyota to Tooy's house. Once inside, he brings out some glasses—a beer mug, a champagne flute, a wine glass, a shot glass, a water tumbler—and places a generous wad of dried herbs in the bottom of each, saying, "Each person must kill himself." So we each pour in a measure of rum from the bottle he offers. As Kalusé leans over to clink glasses, Tooy stops us—"That's not allowed. And you have to stand up when you drink this mixture!" So, without further ceremony (no libations allowed, either), that's what we do. Tooy tells everyone to swallow the herbs, which go down with difficulty. (I see Kalusé spitting the residue outside the door and I follow suit, discreetly. Sally doesn't notice but somehow manages to get it all down.)

★   ★   ★

For years, Tooy has lived at the edge of the city, where Cayenne meets the forest. The neighborhood just preceding his, as you travel beyond the market and over the stinking canal, is called Chicago, because of its frequent crime and gunfire. That's also where, even during the day, women and girls from various nations peddle their bodies in front of frail wooden shacks. The occasional Chinese store, stocked with liquor and a few staples, is the only other local commerce. (A decade earlier, we'd described that neighborhood in a phrase that still works: "a mean-looking area of mixed Chinese, Creoles, Maroons, and some longer-established Haitians, as well as some dreadlocked immigrants from Guyana, where recorded reggae, kadans, zouk, merengue, soka, salsa, and kaseko pour from various doorways.")[1] Beyond Chicago, you turn off the last paved street onto a deeply rutted track that winds its way through a vast complex of single-family structures crammed with recent Brazilian immigrants. Tooy's place is at the very end of the road, next to a fetid canal he generously calls a creek.

Tooy's lived in this spot for almost twenty years, since the government drained the mangrove swamp on which it sits. (Before that, he lived nearby, at the edge of the swamp.) He pays off the property year by year—a long-term loan from the French State. From the front, a sliding iron grate leads into an open space of packed earth covered with rusting corrugated metal. There's an old beaten-up sofa against the front wall of the wooden house, a shrine to the ancestors in a corner, a plastic tricycle, and in the center, a sawed-off tree trunk for butchering meat, and a couple of large pots. Indoors, there's a tiny kitchen with stove, refrigerator, and sink and pots hanging on the walls, a grungy bathroom with flush toilet and ancient washing machine, and a living room-dining room painted green and blue. A steep staircase leads to a sleeping loft. Off to one side is a room just big enough for a double bed. Everything is dirty, with spiderwebs and frayed electrical cords hanging all about. Aesthetically, it is a man's house, though the kitchen pots are sparkly clean and shiny when his wife's around.

Behind the house proper is where most of the action takes place. My field notes describe

a lush calabash tree with lots of beautiful fruit growing next to a fetid creek with sewage pouring into it from a concrete pipe. Tooy's waiting room added on to the back of the house is 9 × 5 meters, with a concrete floor and zinc roof. There's junk all over—a large plastic cistern, a Chinese bicycle, a broken-down gold-mining pump, nine drums—an *agidá* [large snake-god drum], several *apíntis* [talking drums], a few *déindéins* [small drums beaten with sticks]—old bike tires, several dozen buckets, plastic and metal basins of all sorts, clotheslines strung here and there. Over the door is a Komantí [warrior-god] staff, a *kándu* [a protective charm made of a tiny bow-and-arrow], an *óbia* package wrapped in black cloth with a red ribbon, and a ritual fire fan [to blow away evil]. There are two pewlike benches and seven chairs in bad repair, each one different. Large table with oilcloth. A couple of rum bottles and one of sugarcane syrup. Two or three others with leaves in the rum. Some empty beer bottles. In the corner, a synthetic Christmas tree decorated with paper, balls, and tiny electric lights. A smaller table with a bottle of champagne covered with *keéti* [kaolin]. Two large Komantí staffs alongside a hoe, a pair of old leather sandals, various auto engine parts, a large jerrycan for gasoline. Plastic bags, including one of sugared almonds, hanging from rafters. Two large hairy spiders crawl on the ceiling. In a corner, one lifeless dog. There's a rusty straight razor on the table.

Inside, in the dining room, there are four clocks: one marked "High Class Quartz Clock," one with a revolving pendulum, one with a swinging pendulum, all set for different times. TV with "Made in Europe" sticker affixed to the screen. There's a chainsaw, a broken electric fan, mosquito coils, and an outboard motor under the rickety stairs leading up to the sleeping loft. There are ritual objects here and there: white flags, *óbia* packages, a black ball of compressed leaves, a basketry *óbia* bottle hanging on the wall. There are two old stereo systems, neither of which works. On the floor, a Barbie doll, another pink doll, a large stuffed turtle. A cassava squeezer made for tourists hangs on the wall. Christmas decorations are strung around. Various bottles of French pharmaceuticals near the TV. Lots of Chinese calendars (different years) on the walls. Under the TV table (which is actually an old metal office desk) some twenty-five widely varied and partly consumed liquor bottles. There's a great big wooden dishware cabinet with a glass front holding pots, pans, photos of Tooy drumming, dancing, and doing *óbia*. An old sofa and a stuffed armchair. There's an eating table in the center covered by oilcloth, with 4 chairs. Just outside the one shuttered window is a pigeon house with several birds. Electric wires hang everywhere. Walls are pastel blue and pastel green. There's a telephone with a long cord set on the armchair.

Up the stairs—more like a ladder—is Tooy's double bed. It's covered by a mosquito net and flanked by a heavy armoire on which are piled ten old valises holding clothes, photos, papers, and who knows what else.

Off the waiting room, behind the house proper, separated by a corrugated zinc wall, is a dirt-floor, zinc-covered consulting room where Tooy administers ritual baths and stores his leaves, roots, vines, and other ingredients, piled more or less neatly all around the walls and shelves. On the floor there's a hose, various plastic buckets and basins, some plants in pots, a mortar and pestle, a couple of machetes, metal graters, knives, and cutting boards. On the rough shelving there are commercial lotions and perfumes, small seashells, conch shells (which Wéntis use to call each other to council meetings under the sea), barks, roots, bottles of bleach, starch, and Crésyl, some eggs, balls of kaolin, seedpods, lots of candles, matches, and a lightbulb in its packaging. There's a tangle of electrical connections and relays and whenever a wire gets loose, the house plunges momentarily into darkness.

Off of this space are three smaller ones—the first chamber, where Tooy consults tarot cards with his clients, is devoted to the Wéntis. Lit by a small window and bare bulb, the tiny space, floored in concrete, contains among other things a table or altar with two folding chairs before it, along with several decks of Marseille tarot cards, various bottles of beer, champagne, and Coca-Cola, plant medicines of different kinds in calabashes, a Black Forest-style gingerbread house of wood, Christmas wreaths and gold tinsel decorations, a large Chinese-made clock, various porcelain figurines, boxes of candles, plastic flowers, and on the walls and draped from the ceiling a terry-cloth image of Jesus, embroidered Saramaka textiles, a couple of chromolithographs of saints, a "tapestry" with sheep grazing and another of the Virgin Mary, and a model ship in gilded plastic. On a wooden rack sits a cordless phone. The altar also holds two similar liter bottles, elaborately wound about with white cloth and embroidered neckerchiefs and topped with braided red-and-white cloth necklaces and cloth-covered biceps rings—these are the "seats" of Tooy's possession god Dúnuyángi and his wife, Ma Yaai's, possession god Yontíni. To one side of the altar, in an almost hidden alcove at the rear of the tiny room, are the clay pots of several sea gods—Dígbeónsu, Adjéunsu, Yowentína, and others—alongside conch and other seashells and several bottles of beer. One large white platter holds a white stone not much smaller than an American football, bathing in herbs. On the floor is a pitcher containing a yellow liquid.

The second small back room is more private—permission to enter must always be asked by knocking and inquiring, "Father, may I come in?" This is the shrine of Dúnguláli-Óbia. The red door is marked with darker-red bloodstains. The dirt-floor chamber—2½ by 3½ meters with a low ceiling—is windowless and has a two-foot-high post, representing Akoomí, whose top half is stained with blood, flanked by two rows of crusty bottles of rum and beer, and iron and clay pots filled with medicinal leaves and sacrificial blood—the iron pots are for Gisí, Dankuná, and other óbias we'll meet later on. There's a bull's horn, ritually prepared cutlass blades, and balls of kaolin before the altar and along one wall. A wooden plank with an oracle bundle attached is on one wall, waiting to be taken down for divination. All around the walls a forest vine is draped. Whenever friends gather to eat a meal with Tooy out in the waiting room (which is cooler than the indoor dining room), Tooy always dishes out a plate of food and brings it into the Dúnguláli chamber so the óbia can share the meal. The room is always kept pitch dark, unless Tooy is inside.

The third room contains an óbia boat, a four-foot-long, two-foot-deep "canoe" that holds a solution of whatever leaves, barks, vines, and roots were prepared for the last ceremony that took place in the house. This is where Saramakas, rather than other clients, come to bathe, using calabashes to pour the water over their bodies.

*   *   *

Tooy may well be the best-known curer in Cayenne. At the time we got to know him, he had a large and varied clientele as well as a group of eager apprentices who helped him find forest leaves, roots, barks, and vines and then grind them up according to his instructions, to be made into baths for patients. On a typical day, there were always clients waiting their turn—

The back door (clients' entrance) to Tooy's house—the low structure at right. The taller concrete-block structure is the neighbor's house.

Brazilians, Haitians, Martiniquans, Guadeloupeans, Creoles, East Indians from Guyana, Amerindians, Paramakas, Alukus, and Saramakas, sometimes a couple or a family group, and even the occasional French metropolitan woman or man.[2]

The telephone rings frequently, with Tooy answering in Saramaccan, Ndyuka, or Creole, as appropriate, and the general atmosphere is lively, relaxed, and welcoming. The young apprentices joke among themselves, and we often have the sense of being at a spontaneous theatrical performance. "Who's the boss, sugar or salt?" "Who else thinks he's boss—water, blood, fire? . . ." "What part of the body is boss?—feet, because they carry all the rest." Once we heard an hour-long debate in Saramaccan about this exotic thing that the French call *salade* (meaning both "lettuce" and "salad"). The question was: could you have a *salade* if there is no lettuce in it? And then, could you be considered an authentic Saramaka if you ate *salade* more often than rice?—which one of them claimed he now did.

Most of Tooy's consultations are part of an ongoing set of cures for a person who comes with a physical ailment (stomach pain, arthritic troubles, what is now called on American TV "erectile dysfunction" . . .) or a problem with a job, a lover, or a spouse. For routine visits, Tooy charges the equivalent of twenty bucks. But for serious cases, the costs quickly mount.

Two of the salad debaters.

Tooy now has two wives. Ma Yaai, his Ndyuka wife of forty years, is short and rather round, her face generously embellished with decorative scarifications. She suffers from diabetes (for which she receives two injections a day from a nurse who works for public health), and she has difficulties attending to her household chores—the two children she's adopted from sisters are Mireille (five) and Sammy (nine), too small to be much help, but both are as fond of Tooy as he is of them. She's recently begun to get a small old-age pension, having reached the age of sixty. When she gets dressed to go out, for example for a doctor's visit, she chooses one of two stylish wigs. For the past four decades, Ma Yaai has been the medium of an important sea god, Yontíni. When her god and Tooy's come into their heads together, they sing the most beautiful songs you've ever heard.

Tooy's second wife, Céline, is a fifty-year old Guadeloupean who looks younger than her age. Divorced, she works in a copy center downtown and lives with her two daughters about a mile from Tooy. He spends almost every night with her, leaving Ma Yaai with the two young kids at home. Even though they've been together ten years now, Céline's never learned any Saramaccan, and she and Tooy speak to each other in Creole. She's wildly in love with Tooy and blushes as she confides to us he's at once a husband, a father, a friend, and a lover to her. Ma Yaai isn't happy that Tooy spends almost all

Tooy and Yaai.

Tooy and Céline.

his nights with his younger wife, even though she's grateful that Céline is so generous to her, helping her fill out her welfare and medical papers, driving her to the doctor, and coming to visit when she's ill. From time to time, to show her pique, Ma Yaai goes off for weeks or even months at a time to her house in Saint-Laurent, where many Ndyukas live, on the border with Suriname.

★   ★   ★

Sitting in the house one day, Tooy tells me about an incident that happened a couple of years earlier. His older brother Sensiló, who'd recently gone blind, was visiting from Paramaribo. (Tooy explains to me that his brother's possession god, Flibánti,[3] is extraordinarily jealous about Yowentína, his wife in Wénti land—if you tell her you want her, no way Flibánti won't kill you!) Tooy went off to Chicago to buy some nails for a canoe he was building out behind his house, leaving Sensiló alone on a stool. He bought his three kilos of nails and had come out on the sidewalk when two beautiful women, one tall and one short, and one of their children came along and greeted him in Creole. He describes an animated conversation with the two of them, all in Creole. It's both playful and flirtatious—they tease him about whether he doesn't really know them, leaving him confused but intrigued. Finally they part, saying, "Bonne route," "Meci Mesdames," "Meci Monsieur," and so forth. Arriving home, Tooy (before he says a word) is confronted by Flibánti, who scolds him, "It's damn lucky I love you, because otherwise I'd have hit you over the head with a two-by-four!" and teases him about the identity of the women he met, letting on that the shorter one was in fact his own wife, Yowentína, and that Tooy had better watch his ass. Two days later, when I'm driving to the market with Tooy, he has me stop the car and get out, and he shows me the Chinese store as well as the exact place on the sidewalk, next to a vacant lot in Chicago, where he met the two Wénti women and their child.

Tooy likes to tout Flibánti's powers.

Once, at the village of Gódo during a Komantí "play," they summoned Flibánti to come join them. While he was dancing along with the others, a man from the village of Akwáukôndè came up to him with a hen's egg he'd specially prepared with óbia, saying, "Handsome fella, I like the way you dance. Here's a little gift from me!" Flibánti said, "I don't think I'll take that egg. [he recounted his praise name:] Peesi en koko hen kwátaki fu hándugbáu—Man, you're trying to mess with me! I came to dance, not to fight!" Then he took the egg and slammed it down and jumped right up on top of the shrine of the biggest avenging spirit of the village! "You know who you're messing with here?!" he asked. The house collapsed! It was the house of the kúnu [avenging spirit] called Djakái. Djakái showed up and asked, "What's going on here?" Flibánti said, "You know me, kid. And I know you too." [He says some esoteric words.] Djakái said, "Leave off! Calm down!" Flibánti replied angrily, "Quick now! Twelve lengths of cloth, twelve bottles of rum, twelve bottles of cane syrup, twenty-four bottles of beer—bring them quick!" The man who'd insulted Flibánti had already fled, so the elders of the village quickly ran off to together the payment to finally calm things down.

Another time, Gaamá Agbagó was staying near Afobaka on some business, and almost every morning he'd hear a loud unpleasant noise. When he finally complained and was told that it was Sensiló's óbia calling out, he quickly assembled and paid the óbia twelve lengths of cloth, three bottles of rum, twelve parrots' feathers, and twelve cowrie shells.

More recently, during the Suriname civil war, a Javanese officer, with "160 soldiers in seven trucks," ordered thirty-seven Saramaka women to lie belly down on the ground at Wéti Sándu, south of Paranam, but Flibánti stormed in, machete in hand, and the commander told his men to run for it—they threw down their weapons, jumped in their trucks, and on the road, six of the trucks overturned, killing them all. Ronnie Brunswick—the leader of the Jungle Commandos—was an eyewitness, says Tooy.

★　★　★

The day before we leave for Martinique, after our first visit to Cayenne since we've known Tooy, he tells us he's making identical óbia bottles for me and Roland to take back with us. It's a man's thing—don't share the bottle with anyone, he warns. Into two empty rum bottles he loads shavings, which he

makes with a knife, of selected *biyóngo* (ritual spices or power objects)—
quartz crystals, mica, vulture bone, and the claw of a giant anteater, to
which he adds some *komantí sangaáfu* (the plant he showed us in Martinique
that when drunk properly in infusion allows you to hear "the sounds of
the universe"), some long black weeds, various roots and leaves, some salt
and sugar. Each bottle is topped with a cowrie shell with a parrot feather
stuck through it pointing downward. I'm told that when I arrive back home,
I should load the bottle up with a mixture of molasses and water, spray a
mouthful to the left, then to the right, and then drink a bit, and give Roland
the same instructions. The cork, he warns, should be fitted only loosely—
otherwise, the bottle will explode.

TOOY POSSESSED

✴ 2000/2006 ✴

He slips into possession so gently that it's only by the way he addresses Sally (as "Madame," rather than his usual "Sister-in-Law") or Kalusé (as "Bási Ronal" instead of "Father"), or the distinctive way he laughs or the way he goes on about the man he calls Stupid-Head, that you realize it's no longer Tooy who's speaking. But he never waits too long to erase all ambiguity by calling out one or another of his praise names: "I'm Sáki-awángba-djíngmbe, Big Man of the Water! I'm Maníng-awúsu-djíngmbe, Big Man of the Forest! But you can just call me Maníng," he laughs. And then he gets right into his teaching and preaching, boasting and cajoling.

Here's a transcript of a recording where he's talking to me in 2004, after Sally and I had helped get him out of jail:

> Man, the goddess called Dígbeónsu of Olóni, heh heh heh! She bore that whole lot of Wénti women. She's in the water, she's in the air. How could you begin to measure yourself against her? Man, when Death comes to take you, you simply have to go. Your ultimate destiny in life is death. I know you can't live forever and that you don't want to die yet, so I'm going to beg the Great God that he let you live. But there's no one on earth who won't die, so you'll die one day too, heh heh heh. I'm Awángbadjíngmbe! I'm Kási-fu-wámba! Man, come embrace me, come give me a big hug, Brother! I'm Awángbadjíngmbe, I'm Kási-fu-wámba! [We embrace.]
>
> The animal called Bush Hog, it says that its secret name is Gungu-vuláng-mammbá.[1] It's also Sosóo-gídigídji—that's its play name. [He sings:] *Sosóo-gidi-gidjí, Ma Yêndjila. | Sosóo-gidigidjí, Ma Yêndjila.* And what Bush Hog tells us is *mbêmbe-na-sabánga*—which means, "The thing we were talking about yesterday is still with us today." That's what the song says. And when those animals stampede through your village, you can't tell me that you don't shake with fear. Any man would wither! That animal has the whole world frightened of it! (I'm so happy you're here again today!) The bush hog—it's also called Bataa-a-kú (that's what forest spirits call it). And Frenchmen call it cochon bois. Don't be afraid! I'm the one teaching you this. I'm Awángbadjíngmbe! I'm Kási-fu-wámba! Big Man of the Forest, Big Man of the Water! If you try to

trick me, you'll just be tricking yourself, my brother! If you ever try to trick me, you'll just be tricking yourself. Mother Dígbeónsu, she's in the air, she's in the water, heh heh heh.

Because of the wonderful deed you did for me, I'm going to give you something special today. The others won't like that but I'm going to do it, because of what you did for me. Had you done it for Flibánti [Tooy's brother's god], he'd have given you the very same gift. I'm telling you straight! When you go home, find yourself a bit of nutmeg, in the shell. Get four sticks of cinnamon. (Brother, I'm giving you some heavy witchcraft! Serious stuff! Make sure you don't tell Stupid-Head about this. Stupid-Head mustn't hear that I'm telling you this. This is something that only you and I should share. And you'll have to pay me twelve coins for it!, heh heh heh.) That nutmeg, it's Akoomí's nutmeg! [The spirit who brought Dúngul–áli-Óbia] This is a really big thing for me, Asáki-awángba-djíngmbe. I'm also Kási-fu-wámba. And Akumbulá-dênde. I'm Pakatá-fu-adjú. I'm Kuláng-káma-bulá-dembu. Heh, heh, heh, heh, heh!

Well, you take those things and you pound them in a mortar, púm púm púm, mash them up. Find four biscuits, two male and two female. Put them in and mash them, púm púm púm. (I'm really giving it to you now! So do it! It's your work! You can't go back now.) OK. There's one more ingredient, but I don't know if you can find it anywhere near here. When the wind blows, there's a certain tree that cries out [high-pitched] kwéén-kwéén, kwéén-kwéén, kwéén-kwéén! [to Sally] Haven't you heard that, Madame? . . . [She says yes.] You know it! [He laughs with pleasure . . .] Well, you pound the bark, you take two pieces of the bark, put them together and pound them in the mortar. Then take some konsáka leaves, man. And you put them in a large clay pot with the rest. Get three bottles of beer. (If you don't have any, just ask Stupid-Head for them. The man who lives here, he's Stupid-Head. He makes out that he knows things, but what does he really know? If he doesn't watch out, I'll cut him to pieces! I've already cut him up twice. Brother, haven't I cut him up twice? He pretends he's "ripe"—what kinda ripe? But I won't cut him up again, not yet, anyway. Brother, you needn't be afraid of me.) Now, go down to the sea, wait for the third wave that rolls in, catch a bit of it in a calabash and bring it home. Open three bottles of beer, man! Put it all in the pot. Then wash in it, Brother. And watch how things go for you after that! (But don't tell Stupid-Head—or anyone else. This is between you and me.) Ma Yowentína and her father Adjéunsu and her grandmother Dígbeónsu of Olóni, heh heh heh. The big man who's master of the sea—do you know his name? (The man, not the woman!) [I say: Adjéunsu.] That's right! So, you call his name. You stand before your doorway. You open one more bottle of beer and you pour a libation to him right in front of the clay pot. Then you wash yourself with what's in that pot until you're clean all over. The woman can wash, too—you needn't be afraid. Other men will desire her but the man who takes her will drop stone dead! Don't worry. It's me! I'm telling this woman, whether she sleeps with a man on

Stupid-Head's watch or she doesn't, he couldn't help you out either way. But from now on you're dealing with me! The man who tries to seduce her will collapse in his tracks! Time for me to leave, now . . . [and he sings a strange song, *Wayo, wayo, tjala, tjala* . . .] I'm still here, man! I want to thank you for what you've done. Only the Great God himself can really thank you in a fitting way. But I walk with Olóni. The things I've given you today, take them, hold them tight! *Wayo, Wayo, tjala, tjala* . . .

And the god sighs very deeply, and leaves. Tooy looks up, wearily, and asks Ma Yaai to bring him some tobacco.

∗   ∗   ∗

From the time I met him, on our first visit to Cayenne after Roland's lumberyard cure, Tooy's god, Dúnuyángi, has displayed special courtesies to me, explaining that he'd been to our home in Martinique and had been treated with respect. Do we happen to know, he now asks slyly, what he'd seen out in front of our verandah? I say I have no idea, so he elaborates. "If you seek me, you shall find me," he sings. "If you seek me, you shall find me."

I'm Master Djidjíngmbe, I'm Sáki-awángba-djíngmbe as well. Now, you and Stupid-Head, you're like two brothers—but don't forget, I ain't no relative of yours! If you enter the forest and curse it, it's me you're cursing! If you go in the water and curse it, it's me you're cursing! Because I'm Sáké-awángba-djíngmbe and I'm Maní-awónsu-djíngmbe, too! So, I'm going to tell you some lies, and you'd best listen up!

In front of your house, near the edge of the sea, where the water doesn't even think about trying to be cool anymore, there's an old man out there. His eyes are here, right in the middle of his head! [He points to the top of his skull.] That's not his home, just a place he likes to rest. You know that little cove behind the mountain? That's another place where the old fellow likes to relax. In fact, those are his two preferred places.

Now, when this guy looks up at you, it's from the two eyes on the top of his head. It happened like this: He had a daughter named Zoofayaúnde who was one beautiful girl. People were coming from all the underwater villages for a fête at his place. The man is in a house over here, his wife is over there. The "play" really heats up. And then the visitors notice Zoofayaúnde. "Oh, that woman there, we want her! We want to take her away with us!" There were two brothers who came to the fête. One said, "Brother, I'm going to start drumming. You go dance with the woman." He grabbed the drum and began playing, [he sings] "I'm drumming my heart out, I'm drumming my heart out in *ayaónde* [repeat]." The place was really on fire! One of the boys jumped on the father, grabbed his face with his fingers, and put out his eyes. Meantime, the other made off with the daughter. (I was there, but I wasn't the one who took her.)

A long time later, she showed up at her parents' village and sang out, [he sings] "I've come to see how you're doing, I've come to visit. I'm Zoofayaónde, and my mother's Ahómedjí. (Now, her father is Konkí-fu-Azô, the King of Azô. Her mother is Ahómedjí. The village is Azô.)

The old man, you can see him coming up for air just off the point to the south of your house. But he has two gardens—one, where you see the fire-flies at night on the hillside, and another on a hill called Zeeagbagóbúka. You should pour offerings of beer—not rum—to him, calling him by name: Konkí-fu-Azô. He owns that part of the sea. He's the king there. His eyes are in the middle of his head. He's looking up at you from down below the sea with his eyes on top. Because the boy jumped on his head and struck out his eyes so the other one could make off with the daughter, Zoofayaúnde. (Man, was she a looker!) By his powers, the king grew back his eyes, but they came up on top of his head.

And he concludes, "Come embrace me, man, come embrace me, woman. We've talked a long time . . ."

Before he leaves, I ask the god what *ayaónde* means. "It's underwater lan-guage!" he chuckles. "*Ayaúnde* is the name of the gong, the great gong un-der the sea. They have one in the meetinghouse of each of the towns down there, Gaánlolo, Olóni. . . . When it rings, the whole world of Wéntis hears it." And then he confides, "If I hear it ringing—even though I'm not a 'wa-ter person' myself, I can dive in and go to the meeting, too." Another time he tells me *ayaónde*, or *ayaúnde*, is the way Wéntis speak of a great rocking motion—sometimes it refers to the tides and sometimes to the ringing of the great underwater bell, back and forth. Perhaps, I suppose, they're one and the same (Dúnuyángi's hermeneutics of depth . . .).

★   ★   ★

"Give me some tobacco," Tooy's god orders me another time, suddenly add-ing, "There are words in this world that you've never once heard! Heh heh heh." And then he regales me with a few of them.

The creature called Papágádu, have you ever heard of it? [I allow as I've had some experience with these snake gods.] OK. But I'll bet you don't know how it says its praise name. It says, "I'm Adjí-kódo-gidi-únzu-moyon. If the wind blows, I coil up, if the wind doesn't blow, I coil up." But this isn't just any Papágádu! It's the one that lives underneath the earth—The Great Papágádu,

The Earth Mother, The Big-One-of-the-Forest, it's all black without any stripes! And it's got an agouti's head! [sort of like a rabbit] It doesn't have a snake's head! If you travel till you come upon it, you've seen the face of Evil. You'll die. Here's how he says his name: "I'm Adjí-kódo-gidi-únzu-moyon. If the wind blows, I coil up, if the wind doesn't blow, I coil up." . . . Brother! When I shoot the breeze with you, you must remember it all, and when you repeat it, don't be afraid! Don't be afraid, man. I know what I'm telling you. This is exactly what that Papágádu says: *Adjí-kódo-gidi-únzu-moyon.*

Brother, the forest—that's what they call *zumê.* The secret name for "forest" is *zumê*! (Man, I just love to talk with you, because we understand each other, not like when I talk with those young folks who don't understand a thing.) Man, the secret name for "forest" is *zumê*! If you're in the forest, don't ever say that word! If you say it, you'll never come out! (Now, it's really *kwamá* reeds that have that secret name. *Kwamá's* secret name is *zumê.* They use it in Papá songs, they play it on the *apínti* [talking drum], but they use it as the secret name for the whole forest as well.) That's why both Papágádu and Howler Monkey have the same praise name. They say they're "Zúmê-koko-kudjumê, the child of the forest, the mother of the forest." (I don't care what you do with Stupid-Head, but when you and I are talking, don't forget a word I tell you, Brother!)

That great snake who lives at the base of hills. He's the one who gives Wéntis clothes when they come ashore to walk among humans. Just the way the police give you a visa to walk in a country when you cross the border. That snake lets the Wéntis come onto shore. One of these snakes was called Asodátan, that's the name already! People from the Matjáu clan killed him. I worked four years with a Matjáu man and learned all about it. That god, Asodátan, has the agouti head. He gave me three words to say, but I don't use them anymore. They're too dangerous. Howler Monkey says his name is Zumê-koko. He has the same name as that thing. They both say their praise names the same way. It means that he's the child of the forest, the mother of the forest. Asodátan says his name is Gwesíalíngi, or Zumê-koko-fu-zúme. The great money *óbia* of the Matjáu clan, this is its god! I made that *óbia* seven times with my Matjáu-clan friend. He didn't hide any of it from me. This is the *óbia* that Chief Agbagó used to get his money!

Yet another time, in the midst of some other story, he adds more about bush hogs, sharing some esoteric hunting lore that he still hasn't told me the end of.

The woman called Gwágasa-Gwandímbo, [loud, high:] heheheh! heheheh! heheheh! [to Sally] Madame, the woman called Gwágasa-Gwandímbo [loud, high:] heheheh! heheheh! heheheh! [he almost loses control, beginning to sob but catches himself] Oolo! [to me:] Man, I'd better snort some tobacco . . . The

Tooy Possessed

woman called Gwágadja-Gwandímbo has a daughter who is guardian of the savannah called Tjéntji-mbéi-na-tjéntji. She watches over all the bush hogs, and
her name is Ma Gumbá. You need to know exactly how to call on her to get her
to let them out of that savannah. If you don't do it right, Brother, watch out!

Sometimes, he teaches us moral lessons.

Man, you go to a large "play." You're there for quite a while, watching the action. Then a young man has cramps and feels diarrhea coming on. He has no
idea where people go to shit in that village. So he walks out the main path, as
fast as he can without attracting attention, pulls off his loincloth, and squats
next to the path. He shits right there, but before he can straighten up, pieces
of shit stick on one side of his cheek. The path says to him, accusingly "You've
come to the 'play' to ruin my reputation?" He answers, "No, I didn't come
with that intent. But I couldn't help myself. I just had to go." "You just had
to go?" asks the path, sarcastically. "Well then: *Zuunzjé dê kwayán, kwayán sa*

kó záádome." That's what Main Path says to Living Person. The guy gets back to the crowd and people begin asking, "What smells exactly like shit around here?" The crowd parts until the guy is standing all alone right in the middle, with the shit reeking on his body. That's what this means: *Zuunzjé de kwáyan, kwayán sa kó záádome.* You come to ruin my name, and you've got shit sticking to your own body!

This, the god tells me when I ask, is "*kôndè* ['country' or 'old-time'] talk," not a particular esoteric language.

On another occasion, after he'd been with us for an hour, the god said:

Man, let me snort some tobacco . . . Time for me to go, heh heh heh. Woman, [sings to Sally] "If you deceive me, I'll deceive you, too. I'm one smart guy. If you love me, I'll love you, too. You're one shapely gal!" [addressing Sally:] Madame? If you forget me, it's no one's fault but your own. But I'm not the kind of guy someone ought to forget, or else! When you see me, be sure to greet me, 'cause I'm Sáki-awángba-djíngmbe, I'm Kási-fu-wamba, I'm Agún-gula-bitjêmbe-who-pays-for work, I'm Gulán-káma-gulán-beyimbó. Eh, heh heh heh heh heh heh! Woman, I knew my father, I knew my mother, I knew my grandparents. [sings, almost as if in pain:] "If you deceive me, you're only cheating yourself. If you deceive me, I'll deceive you, too."

The god then calls out to Céline, Tooy's Guadeloupean wife, who has driven over right from work downtown.

Woman, you just walk by without even greeting me? Heh heh heh. Woman, how is Yowénza doing? Céline, I'm talking to you! (That's what I've heard Stupid-Head call her: Céline.) How's Yowénza? [Céline comes up and hugs him from behind, saying in the few words of Saramaccan she knows, "I don't understand."] You don't know who Yowénza is? You and he sleep in the same hammock every night and you don't even know his name? Well, why do you sleep with him then? [I translate for her and she giggles.] I'm talking about Stupid-Head! [He laughs.] Let's split, Brother. Let's rest.

And suddenly the god is gone.

ENSTOOLMENT

⋆ 06302001 ⋆

Since before we've known him, Tooy has been reluctantly but inexorably pulled into the vortex of Saramaka politics in Cayenne, his name pushed forward by the younger men who surround him to stand as their representative to the French State. The choice is in some ways paradoxical, since Tooy cannot read or write, and they know that's a gamble. Yet for many Saramakas in Cayenne, he represents the epitome of traditional wisdom as well as a generous sociability, and that's a face they'd like to show to the authorities at a time when more and more young immigrants are having run-ins with the law over issues that range from immigration papers to drugs. They reason that if anyone can help smooth over the problems of the rapidly growing population of Saramaka immigrants in the city, now some 4,000, it would be Tooy, who has carved out a firm niche for himself over a forty-three-year residence in Guyane. (Tooy holds a renewable ten-year residence permit—something like a U.S. green card—and receives welfare benefits from the State.) Against his better judgment, Tooy has let them plead their case with the Guyanese and Saramaka authorities.

Saramakas have had captains in Guyane for over one hundred years, men who serve as official buffers between the migrants and the French administration. During the heyday of canoe transport, there was a Saramaka captain on each of the major rivers: the Mana, the Sinnemary, the Approuague, and the Oyapock; and in the 1970s, a decade after Saramakas poured into Kourou to help build the European space center, a new captaincy was created there. Each of these positions (like village captaincies in Saramaka territory) is a combination of political and spiritual authority and is subject to the Saramaka *gaamá* in Suriname. A man becomes captain for life, and his successor is chosen by divination with the coffin of the deceased officeholder. Captains in Guyane get paid 30% of the official minimum wage and are given two sets of official uniforms for public events.

Following the official go-ahead from both Guyanese and Saramaka authorities, the date of June 30, 2001, was set for Tooy's enstoolment as the first Saramaka captain of Cayenne. We flew down from Martinique for the occasion.

* * *

It's a typically hybrid event. Part One's in the Place des Palmistes, Cayenne's main square, on a Saturday night. A delegation has come over from Suriname, including the premier Saramaka dance troupe. In the bleachers are five hundred onlookers, Saramaka immigrants and curious citizens of Cayenne, who drift in and out throughout the evening. Lots of waiting. The lighting system has failed, and in the end the mayor of Cayenne doesn't show up for his speech, which is given by an aide. I follow up on the stage with a speech the Saramaka organizers had asked me to prepare about their people's contributions to the development of Guyane. Aniké Awági, Saramaka Headcaptain from Suriname, then makes a presentation of gifts from the Saramaka people to the town of Cayenne (a carved stool, a model of the canoes Saramaka men used when carrying gold miners up and down the rivers). A Creole MC, provided by the municipality, introduces performances by various Guyanese folkloric dance troupes, who lackadaisically go through their routines. Finally, around midnight, the visiting Saramaka group performs, ending with the traditional

Djangilí dancing at the evening event. Tooy sits at left, Headcaptain Aniké Awági (with cap) in center.

"fire dance," in which warriors dance barefoot in the flames and burning embers.

Part Two the next day is more fun, a more purely Saramaka event, in the ample yard of a house that Tooy inherited from a brother and now lets younger relatives live in. Tables are decked out with colorful textiles, everyone's wearing fête clothes. Lengthy libations to ancestors and former captains. The Association of Young Active Saramakas of Guyane, which has been the driving force behind Tooy's designation as captain, directs the event, performing Tooy's actual enstoolment, then draping the new captain with various gifts: an embroidered hammock, stylish neckerchiefs, loincloths, and many handsome capes, all embroidered and fringed with crochet. Others, including ourselves, follow suit, and Tooy is nearly buried under the textile gifts. A bottle of champagne is presented. Drinks and toasts. And then celebratory dancing, both by the troupe from Suriname and by local Saramaka girls, who really know how to shake their thing. The crowd of one hundred or so Sunday celebrants is appreciative and involved.

Back to Tooy's house, where Ma Yaai and other women have made peanut rice, ginger drinks, coconut sweets, and other festive dishes. Headcaptain Aniké Awági, Tooy's brother Sensiló, other dignitaries, and ourselves get pride of place at the table in Tooy's waiting room.

The next morning, when I greet him as Captain, Tooy confides that he's not at all sure about this captain business, but he's resigned to waiting to see what comes of it. He acknowledges that he's worried about envy and the sorcery it inevitably brings.

MOTHER AFRICA

★ 1690/1712 ★

In the 1960s, living with Saramakas for my dissertation research, I kept in our tiny house a small shelf of anthropology classics including *The Nuer,* with its photos of lanky leopard-skin chiefs and other Nilotic men with their lengthy male members. Saramakas, examining the photos, remarked to a man, "We've lost it! Look at how those Africans were hung!"

What is Africa for Tooy? A land of men's men. Where those who prepared themselves properly could take off and soar like eagles. Where others could dive into the river in the morning and commune with the spirits underwater till nightfall. Where men had gods and *óbias* who could cure any disease that ailed their fellows—a land of warriors impenetrable to spears or bullets, men who had never eaten salt or ever shaken hands with a white man.

Tooy's first remembered forebears, like those of most other Saramakas, are those Africans who came on ships, those who experienced the Middle Passage—in Tooy's case, Gweyúnga, his wife Béti-Kadósu, and her brother Wíi. "Bavíli," says Tooy, "is where they came from—but they called it Bavíli Luángu." He adds, perhaps to see if he can get a rise out of me, "In that forest, there were people who ate other people—I've seen it at the movies, but I'd already heard it from my elders long before." "Bavíli," he says with a guffaw, "is a place where there were naked cannibals!" And indeed, though images of Tarzan—who was popular in Suriname, as elsewhere in the Caribbean—may play some role here, Central Africa was home to the Imbangala and others whose ritual consumption of human flesh, and tales thereof, was part of a broader political idiom that ebbed and flowed through the region during the sixteenth and seventeenth centuries. So I tell Tooy, when he asks my opinion, that indeed it might have been so.

★   ★   ★

Throughout the Americas, slave masters pinned labels—something like brand names—on the newly arrived Africans they purchased. (Often, they were merely accepting labels that had been devised by traders, whether in Africa or on shipboard.) In particular colonies at particular times, Africans' imputed behaviors directly determined prices: Congos and Loangos, Ibos and Coromantees, Nagos and Mandingos—each had their characteristic work habits and temperament (so the planters believed). For a long time, Western historians associated such labels with African ethnicities or tribes or kingdoms, though more recently they have been realizing the complexity of the ethnogenetic processes that made, say, a "Congo" out of people coming from scores of different ethnic and linguistic groups. As historian Joseph Miller puts it, regarding the case at hand, in Loango "traders known as [Ba]Vili mediated between European slavers and a partially distinct network of trading villages dispersed eastward toward Malebo Pool and southward across the Zaire as far as the Ndembu region."[1] And he describes how the enslaved Central Africans would have discovered new social identities beyond the local and already multiple ones that they had when they began what he calls "their tortured ways toward the coast":

> Yoked together in slave coffles with others of unfamiliar linguistic and cultural backgrounds, they must have gained a sense of familiarity with one another and would have created alliances out of it, which the Europeans labeled "Congo" [or "Loango"]. They would have extended these characteristics as bases for collaboration for sheer survival while being held near the shore, amidst many others, awaiting transfer to the ships. Entirely separate European and African inventions, building on different aspects of the same cultural background, thus converged to stimulate "ethnic" communities out of the dehumanizing confrontations of enslavement. The slaves' further experiences of confinement during the Middle Passage and the specific circumstances they encountered in the Americas created changing incentives for Central Africans to draw on differing aspects of their home backgrounds as they searched for a morally restorative sense of humane community among themselves. The meaning of being "Congo" [or "Loango"] in the Diaspora changed accordingly.[2]

The enslaved peoples who arrived at the West Central African port of Loango, accompanied by the BaVili traders who sold them for transshipment to Suriname, came from an increasingly diverse catchment area in the densely inhabited regions of the interior: "The Dutch were more partial to Loango, where forest peoples from modern southern Gabon would have been prominent among the slaves they boarded."[3] But after 1670, more, and ever more distant, parts of Central Africa were being exploited, and BaVili traders assembled peoples of increasingly diverse origins. Miller concludes that the cargos brought by the BaVili to Loango in the early years of the eighteenth century—when Tooy's remembered ancestors arrived on that coast—were notable mainly for "the extreme diversity of backgrounds they brought onto the ships."[4]

In Suriname, Tooy's newly landed ancestors took as their collective identity the brand name Bavíli Luángo, perhaps the main thing up to that moment that they shared, besides their suffering. Two of them, Wíi and his sister Béti-Kadósu, are among the honored founders of the Saramaka clan called Lángu, which still holds sway over the Gaánlío in central Suriname today.

* * *

But, according to Tooy, his African ancestors didn't hail only from Loango. He's told me that "the name of the country was actually Dahúmbe, though Saramakas later changed it to Dáome [the name of one of their villages today]. Dahúmbe and Bavíli are like brother and sister." That Dahomey and Loango lie more than one thousand miles and several nation-states apart on white men's maps does not matter one whit to Tooy—and in fact, he surely has many ancestors from both regions. But he expresses this mixed heritage through a merged geographical image I've heard only from him: "The man called . . . [long hesitation] . . . He doesn't want me to say his name. . . . The first man in Africa who made peace with whitefolks, the first one to eat salt. . . . He still doesn't want me to say his name. . . . It was . . . Djasíbumbú! He was from Dahúmbe and Bavíli!"

Nearly 90% of the Africans arriving in Suriname in the early eighteenth century—when Tooy's remembered forebears stepped ashore—were either from Loango/Angola or from Togo/Dahomey (see "Reflections from the Verandah," later in this book). So, Tooy's merger of Loango and Dahomey nicely captures historical reality, as long as we take it as metaphor. Other Saramaka stories about ancestors, as well as songs, drum rhythms, and prayers, preserve a much larger array of African place-names: Aladá, which Saramakas also call Papá country (from the names of the major slave-shipping ports of Allada/Ardra—the coastal kingdom of seventeenth-century Dahomey—and Grand and Little Popo, in neighboring Togo); Anagó (the Ewe word for Nigerian Yorubas); Asantí and Afánti, also called Komantí (from the name of the central Gold Coast kingdom, the southern Gold Coast confederacy, and the Dutch fort at Koromantin);[5] Púmbu (from Mpumbu, the Kongo word for Malebo Pool, on the Congo River, and used in colonial accounts to refer to a large region in the interior of the Kongo); and many more, flickering like stars light-years distant in the firmament of Saramaka collective memories.[6]

With the help of a New World mnemonic, Tooy's African geography can get still more detailed. Along the Oyapock River, half a day's paddle upstream from the first rapids, lies Dadíafê, which we have often discussed together. It's apropos of that mystical place, so central to Dúnguláli-Óbia and its messenger, Akoomí, that he tells me one day, almost dreamily:

> Dadíafê—that name comes from Africa. It's a creek just upstream from Dahúmbe. Right below it is an island, with a dwarf silkcotton tree in the middle. When a branch falls off that silkcotton tree, a child is born or a person dies. That's where they shot the guns! The island's full name is Bom-sêkele-meedji-kánka-somaní-dadíafê. Or rather, that's what that silkcotton tree says to you. It warns you, "You must not come too close to me, or else!" That's what *Bom-sêkele-meedji* means. It's also rendered as *Kánka-somaní-dadíafê*. This place is in Africa. It's Dadíafê Island. The creek is also called Dadíafê. The ship that left from there carrying the slaves was called Sanfómaíndi (some people say Sanfómaíngi).[7] It left from the place called Dadíafê.

And then Tooy tells a story that a couple of the younger men in his entourage, sitting around after a meal of rice and pig meat, contest vigorously—how could slaves have carried anything at all, they ask? Tooy insists on his version.

> The men boarded the ships with their magic pouches. The whitefolks couldn't see them. Every great man had his pouch on his side. Each carried his *biyóngos* [magical ingredients]. Gweyúnga's Tonê-god—he brought the *biyóngo* for it. He and his wife. Gweyúnga didn't leave his wife behind when he went to the "play" [the fête the slavers threw to trick the Africans onto the ships]! He brought her along! Béti-Kadósu. They came together. On the one ship. They'd already had kids together in Africa. Wíi must have come on the same ship with his sister and her husband.

This is vintage Tooy, laying the groundwork of who he is: the child of enslaved Africans from Dahomey and Loango, two great men (Wíi and Gweyúnga) who arrived with their magical powers in their pouches, and the woman (Béti-Kadósu) who was sister to one, wife of the other.

NEW WORLD BEGINNINGS

★ 1712 ★

"They landed during a war," says Tooy—which, for reasons too complex to outline here, tells me that his ancestors landed in 1712, when French admiral Jacques Cassard assaulted the Dutch colony of Suriname with eight men-of-war and thirty smaller ships.[1] Eighty-five years earlier, another Saramaka captain descended from these people gave a similar version of the story to a Dutch official:

> We were brought to the colony during a war. A man named Cardoso had purchased the whole shipload of Africans. Afraid that we would fall into enemy hands, since the colony was under attack by large ships, he sent us into hiding in the forest near Puupangi to await their departure.[2] Among us was a man named Wii, who had been a chief in Africa. In the forest he had contact with runaway slaves who told him about the terrible things that awaited him on the plantations. Wii spoke with his sister Beti, and they both decided to run off with any others who wished to join them.[3]

This account also explains the second part of Béti's name, Kadósu—from their Sephardic Jewish slave master—which Tooy uses anachronistically for her even in Africa. Today, Tooy's natal village of Bundjitapá is the seat of the Kadósu branch of the Lángu clan.

Tooy's version follows Gweyúnga, the newly landed rain priest (who had the Tonê-god), and his wife, Béti-Kadósu, during their first year in Suriname, when they were kept on an island near the mouth of the great river and then moved to the nearby site of a large plantation owned by the Commercial Society of Suriname. The signal event is the birth of Antamá, Tooy's favorite First-Time ancestor, who during the second half of the eighteenth century was a larger-than-life political and religious leader, heir to his father Gweyúnga's rain-making powers and his uncle Wíi's *óbia*s.

> It was at Zezéku that Gweyúnga got Béti-Kadósu pregnant, but it was at Saáf-ugoón [Societeits Kostgrond] at Nyufóto [Fort Nieuw-Amsterdam] that she

gave birth to Antamá. (When you're at Nyufóto and look toward the sea, there's a kind of island—that's Zezéku. That's where they were in slavery at first, all together. When they moved them from there, it was to Nyufóto.)

Characteristically, the geography is remembered with precision. As are other events that occurred during the months (or might it have been a year or two?) that Tooy's ancestors lived and worked at "Slave-grounds," the Societeit plantation near the future Fort Nieuw-Amsterdam (built 1734–47).

> There was a shortage of women there, so the men went to find wives at the Indian village across the river at Blauwgrond. They went to Chief Pama and his wife Ma Libo. Kwadjaní and the others asked the *íngis* for women. Then Ma Libo laughed [a high-pitched stereotypic Indian laugh] in their faces, saying, *Adúmakúku án sa kó ku kangwéla!* [Tooy explains that in esoteric language, *Kangwéla* means "black person," *Dúmakúku* means "Indian"—"Indian women are not for black people."] The men said, "Is that so?" And then they added [speaking an esoteric language of their own]: *Fu kêke mulêle kóti kwanzambí, u sa yéi fuámba!* ["That may be so, momma, but by the time the stars have shown and the sun comes up once more, we'll see if what you say is true!"—*mulêle* is an esoteric word for "stars," *kwanzambí* for "Venus."][4] And they left. Later they came back and caught as many Indian women as they could—the rest had fled into the forest.

"And that's why," concludes Tooy, "among Saramakas today you'll hardly find any clans that don't have Indian 'mothers.' And it's how my ancestors incurred the wrath of the Indians."

It was not long before Wíi led his fellows in their escape and decades-long trek southward through the forest, with various encampments and villages and battles still remembered today.[5]

THE PINK HOUSE

* 05081986/06071997 *

For most of the last thirty years, until their recent separation, Kalusé and his wife Juliana lived in a bright-pink concrete house he'd built in one of the rougher neighborhoods of Cayenne, just a street away from a sprawling slum in which recent Haitian immigrants put together shacks from corrugated metal and cardboard in an area that turns into an inland lake of mud and muck during the rains. Shielded from the dirt road by a makeshift barrier of rusting corrugated metal, the house was set up in bourgeois Creole style and impeccably maintained by Juliana—"Yayunn" to most everyone. A large cage on the front porch was home to a spider monkey Kalusé caught in the rain forest. The yard out back served as a kind of community center for migrant Saramakas, who would come for divination sessions, political debate, or just to hang out, listening to music cassettes from home. The formal sitting room overflowed with heavy wooden furniture covered with embroidered doilies, displaying carefully chosen bottles of liquor, a massive TV, pin-up calendars, and an impressive number of gilded trophies won by the soccer teams Kalusé captained. Bustling with activity and children of all ages, there was always something going on—women's and children's activities during the day, men's affairs in the afternoon and evening, once work let out. Kalusé's strong physique, quick mind, and ten-year residence-work papers made him a popular construction worker with both Creole and metropolitan bosses, and he was often asked to bring along a dozen other Saramakas without papers who were grateful for day work at half the minimum wage. In the mid-1990s, he was excited to be working on the construction of the enormous new penitentiary going up just outside Cayenne. "It's got two restaurants, a basketball court, and a swimming pool—just like a hotel in the movies," he told us.

Because of the ample space under the eaves, the house was a frequent venue for Saramaka wakes, where men would come to pay their last respects to one of their fellow immigrants with dominos, folktales, and drink. Once, at such an event, I discreetly asked about a man I'd never seen, sitting a few places down on the long bench that ran along the outside wall—a man who'd said nothing all evening. "He's an 'After-Seven,'" whispered the always po-lite Kalusé. A moment's thinking and I was with him. Saramakas count "six, seven, eight"—*síkisi, séíbi, áíti. Áíti* also means "Haiti." Kalusé was telling me the man was Haitian. (Using similar logic, other Saramakas call Haitians "Four-plus-Fours.")

Yayunn is jovial, occasionally hot-tempered and histrionic in domestic conflict, a lively manager of the household scene. By Saramaka standards of female beauty, which call for ample amounts of flesh on the bones, she's a real prize. Like many other Creole women from the Oyapock region, Yayunn is "half" Saramaka, via her father, who was a migrant canoeman. Like her Creole mother, she and her sisters speak Saramaccan as easily as they do Creole and French. On the other hand, many of Kalusé's children with her have only a passive understanding of Saramaccan. Once, we saw the house decorated with pink satin window dressing over the doorways and bottles of champagne tied with pink ribbons all about—a baby of one of their daugh-ters had been baptized the previous Sunday. Other times, we share Kalusé's sadness and frustration—one of his younger brothers was shot dead in Cay-enne by some Hmongs who mistook him for a man who had stolen from them, and another whom we particularly liked died from AIDS, which like crime is rampant in Guyane.

In recent years, Kalusé and Yayunn frequently fought. Most of their kids were grown—one is a police inspector at the airport. In 1997, when we ar-rived, Yayunn told us Kalusé had moved out. We found him several miles away, living with a sister's son next door to a house he was building for him-self, his head heavily bandaged from the wound he'd received when Yayunn hit him with a frying pan. He was out of work but getting unemployment payments. The yard he was staying in had younger, newer migrants: a Sara-maka woman playing a handheld video game, another sporting the tough, current Paramaribo style—hair stiffly coiffed with red highlights, gold teeth, pointy bra.

When we asked about changes in Saramaka—he'd visited Suriname recently—he said that women were keeping up traditions more than men. Monetization is rampant and destroying the social fabric. Men come back from hunting saying they didn't get anything and then sneak the game in after nightfall, when no one will see, so they can sell it rather than share with kinsmen. Paramaribo has discovered offshore oil and the city has undergone a cleanup campaign—people picking up litter, streets impeccably clean. Dési Bouterse, the former military dictator, is running things from behind the scenes with his drug money—what can you say? He's the only one who gets things done, claims Kalusé.

GWEYÚNGA, THE
RAIN PRIEST

1690/1754

According to Melville and Frances Herskovits (our anthropological ancestors in Saramaka), who spent six months in West Africa in 1931,

> In Dahomey there is a legend that when the first kings of the last royal family conquered the plateau of Abomey, the priests of the river cult fomented rebellions against the new rulers, and were all sold into slavery. Nothing of their cult is said to be known today in Dahomey, and the old gods they worshiped are left to trouble the Dahomeans. Today there are places in Dahomey where no Dahomean dares to go. Sometimes, it is said, they hear drums beating from the river bottom, and sacrifices are given to the rivers, although the proper invocations to appease the gods are no longer known.[1]

In the 1970s, elderly Saramakas told me elliptically and with reticence about a spiritually dangerous incident that occurred inside Wet-Eye Creek during the eighteenth-century wars against the whites.[2] The protagonist is Tooy's ancestor Gweyúnga, the African-born runaway slave who was priest of the river goddess known as Tonê. In the story, as the colonial army tries to forge the broad creek, Gweyúnga, who had the power to "bring down the rains," sinks the whites in their tracks, and large numbers drown.[3] Even earlier in Saramaka history, another African-born runaway, Kwemayón—also remembered as a priest of Tonê—sang to Gánsa, the goddess of the Suriname River, *Gánsa, mi yánvaló, mi yánvaló nawé*, and then, in the words of the great historian Tebíni, "Kwémayón descended into the river. He slept right there, underwater at the foot of the falls. The African!"[4]

My own acquaintance with Tonê predates my hearing these historical fragments. When we lived with Saramakas in the 1960s, our closest neighbor was Naai, the nonagenarian sister of Gaamá Agbagó. Born with a caul, Naai was herself a Tonê child, a special being sent by the river goddess.[5] During our stays in her village, Naai several times participated in rites for Tonê held in the village of Malobí, where many of the descendants of Gweyúnga live. She told us once how a man named Galimo, possessed by a water spirit, swam out to the middle of the river and went under until everyone panicked, thinking him drowned, but how he then emerged ever so gently, not even panting, and swam ashore, saying he'd seen Gánsa and that she was getting herself ready to come ashore. The multitude led by a priest of Tonê then carried Gánsa ashore in a calabash amidst great celebration and placed her in a clay pot in the Tonê shrine.

Tooy inherited his relationship to Tonê from his forebear Gweyúnga, and conducts periodic rites for Gánsa, Mother of Waters. When he sings to her, he begins: *Tonê Gánsa, so dê adáni Sokoto*—"as it is in Sokoto," a river that flows into the Niger but also the name of a city in northern Nigeria, a town in northern Côte d'Ivoire, and more especially a town in northern Ghana near the border with Togo.[6]

Once Tooy told me about a great famine whose memory is preserved in Tonê language. "People decided to present offerings on an altar at the top of a great silkcotton tree. But the rule was that you had to carry your gourd with manioc dumplings in one hand and climb the tree using only the other hand and your feet.[7] No one was making it all the way up. But Chameleon [called *agama* in Saramaccan] started up and said this prayer to Tonê: *kúte kúte kaláɓo, kúte kúte kaláɓo, kalékwé domó yogó domó asidá hóló gwêgede agáma líba hêngi-e*. That's the language of Tonê! And he climbed right to the top! Then he sang out [sings:] *Bóluwé, bólué-wé-wé-wé-wé-wé-wé, gaán másu dendé, sêgbenu sêgbenu kaakbo kaakbo íni-we adánuwe bóluwe, agámasu dendé bóluwe-o, gánsa-e, adáni vêse yême*." Tooy explained that *kúte kúte* means "he's climbing"; *kaláɓo*, that he's arrived. "The Old Ones used to teach me these things. They knew I wouldn't forget!"

Tonê lore is so thoroughly integrated into Saramaka life that it even appears in the folktales told at wakes. Tooy taught me the drum rhythm that Anasi, the spider man, uses in a tale to call Tonê from the river and bring her ashore to her shrine: the drum says, *Bandámbalá bandámba gákili bánda, bandámba gákili bánda, don don i dón, búnuyên*. Tooy assures me that he knows this drum rhythm only from the folktale![8]

*　　*　　*

The Herskovitses tell us that in Dahomey, the sons of Agbe, the God of the Sea (himself the son of the Sky God), include Saho and Gbeyongo.[9] Saho rules over the waves of the sea as they advance, and Gbeyongo has charge of them as they recede. These gods are in the sea and in the sky, and when they desire rain they must first send water from the sea into the sky. Dahomeans say that it is Gbeyongo who causes boats to sink and people to drown.[10]

Saramaka Tonê shrine.   Inside the Tonê shrine.

A continent away and separated by three centuries from his Dahomean forebears, Tooy tells me one day that

> there's a place in the middle of the sea called Godolyú-lúmadu. That's where the sea gets pulled up into the sky and then pours back down. That's what makes the tides. When the water whooshes up, the tides recede, when it pours down, the tides are full. Not a single airplane goes near that place! Not a single ship! The saltwater Wéntis who live there call the place Godolyú-lúmadu or Hwémado. When it pulls up the sea, almost the whole sea goes up! Brother, if you're ever on a ship at sea, don't call that name! You'll never return alive. Different priests call it differently. One says "Tjololo Máwa." But as far as Ma Yowentína is concerned, it's the other words that you use for it: Godolyú-lúmadu-hwémado.

Not only that. In Dahomey, the Tòxòsu—"the abnormally born who become spirits of the rivers and guard the approach to the kingdom of the dead"— are recognized as "kings of the water."[11] "Dahomean practice, during the native regime, was to give to the river all children who were born with hair or teeth, or those who were hermaphroditic, or had other anomalous characteristics, since the belief was that these were spirits who belonged to the rivers." And the term Tonê, the Herskovitses suggest, is Dahomean.[12]

Neither Ndyukas nor other non-Saramaka Suriname Maroons, whose ancestors in general escaped after those of the Saramakas, have significant cults for Tonê.[13] It would seem that some of those rebellious Dahomean priests, sold into slavery in the late seventeenth century, found their way to Saramaka but not to the other nascent Maroon peoples. And among them was Tooy's progenitor Gweyúnga, who bore the name of the son of the Dahomean God of the Sea.

ANTAMÁ AT WAR

✳ 01201753 ✳

Although in some storytelling contexts Tooy notes that Antamá was Gweyúnga's son, much of the time Antamá stands alone as Tooy's progenitor supreme—often he refers to him in whispered conversation simply as "Father." In Saramaka historiography, Antamá first emerges—after his birth at Slave-grounds, near the mouth of the Suriname River, a year or so after his parents were landed there—as a precocious warrior. In the 1970s, the oldest living Lángu man named four of his clan's war heroes and spoke Antamá's esoteric warrior name:

> There was once a really big battle near Victoria. They completely finished off the whites! Bákisi, Antamá—his warrior name was Odínko Kánkánkán!—and Kaásipúmbu. Those were real men! Antamá and his younger brother Makambí. Men's men![1]

For Tooy, one of the signal moments of the wars against the whites came when Antamá lost his brother Makambí in battle, an event I can now date to 1753.[2] In the wake of the breakup of the large village of Kumakô, which the whites finally defeated in 1743, there were continuing battles in the area around Victoria.[3] Tooy's graphic version centers on Antamá.

> Antamá's brother Makambí went off to fight at Victoria. He and Bákisipámbo [another Lángu leader], Kwakú, and Kwadjaní [two leaders of the Nasí clan]. They had made a camp at Gaán Paatí. (It was near the railhead at Kabel. You pass Makambí-kiíki landing, before you get to Wátjibásu, on the east side, that's where Makambí and Bákisi and Kwakú lived. That's where they left to walk on the footpath to go fight at Victoria.) After they had fought for a time, Kwakú and Bákisi called Makambí and said, "Let's go, we're tuckered out." Makambí said, "It's not time to be tuckered out yet." Three times they called him to leave. Three times he said no. So, they left him there to continue fighting. That's when the Indian hidden up in a tree shot him with an arrow! So, he took the arrow and yanked it out, but his guts poured out, too. He bent

over and shoved his guts back in with his fingers. He left Victoria and went up Company Creek and across to Makambí Creek and went up it until he got to a stone called Tósu-gbéne-gbéne. When he got there, Kwakú and Bákisi were already resting at their camp at Gaán Paatí. Makambí couldn't go on, so he lay down on the stone. He began snoring there. The others heard him and went all the way to him. He died just as they arrived. They buried him there in a cave. That place had been Nasí-clan territory, but it became Lángu's. And that's why it's called Makambí Creek. Well, they sent a message to Antamá that Makambí was dead, and you can imagine the *sangasanga* that he did!

Sangáa—Antamá's *sangasanga*—is a ritualized display of emotion involving rushing around almost madly. Today, it's restricted to the final morning of second funerals, when the ghost of the deceased is definitively chased from the village in a wild melee led by youths. But as late as the first half of the nineteenth century, it was still an explicit rite of commemoration, as Johannes King, a literate Maroon, explained at the time:

"Sangaa," means many people with guns, machetes, and spears in their hands running all over the place exactly the way that the warriors used to fight in Africa, and with many war cries. And the older men showed the youths and young girls how they had fought with the whites and how the warriors raided and destroyed whitefolks' plantations, carrying off people to the forest. While they were running around like this, they would shoot many, many salutes, just like the government soldiers do in the city square. Then many people would shout together: "Battle! Battle! The battle's on!" And then they would fire guns, play drums, and blow horns, just like warriors going off to raid a plantation.[4]

Pero Rodrigues, a missionary in Angola in the sixteenth century, as well as Father Lorenzo, a Capuchin in Central Africa in the eighteenth, described armed war dances known as *nsanga*—"to jump from one place to another with a thousand twists and such agility that they can dodge arrows and throwing spears aimed at them" . . . [and] "to make contortions to demonstrate their force and their dexterity"—which "involved dancing out large-scale encounters during ritual contexts such as Imbangala initiation ceremonies . . . or prior to war."[5]

In any case, Antamá was stricken by his brother's death—to the degree that his warrior buddies decided they had to act. As Tooy tells it,

They went all the way back to the plantation zone and liberated Djakái, a youngster, and they brought him straight to Antamá. He'd been a slave. Now,

Antamá raised him in freedom. He never called him Djakái. He always called him "my brother." So we've heard.

As he grew older, Djakái, as we shall see, became a trusted member of Antamá's most inner circle.

THE SOLDIER'S TALE

* 10051939 *

Over the past several years, I've been able to piece together, from Saramakas and from archives, a good bit about the Saramaka soldier, Kuset Albina, who survived the war thanks to the magic paper Tooy gave Roland to protect his lumberyard. For Saramakas trying to make a go of it today in often-hostile French Guiana, his story—however fragmentary and undocumented—has assumed mythic proportions, serving as concrete evidence of their people's collective contribution to France. It's my hope that this expanded, documented version may further serve their cause—for Saramakas, knowledge is power.

Aniké Awági, Saramaka Headcaptain now in his eighties, told me how, as a teenager, he had been part of a group of men including Kuset who gathered in the sacred Saramaka village of Dáome to be washed in the Great Óbia in preparation for going off to work as canoemen on the far-away Oyapock River, bordering Brazil. He remembers that two women from French Guiana (one Chinese, named Pundu, and one Creole, named Bemai, both pregnant), who were visiting in Saramaka, came with their husbands and pounded the rice for the ceremony—"right there under the big mango tree." After the ritual washing, the whole group paddled downstream toward French Guiana and, when they arrived days later, heard the news that "the War of '39" had been declared. Stopping at the provincial town of Mana, where many Saramaka migrants worked as canoemen for the gold miners upriver, several men went straight to the gendarmerie and offered to volunteer; but only Kuset, another Saramaka, and a Ndyuka who happened to be there were in the end accepted as fit for service.[1] Kuset had his reasons for going to war— Sensiló, who spent his childhood and adolescence in Guyane, told me that Kuset's father, Aféifi (who had been prospecting for gold on the upper Kourou River), was among the scores of Saramakas working in French Guiana who'd been killed over the years by prisoners escaped from the *bagne* (penal colony) and that, when offered the chance to "go kill whitemen," Kuset said he'd be happy to take his revenge.

Tooy told me what happened next, which he says he heard directly from Kuset, years after his return from the war. The three recruits were put on a ship to take them from Mana to Cayenne to officially enlist. One, a Saramaka, when he heard what service would really entail, became terrified, climbed the mast, and dove off, killing himself instantly. The Ndyuka, who felt similarly, somehow managed to dive overboard and escape into the forest. Only Kuset arrived in Cayenne and enlisted, confident of his warrior prowess.

Precious documents in the French military archives at Pau, in the foothills of the Pyrenees, which I managed to retrieve after years of frustration and with the generous help of archivists both civilian and military,[2] provide the proof that Tooy and, particularly, his younger Saramaka friends who know at first hand the importance of official "papers," want so much to have in hand. These papers attest that Kuset "enlisted as a volunteer from a foreign country for the duration of the war on 5 October 1939 at Cayenne," that he joined the Twenty-third Regiment of the Colonial Infantry in February 1940, that he was sent to the front in May 1940, and that he was captured by the Germans near Soissons, with the Sixth Company of the Twenty-third Regiment of the Colonial Infantry, on June 8, 1940.[3]

Kuset lived through the very worst moments of the war. From May 10 to 13, his regiment made a heroic stand in the area of Stenay-Montmédy near the Meuse (northeastern France): "Despite the violence of the bombardments and the assaults that continued for days, despite the enemy's superiority in numbers and materiel, the 23rd RCI managed to hold the position that it was responsible for."[4] Then, between May 16 and 19, they defended the last fort on the Maginot Line at Villy-la-Ferté during the Battle of the Chiers, suffering very heavy bombardments and retreating only just before the remaining 105 troops in the fort were killed to a man by the Germans. On May 13, only kilometers to the north at Sedan, the German army, with its frightening Panzer divisions, had crossed the Meuse, and Kuset's regiment seems to have retreated west from Villy, continuing to suffer heavy bombardments and to engage in counterattacks into early June.[5] On June 5–7, the Germans finally broke through the Somme-Aisne line, which Kuset and his comrades were then defending. Shortly thereafter, an officer noted that "the 6th company [Kuset's] is now commanded by S/Lt Lefenvre. Lieutenant Midan has just been killed and Lieutenant Bounard, seriously wounded, has been taken prisoner. One whole platoon has vanished."[6] On June 8, near Soissons, Kuset was captured with most of what remained of his company.[7] (By June 10, the French government had fled Paris, which fell four days later.)

By the time Kuset was captured, "soldiers who had experienced German air attacks in early May" had, apparently, "become partially inured to them, at least to the shrieking of the Stukas,"[8] but that can hardly have been much solace to Kuset and his inexperienced companions from the far reaches of the French empire. Nevertheless, they fought valiantly.

> No less remarkable was the tenacity with which the French army continued to fight in the first two weeks of June, despite the terrible blows that it had suffered in the previous three weeks. . . . The Germans themselves were impressed by how hard the French fought on the Somme and Aisne. This battle was almost certainly lost in advance owing to the Germans' quantitative superiority, but the initial French resistance was so strong that [General] Weygand briefly wondered whether the line might after all be held.[9]

The losses were monumental. "The French armies holding off the Germans in May–June 1940 suffered 124,000 dead and 200,000 wounded in six weeks, more than America did in Korea and Vietnam combined."[10] So, too, for the captured—indeed, "The number of French prisoners was very high—something like 1.5 million" over the course of the battle for France.[11]

Nazi policy singled out black troops, and Kuset's story must be understood in this context.[12] The SS sent orders that, on the battlefield, blacks (who, mainly in the form of "tirailleurs sénégalais," had haunted the German imagination since WWI and the occupation that followed the Treaty of Versailles) were to be summarily shot rather than captured so that there would be no risk of contaminating the Master Race—and many were, including in one murderous moment some six hundred men of the Forty-Fourth Regiment of Colonial Infantry whose ammunition had given out.[13] (According to these orders, a small number of blacks were to be captured specifically for use in medical experiments, particularly to develop tropical medicine for the planned German colonial expansion in Africa.) Yet, despite these orders, perhaps because of the fog of war, large numbers of the black colonial troops used by the French as cannon fodder—estimates run as high as 25,000—were captured and sent to prison camps inside Germany in 1940. (Still other black troops captured that year, including Léopold Sédar Senghor, were interned in camps in occupied French territory.) After some months, however, Nazi policy shifted, decreeing that those held captive in Germany be sent back to occupied France as a prophylactic measure for the Fatherland—and by 1942, there were 44,000 black prisoners being held on occupied French soil.[14]

From the time of their capture, those blacks headed for camps in Germany received special treatment. One account, from an African captured like Kuset with his colonial regiment in the Battle of the Somme in June 1940, is worth citing at length. Edouard Ouédraogo, who held the rank of *adjudant* (noncommissioned officer) in the Seventh Regiment of Tirailleurs Sénégalais, remembered:

I shipped out from Port Bouet [Côte d'Ivoire] all set to show the Germans that not only did I hate them as a Frenchman but that *Mein Kampf*, which I'd read in Ouagadougou, had turned me forever against Germany, for whom I was and would always be a monkey. So, I found myself at the front with the Germans coming at me first with machine guns, then with bayonets, and then with daggers. After a number of days of weariness and one of deadly combat, Captain Thomas ordered us to surrender. . . . Wounded in the face and thigh, I came out of the forest like the rest, surrounded by savages screaming their heads off. . . . I immediately recognized Hitler's men, legs spread, machine guns poised, doing the work they'd been taught from childhood: killing. The wounded were dispatched on the spot with a solid kick for good measure, the healthy were shot after first having their teeth knocked out with a gunstock. . . . My buddies fell, rewarded for having surrendered with a bayonet through the body, for the Germans aren't satisfied simply to kill—they need something more horrible to satiate themselves.

During all this, we were separated from the white Frenchmen. . . . Then a few wounded Germans were hauled out and they pleaded for revenge, which was quickly administered on several dozen prisoners who paid for their surrender with their lives. . . . We were shoved into trucks to be taken to Doullens. There, in a room the size of the one I live in today, they squeezed in hundreds of men. In the morning, all those who were small or weak and unable to resist the surrounding pressure died by serving as mattresses for the others, whom the S.S. dragged out in the morning, half-asphyxiated from the lack of air.

In this state of extreme weakness, we were forced to march at the speed of the cyclists who accompanied us across the Somme, the Pas de Calais, the North, Belgium, Holland, and toward Germany. We did sixty or seventy kilometers a day at a trot, and those who fell behind were killed. Interpreters were sent ahead to tell the people in the cities and villages we went through that it was formally prohibited to give Blacks either food or water. We marched in the following order: English, French, Arabs, and Blacks. Accompanying us on our march, there were always pistol shots, machine-gun bursts, and cries that sounded like mad dogs.

The Germans decided to go after tall Blacks . . . and I was pretty tall. So, I had to march bent over for days and finally switched to a column of Sudanese, where I had another surprise because the Germans had decided to kill all men with scarifications, since they believed they must be cannibals. Unfortunately, I had a large scar on my face and it made me curse the customs of my country. . . . The Boches truly have their own idea of fun and games: when we got to a stopping place, they knew that the Blacks, who'd been closely guarded during the day's journey, were dying to get a drink, so they placed us near a fountain in order to encourage our desire to drink and they left a machine-gun near by unattended, as if they were giving us some time on our own. Pushed by our tremendous thirst and thinking the guards inattentive, we made a rush for the fountain. The machine-gun opened fire, the first arrivals were mowed down, the others ran back, and the bastards fell over laughing at their little game. . . .

We arrived at the mouth of the Escaut in Holland, where barges awaited us. . . . After four days on the water without any food, we were offloaded at Wesel [Germany], where the Nazis were all waiting—men, women, and children of all ages—to spit on us, yell at us, and make signs that we would soon have our throats cut, in the meantime kicking us as we went by. . . . After two days of travel in cattle cars holding as many men as could be squeezed in shoulder to shoulder, with doors that were probably sealed with lead, we were brought to Stalag VI-C, where we were photographed and washed.

That's when I understood the German genius about "the master race"—they thought that since we were black, it was because the French colonizer hadn't sufficiently cared for our bodily hygiene. . . . We were beaten, stomped on, rolled, and dragged around by the feet. Every day, people would flock from the nearby villages to stare at us, like the animals in *Mein Kampf*, monkeys in a cage. They photographed us, forced us to smile, to show our filed teeth, and turn our faces so they could photograph our scars. They photographed us going after our lice and they'd throw us a cigarette in order to film what would happen. . . . At the hospital, Blacks were treated through a window and no matter what you suffered from, you'd be given the same pill through the window. They forced us to work in the canal up to our knees in water without boots. . . . When we returned, tired and famished, they forced us to dance and play the buffoon for them, so their films could be sure to be both hilarious and have that human touch.[15]

For black prisoners, then, things seem to have been especially awful. (Not that this wasn't also true in practice in the French *bagne* of Guyane, not to mention U.S. prisons.[16]) The Nazis are said to have enjoyed depriving them of food and watching them slowly die of hunger. Or worse: in the same stalag that was Kuset's home for a year, a black American GI was pulled out of the ranks one day on a whim and summarily shot in front of his comrades by a member of the SS.[17]

★   ★   ★

Kuset told Tooy some of what it had been like for him on that faraway battlefield. He and his commander, an "Englishman" (probably from the West Indies, perhaps a St. Lucian or Dominican, since he seems to have spoken French Creole and is described as being "black"), were down in a trench, hiding. All around them men were getting shot. Kuset told Tooy, "The war came to us three times"—there must have been three waves of attacks. Each time, all around him, he said, men were crying out for help, no one knew what to do. There was gunfire everywhere, dead men falling right on top of him. When he was hungry or thirsty, he'd take bread and water right off the body of a man he'd seen alive the day before. They fought, he said, with guns, with bayonets, and with daggers. Blood everywhere. There were two times he was sure he was going to die. One was when they began using him as messenger to carry papers behind the line. He did it three times but refused the fourth, saying he wasn't the only expendable body, so they sent another man who never returned. The second time was after he'd surrendered. He'd stood up in the trench to shoot, but the Englishman said, "Don't fire, they'll kill you," and they both threw down their rifles and raised their arms high in the air. The Germans took them off, beat them with rifle butts, and tied them up. And then they marched them toward the train that would take them to Germany.

At the railhead, they waited for several days as bombs dropping from the dive-bombers burst all about. When the train finally arrived, the Englishman said, "From here on out, it's every man for himself. You'll have to do whatever you must to survive." The Englishman managed to board the train. There were men everywhere pushing and shoving to get on. The Englishman called out to Kuset that he should try to get aboard. He had to climb on top of a whole lot of other men to make it. The place was packed and he literally vaulted over a crowd to get on. And then, when the train had gone a hundred meters or so, he looked back and saw the dive-bombers swarming down and then a bomb bursting, killing every single man who'd been left behind in the crowd.

Kuset continued his story, telling Tooy that the train took them all the way to Germany. They were kept there a whole year in a prison camp, where they were forced to wear an iron *mutête* (some sort of iron cage) on their backs, day and night.[18] They slept with it on. He and his English commander bore these iron cages for a whole year. When you slept, the edges of the cage cut deep into your skin. (When Kuset came back, he still had the scars—"I saw them," said Tooy.) They also pulled out all his fingernails and broke several fingers (as Saramaka Captain Antuáni, an intimate of Kuset after his return from the war, told me). The day they took off his iron cage, the prison guard came to see him and said, "The only thing to do now is escape. The next thing they're going to do to you is cut off your balls, because they don't want other 'nations' to make babies here! I can't open the prison door

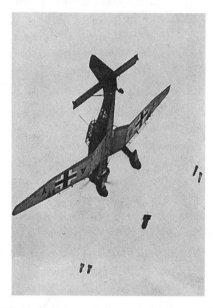

"The German Junkers JU-87 dive bomber, popularly known as the 'Stuka.' The pilots would swoop down at 70 to 80 degrees from an altitude of 10,000 feet and pull out of their dive at 3,000 feet or lower. The aircraft were fitted with sirens which emitted a high-pitched shriek."[1] This photo was taken from a following aircraft.

"I can only say what I saw, heard, lived and have kept in my memory. . . . I saw very well, about 800–1000 meters to my left, an artillery battery . . . which never stopped firing at the diving Stukas which ceaselessly attacked it: I can still see the little round clouds which its guns created in the sky around the swirling planes which continuously dispersed and returned." [Testimony of Paul-André Lesort, whose detachment found itself manning one of the defensive points in the hills above the Meuse. German air bombardment started at around 10:00 a.m. on the morning of May 13, 1940][2]

Another soldier, Gustave Folcher, with the Third North African Infantry Division, part of the Second Army, was on the high ground above the Meuse, slightly to the southeast of Sedan, when the aerial bombardment began that day: "Plane after plane, flying at the speed of a meteor, poured down bombs and bullets on us. It was terrifying to see those machines diving at us, spitting out their bombs with a shrieking which, we assumed, was made by the bombs as they fell. In any case the noise was terrible. . . . Each time the planes came back we emptied our guns at these balls of fire which seemed to mock our poor rifles."[3]

for you. But if you manage to get out of the building, you'll be free. It will have to be through the window." They were on the fourth floor. ("That's what Kuset told me," said Tooy.) After seven or eight in the morning, after the guards made their daily rounds, they began preparing their bedsheets to make them into parachutes. Once night fell, the Englishman said, "I'll go first. When you look down, if I made it, then you follow. But If I don't make it, don't come. Just stay and continue to take the punishment. Even without your balls, at least you'll be alive." So, the boss went first, bedsheet attached to his wrists and ankles, gliding all the way down. Then Kuset followed, gliding right down. . . . They got rid of the sheets, hid them, and walked all night, till dawn. Three days and three nights walking, without a bite of food, drinking from mud puddles. Then they came to a rail line that went all the way to . . . what do you call that country . . . Canada? (Tooy's memory seems to be reaching its limits . . .)

But Kuset's sister's son Seduáni, whom I met in 2004, picked up the story for me here, telling how Kuset and his comrades hijacked the first train that came along. "Kuset was the one who killed the engineer and drove the loco-motive." They traveled for three days and three nights before they got to the seashore. They knew they had to get to England. Luckily, the commander had a friend who worked on a ferry that could take them across, even though they had no money. He said to the commander, "You're still alive?" and they embraced. He told them, "Come back at three in the morning when everyone is asleep and I'll get you on." So they traveled on the ship for one night and one day. And they arrived in the commander's own country—England.[19] They kept Kuset and his commander three months in the hospi-tal there. Then they sent him back to France. He spent something like four years there before they sent him back to Guyane. It was on a ship called the *Saint-Domingue*. Tooy told me that Kuset's commander had given him some advice. He'd said, "If they offer you a medal, don't accept it. But if they offer you a paper, take it." (To me: "That's what you've found in the archives!") "As far as money goes," concluded Tooy, "they never paid Kuset a penny, he never got a single thing from France—and this was a man who took gunfire, the real thing, guns with a 3-kilometer range, you couldn't even see the men who were shooting at you!"

*   *   *

From the documents in the archives, I can reconstruct only a skeletal ac-count of Kuset's trajectory once he fell into German hands, though it is suf-ficiently evocative.[20]

"Wir sind die Moorsoldaten und ziehen mit dem Spaten ins Moor . . ."

(We are the peat bog soldiers, we're marching with our spades to the bog . . .)

We walked many miles to Stalag IV-B near Muhlberg in deep snow. No food or water for days. Most every one in my group was wounded and had trouble keeping up with the main body of prisoners. By the time we made it to Stalag IV-B we were in bad shape. Arrived at Stalag IV-B on January 10, 1945. We were sick, cold, hungry and bad, bad cases of dysentery. It got worse as time went by. We were in a very bad condition. Here I became Prisoner of War # 316538.[4]

My most vivid memories of our barracks were of the nights. . . . There was just room for all the exhausted men to lie down in the unheated building. We lay in groups of three to preserve warmth. . . . Very soon we learned to pull our tortured feet close to us because some dysentery victim was always staggering through the darkness toward the door trampling over frost-bitten and trench-foot-afflicted feet. I believe I have known no pain greater than that suffered for ten minutes following the mauling of one's frozen feet by a stampeding, dysenteried P.O.W. Older hands at the game would have known to nest down as far from the door as possible. We actually had no choice, coming in as we did at night to an already crowded barracks.

Very early in our stay we were processed through a shower and delousing unit common to German prisons. There bare brick and stone structures had a waiting room where we completely disrobed, leaving our boots stashed in the room, but tying our garments all in one bundle to be sent through a steam delouser. Two things were luxurious about the whole procedure. One was the hot shower where we could observe our flattening bellies but still muscular limbs, and let the warm streams of water splatter over our blue frost-bitten feet. The other was picking up our bundles of steaming clothes after shivering stark naked for a half hour in the waiting room. It was fortunate that one did not know until later how similar the procedure was to the gas chamber executions of the Jews.

The first day or two in the open air of [Stalag] IV-B convinced me of the drabness of the place. The sun seldom shone and the sky maintained a perpetual Baltic grayness. . . . Every day a workman came into the camp to pump liquid from a great open urinal near our barracks. It was hand-pumped into a horse-drawn tank wagon. This we could see being spread as liquid fertilizer in the fields beyond the fence. Thus, as the protein left our shrinking bodies it was pumped onto German fields as nitrogen fertilizer. I was impressed with the macabre quality of German efficiency in using their dwindling resources.

On the second or third day in IV-B a large number of us Americans were marched to another portion of the camp to await more processing. . . . We were photographed and numbered, much as a convict, and issued a P.O.W. tag bearing the number. This we wore like a dog tag.[5]

· captured June 8, 1940, near Soissons, in the valley of the Marne, with the Sixth company of the Twenty-third Regiment of Colonial Infantry
· listed as prisoner number 46,095 in Stalag IV-B, Mühlberg, Germany. (He would have arrived at this gigantic camp, close to the Czech border, after several days of rail travel packed into a cattle car. Built on 30 hectares to hold 10,000 prisoners, the stalag held over 25,000 when it was liberated in 1945—hundreds of thousands of men had passed through it, and several thousands are buried there. Prisoners were sent out in Kommandos to do various kinds of hard labor: harvesting potatoes, digging ditches, and similar farmwork in the bitter cold. The standard diet was one boiled potato per day. It appears Kuset stayed about a year.)
· transferred to Stalag IV-D, Dortmund, Germany
· transferred to Fronstalag 232, Luçon (Vendée), occupied France (and probably to the new Fronstalag 232 in nearby Savenay, when the Luçon camp was closed in August 1941)
· transferred February 1, 1942, to Fronstalag 133, Rennes (Ille-et-Vilaine), occupied France
· liberated from Fronstalag 133 on June 8, 1942 (after exactly two years of captivity) because of illness—another document contradicts this information, saying instead that he was repatriated from Germany to France for health reasons on May 6, 1942
· his name appears on a list of wounded and ill soldiers at the Supplementary Hospital of Decorative Arts of Limoges (Haute-Vienne) on July 24, 1942
· transferred October 26, 1942, to the Centre de Regroupement et Réadaptation at Fréjus and then to the Centre de Transition des Troupes Indigènes No 4, in the Hers Rang Company, on October 30, 1942
· transferred to the Centre de Regroupement et Réadaptation, sous-groupement 15, on April 1, 1943, then to sous-groupement 13 on August 1, 1944, and finally to sous-groupement 14 on October 1, 1944.
· on October 16, 1944, the C. R. R. became the Centre de Transition des Troupes Indigenes Coloniales no. 17
· promoted to the rank of private first class on January 12, 1944
· transferred to the camp of Souge on January 1, 1945
· as former prisoner of war, debarked at Cayenne aboard the S/S/ *St. Domingue* on June 11, 1945, and immediately transferred to the Bataillon d'Infanterie Coloniale de la Guyane.
· on February 3, 1946, demobilized and free to leave.

Tooy told me that after Kuset—whom Saramakas call simply Nyámísi ("Yam")—returned from the war, he lived for years in Saint-Laurent-

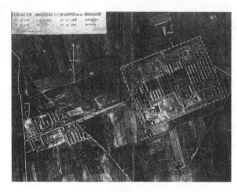

Aerial view, Stalag
IV-B, Mühlberg (Saxony),
Germany, where Kuset
spent a year.

Stalag IV-B. Guards
on parade inside
main gate. Copy-
right Barry Seddon.

Stalag IV-B.
The delousing
block. Photo by
N. Uchtmann, a
Dutch prisoner.

Stalag IV-B. One
of the six watch-
towers. Photo by
N. Uchtmann.

du-Maroni. At nearby Mana in 2004, I met Kuset's eldest son, Nokó, who said he was one of seven children Kuset had fathered on French soil with his mother, and that there were fourteen "outside children" there as well. After the war, to the general disapproval of Saramakas, Kuset refused to return to his home territory to be ritually purified. He adopted a Creole lifestyle, acting "French" as much as Saramaka, speaking to his children only in Creole. Sensiló told me he once accompanied Kuset on a visit to his friends the gendarmes of Mana, where Kuset impressed him by telling him that one of the bottles on the table was "vin de Bordeaux" and the other "vin de Paris"—he knew all that! Saramaka Captain Antonísi of Saint-Laurent told me how, each year on Bastille Day, he would accompany Kuset to the local meeting of Anciens Combattants.

Everyone who knew him said Kuset resisted speaking about the war. As for most others who had lived through its horrors, it was simply too painful for him to revisit the experience. What they learned from Kuset had been extracted by cajoling and insistence. Had it been up to him, he'd have told nothing of what had occurred.[21]

By 1974, when he finally did return to Saramaka quite ill, it was too late. The gods whom he had called on in battle—particularly the great carry-oracle of his natal village of Béndiwáta—had long since given up on him, and they simply let him die. In fact, the day Kuset died, while being ritually washed by the Béndiwáta Mother, Sensiló happened to be present; and he told me how Kuset had confided that once, on that faraway battlefield, another soldier had told him he really liked the foxhole Kuset had just dug and Kuset had given it to him, and how that night Kuset, in a foxhole some distance away, had watched in horror as a bomb killed the man. The Béndiwáta goddess had saved him, he was sure. But he'd never returned to thank her during all those years.

For Saramakas in French Guiana (which today means one-third of all Saramakas), Kuset is a special kind of hero. Indeed, when Tooy told me at Roland Legros's lumberyard, the first night I met him and the first time I'd ever heard of Kuset, that this man had fought in the war "for fifty-five years" and returned unscathed thanks to the charm he wore next to his heart—the charm that includes, as we have seen, venerable Christian spells against spears and arrows and invocations for divine intervention with sword and shield, many written by the pope, Saint Leo III, explicitly for Charlemagne, Emperor of the Occident, who used them in battle in the ninth century—Tooy might have had in mind an image of his warrior-hero that resembled, in its symbolism and power, another image that depicts an event at Mühlberg, one that this sleepy town would much

Titian, *The Emperor Charles V at Mühlberg* (1548). Oil on canvas, 332 × 279 cm. Museo del Prado, Madrid.

rather be remembered for than the stalag: the signal victory of the Holy Roman Emperor (who would have understood those spells better than most of us today) over the Protestant princes led by John Frederick, Elector of Saxony, a victory that took place almost exactly five hundred years before Kuset, on that same faraway frozen spot of earth, triumphed over the iron cage.

As Tooy and his friends never tire of saying, not a single Maroon from another group—no Ndyuka, no Paramaka, and, especially, no Aluku (despite their being French citizens by birth)—volunteered to fight for the Mère Patrie in France's darkest hour. Only a Saramaka, Kuset Albina. Today in the Saramaka neighborhood of Sable Blanc, on the outskirts of Saint-Laurent-du-Maroni, Captain Antonísi lives on the street officially named in his memory.

THUNDER AXES

⋆ 00000000 ⋆

On July 21, 1928, Melville and Frances Herskovits were visiting in the home of James Lawton, American consul in the colony of Suriname, when their host "brought out a finely-polished Indian axe-head which . . . Djukas . . . had found in the ground and insisted was a bolt thrown from the sky by the Gods." Melville was excited to find "another Africanism."[1]

Saramakas call them *dóndo-matjáu*—"thunder axes"—and say that they crash to the ground during lightning storms. Such stones have special powers and are kept in Komantí-óbia houses. Tooy once drummed a song during a Komantí session at his house that he later explained to me says, "If you work with the tree Komantí calls 'odú fankáiya,' you'll succeed," adding that this is the only tree in the forest that a thunder axe cannot fell.[2] Another time he sang me the Komantí song in which that tree, whose bark is called *aluangête* in Komantí, boasts of the impenetrability of its skin: *Zau tutú, zau djefelêbe. A kóti a kóti a baanabó, a kóti a kóti a kilínga, a nuwan geke búba, wán búba músu tan búba.*

Tooy told me,

> Busikí [male Wéntis]—they're the ones who have them. Thunder axes fall into the sea, but how could you ever find them? You see them falling into the sea at night [what we call shooting stars]. When a thunder axe falls, it calls out the strong name of Busikí—*Atjá-pêtêpêtê-fu-ádja*. The ones that fall in rivers are different, they call out *Atjá-pêtêpêtê-fu-ámba*.[3]

And then he tells me about a great stone in the middle of the sea. "It's called Sankúimadjú. If you call that name—*Atjá-pêtêpêtê-fu-ádja*—and you hear thunder before three hours have passed, you're as good as dead. Three hours must pass before there's thunder! That's why you must be very very careful with that name!" He also tells me about a stone—is it the same one?—that's under the sea and that's called Nyen-u-nyen. "Every person in the world has his name inscribed on that rock! When the Busikí mother and Busikí father erase your name on that stone, you're dead!"

On other occasions, Tooy tells me of other middle-of-the-sea phenomena. "There's a tree in the middle of the sea, sticking up—it's called Djuntolóbi. When one of its branches falls, a baby is born somewhere, a hunter kills a large animal, or someone dies." Or again, "Busikí sings a song about a great rock in the middle of the sea. When the sea comes crashing up against it, trying to break it, the rock says, 'I was here when you arrived. I'm going to be here long after.' And the sea recedes in a spray of froth." He sings, *Benko! Kaíndjima kaí kántamba-o, kaíndjima-e, mi óbia-e.* "That stone's name is Kaíndjima. This is Komantí language, Brother!"

Tooy tells me how dangerous it is to work with thunder axes. "If you pick one up without knowing how, you're dead! That 'iron'"—he sometimes calls thunder axes "iron"—"there aren't twelve óbia bosses in the world who can catch one as it flies by. [He imitates the terrifying noise it makes zipping by.] But I know three who've done it! By the seaside! If you take one and *wísi* someone [try to kill them supernaturally] with it, they'd better know exactly what to do, or they're dead. When you work with a thunder axe, you and it become *máti* [friends]. If someone tries to use it against you, when it arrives your óbia [your Komantí spirit] will ask it, 'what do you think you're doing here?'" In Georgetown, Guyana, on a visit once, Tooy met an old Amerindian shaman who had his thunder axe on an altar next to a lighted candle. He showed Tooy how when he looked into its polished black surface, he could see the face of the person who was trying to kill him.

On the final day of our visit in early 2005, Tooy took Sally and me into his Dúngulálí house and, amidst the rituals of parting, showed us his own thunder axe, lying near Akoomí's bloodstained post. He whispered that when it flies by, it says that its name is *Hánkuma-nítji* or *Hánkuma-nítji hé bêête bêête súmani.* He reached down and passed it to us to cradle in our hands—heavy, shiny, blue-black, and perfect as the day it fell from the sky.

MASTER OF THE HOUSE

Ma Yaai had been away at her house in Saint-Laurent-du-Maroni for a couple of months, exercising her most effective form of protest against Tooy's devoting too much attention to Céline. They talk often by phone, in part because he is so dependent on her Wénti-god. When Tooy hears that Sally and I are going to Saint-Laurent for a couple of days, he decides the time has come and persuades Ma Yaai by phone to return with us to Cayenne.

Once we've finished our research in that border town, we drive over to Yaai's place, following Tooy's verbal instructions. It's in the strange Maroon ghetto called La Charbonnière, where Swiss chalet and Eastern Maroon architecture were melded together in a 1980s public-housing scheme. She takes us upstairs to a small room she has set aside for her "master," the Wénti called Bási Yontíni. She places his bottle, wrapped in black cloth with a red sash, which had been on an altar, in a special soft valise that also contains other accessories of the god. And then baskets, valises, rice sacks, cassava sacks, okra sacks, machetes, and finally two children are squeezed into the small car, with Yaai's god valise on her ample lap. We set out for the four-hour trip.

An hour out of Saint-Laurent, we see a young man selling a partially butchered howler monkey by the roadside and offer to buy it as a gift. The hunter turns out to be a nephew of Yaai's, and he adds some bush-hog meat for good measure. Before long, the car starts to wobble, as if a tire has a bubble. So, we bump along slowly for a couple of hours until we reach the next gas station, where we're unable to figure out the problem. Yaai is convinced that her Wénti is causing the bumping. It doesn't stop until well after dark, when we reach the outskirts of Cayenne. Now she's sure it was the Wénti.

As soon as we've piled out and the goods are unloaded, Tooy, overflowing with joy at having Yaai back and with gratitude to us for having brought her, ushers her and the two of us into his Wénti chamber, where her god and his join us almost immediately. We've never heard such sweet singing as the two gods greet each other, with the several men who are outside in the waiting room joining in on the choruses. There's talk about how the car bumped around because Bási Yontíni is so "heavy." There's joking about how I "took" Tooy's wife, playfully accusing me of being like Parrot, who, after sleeping with someone else's wife, boasted (in drum language), *Suun fu akí, suun fu andá. Suun fu akí, suun fu andá. Saanfo maíni, suun fu andá.* Tooy's god announces that this house doesn't belong to him, it's Bási Yontíni's. He's the master of the house!

Here are my notes made listening to the tape recording:[1]

Yaai's god begins to sing, as Tooy's joins in, *Aladjímèèdji-e, aladjímèèdji-o, téé na Alosúgbe,* a prayer to Ma Dígbeónsu to protect them after the voyage to a new place [see p. 16 above; the last three words mean "as far as the sun"]. Lots of gentle chuckling. . . . Tooy's god explains to me that "the big man [Yaai's god] doesn't travel without that bottle there," as he places it in the center of the Wénti altar. Tooy's god sings out, *Djúa na bolóbi-o e i fankáiya, djúa téé a mi tatá bolóbi-e, djúa téé na bolóbi-e.* Tooy explains, "That's what happened to the woman [Yaai]. It's Komantí! When you leave your house and go somewhere, nothing should block your path, so that you can get home safely again. Father Bolóbi's children [apparently jaguars] all went out, but they returned "between his legs" safely—this is their prayer that all will go well." And he sings it again, before switching to another Komantí song: *Djúa bête denaí-o-o, miam, djúa bête denái, mi bási-o, bête dê a únu kámba-e* [the last phrase means, "wonderful things are in your room"]. He explains: "'The wonderful things you have, give me some!' But over there in Komantí country, they have guns that really shoot you, machetes that really cut you, clubs that really knock you. So you say [sings]: *Djúa bête denaí-o-o, miam, djúa bête denái, mi bási-o, bête dê a únu kámba-e. Djúa bête denaí-o-o, ná fu toló ná fu taká ná fu ofalá, siisí mámba.* [spoken explanation:] 'I'm praying for good, I'm not asking for a gun [Komantí *otoló*] or a club or a machete [Komantí *ofalá*] or a spear [Komantí *ataká*] but for great pleasure [Komantí *siisí mámba*].'" Tooy's god suddenly says, "Where's that Dángogó kid? [referring to Kalusé] He's supposed to meet us here." Yaai's god sings out, *Mi mandá ódio, mi mandá ódio. Tatá Yembu . . . Gonkíma-o. . . .* ["I send greetings, I send greetings to Tatá Yembuámba," whom the god addresses with the Komantí word for "friend," *agonkíma.*] Her god sings another: *Tangí-o, davié, tangí dê a múndu-e. Tangí dê a mámba-o. Tangí dê a mámba* ["Thanks, blessings, thanks to the universe, thanks to the river"]. And then another (with men in the other room chorusing softly): it seems to have something to do with *"Dagowé, mi gádu"* ["Dagowé"—the sacred snake—"my god"]. Tooy's god sings, *Sináimbo mámbo-ye, óbia Sináibo-i, u dê a Sindyábo kôndè kaa, kamía mbéi waiya-waiya-waiya-o* ["Sináimbo, óbia Sináibo, we've arrived at Sindyábo's village, the sea is rocking"]. Then Sináibo says his praise name, a long string of "language." . . . Tooy's god starts another song as others chime in: *Wenú-ee . . . gádu-ee.* Then another, *Gwemidjé, Gwemidjé, Gwemidjé-lò, Aduné-o.*

Another, *Mi muyêè-ee. Ugwéla-e. Mi ku únu-o, Gwéla-e* ["My wife, Ugwéla, me and you, Gwéla"]. Tooy's god, speaking a bit slowly, slightly slurred, asks Tooy's nephew Frank, "Remember what I told you in the forest the other day?" Frank says, "What did you tell us, Papa?" "I told you [singing], *Wánwan fu wán, nanga wánwan fu djawélu, wánwan fu wán, nanga wánwan fu djawélu, wánwan fu wán, asógáigái fu kôdomè, wánwan fu wán, asógáigái fu kôdomè.*[2] Well, there was a reason I told you that. The thing you were going to do with those leaves. . . . So, that's been said now. Let's have fun!" Tooy's god makes his strange little laugh (heh heh heh heh heh). He starts telling us about how we went all the way to Saint-Laurent and brought Yaai back, but then her god interrupts, singing, *Gádu téi yobekee, gádu téi Gamu tjái* . . . "We're finished," declares Tooy's god. He asks Yaai's god, "Do you want to leave now?" Yaai yawns loudly and Yontíni leaves, as she throws down her head and shivers noticeably. Tooy's god then speaks to her god anyway, saying we are calling on him to help with some work the next day at cock's crow. We can't do the work without him. We're going to prepare a large washing/bath. Anyone who wants to can participate. Anyone who doesn't want to won't. But this is for the kid here [me], who came here from another country, it's to give him pleasure. [This is said to Yaai's god as a sort of prayer.] Then Tooy's god sings a long song, which he says is to give me thanks: *Tangí mi yéi, manamutámbo ó oó oló* ["I hear thanks, *manamutámbo*"]. Interruption by a call on Tooy's cell phone—a client wants an appointment, and he speaks to her normally, in Creole. Then a new song from Tooy's god, *Wemee-e, mi na Tósida, Tósida bígi dá mi e* . . . ["*Wemee*, I'm an anaconda god, water gods are what I like"]. Tooy's god seems delighted with himself, chuckling in falsetto, talking in slurred, slow speech. But he reminds me once again before he leaves us that it's Bási Yontíni who's master of the house.

★　★　★

On July 6, 1929, Melville Herskovits noted in his field journal that he and Frances had bought two "gods" at the downstream Saramaka village of Disión. Of the first, he wrote, "Small—(wenti Nyamusu?) Wata Wentu[.] put Sweeti Sopi on it—women ask of it children."[3] When I asked Tooy if he could tell me anything about this Wénti, he immediately broke into song: *Mamá Nyamútu, Tatá Nyumútu, wáta séki, sómba-we* . . . ("Mamá Nyamútu, Tatá Nyumútu, the water is rough, gods . . . "). And he explained, "Mamá Nyamútu is the god of that place, a true Wénti from the tidal zone. It doesn't belong just to Disión but to all clans—it lives near Jews Savannah."

Another time, Tooy told me how a strange man named Atjúa-Gbéung (whom we'll meet later, in another context), was once paddling upstream from the city. Near the mouth of Cassipora Creek at Jews Savannah, he was cutting from east to west when the water in the rapids became very rough.

Mamá Nyamútu.

He placed a ball of kaolin into the rapids and sang out: *Mamá Nyamútu, Tatá Nyumútu, wáta séki sómba-we.* . . . The water calmed in an instant and he passed through safely.

Shortly before her death in 1972, Frances Herskovits, Melville's widow, told me how the two of them had made a large collection of Saramaka objects for the Hamburgisches Museum für Völkerkunde in 1929. She related that in the late 1940s they had received a letter from a curator reporting that a good half of the collection had been burned in a wartime fire caused by an Allied air raid. They hadn't ever managed to get back there to see what was left, and she urged me to visit. (It was the only time I met her.) When Sally and I finally examined the collection in 1977,[4] we found, among the eighty-six pieces that had survived (of the 193 originally in the collection), the wooden image of this Wénti, Mamá Nyamútu, who guards the rapids near Jews Savannah. With her raffia skirt, bush-hog whiskers, and red and black seeds for eyes, the 36-centimeter-high god image, stained with kaolin, is still in a storage cabinet in Hamburg.

★   ★   ★

Most of the Wéntis that Tooy spends his time thinking about—singing and drumming for, doing rites for—are, like Bási Yontíni or Mamá Nyamútu, saltwater gods, whose home is the sea, though they can swim up rivers or walk among the living when they choose. But there are other Wéntis who live in fresh water and never venture beyond their riverine domain.

Tooy parses Wéntis as follows: saltwater ones are called Tósu-kpêke-kpêke, freshwater ones are Tósu-kédje-kédje. When you give a freshwater Wénti saltwater to drink, she'll vomit. But when you give some to a saltwater Wénti, she will tell stories! He goes further: saltwater Wéntis never work with blood, only sweetwater ones do. Like Dúnguláli-Óbia, saltwater Wéntis don't mix with death or dead people. And like Dúnguláli, saltwater Wéntis don't drink rum. (In Paramaribo, he says, from Combé Creek downstream is the realm of saltwater Wéntis. If you have a freshwater Wénti in your head, you can't cross the bridge at Combé Creek, or you'll die—freshwater and saltwater Wéntis don't like one another.) He draws one final distinction: saltwater Wéntis never possess a second person after the first has died. If a Wénti possesses a second person, you know it's a Wénti "mixed" with something else, for example a god with a saltwater mother and a freshwater father. For Tooy, true Wéntis are the ones from the sea.[5]

★ ★ ★

The Nasí clan makes claims to have been the first among Saramakas to have discovered a freshwater Wénti, a certain "Mása Wénti," a.k.a. Adonkubónsu —an event I can date to the final decades of the eighteenth century. At Balibakúba Plantation on the Commewijne River, a woman named Pikí Efá served as a house slave. Whenever she came down to the wharf to wash dishes, she would see something—she wasn't sure what—underneath, something like a large fish. Frightened, she eventually threw some cassava juice (which contains hydrocyanic acid and is toxic) on it—the way people today often throw gasoline on a sacred snake, to get it to leave without killing it—and it never came back.

Some time later, this woman was liberated from slavery by Kwadjaní and Kwakú Étja during a raid. But another Wénti witnessed their flight. Now, in those days, at the mouth of Cassipora Creek near Jews Savannah, all the Wéntis used to get together for an annual "play." When they were all gathered, the one who saw the abduction reported to the others, and they decided to put a Wénti watchman at the mouth of Mawasí Creek to punish the matrilineage of the woman who had poured poison on their kinsman.

Meanwhile, living with the Nasís who'd liberated her, Pikí Efá bore a son, Matési, a.k.a. Báya, and two daughters, Tjiká and Odukempenú. Once, Piki Efá's husband, who was from the Dómbi clan, one of his kinsmen, and Báya were on their way downstream with a raft of logs when the Wénti watchman saw them and pulled Báya off and underwater. The husband had a god in his head who told them that Báya wasn't dead. So, they began playing Wénti songs and drums. After twenty-one days, they saw the water "boiling" like a rapids and Báya reappeared, rising from the water on a golden mat (some people say it was a golden stool), holding a rattle and a spear and with a metal ring on his biceps. When they went and took Báya into a canoe, the mat (or stool) descended into the river. Later, a Wénti possessed Báya— it was Adonkubónsu. After Báya died, the other Wéntis sent that Wénti's chief officer, who was called Potíi, to possess a man called Mandó. He would dive underwater and, one by one, carry all the Wénti paraphernalia—the spear, the rattle, and the biceps ring that belonged to Báya—back to their underwater village. (Perhaps one of these things—the rattle?—one man told me, is still at the Nasí village of Kambalóa.) All this happened in the Kambalóa matrilineage called Gaánbokió-bêe. Forty or fifty years ago, when they would play Wénti there with the *agidá* (snake-god drum), Chief Agbagó used to come and Todjê, his Wénti, would dance.

★ ★ ★

In conversation, Tooy frequently alludes to connections between Papágádu (boa constrictor gods) and saltwater Wéntis. Besides his ruminations about how a special class of Papágádu—those with the head of an agouti—give Wéntis clothes to wear when they step out of the sea to walk on the earth, just the way, he says, the police stamps your visa when you visit another country, he often tells me these two kinds of gods are just friends. As a man who frequently "domesticates" various types of gods, causing "wild spirits" to become tame, to speak appropriately through their human medium, to tell their name and their needs, Tooy is intimately familiar with the special leaves used for each class of god. And he's told me more than once that, despite significant differences between these two types of gods (Wéntis don't get involved with death while Papágádus do, for example), most Wénti leaves work well with Papágádus and most Papágádu leaves work well with Wéntis. Moreover, Thursday is the day sacred to Wéntis as it is to Papágádus. "In the end," he says, "Papágádus and Wéntis do many of the same things."

Anthropologist Diane Vernon, who has spent years working with Ndyuka Maroons and has written about their money magic, provides some helpful clues.[6] She argues that Ndyukas have two kinds of magic to help them get rich. One is considered predatory and evil, involving supernatural creatures (Bakuu) who are bought from whitefolks in order to trick people into giving you money. This kind of magic, she says, is associated with theft and witchcraft. The other is the magic of Papagadu, which is local and considered benign, and helps Ndyuka men gently seduce money out of whitefolks. This kind of magic is associated with honest labor, whether logging or wage work. Vernon's discussion of how Ndyukas mobilize Papagadus, their possessing boa-constrictor spirits, in the service of getting wealth, suggests to me a functional similarity to Saramaka Wénti practices. Though Papagadus and Wéntis, as Tooy insists, are different in significant ways (snakes vs. sea gods, affinities with death vs. affinities with life), if properly approached and handled, Papagadu spirits can do, for Ndyuka men, something close to what Wéntis do for Saramakas, persuading whitefolks and others who hold riches to open their hearts and purses and share some of the wealth around.

Wéntis remain a remarkable and unique Saramaka phenomenon—like Dúnguláli-Óbia and Mamá-Gádu, part of Kódji's rich spiritual legacy, developed at a moment when Saramaka canoemen were for the first time confronting in really intense form the exigencies of the global economy. In recognizing their functional similarity to Ndyuka Papagadus, Tooy takes nothing away from their specialness, their highly developed rites, songs, and drums, and all that Wénti lore that he never tires of telling me about. "Did you know," he once asked me, "that a normal ship can't go near Wénti country, or it'll catch on fire from the heat? And if Wéntis take you on their own ship, it gets so hot as you near their country that you turn to cinders?" "Well, then, how have people visited there and returned to tell the tale?" I ask. "If you're man enough, when you arrive, you become yourself again. Flibánti told me all about it. He goes to visit his wife [Yowentína, a Wénti] almost every single day! Just remember not to eat cooked food when they offer it. Stick with bananas or mangos."

*　*　*

On the fourth day of Tooy's visit to Martinique, the morning after Roland's bath in the sea, Sally and I showed him a wooden sculpture of the Brazilian sea goddess Iemanjá, which we'd bought in Cachoeira (Bahia) a couple of years earlier when we had Fulbrights to Brazil. Tooy looked at her lovingly, saying, "What a great thing that would be to put in my óbia house!" And in the following days he often asked me to say her name for him. He liked to pronounce it as "Yemánzáa."[7]

Iemanjá in our house.

Two years later, when he was awaiting open-heart surgery in the hospital in Martinique, he sang me a song he'd heard in a dream: *Mamá, mi mamá Yemánzáa | Mi ta haíka i, yôôô | Yéi mi mamá yaaa* ("Mother, my mother Yemánzáa, I'm waiting for you, Do you hear, my mother?"). "I walked north in the dream," he explains, "and went down a big hill and then turned east on an old path up a hill where I saw a very large jaguar, sound asleep." Do you think that's a bad omen? he asks. No, it's good! he laughs. And he sings the song to Yemánzáa again.

In 2003, on our way home from another stay in Brazil, we stop in Cayenne and Tooy mentions he's thinking about making an altar to Yemánzáa. And then finally, on our first visit in 2005, we present Tooy with our statue of the goddess for him to keep, and he sings us a new song to her: *Ma Yemá-e, Mamá Yemá, gaán tangí tangí mi ta bégi únu fu di súti ódi f'i, Ma Yemázála, mi ta méni i-o, mi mamá, Mamá Yemá, mi ta bégi i yéti fu di súti ódi f'i yéi mamá-e, Ma Yemá . . . záa!* ("Mother Yemánzáa, I offer thanks for your sweet greetings, I keep thinking of you, I continue asking you for those sweet greetings of yours, Mother Yemánzáa") He's overjoyed but decides to keep the goddess in her wrapping until Yaai gets back from her stay in Saint-Laurent, so she and her god can participate in placing her on the Wénti altar.

During one of the visits of Tooy's god in 2005, he instructs me to make a Wénti altar at our home in Martinique. "Here's what to do to make sure you have no problems, to make your life the way it ought to be. When you get home, on the lowest terrace facing the sea, where you'd go if you were going to get into a boat, find a short little table and place it there. Cover it with whatever pretty cloth you wish. But be sure it's a Thursday, the Wéntis' day! Then you and Madame [Sally] should sit down there, you and those people will eat together. Go sit down and drink with them. Call on Ma Yemá to come and join you! You and she should work together." And then he adds, "But do watch out on the west side there. There's an Adátu [a toad-spirit Komantí] who has designs on your wife. He's not evil. Let him come to the altar, too. Beer should never be lacking there for the Wéntis, sugarcane syrup for the Earth Mother, a bit of honey for the Adátu. In the evenings go sit down there, in the mornings go sit down there. Drink a little with them!"

On the last day of that visit, Tooy's god, Dúnuyángi, prays as he pours out libations of beer in the Dúnguláli shrine: "Ma Yowentína, take some, Ma Díg-beónsu, take some, Ma Yemánzáa, take some. We're at the seaside! Let's drink together!" And when I ask a few minutes later who the gods are who actually live in Tooy's house, he says there are three women and six men—one of the men stops him as he begins to say his name, but the women, he says, are Ma Yowentína, Ma Dígbeónsu, and Ma Yemánzáa (now fully integrated into his pantheon). Even if he can't for the moment name the men, it's clear that, in addition to Dúnguláli-Óbia and Tatá Dúnuyángi, Tooy's main man remains Bási Yontíni, master of the house.

STORM CLOUDS

A week after his enstoolment, with the visitors gone and life returning to its earlier pace, Captain Tooy ventures out in the evening with his machete and an old rice sack to gather some medicinal leaves a mile or so along the canal. From the brush, three men in ski masks jump him, and though he's able to get in a chop or two himself, they cut him up badly with their machetes and leave him bleeding on the ground.

Tooy's had premonitions. The captain business was never his choice. He knew it would foster jealousy and the sorcery that goes with it. He's known he's been negligent for a long time (and it's nagged at him) about following up on messages from Paramaribo, where a brother's divination repeatedly finds that he needs to make a trip there to appease the avenging spirit called Frenchwoman. He's also had his differences with the Association of Young Active Saramakas of Guyane, who'd like him—at least in certain contexts—to act more "modern," not to go off on tangents about First-Time stories or ritual lore every time they come to him with a matter concerning the French bureaucracy. And there's a festering problem with an Amerindian woman he had a daughter with a decade before, who's after him for child support and is threatening legal action.

So, the assault didn't come completely out of the blue. And the storm clouds continue to gather.

★ ★ ★

We visit Tooy the next morning in the hospital—the first time he's seen a doctor in his life, he says with only slight exaggeration. He's just out of the operating room, where they've stitched up large swaths of his face and shoulder. The assailants had just missed an eye when they slashed his cheek and vital tendons when they cut deep into his shoulder; yet despite the X's they traced on his back, the surgeon tells us he should be fine in a couple of weeks. Through his bandages, the ever-ebullient Tooy describes the assault and then teaches us a proverb in the esoteric language of Luángu (also called Lángu): *Lobangáya dyè a sabánga déndu*. *Lobangáya*, he says, means "tongue"; *sabánga*, "teeth"—tongue lives among teeth, tongue and teeth have fights, teeth bite tongue, but in the end they have to live together, and so should everyone else. (I recall that in the 1970s, my friend Peléki used to tell me that no one knows Luángu like the people of Bundjitapá—Tooy's home village.)

A large wooden house has burned down in the city, and Tooy and some of the visitors to his bedside speculate about the conflagration's origins, invoking an *óbia* called "firebomb." Later, Tooy confides that people from Guyana know this *óbia*. If you do one of them wrong, say, sleep with their wife, they'll throw it upon you. Its particularity is that they can specify exactly what should burn—so, it might burn everything inside your house but not touch the house itself, or it might turn the man in the bed to cinders but not even touch the woman. He assures me that almost every man from Georgetown knows its secret, and he asks me, "Since you travel a lot, if you ever go there, be sure to get it for me."

I consider the wonders of the Caribbean collective imagination. One of the most powerful images of Guyana—etched in people's memory through media as diverse as the Mighty Sparrow's calypso ("I en care if all a BG bun down") or Martin Carter's poem ("Guyana—The Unfinished Tragedy")—is Black Friday (February 16, 1962), which witnessed "the terror, the exhilaration, the intensity, and the extraordinary image of a wooden city on fire on a day . . . that represented a leap across the threshold of racial conflagration from which the society has yet to recover after some four decades."[1] Refracted, transported, reinterpreted years later into the powerful idea among Saramaka migrants in French Guiana that people from Georgetown can throw their firebomb *óbia* at will.

∗   ∗   ∗

It was around this time that I had to give Tooy the news that Roland was pulling out of his status as client. Ever since I'd seen his face when he noticed Tooy's "fetish" in the airport, I'd had my suspicions. Whenever I saw Roland, he'd assure me he would come up with the rest of the money. Indeed, each time we went to Guyane (which we'd now done several times in connection with a book, *Les Marrons*, we were researching), he'd give me 10,000 francs to transmit in cash, and by now he'd paid off half his debt. But things weren't going well for him, and he'd lost confidence in the Saramaka cure. Tooy seemed less worried about the money—he told me to ask Roland for a final payment of 5,000 francs and to forget the rest—than about Roland's lack of confidence. The idea that Saramakas weren't competent to solve a problem such as Roland's was a collective shame, but on the other hand, he reasoned, Roland had never really seemed to understand what he and Kalusé were trying to do for him.

★ ★ ★

The next year, Tooy caught his own version of a firebomb. The Amerindian woman whom Tooy understood to be threatening him for child support was in fact accusing him of having raped her a dozen years earlier and, with the help of a gifted lawyer, got a $33,000 indemnity from the State for herself and a seven-year prison sentence for him.

Inadvertently, she also saved his life. Upon Tooy's entrance into Cayenne's super-modern penitentiary in February of 2002, the prison doctor discovered, during the routine admission exam, that if Tooy didn't have open-heart surgery to replace his aortic valve, he'd be dead within months if not weeks. In France, the State routinely pays all medical costs, and Tooy, escorted by two gendarmes, was soon on an Air France flight to the only place in the French Caribbean that has adequate facilities for this major surgery—Martinique. Though he remained under heavy guard, I was able to get the Court's permission to visit him for a half hour every single day.

SEX, MAGIC, AND MURDER

★ 06212001/1754 ★

Happier times. We were squeezed around Tooy's dining room table—Tooy, his older brother Sensiló, Sally, and me—the TV with its rabbit ears on the cluttered sideboard soundlessly miming a French game show. On the oilcloth, Sally had laid out separate bowls of rice and stewed chicken and okra sauce, with a large plastic pitcher of water. Tooy heaped up his plate as usual, announcing that, as a matter of principle, he never took seconds. He loaded another plate for Sensiló, who had been blind for the past five years but had once been among the strongest and most successful Saramaka canoemen in French Guiana. It was my first meal with Sensiló, who was making a rare visit from Paramaribo—illegally, since he doesn't have French papers. There was no way he would miss his favorite brother's enstoolment as captain of the Saramakas of Cayenne.

As we began to eat, Tooy asked me (showing me off to his brother, as it were) to tell them what I knew about "the sinking at Gaándan Falls," a First-Time story I'd often discussed with him—how the whites sent an emissary during the eighteenth-century wars, how the Saramakas tricked him and stole the goods sent as tokens of peace, and how they sent him and his companions to their deaths as their canoe plunged over the great falls. I obliged, enjoying the occasion, while we wolfed down our food—Saramaka men eat rapidly, as if someone were about to take away their plate. At a certain point in the story I mentioned Kwasímukámba.

With a muffled roar, Sensiló threw up his arms, jumping up from the table, upsetting his plate of food, overturning the water pitcher, and stumbling cane-less through the open doorway. Tooy followed him quickly. I sat stunned.

It would take me two years to learn why I'd caused Sensiló such distress. The next morning, he greeted me as if nothing had happened, and we continued to enjoy each other's company during his occasional visits to Cayenne. Tooy would tell me, when I pressed, only that Sensiló "couldn't hear" that name.

Sensiló.

I was proud of the knowledge I had about Kwasímukámba, the double agent whom Saramakas finally bested in the mid-eighteenth century.[1] For historically minded men, he remains the prototypical symbol of betrayal and his highly secret story a constant reminder of the necessity to be guarded in all relations with outsiders. He stands as a dark warning star at the heart of the Saramaka moral universe. I knew literally hundreds of details about his complex life. But I was clueless as to his special meaning to Sensiló.

★   ★   ★

Cut to the high-security prison wing of the hospital in Martinique. Two years have passed. Tooy's open-heart surgery is scheduled for two days hence. The gendarmes are rougher than usual when they pat me down for my half-hour visit—the pen and folded-up sheet of paper in my pocket don't sneak by today, though the apple I bring as a gift is permitted. Keys turn and the steel door clanks open. Tooy is sitting on his bed looking alone and frightened, in an isolation cell thousands of miles from home, treated like the danger-ous criminal he isn't and about to undergo the dreaded knife. I take the only chair and try some comforting small talk.

The day before, I'd snuck in a photo of an impressive all-white, stylish, vintage yacht (named *Talatha G*) that had anchored in the cove below our house. Now, he tells me he's dreamed a new song, thinking about that Wénti ship and his own predicament. In deep voice, softly, he sings, *Ma Dígbeónsu, Heépi wi-o! | Ma Dígbeónsu, Heépi wi-o! | U dê téé na alónugbe | Tjá u gó a niviélo.* He explains, "This is a Wénti song—we're out here in the world, but we don't know where we are, we don't know where we'll land. In Wénti language, *Alónugbe* means 'sun,' *niviélo* means 'sea.'" (Thus: "Mother Dígbeónsu, help us! We've come as far as the sun, bring us back to the sea.") He looks at the photo, which he's stored under his mattress, and says admiringly, "That ship could really carry you right to the bottom of the sea, all the way to Wénti country!"

Tooy clears his throat and announces he wants to offer me something, though it's something he can give me only in very small doses. "Gweyúnga," he begins, "had a wife named Hwéte—one of Alabi's wife's people." I could tell I was about to receive a rare gift. "Something was coming out of the forest and stealing chickens, dogs, and, one time, even a child from Gweyúnga's village. Who," Tooy asks rhetorically, "was doing it?" He leans toward me and whispers conspiratorially, "Kwasímukámba!" And then he throws up his hands to indicate that the dose is finished.

Now, I knew that Kwasímukámba had posed as a new runaway when he joined the Saramakas in 1754 and that he'd lived for some months with their chief, Ayakô, before escaping back to the city to lead a massive colonial army against them. What I'd never considered was who he'd first encountered when he showed up in Saramaka territory, who—in Saramaka parlance—had "caught" him. Or that he might have had a history in Saramaka before he arrived at the chief's village. This was what Tooy had now started to reveal—a highly charged story that places Kwasímukámba near the center of his own history and plumb center in that of Sensiló.

*   *   *

Over the course of many months, in dribs and drabs, during my hospital visits and my prison visits and finally as a free man once again, Tooy very slowly filled me in.

Kwasímukámba, the wily faithful slave, enacted a daring plan to "escape" from slavery, pose as a runaway, and spy on the Saramakas. From his forest camp at the head of Wet Eye Creek, he would raid Gweyúnga's village in the dead of night to steal a chicken, or it might be a dog or even a child, to sacrifice to his óbia.

Gweyúnga decided to act—who could be ruining his village? He went into the forest to set a trap. First, he built himself a shelter on a hillock and then, with his Tonê pot, brought down the rains. Just before dawn, Gweyúnga heard the forest begin to tremble: Kwasímukámba appeared at his doorstep seeking shelter. Gweyúnga just sat there, puffing away on his Tonê pipe, softly singing Tonê songs. Kwasímukámba stood transfixed. And then suddenly he collapsed with a thud. Gweyúnga had "smoked" him—his óbia had put him to sleep!

When Kwasímukámba awoke, Gweyúnga invited him back to his village—but he had miscalculated Kwasímukámba's powers, for by the time they arrived, Gweyúnga's strength was already ebbing. "Kwasímukámba," Tooy concludes, "was simply riper than he was." And Gweyúnga was to pay the consequences.

It began with sex. Gweyúnga had two wives: Béti-Kadósu, who'd come with him from Africa and given birth to their son Antamá, and the much younger Hwéte. By this time in his life, Gweyúnga was, as Tooy puts it, having trouble getting his cock to crow. (It's not just that he was well into his sixties—Kwasímukámba had also been working him over with óbia, Tooy explained.) So, whenever Gweyúnga went to spend the night with one wife, Kwasímukámba would pay a visit to the other.

What happens next is recounted in rival versions, though both pin full blame on Kwasímukámba. Tooy is persuaded of the truth of his own account, because he heard it right from the mouth of Sensiló's óbia (who, as we shall soon see, has special reason to know)—Hwéte informs Kwasímukámba that she is pregnant with his child, and he decides to make an óbia to kill Gweyúnga before he finds out. He sends Gweyúnga off to set fish traps, empties out his Tonê pipe, lines the bowl with iguana skin (the strongest taboo of Tonê), and loads the tobacco back in. When Gweyúnga returns and smokes his pipe, his belly roars, and it is only hours before Death kills him. The other version, which I heard in the 1970s from Mètisên, a man brought up in Tooy's natal village, depicts Hwéte as Gweyúnga's new wife who begs Kwasímukámba to make her a love potion to bind her husband more strongly to her, but the jealous Kwasímukámba, instead, prepares a death potion, which she then innocently feeds her husband. In Mètisên's words,

> Hwéte peeled some very ripe plantains and cooked them until they were just right. Then she mashed them with peanuts, and while she was mashing threw the óbia in with them. Then she added palm oil. If you saw it, you just knew it would be sweet! . . . As soon as Gweyúnga had taken the first bite, his belly roared *huun!* And it began to hurt him terribly. People made medicines and performed rites till they were weary. All night long! And then, around five in the morning, he breathed his last.[2]

There's no disagreement about what happened in the aftermath of the great man's death. Rumors were flying. Palavers were held. And when they raised Gweyúnga's corpse in divination, it made it clear that his wife, Hwéte, had killed him.

Hwéte knew nothing of the verdict and remained in mourning confinement. Meanwhile, the villagers decided to build a coffin big enough for two, Gweyúnga on top, Hwéte on bottom. Tooy told me it took them two full days to cut enough planks for that coffin.

Some people hoped that Antamá would avenge his father's murder by finishing off Hwéte. But Antamá never accepted the verdict—how could Hwéte have done such a thing? (Tooy told me that according to his brother's god, Flibánti, who was an eyewitness to these events, Antamá used his powers of flight to go up and visit his mother's brother Wíi in Lángu, to make sure it was all right to bring the woman upriver. Wíi told him to go ahead.)

Antamá snuck in at midnight to see her, told her what was going on, and loaded her and his half-sister Afaata—Gweyúnga's daughter with Hwéte—into his canoe for the upstream journey to his village far up the Gaánlío. By the time Gweyúnga's village had discovered Hwéte's absence and determined that she hadn't simply gone off into the forest to kill herself, it was too late. There was nothing left to do but bury their dead leader.

Hwéte, heavy with Kwasímukámba's boy-child, and her daughter Afaata arrived the next day in Antamá's village—where Tooy today looks back on them with affection as the founders of his matrilineage.[3]

* * *

Some months after these events, Kwasímukámba stayed for a time in Antamá's village, where the two became very close. The wars with the whites were still raging, and Kwasímukámba shared much of his ritual knowledge with his new friend. And as Antamá prepared to go off to battle near the coast, Kwasímukámba taught him one of his trademark powers—the óbia that permits men to fly.[4]

When there had been no word of Antamá for many weeks, his people charged Kwasímukámba with witchcraft. At which point he used his óbia to summon Antamá, who alit in the center of the village in the form of a vulture. As Tooy tells it, Kwasímukámba addressed the bird, saying, "Antamá, I taught you to fly, but your people doubted me. So I'm taking the flying óbia away from you and giving it to my son, Gisí" (the fruit of Hwéte's pregnancy). That's when Kwasímukámba himself flew off to the coast, soon to lead a great army against the Saramakas. "And it's why," says Tooy plaintively, "my people no longer have flying *óbia*."

★ ★ ★

What, then, is the special connection with Tooy's brother Sensiló? The short answer is that the most powerful ritual possession of Antamá—who became the greatest Saramaka *óbia*-man of the second half of the eighteenth century—was the *óbia* called Flibánti, which he learned from Kwasímukámba. Tooy tells me that during the epic battle with the army brought by Kwasímukámba, Antamá ritually "boiled" him and managed to shoot him, after which Kwasímukámba turned himself into an armadillo. "If you ever tell this story to anyone, close the door first!" he says. "It's very secret! That's why they call that place Armadillo Creek [Kámbakiíki]. The animal's hole is still there." And then he adds, "Sensiló can't go anywhere near that place!"

Tooy tells me that, after Antamá's death, his *óbia* passed to his sister Afaata. And he can trace its further descent with precision, from one person to another—until it finally possessed Sensiló.

If Kwasímukámba is a dangerous figure for all Saramakas, he is the gravest of dangers for Sensiló. Kwasímukámba betrayed and murdered Antamá's father. Later he befriended and betrayed Antamá himself. But in the end, with the help of his ritual powers, Antamá turned the tables on Kwasímukámba, "boiling" and shooting the traitor.

The *óbia* I have chatted with during Sensiló's visits to Cayenne, who once assured me he was "here before Noah," is then none other than Flibánti, Kwasímukámba's personal *óbia*, which he taught to Antamá. Eyewitness to Kwasímukámba's exploits as well as the power behind his ultimate defeat, this *óbia* is intimately linked to the lives of both the great spy and his friend and later nemesis Antamá.

Indeed, when Sensiló, who had been a proud and powerful man, lost his sight five years ago, it surprised no one that divination found it was Kwasímukámba taking his revenge.

No wonder Sensiló startled at the very sound of his name.

FRICTION

We might locate Roland's doubts and fears about Saramakas somewhere within that murky realm of intercultural connection that Anna Lowenhaupt Tsing has labeled *friction*—what transpires in "zones of awkward engagement, where words mean something different across a divide even as people agree to speak." As she suggests, such zones are becoming increasingly commonplace as the world globalizes.[1]

Since the early 1960s, I had understood that much of the magic that affected the everyday lives of Martiniquans had its roots in medieval Europe. In the Caribbean, there had clearly been what Michael Taussig describes as a "folding of the underworld of the conquering society into the culture of the conquered . . . as a chamber of mirrors reflecting each stream's perception of the other."[2] When I studied the lives of fishermen and the ritual specialists they patronized to assure that their catch would be larger than their neighbor's, time and again I stumbled on recipes from *grimoires*—and on talk of the Devil. Fishermen instructed me, repeatedly, that when walking at night in the unelectrified village, if I felt a tingling and my hair stood on end, it meant there was a *bête infernale* in the vicinity and that I must quickly pull the pockets out of my pants, take off my shirt and put it back on inside out, and open my pocketknife. On the trail that ran through the village—there was no road yet—nighttime brought dangerously alluring sights (fiery automobiles streaking by, unimaginably beautiful women bathing in the sea, gnarled old women nursing babies on a rock, strange children wandering and crying out) as well as more obvious dangers. One man, known for his courage, had seen the Devil more than once. In fact, when he went to wake up his crewman not long before, a giant horse-with-three-legs—Lucifer himself—fell out of the mango tree under which he was standing. And coffins were often sighted at crossroads. When another man known for bravery came upon one in the middle of the path, he opened his knife, sat down on the box, and boldly asked, "Who's inside?" "Heat, heat," came the first answer. When he pressed, the woman's voice asked him if she sounded like thunder. No, he said. Like wind, then? No. Perhaps like running water? When he said yes, the coffin dissolved into a rivulet slanting off to the sea. No one who has close acquaintance with Antillean culture is surprised by the prevalence of ritual, by the everyday preoccupation with protective action against the forces unleashed by enemies. And the Devil, in all his forms, is a constant potential menace.

Roland's first assumption, once he'd seen Tooy in action (and caught that glimpse of his "fetish"), was that he worked with the Devil—certainly the farthest thing in the world from Tooy's mind. Roland feared becoming *engagé*—being forced to make a pact with the Devil. In the larger Creole world, the rise of politicians and rich men is widely attributed to such supernatural "engagements." In Haiti, the instruments are *baca* and *zonbi*. In other places, they take different names and shapes. But there's always the possibility of getting some sort of spirit to work for you in return for selling your soul. Take Suriname and French Guiana, where store owners are said to buy *bakúlu*, spirits in the form of tiny people who can fit in your pocket and do your bidding in return for payments and other obeisance. They make the money for you, you become their slave.[3]

*   *   *

Roland began to express his reluctance to me just days after Tooy and Kalusé returned to Guyane from Martinique. At first he says it's money—he has cash flow problems and can't yet come up with what he owes to complete the cure. One municipality owes him 400,000 francs for lumber and cement, someone else has written a bad check for 370,000 francs. But soon he admits he simply isn't sure that Saramaka ritual, no matter how effective in principle, is going to be right for him. It's like when the priests came: things looked up for a few days but soon continued their downward spiral. He's pretty sure it's the thing in the ground at the lumberyard. After all, he says, Tooy confirmed this when he told him he hadn't properly taken care of the *"esprit"* who lives there. (Roland conflates Tooy's concerns about the god-who-has-the earth at the lumberyard with his own ideas about the evil spirit of the human sacrifice.) Roland says he's sliding down into a hole but doesn't sense he's yet hit bottom, so how can he begin to climb up the other side? He's spending a lot of time praying—he knows people are using "voodoo" against him—so he feels he has to do something, but what? I suggest that maybe Tooy would be willing to work on credit, with payment only after things go well. Roland says not to worry, he'll pay, he always assumes his responsibilities. But he's unsure that the Saramakas are compatible with his needs.

Two weeks later, I stop by the lumberyard, having spoken by phone with Tooy and Kalusé in the interim. (When I'd called Tooy, a girl answered in French, but I could hear Tooy singing enthusiastically in the background. When he got on the phone, I asked what he'd been singing: Komantí!) The place is humming with activity, forklifts moving around piles of lumber and pallets of cement sacks, secretaries carrying papers between rooms. Inside his air-conditioned office, Roland asks me if, on my next trip to the USA, I could obtain for him a few vials of a certain growth hormone that's illegal in France—something he wants to feed his cocks. (When I check the label of an old bottle at his house the following week, I see it's manufactured in a small town in Texas.) He also tells me about a recurrent dream and draws a sketch as he speaks. The familiar dream woman leads him into the cock pit, where he comes upon the plate in the exact center of the circular arena. He is able to lift it up and get it out of the way without a problem. Then she leads him underneath the grandstand—there's another plate right in the center of the space. But this one is heavy! He's unable to budge it, hard as he tries. *That* is the problem, he says. Someone has to be able to take that and get it completely out of his way, forever. He says he's keeping after his debtors and hopes that in ten days' time he can make a definitive decision about going to Cayenne.

A few days later, he seems optimistic and says to explore plane reservations for a couple of weeks hence. I call Tooy, who's enthusiastic and will go into the forest to begin getting together the necessary leaves the following week. The next day, we meet Roland by chance. He's come over to our side of the island for a cousin's funeral and, as is customary after the visit to the cemetery, is having a few drinks with the men. A bit wobbly, he takes me aside to say, straight out, that the real problem is that he's afraid of becoming *engagé*.

★   ★   ★

Back on the verandah, I reread the pages of Eugène Revert's classic *La magie antillaise* (1951) on *engagement* (a topic I've discussed often enough with fishermen and neighbors since the 1960s). It's described as any pact with the Devil—whether Lucifer, Beelzebub, Astaroth, le Grand Ravocal, or Aglamaton—who agrees to do your bidding. The request is normally written on parchment, signed in blood, and left for the Devil under a silkcotton tree at noon or in a stand of bamboo at Christmas midnight. Alternatively, the parchment can be placed in a bottle, neck down, under the eaves of your house. These contracts, says Revert, are very common in Martinique, and the success of many "big men" is explained by them. The truest devotees set a place at the table at each meal, with a plate of food and drink for the Devil. In return, they get such things as the gift of night flight or the ability to turn themselves into the animal of their choice and do their will. No wonder Roland, who is a devout Catholic, is afraid!

Several days before our planned trip together to Guyane, Sally and I visit Roland in his lumberyard. He professes confusion about what to do. His first priority, he insists, is to honor his financial obligations, and toward that end, whatever he decides, he will get together 20,000 francs in the next few days to give Tooy. ("With these kinds of people, if you don't pay them, watch out, you never know," he remarks.) Under his breath, he says that he's more than a little afraid of the Saramaka "voodoo" and of becoming *engagé*. I make my best ethnographic presentation about how it isn't a matter of "engagement"—but he seems unconvinced. He tells us that a woman came to him and said she sensed there was an *"esprit"* in the lumberyard and offered to exorcize it gratis, but he hesitated to trust her. In the end, he tells us he'll be able to make a final decision about whether to continue the rituals in Guyane later, perhaps in two months. There's something inside him, he feels, some sort of *"esprit"* ("everyone has an *esprit*," he says) that is preventing the rituals—whether by Saramakas or Catholic priests— from working. The *"esprit"* is also making him feel hesitant about doing the thing. He's genuinely ambivalent and scared and unsure what the right thing is to do.

*   *   *

As the months roll by, I occasionally visit Roland's lumberyard, in part for such mundane matters as buying some boards to build a shelter for our seventeen-year-old Nissan pickup. But he always takes me inside his private space to report on his situation—for me, it feels like being the priest inside the confessional. He insists he's telling me things he tells no one else. He remains unsure whether Tooy's rites are right *for him*, though he doesn't doubt his honesty or competence. "There's a woman," he says, "who appears to my daughter sometimes when she's in church. I sometimes see her in my dreams, too." This person advises against his going to Guyane. But might it be, he asks, that the evil spirit of the lumberyard is actively trying to prevent him from going to Guyane and thus to find a solution? Roland concludes he's "on standby" (he uses the English words) with Tooy. Perhaps, he says, he'll time a visit to Guyane just after the new year.

He tells me a recent dream in which three snakes are crawling into three holes at the base of his house in town. His dream woman came to him and told him to sprinkle ammonia on them. When he awoke, he went down to the place he'd seen in the dream, and there were no holes in the house at all, but he sprinkled the place where they'd been in the dream in any case. Then he went up to his terrace and rested for a moment, looking over the balcony, when he saw three little piles of sand arranged in a perfect triangle in the lawn he said he is trying, rather unsuccessfully, to grow. When he went down to examine them, he saw they weren't formed with normal beach sand—there were little bits of shell in them, indicating cemetery sand. He asks, rhetorically, whether people might be trying simply to frighten him— or, he asks me, is this a sign that someone is seriously working against him? He took an empty paint can and a trowel and scooped up the sand, capped the can, and threw the whole out to sea, saying as he did so, "Get out of here, you evil things!"

One day Roland drives me back from the lumberyard, after our truck's electrical system has died on the spot. On the road, he tells four stories that mix magic and cockfighting. ("Combats de coqs" are one of the longer entries in Geneviève Leti's recent book, whose title translates as "The ABC of Beliefs and Superstitions in the Magico-Religious Universe of the Antilles." Another book describes one of Roland's specialities: personally marking on each egg the degree of auspiciousness of the day it was laid.)[4]

A couple of years ago, Roland told me, he learned that his cockfighting rival's main óbia-man was a Rasta originally from St. Vincent who wears several rings on each finger. When Roland discovered his identity, he went to see him. At first, thinking he was a normal client, the man started laying out his tarot cards, but Roland explained who he was—and the man began to weep, saying he was just doing his job. Roland explained to him that all he wanted was for him to undo the things that he'd already done against him.

His rival also frequented a coolie *quimboiseur* in the north, whom Roland decided to visit. The man spoke to him in Tamil, took him into a little "Hindu temple" he had next to his house, and admitted he worked for his cockfighting rival.

Some years ago, Roland traveled to Guadeloupe to seek help, but he knew no one. At the airport, he asked a taxi driver, who took him to a specialist. The man was a coolie with silver teeth and slick hair. He called over a Chabine woman, and they prayed together for a while. As he spoke, he tapped the ground with a walking stick. He went into trance and told Roland he was traveling to Martinique. He arrived at Mt. Pélée and said it was very cold, asking Roland to guide him, since he didn't know the country. So, Roland guided him to the airport, then to his hometown near the southeastern mountain, where the man said he saw the church, and Roland finally guided him up the street to his house—the man recognized the beige walls and red corrugated-metal roof. In the end, he gave Roland some simple instructions: have a mass said and sprinkle some holy water at the entrance to the cock pit.

In another town in the north, he regularly visits a man who was once a powerful *quimboiseur* but now only "sees" things—he doesn't really make things happen, as he did before. He's one of the people who's been warning Roland lately about going to Guyane to work with Saramakas.

* * *

The following year, Roland phones to tell me he is working long distance on the lumberyard problem with an African priest. If Tooy still wants to "pray" for him, that's fine, but he no longer wants him to undertake any serious work on his behalf—that would be too much of a "mixture," he says.

When we next meet, Roland explains that Tooy was surely right about one thing: he did have an "*esprit*" in the lumberyard, and it needed to be talked to—which he'd never done before Tooy's visit. The problem, Roland says, is that people who've tried to help, from Tooy to Haitians to Africans, have always (he believes) wanted to replace the "*esprit*" with something else, and he is afraid of that. He wants a more "natural" solution, simply chasing away the "*esprit*." So, he's been praying a lot, especially using the books of Abbé Julio (which are common French *grimoire* booklets). He is considering bringing over a Greek Orthodox priest from Burkina Faso who regularly prays for the children of his brother and his African wife. He also says he's thinking, vaguely, of Mexicans, because he's heard they're "powerful"—or of this Cuban religion, what's it called? Santourita or something?

Later, Roland confides that a priest in France has also been helping him long distance. The burning issue is whether, as he's always thought, the "*esprit*" in the cane field should be chased or whether, as he understood Tooy to be telling him, it should be placated and prayed to. (He misunderstood Tooy, who was talking about the god who lived there, not an "*esprit*" that had been killed there.) Now, the long-distance French priest and a former *quimboiseur* who has become an Evangelical minister (and given up all his *quimbois* things) agree that what needs to happen is that the "*esprit*," which met its untimely end in the cane field, be "properly" buried. I asked if he meant a Catholic burial. He answered, "Whatever." "But where," he asked plaintively and rhetorically, "am I ever going to find a priest in Martinique who would be willing to perform such a burial?"

* * *

From Roland's perspective, little has changed in the four years since Tooy and Kalusé arrived to cure his lumberyard. Once again, his hens haven't been laying to his satisfaction and his cocks have continued to lose; and when I go in to pay the bill I owe for some sacks of cement, he looks discouraged and gray. "Things have never been worse," he confides. "These days, the stacks of treated pine I order from France end up in Morocco."

SÁNGONO MI TÓALA!

⋆ 1760/1763 ⋆

When Tooy really gets going with the singing and storytelling, there's nothing he likes better than to recount the exploits of his earliest remembered ancestor, Wíi, and how he was the one who "brought the Peace"—brought lasting freedom—to Saramaka. (I remember how Tooy kept us awake with a lengthy version beginning around midnight, only hours before his early-morning departure from Martinique the time he came to cure Roland's lumberyard.) Lángu-clan pride is wrapped up in this story as in no other.

Tooy begins with Wíi's song of victory, in Luángu language:

> *Sángono mi tóala!*
> *Mapána nêngè tjá lówe kó!* [Mapána people brought escape!]
> *Sángono mi tóala!*
> *Bavíli Luángo tjá lówe-e* [Bavíli Luángo people brought freedom/peace]
> *Sángono mi tóala, vié, tjátjá, hanhanhanhan.* [This last "word" is made by pushing on the Adam's apple with two outstretched fingers.][1]

And then he tells how the Saramaka chief, Ayakô of the Matjáu clan, had just finished his afternoon bath in the river and rehung his *óbia* hammer, with its tie around his neck, on his back. "That *óbia* is no good!" Tooy remarks parenthetically—"He's the one who's wearing it and, if anyone happens to see it, he, and not the person who saw it, is the one who dies!"

Well, there was old man Wíi, visiting in his wife's village. (He was married to Ayakô's daughter, Yáya-Dáunde.) In the late afternoon, he went into the reeds to bathe and, by accident, happened upon his father-in-law, who had just finished his bath. He saw the hammer! Ayakô didn't notice him, and Wíi quietly withdrew. Wíi stayed for three days in his wife's village. Then Ayakô had a collapse. Wíi went back to his village. The Matjáus did divination, and it said that Wíi had thrown witchcraft at him. Ayakô, very feeble, called his son Dabí to him. "When I die," he said, "put a musket ball in my mouth, take it out, and then shoot Wíi with it. If he really caused my death, he'll die. Otherwise he won't be hurt."

When Ayakô died, Dabí took the musket ball, did what he was bid, and hid it away. Wíi came to the funeral with his sister's child Tjámbaluángu, a young girl. Dabí went and told Yáya-Dáunde that he was going to kill her husband, but if Yáya warned Wíi, he would kill her instead. Yáya was in tears, for her father and for her husband. During that evening's "play," Yáya knew that Wíi would dance over and sing, asking her for water. (In those days, if you were visiting a village and someone offered you a calabash with warm water in it, you knew you were going to be killed, you'd better escape if you could.) So, Wíi asked for water. (In those days, it wasn't in a calabash like we use today, it was in a *totowítu* calabash! There's a tree in the forest called *zéntete*. Monkeys knock the fruit on a branch to split it open—that's the *totowíto*. That's what they drank from back then.) So Yáya went and warmed up some water and served it to her husband as a warning. (This is the way Lángu people will tell you the story.) Wíi left the scene and went to the river to bathe, but the thing that saved him that night was that he didn't take off his *óbia* sack even once. (In those days, you slept on *wándji* bark, that was our mattress.) He went into the open-sided shed—in those days they didn't have houses with walls—unrolled his bark mattress and called his sister's child, and they both lay down there. Yáya-Dáunde came and lay down with them there, too. Dabí wandered around until he found them, but luckily, Wíi hadn't taken off his sack. Dabí shot him right in the chest, but Wíi caught the bullet with the thumb of his right hand. He jumped up and took his sister's child and called to his friend Kofíkióo from the forest's edge and asked him to bring him a bunch of bananas. And they took off! They ate those bananas all the way to Ndyuka, where he met his friend Tatá Agumasáka and found the Peace.[2]

When Wíi left Saramaka, he walked up Doisanumaa and Avo Creeks until he got to Djaai Creek, which flows into the Tapanahoni. He came upon a garden, where he saw an old woman and three girls. "Don't be scared," he told them. "I'm not a runaway slave!" He greeted the old woman, "*Bakuí bangóni.*" She replied, "*Batjêtje bangóni.*" And then he said "*Bayáka bangóni.*" (That's the way everyone talked in those days. It was their "bonjour." *Bangóni* means "person.") She took him to the island where his friend from slave days, Agumusáka, lived. (In those days, Ndyukas lived on islands.) Big greetings between Wíi and Agumasáka!—"*Bakuí bangóni . . . Batjêtje bangóni . . . Bayáka bangóni.*"[3]

"I heard this all from Sibên's very mouth," he adds, alluding to the great avenging spirit of Béndiwáta, who had once been in Pobôsi's head. Then he continues his story:

Now, the whites had tried to make peace with the Saramakas three times already. The last time, Tatá Bákisipámbo shot them at Sisabo, on the Upper River. The second canoe, which was just below Pétodan Rapids, heard the shots and tried to get away downstream. But Tatá Bákisi turned around and cut them off at Gaándan Rapids [about 30 km from Pétodan Rapids]. The African guide at the head of the whitefolks' canoe warned them, "That wasp's nest up in the *kupawá* tree there—it's not a wasp's nest, it's a person!" So the commander of the boat said, "*Poti leti*" (Straighten out the canoe). And they crashed over the rapids. The African guide grew his wings and flew off towards Africa, singing [Tooy sings], *Déé neniángo sondí u mi-o-o, kêngivè-o. Un déé awó sondí u mi-o, kêngivèvè. Ma un déé ni awó sóndi u malúngu loángo, kêngivè, un de heee, kêngivè-o.* [Tooy says to me, "His wings have already opened!" and continues singing:] *Déé awó sóndi u mi-o, biká malúngu mi mi mi mii. Un déé ni alándi gánga u mi-e, biká mi malúngu ózila-e* (This is an Apúku song—there are other Apúku songs about the sinking too!) All the whitefolks in the boat drowned and washed up at the place called Maata Sandu. That was the last time whitefolks came to make peace before Wíi went off to Ndyuka.[4]

Tooy then tells how Wíi was returning from Ndyuka, carrying salt to prove that Peace had come, when at the mouth of Lokotí Creek, where it meets the Suriname River, he saw his friend Kofíkióo, on his way to a raid of whitefolks' plantations. Tooy explains, "Kofíkióo and Wíi had a special greeting. One would say, *Mi aliábosu*, and the other would answer, *Mi akwábosu.*"

Kofíkióo and Dabí and some other men had come down from the Pikílío and were going on a raid when they met up with Wíi coming back from Ndyuka, right at the mouth of Lokotí Creek. Dabí was in front, Kofíkiío behind, and it was Kofíkióo whom Wíi saw first. Wíi called out, *Mi aliábósu.* He didn't answer. Wíi said, "What's going on? There aren't two people with whom I call that name. I'm the one who's calling you here!" Kofíkióo said, OK. And he answered, *Mi akwábosu.* He called Wíi to him and Wíi asked where they were going. (Dabí was already way ahead.) He said, "We're on our way to the whitefolks' plantations, to go fight and take things." Wíi said, "Don't do it. Peace has come. He showed him the salt, and he said something in Luángu [which Tooy doesn't say]: it meant, "Turn back!" Dabí didn't see the others following him, so he came back to see what was happening. He asked Kofíkióo, "Where've you been?" Kofíkióo said, "My belly's been giving me trouble [diarrhea]. That's why I was hanging back." Dabí said, "Really?" Then Kofíkióo asked him, "Just imagine that we were going along here and suddenly we met up with Saa Uwíi [Wíi]. What would we do with him?" Dabí said, "Brother, me and Saa Uwíi don't have a problem anymore. I was just helping my father. Me and Saa Uwíi have nothing between us. I shot him because my father told me to, not because I wanted to." Kofíkióo said, "Well, I've seen him. And he says that Peace has come." "Well where is he, man?" So they walked back to the mouth of Lokotí, right at the big stone just inside the creek. The embrace they gave each other—it was as if Jaguar had met with Jaguar! So, they all turned back upstream.

Tooy sings out, just as had his ancestor Wíi, once he and Dabí had embraced: *Mapána nêngè tjá lówe kó! Sángono mi tóala!* | *Bavíli Luángo tjá lówe-e* | *Sángono mi tóala, vié, tjátjá, hònhònhònhòn* [this last made by tapping the Adam's apple with one's fingers].

★ ★ ★

Whitefolks' documents closely mirror Tooy's account. They describe how Wíi was accused of witchcraft in Saramaka, sought refuge along with his sister's daughter in Ndyuka, and arrived just in time to witness the final peace negotiations between whitefolks and that nation. Then, about a year later, the whites received a message from Ndyuka—originating from Wíi—that the Saramakas also wanted peace. Toward this end, the Council in Paramaribo decided to send Quakoe, a Ndyuka headman then serving as official emissary to the whites, to Saramaka. With a solemn handshake, he promised that he would undertake the mission, and he accepted in advance a reward for this service. But instead of going to Saramaka, he simply returned from the city to Ndyuka, making clear to his compatriots that he had no intention of actually making the trip. The Ndyuka headmen claim to have tried to force him to go, but to no avail; and they finally "summoned Wíi, who some years ago had fled from Saramaka . . . and they persuaded him to go [instead of Quakoe], and they gave him four men [another document says it was eighteen men] to accompany him. Wíi accepted"[5] Wíi's expedition from Ndyuka to Saramaka left in late 1761 (after considerable discussion among the Ndyukas about whether or not Wíi was in fact a witch). Its successful return to Ndyuka took place in February 1762. Some forty Saramakas, including six headmen, accompanied Wíi back to Ndyuka, all seeking peace with the whites. (A postscript to one of the letters written from Ndyuka to the governor to describe the expedition reported that on their way to Saramaka, Wíi's group had intercepted a group of Saramaka men on their way to raid the governor's own plantation, and that they were successful in convincing the would-be raiders to return to their villages.[6] This postscript, then, points directly to the event described by Tooy: Wíi's journey from Ndyuka down the Lokotí Creek, at the mouth of which he met a group of Saramakas heading downriver on a raiding party, showed them evidence that peace had come to Ndyuka, turned them back, and thereby set the final peace negotiations in motion.) Indeed, according to the documents, Wíi was among the Saramakas who participated in the final oath-taking with the whitefolks on September 19, 1762—the Saramakas insisted they drink each others' blood from a calabash—and Wíi made sure that his sister's son Antamá was one of those officially recognized as captain.

Taken as a whole, the whitefolks' documents, like Tooy's account, tell us that Wíi was a refugee from Saramaka harbored by the Ndyukas; that he was involved in troublesome relationships with both Saramakas and Ndyukas that included frequent accusations of witchcraft; that he successfully communicated to the whites the Saramakas' wishes for peace; that he led a peacemaking expedition from Ndyuka to Saramaka (and that it met on the way a party of raiders whom he turned back); and that, as a result of the subsequent negotiations, peace finally came to Saramaka.[7] Born in Africa, an early maroon leader of the Lángu clan, a refugee among the Ndyukas for alleged misdeeds in Saramaka, Wíi in his own complicated way—as Tooy insists—indeed "brought the Peace." *Sángono mi tóala!*

*   *   *

"Wíi," Tooy once told me, "never died—they didn't find him to bury."[8] Indeed, he became a "dangerous thing." "There's a savannah at the head of Péto Creek," he says. "If you go there on a Friday, you'll die. I myself saw a man who went hunting there on a Friday. After a while, the bush hogs came, as many as seven, and they killed him!" At which point one of Tooy's young assistants, Asántikálu, chimes in that he was once in a single-engine missionary plane, momentarily lost over the upper Gaánlío. As they overflew a vast savannah, he saw a giant animal, "something like a lion," jumping up and brandishing his claws in the direction of the plane. It was as big as a house, jumping and jumping! With a wave of his arm, Tooy warns him to stop talking and sings a calming song. He tells us quietly that that's where the old man lives.

THE NAMESAKE

* 1848/1931 *

For Saramakas, every human is formed by three people: a father, a mother, and a *nêséki*—a spiritual genitor, or "namesake." All three participate in the physiological process of conception. When a baby has its first illness, specialists perform divination to discover its namesake, who usually turns out to be a recently deceased relative, though it is sometimes a figure from the more distant past or, in rare cases, even a dead hunting dog or forest spirit. (When Kuset miraculously made it home from World War II and had his first child, the red birthmark that ringed her neck showed that one of her father's battlefield commanders, whose throat had been slashed by a German bayonet, was her namesake.) As the parents consult diviners for childhood ills, they learn more about the namesake's taboos and desires, and the child gets used to invoking it when in need. Most people have a close relationship with their namesake throughout their lives. Tooy's identification with his—a man named Pobôsi—knows few bounds.

Pobôsi was the father's brother of Tooy's father Méliki, whom he raised from early childhood. From Méliki, Tooy heard countless stories about the man he called his father. But Pobôsi is sufficiently famous—as an early twentieth-century prophet and *óbia*-man and intermediary with the world of whitefolks—so that, even without his father's relationship to him, Tooy would have heard a good deal about him.

Before I ever met Tooy, I'd run into Pobôsi on a number of occasions—in stories Saramakas told me in the sixties, in a Dutch account of a 1908 geological expedition, in a priest's report about the Catholic Church's first mission to the Saramakas in the 1920s, and in Melville and Frances Herskovits's *Rebel Destiny: Among the Bush Negroes of Dutch Guiana*, published in 1934.

In the 1960s, my friend Asipéi, already well past middle age, liked to regale me with stories about his "grandfather" Pobôsi, a larger-than-life figure he'd known in his youth. Early in the reign of Gaamá Djankusó (who held the office from 1898 to 1932), he would tell me, a white man had come to the chief's village, asking permission to explore the upper reaches of the Gaánlío. (For

Saramakas then, as now, every creek, each large rock, even many large trees had a specific meaning and history related to former villages, gardens, and hunting camps that once dotted the area—but for colonial whitefolks, this was virgin territory that had to be brought under rational control, part of what Conrad's Marlow famously called the "blank spaces" on the map.) The chief warned him off: "There are things on the Upper River that haven't yet made peace with me, Djankusó. So all the more so for you, white man!" But the explorer persisted, and the chief was forced to yield. Djankusó chose Pobôsi, one of his most trusted associates, to guide the group upriver, making sure they avoided the sacred battlegrounds where, a century and a half before, Saramakas had, with the help of their *óbias*, defeated the colonial armies.[1] Far upstream, Asipéi told me, a bug flew into the white man's mouth, he took ill, and he was forced to return to the chief's village, leaving his mission unfinished. "I told you so," said Djankusó. "Now, get yourself back to the city!"

Years later the white man came back, saying he wanted to find a route from the Gaánlío to the Corantijne River and put that on the whitefolks' map as well. Again, Djankusó selected Pobôsi as guide. Far upriver, as they traveled west, the white man fell sick and died. Under the forest canopy, Pobôsi and his sisters' sons gave him a decent burial, Asipéi told me—but then they made off with all the expedition's goods. When the *gaamá* heard that the white man was dead, he dispatched a canoe to bring the news to the city. And the city sent police to investigate. Pobôsi led them upstream to the place where he'd buried the Dutchman, and the city men dug up the corpse, placing it in a wooden coffin and then placing that one in a coffin made of steel—a fact that singularly impressed the Saramakas—and transporting it all the way to Paramaribo, where the autopsy cleared Pobôsi of foul play. In a nutshell, that is what Asipéi told me about the expedition designed to put Saramaka territory on the map.

A long report, published in the *Journal of the Royal Dutch Geological Society* in 1910, presents the whitefolks' version and preserves a precious photo of Pobôsi in his prime.[2]

The expedition report also attests to Pobôsi's early interest in the trappings of Christianity, though the explorers seem to have taken it simply at face value. On November 2, 1908, when after some heavy going through the forest the group was at last ready for the relatively easy return voyage downstream, the daily entry records the following:

> Toward sunset, the workers came together and under the leadership of Bosk [Pobôsi] held a prayer-meeting. The psalms rang out louder than usual. They praised the Lord, who had supported them on the long journey through the

"Eilerts de Haan and Dr. Tresling with their Guides." Pobôsi is at the right.

forest and their safe return. . . . The rest of the evening was marked by high
spirits, and till midnight psalms and more worldly songs followed in quick
succession.[3]

Asipéi had told me that, sometime before that expedition, Pobôsi had
founded an idiosyncratic "church." Though nonliterate, he would "read"
prayers from his open palms and lead his band of followers—mainly wives
and children—in singing "psalms." Later, after the death of Eilerts de Haan,
Pobôsi was possessed by a god who said he was Mása Heépima ("Master
Helper"), a common Saramaka name for Jesus, but most Saramakas opined
that the possessing spirit was, rather, Eilerts de Haan, taking vengeance for
Pobôsi's having made off with his goods. Asipéi also told me—and this was
Pobôsi's main fame for him—that he was the greatest óbia-man of his day, the
master of gods of land and sea, an unrivaled diviner, and Gaamá Djankusó's
favored ritual advisor. In matters spiritual, this man of many gods was simply the most powerful Saramaka of the early twentieth century.

Which is where Tooy, who models himself closely on his namesake,
comes in.

* * *

"Pobôsi," Tooy often says in admiration, "had six wives and six dogs [for hunting]. . . . And thirteen 'things' in his head."

Those "things," as Tooy has described them to me, include, among other gods and óbias, a Wátawenú called Mênde, the giant anaconda who owns the river beginning at "Stone House"—a rock formation that he himself is said to have made, not far downstream from Eilert de Haan's grave, where great flat stones block the Gaánlío for 50 meters and the water whooshes underground—all the way downstream to the fort in faraway Paramaribo. Mênde is among the oldest of avenging spirits in the Lángu clan, having been inadvertently killed during one of the primal acts of Lángu history, when their ancestor Kaásipúmbu "purified" the river, making it possible for Saramakas to settle along it.[4] Once, Tooy told me a deeper, Lángu-clan version of the incident: when water lilies (tokóógbagba) choked the river, making it unusable, it was actually Kaási's brother Adánibósu who did the work, using his basket called apatabúi with magical fish drugs inside. He said some words which no one knows anymore, and he sang a song. And then "the fish were drunk in the swamps, the fish were drunk in the river!" (Tooy adds that Saramakas hid Adánibósu's name from whitefolks and rarely pronounce it still, which is why people talk only of Kaási—"You have to dig deep before you hear that name!") "And this," continues Tooy, "is the song that Mênde sang to tell his children to come and snuggle under him that day, to warn them that danger was on the way" [he sings]: Kwalo, nundeonê. Kó kolondeonê, nómò . . . "The Lángu clan," adds Tooy, "are the masters of Wátawenú gods, ever since they troubled Mênde." Mênde was the first of Pobôsi's possession gods.

Another was an unusually strong Komantí called Sáka-Amáfu (a.k.a. Ándo), who, when he came into Pobôsi's head, would boast that he was "Kantiánkáma-u-Súduantjí ['giant tree' from Súduantjí]," adding that "when tjembê-uwíi [a fast-growing medicinal plant] grows, I grow, too, and when women have their menses, I have mine, too!" Sáka-Amáfu had quite a pedigree. He had arrived in Saramaka, summoned by a wooden horn shortly before the end of the wars with the whites, which he helped the Saramakas win, and soon became one of Antamá's favorite óbias.[5] (Because he never actually went into battle, he is served with the red juice of the annatto plant rather than with blood.) When Ma Kiinza, Antamá's daughter, had her first menses, Antamá ritually prepared her so she would never menstruate again (Komantís still call her Woman-Like-a-Man), and he gave her Tatá Wíi's war óbia, which is still in Tooy's natal village today. But he also made sure she would be possessed by various of his óbias, including Sáka-Amáfu. After her death, Ma Kiinza became the namesake of Agwadá, a blind Tonê child who was eventually possessed by Kiinza's Tonê-god as well as by Sáka-Amáfu. It's no wonder that when Agwadá died, Sáka-Amáfu possessed his son, Pobôsi, whose namesake was none other than Ma Kiinza herself.

Tooy likes to tell me, with scant exaggeration, that every person really has two namesakes—his own namesake and his namesake's namesake. (And I've heard him pray at the ancestor shrine, addressing "my namesake Pobôsi, my namesake Kiinza.") In his own case, this reasoning strongly reinforces his blood relations to Antamá: Tooy's namesake, Pobôsi, had in his head Antamá's Komantí, Sáka-Amáfu, passed down via Antamá's daughter, Kiinza, who was Pobôsi's own namesake. Tooy's relationship to Pobôsi's gods could hardly be more intimate. "It's only thanks to Ofilíbaní [a.k.a. Flibánti, Sensiló's óbia] that I can have women at all," Tooy tells me one day. "He freed me from that part of Sáka-Amáfu that 'can't see women.' If not for him, I'd have to be a bachelor!"

Sáka-Amáfu, Tooy says, didn't call out "Hói, hói, hói" like other Komantís. Instead, he went "mumumumumu" (moving his lips up and down). Once, in Bêndêkôndè, they wanted to test that he was for real, so they took a chicken's egg and colored one end black with soot and the other red with annatto—it was white, black, and red. Then they gave him a small bottle of rum and said three prayers to the Great God. He flung the egg through the open doorway and it burned down the house it hit, the shrine to the great avenging spirit of the village! He said, "Who's playing with me here? What child thinks he can test me? Where is that kid? Get outta here!" He strode around, in and out of the ancestor shrine, breaking things all over the village. He caused thousands of guilders of damage!

Komantí gods come in several varieties: Sáka-Amáfu was a Busikí, the kind that travels by sea. This óbia was so powerful, says Tooy, that menstrual pollution posed no hazards to him—a woman having her period could come and sit down on his lap! Not that he liked women—he didn't even like to see them—and his strongest taboo was seeing a woman's teeth (seeing her laugh). Sáka-Amáfu worked with, among other óbias, one called Sokotíóbia, which is grilled rather than prepared in a pot. Also known as "Dêdè básu fútu" (the Bottom of Death's foot), it functions much like Dúnguláli-Óbia—a person you've killed can't come back to get you. Pobôsi was past master.

Pobôsi was also the very first person on the river to get a Wénti-god—a sea god—in his head. As we have seen, sea gods were not discovered until the end of the nineteenth century, by Saramaka men working on the coast. But soon after their first appearance there, Pobôsi got one of his own, the first to possess someone upriver—a Wénti known as Tatá Yembuámba or Bási Sikeneyí or simply The Big Man of Olóni, after the great underwater city in which he lived. Once, Tooy told me, Yembuámba took Sensiló's *óbia* Flibánti for a visit to this magical place, and later Flibánti told him about it—how, for example, if you don't know the password they won't even let you step ashore! (Tooy confided that to enter the realm, what you need to say is [nasalized] "*Senòò, senóó*" plus the name of the Wénti-god you're coming to see.) Flibánti also told Tooy about a special pool they have down there called "kibámba-wáta" (whitefolks' water). If you're a man of sixty and they throw you in, you emerge a youth of seventeen. Another time in Cayenne, Flibánti himself told me, almost dreamily, that "Tatá Yembuámba is the whitest of white. He walks on the earth till he's finished and then he travels undersea." His brothers and sisters in Olóni include Todjê, the tutelary spirit of the late Gaamá Agbagó, and three beautiful sea-god sisters with musical names: Yowentína, Korantína, and Amentína. Tooy's relations with sea gods are multiplex: Yowentína is married to Flibánti, the god in Sensiló's head, and Tooy's Ndyuka wife, Ma Yaai, is the master of a particularly powerful Wénti named Bási Yontíni, who is their son.

Pobôsi later got a sweet-water Wénti, an anaconda god named Sobéna, who was one of Yembuámba's wives. Yembuámba brought her to Pobôsi. "Could she dance and sing!" exclaims Tooy. The way they found out she was a sweet-water Wénti was by giving her some seawater to drink. When she vomited, they knew she wasn't from Yembuámba's country.

Once, Tooy told me, there was a big underwater "play" where many anaconda gods gathered. Sobéna saw one she fancied, Kítuwátaménu, and introduced him to Yembuámba, who in turn brought him to Pobôsi and put him in his head. Long after Pobôsi's death, Tooy tells me, they continued to play for that god; in fact he himself has played the *agidá* (the large snake-god drum) for him. But if Yembuámba arrives at the "play," Kítuwátaménu (also called Baakaómióto or Tjakítjaíbénu) immediately leaves and the dance ends. He's uncomfortable even seeing Yembuámba—understandably, since he slept with the latter's wife. (In similar fashion, Yembuámba didn't like to share the stage with Sáka-Amáfu. If Sáka-Amáfu came into Pobôsi's head when Yembuámba was present, he'd summarily throw him out.)

By dint of his father having been a blind Tonê child (and having Ma Kiinza's Tonê in his head), and also via his namesake Ma Kiinza (the daughter of Antamá) herself, Pobôsi was intimately familiar with the rites and leaves and songs for these river gods, originally the domain of Antamá's father, Gweyúnga of Dahomey. Pobôsi is said to have had a Tonê god in his head, but I don't know its name.

Another of Pobôsi's gods was the bird god Alêmitjé (sometimes Alemité), known for his playfulness, who took the form of a macaw. No one ever figured out exactly what kind of god he was, but he brought Pobôsi another god who he said was his own son named Zainú. Both these gods "could speak to the forest and the water." Alêmitjé was a real man, Tooy told me. Once Pobôsi went to the lower river for a big "play." Now, there's a very powerful god in Makambíkiíki whom Apúkus call Bedékimana (because he had powers as strong as the old man in Apúku country who has that name) and Komantís call Osáaboní. He was in the head of a man named Daní. Alêmitjé was going to meet with this god at the "play"—but it rained a whole day and a whole night, so they decided to postpone it. Good thing, too, says Tooy, or the whole world would have shaken—those gods!

Pobôsi had another mysterious god called Ataába. An Adátu—a toad spirit who accompanies strong Komantís and serves as a kind of bodyguard or watchman—it was so nasty that people tried several times to ritually separate it from Pobôsi. The final attempt ended with their deciding to simply leave the god be, after it came into Pobôsi's head and sang out: *Nêne nêne nêne nêne nêne kêlewa-e. Kêlewa-e. Nêne nêne nêne nêne kêlewa-e. Akêlewa-e-o. Akêlewa-o. Sábi dê a Nána-e-o.* No one ever figured out exactly what it was—a Komantí, an Apúku, or what, but from its speech and movements, it seemed most likely to be a particularly rough Adátu.

Pobôsi also served as the medium for the great avenging spirit of his father's matrilineage, a ghost-spirit called Sibên, who is the reason the great village of Béndiwáta has become so depopulated. Tooy told me that, when he was alive, Sibên's sister had accused him of witchcraft. They summoned him to the council house of Béndiwáta, where the whole village awaited. They offered him a stool and told the sister to speak her accusations. They asked his response, and he said he knew nothing about it. The sister had prepared a piece of firewood, a rice-pounding pestle, and an axe and secreted them by the side of the council house. When he arose, she knocked him with the piece of wood, then with the pestle, and finally split his spine with the axe—right in front of everyone. He tried to run but collapsed in the brush by the village, where they left him till the following morning. He became a really strong avenging spirit! Whenever he came into Pobôsi's head, they'd pay him three striped cloths, three white cloths, and 3 liters of rum. Tooy has seen Sibên in the head of Pobôsi's successor. One day, after telling me the drum name of Paánza, the founding mother of his father's clan—"you play *Avó Kêteke imisí a gángán, misí gangán hampê*," Tooy said—he asked me, "Do you know who taught me that? It was Sibên!"

Pobôsi also had the god he called variously Mása Heépima, or Mása Líbiman, or Jesus, or Jesus-Maria, who many of his contemporaries thought was the spirit of the white man he had led to his death on the Upper River. As

Pobôsi grew older, this god exerted ever-greater weight on his life, persuading him to renounce much of his traditional beliefs and practices shortly before his death in 1931.[6] Tooy told me that when they raised Pobôsi's corpse in divination, it revealed that what had killed him was Mása Heépima.

*   *   *

By 1920, Pobôsi was master of numerous gods and spirits, including Mása Heépima, and had a flourishing *óbia* practice. But he still sought to add a more official Christian arrow to his bulging spiritual quiver.

In 1921, he showed up in the downriver Saramaka village of Ganzee, which belonged to the Moravian Church. An excited German missionary recounted that

> Pobosie was a famed magician among the Saramakas. He described how in the wake of a dream, he had lost trust in his gods, taken his followers to an abandoned village, built a wooden house, set up a table and benches, and gathered his people to pray to the true God. But he knew he was feeling his way in the dark. So he went to Paramaribo and visited various churches. The Roman Catholics' service impressed him the most, and he decided to call his god Jesus-Maria. He told all this to the missionaries in Ganzee and asked them to visit his village and instruct him.[7]

And the next year they did. After three days of hard canoeing upstream from the *gaamá's* village, Moravian M. Schelts arrived in Bakrakondre (also called Lántiwéi), Pobôsi's domain far up the Gaánlío. Pobôsi told Schelts he'd been praying to this new God "for the past four years" and had made several overtures to whitefolks in the city, but that given their apparent lack of interest, he'd concluded that they didn't really want him to pray to their God—the missionary wrote that "this last statement felt like a sword plunged into my heart." Pobôsi also confided that his people were leaning more toward the Catholics, because they'd been told that Moravians had days on which they wouldn't be able to eat meat. The missionary was quick to assure him that, quite to the contrary, it was the Catholics who maintained meatless days. "If that is true," Pobôsi is said to have told him, "we'll gladly follow the Moravians." The missionary wrote that the village had eight adult men and numerous children. Some men, he noted, had more than two wives. "And Pobosi has five." He concluded, "The Lord has left the door wide open for our mission-work," but problems remain: "We shouldn't assume that they have told us about all their Heathen things and there will surely be other ones to extirpate." Moreover, "While we must thank the Lord for Pobosi, the man has had to swallow a very hard stone—when he was a Heathen, he was feared and respected, but now he is scorned and ridiculed."[8] Or so the missionary imagined.

Meanwhile, Pobôsi continued his role as guru to a growing band of followers, a man of many gods (and many wives), following Jesus-Maria on some days, and his Komantís and anaconda gods on others. He remained a staunch advisor of Gaamá Djankusó, for whom he divined on numerous occasions during the period. But he was still seeking stronger whitefolks' support for his homegrown church and felt he wasn't getting it from the Moravians.

One fine Paramaribo morning in March 1925, Father Franciscus Morssink, celebrating his twentieth year as a Catholic priest in Suriname, came upon "a very strange-looking troop of Bush Negroes" milling about near the door to the cathedral—seven men and three youths who made up a delegation sent "by Papa Boboshi to the whitefolks of the Catholic Church" and handed him a letter written by a confrere upriver.[9] The group was shunted from one Church office to another, and Morssink crossed them several times in the course of the day as they wandered the city "like ships without a rudder," until finally, with the bishop's permission, he took them under his wing. "Each day," he wrote, "they come mornings and afternoons to learn the catechism. But for men who've never once in their lives sat on a school bench, it is a quite a chore." By the time the delegation set off upriver, Morssink had developed a plan for a new mission field on the Gaánlío, ten days upstream from the railhead at Kabel, where he would fulfill Pobôsi's dream: a church and school for his followers. Within months, the bishopric had dispatched a local schoolteacher-catechist, Marius Spanning, to Lántiwéi.

Two years later, Morssink made the upriver voyage from the railhead at Kabel for his first visit to Pobôsi's village, where he found most of the seventy inhabitants gathered with the catechist to greet him by the shore. In front of Pobôsi's house, he saw the "nineteen-foot-tall idolatry-pole"—the shrine where he made offerings to his gods and ancestors. At its summit was "a platform, a sort of table, decked out with bottles, bowls filled with kaolin, boxes filled with coins, etc. etc." As well as an aged bottle of beer that someone clambered up to retrieve to serve him with his midday meal.

Morssink hatched a scheme. After the weekly Sunday "procession" through the village, led by drummers and dancing people, with children dancing round Pobôsi's pole, Morssink threw them candies, after which they all dove into the river to refresh. "I explained to them," Morssink wrote,

Pobôsi's "idolatry-pole" and house, before Father Morssink's transformation, 1926. To enter the house, one had to pass between two Komantí(?) figures, a feature I have never heard of except in this case. Two jaguar skins—also associated with Komantí—are attached to the house front. Used by permission of Moravian Archives, Herrnhut, Germany (LBS 05302).

"that I would transform their 'idolatry-pole,' which had up till then served the devil, into an object that would serve our Lord." And he asked them to bring him a sturdy ten-foot-long beam by the next morning. Although "the pole had dried out over its twenty-year life and the people had no ladder," the intrepid missionary shimmied up and with the help of some young men fixed in place "a gigantic and beautiful cross whose broad arms stretched out over the still-heathen Bush Negro village."

During the next few days, the villagers agreed to Morssink's plan to destroy most of their remaining six god houses, though they refused to throw their contents in the river as he commanded—fearing pollution of downstream villages—and instead threw them into the bush. Including, it would seem, a "realistic, 12-foot-long full-masted ship, that was placed there to await the coming of a particular 'kromantjing' god, who years before had informed them that he would appear to them some day—whether he would arrive by air or water they couldn't say but they'd prepared the ship for his coming." This ship, in fact devoted to Pobôsi's Wénti-god, Tatá Yembuámba, was hauled out by many hands, along with the god's "óbia rattles, pieces of kaolin, iron armrings and other filth, to begin its long process of decomposition in the forest."[10] Morssink compensated the villagers by placing a statue of the Sacred Heart, which he had brought from the city, above the door of the little school-church. And he reported that women seemed eager to take holy water from the font whenever they passed.

Tooy tells me that he himself once rode that ship. "There was no one left in the village by then, but the ruins of the houses were still there. I was old enough to go hunting by myself. I passed through the village and saw a large rotten trunk, which I stood on. I took four shots at a deer, but each time the gun misfired. I ran after the animal and looked back. It was Yembuámba's ship I'd been standing on! Pobôsi's son Lógofóu used to tell me that when they'd 'wash óbia' there, the great snake—Mênde—would slither in and curl up to sleep right there in the leaf water." Tooy also tells me that the name of Yembuámba's ship was Ditú—when it was at sea it stretched to more than 100 meters long, but when it was in the river it shrank to only a couple of meters.

At Morssink's insistence, the villagers did put two things into the river. Tooy told me that they took the pot and the necklace of Yembuámba and placed them at the water's edge. On each of the next three days, those things went downstream and then returned right back to the landing place—after that, they never saw them again. "Tatá Yembuámba's pot! Its name was Yankínápu. If anyone else tried to lift it, he'd just fall over—only Pobôsi could do it. And his óbia necklace called Antíafon. When you took it and tied it on, the dog that had the nerve to run up to you and bark would fall right over on the ground dead! Yembuámba, he was the Big Man from Olóni, a true saltwater person!"

A year later, Morssink visited Pobôsi once again. Indeed, this time the train he took from Paramaribo to the railhead also carried anthropologist Melville Herskovits, who noted that his bush guide spent the whole trip in "a long and hot argument with [Morssink] about the iniquity of the Moravians and their missions."[11] During this 1928 visit, Morssink conducted forty-six Catholic baptisms, twenty-four first communions, and four marriages—the first ever on the Upper River.[12]

Tooy wasn't surprised when I told him that the first man married by Morssink—how could it be otherwise?—was his namesake, "the patriarch

"Thomas Poboshi and Juliana Miki, my first married couple." Pobôsi is at right.

Poboshi," who, Morssink writes, insisted, with considerable mystery, on donning one white sock and one black one for the wedding picture. (Tooy really got a kick out of that one!) Albeit under pressure, Pobôsi had agreed to choose one of his five wives to marry, though he assured Morssink he would continue to look after the others.[13] Tooy's eyes teared up when I told him about Father Morssink's second marriage and gave him the photo—his father Méliki, his half-brother Otto, and his father's wife, captured on film several years before his own birth. When dealing with whitefolks, Tooy uses as his given name "Alexander."

Between 1928 and 1930, Morssink supervised the construction of a new village downstream from Lántiwéi, Ligólio, named after Saint Alfonso de Ligorio, founder of the Redemptorist order. Pobôsi moved his people there shortly before his death. Half Christian and half heathen, the village dissolved some years later, as most of the children educated in the school moved to Paramaribo.

"The second married couple of the Lángu-clan: Pobosi's son Alexander Merki, his wife Cecilia Atjamau, and their child."

* * *

History in Saramaka (as everywhere) is actively under construction. Events in the Saramaka world may not be revealed for generations. Just as bursts from exploding stars arrive in the nighttime sky light-years after the actual event, news of everyday events in Saramaka often arrive only after several generations have passed. Pobôsi's mother, Awóyo, was the vehicle for one such revelation, regarding a domestic tragedy that had occurred some seventy-five years earlier. When she became possessed by a water god that lived at Kaakapúsa Rapids in the Pikílío, it told how her mother's mother had a husband who spent his time working near the coast, and how that woman's sister had a husband who was a great hunter. Their matrilineage preferred the hunter, and the other man was jealous. One day, the god revealed, the jealous one invited his brother-in-law to go set fish traps. On the way, the hunter said he'd forgotten his tobacco and asked to borrow the other man's. As he bent over to snort it, his brother-in-law knocked him over the head with a club and killed him. Then he tied him up, attached some stones, and sank the body at Kaakapúsa Rapids. On hearing the god's account, one old man rejected it publicly; but the god sang to him persuasively, and eventually it was accepted by all. The rest was already known to the family: the woman with the surviving man bore three stillbirths with him. Eventually she bore another child, Mônimáu, who was the mother of Pobôsi's mother, who had the god who told the story in her head. After Pobôsi's mother died, the god possessed one of his sisters.

* * *

During 1929, Pobôsi spent a good deal of time with his friend Gaamá Djankusó and seems to have been present during the Herskovitses' brief visit. Melville's diary anxiously recounts, "After dinner we had another short krutu—two men and a woman, certainly workers of magic—from Luango, were presented, and probably tried stunts afterwards." He and Frances expand the account in *Rebel Destiny*:

> The older man had several broad stripes of white clay from wrist to shoulder of his right arm, and from knee to pelvis on the inner left thigh. Slung from one shoulder and reaching across to the opposite thigh was a white obia made of native fiber, and on his neck were several others. To these obias were added iron bands on his arms, while below his right knee and at the ankle of his right foot were other obias made of fiber and twisted black thread. . . . Late that afternoon the obia man who had appeared at the first council meeting with wide stripes of clay came again, and his wife accompanied him. They were the best diviners on the river.[14]

Forty years later, I caught a glimpse of Baala, Pobôsi's sister's son, who inherited most of his *óbias* and lived as a hermit near the abandoned village of Ligólio. My field notes record that he was "hung all over with *óbias*, smeared with broad bands of kaolin, the most ritually prepared man I've ever seen." Tooy tells me that when he reached the age of manhood, it was Baala who bestowed on him his ceremonial loincloth in the family's ancestor shrine. And not long afterward, it was Baala who taught him how to use the esoteric *paiyá-paiyá-óbia* fan—the two-sided, hinged divination affair that he had shown me in Martinique—for hunting.

Tooy once described to me the death of Pobôsi. His son Lógofóu and sister's son Baala were by his hammock in the evening. They called on his gods three times. The first summons brought Alemité, who said, "Man, what do you want of me?" but they said it wasn't him they needed. He said, "Man, don't fool with me like that!" and left. They called again, and Yembuámba came. Yembuámba asked him, "Man, what do you want of me?" They said, it wasn't him they needed. He said, "Man, don't fool with me like that!" and left. They called a third time, and Sáka-Amáfu came. He said, "Man, what do you want of me?" They said, it wasn't him they needed. They needed someone else. He said, "Man, don't fool with me like that!" and left. So they called once again, and "The Mother herself came"—the Béndiwáta Mamá. She came into his head with great violence. She told him, "You're as good as dead already," and started to divide up his possessions until by morning he was stone dead. "That man," concluded Tooy, "was really something! He knew forest leaves better than anyone in the world, and then he left them behind to found a church!"

Another time, Tooy told me that when they went to bury Pobôsi, he kept knocking on the coffin. Yembuámba tried to take him off to Wénti land, but the Béndiwáta Mother stopped him. Sáka-Amáfu tried to take him off to the forest to become a jaguar, but the Béndiwáta Mother stopped him. Alêmitjé tried to take him off to become a world-traveler, flying wherever he wished, but the Béndiwáta Mother stopped him. She said, "Let him go to the land of the dead like the other ones."

The day before his open-heart surgery in Martinique, Tooy offered me a fragment about the aftermath of Pobôsi's death. His god, Sáka-Amáfu, flew off, intending to get to Africa, but first touching down at Sotígbo on the upper Gaánlío, then at Naná (near Gaán Kiíki), then at Gaán Paatí (near the Kabel railhead), and finally at the great savannah near Moiwana on the coast. There, in the midst of a raging rainstorm, he saw a Ndyuka named Wensi whom he decided to kill, but the gods-who-had-the-place persuaded him to possess Wensi instead. Tooy once saw Sáka-Amáfu in the head of Wensi's Ndyuka successor, going into the polluted menstrual hut and carrying out bloody rags, which he'd throw on the fire when he wanted to stop other Komantís from dancing—as when he was with Pobôsi, Sáka-Amáfu, who was once in the head of Antamá's daughter, remained immune to women's pollution. The Saramaka god had crossed over to the Ndyukas and, for some years, created quite a stir among that nation.[15]

Tooy's namesake lived life to the hilt. A "many-wife-man" with "thirteen" gods in his head, a famed hunter and óbia-man who lived surrounded by admirers and clients whom he often led into uncharted waters, Pobôsi was forever fascinated by whitefolks' powers, from reading to surveying instruments to Christian prayer. Like Saramaka culture more broadly, Pobôsi strongly embraced additivity, constantly integrating novelties into his ever-expanding spiritual repertoire. Morssink, perhaps for reasons of his own, didn't mention it, but the "idolatry-pole" in front of Pobôsi's house, which the priest so proudly transformed into a cross, was already topped by a tiny cross, set into an object that looks very much like the chandeliers in Paramaribo churches. Check out the 1926 photo. Pobôsi never missed a beat.

FRENCHWOMAN'S REVENGE

⋆ 1920/2005 ⋆

One of Tooy's younger friends, Ben, who'd recently traveled to Paramaribo, brought Tooy a stern message from his relatives. Divination keeps telling them that the Frenchwoman spirit is behind all his troubles—his getting cut up by the masked assailants, his going to jail. It's imperative that he get himself over to Paranam (Alcoa's company town, not far from Paramaribo), where the avenging spirit is in the head of one of his granddaughters, and make things right again—or else.

When a Saramaka commits a crime against a person, it's usual for the victim, after death, to haunt the perpetrator's matrilineage forever in the form of a *kúnu*, an avenging spirit. Every Saramaka is subject to a number of such spirits from the past, and divination in the case of illness or misfortune often instructs a person to enter into contact with one of them and make offerings to soothe its anger. It has been some time now that Tooy's matrilineage has been "finding" that Frenchwoman is at the root of his problems and that he is being more than negligent in ignoring her.

Frenchwoman has been troubling Tooy's people for only a few decades. But her story weaves backward and forward through the last two centuries of Saramaka history.

Let's begin smack in the middle, with a man called Sansimé, an ancestor of Tooy's who was quite a character. In 1968, my friend Asipéi described seeing him decades before in Mana, possessed by Mavúngu, the quintessential Saramaka forest spirit. Sansimé, Asipéi told me, had feet that were curled under and pointed backward. One time, a great *óbia*-man, Dáomi of Kapasiké, came upon him walking on all fours, as he habitually did in his youth, and ordered him to stand up. Sansimé did—and he never walked on all fours again. Asipéi saw Mavúngu speak through him many times at Mana. He'd say, "Everyone should go hunting on such and such a day next to the river at such and such a place," and five men would, and they'd kill a tapir immediately. Whitefolks gave Sansimé gifts whenever he passed—whole crates of Marseille soap! "He was a great singer and he finished off those Ndyuka women," Asipéi continued. "They couldn't get enough of him!" Once, the Ndyuka men who lived at Mana decided to beat him up for having slept with their wives, but he stood up and sang a song—"Sansimé's back doesn't mind being beaten . . . "—that was so sweet they let him go. When Sansimé died, Asipéi said, they buried only his clothes—his body had already gone back to the land of forest spirits.

Frenchwoman is closely linked to Sansimé—indeed, she died in his village—ultimately because of his charms. But before we go there, let's learn more about Mavúngu, since it provides the key link between Tooy, Sansimé, and Frenchwoman herself.

Any Saramaka can tell you that Mavúngu is the gaán-óbia of the Dómbi clan, and that its special gift is to be able to locate people who've lost their way in the forest, as well as to cleanse the forest when a death has sullied it (whether from a hunting or agricultural accident or a murder or suicide). One of its distinctive features is the use of a sakúsu, a bellows that serves to disperse the medicinal smoke it uses in its cleansing ceremonies. Another is that it plants a tiny silkcotton tree at the spot where the óbia ceremony has been performed—Saramaka territory is dotted with the distinctive trees that were planted during a Mavúngu ceremony at some time in the past, each commemorating a particular unfortunate event. All this I learned early in our stay with Saramakas in the 1960s—it was public knowledge.[1]

In 1975, the great historian Tebíni told me, "Malúndu made Mavúngu"— a formula I heard several times after that as well. A woman named Efadámba of the Papútu clan, he explained, had been lost in the forest but emerged days later with a pot on her head containing Malúndu. The Dómbis were called in to help domesticate the forest spirit who had possessed Efadámba. That spirit told them much about the place in the forest she came from and made a second pot for them—this was Mavúngu. The Papútus kept Malúndu and the Dómbis went off with Mavúngu, after agreeing to pay the Papútus a large sum for it: a demijohn of rum, a homemade cotton hammock, and "something else." (As is standard whenever an important óbia is bought, the payment was only partly transferred at the time of sale. In this case, there remains the cotton hammock and "the other thing"—whose identity is either secret or forgotten—still to pay.) Mavúngu, Tebíni insisted, is not as strong as Malúndu, but nobody knows Malúndu anymore. Its shrine in the Papútu village of Gódo lies in ruins—the old men who were its priests didn't pass on their knowledge. Meanwhile, the Dómbis claim that they are the ones who really found Mavúngu—but if that were true, asks Tebíni, why do they still have those debts to pay off to the Papútus?

Around the time I was speaking with Tebíni about such matters, Otjútju (who became *gaamá* of all Saramakas in 2005) told me, similarly, that Malúndu was the very first Apúku to possess a member of the Papútu clan and that the Dómbis came and got Mavúngu from this Papútu spirit. Efadámba, he said, had been lost in the forest; when she emerged, Malúndu possessed her and told them of her stay in the village of the forest spirits. It was Malúndu, he said, who made Mavúngu for the Dómbis—and they still haven't finished paying.

Tooy's rather different version—more nuanced, more detailed, and involving his own Lángu kinsmen, including Sansimé—was told to me in fragments on different occasions. It's really two related events, he says. The first involves a girl named Yáisa from the Lángu-clan village of Kayana, who wore the adolescent apron of an early teenager. She and two sisters went off to the forest to drug a creek for fish. The Apúku named Musánse saw her, took a liking, and threw her over his shoulders and carried her deep into the forest. Her kinsmen had long since "smoked" the forest and given up hope of ever finding her when, one day, Musánse accompanied her, nine months' pregnant, as far as the edge of her village. He told her not to let anyone wash her in even a single leaf—he'd already prepared her to give birth, not wanting this to happen in the forest. Ten days later, she bore Atjúa-Gbéung, whose feet were curled under and pointed backward and who had but three fingers on each hand and foot. The boy was good at everything, except where his feet were concerned. He slept on the great stone in the river just below the village of Kayana; he didn't sleep onshore. Tooy says that one of his Bundjitapá kinswomen took him as her husband, but soon found out that he already had another wife—an anaconda. But she stayed with him, though they never had children. And then one day, Atjúa-Gbéung went around saying his goodbyes to the whole village—people thought he was going to his wife's village for a visit—and he simply vanished. They never found him to bury. Well, he was Mavúngu! The whole thing all rolled into one! The embodiment of Mavúngu! And he's the one who "made" Sansimé—Atjúa-Gbéung is Sansimé's namesake! So, that's how Mavúngu came into my matrilineage, says Tooy.

The second part of the story again involves Ma Yáisa. When she was older, she took a husband at Papútu, and they lived in a garden camp way up the Gaánlío. They were on the way down to Papútu one day—there's a creek mouth called Fínu-sándu, just above the village. She went there to get some water, and that was the second time she got carried away. Mavúngu took her off into the forest, but this time she was a middle-aged woman. Her people smoked the forest and did all sorts of rituals, but to no avail. And then, long afterward, some girls near the riverbank saw her emerging with one clay pot on her head and another under her arm. One was Mavúngu, the other Malúndu. They told an old man who was weaving a basket nearby, but he said, "Get out of here with that crazy talk." They went and told others, who found her, tied her up (because she was violent, in the early stages of possession), and brought her to the council house.

The Mavúngu pot stayed at Papútu—until the Dómbis came and bought it. (They still haven't finished paying, Tooy tells me—they owe a machete, a hammock sheet, and a bottle of black gunpowder. Once that's paid, he says, the Papútus will pass along a share to Lángu, where the woman came from.) There's a tiny island in the river just below the confluence of the Gaánlío and Pikílío. That's where the Papútus stored the pots while they investigated the case. Today, no one ever goes ashore there.

But the Malúndu pot came back to Kayana. Neither of the gods had fully possessed Yaísa at Papútu, so it was decided to bring her back to her village. As they were going up through Gaándan Falls, she began to menstruate. They put the Malúndu pot on a river stone, surrounded her with *sangaáfu* fronds, and brought her home. Kayana got the pot and the god. That's how Malúndu came to Lángu. That's what my oldfolks told me, says Tooy.[2]

The Nasí clan tells yet a different story about the origins of Mavúngu.[3] They describe how when the two Nasí warrior-hero brothers, Kwakú Étja and Kwadjaní, each captured an Amerindian woman in the forest—we can date this event to 1759[4]—one of the women was carrying Mavúngu-óbia, while the other carried another important óbia of the Nasís, Anía-óbia, in a pot on her head. Not long after, according to these Nasí versions, the clan agreed to sell Mavúngu to the Dómbi clan, which was having problems with the fertility of its women and risking extinction. And as is customary, only part of the payment, which consisted of "a demijohn of rum and a cotton hammock and something else," was transferred; the cotton hammock and the other thing (whose exact identity no one seems to know anymore) is still outstanding. And, according to these Nasí historians, it was only some time after the sale of the óbia that a Dómbi named Agba Nangba constructed the first *sakúsu* bellows for dispersing the smoke—that is, this was a late addition, not part of the original óbia.

*   *   *

As a historiographical aside—one with considerable theoretical import—it is worth underlining that whether it was Lángus, Nasís, Dómbis, or Papútus who first found the Mavúngu-óbia pot carried out of the forest by a woman, *all* Saramaka stories of the origin of this important *óbia* place it in the interior of Suriname.[5] (Because of collateral information about where the various clans were living at the time, I can confidently date the event itself to the final years of the eighteenth century, several decades after the Peace treaty.) This does *not* mean that the ideas or the specific rites relating to Mavúngu were not brought from Africa. Indeed, Papútus were a late-coming clan who arrived shortly before the Peace, and some of the participants in the finding of Malúndu and the making of Mavúngu may well have been African born. However, I would suggest that Saramakas' insistence that these *óbias* are of local, not African, origin is part of a broader and significant discourse shared by Saramakas. Their ancestors chose to systematically downplay African identities and origins in favor of New World ones as part of their nation-building project.

Discourse grows out of social circumstances, social relations, and institutions. If, for example, Brazilian Candomblé stresses fidelity to "African" ways, it is in part to create an "alternative space of blackness" in which subjugated people can cultivate a sense of individual and collective identity, what Rachel E. Harding calls "a refuge in thunder."[6] But for early Saramakas, it was collective identities as members of rival groups that were in question, as bands of slaves from various plantations escaped and formed the kernels of new social groupings, which would become, through time, matrilineal clans. Saramaka discourse, then as now, stressed group solidarity, and that meant the downplaying or soft-pedaling of diverse African origins in favor of those things that the members of each particular group had in common—collective property, practices, and knowledge. So, the "discovery" of an *óbia* in the forest by the members of a clan (Lángu, Papútu, Dómbi, or Nasí) served to bind it together and distinguish it from other clans. The discourse of Saramakas regarding, on the one hand, African and, on the other, New World identities—in the form of origins, magical powers, and much else, then as much as now—was part and parcel of a rapid process of creolization, of the formation and maintenance of an ordered social life and a meaningful identity in the here and now. End of sermon, back to how "the Frenchwoman" became an avenging spirit.

★ ★ ★

Tooy told me that while the talented but handicapped Sansimé (who was Tooy's mother's mother's brother), the very incarnation of Mavúngu, was living in the French Guiana town of Mana in the 1920s, a man from Dángogó approached him, seeking help for his Creole wife, who was being troubled by a forest spirit. (The woman's name was Equinet, but Saramakas called her Akákibúka.) Some time after Mavúngu, via Sansimé, succeeded in domesticating this spirit, the husband returned to Suriname.[7] Years passed and the woman, pining for her husband, finally bought a large canoe. Along with a group of homebound Saramaka men, she journeyed to Suriname. On their way upriver, the group stopped at Kadjú, Sansimé's village. They greeted each other and talked about old times. Then the woman asked Sansimé to "wash" the god he'd domesticated in her, and one thing led to another. Soon she was living with him and had forgotten about her husband way upstream in Dángogó. After Sansimé's death at a ripe old age, she remarried in his village and remained there until she, too, finally died. At which point there was a problem: although she spoke excellent Saramaccan, lived just like a Saramaka, and—according to some people I've spoken with—had even cut decorative scarifications, she was still a "Frenchwoman" who had been baptized in the Roman Catholic Church. How could she be buried in a Saramaka cemetery? (This is a perennial problem for Saramakas. Captain Kala of Dángogó often asked rhetorically, as he prayed at the ancestor shrine for Sally's and my continued health in the 1960s, "If they died, how would I know how to bury them?") So, on the urging of a couple of elders, Abegòò and Buítatá, they wrapped her body and laid it to rest in the riverbank, to be carried away by the waters. Which is why she became an avenging spirit for Sansimé's (and Tooy's) matrilineage. After all, sighs Tooy, when Saramakas die in French Guiana, they get buried like everyone else in the municipal cemetery.

★ ★ ★

In Tooy's house in Cayenne, inside his Dúnguláli chamber hangs a carry-oracle (sóói-gádu) called Luégan or Luégan Ndjwézan, an anaconda god discovered on the Approuague River shortly before Tooy's birth. It was this god that Tooy raised and questioned before his court appearance, to decide whether he should flee to Suriname or stay and stand trial. He cherishes its opinions. The man who discovered it was Sansimé.

Given these connections, if Tooy had asked my opinion back in 2001, when the storm clouds were gathering, I'd certainly have suggested that he get himself over to Paranam, where Frenchwoman speaks through her medium, and do whatever he must to settle his scores with her and get on with his life. But Tooy's never been one to pay much attention to what other people think he should do.

TAMPÁKI

★ 1900/2005 ★

From the perspective of the Saramaka village of Dángogó where we lived in
the 1960s, Tampáki seemed a mythical place. One of the wives of our friend
Headcaptain Faansisónu was named Tampáki. We knew that Wénti gods
and Dúnguláli-Óbia, as well as Mamá-Gádu, a carry-oracle we often consulted, and *palipú* palms with the fruits we'd grown to love, had all been
brought back to Dángogó a half century earlier from that far-away village
on the French Guiana–Brazil border. And older men we knew waxed lyrical
about the beauties of Tampáki women—they would tell how young women
would compete to be the companions of any Saramaka man with gold in his
pockets. A number of men from Dángogó had in fact gone off to Tampáki
decades before and never returned.[1]

It wasn't till shortly after New Year's 2001 that we were able to visit, taking
the biweekly Air Guyane flight from Cayenne to Saint-Georges-de-l'Oyapock,
since the road under construction still wasn't passable. The region had long
been a backwater—it was only in 1968 that Saint-Georges, the only town,
got its first car (a Jeep for the gendarmerie). Now we found a number of
paved streets; hundreds of houses; scores of cars; a few stores that stocked
guns, outdoor equipment, groceries and clothes; a couple of small hotels;
a church; and the other trappings of a remote French *commune*. And an
active landing place where motorized canoes came and went to the Brazilian town of Oiapoque (in Creole, Matinik ["Martinique"]) across the broad
river.

We soon recognized an old man as being Saramaka (by the way he walked
and other intangibles), and he led us to Léon, a pillar of Saint-Georges, who
greeted us in Saramaccan. Léon's father, to whom he'd been close, was a
Saramaka from Tampáki, his mother the daughter of St. Lucian immigrants
(gold miners)—they'd met when his father was called in to use a special
Saramaka *óbia* to save the life of his mother who'd been bitten by a venom-
ous snake. Léon himself had never been to school but had learned to read,
write, and do sums working as a boy in a local Chinese store and had taught

Mamá-Gádu, Dángogó, 1968.

himself electricity by correspondence course (with an outfit all the way in France). He now directs the local branch of Electricité de France, running the computer-driven hydroelectric generating station a few kilometers upstream from town and owning a sizeable house, with his Creole wife Julie and various children, as well as numerous other properties around town. We were their guests for our stay, and Léon took us around to talk with the only three Saramakas who still live in the place.

We first visited Anatól, in his late seventies, who hadn't returned to Saramaka since he arrived in Saint-Georges as a teenager. He lives in an old wooden house from which he sells homemade Popsicles—he told us he has eleven children in the region. Next, to the substantial home of Roger Joly, who came as teenager in 1951 and has never returned. He too has eleven kids here and quite a reputation as a curer, not only among Saramakas but among Creoles, Amerindians, Brazilians, and other residents as well. (Tooy has told me he has three gods in his head: a Wénti named Záiwa, a Komantí, and an Adátu.) His Creole wife gets along in Saramaccan, switching easily with visitors between French, Creole, and her husband's tongue. And finally, there's Sité, the old man we'd first seen, who is Léon's father's brother. He has been in Guyane since 1939, with one brief trip back in the 1960s, when he claims that he saw us in Dángogó while visiting for an óbia. He had raised Léon after his brother died, and now Léon has set aside a room in his house for him. Sité proudly showed us a photo album of women—his "wives," he boasts—

Amerindians, East Indians, Chinese, Alukus, Creoles, but not a single Saramaka. (There was, however, a comely, married Frenchwoman.) With French papers, Sité receives an old-age pension worth some $700 a month. And he pays to have his clothes ironed—even his underwear.

Léon, in his late fifties, lives life to the full. Besides running the region's power station, he hunts, cooks, and maintains a large garden outside of town, which he pays young Brazilians to keep weeded. Two years earlier, when he and Julie (who is an assistant in the local preschool) officially married, they celebrated by taking a Carnival Cruise Line honeymoon through the Caribbean—they proudly showed us the snapshots. But this is Saint-Georges: Léon, who loves to tool around in his shiny SUV, doesn't have a driver's license—nor would anyone think to ask him for one.

*   *   *

It was at the cusp of the twentieth century that Saint-Georges became a magnet for Saramaka canoemen. The boom began when the Carsewene gold fields, where thousands of men had been prospecting, were officially declared Brazilian, and many of these adventurers returned to explore the Oyapock basin from the town of Saint-Georges. Saramakas, who had already monopolized transport on most of the rivers of the colony, quickly made that river their own as well.

Saramaka canoemen in Guyane, early twentieth century.

The Franco-Brazilian "contested region," today part of the Brazilian state of Amapá, had long been an ambiguous borderland, filled with marginal peoples and rocambolesque events. In 1841, Brazil and France had signed an agreement to allow settlement of the area between the Araguari and the Oyapock, with neither nation having jurisdiction. In 1884, in a moment of revolutionary farce, a young *lycée* teacher from Cayenne (Henri Coudreau), a Paris-based novelist (Jules Gros), and the colonial authorities in Cayenne proclaimed "The Republic of Cunani," with a territory that stretched from the Araguari to the Oyapock, and its capital in Cunani, a town that "had at the time 600 residents—basically, escaped slaves, criminals, and deserters."² And in 1895, an expedition from Cayenne invaded Amapá, with a number of soldiers killed, causing international tensions that led to the final adjudication by the Swiss government, appointed to resolve the dispute, in Brazil's favor in 1900.³

The 1890s gold rush in Carsewene had involved an unusually large number of miners. One author claims that twenty thousand men streamed into the region in the wake of the discovery of gold in 1894.⁴ The next year, a Brazilian expedition to the Carsewene reported:

> The Creoles of Cayenne, Martinique, and Guadeloupe number in the thousands; all commerce is in their hands and only gold and silver are accepted—never Brazilian money. Besides these French, there are English, Americans, Chinese, and Suriname Dutch, and each nation lives apart. Commerce is on a grand scale with everything arriving from Cayenne on the steamships that dock once or twice a month, bringing new adventurers from various nations in astounding numbers. . . . Everyone agrees that insecurity is endemic. In the mining district, it's a rare night that doesn't see two, three, or four murders among the miners, particularly by the Creoles of Cayenne, Martinique, and Guadeloupe, who then escape downriver. . . . All gold goes to Cayenne.⁵

But the great majority of this rough crowd left precipitously in 1900, when the area was declared Brazilian, moving into the Oyapock and Approuague basins in French territory, where there was plenty of gold to dream about. In a stultifying chronological list of the major events in the history of French Guiana—for instance, "1897, 14 July: Inauguration on the Place Victor Hugo of a Monument raised to the memory of Victor Schoelcher"—we come to "1901, April: Léon, known as 'the baker,' renowned throughout Cayenne for his *petits patés*, with a companion, discovers gold on the Inini Creek [on the Approuague]. Three months later, they return to Cayenne, each possessing 42 kilos of gold."⁶

* * *

"Ladies of the Placers."

In the wake of this reflux from the Carsewene, Saramakas built their village of Tampáki, a few kilometers downstream from Saint-Georges. Of all the towns in Guyane, it was Saint-Georges that developed a reputation as the place where women were most available to Saramakas as wives, and soon Tampáki was a thriving settlement of three hundred (some sources say four hundred) residents: Saramaka men, their Creole wives, and their children.

By 1910, Tampáki was said to have the largest ancestor shrine of any Saramaka village in the world. One document attests that between 1901 and 1934, 470 children were born there to Saramaka fathers and registered at the *mairie* of Saint-Georges.[7] And a Saramaka resident told me that when he first arrived in 1939, there were still a good three hundred people living in Tampáki, and a rosewood mill was working around the clock. (During the 1920s and 1930s—until the trees were depleted and the industry moved to the Brazilian Amazon—French Guiana was the world's largest producer of rosewood oil, the essential ingredient of Chanel No. 5.)

Headcaptain Aniké Awági, now in his eighties, who lived in Tampáki from age nine until well into his thirties, told me the early history of the place, forever associated in Saramaka consciousness with the deeds of Kódji, its first captain, the medium of the Wénti Wánanzái and other powerful spirits, and the discoverer of Dúnguláli-Óbia.[8] But, Aniké told me, it was a man named Tuálo, who had been working in Mana, who was the real Saramaka pioneer on the Oyapock—and also the very first man to take a Creole wife. Arriving in Cayenne from Mana at the end of the nineteenth century, Tuálo found a number of Saramakas already working around the capital. His wife Marguérite suggested they move on to the Oyapock, where the couple formed a river transport team, Tuálo poling the craft at the prow, Marguérite steering at the rear, bringing goods up as far as Camopi and from there to the placers of Bienvenue. ("I myself helped Marguérite grate cassava," Aniké reminisced—her husband was long since dead.) Soon, Tuálo returned to Cayenne and told others about the opportunities on the Oyapock, and he was followed there by Abelíti, Kodjóbii, and Kódji (the famous curer who had just arrived from Haarlem, on the Saramacca River in Suriname), as well as a group of men from Dángogó: Gasitón, Kositán, Agbagó, Wênwèkaká, Gidé, and Kódjo.[9]

Aniké told me how a "French officer" in Saint-Georges who was about to be sent to Cayenne to have his leg amputated was instead cured by Kodjóbii's *óbia* ("they had him run around Saint-Georges three times to show off the cure!"), at which point the French authorities encouraged Saramakas to settle the area. They'd offered Kodjóbii the first captain's position on the Oyapock, but he declined in favor of his elder, the already-respected Kódji. According to documents in the archives, Kódji served for two decades until his death in 1923. Then his son—today remembered as Kómandán Kódji—who died in 1972, took the position and in 1942 was named by the French colonial government the first *commandant* of all the Saramakas in French Guiana.

*　*　*

Kódji appears to us as one of those larger-than-life figures, a man of outsize appetites and accomplishments, rather like Tooy's namesake Pobôsi. Born about 1850 in the Lángu region of Saramaka, he was by the 1880s part of the sizeable workforce engaged in logging around Haarlem on the lower Saramacca River, where Saramakas mingled with Ndyukas and Matawais. There was tremendous religious effervescence under way in the region, as a Matawai prophet's version of Christianity was doing fierce battle with local river spirits, and as the new Ndyuka god, Gaán Tatá (or Gaán Gádu), was gaining followers by the hundreds, urging people to destroy and abandon their other gods and establishing a hierarchical, nonegalitarian system which identified "witches" and, upon their deaths, appropriated their belongings and distributed them to a small coterie of priests.[10] Kódji, already famed as a healer, was actively working with two different carry-oracles: a branch of the Béndiwáta *sóói-gádu* (for which his father was head priest in Lángu) and a new *sóói-gádu*, Mamá-Gádu, which "came to him" when he was on the lower Saramacca. (It is said that when he wanted to call on it, he also used the Ndyuka oracle Gaán Tatá.) A man of many gods, adding new ones throughout his life, while in Haarlem Kódji was possessed by a powerful Komantí called Amáfu, which he integrated into his curing practice. And he found the most spectacular of all his gods, the Wénti Wánanzái, while there, near the mouth of the Coppename, where Tooy's brother Sensiló told me he'd once happened upon an edenic Wénti realm, with pools filled with fish, rapids with beautiful flat white stones, and magical pineapples.

It is hard for me not to imagine that whatever else they may represent on the plane of the Saramaka *imaginaire*, Kódji's Wénti, the first sea god ever to possess a Saramaka, and Mamá-Gádu, the *sóói-gádu* he discovered, are in some sense one energetic Saramaka's reaction against the local dominance, on the one hand, of Matawai Christianity and, on the other, the coming of the all-powerful Ndyuka Gaán Tatá. After all, Wéntis and Mamá-Gádu (who works with them)—in contrast to Gaán Tatá—are above all egalitarian and beneficent. Wéntis' collective genius is to provide good things to anyone who asks: money, whitefolks' goods, and children. And no one ever dies in Wénti land.

Kódji's reputation had preceded his 1901 arrival in Tampáki, and after quickly being named the river's first Saramaka captain, he entered into a period of remarkable spiritual discovery as the village's population exploded.[11] Kódji's Wénti Wánanzái would return from the deep with remarkable tales of the undersea realm, and he brought back other Wéntis, who quickly possessed other newcomers to Tampáki. It was these gods who taught residents about Gaamá Lajan and Mamá Dimanche, about the various Wénti towns under the sea and in the floodplain of the Oyapock, and all the rest. And it wasn't long before the Nêngèkôndè-Nêngè called Akoomí possessed Kódji and began to teach him the secrets of Dúngul* áli-Óbia, which he himself had learned from his father-in-law in the land of the dead. Tooy tells me that whenever Akoomí appeared in Kódji's head, he would recite his praise name, "Mi da Hédi, Mi 'Hédi sumaní kasángelé.' Mi 'bánya fútu tetéi'" ("I'm the head. I'm 'Hédi sumaní kasángelé.' I'm what's worn around the leg"). And whenever Kódji got dressed up to go somewhere, he'd tie on Akoomí's magical protection above his calf (some say around his ankle). As Tampáki grew and prospered, Kódji remained its guiding light.[12]

Much else was going on in and around Tampáki, as Saramaka men amassed gold in the river transport trade and built Creole families with the belles of Saint-Georges. Escapees from penal colonies—both French and Brazilian—caused frequent problems. Some Saramakas served the French as bounty hunters. In one celebrated case, a Saramaka named Voisin—probably the man brought up by Kódji who inherited many of his powers—successfully brought in a recidivist escapee in 1939.[13] And Saramakas—some thirty, according to old men today—often lost their lives in this activity, as did innocent Saramakas who were attacked by escaped prisoners in the forest. Escapees were often starving, and Saramakas preserve numerous stories of their attempts, sometimes successful, to ambush, rob, or kill Saramakas who happened to cross their path. Something of the excitement of this period was expressed to us when we lived in Suriname, where old Saramaka men used to tell us about their tremendous fear of escapees from the *bagne* (penal colony). Well into the 1970s, Saramaka mothers still frightened their children by repeating the adage "Little children cooked up with dasheen, that's the escaped convict's favorite dish!"[14] Books on the *bagne* recount how four particularly fierce North Africans, who had been sowing mayhem throughout the colony in the several months since their escape in early 1934, fell upon a Saramaka garden camp near Tampáki and killed a woman. But before they could cross the border to Brazil, they were captured by Saramakas and, in return for a reward, turned over to the authorities on the other side of the colony in Saint-Laurent-du-Maroni. Another account suggests that the Saramakas lynched them with machetes and clubs. Saramakas still say that *alábi poité* (Arab prisoners from the French North African colonies) were "the worst of the lot."[15]

Saramakas also had to deal with escapees from the Brazilian penal colony of Clevelândia do Norte, just across the Oyapock, where large numbers of rebels and anarchists from the 1924 revolution in the south of Brazil as well as others from a revolt in Amazonas had been sent.[16] Elderly Saramakas still remember bloody encounters with these escapees during the late 1920s. Tooy described to me how his father and three others (including Pobôsi's son Lógofóu) were attacked on the Brazilian bank by men who captured them, tied their hands, put them up against a tree, placed long guns to their bellies, and threatened their private parts with a razor before the Saramakas succeeded in escaping back to Tampáki. Lógofóu, who was particularly "ripe," saved them.[17]

With the opening of the Guiana Space Center at Kourou in the 1960s, work opportunities shifted and the Saramaka population of Tampáki never recovered. When we visited in 2001, there were only seven elderly men who remained (plus the three in Saint-Georges), including Saramaka Captain Laláni, who is the successor to Commandant Kódji. The village is increasingly populated by Amerindians from Brazil, though a very recent development plan has begun to attract young Saramakas from elsewhere in Guyane. Yet, by any measure, the Saramaka imprint on the region of Saint-Georges remains major. A significant portion of the Creole population has at least one Saramaka grandparent or great-grandparent. For example, Georges Elforth, the mayor of Saint-Georges, is proud of his Saramaka grandfather who taught him to "snort tobacco" in the Saramaka fashion,[18] and a number of Creole women with Saramaka fathers still speak Saramaccan. Today, the Oyapock remains the spiritual center of Saramakas in French Guiana. The river is speckled with sacred sites where the deeds of Saramaka pioneers in the region, and their gods, are periodically commemorated.

★　★　★

In 2001, we spent a few days in Tampáki with the Saramakas elders who call it home and also with Léon and other children of Saramaka men who maintain houses there and were visiting from Saint-Georges for the weekend. January is the moment for Wénti commemorations, and we had the chance to participate, on successive days, in the annual rites at Gaamá Lajan ("The Mother of All Money") and Mamá Dimanche ("Mother Sunday").

When we arrived at the landing place, where a tattered French flag waves next to a shrine for the Béndiwáta Mamá built by Kódji (whose father was the priest of this all-powerful god in Lángu), we were immediately taken ashore to the Wénti house in the center of the village, marked by a flagpole with a long white pennant. Soon, six elderly men joined us on the built-in benches along each side of the house for introductions and prayers. Then to the ancestor shrine. And finally to the wooden house that had been prepared for us to sleep in. The village was decked out for the coming ceremonies, with fresh palm fronds hung across doorways. There seemed to be some fifty wooden houses topped by corrugated metal, most with indoor plumbing (or at least an indoor hole-in-the-ground). Random calendars from Chinese stores, pin-ups, and old electoral posters adorned the walls. The village is dotted with fruit trees—soursop, mango, breadnut, cashew, orange, lime, coconut, and *palipú* palm. Out behind the settled area in a forest glen, I soon learned, was

Wénti house, Tampáki, 1982.

the mother shrine of Dúnguláli-Óbia, where the *óbia* is buried in several de-
pressions in the earth. At various moments during the next few days, the old
men repaired to that glen to consult Mamá-Gádu, the carry-oracle that, as in
Kódji's day, shares that space with Dúnguláli and directs the village's com-
ings and goings. Outsiders, including me, were not invited. I decided not to
try to persuade the old men that, despite the way I looked, I'd already had
serious relations with these powers elsewhere in the Saramaka world.

★   ★   ★

Saturday morning early, the flotilla of seven motorized canoes set out for
Gaamá Lajan, the lead boat bearing a white flag embroidered with red ini-
tials: *G.M.L.* Several kilometers downstream, we pulled in on the left bank—
a steep rock incline topped by an open-sided palm-roofed shed built over a
natural stone basin. Giant mango trees all around. A blank white pennant
is raised. Two of the old men separate several varieties of leaves that had
been brought in a basket and then mash them, place them in a porcelain
vessel, and add kaolin and water. The shed is purified by tossing some of
this solution all around. Meanwhile, some of the Amerindians help out by
clearing the high grass with machetes. Both Saramaccan and Creole is being
spoken all around. There are more than one hundred people: some fifteen
Saramakas, seventy of their Creole descendants, and fifteen or so Amerindians who now live in the downstream end of Tampáki.

Prayers are said and songs are sung as libations are poured by Léon and a
young Saramaka visitor—some two hundred bottles of beer, sparkling wine,

and cane syrup. Half of each bottle is deliberately poured out for the gods and the rest set aside for drinking afterward. The Wéntis are asked to bring wealth, health, and children. There are special songs for the Wénti women who guard the gold amongst the river rocks down below us, as well as songs for Kódji's other gods, including Akoomí, who taught him Dúnguláli-Óbia. But the singing is halfhearted, as the old men are really frail and not many people know the words.

Once the tide has gone out and the river fallen sufficiently to expose the rocks that mark the sacred spot, everyone wades out to chest level and is washed, women and children first, as the water is beaten with leafy branches by three or four younger men amidst much shouting.

As we board the canoes to return, a young man gives each person a ribbon of palm fiber to hold, which is then given back to him as we arrive in Tampáki. At the landing place, the whole group is lined up to follow a trail being made by one of the old priests with beer and kaolin to the Wénti house, where everyone files in and out. Then there is ritual washing, as much as you like, from a large clay pot set up in front of the Wénti house. Each person carries a bucket of water from the river and adds it to the pot before washing himself in the Wénti leaves.

*　*　*

The next morning, Sunday, the flotilla sets out for Mamá Dimanche, this time carrying a white flag decorated with eyelet and embroidered with her full name. There are only half as many people as the day before, but Emilie and Suzette, middle-aged daughters of Saramaka fathers, entertain us with stories of growing up in Tampáki—how the Wénti called Asantéa brought two children to Suzette's grandfather, who had never been able to father children in Saramaka; how she possessed a Creole woman named Antuáni; how Kódji's Wénti, Wánanzái, had stopped World War I just in time so that Saramakas would not be forced to go fight; how Kódji's son Yembá once visited from Saramaka and expressed skepticism about all this Wénti lore, but was whisked away one morning by some messengers who looked like whitemen and took him to Wánazái's underwater village and brought him back in the afternoon, when he emerged from the river carrying cashew fruits and embroidered cloths, all perfectly dry, and he said he'd been served drinks but no food and had had a marvelous time; and how as children they used to gather by the riverbank at night and watch the Wénti ships ablaze with lights dock across the river at Tósuósu. This time, the rites take place on a tiny island in the middle of the border river—the shrine that was once there has been removed by "the Brazilians." (A Brazilian air force base, on the site of the former Brazilian penal colony of Clevelândia, is just downstream.) The scene is spectacular—a beautiful falls under high trees. Just before the flotilla heads downstream, Léon and a few of the old men go off by canoe to pray at the base of the falls to the Wénti mother herself.

On the way downriver, we pass the mouth of Tósuósu Creek, where Wéntis have a large underwater village. One of the old men discreetly deep-sixes an unopened liter bottle of beer from the front of the canoe—no words are spoken. This is the place where people in Tampáki used to see great Wénti ships docking at night. And where a hand normally reaches up to take the offering of beer. Kódji—Emilie and Suzette tell us—always said, "Never forget that place."

*   *   *

Everyone agrees that the Tampáki that we saw in 2001, and returned to several times in subsequent years, is but a shell of the great village that Kódji had settled a century before and which remained, for the next six decades, the center of Saramaka life in Guyane. By the 1970s, Suzette told us, the last real priest of Dúnguláli had died and some men from the village of Héikúun

Tampáki 2005.

had come and taken the *óbia*'s pot back to Saramaka.[19] Tooy told me how he'd gone for a visit a few years ago and confirmed, to his great disappointment, that "Dúnguláli is no longer at the Oyapock."

I'd bought 12 lengths of striped cloth, 12 meters of white cloth, 3 cartons of beer, and 12 bottles of rum. They raised Mamá-Gádu for me, they raised Gaán Tatá [another carry-oracle]. I went to the Wénti house on a Friday morning and unfurled 6 meters of white cloth at Kódji's shrine—it touched the ground! I made an offering of six striped cloths and *bái madjómina* with 5 meters of white cloth, 12 bottles of beer and five bottles of rum. In the Wénti house, I made an offering of six bottles of cane syrup, 3 meters of calico cloth, one white cloth, and 1 liter of rum. They played drums morning till night, for those powers belonging to Akoomí—they played Komantí, they played Wénti. But they didn't play Dúnguláli. There's no one left who can play the Dúnguláli rhythms! I slept there for seven nights before I came back. Now, there's one man there who still knows some Dúnguláli-Óbia songs, but his throat isn't in good enough shape for him to sing them anymore. They haven't lost absolutely everything—they can still "smoke" things—but that's about it.

PALIMPSESTS

✶ 1604/1837/1841/1863/2001 ✶

The forest hides its traces and guards its secrets. Our earliest description of Mamá Dimanche dates from the short-lived English settlement of 1604-06: "The Riuer of Wayapoco is a very faire Riuer, and nauigable, which entreth the maine more then fortie miles. And at the end thereof there is a very great fall of water which commeth ouer great hils and mountaines."[1] In 1863, Frédéric Bouyer, captain of a French frigate, visited Mamá Dimanche and left a romantic description and engraving:[2]

> The falls are curious and worth the visit, fully compensating the three hours of canoeing it takes from Saint-Georges. At their base is a small island, partly submerged, where under the shade of some mango trees one gets front row seats to a marvelous spectacle.
>
> Although the falls don't match the grandiose proportions of Niagara's—only thirty feet high and subdivided into three—the tumultuous waves which boil across a mile of weed-covered rocks, the green islands, the giant trees that push out of the torrent, the disorder of Nature, the power of the currents which overflow and mix twigs, trunks, leaves, and branches—all this leaves the heart filled with a strange and respectful admiration for the Organizer of these marvels.
>
> It fell to me to contemplate this spectacle at a time when it took on an especially moving character, the height of the rainy season. The engorged waters overflowed and angrily ran riot amongst the rocks. Rains fell without respite. Thunder roared. The great voice from the Heavens mixed with the sound of the falls. Through the mist appeared the phantasmagoric silhouettes of trees and the silver-fringed foam crashed against our feet. The elements seemed to have run wild, as in the days of the Flood, as in Chaos.

And then he adds a note about an incident that occurred there twenty-five years earlier.

> Just below the falls lies the tiny island of Cafésoca, only a few centimeters above waterlevel, with just enough space to build a tower and a house. This

tower is a singular fortification, created in order to stop the invasions of the Bush Negroes of the Maroni who, having descended the Oyapock, attacked some Indians who then asked for our help, and our warrior spirit seized the occasion to play at being soldiers. . . .

A somber drama once took place on this little spot of earth, but I choose not to speak of it. We did not play a pretty role. Indeed, it is sad to have to admit that when it comes to the relations between civilized Christians and savages, honor is not always on our side.

The "it" Captain Bouyer chooses not to speak of is the 1837 summary execution by firing squad, ordered by a colonial governor panic-stricken by the prospect of an impending Aluku Maroon "invasion," of four Alukus who had come to ask permission for their people to settle the area. (After an official investigation, the governor was relieved of his post.) And "it" also includes the aftermath of 1841, when the Alukus once again attempted to persuade the French of their peaceful intentions and sent a new delegation to the Oyapock. Alerted to this new "menace," French troops based in the tower at Fort Cafésoca set out upstream and took the Alukus by surprise. In the ensuing melee, all but one of the Aluku delegation died, including their Paramount Chief Gongo.[3]

* * *

Mamá Dimanche, then, is at once a Wénti site commemorated each year by Saramakas and the site of two separate massacres of Alukus in the nineteenth century—without, as far as I know, the two being connected by Saramakas (or anyone else?). The forest guards its secrets.

* * *

Bouyer concludes his description by noting that "these days, the tower is inhabited by twenty-odd convicts who work in the surrounding forest," and that

the island, the tower, the house, the twenty prisoners, and the guard were all recently attacked by two frightening alligators, though the law of force held sway in the end. One of the monsters perished on the spot and is today the centerpiece of the Museum of Grenoble. The companion of this colossal saurian disappeared into the depths, staining the waters with its blood, depriving the naturalists of their spoils.

* * *

Engraving by Riou, after a sketch by Frédéric Bouyer, of the site known to Saramakas as Mamá Dimanche.

Engraving by Riou, after a watercolor by Frédéric Bouyer, of the Island of Cafésoca.

Fifteen years later, the French explorer Jules Crevaux set out to explore the Oyapock, with his Aluku Maroon guide whom he always referred to as "le fidèle Apatou."

> At 8 AM we passed by the little island of Cafésoca on which stands an old tower that would have collapsed long ago were it not held up by trees and vines that completely mask its stones. This fort used to serve as an outpost inhabited by soldiers charged with defending the lower Oyapock against the Aluku Maroons, whose reputation as warriors, which they'd acquired in their wars with Suriname, caused considerable fear. It was here that a French officer directed a massacre of unarmed men and women of the Aluku tribe who had approached with peaceful intentions. I console the faithful Apatou, who showed his feelings of rage as soon as he saw the tower, by telling him that the officer who commanded the post had been officially disgraced.[4]

ANTAMÁ THE ÓBIA-MAN

⋆ 1771/1800 ⋆

For Tooy, it's Antamá's "fierceness" almost as much as his óbias that he's most proud of. Though I know from documents written by whitefolks who were present that Antamá attended the signing of the peace treaty in 1762, Tooy denies any such possibility, holding on to Antamá's image as a warrior "who never ate salt and never shook a white man's hand."[1] Tooy's right, of course—at least in spirit. Eight years after the Peace, when the German missionaries finally managed to baptize their first Saramaka (Alabi/Johannes Arrabini), it was Antamá who stormed down from Lángu to protest.

> Soon after the service, Captain Antamá, accompanied by another negro, arrived in great anger, holding a musket in one hand and a saber in the other. The captain, with great passion, asked us if we did not know to whom this land belonged and what we thought we were doing with Arrabini—or was it our intention to kill him? He feared that the gods would kill Arrabini. They had different gods from the whites, and each must remain true to his own. We allowed him to speak his mind, but when he had finished we related to him the Truth.[2]

The missionary's wife added that Antamá's musket was "fully loaded" and that he had "brandished his drawn sword over my husband's head."[3] During the following months, it was Antamá who continued to lead the anti-white resistance.

> On the 10th of March [1771], we were truly inconvenienced by the frightening shouting which the local people made in the midst of their heathen service to their idols. The Devil is surely very busy trying to make Captain Antamá his special servant and a leader among his people.[4]

Antamá, already one of the most powerful of all Saramaka óbia-men, was busy building a new shrine for his óbia. "He pretends that he is revering the Great God there and that the whole village must be absolutely silent. Nor may anyone enter it with a tobacco pipe, axe, or musket."[5]

In writing about this missionary report in the 1980s,[6] I assumed that An-tamá's new shrine—which had tremendous impact during the next several decades—was for Tonê, the river god that his father, Gweyúnga, had brought from Africa. I believed it was Antamá's second Tonê shrine, since I had clear descriptions of another one he had already built. But Tooy has convinced me otherwise. The taboos and the other descriptions I read him from the missionaries' journals are, he says, those belonging to Flibánti—the óbia Kwasímukámba had taught Antamá some fifteen years earlier and which, two and a half centuries later, is in the head of Tooy's brother Sensiló.[7]

While Tooy was in the prison wing of the hospital in Martinique await-ing heart surgery, he slept with a book under his mattress. I had managed to persuade the frighteningly tough gendarmes who guarded him that this book—Pierre Fatumbi Verger's *Orixás*, with photos of Yoruba gods in Africa and the New World, which I'd given him as a present—was the equivalent of the Bible for him and therefore permitted in his cell by French law. During our daily half-hour visits, we often turned the pages together, and he'd ask me to read the captions. Some pictures of Ogoun in possession in Nigeria inspired him to reveal that Antamá's óbia Flibánti, too, likes to eat dog—as well as jaguar! He also relishes an animal I'd never heard of called *zanáu*, which has but one eye. "It's as tall as a room," Tooy tells me, "and it lives on a mountain that has six peaks which you can see from Montagne Tortue on the Approuague. It picks people up in its claws and devours them! There's a cave where it keeps the bones." He adds, "No man's ever gone hunting in that place and returned alive!" When I later consult a map, I see, uneasily, that it's quite near where the new road between Regina and Saint-Georges is being built.[8]

In any case, during the final three decades of his long life, it's clear that Antamá was the most important óbia-man in Saramaka, as well as the de-facto *gaamá* for the Upper River region. And that neither the German mis-sionaries nor the Dutch administrators in late eighteenth-century Saramaka knew quite how to handle him.

As Wíi's sister's son—the official successor of the man who "brought the Peace" to Saramaka—Antamá considered himself entitled to more than the usual captain's prerogatives. Only five days after Gaamá Abíni's death in 1767, he boldly asked the colonial administrator to appoint him in the dead chief's place. Two years later, he sent a delegation to Paramaribo to request on his behalf "four muskets, four jugs of gunpowder, five jugs of rum, one crate of candles, a short sword, and a hat with a silver or gold [medal-lion?]," and he explicitly told them to say that these were in gratitude for the services performed by his uncle, "Wiel." His posture toward the whites was consistently confrontational; the administrator noted that he "comes to no political meetings [with the whites]; says he has nothing to do there; says that when whites distribute gifts he's grateful; he is [by character] impatient." And a message from Antamá to the administrator, "ordering him to come see him in his village," provoked the white official to reply, "You chiefs are always summoning me. Do you think I am a slave or a dog with nothing better to do than run through the forest at your bidding?"[9]

During the final decade of his life, Captain Antamá was still trying formally to wrest the gaamáship from Alabi. The missionaries wrote:

> Grang Adama [= Great Antamá, his sobriquet throughout the late eighteenth century] is a captain but like all other captains is subordinate to Johannes [Alabi], to whom the Government gave this distinction as well as extraordinary presents because of his fidelity and truly great services to the country. Grang Adama now believes that he should be Chief-over-All and, because he was denied this or that thing which he had requested from the Government, the other captains have succeeded in convincing him that Johannes—whom the others consider their enemy—is responsible. In earlier days [at the time of Alabi's baptism], Grang Adama was so agitated that he actually wanted to shoot Johannes.[10]

For a while, it looked as if Antamá might get his way. The missionaries reported in 1792 that "on the second of February, Johannes left for Paramaribo with the purpose of giving up his position as first captain [gaamá], to whom all the other captains in the land are subordinate. It has been a very difficult period for him lately."[11] But Antamá, for complex reasons, lost this official battle, and Alabi maintained his tenuous hold on the office. The documents make it clear, however, that as far as most Saramakas during the late eighteenth century were concerned, it was Antamá, with his óbias and political clout, who really made the decisions on behalf of all Saramakas except those gathered around Alabi and the Christian missionaries.

*   *   *

Tooy has told me a number of fragments about Antamá's activities after the Peace—almost always after I'd first heard some detail he'd alluded to in a prayer or a song and then pressed him for an explanation. Antamá, whom Tooy normally refers to simply as "Father," is enough of a First-Time icon that one can talk about him only with circumspection, and rarely.

Djakái—the boy stolen from slavery, whom Antamá had accepted as replacement for his brother Makambí, who'd been slain in battle, and whom Antamá had raised until he was nearly a man—provides one focus. I had asked on several occasions whatever had become of him, without much response. But I persisted. One day Tooy fixed me with a stare and said, "That boy fucked Antamá's wife!"

> Bákisipámbo [another Lángu hero] went straight to Antamá. He knew that if Antamá heard, he'd kill Djakái in an instant. He called him over using a name that only he knew. He said, "Man, that kid fucked your wife!" Then he laughed and continued, "Go grab him and kill him right here in front of me and then we'll be done with it. He fucked your wife. Kill him right here, now!" Antamá looked at him. "Man, so that's what you have to tell me? All right, I've heard." Antamá called a great council meeting. When everyone was gathered, he said, "Bring me my little sister and my little brother." He sat Afaata down on his left knee. (His little sister, he and she had the same father!) He sat Djakái down on his right knee. (He had raised them both.) He stuck the point of his sword right up against Djakái's chest and said, "Man, since you became big enough and I didn't go find a woman for you, you went after my own wife. I'm not going to kill you. You're going to take your 'sister' here. Fuck her as much as you like. But if you ever go anywhere near my wife again, with this very sword I'll kill you." Then Djakái lived with Afaata. She was his first wife, he her first husband. And the first child they had was Gadien.

Listening over time to Tooy's prayers to his ancestors and participating with him in other rituals, I had begun to piece together a partial picture of this Gadien, to whom I knew Tooy felt close. Here's a transcription of Tooy, in the middle of a long libation to various ancestors, addressing Gadien and giving characteristic simultaneous commentary on the side:

> Father Gadien, we give you rum. (Gadien would say he was *Opéte nyán opéte*, he was *Akótokoí djaíni búa. Káu tjánkontíma béye, a bête djáni kó a bêliwa.* Gadien would say all that. The man called Gadien, he was a short little fellow!—that's what we've heard. Whenever he walked around, it was always with his sword hanging from his waist!) Father, we give you rum. Father we call on you. (He called Tatá Antamá "mother's brother"—Antamá's sister bore him.) Father Malumbái [another name for Gadien], we give you rum! We pour rum on the ground for you, our elders. (They say that when you said your praise name, you'd say, *Opéte nyán opéte, opéte nyán opéte.* And they'd answer that they'd heard you. You'd say again, *Opéte nyán opéte, opéte nyán opéte.* And then you'd say you were *akotókoí djaíni búa.* You'd say *Káu djankotíba [tjánkontíma?] béye, a bete djaki kó a béliwa.* In other words, "The death that killed the jumping animal [toad] won't find it to kill again!"[12] Gadien! He called Gisí "mother's brother." Gadien! He called Bási Antamá "mother's brother!")

When I pressed Tooy on his fondness for Gadien, he filled me in on some of the reasons. "When Antamá was old," he told me, "he worked closely with

Gadien, and when he died he left him everything he had." Another time, he told me, "The *apínti* [drum] rhythms I play here all belong to Gadien—he got them from Antamá." And in another context I got some spontaneous confirmation, as Gadien's drum became the authority for a tale Tooy's ancestors have told at least since the eighteenth century. Tooy was in a teaching mood that day, talking to several younger kinsmen as well as me:

> The Great God once sent down his messengers to announce that young people must kill their mothers and their fathers so that the youngsters could run the world. The message [in drum language] is *odú kwatakí bi de a bímba tála*. (This was the Great God's way of testing them.) So, the youngsters all did it and then they burned the bodies. Except for one kid, who snuck out and dug a deep hole in the forest, built a house in it, and set up his mother and father there, where he brought them food every day. (That's what the drum is saying.) Then the Great God sent his messenger again and told them that they should braid a rope out of sand for him. So they went to the river and gathered sand, but they didn't have any idea of how to braid it into a rope. The one kid snuck out to his parents and asked them how to do it. He told them, "I didn't save your lives for nothing, now it's payback time! Here's my problem . . ." The husband told the wife to tell him. She said, "No way, he's yours, too. I didn't cheat on you to make him, he's really yours! You tell him what to do." So finally he said, "When the messenger comes again, tell him to braid you one meter's length of the rope at exactly the thickness he wants yours to be, and say that you'll add on to it and make it as long as he wants." So, the kid said OK. The messenger came and reported back to the Great God. The Great God said, "This kid didn't kill his parents!" He sent back the messenger. The kid arrived at his parents' in tears. He told them he'd hidden them so that they could live, but now this was going to be their last day alive. The father said to the mother, "Don't cry. The Great God exists." The Great God himself came down and asked his messenger to call the kid. Then he asked him to bring his parents. He did it. Then the Great God said, "You and your parents come and stand over here, on the east side. All those who killed their parents, go over there, to the west." He waved his arm and those people disappeared. But the place where the kid and his parents were standing, that's right where we are today, it's our village. That's what the *apínti* drum says! It says, *odú kwatakí bi de a bímba tála*. Ndyukas play it as *obímba de a bímba tála*. In either case, it means, "Young ones must live amongst older ones. Older ones must live amongst younger ones."[13]

And then he adds,

> An old man once told me that when you drum *asú muná fulú ben konú fulú*, that means, "Young ones must live amongst older ones. Older ones must live amongst younger ones." But as far as I'm concerned, *asú muná fulú ben konú*

fulú doesn't mean that at all! In fact, it means, "Your old folks really used to know things, but now only youngsters are left, and they have it all mixed up." It's a completely different drum proverb. If you want to say, "Young ones must live amongst older ones. Older ones must live amongst younger ones," you play *odú kwatakí bi de a bímba tála.* That's precisely what Father Gadien's drum used to say! That's what I'll take any day!

Several of Gadien's contemporaries also play active roles in Tooy's consciousness: Afaata and Djakái, as we've seen, but also Kwasímukámba's son Gisí and others, including a sister of Gadien who is remembered mainly for having risen from the dead (and who is in Tooy's direct matriline).

Ma Alúmba, who arose from the dead. Afaata's daughter. She'd been dead a whole week. She had a daughter named Míamaa and a son called Peedjekú. They'd held the all-night "play" just before burial. (In those days, it was Adunké and Luángu—they didn't have Papá yet.) At four in the morning, they saw her move. They stopped the "play." Only her two children stayed with her. They began to unwrap the body. She was lying there on a banana leaf. (That's the way they buried people in those days, without coffins.) Her first words were "Míamaa!" Three times. The daughter finally said, "Mother?" She asked Míamaa to come and put her hand on her belly. She pulled out three seeds of the gourd that we call "alúmba-gourd" to go plant. (It hadn't been in Saramaka before that.) She called Peedjekú and told him exactly what leaves to go gather in the forest to come wash her with. They did it and took the cloths she'd been wrapped in and the sticks and planks that had supported the corpse and threw them into the grave in the cemetery and covered it over. Then they swept her three times with the broom *óbia* she'd taught him to make. Flibánti still has the *óbia* that they used to cleanse Ma Alúmba when they took her off the banana leaves—it's kept over the door to his house. Ma Alúmba lived another five years!

Gisí (sometimes Djisí) was Afaata's half brother. Hwéte was their mother, but Kwasímukámba was Gisí's father and Gweyúnga Afaata's. So, Gadien called Gisí "mother's brother." When Gadien got big enough, he asked Gisí to teach him the *óbia* that his father Kwasímukámba had left him. But Gisí didn't want to work with it. He said, "Let's just work with the ones we already have." Gisí was a strange man, says Tooy. As he grew up, he never carried a gun and he never had a wife, nor did he work with money. When he went to the city, he'd go into any store he liked and just take the goods and put them in his canoe. The whitefolks would shoot at him, try to hit him with clubs or cut him with machetes. But nothing could hurt him. His *óbia* was at the front of his canoe. When he died, they held a three-week-long celebration in Paramaribo, they were so glad to be rid of him! Today, Komantís call Gisí

Bási Aliá, Apúkus call him Kwángu. A piece of his war óbia, Kokobéngu, remains in a special shrine behind Tooy's natal village of Bundjitapá.

Djakái, Afaata's husband and Gadien's father, eventually left Lángu to take a wife in the Papútu clan, where after his death he became a major avenging spirit. (Whenever I've asked, Tooy has denied knowing how this happened, but I suspect he feels it's simply too dangerous to speak of.)

Tooy did tell me about the death of Afaata, the woman who—as a refugee from downriver where her mother had been falsely accused of murdering her father—effectively founded his matrilineage in Lángu.

> When it came time for Afaata to die, they really played those Luángu drums for her! But when they raised her corpse in divination, she said she wasn't ready to be buried. Gadien said, "No way. Let's bury her." A great rain fell. [Tooy lists the various rocks and sandbanks and other geographical markers they passed on the way to the cemetery.] There's a stone called Afaata-peeká [Afaata stuck here], because the canoe sank on the way. Gadien rescued the *apínti* and played it, all wet, on [he says the name of a boulder]. Finally they were able to bury her.

✷ ✷ ✷

Antamá, however large he loomed on the eighteenth-century Saramaka stage, probably spent much of his time the way Tooy does, engaged in routine acts of curing. The German missionaries and Dutch administrators make various allusions to such rites, though their understandings are fuzzy at best—here are two that may serve for all the rest.

> [27 March 1771] In the village of Kwama, a woman had a miscarriage and Captain Antamá came to her to say that a god must be summoned or else she would have nothing but repeated miscarriages. But if she paid him he could "make" [domesticate] this god. The poor heathen, knowing no better, let him talk on, and the god was "made." [14]

> [3 March 1774]. I have heard that toward the end of last year . . . in a certain village there had been a miscarriage. But afterwards, the woman still seemed pregnant, so her family called on Captain Antamá, who was the biggest godmaker, to ask him to "make" the gods so the woman would not bring another still-birth into the world. Antamá said "Yes, I shall do it," but first sought payment. Such lads say that if they are not well paid, the gods will not work. The fee for such godwork or óbia is 40 lengths of cloth. He took his payment and began his work. Then he said to the person who had hired him, "You needn't be afraid any more. The girl will no longer have miscarriages nor bring into

the world unnatural fruit." Some time later, the woman's time arrived. She was duly delivered of a child which was half human and half monkey or ape. Then was the good Antamá, along with his god, in some difficulty. They summoned him immediately and asked him what kind of a child this was. He was more than a little embarrassed by all this, and afraid that he would lose his good name and the earnings he got from them. He called his gods together and begged them to make him [the child] normal, but his pleas were in vain. Antamá told the people that the time had not yet come for the god's powers to transform him into a natural human posture. "I have never seen such a thing. The gods cannot help with it." I was not told what they did with that child but I will try to find out more.[15]

Before the aged Antamá died, which we can date to about 1800, since the missionaries last mention him in 1798, he divided his many *óbias*, including those he'd learned from his mother's brother Wíi. His sister Afaata got Flibánti, which he'd learned from Kwasímukámba. (Tooy tells me that a woman named Logoso-óbo, who was married to Afaata's mother's brother Aségogó, warned her strongly at the time: "Flibánti is too powerful, you shouldn't take it on!" But she took it.) Antamá gave the Tonê *óbia* he'd gotten from his father, Gweyúnga, to his daughter, Ma Kiinza, along with his powerful Komantí, Sáka-Amáfu. These eventually found their way to Tooy's namesake, Pobôsi, since, as we've seen, Kiinza was the namesake for both Agwadá, Pobôsi's father, and Pobôsi himself. Antamá gave the rest of his varied *óbias* to his sister's son Gadien. As a matrilineal descendant of Antamá,[16] Afaata, and Gadien, and the spiritual successor of his namesake Pobôsi, Tooy claims intimate knowledge of all of these powers. He often tells me how grateful he is that his brother Sensiló was the one possessed by Flibánti—"if it hadn't been him, it would have been me!" So that's one burden he doesn't have to bear.

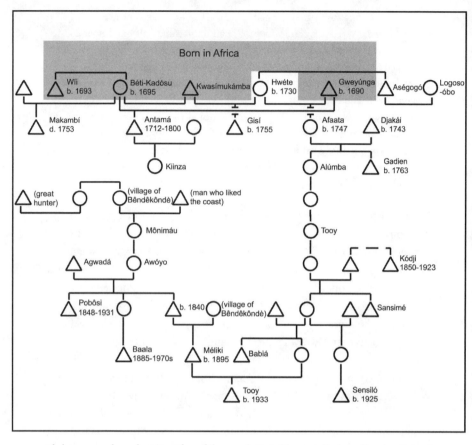

Skeleton genealogy showing a few of the people Tooy likes to talk about (for simplicity, I have not put in names that are not mentioned in this book).[17]

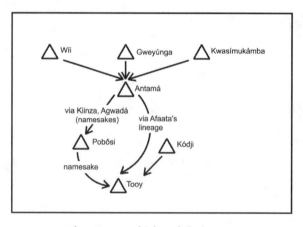

Where Tooy gets his knowledge/powers.

CHRONOLOGY

∗ 1933/1970 ∗

On various occasions, sometimes in reply to my questions, Tooy has put aspects of his life in some semblance of chronological order. "I barely remember my mother," he once told me wistfully, "and I hardly remember my father, either. You could say that mango and orange trees raised me there in Bundjitapá. I had two older sisters, but neither really took me on. I hung around with anyone and everyone. And once I got old enough, all I cared about was playing drums and showing off to the girls—drumming and women." Which means that, besides the many dalliances he likes to boast about, Tooy spent a lot of his early years with ritual specialists. The drums (and songs) he mastered would serve him for the rest of his life.

His first trip outside Saramaka territory was with a mother's brother in the early 1940s, building the American air base that later became Suriname's international airport. (During World War II, the United States constructed a string of airfields all along the eastern coast of South America as potential stepping-stones to Africa and Europe.) Pay was good and the work tolerable. By the time he was fifteen, Tooy boasts, he could handle a lumber raft with logs he'd cut all the way from Bundjitapá—the most upstream village on the Gaánlío—down through the rapids to Berg-en-Dal, in the coastal floodplain. Once he brought his ill sister all the way down to the hospital there, after which she recovered and had several children. (One of her children, Frank, now helps Tooy in his curing practice in Cayenne.)

By the 1950s, Tooy was spending an increasing amount of time around Haarlem, on the Saramacca River, where there were logging opportunities as well as a cooking-oil factory that offered cash for bundles of wild palm nuts. "The first time it was with my cousin Konyáki. We stayed seven months. After that, I was always on my own." It was on that first trip that he became involved with the legacy of Kódji, the man who'd preceded him in Haarlem by some sixty years and had left from there to live out his extraordinary life on the Oyapock. Tooy had a cousin, Awénke, at Haarlem—each is a

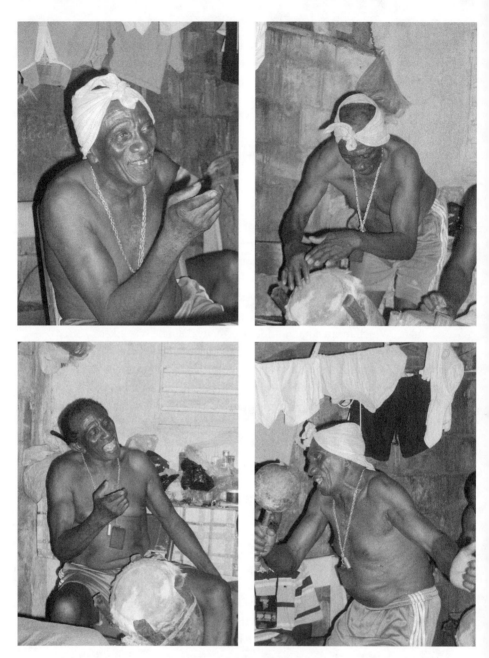

Tooy singing and drumming Apúku, 2003.

(classificatory) sister's daughter's daughter's son of Kódji. But Kódji was also Awénke's namesake, and while Tooy was living at Haarlem, Awénke made the journey to Tampáki to bring back some of Kódji's powers that had remained on the Oyapock. It was in the aftermath of this trip that Tooy became involved for the first time with Kódji's spiritual legacy, particularly Dúnguláli-Óbia and Wénti-gods.

In 1958, Tooy crossed over for the first time to Guyane, taking the bauxite ship from Paranam to Moengo, continuing by truck to Albina and then across the Marowijne by canoe, to stay with a mother's brother, Jozef Babiá, in Saint-Laurent-du-Maroni. His late arrival in Guyane at the age of twenty-five contrasts with that of his brother Sensiló, who's told me that Babiá brought him over to Mana when he was only five years old—which would place it in the late 1920s—and that he stayed for fourteen years without returning to Saramaka. More remarkably, Sensiló says he lived during that period at a placer called La Patience, far up the Mana River, with a group of Creole-speaking gold miners originally from the island of Dominica. "I hardly knew how to speak my own language anymore when I finally returned to Saramaka," he says.

Saint-Laurent, where Tooy settled down, was until the 1940s the headquarters of the infamous *bagne* (penal colony)—the place has never had a good press. Guyane's most famous writer, Léon-Gontran Damas, said simply, "Saint-Laurent is a veritable Sodom,"[1] and an American journalist years later concurred:

> Saint-Laurent is not much of a place. It never was to begin with. Four or five rat-infested streets of decaying wooden houses in the old colonial style— some occupied, some deserted. You can see it all in ten minutes. The whole place reeks of decay. Old Creole women peer out through the windows of their crumbling structures at any stranger who walks the streets. The open sewers are clogged with filth and drowned rats. Stray dogs paw hungrily at the rodent carcasses. The stench is sickening.[2]

With his uncle, Tooy got a job in public works—road construction on the infamous Route of Death between Saint-Laurent and Cayenne, which generations of convicts had never been able to finish. In 1923, journalist Albert Londres wrote, pen dripping with sarcasm,

> What a magnificent road! It's supposed to cross all three Guianas. Nobody's been counting the corpses. They've been working on it for more than fifty years. And it's twenty-four kilometers long!
> On all sides, the marshes; everywhere, the wavy-grass savannahs. We arrive at kilometer 24. It's the end of the world.

And for the first time, I see the *bagne*! There are a hundred men there, all with sickness in their gut. Some are standing, some lying down, some moaning like dogs.

The bush lies in front of them like a wall. But it's not they who will break down that wall; it's the wall that will be getting them. . . .

But the real question is whether the intent is to build a road or to kill convicts. If it's to kill convicts, don't change a thing! It's all going smoothly! But if it's to build a road . . .[3]

And another journalist wrote more dryly,

The investigator can see emaciated men breaking rocks and digging ditches, naked in stagnant mud contagious with death, naked in the glaring sun. It's a maintenance detail. Once in a while a pickaxe uncovers a tibia or a humerus. The edges of the colonial road are a cemetery.[4]

By the time Tooy got to it, the final stretch of road—the 68 kilometers separating Saint-Laurent and the Mana crossing at Saut Sabbat Rapids—was all that remained to finish properly of the 260-kilometer total. "It was a dirt road back then and when a vehicle arrived at the Mana, Saramakas would hitch two canoes together to carry it across." As for the work,

They'd bring us out in a truck and leave us by the river for two weeks. We'd bring a supply of rice, and in those days there was game everywhere—bush hog, howler monkey, tapir! We were paid by the day, from 7:00 a.m. to 2:00 p.m., but we could do pickup work after that. We'd cut *kupi* [hardwood] trees and saw them into planks—usually 5 meters long, 30 centimeters wide, 2 inches thick. What a job to get those planks into place! For bridges over some of those creeks, we cut planks that were a good 15 meters long! I stayed a year and five months before I was let go.

Tooy also learned a good bit about the region from the old-timers he worked with—the Mana, a long river cut by scores of rapids, had been the very first settlement site of Saramakas in Guyane, in the mid-nineteenth century.[5] Tooy heard tales of the pioneer Saramakas who "opened up" French Guiana for their fellows—about, for example, Asímadjô from the village of Dángogó, who left Saramaka in haste in the wake of the scandal caused by his having slept with a mother's brother's wife.

He walked east for days through the forest until he arrived at the Ndyuka villages on the Tapanahoni and was welcomed by his Ndyuka friend Hansibai. He and his friend each made a canoe and, accompanied by the sons and sisters' sons of Hansibai, paddled down the Maroni to its mouth and entered the Mana. In the town of Mana, Asímadjô learned to speak Creole and saw how Creoles from French Guiana, along with a handful of Ndyuka and Aluku

Maroons, controlled the river transport trade. He saw that Creole canoes were far smaller than Saramaka ones, holding only six barrels (compared to Saramaka ones that held up to forty-five), and that the Creoles maneuvered exclusively with paddles, rather than with the poles Saramakas used at the prow of their canoes to get through the rapids. The Creoles were dying in the water and the goods weren't getting to their destination . . . and neither the Alukus nor Ndyukas were up to the task. Hansibai and Asímadjô succeeded in the transport trade, working the lower river for some time. And when Asímadjô made his triumphal return to Saramaka, bringing back a case of fancy French soap and a magnificent French sword, large numbers of men were ready to follow in his footsteps.[6]

Older Saramakas still like to describe the rigors of the transport trade.[7] They tell about Akóni, another pioneer in Mana and the first to try to bring a load all the way up to the mines at St. Léon, on the Upper River. Unable to get through the rapids at Saut Continent, he and his crew built a platform in the forest, stocked the merchandise there, and went downstream to seek help. His father-in-law, who lived in Mana, went upriver, found the load, and was able to bring it up some distance further, but when he got to the rapids called Saut Par Hasard he, too, was stymied, so he and his crew built a platform for the goods and went back downstream. Tatá Agáduhánsu, who was at the place called Délices with his sisters' sons Asántifútu and Akaaso and with Tatá Kogá, said they'd do it. And they did. They found the goods and, using their poling technique, brought them way upstream. At the mouth of St. Léon Creek, a tremendous *posontíi* tree had fallen and blocked their entry. They cut at it with their axes for a whole week but couldn't get through, so they unloaded the canoes, made a camp, and called their gods for consultation. Tatá Kogá had a god called Ma Kambó, and Agáduhánsu had an Apúku called Misíi (short for *Mi si lóngi*—"I see far"). The gods said, "If you give up and go back now, you'll die. Cut the tree." They worked at it for three more days and called the gods again. This time the gods said they would work with them the following day. As the men were cutting at the tree, they saw two ducks and shot them. (It was the gods who'd brought the ducks.) The Creole gold miners upriver at St. Léon heard the gunshots and figured the Saramakas didn't know where to find them and were signaling with their guns. So they answered with their own guns and went down to meet them—a moment of joy still recalled with emotion. As Saramakas say, "Honors for opening up the upper Mana go to Tatá Agáduhánsu and Tatá Kogá, and those for the lower Mana go to Asímadjô, but not to him alone, for it was his Ndyuka friend Hansibai who first told him there was a river over there with work to be had."

Tooy heard all this and more during his days and nights by the Mana. He heard about the marvelous Wéntis that inhabit the mouth of that river, including Teefón ("Telephone"), which Tatá Agáduhánsu himself had in his head.[8] And how there were so many Saramakas working the river that the French government decided to create the first Saramaka captain's position at Mana, offering it to Agáduhánsu, who deferred in favor of Samuel.[9]

Saut Sabbat Rapids, where Tooy spent much of his time bridge building, had a bloody past as the first stopping-off place for escapees heading east from the *bagne*. He heard, for example, about a Saramaka called Suwí (or Lepetjá) who was going up through the rapids when the escapees shot the man at the head of his canoe. There were thirty-five whitemen, Tooy says. Suwí stormed ashore and killed five with his machete and managed to tie up the other thirty with vines and bring them in to the authorities at Mana. Tooy also heard about Tatá Maayani, who met up with a group of escapees just below Saut Tamanoa Rapids, upstream from Saut Sabbat, where he had his camp. The six of them were trying to steal his canoe and his gun. But his Komantí warned him! They were headed for Brazil, so he told them he'd show them the way. Just above Kakioko Creek, when they got out of the canoe, Old Man Maayani killed them all, cut off their heads, and threw their bodies into the forest! He took the heads and his gun, got back in his canoe, and came home. And he put those skulls in his *óbia* house!

* * *

After leaving his public-works job, Tooy spent a year in eastern Suriname, working in a timber camp near the Ndyuka village of Moiwana, then doing day jobs around Moengo, and finally going back to Saint-Laurent—but there were no salaried jobs, just sawing logs and day work. And then Alcoa began to build the great dam at Afobaka, and from 1960 to 1962 he was right in the thick of it. The end came suddenly, when a steel beam dropped 7 meters and he was unconscious from Saturday till Tuesday. So many men were dying in accidents—"people drowning, machinery killing them, every sort of death you can imagine!" He decided just to quit, and went to live in the nearby Saramaka village of Balén.

During this time, Gaamá Agbagó came down from the Pikílío and lived in Balén for several months. There were repeated council meetings about damming the river, one including the *gaamás* of all the other Maroon peoples. They concluded that it wasn't Agbagó's fault, he couldn't be held responsible. And the day they poured libations for Gaamá Agbagó, to ask the ancestors to exonerate him, it was Tooy who played the *apínti*—the drum of Gadien!

Every morning, it was Tooy who woke up the *gaamá* with the appropriate drum rhythms, playing his drum name *Naná-u-Kêlempé Kílintínboto-fu-Lámbote*. He had been hesitant to do it, but Flibánti, who was there with Sensiló, urged him to play Gadien's drum. He'd wept and then decided to do it. He described how Tatá Dooté of Dángogó (our old friend from the 1960s) sat down on his left, the *gaamá* on his right. They brought out the *gaamá*'s drum. "Is the Bêndêkôndè kid ready?" the *gaamá* asked, playfully referring to Tooy by the name of his father's village. "Yes, I'm ready." "Well, here's the drum . . ." Later, said Tooy, the *gaamá* asked Basiá Bótokoósu to summon him to his residence. Captain Kala was there, Headcaptain Faansisónu was there, and the latter poured the rum onto Tooy's hands before it reached the earth. The *gaamá* asked him if he wanted to become a captain. He said no. Then he asked if he wanted to be a *basiá* (assistant headman). No. So they made an older brother of his captain of Bundjitapá. That was Tooy's first brush with a captaincy.

While in Balén, he lived with a woman from Ndyuka, a distant relative of his father's. "She was quite a case!—always 'testing' me, trying to find my weak spot."

> When I was out working, she'd eat my food, take my clothes, drink from my rum bottle. I was as good as dead! Then a guy started telling his wife that he knew that I had sent my wife as go-between to ask her to sleep with me. I held this thing in my heart for one whole year without doing anything about it. And then one Saturday night, I slept in two different houses, with two different women—neither my wife. Before I went out, I'd told my little brother where I'd be so if he heard a commotion in such-and-such a place, he could come running. I left the first woman whose house I visited around midnight. Then I went on to the second. I was quite a guy—but guess what? The very next day, that woman's husband died! Baad! When I'd arrived in the middle of the night, I'd knocked on the door and she opened it, and just then a giant bat flew out and nearly knocked me over. I should have known to go home, Brother! But I went right on in and stayed till half-past five, just before dawn. As I arrived back in Balén, I came upon a niece of mine who told me that the woman's husband had returned home from work during the night (the evening shift at the dam let out at midnight) and had carefully opened the door and had seen me with his wife! After I left, I learned, he came back and really beat his wife—all because of me. The next night, his people showed up to beat my little brother and were just getting started when I showed up and stopped them. I went into my house to change out of my work clothes and the fifteen men blocked me in my house. They accused me of this and that. They kept saying I should come on out of the house. I denied the whole thing. Back and forth. Lots of threats. Finally, I jumped out and said, whoever wants to hit me,

let him try. And I walked right past them and into my father's ancestor shrine. I called the strong name of the ancestor shrine. I called the strong name of the jug used to pour libations. I called the strong name of the palm-leaf fringe around the shrine. I called the strong name of the Earth Mother. I told my father I needed his help. And I told them all sorts of things about their matrilineage [including allusions to various cases of sexual misconduct that brought avenging spirits]. And the men just took off! Though I don't dare go back to that village, they never beat me. I bested them with my knowledge![10]

Tooy would have been nearly thirty when he took up curing on a steady basis, near Balén. "I began curing people, but not for sickness. It was to make gods, domesticate them, settle them in people's heads—Apúku [forest spirits], Papágádu [boa-constrictor gods], Komantí [warrior/curing gods]. The main thing I did was make Komantís—and play Papá and *apínti*." He also used to work with his *paiyá-paiyá-óbia* fan, also called *wómi sáku*—the óbia fan he'd used at our house in Martinique, which his father's brother, Baala, Pobôsi's sister's son, had taught him to use for hunting, soon after he'd bestowed his first loincloth on him in the family's ancestor shrine.

It was there that a group of Ndyukas brought him Yaai, who later became his wife, to "make" her mysterious god—seven Ndyuka priests had already tried without success. "I'd never seen her before. But I built a little house in the forest by a creek where I could take care of this work. It wasn't a shrine for a god, it was a shrine for the god-who-has-the earth"—in other words, the kind of god Tooy had prayed to in vain at Roland's lumberyard.

One day I was with this woman in a consultation—I was reading tarot cards and a "jumping animal" walked right up to the house. She saw it and cried out, "You have a visitor! You have a visitor!" One of its legs was cut off! The animal came and sat down right in front of the woman. I went and sat down behind her. That woman was carrying a pregnancy she'd had for two years without being able to give birth! When the animal sat down and fixed her with a stare, right then, *yòòòòòòò*, her waters broke! I said, "Trouble!" and went and got some water and sprayed her belly several times with my mouth. The animal took off down the trail and disappeared into the forest toward the west. You know who that woman was? It was Yaai—that's how I met her.

He cured her the next day.

I prepared a clay pot. (My apologies to Dúnguláli!) That pot—three times it refused to boil. How could this be, I said. I went off and broke some leaves off trees. Don't ask me what they were, because I still don't know! We mashed them up and finally the pot boiled. I went and washed my hands. (I still don't know what weeds those were.) I took the pot off the fire, cooled it, and gave her some to drink, three times, and she kept crying out that her belly was killing her. I had her drink yet again. That's when the "father" [the god] arrived. She gave birth to seven snakes. I washed her with leaves. I kept giving her to drink from that pot. Eventually, her people sent a message for me to bring her home. I couldn't, so they came back to get her. By that time, the end of the month, her belly was absolutely flat. We consulted divination. It said that there was a god whom her people had troubled, and that was what had been in her belly. They'd had seven specialists try to "make" it, but none could. Three days later, I went to see the garden I'd made with my older brother, where we'd planted more than one thousand orange trees, to say goodbye. And then I left and never went back.

Tooy moved back to Saint-Laurent, where Yaai joined him from Ndyuka, and this time he settled in, building a large house—"9 meters by 10 with two stories, right near the municipal water tank." [11] He took a night job to earn money, serving as watchman at the sawmill, and set himself up for both Saramaka-style and Creole-style curing during the day. The god who'd begun coming into his head with increasing regularity, Tatá Dúnuyángi, taught him how to "see things" in a mirror as well as how to better manipulate his tarot cards. ("You have to have a strong stomach to do divination with cards," he remarks to me.) [12] And he built his first Dúnguláli-Óbia shrine, with help from a close friend, Seduáni, whose father had been the priest of a branch on the Suriname River. (During Tooy's time in Haarlem, he'd learned much about the óbia from his cousin Awénke, Kódji's "namesake" and priest of the óbia there.) A few years later, he traveled to the Oyapock to make offerings at the mother shrine. "I made my offering to Akoomí, raised a flag in his honor. I said I wanted to work with his óbia, and I gave him 3 liters of rum and three cloths. There's nothing about that óbia I don't know! But no one can say that I stole it."

During this time, Tooy worked diligently to settle Yaai's god in her head. He went to her village in Ndyuka, far up the Tapanahoni, and spent six full months presiding over the final rituals that removed the god from the forest to her village. "Thirty-one people went to the spot to help bring it out—all of them came out of the forest weeping, but no one could figure out why." Eventually, he was able to determine that Yaai's kinsmen had cut a garden in the domain of this god's father without asking proper permission. But what he found out next, as the god began to speak through Yaai, was the real shocker: the god's father was none other than Flibánti, the African-ghost-spirit in the head of Tooy's brother Sensiló—the óbia that Kwasímukámba had given to Antamá. It was Flibánti who had brought Yaai's god out of the sea, where it had lived with its mother Yowentína, Flibánti's wife in Wénti land, and it was Flibánti who set up a garden for this son of his near a creek in Ndyuka. Tooy brought Yaai back to Saint-Laurent, where they set up a shrine for her god, who had told them his name was Bási Yontíni—a genuine Wénti from Gaánlolo, under the sea, though he has an African-ghost-spirit for a father and a Papágádu (snake spirit) named Asináia for a wife.[13] From that moment on, Yaai's Wénti became a centerpiece of Tooy's life.

During his time in Saint-Laurent, Tooy was shot in the foot in a hunting accident. "I walked 7 kilometers with that shot-up foot. I felt nothing, and it stayed swollen for months. Finally, Yaai's god came and told me what to do. I sacrificed two fowls to Dúnguláli. But the foot has never healed completely."

All this time, the brother of Tooy's mother, Jozef Babiá, lived nearby and they spent a great deal of time together. Babiá was quite a guy. Called by everyone Losión (perfume), he had been in Guyane for decades. Tooy loves to tell how "ripe" he was, even though he had no gods in his head. Once, for example, some of his enemies decided to get together and kill him by sorcery. In the savannah, near the customs house, they made an óbia, digging a hole and putting in various leaves and a new unwashed length of cloth. Then they ritually shot him, buried him there, and sang Papá, just the way they bury a real person, and then covered up the hole. But a friend—a Creole—who was on the balcony of his two-storey house saw this and, very upset, went to tell Babiá. Babiá comforted the friend and said, "That's all those people did? Not to worry. We'll eat them for breakfast!" (Saramakas say, "We'll drink their coffee!") Then Babiá asked his friend to show him the exact spot. The man took him near and pointed to where it was—he was too scared to get closer. Babiá went and emptied the hole, pulled himself right out! Seven days passed, and the man who'd directed the óbia was struck with a tremendous fever. His wife, who was Babiá's niece, had also washed in the óbia, and Babiá told her, "Go back to Saramaka, or you'll never recover," and he offered her 40,000 (ancien) francs for expenses. But instead, she took her husband up the Marowijne to the village of Apatou. Two days later, he was dead. Five weeks later, she died, too. That day, she'd prepared some kwaka (grilled cassava flour), she'd swept the house, and she put a little kwaka in water. The first mouthful she took, Hwoii! (dead). Later, another girl who'd washed in the óbia came to beg him to protect her, but he said, "Get outta here! You knew full well what you were doing!"

Another time, Babiá was bringing a canoe filled with railroad ties made of lókísi hardwood across the broad river to Albina, on the Dutch side. In those days, they sold for 50 cents (a half guilder) each. He had twenty of them. Babiá took a sack of okra and put it in his canoe with his gun and hunting sack. During the crossing, the canoe overturned, and he found himself swimming with his okra sack, his gun, and his hunting sack. Three times as he was about to go under for good, he called out to the Béndiwáta Mamá, who each time lifted him up. (He had an *óbia* in the okra sack.) You can stand on her back for a whole hour—as long as you don't move at all. The god brought him right to shore.

Babiá got some of his *óbias* from an unusual source—three strange Africans who lived with him for years in Mana. Tooy now works with a few of their *óbias*, which his uncle passed on to him. I'd first heard of these characters in the 1960s, when Asipéi, who'd spent the 1920s in Mana, reminisced about how one of these men had an *óbia*-necklace he used in divination and offered to make one for him. It told you instantly when your wife was so much as flirting with another man. Asipéi told him thanks anyway. He was afraid of it; there are some things it's better not to know. Tooy described the Africans—all of whom lived in Mana before his time—more fully. Their names were Sêbede, Kodjáko, and Ahóntodji. Sêbede brought up Babiá, took care of him like his own son. The three of them had an *óbia* post in a shrine. If you came near there with another *óbia*, you were a dead man!

Each of those Africans had a matchbox, and once a year they'd take out a match and use it for the whole year. When Ahóntodji's was almost empty—there were only two or three matchsticks left—he said he couldn't stay till the box was empty; it was time to go home. The next morning they went to look for him, and he was gone—he'd flown back to Africa! But Kodjá and Sêbede stayed on. Kodjá died first, and when Sèbede died, people said he was a witch and wouldn't help bury him. Babiá lifted his coffin on his back and carried it all the way to the cemetery! Sêbede, says Tooy, had an *óbia*-in-a-calabash. Every week he'd light a candle in front of it. Those men had a matchbox where one match would strike for an entire year! They taught Babiá some African "language," according to Tooy's god Dúnuyángi, who one day tells me a "dangerous" phrase that they said was from the Anagó people: *Selebóbo selefála, anatá djóbidjóbi, bêtele djóbidjóbi, abeyé beyówa.* Dúnuyángi explains, "If you buy a hoe blade, and set it on a wooden handle, you can't be the first to cut the earth with it—if you do, you'll die! Give it to someone else to cut the earth with first. That's what these words say. 'If you're looking to kill me, you'll kill yourself!' Tatá Sêbede and Kodjá and Ahóntodji, they brought that talk to us. Saramakas hadn't heard it before." There was only one thing, Babiá told Tooy, that the three Africans promised to give him that they didn't—the identity of the leaves they used to drink in a calabash, that's what they didn't give him.

I ask Tooy if he's ever heard of other Africans whom Saramakas knew—on the Oyapock, in Paramaribo, or elsewhere. (I certainly haven't.) He says only those three. And for him, their legacy—what they taught Saramakas—is pretty small change. So any local openings I might have hoped for toward Randy Matory's master narrative—which seems to work for Candomblé and, to a lesser extent, for Santería—that New World Afro-American religions bask in an ongoing, centuries-long interchange with African motherlands, may be laid to rest in this case, at least as far as I'm concerned.[14]

★   ★   ★

"I didn't mean to leave Saint-Laurent for Cayenne," Tooy told me. (He'd been living there some five years by this time.)

> The big man of Cayenne called L. had been in two accidents; he was dying. Seduáni, who knew us both, came to me for advice. I "cut cards" six times to see what needed to be done. On a Good Friday, they brought me to Cayenne (I don't know what year). I was supposed to meet him just across the creek from here. I boiled a pot of leaves for him, three weeks' worth, and told him he couldn't eat food cooked by women or go anywhere near women during those three weeks. He asked me how much he owed. I said I didn't know—he could pay me 300,000 [ancien] francs. He said, "I want to live! Three hundred thousand francs couldn't even buy my coffin!" In fact, he paid me 1,900,000 francs. I didn't ask for it—it's what his heart told him to give. And L. is still alive today!
>
> Once I was in Cayenne I began to spend time with my older brother Payei, whom I'd never met before. We'd each take our wife to his forest camp in Roura, a fine place next to the river but far from the road, where we worked in his garden and sold kwáka [roasted cassava granules] at the landing place. Yaai was very sick there. I brought her down to the hospital in town, where she stayed for two months—she was almost dead.
>
> A man named Docile St. Clair had taken care of my brother when he was young—he'd had him baptized. He had bought that piece of forest, and he and my brother worked gold there for fourteen years. When he died, he left Payei 450 hectares in his will. That's where I worked until the police stopped me just a few years ago. It turns out that the man hadn't made the papers correctly, and after my brother's death, they said I had a different name from him, so how could I be his brother? But the police knew that land was my brother's, and in the end, they gave me title to 5 hectares there. The rest is vacant land. You can only get there by canoe.

★   ★   ★

Given the rest of the chronology, Tooy's move to Cayenne must have come around 1970.[15] That's when he would have set himself up with Yaai in the house at the edge of the city, with an altar for Bási Yontíni and a chamber for Dúnguláli, next to the swamp that was later drained to make space for his current home. And it's when he began working in the capital as a full-time curer.

MY FIRST-TIME MUSEUM

✶ 1690/2007 ✶

I try to envision what a *musée imaginaire* of Saramakas' history-with-white-folks might look like, a museum of words and images rather than objects. (By this point in the book, the reader should be able to fill in this skeletal plan with additional appropriate words and images.) It might begin with the Saramaka adage "First-Time isn't dead yet," and would certainly be dominated by continuities of whitefolks' oppression and by vast imbalances of power. But it would include, just as surely, ever-changing creative responses from Saramakas refusing to accept the whitefolks' definition of the situation and successfully building separate worlds quite their own—perhaps this whole book might be read as a testament to that.

The rooms could be arranged chronologically.

EARLY EIGHTEENTH CENTURY. We begin with the iconic image of whitefolks' control over Africans' bodies—Joosie hanging from his gibbet—bespeaking everything from capture and enslavement in Africa, through all the horrors of Suriname slavery, to the recapture of Saramakas in battle followed by their torture and death. Joosie was one of twelve members of Kaásipúmbu's "Lángu" community who were captured by massive military expeditions in 1730. Before the end of the year, eleven of them are "brought to justice . . . in the hope that it would provide an Example and deterrent to their associates, and reduce the propensity of slaves to escape."[1] Their sentence, administered by the Court of Policy and Criminal Justice in Paramaribo, reads as follows:

> The Negro Joosie shall be hanged from the gibbet by an Iron Hook through his ribs, until dead; his head shall then be severed and displayed on a stake by the riverbank, remaining to be picked over by birds of prey. As for the Negroes Wierrie and Manbote, they shall be bound to a stake and roasted alive over a slow fire, while being tortured with glowing Tongs. The Negro girls, Lucretia, Ambira, Aga, Gomba, Marie and Victoria will be tied to a Cross, to be broken alive, and then their heads severed, to be exposed by the riverbank on stakes.

"A Negro hung alive by the Ribs to a Gallows." Engraving by William Blake after a drawing by John Gabriel Stedman, based on an eyewitness account from 1773.

> The Negro girls Diana and Christina shall be beheaded with an axe, and their heads exposed on poles by the riverbank.[2]

But even while Joosie twists in the wind, his brothers and sisters are carrying on with their remarkable project of nation-building. So, this first virtual room is dominated by the whites' attempts to exercise violence as a means of control and by the resulting war between unequals, during which Saramaka men, women, and children quietly create a whole new culture and society—language, political and economic systems, rituals and beliefs, and all the rest—based firmly on their collective African knowledge and experience, with much smaller contributions from their limited contact with European and Amerindian peoples.

MID-EIGHTEENTH CENTURY. The process of formal peacemaking deserves a room of its own—the whites' continuous perfidy, the Saramakas' ultimate triumph, thanks to their óbias and their skills in guerrilla warfare. We would see the whitefolks sending in their spies, including Kwasímukámba, to learn Saramaka secrets, but Saramaka óbias helping the rebels to triumph in the end. And once the Peace was tentatively set, whitefolks, thinking the Saramakas childlike, trying to trick them with baubles (Ensign Dörig at the tribute distribution: "I had arranged all the shares in such an attractive way that they would think that there was three times as much as there actually was"), but the Saramakas hanging tough and insisting on "53 kegs of gunpowder, 13 muskets, some light guns," and other such instead.[3] For Saramakas, *nouná* now becomes the watchword—it's time for ruse and avoidance.[4]

LATE EIGHTEENTH CENTURY. Colonial postholders and Moravian missionaries dwell in Saramaka villages, trying to win, on the one hand, recently escaped slaves whom they can return to servitude, and on the other, Saramaka souls for Christ. Saramakas resist magnificently, playing a shell game with the many new "runaways" they are harboring, and under the charismatic leadership of Tooy's ancestor Antamá, refuse Christian conversion almost to a man (and woman).

MID-NINETEENTH CENTURY. Slave emancipation on the coast and the gold rush in French Guiana bring wage-labor opportunities and increased contacts with whitefolks for Saramaka men. Keeping First-Time ideology alive becomes the watchword. The folktale about King Nothing-Can-Hurt Him speaks to the order of the day: so long as you never accept the whiteman's definition of the situation, you'll triumph in the end.[5]

EARLY TWENTIETH CENTURY. Whitefolks step up the pressure, trying to bring Saramaka lands under rational control (for purposes of granting mining concessions as well as for more abstract, empire-building reasons) through surveying and mapping. Saramakas, including Tooy's namesake Pobôsi, pick and choose from the offerings of whitefolks but largely resist, mainly through ruse. Saramaka men become increasingly dependent on migrant labor as canoemen in French Guiana, where their newly discovered Wéntis help them succeed.

MID-TWENTIETH CENTURY. The colonial state and Alcoa get tough and unilaterally appropriate one-half of Saramaka territory for a hydroelectric dam and lake. There is no international outcry (from anthropologists or anyone else)—only a feel-good project to save the displaced animals. Beyond the affected area of the lake, Saramaka life goes on much as before. (We begin our anthropological fieldwork on the Pikílío.)

LATE TWENTIETH CENTURY. The postindependence Republic of Suriname wages war against Maroons. The killings of Saramakas at Atjóni might be the emblematic centerpiece here.[6] After a protracted trial, the Inter-American Court for Human Rights forces the Republic of Suriname to accept responsibility and pay the relatives of the murdered Saramakas nearly half a million U.S. dollars. Other exhibits in this room could include eyewitness accounts of what happened in the Ndyuka village of Moiwana on November 29, 1986: "The soldiers rounded up another group of seven people: six children and one woman. They lined them up in the middle of the village. They begged for their lives, but the soldiers shot them all to death. . . . Before the soldiers left, they burned down the whole village"[7] Or more general accounts of the period: "In June 1986 [Suriname Head of State] Bouterse . . . unleashed his military—including field artillery, aerial bombardment, and tanks—on the defenseless village of Mongo Tapu. . . . In the following months similar violent actions were taken against other Maroon villages. In December 1986 the *New York Times* reported that 244 Maroons had been killed. . . . The immediate challenge concerns the fate of the more than 14,000 [Maroon] refugees. At least 10,000 of them . . . have fled across the Maroni River into French Guiana."[8] In June 2005, in a sweeping ruling, the Inter-American Court for Human Rights found Suriname guilty of having violated the human rights of 130 named members of the village of Moiwana (including killing at least 39 people, mainly women and children, and wounding many more; covering up the crime and failing to investigate it; and effectively exiling the whole community from its traditional lands). The court ordered Suriname to pay a total of nearly three million U.S. dollars to the surviving members of the community, to grant them collective title to their lands, to bring the perpetrators to justice, to erect a memorial, and to make a public apology. As this book goes to press, Suriname has already paid survivors their money, erected a memorial, and made a public apology, though the collective land grant and prosecution of the perpetrators remain unfinished business.

TWENTY-FIRST CENTURY. In Suriname, there are yet more blatant attempts to abrogate unilaterally the eighteenth-century Maroon treaties. The government in Paramaribo cuts up the bulk of Saramaka territory into parcels and leases them to Chinese, Indonesian, Canadian, American, and other multinational logging and mining companies. Logging roads are cut through First-Time village sites; game, birds, and fish disappear; vast expanses of red mud and white sand replace tropical forest; thousands of tons of cyanide- and mercury-laced gold-mining slag bury watercourses. The Association of Saramaka Authorities (the traditional captains and the *gaamá*) bring suit before the Inter-American Court for Human Rights, seeking collective title to the lands on which Saramakas have lived, farmed, and hunted since the eighteenth century and, potentially, establishing far-reaching legal precedent for indigenous and Maroon peoples throughout the Americas. The outcome is pending at the time this book goes to press.[9]

Meanwhile, in French Guiana, where one-third of Saramakas now live, most without French papers, the government in Cayenne has turned a blind eye to massive ecological depredations caused by multinational and local gold mining in Aluku territory. And Saramaka captain Tooy is sentenced to seven years in prison for a crime he did not commit.

First-Time isn't dead yet.

THE TRIAL

✶ 02202002 ✶

If February 20, 2002, ranks up there with the worst day of my own life, imagine what it must have been like for Tooy.

This is not a pretty story, and it has no heroes. Even writing about it runs multiple risks, real and imagined, including the loss of previously sympathetic readers. But for all that, it's probably worth trying to get down the events as best I understand them. For it is part of Tooy's story, as well as part of my own.[1]

✶   ✶   ✶

Of the seven deadly sins, there's little doubt that the favored choice of most Saramaka men has always been lust. Since earliest recorded history, having what they call "long eyes" about women, married or not, has landed them in trouble. Around midnight, the Suriname River is dotted with the lanterns of men in canoes making their way upstream or down, often stopping at a landing place to exchange a canoe for another that happens to be there and continuing to the target village in this borrowed craft, which will be returned before dawn, the owner none the wiser—stealth and caution are part of the local mating game. Adultery is by far the most common "crime" in Saramaka jurisprudence. Normally, the adulterous man (if caught) pays the husband's lineage a fine or suffers a severe beating or both. Most men have had to pay fines or have received beatings numerous times in their lives—and that's only for the times they've been caught. The introduction of Casio digital watches was a major breakthrough in the 1960s, as men visiting married women for a night had previously assured their predawn exit with large wind-up alarm clocks that risked alerting neighbors to the affair.

Adultery may lead to more serious sanctions for the man: in certain cases, his matrilineage suffers eternal vengeance from the spirit of the woman's deceased husband. Indeed, one of the two major lineages of Tooy's Lángu clan has its origin in just such a domestic event, which must have happened nearly three hundred years ago. As Tooy summarizes it,

> Tatá Kaási [the earliest of the great First-Time Lángu leaders], his brother-in-law Piyái, and Tatá Amúsu went off through the forest to bring back Olíko, because Piyái wanted her as a wife. (Kaási had two wives, Amímba and an íngi [Indian] woman named Talí—Piyái was her brother.) Ma Olíko, she was an íngi. (Her name is really "sweet," and they say she was quite a looker!) These men—night was their day. They'd walk through the forest at night! They waited for her near the creek at the íngi village, where she would come down to wash; then they would take her away. They hid there. Then two young girls arrived. Kaási took Olíko with his óbia. She was carrying a gourd to get water—still a little kid. They brought her back to their village to raise. After a while, Piyái told Kaási she was big enough to be given to him in marriage. Kaási said no, she wasn't big enough yet. (That's what brought the avenging spirit!) One day they saw that Olíko was pregnant. Well, who do you think had knocked her up? Of course it was Kaási! Piyái didn't say much and didn't ask for reparations. He simply took his sister and the better part of Kaási's óbias and walked off into the forest, never to be seen again. (The children of Kaási and Olíko are the Pikí Kaapátu subclan of Lángu. Piyái became the great avenging spirit for the Gaán Kaapátu subclan, the children of Kaási and Amímba.)

Saramaka men like their women young. I once overheard a man say, "The two greatest gifts of God to man are all-night 'plays' [the large celebrations that culminate funerals] and young adolescent girls." And, indeed, thirteen- or fourteen-year-old girls have always been the most actively sought partners. Girls marry young—fourteen would be about the norm. And sex is considered an untrammeled joy by men and women and is unaccompanied by anxiety, except as regards jealousy, which is a strong Saramaka passion.[2]

* * *

In February 2002, we had arrived in Guyane for a month of research aimed at finishing a general book about Maroons in Guyane.[3] When we visited Tooy on the day of our arrival, he told us, "They're talking about putting me in jail because of that íngi girl"—shades of Tatá Kaási!—and he showed us a fistful of papers he'd recently received. As we read through these documents—a series of legal forms, a psychiatrist's report, various depositions—it dawned on us that Tooy was being summoned to appear the following week before the Criminal Court of Cayenne to defend himself on a charge of rape.

When we ask, Tooy says the Indian woman left him around 1988, after they'd lived together several years, and that she surprised him three years later by showing up with a little girl, asking him for money. He was angry she hadn't told him about the child earlier, but he gave her some cash. He continued to give her money over the years, once, he says, even buying a bicycle for the child. And then in 1998 she showed up again, this time with her mother, demanding the equivalent of thirteen thousand dollars and threatening that if he didn't pay she'd take him to court. Since then, he's been summoned repeatedly to the police station and the courthouse, questioned, and then released. He says he is getting tired of this harassment.

It's Tuesday, February 12, and—according to the documents Tooy's showed us, which of course he can't read—the trial is set for Wednesday the twentieth. We ask Tooy if he has a lawyer. He searches through his papers and finds a slip with a handwritten name—the court-appointed lawyer is one Antoine Auguste, Esquire. Tooy says he's never met him. We hurry back to our hotel and find the name in the phonebook. We call, explain ourselves, and are given an appointment first thing in the morning. We're one week from the trial date.

On the way to the lawyer's, we stop by Tooy's to say good morning. He takes us out behind his house, breaks off some *gwáyamáka* leaves, and tells us to masticate them and hold as big a wad as we can in the back of our mouths while we speak to the lawyer. It guarantees, he explains, that our words will have their intended purpose—it's a specialty of the Kaapátu (Béndiwáta) people, who learned it from Amerindians (that is, from Kaási's brother-in-law Piyái).

Downtown in Cayenne, we find Mr. Auguste in his tiny office cluttered with stacks of folders. We do our best to speak above the radio behind his desk blaring carnival music—it seems not to occur to him to lower the volume. We introduce ourselves as anthropologists who have long worked with Saramakas and give him two of our books in French, in the hope that they will help him better contextualize the life of his client before the court, especially as concerns matters of sex and family.

Mr. Auguste's face breaks into a broad smile: "It's God himself who brought you to this modest office. I know I'm going to lose this case, but now that you are here, we have a fighting chance to get a lighter sentence." He tells us that the maximum sentence for rape is twenty years, and that's exactly what he'd been expecting the jury to hand down. We spend the next half hour giving him a minicourse in Saramaka culture, explaining that girls begin sex at a very early age, that husbands are often far older than their wives, and that most men have several wives. As he lingers over the photos of bare-breasted Saramaka girls in our books, he leers at the idea of having more than one wife, particularly young wives, saying what a shame it was that he hadn't been born into that society. When we inquire, he suggests that it would be best if he and Tooy did not meet until the day of the trial: "It's better not to try to 'program' those people—it just confuses them, and they end up contradicting themselves when they take the stand." We explain that Saramakas consider Tooy a leader of his people, a scholar, and a priest, and try to show him the four-page newspaper spread about Tooy's enstoolment as captain. Auguste doesn't seem very interested but thanks us for the information. As we leave, the radio is still blaring carnival songs.

Back at Tooy's, the young apprentices tell us that an old client of his, the honorary consul of Peru in Cayenne, has hired a second lawyer named Richard Lamartine. Meanwhile, Tooy has found some additional papers delivered by court courier and asks us to read them for him. We telephone Lamartine and make an appointment. Tooy says when we ask that he's never met him either.

We are becoming increasingly concerned about the seriousness of Tooy's situation. Alone in our hotel room, we try to analyze the options, wondering whether Tooy shouldn't consider escaping to Suriname, which has no extradition treaty with French Guiana and is just a quick canoe ride over the open border from Saint-Laurent, four hours away. Even if the chances of being convicted and ending up in prison were only 50-50, wouldn't we be tempted simply to go home to Suriname, if we were in his place?

Later that evening, roughly sixty members of the Saramaka community, many of them relatives of Tooy's, meet to discuss the case and ask us to explain the stakes. (All these people are immigrants, many of them without papers, and few of them can either speak French or read and write.) Auguste has told us that he has the right to call five character witnesses, but that we have only until the next morning to submit their names to the court. So together we agree on a list: the two of us, a journalist friend who had written an article about Tooy when he became captain, Ben Amiemba (president of the Association of Young Active Saramakas of Guyane), and our old friend Kalusé, who is Tooy's assistant captain.

The next day we meet the second lawyer, whose office is a considerable step up from Auguste's. He shows us his copy of the French edition of *First-Time*, which he'd bought a couple of years before to try to learn something about the Saramakas he was seeing with increasing frequency around Cayenne. Like Auguste, he feels that our presence provides a ray of hope where there had been none before. But he cautions us that the presiding judge is a militant feminist who has told him privately that she's had it up to here with the recent plague of rapes in Cayenne and thinks the only solution is to get all the bastards firmly behind bars.[4]

★   ★   ★

Though Tooy clearly didn't enjoy speaking about it, we told him it was important that he tell us everything he knew about the events leading to his current dilemma. His version (corroborated to us independently by his wives and various other Saramakas) is a tangled web.

Some twenty years ago, he said, when he was living in a two-room shack at the edge of the mangrove, not far from his present house, he took in a family of íngi from Maripasoula, far up the river that borders Suriname. The mother, he further specified, was pure Indian, while her husband was a Creole from Guadeloupe, and there were three young-teenage daughters—Annette, Cathérine, and Brigitte—as well as a still younger son, Jean. Cathérine had been having serious health problems—headaches, earaches, and occasional convulsions—and her mother had taken her to a Saramaka curer in Maripasoula, Thomas Ngwete. Divination told Ngwete that Cathérine's problems stemmed from an Apúku forest spirit who lived in a boulder that had been singed when Cathérine's father had cut a garden near its abode. Ngwete worked to cure Cathérine over several months without success. In the end, he suggested they travel to Cayenne to consult Tooy, who had stronger powers.

On Ngwete's advice, the whole family took the biweekly plane to Cayenne and squeezed into Tooy's tiny house, where they stayed for several months as he commenced his curing rituals for Cathérine. Ma Yaai, Tooy's wife, was at her home in Saint-Laurent during the period, and he visited her occasionally on weekends. At the outset, Tooy requested 2,000 francs ($325) from Cathérine's father for the cure—he never asked for additional money from them. Tooy recalls that Cathérine's father and mother were having conjugal difficulties at the time. He thinks it may have had to do with the father's strong adhesion to the Evangelical Church, in which he tried to enroll his daughters as well.

Before long, Tooy says, he began sleeping with Cathérine's younger sister Annette, who—though only thirteen—was already sexually experienced. The parents made no objection, and the couple stayed together for the next five years. After the first months with the whole íngi family at Tooy's, the parents went back to Maripasoula, leaving the three daughters and the son in his care. Before long, he says, he began sleeping with Annette's sisters,

Cathérine and Brigitte, who would climb up to his sleeping loft while Annette was having her period and therefore sleeping downstairs, separately. (These two girls, he says, were also experienced with men by the time he first slept with them.) The girls played a game of competing for his favors. Whenever Annette was sleeping on the bench downstairs, Brigitte would scamper up the stairs to be the first in bed with him. He was having great fun with the three girls, going everywhere with them, making a large garden at his brother's place at Roura, where the four of them worked together and stayed during school vacations. He also took them on vacation trips to Saint-Laurent, where they all stayed with Ma Yaai. And he once took them on a memorable trip to Suriname, where they visited his relatives, did some curing for Cathérine, and enjoyed the change. Back in Cayenne, Tooy tried, several times, to fix up Cathérine and Brigitte with young men he knew, thinking that it would be good for them to have more permanent relationships. Several young Saramakas took advantage of this opportunity, though none of the relationships lasted long.

Tooy told us that after a couple of years of this, Cathérine and Brigitte moved out, lodging at the home of a state-appointed "guardian" while they finished school in Cayenne. Tooy continued to see them frequently, since they lived nearby and often visited their sister Annette. Then, after five years of living together, Tooy and Annette decided to part ways, and she returned to Maripasoula. Before she left, Brigitte visited in the house for a few days.

For the next three years, Tooy didn't see or hear from any of the sisters. Then, out of the blue, Brigitte and her mother showed up with a three-year-old girl, telling him the child was his. Tooy was shocked—when a Saramaka woman becomes pregnant, it is considered crucial for the health of the child that the father have frequent intercourse with the mother. But he offered to recognize his daughter. Brigitte said that that was not why they were there, they just wanted him to know about her. He gave them some money to buy her things. After that, Brigitte visited periodically, asking for money for the child, which he gave, and occasionally having sex with him. At one point, he bought the child a bicycle as a present. When we asked, he said her name was Agnès.

For a few years, he says, Brigitte stopped coming. And then, suddenly, she showed up with her mother and said that if he didn't pay her 80,000 francs, she would bring a lawsuit against him. Over a period of several months, she came back three times—and phoned several times as well—each time threatening a lawsuit if he didn't pay the 80,000 francs. The final time, he tells us, she had already filed her complaint with the law but said she would withdraw it if she were paid. Each time, he said he didn't have the money.

Tooy felt terribly abused by this situation—here he was, having taken in the whole family for several years, always treated them well, been kind to the extent that Brigitte allowed with their child, and now she was threatening him for money. He performed rituals as best he could to ward off this unprovoked attack, but worried that mysterious French laws were somehow closing in on him.

Tooy began to receive summonses from the police and the courts and went, he says, "seven times" (which in Saramaccan means simply "many") to the police or to the courthouse and once even to the hospital, each time answering their questions as best he could. In the most recent of these encounters at the courthouse, he was warned that he was currently in the status of "liberté conditionelle" (something like being out on bail—without having to pay bail).

*   *   *

On the Saturday before the trial, we pick up Tooy on our way to the meeting we have arranged with his two lawyers and the others who will serve as witnesses, so the lawyers can explain to all of us what we should expect to happen in court. Outside his house, Tooy prepares us each ritually and, again, gives us the wad of *gwáyamáka* for our mouths—he places a large plug in his own cheek.

The days before the trial are filled with rituals of many kinds. Oracle bundles are interrogated three times, and each time give the same answer: Tooy will be found innocent at the trial and should not flee to Suriname. A Saramaka priest of the Béndiwáta Mamá who lives in Saint-Laurent is consulted by telephone and prepares an *óbia* in the form of a large calabash filled with ritual ingredients and tied with a cloth, which we go to pick up—it's an eight-hour drive round-trip—and bring back to Tooy for him to use as a ritual bath. Tooy directs a young client, who is also a friend (and who has a Haitian father and a mother from Guyana), in making an *óbia* for winning the trial—he explains to us that you can't make an *óbia* for yourself. They use the king, queen, and jack face cards from a normal deck, some fingernail shavings Tooy makes with a penknife, an insole from one of his old shoes, and a photocopied page from a *grimoire* containing spells about trials. They carefully measure thirteen paces in front of the back door to Tooy's house and dig a hole in the middle of the dirt road with a pickaxe. In the hole, Tooy directs his acolyte to place the photocopy, the insole, and the nail clippings, then the queen (Tooy says, "That's Brigitte") facedown, the jack facedown (Tooy says, "That's Brigitte's lawyer"), and then the king faceup (Tooy says,

"That's me!"). Next, he prays, saying his "soul" should leave the hole, but hers and her lawyer's should stay right there; and at the trial, their mouths should be stopped up and he should go free. Tooy bends down and uses his bare hands and feet to push the loose earth back into the hole until it is completely covered, as if nothing had happened there. That same afternoon, he goes into the forest to do a much larger "throwing-away" ceremony. He takes with him five scraps of paper bearing the name of Brigitte's lawyer or Brigitte herself, which he had Sally write out.

*　*　*

Much of our own time is spent trying to make sense of the sheaves of documents Tooy has given us. We realize they're missing crucial elements—Brigitte's deposition as well as his own—on which the court will rely for its decision. We also realize that the whole investigative stage of the trial, which took depositions from various members of Brigitte's family, never once interviewed a relative of Tooy's in order to corroborate his version of the facts. But we still have a lot to work with. Annette's deposition is there, as well as the psychiatric reports on both Brigitte and Tooy.

Annette's sworn deposition, given before a gendarme in Maripasoula, describes how in August of 1983, she and her family took up lodgings in Tooy's two-room shack while Cathérine was being cured:

Annette: "Pretty soon I started having sex with Mr. Tooy, but I want to make clear that these were consensual relations. I was never forced. I was never threatened. Mr. Tooy was 48 years old, I was 13 years old. I was no longer a virgin, I'd already slept with other men. Tooy and I had relations on the sly, so my parents and sisters wouldn't know. This continued throughout the month of August. . . . I swear that I was never forced to have relations with Mr. Tooy nor forced to stay with him. I should make clear that at the beginning I was in love with this man . . . "

—And then she stopped to ask the gendarme:

"I am stopping my deposition here to ask you if this will be read in court."

The gendarme: "Yes, of course, by the judges. That's why you're giving the information."

Annette: "Then I'd like to change my story."

—The gendarme notes that Annette began to weep and then wiped away her tears before continuing.

"The first night, my mother and sisters were asleep in one room and I was alone in an alcove in the second. . . . During the night, I felt Mr. Tooy slipping into my bed. He mounted me and we had sex. . . . I didn't scream because I was embarrassed and didn't want to wake up my mother or sisters. I was only thirteen. It's true that I'd already had other boys, but by choice. . . . The next night he asked me to come to his bedroom and I accepted. . . . I was surprised to find that my sister Cathérine was there too. Mr. Tooy had sex with us both. I'd say it was consensual in that I didn't object. He didn't take me by surprise or by force. . . . We had sex just once that night. Then he did it with my sister Cathérine. . . . After that, it was every night, Mr. Tooy, my sister, and me. Just as I've described it to you. I can't say how many times but, believe me, it was many. . . . In April 1989, I learned that my sister Brigitte was pregnant by my companion, Mr. Tooy. I was surprised, because I had figured it was her boyfriend who'd gotten her pregnant. But Cathérine told me it was Mr. Tooy who had done it."

The French psychologist's report on Brigitte, which described her as "a 28-year-old young woman of mixed parentage," was based on scientific tests and clinical interviews. It tells the story of a rape committed on a sexually inexperienced sixteen-year-old schoolgirl who did not understand later that she was pregnant. It relates how the young woman, despite her trauma, persevered in her studies and then volunteered for military service in the *metropole*, leaving her young daughter Agnès with her parents in Maripasoula. It continues: Brigitte returned to Cayenne and found employment in a restaurant, where she met a Frenchman nine years older than she. After two years together, she became pregnant and they married. And then some two years ago, speaking on the phone to Agnès (who was still in Maripasoula), Brigitte learned that a curer there, a friend of her parents, had sexually abused the girl repeatedly. Brigitte decided to bring her daughter to Cayenne and to bring suit against the aggressor.[5] The psychologist tells how she was asked by the court at that time to undertake the psychological evaluation of Agnès and that, in the process, she learned that Marie, Brigitte's youngest sister, had also been sexually abused by this same man. Later, yet another sister, Silviane (then seventeen), confided to Brigitte that her husband had engaged in "lascivious touching" of her during Brigitte's pregnancy, while he was supposedly coaching her for some math exams. Silviane decided to bring a lawsuit against him, eventually leading Brigitte to file for divorce. The report mentions that more recently "Brigitte (and, according to her, two of her sisters) were also sexually abused by a brother-in-law who pretended to be a curer, in conditions very similar to the rape of one of her younger sisters and Agnès." And the psychologist concludes that, on the basis of her scientific tests (Rorschach, Szondi, and Raven IQ [the psychologist's divinatory instruments]), Brigitte will never escape this extraordinarily vicious cycle of abusive sexuality until she exorcizes the original traumatism (her rape by Tooy). This process, the report states, must involve his punishment.

Sally and I try to make sense of the document. It makes it clear that during the past couple of years, there have already been at least three lawsuits for sexual abuse brought by members of Brigitte's family—her daughter and two of her sisters—all with verdicts favorable to the plaintiffs, and apparently with financial damages paid to them by the State. We can't tell from the report whether there have been additional lawsuits regarding the abusive brother-in-law, though the psychologist says all three sisters were his victims.

We move on to the psychiatrist's report on Tooy himself. Written by a monolingual French psychiatrist at the hospital, it began by noting that he had sent away the three relatives accompanying Tooy to the interview in order to have only Tooy and the official interpreter present. (The interpreter did not speak Tooy's language but rather what the court calls "Taki-Taki"—more properly called Sranan-tongo, the Creole language of coastal Suriname—and Tooy was obliged to communicate as best he could in that language, which he speaks poorly, so the interpreter could try to put his words into French.) The official report states, "The only language spoken by Tooy Alexander is TAKI-TAKI." It goes on to declare that Tooy cannot give either the names, ages, or sexes of the children being raised in his house by his wife, that he says all of his brothers and sisters are dead except for him, that he doesn't know how many are male and how many female, that he doesn't know their names, and that there was "a generalized madness (insanity) in his family." It concludes that Tooy suffers from "confusion, vagueness, and contradiction in his memories and declarations," and that he experiences "difficulty in situating events in time and space, as every human being must do." The psychiatrist also concludes that, "despite his advanced age, declining sexuality, and heart disease, Tooy continues to present a danger were he placed in contact with underage girls in a social environment that ignores the laws and prohibitions of our society," and that if incarcerated he would at least have a "moderate" potential for rehabilitation—although "his understandings of sexual relations are based on cultural, social, and traditional rules which are not compatible with those of French society."

* * *

Trial day, we're up at dawn and dress as respectably as we can. Nervous and fearful, we drive to Tooy's. He takes us into the Dúngulāli chamber where we greet the Father and are given some liquid to drink and rub on our hands. Then we squeeze into the other chamber, where Yaai's Wénti holds sway. Tooy prays and sings as we drink some liquid from the god's clay vessel in a tiny calabash. We reassure Tooy (and Yaai, who's fussing with his clothes) that it's all right for him to put on his multicolored cape, the one he wore for his enstoolment as captain of the Saramakas of Cayenne, on top of his Western suit.

Soon after 8:00 a.m., the jury has been selected (all Creoles except possibly one Frenchman, as far as we can tell) and the court declared in session. A great deal of time is then spent by the bailiff passing out, explaining, and then collecting forms to compensate the witnesses and jurors financially for their loss of time, their mileage, and their air tickets. The cavernous courtroom consists of the raised dais where the Présidente is flanked by two other judges in formal robes, the jury box on the right, the public prosecutor (also in black robes) in a box on the left, a witness bar in the center facing the judges, and a series of pewlike benches filling the rest of the hall. Tooy is alone (later joined by the translator) up front, with his lawyers (in their robes) sitting behind him. We and Tooy's other supporters sit in the rows behind them. These include Saramaka friends and relatives, a certain number of Creole clients and friends, and a few Haitians and Brazilians. Across the aisle to our left, Brigitte's camp is similarly arranged. Her lawyer is a young, attractive, articulate Guyanaise, also in robes.

The first argument made by Tooy's lawyers, at our behest, is to ask the court that Tooy be permitted to speak in his own language rather than in "Taki-Taki," explaining that this language is about as distant from Saramaccan as Spanish is from French. (They don't explain that making him speak "Taki-Taki" also means that his words must pass through an interpreter who comes from a culture, that of urban Suriname, that absolutely disdains Maroons.) The three judges retire to consider this request and return a few minutes later to pronounce a refusal without recourse, saying that Tooy has never asked for this before in all the preliminary proceedings, that they wouldn't in any case know where to find such an interpreter, and that the trial must go on. "We are in France," says the Présidente, "not in Saramaka country."[6]

Tooy is called to the bar for purposes of identification. The first thing he's asked, via the interpreter, is his name and his age. After saying his official French name, he says he doesn't know his age (bringing a broad smile of condescension to the Présidente's face). As he begins fumbling with his money pouch under his dress shirt to find his residence card, which has his official birthdate, the Présidente interrupts to say, "I already have a copy of *that* before me here." "You don't even know your age?" she mutters, shaking her head, and tells him to go and sit down on his bench. Tooy looks defeated, alone, and lost.[7]

Then, as witnesses, we are ushered out of the hearing room until our time to testify, so we miss the first hour or so of the trial, during which the psychiatric expert gives his professional assessment of Tooy and his capability, despite his "mental confusion," to take responsibility for his acts and stand trial.[8] I am the first of the witnesses to be recalled to stand before the court.

At the lawyers' suggestion, I've prepared a twenty-minute presentation covering my own bona fides and then offering nutshell summaries of Saramaka culture and society, the history of Saramakas in Guyane, Tooy's central importance as person and symbol to the Saramaka community in Cayenne—his role as "man of knowledge," "historian," and religious leader; his political and judicial role as traditional captain—and the claim that the language he is being forced to use in court is not his own. The court treats me with considerable respect, the public prosecutor making a point of having read my books with great interest, until the moment when I begin citing errors and misunderstandings in the psychiatrist's report on Tooy: the fact that Tooy has forty-three children whose names and residences he doesn't know, that two of his siblings drowned, that there was frequent mental illness in his family. The Présidente interrupts, asking, "Where in the world did you gain access to Tooy's dossier? You have no right to see those papers! You are here solely as a character witness!" I reply that since Tooy cannot read or understand French, he had no idea what was in the pile of papers that had been sent to him by the criminal justice system, and he had asked me to read them and translate them for him. The Présidente repeats that I have no right to see or cite these materials, as I am there solely as a character witness. (After my testimony, Tooy's lawyers lean over to me, also somewhat disturbed that I referred to materials in the dossier.) I clash with the Présidente again when she asks me, "Can you tell the court why in the world a beautiful young girl like Brigitte would be attracted to an old man like *that*?" pointing her pursed lips in the direction of Tooy. In retrospect, I realize I should have answered that she ought to pose that question not to me but to Annette, who was thirteen when she fell in love with Tooy—but I wasn't sufficiently quick witted.

Sally is the second character witness. She presents herself as a scholar who is there to try to introduce the court to a world in which sexuality is viewed very differently from the way it is in France. She begins by showing the three pictures on the dedication page of her *Co-Wives and Calabashes*, winner of a national women's studies prize, which she intends as testimony to her feminist sympathies: a girl named Moina first at age six, then at ten, and finally at fourteen, holding her first baby, the point being the normalcy of sexual precocity among Saramakas (and, she adds, on the basis of the anthropological literature she's read, Amerindians). She speaks of Saramaka polygyny—the fact that most men have several wives. And she speaks of how, when a man's wife has her period, he normally sleeps with another. By the time she gets toward the middle of her prepared lesson, which is all about the need for respecting cultural difference, she has been interrupted so many times by the Présidente that she finally gives up. The Présidente and public prosecutor say that those cultural arguments are all well and good, but this trial is not taking place in Saramaka country but in France.[9]

The other two witnesses we have arranged for Tooy—Ben Amiemba, an articulate young Saramaka who speaks French, and a Senegalese journalist who had covered Tooy's enstoolment the previous year—testify briefly about Tooy's character.[10] (Later, Ben points out to us that Tooy's witnesses all being foreigners certainly didn't help his case.)

Brigitte's character witnesses address the court next. There's a gendarme in a spanking white uniform who was flown back from the *metropole* for the trial (he was the one who had taken Brigitte's deposition), the policeman from Maripasoula who took down the deposition from Annette, and Annette herself. The policeman, who has clearly been prepped by Brigitte's lawyer, gives a detailed account of the part of Annette's deposition that followed her asking whether it would be read in court, that is, the version she wanted the court to hear. While the gendarme, relatively taciturn, is at the bar, the Présidente takes the opportunity to read long passages from Brigitte's deposition, particularly the parts detailing the "pénétration"—how Tooy allegedly slipped his index finger inside her underpants—and further prurient details. When Annette is called to the bar, well dressed, sure of herself, she recounts that Tooy raped her when she was but thirteen, after which she stayed with him for years out of fear. She speaks softly and weeps repeatedly during her fifteen-minute testimony. Then Brigitte, chic and confident, tells her story, also weeping profusely as she speaks. Several women of the jury take out their own handkerchiefs to wipe away tears. As Brigitte finishes, the Présidente tells the court she would like "to personally congratulate the victim," who came from such humble circumstances, for having—despite the difficulties she's encountered—completed her military service and received her M.A. in modern languages. And finally the psychologist testifies, reading passage after passage from her report about Brigitte. At one point, one of the judges, a woman, asks whether Brigitte's testimony about what happened thirteen years ago could be the result of reconstructed memory. The psychologist thanks her for the excellent question and says that the tests she has conducted absolutely preclude that possibility. All the scientific indicators show that Brigitte experienced an original sexual trauma that returns each time she sees Agnès, and that her wound will never heal without the incarceration of the rapist. Nor will Agnès's wound from having been born of a rape and raised without a father—having a father, she says, is every human being's right. Furthermore, there is absolutely no indication that Brigitte is "mythomaniac" or "hallucinatory," and therefore she could not be lying or imagining the event post facto, even though more than a decade has passed.

★   ★   ★

By 8:00 p.m., the trial has been proceeding for twelve hours, with a one-hour recess at noon. Tooy is finally called to the bar to tell his version of the facts. His lawyers had told him simply to tell the truth. He begins by describing how Cathérine's parents brought her to him to cure, and how he took the whole family under his roof. The interpreter translates as best she can. The Présidente interrupts him every few sentences, and his voice gets smaller and smaller. When he describes how Brigitte would sneak up the stairs to his bed when Annette was having her period and sleeping downstairs, the Présidente cuts in to ask, "Are you trying to tell us that SHE was the one who raped YOU?!" The interpreter whispers something to him and he hesitates, then nods in confusion. The Présidente and others in the court erupt in loud guffaws. Tooy seems lost, not knowing what straws to grasp, not understanding the subtleties (not to mention the substance) of what is being said. He looks—he has been made to look—pitiful, ridiculous . . . and above all guilty. His testimony lasts only a few minutes.[11]

Then come the lawyers' summations. Brigitte's lawyer is limpid and direct: an innocent young virgin was penetrated by force by a dirty old man. The victim, born in modest circumstances, has since persevered in her studies, struggling though everything was stacked against her, to better herself. At an age when she was still a minor, her virginity was cruelly snatched away and her life turned into a daily torment that has still not ended and will never end until the perpetrator is locked up behind bars.

Then it is the turn of Tooy's lawyers. Auguste argues, without much conviction, that Brigitte made up the rape story in order to extract money from Tooy. Lafontaine claims rather more grandly that what we have here is a "clash of cultures," that both Brigitte and Tooy see themselves as telling the truth, and that the court should therefore be lenient with Tooy.

Finally, the public prosecutor addresses the court to say that, in his long career, he has never been so personally touched by the testimony of a rape victim. He is going to request a sentence of "only" eight to ten years, saying that in asking for this light sentence, he has taken into consideration everything that the two distinguished anthropologists have said on behalf of Tooy.

As the jury and the magistrates file out to begin their deliberations, six heavily armed gendarmes take up position at the back of the hall, ready to haul away their prisoner once the verdict is announced. I've rarely felt such fear and alarm, seeing these burly white giants clanking their handcuffs and chains. After an hour of deliberation, the jury emerges and pronounces Tooy guilty as charged, with a sentence of seven years behind bars.[12] Brigitte's law-yer then rises to ask the court for damages for her clients' pain and suffering. She requests 35,000 euros (nearly $50,000) for Brigitte and her child. The jury again retires, coming back at midnight to accede to the reduced sum of 25,000 euros: 15,000 for Brigitte and 10,000 for Agnès. Since Tooy has no financial resources, the French State will pay them directly from its special victim's fund.

The gendarmes swarm up to take Tooy, cuffs and chains in hand. We in-tervene, emotionally, pleading with them not to humiliate our friend further and assuring them he'll go peacefully. Amidst the yelling and screaming and weeping of some of Tooy's supporters (Saramakas, Creoles, Brazilians, Hai-tians), they hold off on the manacles and let him walk stiffly down the broad stairway to the waiting paddy wagon.

GROUNDS FOR APPEAL?

02202002/03012002

The days following the trial have, at this remove, become something of a blur, a flurry of all-day/all-night worry and activity. Before the verdict was announced, Tooy's lawyers told us they would have ten days to file an appeal and would await our instructions before proceeding. An appeal would mean a new trial that could, depending on the jury, free Tooy, render the same verdict as before, or hand down an even heavier sentence. Tooy's family and friends agreed on one thing—Tooy would never survive seven years in the pen.

We knew we needed professional advice, and so spent the first day writing a thirty-page fax to a friend, Raphaël Constant, Martinique's leading human-rights lawyer, who turned out to be in Tanzania participating in the Rwanda genocide trials. His return fax said that never in his career had he gone near a rape case, but if we were sure of Tooy's innocence, he would help us think about it from a human-rights perspective—an immigrant Saramaka leader caught in the maw of the French justice system. Over the coming days, we had several multipage transatlantic exchanges, we supplying copies of documents and our commentary, he generously sending us opinions and a barrage of further questions. Our own common sense, unfettered by legal knowledge, was often at odds with what Raphaël told us.[1]

* * *

In retrospect, we were enormously naive. But at the time, we felt convinced that if we could just find enough witnesses to confirm Tooy's story, he'd have a fighting chance in a new trial. So, like tropical Columbos, we snooped around Cayenne trying to build a case.

Within two or three days, with the help of Tooy's wives and relatives, we managed to locate witnesses who could corroborate the key elements of Tooy's story: the *ménage à quatre* that he lived for several years with the sisters, the fact that Brigitte was far from having been a virgin at the time of Agnès's conception, and that Brigitte had approached him with the demand for 80,000 francs or else. But we also ran into problems. The three men who assured us they'd slept with Brigitte when she was thirteen or fourteen, well before the alleged rape, were unwilling to testify in court—none had French papers, and all feared imprisonment should they proclaim before the court that they had, in effect, committed statutory rape by sleeping with a woman under the age of fifteen. Tooy's wife Céline gave us a tape recording of Brigitte's state-appointed guardian, who was a friend of Céline's, telling her what a wild teenager Brigitte had been before her pregnancy, but we were far from sure it would be admissible in court. Céline and another Creole friend of Tooy's were ready to testify that they had been present when Brigitte came to extract her blackmail, but given their personal interests, would they be believed by a jury?

Meanwhile, in his faxed messages, Raphaël reminded us that proving that Brigitte was not a virgin, however much it might weaken her "character" before a jury, hardly proved that Tooy hadn't raped her on the occasion in question. And even if it turned out that we could prove by DNA evidence that Agnès wasn't Tooy's child, he said, that still wouldn't prove he hadn't raped her. We wondered whether Brigitte's having waited to file her complaint until one month before the ten-year statute of limitations kicked in might not weigh against her. And how about all those other recent rape trials in her immediate family, each time netting considerable damages? Couldn't a skilled lawyer persuade a jury that, through her education, Brigitte had learned to apply a French conceptual grid to what were common Saramaka (and íngi) sexual relationships, which at once criminalized them and allowed her enormous personal profit? Raphaël patiently explained that it is widely accepted among psychologists that the shame of rape can make victims wait years before being able to face the event. Moreover, other cases of rape in the family and their judicial consequences would not be admissible as evidence in this one. What if, we asked, we were able to prove beyond a doubt the veracity of Tooy's story about having lived with both Brigitte and Annette for years, beginning when each was around thirteen? That, Raphaël assured us, would hardly add to his stature in the eyes of a jury, even if the statute of limitations for statutory rape had long since expired. The bottom line, he suggested, was that any jury in Cayenne would fit this case into a familiar story line—an elderly *guérisseur* (a curer, which is how everyone on the jury would see Tooy) had been given responsibility for these girls by their parents and had abused his power. In the Creole world of Overseas France, it was all too familiar.

* * *

In the modernizing society of Guyane (which is trying so hard to replace its image as a penal colony with that of gleaming Ariane rockets), to consult a curer has become at least to some extent "shameful." The media—and ultimately, the State—has played a major supporting role in this transformation of consciousness. My collection of clippings that chronicle this attitude come from Martinique, where we live. But these four examples from the newspaper *France-Antilles* could as easily be from *France-Guyane* (owned by the same French company), and they give the flavor of these everyday assaults on local practice. (Local television "specials" also periodically present such perspectives, a combination of sensationalist fascination and downward-gazing ridicule.)

A "VOYANT" TAKES ADVANTAGE OF HIS CLIENTS

Yvon Varasse, nicknamed Django, plied his trade near the church of Sainte-Thérèse in Fort-de-France. Until the day the gendarmes discovered that Varesse had swindled a family from the south of Martinique, receiving a considerable sum of cash plus seven gold Napoleons against the promise of better fishing results. Not satisfied with having cheated these people, the so-called "*voyant*" also took advantage—twice—of the youngest daughter of the family, age sixteen.

The "*gadé zaffé*" had threatened the adolescent that he would put "spirits" upon her if she spoke to her parents about these goings-on. According to the victim, she was told that the sexual relations forced on her by the voyant were necessary for the success of his "work."

This new affair demonstrates once again—as if it were still necessary—how very numerous are the charlatans who do not hesitate to extract the maximum profit from the credulity of people who are already in dire straits. The victims, who believe they are going to better their situation, end up, as always, with nothing but disappointment.

ABUSE OF POWER: SETTING HIMSELF UP AS VOYANT, OLIVE IVRISSE TOOK ADVANTAGE OF HIS CLIENTS

It is one of the most lucrative professions. And of a disarming simplicity, as long as you are a fast talker with a fertile imagination, and you're graced with the gifts of a conman and enjoy taking advantage of people, without worrying about where the necessary means come from or where it all might lead. In order not to hurt anyone's feelings, let's just say we're writing about men and women who, one day, decide to put their very ordinary gifts at the disposition of the public, in order to "fix up" their problems of all sorts—emotional, physical, or moral. It takes no diploma to get yourself set up as *quimboiseur, sorcier,* or *gadé d'zaffè*. Any place will do, as long as you're ready to take advantage of the misery, distress, credulity, and naiveté of ordinary men and women.

Women—there's the achilles heel of these pseudo-sorcerers. By nature rogues, they cannot resist the temptations of the flesh. By simple means of medicinal interventions, which destroy reflexes and create a sense of lethargy in the victim, they go on to take full advantage of her body.

It was after reading in this newspaper, twice within the space of several weeks, about sexual abuses committed by two pseudo-sorcerers, that a young woman presented herself to the detective bureau of the Fort-de-France police. A man claiming to be a *quimboiseur* had taken advantage of her when she went to consult him. Following up this complaint, the gendarmes arrested Olive Ivrisse, who had set himself up as *gaded'zaffè* in Fort-de-France. The details of the rape, which occurred in 1988, included the administration of some sort of noxious vapors which rendered her helpless and allowed him to have his way with her. . . . Ivrisse . . . was arraigned on charges of illegal practice of medicine and indecent assault and imprisoned in Fort-de-France.

THE QUIMBOISEUR TOOK ADVANTAGE OF
HIS FEMALE CLIENTS

He was leading the good life, this *quimboiseur*. Thanks to his little office, which was rarely empty, the money flowed in and the 'voyant-guérisseur' had accumulated a nest egg of nearly one million francs. And even better, this quimboiseur practiced therapeutic methods that were just a bit unusual when his clients were female.

If, to take an example, the woman was young and good-looking, he would frighten her by saying she was possessed by a *dorliss* [incubus]. And to exorcize it, he would suggest a method both radical and efficacious—sexual intercourse! With him, of course, and for the measly sum of 1700 francs. . . . This is how Sylvie R was forced to submit three times to the assaults of the quimboiseur.

But in the case of Madame G., a woman of 65 who sold candies for a living, the treatment was different. He contented himself with offering her a miraculous lotion for 25,000 francs. . . .

The criminal court sentenced him to five years. . . .

THE PERVERTED HEALER

The police have just put an end to the practice of a 59-year-old man who profited from his "consultations" to take advantage of his young victims. Three girls aged ten and fourteen have confirmed that they were abused by this man. Their parents had brought them to this "guérisseur" believing they had been bewitched, and having full confidence in F. Unhappily, once the girls were alone with him, he allowed himself all sorts of liberties. . . . Following up on the complaint of one of the parents, the police were able to arrest the man and charge him with corrupting a minor.

It is worth underlining the uncomfortable ambiguities of such media reports, which write so disdainfully of "pseudo-sorcerers" and "so-called
voyants," but suggest by the same token the existence of genuine *sorciers,*
voyants, and *quimboiseurs.* It is worth noting also that on the same page of
the newspaper as, for example, "Abuse of Power," there are no less than five
large, boxed ads, two with pictures, for a "voyant," "grand voyant," "grand
médium africain," "méthode égyptienne," and "parapsychologue." Local
curers like Tooy, in contrast, hardly need to advertise in the papers, drawing
their clientele by word of mouth from every layer of society.

★   ★   ★

And then there was the question of ethnicity—a Creole jury judging a Saramaka man. French Guiana is run by Creoles under the tutelage of Paris—a
neocolony if ever there was one. Not officially a nation, it is a distant append-
age of France in which the small Creole elite holds nearly all local reins of
power, and in which even the awesome force of the French State (including a
sizeable Foreign Legion presence) appears increasingly impotent against the
massive incoming tide of illegal immigrants (largely Haitians, Brazilians,
Surinamers, Guyanese, and now even Peruvians). During the past twenty
years, as the wave of illegal immigrants has swelled, the Creoles have become increasingly apprehensive. The latest census shows far more people
who were born outside Guyane than in Guyane (and it's surely missing yet
greater numbers of illegals). Nearly all the immigrants are poor, barely literate, and non-French-speaking—the antithesis of everything Creoles ideal-
ize. There is a strong sense, both in Cayenne and the outlying communes, of
a loss of control. As early as 1990, Michel Rocard, the French prime minister,
tried hard during a visit "to calm the fears of the population, and especially
of the local [Creole] politicians," boasting that "with 2400 people escorted to
the borders in 1988, Guyane was the leading *département* of France in this regard." In that same speech, however, he had to admit that actual "clandestine
immigration is probably ten times this figure." "Although Guyane is vast and
underpopulated," Rocard went on, "it should not be made any more responsible than the rest of France for welcoming the flotsam and jetsam of its poor
neighbors."[2] And he promised help. In 1992, the French military command
in Guyane was strengthened, according to official explanations, not only to
better protect the European Space Center but in particular to fortify the borders with Brazil and Suriname. Additional Foreign Legion and regular army
troops were flown into what was already a heavily militarized environment.
For the past twenty years, the crime pages of the local newspaper highlight

in each edition the activities of new immigrants—from drugs and prostitution to armed robbery, murder, and rape. And in 2006, an elected official from Guyane expressed his anxieties at a meeting in Paris: "There are strong feelings of xenophobia in Guyane and they are getting worse. Until now, the people of Guyane have respected the laws of the Republic. But the day is coming when they will be tempted to take justice into their own hands. It is time to reestablish the authority of the State in these territories!"[3]

Maroons are near the bottom of the Creole's hierarchy. "I was standing in a shop in Saint-Laurent, looking at magazines," writes anthropologist Ken Bilby, "when a Creole woman walked in; seeing a group of Ndjuka [Maroon] women in one corner of the store, she said out loud, 'Bosch, c'est la *dernière* nation!' [Maroons, they're the *lowest* nation!]; she then did a rapid about-face, and walked out."[4] For the Creole elite, there remains a central unresolved tension between a wish to honor, and identify with, the heroic Maroon warriors of the foundational Guyanais past (whom they've read about in books or heard about in the media), and a deep disdain for their downtrodden, imperfectly modernizing descendants. Sociologist Marie-José Jolivet, who has written at length about Creole life and culture, suggests that those Creoles who have any positive attitudes at all toward Maroons are either rural people or those who have lived a long time in the interior: "In the city [Cayenne], the disdain of Creoles for Maroons loses all ambiguity."[5] Jean Hurault also accentuated the negative: "Permit me to insist on this point: the Creole population of Guyane has nothing but disdain for the tribal populations, about which it nevertheless knows almost nothing. . . . The Creoles are divided about how to handle them: whether to destroy them by assimilation or to exploit them economically, especially through tourism."[6] Bilby tells us that lower- and middle-class Creoles from Saint-Laurent call all Maroons—whether Alukus, Paramakas, Ndyukas, or Saramakas—Bosch, while their counterparts in Cayenne call them all Saramaka. In either case, what is implied is "'uncivilized' inferiors, people not yet 'évolué.'"[7] And he gives extended examples of popular Creole "ethnic jokes" about Maroons, all of which attribute to them childlike simplicity and an inability to deal with the modern world.[8] In their everyday encounters with Maroons, many Creoles display open prejudice, and the epithet *macaque* (monkey) is not infrequently used in anger—just as bourgeois Creoles complain that white Frenchmen in Guyane sometimes call *them* "*macaques*." In twenty-first-century Guyane, *Saramaka* has become the epithet of choice with which to insult Maroons. For this reason, Saramaka schoolchildren sometimes hide their specific origin (associated with backwardness and considered shameful) and, when asked, simply say they are Maroons.[9]

Saramakas fight back, at least symbolically, from time to time. When Kalusé ran a Saramaka cultural association from his pink house in the early nineties, he helped organize a several-day visit by the mayors of Cayenne, Saint-Laurent, and Kourou to the Saramaka heartland in central Suriname, in order to show them, he said, that "Saramakas are neither Alukus nor Ndyukas but have a separate culture of their own," and that "Maroon youths are not necessarily delinquents." And more recently, as a delegate to a meeting in French Guiana's second-largest and most modern town, Kourou, he responded to the government announcement that Saramakas would have to pay rent for the public housing being built to replace the shantytown "Village Saramaka" at Kourou:

> If we're to start paying rent, it *must* be applied toward the house's purchase. In 1962, when I came to Kourou, I myself shot howler monkeys out of the tree that was standing right where they've made the big BNP [Banque Nationale de Paris]! It was Saramakas who built this whole town—the bridges, the roads, the houses. Whatever plans the State makes for us now, that contribution must be recognized.[10]

But the Creoles (and the French) continue to hold the cards. Saramakas can express pride publicly—and sometimes even have their heroic past paid lip service to by Creole politicians—but they remain, for the most part, immigrants who are best served when they stay below the official radar.

★   ★   ★

Raphaël, wearing his political activist's hat, faxed us that Tooy's only chance, were he to be granted a new trial, would lie in the mounting of a massive media campaign, with the unwavering support of the Saramaka immigrant community, to underline the difficulty of his receiving a fair trial. The witnesses we had found would have to agree to testify. There would need to be marches and petitions. Only then might the State blink.

But when we met with them each day, neither the Saramaka community nor Tooy's Creole supporters spoke with a single voice. And there was considerable anxiety that Tooy's sentence might be increased on appeal. Women asked whether, once people had seen how much money a woman could make by getting a jury to believe that she'd been raped, other women mightn't step forward to make similar accusations. After all, it was widely rumored that Tooy sometimes allowed professional consultations, especially with Creole women, to be paid for by sex. And some of these women would surely be willing to come forward and claim they'd been raped if there were 25,000 euros waiting at the other end. All they'd have to do would be to contact Brigitte's lawyer. Tooy might get 100 years, they speculated.

We felt powerless. In the end, along with Tooy's Saramaka friends and family, we made the decision not to file for appeal but to seek other ways of freeing our captain. Saramakas began a slew of rituals, since they were convinced that Tooy's incarceration stemmed ultimately from the French-woman spirit whom he'd been neglecting and other complex machinations in the invisible world, as well as his unfortunate propensity—unlike traditional Saramaka *óbia*-men—to mix sex and curing (à la Créole), which powers like Dúnguláli-Óbia certainly did not appreciate. Seconded by Tooy's trial lawyers, Raphaël had pretty much convinced us that the outcome of a new trial would probably not be different, no matter the evidence or witnesses. At the end of the day, all the jury would see would be an old Saramaka curer who couldn't speak French (the perfect savage) accused of rape by an accomplished young woman (the perfect fruit of the civilizing mission).

With Raphaël's counsel, we began to plan a campaign to obtain Tooy's release on medical grounds, based on a law that was being actively discussed at the time in the press (and which was finally enacted by the French parliament in March 2002), designed to free the notorious Maurice Papon from a prison in France before he died of illness.[11] We'd meanwhile found out that Tooy was the oldest prisoner in the whole penitentiary and that he was gravely ill (though asymptomatic) with degenerative heart disease. While Tooy was in Martinique for his open-heart surgery, we were able to arrange a bedside visit by Raphaël, who spoke with him in Creole, and agreed to become his lawyer. By September 2002, when Maurice Papon was released in France, Raphaël was filing papers in Cayenne, reasoning that if a highly placed violator of human rights could be freed on medical grounds, perhaps a poor immigrant could, too. At the same time, we were lucky enough to become friends—at her invitation, because she'd read some of our books—with the Procureur de la République, the Paris-appointed head of the justice system in Guyane. Over dinner and some excellent wine at her home, we told her Tooy's story in detail. A year later, she would take part in the final hearing that set him free.

THE PRISON

⋆ 02202002/06022003 ⋆

For many people in France, *Cayenne* still means "prison."[1] Everything that Americans conjure up when they hear *Devil's Island* (from the Dreyfus Affair to Steve McQueen playing Papillon)—in short, the world's most infamous penal colony—is signaled in French by that single word, *Cayenne*.[2] Lafcadio Hearn, in his literary way, captured the flavor a hundred years ago:

> It is the morning of the third day since we left Barbadoes, and for the first time since entering tropic waters all things seem changed. The atmosphere is heavy with strange mists; and the light of an orange-colored sun, immensely magnified by vapors, illuminates a greenish-yellow sea,—foul and opaque, as if stagnant....
>
> A fellow-traveler tells me, as we lean over the rail, that this same viscous, glaucous sea washes the great penal colony of Cayenne—which he visited. When a convict dies there, the corpse, sewn up in a sack, is borne to the water, and a great bell tolled. Then the still surface is suddenly broken by fins innumerable,—black fins of sharks rushing to the hideous funeral: they know the Bell![3]

For the one hundred years that it functioned, the *bagne* of French Guiana may well have been the worst prison on earth. By the twentieth century, it had become a veritable machine to use and break men, and had taken on a life quite its own. Only one in four convicts survived for twenty years, earning the place its best-known nickname, "the dry guillotine." Doctor Louis Rousseau, who ended his term as chief prison doctor in 1932, concluded that

> the *bagne* is a charnel house, a mass grave, running from syphilis to tuberculosis, with all the tropical parasites one can imagine (carrying malaria, ankylosis, amoebic dysentery, leprosy, etc.), all destined to work hand in hand with an administration whose task it is to diminish the number of prisoners consigned to its care. The fiercest proponents of "elimination" can rest satisfied. In Guyane, prisoners survive on the average five years—no more.[4]

Prisoners were subjected to a highly rationalized system of dehumanization.

> In the *bagne*, everything was dictated by texts, with a staggering meticulousness. Every aspect of the daily life of *transportés* and *relégués* was precisely described and programmed. . . . As one tries to comprehend the accumulated mass of texts, rules, and decrees, one enters an almost surrealistic universe in which everything is prescribed and foreseen. The manual for guards . . . specifies "the knife commonly called 'pocket-knife' is permitted for prisoners as long as the blade is folding, ending in a right angle without convexity or a point, and is sharpened on one side only." . . . And the rules for punishment go on for pages: giving bread to a man in punishment = 30 days prison; giving tobacco to a man in punishment = 60 days in prison; complaining about the quantity or quality of food = 30-60 days in prison; wearing a non prison-issue hat = 15 days in prison; talking back to a guard = 8-30 days in prison; not completing the daily work quota = complete privation of food.[5]

Arrival in the penal colony was marked by well-practiced rites designed to strip off whatever traces of civilian identity still lingered for each prisoner. Every inmate received a number, recording his order in the list of prisoners logged in since the *bagne* began. From the registration office, where verbal formalities were completed, he was taken next door to the Anthropometry Bureau, "a vast room . . . with desks for different specialists, a height gauge, a scale, a camera mounted on a tripod, and a table with ink pads for fingerprinting." As one author described the generic scene,

> The dreadful day when he had stood stripped in the office where the authorities registered finger prints and made inventories of men's bodies, recording every distinguishing mark, every wart or mole, every birth blotch and every tattooed design, making measurements, and adding these things to ones name and age and birthplace, and to the individual crime histories and sentences sent over by the French courts—all indexed and cross-indexed to facilitate emergency reference.[6]

Also photographed, both full face and profile. Everything written down or pasted into a little book.

There's little need to go into further detail: a voluminous literature bears witness.[7] But it's worth remembering that it is this legacy, the heavy burden of Green Hell, that every development project in modern Guyane, from the Space Center to what was said to be the largest high school in all of France, is designed to erase.[8] Guyane waited fifty years after the closing of the *bagne* to build a new prison. And when it finally did, there was certainly the hope that it might forever wipe out the memory of Cayenne's stain on History. One brochure proclaimed, "The emblem of the *bagne*, a man in prison stripes with manacled feet—that's what we want to make our visitors forget."[9]

It would be hard to conjure up a more modern prison than the Centre Pénitentiare de la Guyane, built just outside Cayenne a few years ago with manual labor provided by, among others, Kalusé and his undocumented Saramaka construction buddies—a tropical adaptation of the cookie-cutter French model that was being built at the same time in Martinique, Guadeloupe, and other parts of France. On a flat plain carved out from the jungle, surrounded by the latest type of razor wire, the main buildings, office blocks, and parking lots are tidy, sterile, and rationalized, baking in the sun. (Imagine the opposite of, say, a Mexican prison as Americans know it from newspapers, films, and books, where inmates and corruption rule.) Our world being what it is, however, this modern penitentiary was quickly overwhelmed by the rising tide of crime and incarceration. By 2002, when Tooy made his entrance, it held nearly seven hundred inmates, 50% more than its official capacity. By 2005, the government was planning a second prison in Saint-Laurent-de-Maroni, next to the Suriname border, designed especially for Maroon inmates.

★　★　★

The presence of one young man helped make Tooy's time inside more tolerable. Since 1999, Moesoela "Ben" Amiemba, an ambitious, bright Saramaka, had been working in the prison as "cultural mediator," the link between the several hundred Maroon inmates—many of whom spoke no French or Creole—and the guards, doctors, and wardens. Ben is very much self-fashioned. Born in the Nasí-clan village of Kambalóa in 1970, he was given to his much older brother Mandó to raise and taken to Paramaribo when four years old. His schooling consisted of a three-year stretch back home when he went to elementary school, and then, when he was in his early twenties in Paramaribo, a vocational school for another three years. In 1994, he moved to French Guiana, joining Mandó's highly successful woodcarving atelier and learning French by taking courses at a Catholic relief agency. His prison employment came thanks to a French scheme to add people to the employment rolls—he was hired on a special contract called "*emplois jeunes*," where the State hired young people.[10]

Ben is a motivated learner. Since we first met in 2000, I've given him copies of all our books, and he's done his best to read them, studying those on Saramaka history with great intensity. While I'm sitting shooting the breeze

RP and Ben, 2005.

with Tooy, he often shows up with a copy of *Alabi's World* or *Les premiers temps*
and asks me to translate particular passages into Saramaccan, so he's sure
he understands the details. His interest, like most Saramakas, is largely in
the history of his own clan, so he rarely asks me a question about one of my
books that doesn't concern his own specific ancestors. Ben has also mobi-
lized a schoolteacher friend who happens to be the spouse of the director of
the archives to make copies for him of large numbers of documents, mainly
from the early twentieth century, about Saramakas in Guyane; and Ben has
shared these with me. When Sally and I were writing *Les Marrons*, a book that
covers both history and present-day concerns of Maroons in Guyane, we'd
often ask Ben for his thoughts on a particular issue. He has asked my help
with writing a history of the Nasí people.

Ben is the president and founder of The Association of Young Active
Saramakas of Guyane (AJASG), the organization that was instrumental in
getting Tooy his captaincy.[11] Much of its efforts over the years have gone
to helping several hundred Saramaka immigrants get French papers. Ben
learned the procedures, made friends with the appropriate civil servants,
and was able almost single-handedly to get these people through the complex bureaucratic process. (For all that, he receives significant abuse and
jealousy—from the many people whom he has, for one technical reason or

another, been unable to push through the system.) At the same time, the association has other projects: a "fête Saramaka" that it holds each November in the central square of Cayenne to promote Saramaka culture (Saramaka dance groups, Saramaka cuisine); a "Village Saramaka" housing scheme that it hopes to build in the rural commune of Roura to permit Saramakas dispersed around Cayenne to own decent housing in a community; and a "Maison de Culture Saramaka," a building in town that could serve as a meeting place, cultural center, and museum. All of these projects involve close collaboration with various state agencies, all are eminently political. And Ben has involved Sally and me in all: to give speeches at the fête on the Saramaka contributions to Guyane, to write supportive letters to mayors, the presidents of the Conseil Général and Conseil Régional, the prefect, and others, lauding the Village Saramaka and House of Culture schemes—even to write the historical introduction to a DVD of one of the fêtes that the association is marketing. So, he keeps us busy for a few days on these projects during each of our visits.

During Tooy's incarceration, Ben managed to see him every couple of days and could report to us and his relatives on his spirits and his needs. More important, he could carry messages to Tooy about our efforts to get him released. I have no doubt that Tooy's knowing that Ben was in the building most days if he needed him made doing time a little bit less awful.

★ ★ ★

Doing hard time, like fighting in battle, isn't something most people, including Tooy, like to talk about in retrospect. Better to forget the nighttime wildness of youngsters high on crack or dope. Better to forget the knife fights and screaming. Even the few ironic pleasures—meeting a Haitian (in for eleven years), a Brazilian (in for eight years), and even a metropolitan Frenchman, all of whom had been put behind bars by Brigitte's family for rape. Everyone counting the hours and days and weeks and months and years. All better put far in the past.

Three days after the trial, I got the court's permission for my first visit. Sitting on a bench in the waiting room, I was amazed that among the fifty or so visitors waiting for the hour to strike, there was not a word of French being spoken—only Brazilian, the Creole of Georgetown, Haitian Creole, Sranan-tongo, and a bit of local Guyanese Creole. I later learned that some 80% of all those incarcerated are foreigners who cannot speak French (many, unwitting testimony to a justice system in disarray). Only three visitors are permitted on each week's visiting day, so Sally had reluctantly ceded her place in favor of Ma Yaai and Céline. When we finally got through the metal detectors, the pat-downs, and the sliding steel grills, a door opened and Tooy walked in, looking gray but stoic. Each woman embraced him, then it was my turn. We had thirty minutes for the three of us. Tooy told Yaai to make sure that the Wénti pots in the shrine had water in them. (He's especially concerned about the pot belonging to Yowentína.) Yaai, characteristically, spent her few minutes complaining to Tooy about money and the childrens' disobedience and the broken washing machine and how in the world was she ever to make it without him. Céline, equally characteristically, focused on sweet talk and cheering him up. I told him what we were trying to do with the lawyers to get him out. On the way home, shaken by seeing our captain behind all those clanging metal doors, Yaai commented (in Ndyuka, of course) that being in prison is just like being in the hospital. (Who needs Foucault or Goffman to understand what total institutions look like from the inside?)

THE WETLANDS AT KAW

⋆ 07152004 ⋆

There are no useless leaves/plants—only uninformed people.
TOOY to Sally, in the wetlands at Kaw

It had been a year since Tooy phoned us, laughing and crying at the same time, to say he'd just been released from prison—we've been able to get down to Cayenne twice to celebrate with him. The first time, he played his *apínti* (talking drum) for us, *kotoko i kotoko tjim tjim mam têne búa*, explaining that you play this to give Sky and Earth thanks: you parted and thought you'd never see one another again, and then suddenly you do.

> A man once set a fish trap just below the deep called Sotígbo [far up the Gaán-lío, way past the southernmost Saramaka village]. He saw a large leaf fall into the water and studied its markings [Tooy said "its writing"] very carefully, until it was carried under his canoe by the current and sank. He stayed up there twelve days, twelve weeks, twelve months, and twelve years, and then he went all the way down to the mouth of Cassipora Creek [in whitefolks' territory]. He was stirring up some weeds at the edge of the water, and what did he see but that very same leaf! It's like the way they caught me and put me in prison—I didn't think we'd ever meet again! So when we meet, you have to be amazed. So you play: *kotoko i kotoko tjim tjim mam têne búa.* So many years have passed and you never thought you'd see him again and then it happens, so this is what you play to give thanks.

Now, on our way back to Martinique from a human rights conference in Brazil, we make a stop in Cayenne.

I give Tooy an Amerindian pipe we'd bought him in São Paulo, with a spiky-rough bowl clearly made from forest wood. He leans over and says, "Aláka, that's the name of Kaási's pipe. Aláka." And he sings, *Gweúngéé, gwéung. Aláka báii gweúngéé, gwéung.* . . . "People don't say the name of that pipe anymore," he confides. "It's too heavy for the mouth. So they call it Aladí instead. They still smoke it at Béndiwáta [where Kaási's descendants live]. Ask me how that pipe got its name," he says. I ask.

> Father-in-law Kaási left his wife Amímba near Bookopondo on the island called Logotabiki and went up to Tuído at the head of the Saramacca River.

An Indian came to her—just stood and watched her, he didn't touch her. She called to father-in-law Kaási [with magic]: *Mukúla mukúla. Mukúla mukúla. Mukúla mukúla.* Kaási heard and said *Apúlu du mádji.* Five minutes later, and he'd already flown in. "Woman, why'd you call me?" She said, "There he is," pointing at the Indian. Kaási asked, "Where's my pipe, where's Aláka?" She gave it to him. He took his flint, lit the pipe, and starting blowing out smoke. [Tooy sings again] *Gweúngéé, gwéung. Aláka báii gweúngéé, gwéung. . . .* The Indian took off and is still running as far as we know! *Gwéungbíí, gwéunglala,* he lit the pipe! *Gwéungbíí,* the smoke came out!

Most of the esoteric knowledge that Tooy has shared with me comes just like this, in the course of our interaction, when something happens to spark the exchange. The next day, when we spot a paca (a large edible rodent) in the wetlands, he asks if we know its esoteric name (we don't)—*gwenenzíí*—or that it has an *óbia* called *bumbatjá.* When I look surprised, he asks whether, when hunting, I haven't seen that animal sitting up and knocking its front paws together (I have) in a motion very much like Saramakas doing the two-handed divination called *máfiakáta*—when pacas do it, he says, it's called *bumbatjá!*

★ ★ ★

When we arrive at Tooy's early the next morning, he's already holding a consultation. A gleaming BMW is parked outside. He invites us into his consulting room, where a stylishly dressed Creole woman of around thirty sits coyly as two young assistants follow his orders to twist and squeeze the juice from certain branches, find a hen's egg, chop up vines, and rip up leaves. Tooy works with his well-worn calabash of *biyóngo* (ritual spices or power objects), slicing off bits of mica and rock crystals, fish scales, vulture claws, giant anteater claws, and other esoteric products into a plastic bucket the woman has brought. Everything has a prescribed order. Tooy tells them what to place where and what on top of what and how to place the egg, explaining to them that an egg has a head and a foot, and you can't just put it in any which way. At a certain point, Tooy asks them to find a piece of paper that he'd placed in the Wénti chamber during a previous consultation. They rummage around in the tiny room until they find it—I can see two names written on it. Tooy passes the slip of paper to the woman, asking her to place it in the center of the bucket. I realize this is a love *óbia*, to bind the woman and her partner together. Finally, Tooy sprinkles *keéti*—kaolin, white clay—over the whole top, as in most *óbias*.[1] Tooy tells her that she must add water and use this bath for the first time in the morning—today would be fine. But she says

A client has parked his Mercedes behind Tooy's house.

she's on her way to the office and can't till tomorrow. He says, OK, tomorrow then. But after that, every morning, noon, and night. She goes out and puts the bucket in the trunk of the BMW.

We hear shouts and run outside to have a look. Some relatives of Tooy's have remade his wash house across the road with new planks and are living there, parents plus seven or ten children and adolescents. The kids have seen an anaconda slithering up out of the slimy canal. The teenagers threaten it with a pole and try to push it back in. Tooy comes out and draws a line in the mud, commanding the beast not to cross. But the snake keeps coming. It's a young one, about 12 feet long and as thick as a man's thigh. We go back indoors with Tooy, leaving the kids to deal with the snake as we make plans for a leaf-collecting expedition to the wetlands of Kaw, a couple of hours by car to the east. A Creole friend of Tooy's, driving a new Toyota pickup, shows up. By the time we go outside again, he's got the snake onboard, alive but bleeding and weak—he's knocked it over the head with the pole. He tried to shock Tooy by joking with him that he'll make a *colombo* (curry stew) with it. And he tells us, when we ask a few minutes later what he's really going to do with it, that he'll drain off the oil to use medicinally, sell the skin, and eat the meat *en brochette*. Tooy tells us he's resigned himself to the fact that Creoles do that stuff—for him (and other Saramakas), anacondas are Wátawenú gods, and harming one brings eternal vengeance.

Two of Tooy's "grandsons" visit—they've just come over from Paramaribo to see their mothers, who live nearby. One sports a white, furry, oversized pimp cap, a gold necklace, red shades, baggy jeans, and Nikes; the other has Rasta-inspired tresses and dark shades. Tooy gives them an affectionate dressing-down about how they're stashed, telling them he knows this country and they don't. Unless they change their looks, he says, the police will pick them up for sure, thinking they're from Georgetown. They do have that cultivated hard, urban Kingston bad-boy look. But they're sweet kids. They smile and say, "Yes, opa" ("grandpa" in Dutch). Two teenage girls from the house across the street join us. Tooy goes on about how if the boys are standing on the street with the two girls (who are dressed in the proper style for Saramaka girls in Cayenne), the police will only be interested in them, not the girls—especially since they don't have papers of any kind. Then he takes out after the girls, scolding them for not walking across the road and asking Ma Yaai how she'd slept and telling her, "We're here, what jobs do you have for us this morning? Clothes to wash? Dishes to wash?" They protest that though they don't go and ask her each morning, they always do the dishes when they see them in the sink. One of the girls tries on her cousin's red shades and looks quite stylish. It's sad to think that Tooy is right, that these guys are more than likely to end up in jail. Tooy tells them things are tough in Cayenne, that there's no work, that there's no pity for kids like them. Undoubtedly he's thinking about Lowell, who was his assistant when we visited a couple of years earlier—a sweet, very bright kid who got caught by undercover agents selling seven kilos of cocaine on the Place des Palmistes with his younger brother. Lowell got away, but his brother is in jail—not yet sentenced but when he is, it will be for many years. Lowell has apparently escaped, via Suriname, to Holland. But what can he look forward to there? This in-between, semischooled "cool" generation seems headed for big trouble.

*　*　*

Around ten in the morning, Tooy, his assistant-for-the-day Asántikálu, and Sally and I pile into our rental car for the trip to Kaw. We stop at the last Chinese store before we hit the forest to buy bird-shot shells for the 12-gauge shotgun Asántikálu has brought along, but all we can find are shells filled with buckshot—in any case, we never see the toucans they'd assumed would be feasting on *pína* palm fruits at this season.

When we finally arrive at the edge of the vast wetlands (small islands of reeds amidst an expanse of labyrinthine water passages), Tooy points out the old cemetery for those who died in the swamp. At the cemetery path, he gathers some *yoóka fési* (ghost's face, a weed also called *nêngè áti* [Creole's heart]), telling it out loud as he takes it: "The evil must stay here, it mustn't come with us!" Tooy whispers to Asántikálu that when he gathers that plant, he must say this, too. Then we gather *pindá-pindá* (which he tells me Creoles call *pistache sauvage*) and another called *téé gádu dêde mi dêde* (when god dies, I die; Creole *adje kopo*); he shows us a plant called *pípa páu* (pipe stem), which he doesn't gather but tells us is good for toothache when taken with salt; and a broad-leafed bush called *atósi koyó* (Atosi's pubic apron), which, he whispers to us, is what Adam and Eve used to cover their shame in the Garden of Eden.

Back in the car, Tooy scans the underbrush for what he needs, and we stop several times. Lots of *sangaáfu*, including some roots of that all-important Saramaka ritual plant—we spot it from afar by its red flower. He shows me a vine used to stop menstruation that has lasted too long—the woman drinks it and puts it on the back of her wrist. Also a couple of others he doesn't take: *boóko koósu* (Creole *tet neg*) and *ti bom* (Creole *barbe chat*). Later we stop for small branches from a giant of a tree called *gaán páu* (big tree), but also

Tooy and RP at Kaw.

known as *kwátakáma* (spider monkey's bed) and by forest spirits as *gwindá* and in Komantí language as *kántiankáma* or *kwakwádabankáma*. Tooy reminds me that it's the name of this tree that Pobôsi's Komantí Sáka-Amáfu took as his own when he'd boast that he was Kantiánkáma-u-Súduantjí, the largest tree in the forest. We stop again for a runner vine called *dòôngòma*. Once home, Tooy has his assistants carefully separate and range the materials along the walls of his consulting room.

Tooy decides to give thanks to his ancestors and pours a libation of rum. Somewhere toward the middle of the ten-minute prayer, he says:

> Gaamá Akoósu, Gaamá Djankusó, Grandfather Akonomoi, take rum! My grandfather Oké-fu-andiási, please take some rum. May the days be bright and the nights, too, on the side of Good! Bush Hog says *Kiingó ta gundámba. A bungu yó, i músu tjángini kó. Tjángini kó, tjángini kó, tjángini kó.* All prayer is asking for pardon.

The several people present—Asántikálu, Ma Yaai, the two girls from across the road, and Sally and I—say "Great thanks," rhythmically clapping our hands, as Tooy turns to me and says, "Béndiwáta [a Lángu village on the Gaánlío] has those words. Take that doorway over there, you're getting ready to go through it. But there's a round log poised to drop from up above . . . various things are looking to kill you. You need to get through—before the *kiingó* drops on you. *Kiingó ta gundámba. A bungu yó, i músu tjángini kó.* 'You up above, let me pass, that's where I must pass!' That's what it says. In Púmbu language! 'Despite the danger—despite the *kiingó* poised to drop—I must get through, please let me pass through.' That's what this prayer asks for."[2]

In the evening, there's a formal council meeting in which some relatives gather to thank Sally and me for having helped get Tooy out of jail. The rhetoric is the same as on the several other occasions during the past year that thanks have been formally proffered.

> The thing they did is so big that we can never thank them. We have nothing appropriate to thank them with. If we had money, we could thank them with that. But we don't have money. All we could do is go out and rob a bank. But then we'd end up in prison again. If only we had "thanks," they would see it. But we don't have "thanks." If the canoe full of "thanks" had arrived here, we'd have long since unloaded it and given everything in it to them. But "thanks" is like the wind, you never get to see it. The wind shakes the trees, *waya waya waya* and you search for the wind until you don't know where to look anymore—you never get to see it. "Thanks" is just the same. We can't find it and give it to them so they can really see it. Our mouths can give them thanks— that's what we're trying to do here—but the thanks itself can never be given.

So, we give them thanks with everything we have, along with the gods and the óbias. The Great God himself must pray for them. They must live for 350 years—without injury, without getting weak, without getting sick!

But it doesn't stop with thanks for what we've done. There's something else they want of us. Although Tooy was enstooled as captain in 2001, the French Guiana government still hasn't given him an official uniform, nor has it started to pay him his captain's salary.

> Saramakas would say that we tied a bone around their necks. What's the bone? [the speaker prompts and others ask, "What's the bone?"] With all the work they've done for us, are we in a position to ask them to do something else for us now? [laughter] Saramakas say that if a man goes hunting on a certain day in a certain stretch of forest from morning till night and sees no game, and then does the same thing the next day, and the same a third day, do you think he'll ever go back there again? But if he goes hunting and sees a howler monkey, boom! And a little later sees an agouti, boom! And a little later a deer, boom, boom!—don't you think he'll go back the next day and the next and the next? That's the way it is with these people. They helped us with the one thing [prison], now we're coming back to them with another.
>
> The old man here [Tooy], he's like a bull without horns. [someone else: "How is he like a bull without horns?"] Well, when you see a bull, it always has a pair of horns stretching up from its head. If it's called a bull, it's always got horns. If you call an animal a bull but it doesn't have horns, it's not a bull. Well, the old man here, Saramakas call him captain. But if you see him, you'd think he was a beggar. Let's say you're standing on the street and he comes along—if it was written right in the middle of his forehead you could say, "Oh, here comes the captain!" But it's not written on his forehead. He's still a bull without horns. Other people have tried to help—we won't mention their names, because we're not here to criticize anyone. But we're here to implore these people to help us get the man officially recognized by the government. When you see a policeman on the street, you know him by his uniform. That's what the old man needs. We beg these people to help us get it for him. A bull can't remain without horns.

★ ★ ★

As happens often enough among Saramakas (not to mention academics), two close friends are no longer on speaking terms. Since some months before we arrived in Guyane, Ben has split with Tooy. In such situations, it's not easy to tease out the causes. Tooy's wife Céline, whom Ben has never been civil to, tells us that during a several-week period after Ben totaled his car, he stayed at Tooy's, recovering and being "cured." There were words about the large phone bill Ben chalked up, and his refusal to pay, and when he walked out he never returned. Neither wants to talk with us about it, but Ben is adamant he won't see Tooy. Sally and I, who spend a good deal of time with Ben on his projects and ours, work toward a reconciliation and, on our penultimate day in Guyane that trip, finally get Ben to sit down with Tooy and talk it out. They seem to be back together once more, ready to discuss common projects—getting Tooy recognized as captain by the government, working on the Saramaka fête and the Village Saramaka (the latter two Ben's projects rather than Tooy's).

*   *   *

Late in the evening, after everyone else has left, we are ready to say farewells until our next trip. Tooy presents Sally and me with a lovely embroidered Brazilian hammock and ushers us into the Dúngulâli shrine, where he sits us down next to him. He prays, "My master Dúngulâli, óbia that parts the paths! *Awíí, awíí kándikándi!* The path to the land of the dead must stay dark, the path to the land of living must stay light! The *óbia* must eat meat! . . . We ask for long life. We ask for two hundred years, three hundred years, without illness. . . ." He asks me to pray, then Sally. I notice that there's fresh blood from a sacrifice on the stone in front of the altar. He reaches over to a clay pot and removes a biceps ring, which he presents to me, saying its taboos include never wearing it to a funeral and, when I go to a wake where there's food set out, turning my back to the table and sitting down and standing up three times before facing the table. Then he passes a calabash of Dúngulâli liquid to us, telling us to hold it palm down with our left hand, touch it to the earth three times, and take three swallows. He gives me a generous handful of "Dúngulâli tobacco" (made, he explains, from the dried leaves of a First-Time variety of banana tree[3]), saying I should buy a pipe and smoke it as often as I want—that pipe is called *Anánagóa*, he says, and he sings the song that's sung as men pass the pipe from hand to hand during ceremonies: *Pípa, pípa-e, pípa lóntu, pípa-ya Anánagoá.* Akoomí has this talk! With that pipe he would kill people who came to harm him! Tooy turns on a tape recording of the big Dúngulâli ceremony they did while we were in Brazil—later he'll give me the tape so I can listen to it as I smoke my pipe and relax back home.

Tooy explains that if you work with Dúngulâli, Death can't kill you—except in one circumstance.

This óbia, if you work with it properly, Death can't touch you. Sickness can kill you. But not Death. When you work with Pásipaatí [a nickname for Dúnguláli], a person might walk up to you and shoot you, boom, or someone comes up to you and cuts you with a machete, djudjudju, or hits you with a stick—but you'll always live. Let's say you're traveling by canoe and you sink, but though you go to the bottom of the river, you'll find a way to get back to shore. Dún-guláli people never drown! But if you "miss" Dúnguláli, if you offend him, Dúnguláli himself will kill you.

The ritual performed while we were in Brazil was designed to renew the shrine after Tooy, having offended the óbia by mixing sex with his curing practices, had served his time and was finally free. It had been a warning from Dúngulálí. Now, Tooy was determined to make things right again.

As the tape continues playing, he explains to us one of the songs as he sings along with it.

Once, Bási Akoomí [the spirit who taught Dúnguláli to Kódji at the beginning of the twentieth century] went off to the land where there are only women. He and eight other men. The women fought them with sticks until they'd killed every one—except Akoomí. Then they went after him with machetes, but his óbia called Tifóu saved him. (That's what this song is about. I've washed in that óbia, but it's not good to make—it makes too many demands on you.) Finally, the chief of those women, Ma Akekóna [once he called her Ma Apeefúnda], showed up and said, "What's going on here, how come one's still alive? Who is he?" They said, "He's called Afeemaónsu" [the name of Akoomí's tutelary spirit]. She said, "Let him be! I know his mother, Ma Íni. His father is Gwánku-sonísa. Take him into your house, wash him, give him food, and cure him." Akoomí stayed there three years before he was himself again.

When Akoomí finally returned to his village, his wife had taken another man! He knocked on the door. She didn't answer (because she wasn't alone). Then she called out to him, "I don't know you anymore. Get outta here!" He said, "Don't talk to me like that. Here I am. If you don't open the door for me, I'll open it myself!" Well, the husband she'd taken, he was ready to finish off Akoomí. (She had taught him much of Dúnguláli-Óbia!) He was hiding be-hind the door with his sharpened machete. Akoomí opened the door. The man cut him heavily. But the óbia called Kadabayí saved him. He shouted, "Dúngulálí-e!"—lightning flashed on his biceps—at which the machete jumped up and cut the man into three pieces!

The tape recorder plays a very sad song that Tooy joins in on: Aíng!, Aíng!, Aíng!, Kwaíng! Ma Íni kó a fin komani-e-o. Aíng!, Kwaíng! . . . This is Akoomí's lament when he came home and found his wife with the other man. "You know what the woman did to him?" Tooy asks me. "She told him to hold out his hands, and she put burning coals in them! That's when he jumped out, cut off her head, cut off the man's head, and cut off the heads of his nine children! (Don't tell this story often—it's very dangerous.)" I ask if this happened in the land of the living. No, says Tooy, in the land of the dead, adding that this is the sort of thing Komantí óbias like to shoot the breeze about.

Thinking about Komantís, Tooy decides to offer me a special nugget and sings, Agódo, agódo séki-e, djámkamísa agódo [repeat]. "This is how Kwasímukámba asked his brother Alúa for the drinking glass. Agódo means 'small calabash,' djamkamísa sugarcane drink. The day had come for them to drink together, and this is what he said." And then he confirms something he'd only hinted at once earlier: "When Kwasímukámba came to Saramaka, he didn't come alone. There were three brothers who walked together. The oldest was Alúa, the middle one Nêngè Kwasí [slave Kwasí], and the youngest Kwasímukámba.[4] Gweyúnga only 'caught' Kwasímukámba—the others went to other villages. After they went back to the coast, only Alúa and Kwasímukámba came upriver again with the whitefolks. It's all in Komantí songs. In fact, when these three men died, they didn't become ghosts/ancestors [mísikôndè] at all. They turned into Komantís! At Kámbakiíki on the Gaánlío, one turned into a thorn tree (djênjênkumáka) and the other a termite hill—both are still there, each topped with a metal soldier's helmet from the days of war."

As we are ready to leave, Tooy takes my hands and says, Nyam-nyam kuvánde, nyam-nyam vála, which means, in Púmbu, "A long trip causes okra to dry on the branch."

> Let's say you plant okra in your garden here and leave for Martinique—your okra will dry on the branch, because you're so far away. You and I have known each other quite a while by now. Even when you're far away, you mustn't forget me. Things happen here that aren't good—they make me captain and then everyone in Guyane is jealous and says I must die. We've got to find a solution. As you've told me, I've already paid with my prison time. Now I lay my head in your hands. You know Saramaka laws, you know whitefolks' laws. Tell me what I should do. I leave myself in your hands. When you go, don't forget me. Nyam-nyam kuvánde.

TEMBÁI'S VILLAGE

We first visited the Saramaka village of La Flêche, two-thirds of the way from Cayenne to Saint-Laurent and a couple of kilometers off the highway on a rutted track, in 2001, and have been back a half-dozen times. The welcome has always been warm, and by now we're privileged guests. Saramakas call the place Tembái-kôndè (Tembái's Village) after its founder and leader, Captain Miséi Tembái Mayóko, a Saramaka now in his midfifties, who settled the spot some twenty-five years ago. Perhaps twenty adults and twenty or thirty children now live there, including Miséi's four wives, and the kids go to school by bus in Mana, an hour away. The village is a healing center for Saramakas and others and is known for the annual fête, in May, of its tutelary Wénti, Djéunsu-Etéunsu.

Miséi, like Tooy, is an extrovert who seems to enjoy life to the fullest. But unlike Tooy, he's very much the public manager and rather flamboyant booster of the two gods for which he serves as medium. Largely uninterested in what we might call the theology of Wéntis or Wátawenús—in marked contrast to Tooy—he focuses on their theatrical aspects. And again unlike Tooy, who has told us that the gods in his house—from Dúngulálí-Óbia to the "hand" of the óbia that Kwasímukámba's son Gisí left his matrilineage to all the Wéntis and others who live with him—could never be photographed for fear that they would refuse to work with him anymore, Miséi positively encourages photography of his gods and their shrines. Whenever we come, he asks us to shoot photos, and he proudly shows us his album of those taken by gendarmes and other visitors. (His Wénti outfit, which he wears when possessed, looks Brazilian influenced [Iemanjá-like]—I've never seen another possessed Wénti in this sort of fancy getup.) Miséi's shrines are more colorful and public than Tooy's—they almost seem set up for display. His curing business includes a kind of showmanship that's entirely absent from Tooy's, which relies rather on a combination of his powerful personality and his unmatched knowledge of ritual.

Some twenty years ago, Miséi told us, a god repeatedly tried to possess him, so they brought him to his natal village of Gódo in Suriname, where a man from the village of Palubásu was able to "lift the taboo" that was keeping the god from successfully coming. It turned out that Miséi's "namesake"—his father's father, who had committed suicide with a gun on the Approuague during the early twentieth century—had had a powerful anaconda god in his head. While they were bringing Miséi from Palubásu, where the ceremony to lift the taboo had been held, to Gódo, Miséi dove into the water and disappeared. Everyone thought he'd drowned, but they later found him lying on the shore at Gódo. The god said its name was Lonzhé, the same Wátawenú that had possessed his "namesake."

Within a year, Lonzhé brought Miséi another god, the Wénti Djéunsu-Etéunsu, who had never been heard of before. Miséi told us that when Lonzhé had been in his namesake's head, he'd brought him an Adátu or Abatútu god—a rough sort of Komantí-like bodyguard or watchman in the form of a toad. And now, instead, Lonzhé had brought Miséi a tutelary Wénti, Djéunsu-Etéunsu. When Miséi dies, he assures us, and Lonzhé possesses someone else, he'll bring yet another helper god to that person.

The *óbia* canoe for Miséi's anaconda god.

Two views of the shrine to Anoenzai Boeski.

Miséi's house, a large wooden structure in coastal style, stands at the center of the village, and there are a couple dozen Saramaka-style houses spread around the white sands of the place. Miséi reserves several for the use of patients, who often spend days or weeks while they are being treated for one or another ailment. (We've seen Guadeloupeans as well as Saramakas convalescing in the village after a cure.) There's a sizeable council house, where Miséi takes visitors and serves them cold beer or soft drinks with the help of the gasoline-generator-powered electrical system that covers the whole village. Miséi, like many of the younger residents, has a cell phone and speaks to friends and relations all over Guyane—and Suriname—with ease. There are gardens tended by the women out along paths leading from the village. Once when we arrived, men had just shot and butchered seven bush hogs and were dividing some of the meat among relatives and carting the rest in wheelbarrows to sell by the highway.

In the central space between Miséi's house and his gods' houses stands an outdoor shrine, covered with thatch, featuring a colorfully painted ship to which large seashells are affixed (reminiscent to us of certain Ghanaian or Haitian shrines for the sea gods.) The meter-and-a-half-long ship, with conchs at either end and carrying an image of its owner, says it's dedicated to "Anoenzai Boeski"—reminding us of Kódji's Busikí, Wánanzái. But Miséi says that Djéunsu had once possessed him and directed the building of this shrine, including the spelling out of the name of the master of the ship, and

Lonzhé's post and necklace (the letters and lightbulb are not part of the display).

Lonzhé's pot on its clay hearthstones. There's an unfinished necklace nearby.

Lonzhé's altar with its *kongoobusí*, canoe, and two blond dolls.

that he wasn't sure that this was related to Kódji's god at all, despite his being a matrilineal descendant of that great man.

Miséi has built two large houses for his gods. The one behind Lonzhé's *óbia* canoe is divided in two—the front half is Lonzhé's, the rear belongs to Djéunsu-Etéunsu. As befits the shrine of a Wátawenú avenging spirit, the front room holds twisted vines and branches, some with embedded cowries, old machete blades, and lots of sacred white clay. The god's "post" holds the necklace he wears when he possesses Miséi—braided red cloth decorated with cowries. On the earth nearby is the iron pot used to "boil" (ritually prepare) biceps rings. The god's altar holds his *kongoobusí* (crooked scepter), a canoe loaded with goods, and offerings left by visitors, including two blond dolls.

The back half of the house, Djéunsu's domain, has an anteroom/corridor which serves as a space for visitors' gifts—on a large table covered with colorful cloth there are several bouquets of plastic and cloth flowers in vases, bottles of champagne, Perrier, Schweppes, and beer, and a life-sized cloth parrot balancing on a perch; a large cardboard cutout of a London Beefeater, originally made for display in a bar featuring the gin of that name, dominates one wall. Once again, the tie-in between Wéntis and a plethora of whitefolks' merchandise.

Inside Djéunsu's shrine. Each bowl contains an egg. Djéunsu's red, white, and blue "belt" is decorated with cowries. Note also Djéunsu's beribboned divination basket, the C.R.S. (police) medallion, and the tall post topped by an *óbia* bottle with an eagle feather attached.

Djéunsu's altar and throne.

The *óbia*'s post and pot.

Close-up of the *óbia*'s post, topped by eagle, macaw, and vulture feathers.

In the back room is Djéunsu's Wénti palace. The ceiling is hidden by swaths of blue-and-white fabric. The floor is tiled in white and light blue. Christmas decorations hang from strings, and there are quantities of embroidered white cloths, cans of room deodorizer, many bottles of cologne and perfume. Terrycloth towels and tapestries with Christian imagery are all bright and clean. There are several Christian paintings and chromolithographs. There are sculptures of wooden animals, ceramic swans, plastic flowers, bottles of sugarcane syrup, champagne, and beer, a 3-foot-tall artificial Christmas tree with decorations, a Santa Claus figurine, candles, a large pendulum clock, several blond dolls still in their boxes (remember Wéntis and babies), a carved wooden armadillo, the medallion of an elite French national police unit, and much else. Miséi explained that most of these are gifts from visitors—though he himself had placed the sixth-grade diploma of one of his sons on the wall. Next to the altar, which is laden with other gifts, is Djéunsu's throne, where the god sits when he possesses Miséi. In contrast to Lonzhé's room, everything here is clean and bright.[1]

A large wooden house next door, which was built under Djéunsu's direction, is divided into a spacious front public room where ritual washings,

Close-up of the *óbia*'s pot.

Miséi Tembái possessed by Djéunsu-Etéunsu, wearing Wénti clothes.

Miséi possessed by Lonzhé, carrying his *kongoobusí*.

divination, and other curing rites take place, and a small back room where the *óbia*—Lonzhé—holds sway and keeps his pot, his post, and his stool (throne). Anoenzai, the captain of the Wénti ship outside, also serves as a carry-oracle, and it's in this front room that they divine with him when people seek help with their problems.

Miséi's son Régis wearing Lonzhé's complex "belt" and posing on the óbia throne, constructed with bull's horns, eagle feathers, vulture feathers, macaw feathers, and the bris-
tles of the giant anteater.

On one of our visits in 2005—whenever we come, we bring offerings of
beer, sugarcane syrup, and sparkling wine to place on Djéunsu's altar—Miséi let us borrow three photos from his album, which we scanned in Cayenne, showing himself in the guises of Djéunsu and of Lonzhé and his son
Régis posing on Lonzhé's óbia throne, which he will some day inherit.

★   ★   ★

In May 2005, we were finally able to attend Djéunsu's annual fête. Four years
earlier when we'd visited, Miséi had presented us each with commemora-
tive tee shirts from the Djéunsu celebration that year. They read (in a white
field surrounded by blue stars): *Vive / 'Djeunsu Eteunsu' / Le 25 Mai 2001/ 1967-
2001 / (34 ans) P.K. 169* [this is the kilometer marking on the road that serves
as street address] / *97350 Iracoubo* [postal code and name of municipality]

/ *Djeunsu Eteunsu;* a pair of crossed machetes—I assume a Brazilian influence—are underneath. We imagined some sort of elaborate Wénti fête and made it our business to be in Guyane at the right moment of the year for the 2005 version.[2]

When I asked Miséi what the "1967" and "34 years" on the tee shirts represented, he said that Djéunsu had announced, when he possessed him not long before, that he was born in 1967, making him thirty-four years old. When I asked Miséi and some of his relatives whether Djéunsu had described his sisters and brothers or even where he came from, they said he hadn't. He is by nature taciturn, which is also the case for Lonzhé, they said, adding that Lonzhé never told about his family even when he was in the head of Miséi's namesake.

The fête, which began at 10:00 p.m., attracted scores of young Saramakas from Saint-Laurent and the settlements in the area, as well as a dozen or so Creoles who were friends of Miséi's and ten or twelve local Amerindians from Iracoubo. Miséi was a gracious host, setting up tables and chairs on the sand for his Creole and Amerindian guests and offering bottles of whisky, cognac, and beer. A makeshift store sold drinks to others. In the council house, a Saramaka band played *kawína* (the calypso of Suriname) as young couples danced tightly in the dark. Female dress ranged from traditional Saramaka wrap skirts to very short skirts and high heels. Most men were dressed to disco. Around 2:00 a.m., a space was cleared outside, and a dozen or so late-teenagers, Miséi's sons and close relatives, filed out of Lonzhé's shrine dressed in loincloths, their legs whitened with kaolin. To the accompaniment of Apúku drums, they danced first upon fire and then upon broken glass before washing themselves thoroughly with *óbia* solutions from an oil drum heating on a fire in front of the shrine. After this half-hour interlude, the pop music struck up again, and it was time for lovers to meet. We retired to the Saramaka-style house and hammock that Miséi kindly provided. So much for Wéntis.

* * *

When I've discussed Miséi's gods with Tooy, he's been faintly dismissive, explaining that these are just Miséi's father's things from Gódo. Djéunsu has nothing to do with Adjéunsu, who for Tooy is the master of the seas, the headman of the saltwater Wéntis, a real *gaamá!* Djéunsu, says Tooy, is a sweetwater Wénti related to the famous Wénti called Tulí, who was active in the early twentieth century and whose master also lived in the village of

Gódo. Both those gods, says Tooy, are mere *kédje-tomé* (sweetwater Wéntis), not *tósu-kpêke-kpêke* (Wéntis from the sea).

Once I asked Miséi what he thought of Tooy. "That man truly knows things! The inside of his head is all filled up. And he doesn't forget things. For the seven landing places of the Lángu clan, there's no one who knows things like him! He knew the Old Ones. His problem is that he won't tell what he knows, he doesn't like to share his knowledge. But he sure does know things!"

FLEEING TRUMPS STANDING

★ 04182005/05302005 ★

Several times during our first visit of 2005, Tooy tells me why he's come to the conclusion that fleeing may be wiser than standing your ground. "We once could have confidence in our óbias," he'd say. "But nowadays, who knows how much of their powers are left? Let's say someone comes running at you with an axe and you have to choose whether to see if your óbias are still worth something or to make your escape. Which makes more sense? I'd say, Run for it!" And he giggles. This tone of sardonic pessimism, the sense of a world on the wane, colors many of our discussions during those weeks, when great, dark sheets of rain are falling on Cayenne.

"Let's say," Tooy tells two sister's sons who are visiting, "that in the days when Saa Wíi used his óbia, there were twelve biyóngos. Well, now maybe seven are left. We still have the óbia, but half its biyóngos are gone! I might promise you that I'll teach you a biyóngo before I die, but what if you're not there when I'm dying? So we lose that knowledge. That's why, as I said, fleeing has its benefits." Or again, he remarks one day,

> People don't really believe anymore. The Old Ones didn't eat onions or garlic. Ashes was their Maggi [bouillon cubes]—it's called adín. You'd cut some sticks, burn them, and whenever you cooked okra or meat you'd take a spoonful of ashes and mix it into the pot. I saw my own mother do this! Nor did the Old Ones eat salt. They burned the sapatí tree—that was runaway people's salt. Do you think any of those great men would have eaten garlic? But look at us now. We used to know about medicinal plants. We used to know leaves that would bend a machete when struck, leaves that could break a stone! The great men used to eat biyóngos and, just before they died, they'd vomit them up. It's all gone now. None of us are willing to keep the taboos. Who's willing to go even one week without touching a woman? Saramakas aren't Saramakas anymore!

"We remain just like Kofímakámaká's dog," an apocryphal animal which Tooy explains was named Ógiten—"Hard Times." "The world," he continues, "is going from bad to worse. Sometimes I look into my divination mirror and can't even report the things that I see. I just haven't got the stomach for it." Tooy remarks that Nélia, his sister's daughter in Cayenne—a bright, attractive forty-year-old whom, he has told me before, he cured of AIDS some years ago—is now on crack cocaine.[1] The girlfriend of one of her sons (Tooy's sweet "grandson" with the red shades), a Frenchwoman who works at the hospital, got her started a few months ago. Tooy says he doesn't think she's started hooking to get the cash, but figures that'll come soon enough. And Nélia's brother Francis, whom Tooy and Yaai had raised till adulthood and who'd been one of his assistants during our early visits to Cayenne, is now in jail awaiting trial on charges of raping a Creole woman—a policeman Tooy knows has told him that he'll be sentenced to seventeen years behind bars. Tooy also reports that a Saramaka man in Cayenne recently shot his Creole landlord and his own wife, after he'd found them in bed together, before killing himself. Ben, who's now sitting with us, adds that Cayenne is rife with "love dramas," and that once Saramakas get involved in local life, they tend to get sucked in. Tooy, laughing, admits to having come within a hairbreadth of shooting a man whom he'd caught sleeping with his *íngi* wife Annette, some twenty years ago. His passion almost got the better of him, in very un-Saramaka fashion.

Learning, he says, is going out of style.

> The gods used to love to teach me things. There was one in Bundjitapá [Tooy's natal village] called Kwebanú-Mutúalála, a Wátawenú mixed with Apúku [one parent of each], but it was Apúku we would play for him. Once, I played for him for twelve days straight—I was pissing blood by the end. He called God Naná Mpúngu, Zámina Mpúngu. My father's brother had a runaway slave called Sépi in his head. He taught me lots of Old Time words, African language—*Paláka*, he said, meant "God" and *étéla*, "I'm going." He'd say *paláka leméla*—"Go with God." He told me that *hú* meant "woman," *wáizaanga* "open-sided house" [Saramaccan *gangása*], *oníabò* "river," *oníabò baasuma akí* "lower river," and *oníabò líbama akí* "upper river."

Tooy imitates the way Sépi used to talk. "I loved to play the drums for them!" he reminisces. "Today," he goes on, "kids come and ask me things, but only when they need some particular knowledge. It's never for the sake of learning, so they'll never really amount to anything. My greatest regret is that I have no one to shoot the breeze with, no one to pass things on to. Young people today just don't have the patience. When I was younger, when you went to a 'play,' if the priest there knew the songs better than you did, it was a real embarrassment. Nowadays, these things don't matter. When I go, I'll take it all with me. My own sister's children don't even bother to come and sit with me. You're the only one who seems to care."

* * *

Aside from these touches of pessimism, by 2005 Tooy seems pretty much back to his old self. His curing business is active, his concerns about getting his captaincy fully recognized by the French authorities continue, and his enthusiasms for gods, women, drumming/songs, and history are as strong as ever. And a problem that had long been weighing on him has finally been resolved: the Frenchwoman avenging spirit has been pacified. (Bási Ofilíbaní [Flibánti], Sensiló's óbia back in Suriname, had gone to see Frenchwoman on his behalf, when she possessed her medium in Paranam, and they had worked out a ritual payment which Tooy has now completed.) Tooy's teaching me things has become in part a substitute for his not being able to teach others as much as he'd like, no matter how different it is. A number of times during our visit, I wonder how many bitter or foul liquids I will have to drink—Tooy plies me with drinks and óbias, seeking to be generous, throughout the stay.

Many of the óbias he offers me, like those he makes for other men in return for money, are for sex. As he gives me a golf-ball-sized hard ball of hashed and mashed leaves, telling me it's *asilapáu kándu* (okra-stem charm)—okras stand up very straight on the stem—he says, "Keep this under your bed, drink a bit with rum. If you drink it three times in a day, you'll be able to have three women that day." Others are to keep me and Sally healthy. He prepares a basin filled with sweet-smelling leaves, telling me to take it home and pour in one bottle of beer before adding the water—this bath puts us in relations with Wéntis, Apúkus, and the Earth Mother. The top is sprinkled with kaolin and when I bring it back to our apartment, it's so pretty that Sally takes a picture.

As for drinks, Tooy's preference during this visit seem to be bitters of one sort or another—bitters so bitter that it is often hard to get down even a few drops. "It's good for worms," he says, as he forces some upon me. (The bark of the white *asúmáípa* tree is for small worms, that of the red variety for large ones, he explains. My remonstrations that I don't have worms only evoke from him that neither does he, but that it is good to keep the stomach clean in any case.) Fortunately, many of his clients have been leaving six-packs of Heineken or Guinness or bottles of sweet Brazilian brandy on the floor of the consulting room, and while drinking at all hours of the day isn't my normal preference, it does help chase the aftertaste of those omnipresent bitters.

Tooy also periodically drinks from a small bottle, and then offers me some, of what he says is "okra-stem charm" (the ball-shaped *óbia* he'd prepared for me earlier). He explains that if a man has made an *óbia* so that if you sleep with his wife you can't get it up (which is quite common, he assures me when I ask), this *óbia* we're drinking ensures that the husband's *óbia* won't work and that you'll do just fine with the lady.

And one day, after a political meeting in his house with Saramaka captain Adaisso of Kourou and his assistant, Tooy gives each of them—and me— as a parting gift an *óbia* to swallow and a bunch more of it to take home, wrapped in brown paper torn from a bag. He doesn't need to specify to these knowledgeable men what it's for—it looks like some sort of rough charcoal mixed with ashes, and it goes down the throat only with difficulty.

There are now three dozen large plastic buckets—red, green, blue, yellow—stacked near the door of the waiting room. When I ask, Tooy explains that they're from clients who paid for part of a cure, then left a bucket for him to fill with *óbia* ingredients for a "bath," but never returned to pick it up and pay the balance. "Clients deceive me because they know I won't harm them. Dúngulái doesn't like [human] blood! So, I'm helpless against them, and they know it." He giggles and shrugs.

On a daily basis, Haitians now seem to be Tooy's most frequent clients, though he continues to see Creoles, Brazilians, Saramakas, metropolitan French, and others. Often, even while Haitians are present, he expresses annoyance to me (in Saramaccan, which they can't understand) at what he sees as their habits. Referring to them out loud as "Hai-*dágu*" ["Hai-dogs," a pun on "Hai-*chien*"—French for "dog"], he tells me that if you do curing for Haitian women, you'd better watch your ass. "They offer you their titties and when you take them, they've got you. Those women may be good-looking, but once you look closely at their habits, you wouldn't want one for a wife here. They'll leave their husband in Haiti, come to Guyane and take another man, and get all that man's money and send it back to their husband in Haiti. Other 'nations' don't live like that! Once they take a new husband, that's the one they think about. But not Haitians. Another thing, when a Haitian's husband dies, she'll have some other man working away on top of her belly while he's still in the icebox at the morgue!" I watch Tooy do a series of tarot-card divinations and make a bucket of leaves for a group of six Haitians—four men and two women—who eventually pay him 20 euros. A second group of three asks how much their bucket costs, and he says ten. They scrape up the money, coin by 50-cent coin, the men scrounging in all their pockets and the woman searching inside her bra. Tooy looks disgusted that they can't more easily come up with the paltry sum.

Tooy receives clients who have varied concerns. One Creole man arrives in his blue work jumpsuit to ask for help with his wife, who has taken to chatting with her boyfriends on the phone right in front of him and their children. (Tooy just shakes his head and tells the man to come back another time.) Two young Brazilian women arrive on a motor scooter and ask him if he speaks Creole. They consult briefly and say they'll return with money the next day. A fifty-year-old Creole shows up with his twenty-five-year-old wife, seeking sexual assistance (and saying he can pay up to 1,000 euros for a true cure). After he leaves, Tooy tells me and his assistants that the man will have to pay at least 4,000 for what he needs. Two years ago, he abandoned his wife of many years for this young woman and hasn't been able to get it up since. Clearly, says Tooy, the (ex-)wife is responsible, and curing the man is going to be heavy work! A couple of young women come in together, one a white Guadeloupean, the other a Guyanaise, both with man problems. Tooy "cuts [tarot] cards" for each and makes an *óbia*-in-a-bucket for each, specifying that one must wash in hers three times a day for five days, the other for six days. He charges each 35 euros for the card work and 30 for the *óbia*, which he tells me is a real bargain. The women express concern about how to wash in their *óbias* at midday without messing up their hair, since they must return to their offices. And one of them is concerned that her man will suspect that she's seeking magical help when he sees her bathing in the evening. Tooy says that's their problem.

When Tooy's telephone slips off its shelf into a basin of water and is ruined, I drive him to Cayenne's new megasupermarket, several kilometers distant, to buy him a new one. As we walk in from the parking lot, the greetings begin: "Bonjour, M. Alexandre," people say with pleasure as he gives out handshakes or kisses on the cheek, like a celebrity or local politician. From the security guards and the store hostesses to the employees loading shelves and the salesgirl who sells us the phone, everyone seems to know him. All are former or present clients. All seem delighted to see him.

While Sally and Yaai are cooking the midday meal together, I join Tooy as he prepares an *óbia* for a Saramaka visitor in the presence of an assistant and an older friend. My notes read:

> There are two yellow rain slickers laid out on the ground, one holding four piles of chopped barks (I'd guess about a kilo of each) and the other, four piles of different barks, four of chopped vines, seven different kinds of forest leaves (still on their stems), and separately, five kinds of "kitchen garden" leaves. It must have taken a couple of hard days of work in the forest to put all this together. Tooy asks his assistant and the older man to "lift the god," and they bring out Luégan, a smallish carry-oracle draped with a red print cloth who had been in the Dúngulúli chamber. The god directs Tooy in the making of the *óbia* from start to finish, being asked which ingredients to add first, whether to add certain other things, how to handle the eggs, etc. Order of things going into the large plastic basin, which the client was first asked to mark in a large X with *keéti* and then place a large beer bottle in the center, was: *biyóngos* of two kinds, one a ball of *keéti*-like stuff (*keéti* with other things mixed into the ball), and then bits from Tooy's *biyóngo-apakí*: vulture's claw, mica, quartz crystals, etc, shaved off with a pocket knife under the direction of the carry-oracle. Then, forest barks, which were in pairs of "western"/"eastern" [side of the tree], with each pair going into the basin in that order; then forest vines, then forest leaves, then kitchen-garden leaves. Within each category, the god instructed which piles to load in first. At the god's instructions, the client then poured in three liter bottles of beer, as we all sipped more beer from a single calabash we passed around. At the end, a small (Heineken) beer bottle and an egg were placed in the basin for each person. A lot of attention was paid to the direction of the beer bottles, the positioning of the eggs, the identification of each person's egg, etc. Bottles and eggs were put to the east so the washing could be done from the west side. (Each was marked with *keéti* so people could find their own.) Sally—who'd joined us from the kitchen—and I included. Then, after we all ate together, we washed, with Tooy presiding. Each person

washed first with his personal egg (used like a bar of soap) and then full-scale washing with the beer mixture scooped out of the basin with a calabash. Then drinking the same mixture and *fulá pfáá* [spraying from the mouth, to right and left] from the calabash. As the washing continued, Tooy and Yaai and the others broke into song, some Komantí and some Wénti. We left at 3:30.

On another day when I arrive, Tooy's wearing his shiny blue knockoff Everlast boxer's shorts, a Brasil tee shirt, and a grungy New York Yankees cap. Three women arrive in succession, and he gives each about twenty minutes of his time. First is Marie-Jo, an amply proportioned woman born in Guadeloupe, with whom he has an off-color joking relationship—she's all over his body, touching and groping and teasing him, and he gives as much as he gets. He takes six very large gingerroots that she's brought, crushes them in a large mortar, cuts up three large limes, takes three grains of *nêngèkôndè* pepper, unwraps three rectangles of laundry bluing (this, he tells me, is the *óbia*'s "*biyóngo*"), and puts it all into a plastic bucket, adding a whole bottle of white vinegar on top. He tells Marie-Jo to lift her skirt (which she does fully and ostentatiously) and sit on the bucket, which is "boiling" pretty fiercely since he poured in the vinegar. Once it quiets down, she's to take it home and wash in it three times a day for three days. She pulls two 20-euro notes from somewhere inside her bosom and places them on the floor for him.

A Haitian woman comes for a tarot session, after which Tooy makes an *óbia* in a bucket she's brought—he tells me this recipe belongs to the Awaná clan—and he adds one egg, some kaolin, and water from the hose and tells her to take it into the bathroom, disrobe, and wait for him in the shower area. The third woman brings a new bucket for him to fill with medicine leaves, plus a six-pack of Heineken and a six-pack of eggs. Tooy goes into the tarot-Wénti room with her. Except for the raucous joking with Marie-Jo, the sessions are whispered, and I sit waiting more or less patiently out in the leaf room. Meanwhile, there's a Haitian woman in the waiting room who, Tooy tells me, has been spitting blood for weeks. Another woman arrives, a good-looking thirty-year-old. He tells her he'll bathe her at precisely eleven o'clock, which is forty-five minutes away. I'm reminded of an American dentist with three or four chairs—Tooy now has one woman in the shower, another in the "wash house," one in a bedroom waiting to be examined, and the one who spits blood in the waiting room. Every few minutes, the telephone rings and he speaks to a client in Saramaccan or Creole as he goes back and forth from one room to another, joking with the women as he adds

Tooy and a client.

sprigs to one bucket, an egg to another. He sits down near me, takes an egg, and carefully marks it with India ink from a bottle, standing it up and making a horizontal almond shape with a line down the middle and two little plus signs under that. He heads off toward the shower with it. A Haitian man comes in, and once Tooy returns, he is told to come back Friday with 25 euros for the consultation—the man is trying to decide whether he should make a return trip to Haiti. Once the man leaves, Tooy asks the sick woman in the waiting room if she happens to know him. She says no—why? Tooy says since he's Haitian . . .

A couple of days later when I'm visiting with Tooy, he keeps falling asleep on his stool. Ben shows up, takes me outside where he's washing his secondhand Peugeot with a hose from Tooy's house, and tells me that the day before, when Sally and I were busy in Kourou, he had spent the day hanging out at Tooy's, and that Tooy had made it with five different women, mainly young and pretty—including a Haitian who, Tooy boasted to Ben, told him that the young men she sleeps with can't hold a candle to him. Ben seems at once bemused, impressed, and morally disapproving—he doesn't seem to know what to make of it, except that Tooy is amazing and Ben wishes he could have such powers. I regard Ben's report as hearsay from an interested party—Ben has been competitive with me about historical knowledge lately and might simply be trying to knock down Tooy in my estimation. But who knows?

* * *

Several times during the visit, Tooy spontaneously talked about his conviction and time in prison. "In Suriname," he mused, "once fifteen days have passed, a woman can't accuse a man of rape. In Guyane, it's fifteen years!" (It's actually ten, though nearly fifteen years had passed by the time he was brought to trial.) He says he can't deny having slept with the fifteen-year-old; after all, he had a child with her. (He talks as if his conviction was for sleeping with an underage girl. The idea of rape isn't salient for him.) He did live with her for five years and never denied it. But he never expected all this trouble. "Is she the only girl in the world with titties?" he laughs. Why would all those men be after her and only her? She's jailed a white man, a Haitian, a Brazilian, and a Saramaka, all for sex—the whiteman, Tooy says, was accused of raping her child. "Are they the only family with breasts? I've been in Guyane since 1958 and never had a problem with the law and never had a problem with a woman," he says.

In jail, the Brazilian told him that when he got out, he'd kill those women. The Haitian, who boasted of supernatural powers, said so, too. And not long ago, when the girl's father returned to Maripasoula from Cayenne, he sat down in a chair and keeled over dead! The mother is now bedridden in Cayenne and needs to be spoon-fed. Tooy says he's not involved in any of this—but that family will get what it deserves. "Meanwhile," he confides to Sally and me, "Brigitte's lawyer has had to stop practicing. She put away four men in a single year for sex with Brigitte or her family! The government decided it wasn't possible!"

A few days later, during a friendly visit with Tooy's lawyer, Lamartine, Sally asks him about this, but he says that Brigitte's lawyer is simply on maternity leave. However, he adds that, thinking back on the case and the others she's been involved in, it now seems pretty clear to him that Brigitte was running a con, that she'd figured out a way to get easy money from the State, and that Tooy was simply in the wrong place at the wrong time, the perfect fall guy for her accusation. And he says that women in Cayenne, who talk among themselves, are now well aware of the potential benefits of bringing men they've had relations with to court for rape. When Sally asks if men are ever acquitted of charges of rape in Cayenne, he says he can think of only a single case (which the State immediately appealed and which is still pending). In today's atmosphere of fear and political correctness, Lamartine pointed out, any accusation of rape is tantamount to a multiyear conviction for the accused and a healthy payment to the plaintiff.

We reflect how, in the guise of Brigitte, Tooy almost met his nemesis. Imagine Tooy as a kind of Greek hero—a charismatic man who is flawed in distinctively human ways and hence doomed to mortal tragedy. Roaming across cultural boundaries, mixing traditional Saramaka knowledge with the tools of Creole curing, he had developed a set of practices that brought him a modest income, frequent sexual opportunities, and a measure of personal power. Meanwhile, Brigitte and her family had crossed their own cultural boundaries and succeeded in mobilizing a different but no less effective set of tools in the service of their own, largely financial, ends. In the ensuing confrontation, Brigitte and her allies successfully manipulated ideas about gender, sex, money, ethnicity, and modernity to bring Tooy to his knees and get their payoff. In this French arena, Tooy's traditional spiritual powers were trumped by a modern arsenal of secular arms. He was not far off the mark when he sometimes thought of what Brigitte and her family did as a curse, for the effect was the same. Tooy's ultimate triumph— really a sort of Pyrrhic victory—depended on a different State apparatus outflanking Brigitte's troops. In the end, a human-rights discourse based on prisoners' rights (a seriously ill prisoner shall not be held . . .) was used to override a human-rights discourse based on women's rights (about rape and domestic violence . . .).[2] We hardly felt proud of the means used to spring Tooy from captivity, but fighting the State with its own weapons had become our only option, once he had been ensnared by its totalizing logic and power. He was free; Brigitte and her daughter kept the money. For Tooy, who most of the time remains philosophical about the whole affair, the denouement is now well under way, as one after another of Brigitte's family suffers illness or death. His pleasure each time another shoe drops is subdued but palpable. He trusts that the gods, óbias, and ancestors will set everything right in the end.

Tooy tells me about several recurrent dreams he had in jail, all of which had him falling into a deep pit and not being able to climb out. But he also describes, for the first time, some of the daily realities of doing time in Cayenne. Whenever he visited the prison doctor, the man would ask if he didn't want some condoms. "What are you talking about?!" he'd object. "There's plenty of AIDS in here," the doctor would reply. Tooy told him to get outta there with that talk. He tells us that inside, he'd actually seen men fighting each other with knives over other men! And how in the showers, he saw something really ugly—búguru (from "boogaloo"?). Men would cut up dominos, file them down, make cuts in the skin of their penis with a razor, and insert the domino pieces. "It's a *makumé* [queer] thing!" he exclaimed. "But women like it too. Hot women like Marie-Jo. She tells me she really loves men with *búguru*." He adds, "Men have died of it in jail—they get infected. Georgetown guys are the bosses of that thing—they all have it. I saw one guy from Cayenne who must have been in his fifties, but he had these big *búguru*. I asked why in the world he'd done it. 'It's the fashion,' he told me." Tooy shakes his head, laughing. "I'll stick with the little thing God gave me."

POLITICS

From the beginning of that visit in 2005, Tooy's status as a bull without horns had been on the minds of Ben, Tooy's close relatives, and Tooy himself. Ben, as usual when we arrived in Cayenne, gave me photocopies of several more letters sent by the Association of Young Active Saramakas of Guyane, which he heads, to the president of the Conseil Général, the political body that officially recognizes Amerindian and Maroon captains, pays their salaries, and furnishes their uniforms. The problems with Tooy's official recognition have only grown more complicated since our last visit eight months earlier. And among other personal losses it's caused is Kalusé's defection to Tooy's rival—Kalusé now says he won't set foot in Tooy's house "as long as he lives." And Kalusé will no longer talk to Ben—his spot as vice president of the association has now been taken by another man.

From our perspective, the situation seems clear. Tooy was selected and installed as Saramaka captain of Cayenne in 2001, according to traditions dating to the nineteenth century. And then in 2003, as part of the complex politics of French Guyana, some members of the Conseil Général who belonged to an independentist party brought a Saramaka (naturalized as French, a trade union leader, and a member of their political party) to the Aluku *gaamá*, who declared him captain of the Saramakas of Cayenne, a status which the Conseil Général quickly approved, leaving Tooy—who was never mentioned—out in the cold, a bull without horns. For Saramakas (and ourselves) the issue was by what rights Alukus could designate a captain for the Saramakas (and after the Saramakas had already enstooled one!). From the perspective of the Alukus, who are French by birth, who have a seat on the Conseil Général as well as the Conseil Régional, and who would like to speak for all Maroons on French soil, it's purely a question of realpolitik. They have the power, to hell with tradition, they can do what they like. Saramakas are in a weak position to object.

Tooy spoke of it with me almost daily, veering between anger and resignation and often asking me to decide whether the issue should be pursued.

On the one hand, he'd been designated captain by all the traditional Saramaka means and not only exercised the office but took all the jealousy and witchcraft that went with it—witness his getting cut up by the masked men, going to prison, and so forth. On the other hand, he didn't really need it. As he told me several times, "Why do I want this extra headache? I have my house here, I have the other one in Cité Césaire [where Nélia and other relatives live], I have my house in Saint-Laurent [where Ma Yaai is currently staying], I have my beat-up car, I have five hectares of forest in Roura [left by his deceased brother]. Why do I need to be captain?" Tooy's conclusion during the visit was that, having come this far, I should help Ben pursue the issue until an outcome was clear one way or the other, and then we should drop it without regrets.

Tooy also told me that his rival is married to the Aluku *gaamá*'s sister's daughter, creating a strong bond. And, perhaps even more important, that the *gaamá* once arranged for Tooy and Sensiló to take an airplane to his village to make an *óbia* for him. (The *gaamá*, it turns out, has a Saramaka father, who was the brother of Tooy's own father.) While Tooy was making the *óbia*, the *gaamá* begged him to set up a shrine for Dúnguláli in his village, to share Dúnguláli-Óbia with the Alukus. Tooy said he'd need the formal approval of both the Béndiwáta Mamá in Saramaka and the Aluku *sóói-gádu*, Tatá Odun. The *gaamá* was unhappy with this response and never pursued the matter.

Sally and I eventually had a meeting with the president of the Conseil Régional, who has known and respected Tooy for years because of having once served as intermediary for a colleague's cure. Several weeks earlier, he had attended the launching of our latest book[1] at the Musée des Cultures Guyanaises, and he knows and admires our work. He grasped the situation quickly and offered to do his best to get Tooy recognized, as we suggested, as a second captain of Cayenne, given that there were now more than four thousand Saramakas living in and around the capital. However, it was the Conseil Général, not his Conseil Régional, that made these decisions, and they were far more concerned with the political stakes (Alukus are citizens who have the vote, Saramakas are immigrants who do not) than with cultural "traditions." The Aluku *gaamá* and the Conseil Général work together on a plethora of issues involving serious sums of money and heavy political power. In that arena, Saramakas do not exist (no matter how dependent both Alukus and, say, the president of the Conseil Général may be, at one time or another, on Saramaka ritual knowledge—these domains are kept quite separate). It was hard for us to feel any optimism about Tooy's chances.

* * *

During that same visit, the choice of a new Saramaka *gaamá* was by far the most frequent and lively subject of conversation. Saramaka Gaamá Songo Abóikóni—widely considered a weak leader, who had been partially incapacitated by a stroke—had died in November 2003. His tumultuous funeral, which dragged on until his burial more than three months later, was marked by the coffin's persistent refusal to name a successor and the *gaamá*s in the cemetery refusing, until the final moment, to "accept" Songo for burial as one of their own. Without awaiting the "second funeral" some months later, after which the successor is normally named, the interim *gaamá*—who cannot himself be a candidate for the permanent position—quickly went to Paramaribo and announced that his own brother, Otjútju (a.k.a. Belfon Abóikóni), had been chosen as the next *gaamá*, and his picture was duly published in the major Suriname newspaper, *De Ware Tijd*. (Since the eighteenth century, tradition has it that once the Saramakas select and enstool the new *gaamá*, he travels to the city, where he is officially installed and given a uniform by the colonial/national government.)

When we'd arrived in Cayenne on April 18, Otjútju's formal enstoolment as *gaamá* six days earlier was, for Saramakas, the talk of the town. Ben returned from a weekend in Paramaribo with photos of the new chief, legs whitened with kaolin according to tradition, head tied in a kerchief, sitting in the ancestor shrine of Asindóópo (the Saramaka capital), and holding the *gaamá*'s staff of office. But only two days later, in the village of Dángogó, another man—Ozéni—was enstooled in the ancestor shrine of that village. Saramakas suddenly had two rival *gaamá*s, and no one knew quite what to make of it. Disputes and rivalries for political office have always been part of the Saramaka political scene. But in the past, it's always been rival clans vying for the office. Here, two men who were closely related Matjáu-clan members of the Dángogó community had somehow split it right down the middle.

Ojútju had never hidden his political ambitions. When I knew him in the 1960s and '70s, he was a close confidant of the wise and respected Gaamá Agbagó Abóikóni and, apparently, his preferred successor.[2] He had long collaborated with outsiders on various projects—he was the first Saramaka to run an airstrip in the interior and one of the few to have a small store. In *First-Time*, I described him as "very much caught between the worlds of the coast and Saramaka" and noted that "he gave me some of my most important leads about First-Time, though his information sometimes turned out upon examination to be spurious"—by which I meant "politically motivated." I knew Ozéni only by reputation, as a man from Dángogó, the village in which we lived, who had chosen to live and work in Paranam, Alcoa's company town on the coast. Allegedly a mild man, Ozéni—I suspected—gained

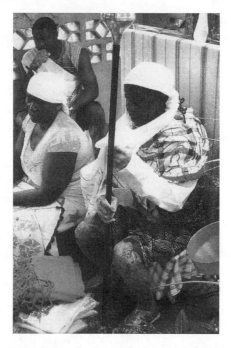

Otjútju's enstoolment, April 12, 2005, Asindóópo.

his support for the office of *gaamá* less for anything he represented than for not being Otjútju. Many Saramakas, and particularly many from Dángogó, didn't really trust Otjútju, whom they saw as too much of a manipulator. Genealogically, both fit the bill.

The talk among Tooy and his friends was, however, of an entirely different nature. Yes, they all agreed that Otjútju was the consummate political animal, and that this made him well suited to the office. But more to the point, Otjútju was not to be messed with. First off, he's what is known as "master of the great avenging spirit"—he has in his head one of the most powerful avenging spirits of his lineage. Second, his namesake is Bôò, the mother of Gaamá Agbagó, and her own namesake was Lukéinsi, the daughter of Adjágbò and Paánza and the medium of the First-Time forest spirit Wámba, giving him a supernatural lineage of great power.[3] Once Otjútju had been ritually enstooled in the ancestor shrine of Asindóópo, who could dare to try and take the office away from him and survive?

Ben plays us a cassette with the audio of Otjútju's installation. Tooy listens intently to the *apínti* and comments on exactly what it's saying: "*Fúndi ofón, fúndi ofón, fúndi ofón, alákatáka fúndi ofón*—the Suriname River is without a headman. The ship has no steersman. The ship turns sideways and drifts dangerously." And then later it plays, "*Séi kúnya, séi kúnya, séi kúnya, alábatáta séi kúnya*—The river has found a headman. The ship has found a steersman." Then, we listen as women sing lively *sekêti* songs composed for the occasion, celebrating the enstoolment of Gaamá Otjútju. "This dispute will have an outcome one way or the other," laughs Tooy. "If a woman's pregnant, if she doesn't have a boy she'll have a girl. Even if she doesn't have a boy or a girl, she'll have some sort of child with teeth in its mouth. Let's just wait and see!"

The next day Ben arrives with what he says is the inside dope—and it soon seems he's on to something. The conflict isn't about personalities or traditional genealogy, it's about the very modern forces of money, corruption, and "development." Ben has heard credible rumors that a certain "Pésé," a Frenchman who runs Guyane's largest gold mine, had made a deal with Gaamá Songo shortly before his death to "develop" Saramaka, with plans to build a five-star hotel across the river from Asindóópo, lengthen the nearby airstrip at Djoemoe, build a road linking the Saramaka villages with the outside world, and open up a massive gold mine inside the sacred Paaba Creek. Songo's death temporarily halted the project, though Pésé sent massive amounts of goods to the funeral as a show of his respect. (I recall having heard at the time of the funeral that a "Frenchman" had sent a plane and a number of canoes carrying thousands of dollars' worth of goods as gifts, from bolts of cloth to cases of rum and soft drinks.) Now, according to Ben's rumors, Ozéni and his supporters plan to continue with Songo's secret plans, while Otjútju wants nothing to do with Pésé.

Tooy surprises us by saying he knows Pésé. "That man's been in Guyane for years, living in Saint-Laurent. He once killed seven *íngi* headmen with that *óbia* of his—he keeps it in a sack he wears over his shoulder. It has an *asamaká* [a dead man's skull] in it. . . . He would go into the forest all by himself and ask his *óbia* if he should sleep in a certain spot that night, and if it said no, he'd move on. He works with it all the time." Tooy tells how Pésé built himself a house in Saint-Laurent, but his wife left to go back to her own country. He asked Tooy if he'd pour libations to bring her back. Tooy did, and a week later she returned. Since then, Pésé has been a fan. But Tooy warns us about the man. He was once up near St. Elie, where Pésé's company mines gold, and learned that Pésé steals Saramaka children from the coast to sacrifice to the devil who owns the gold in the bowels of the earth—diamonds, too, he's heard. Pésé has the children kidnapped and dropped from his helicopters near the gold fields.

Ben mentions that the new Golden Star mine in Saramaka territory (now owned by another multinational, Cambior)—built with the approval of the

Paramaribo government but without consultation with or permission from Saramakas—is already larger than Alcoa's venerable bauxite mine at Para-nam, and that many Saramakas now work there. They're throwing the slag into a sacred Saramaka lake, filling it up. And when they finish with one of their giant machines, they simply bury it in the earth![4] Ben also passes around a clipping and photo, from a small Paramaribo daily, that shows Ozéni's enstoolment and reports on the controversy. As we pore over the poor-quality photo, we try to figure out if Ozéni's legs have been whitened correctly. Otjútju had a better photographer!

One afternoon, Sally and I visit Kalusé. Though he's broken off relations with Tooy, he's as warm with us as ever. Looking up, we see a huge Russian cargo plane gliding down toward the airport[5] and talk about the new Russian presence in Kourou, where a Soyuz launch facility is being built at the edge of the European Space Center, with Saramaka laborers handling the bulk of the work. He tells us that the week before, both parties to the *gaamá* dispute agreed to go to the Béndiwáta Mamá to see what she said: three captains from Dángogó, three from Otjútju's side, all with their cassettes to record the verdict. The oracle tilted in favor of Dángogó, saying that the first person they meet when they returned to the landing place should be the next *gaamá*—and it was Ozéni. Kalusé says he can't see how Otjútju stands a chance, since the only people present at his alleged enstoolment were his brother (the interim *gaamá*), the *apínti* player, and a couple of friends.

A few days later, when we're in Saint-Laurent for another launching of our new book (this time at the town hall at the invitation of Léon Bertrand, France's Minister of Tourism who happens also to be mayor), we pay a visit to Saramaka captain Antonísi, who we've been told is Pésé's middleman with Saramakas. An old friend, he tells us that the man's name is really Alain Pichet, that he owns the St. Elie gold mine, and that he employs dozens of Saramakas. He indeed spent some 10,000 euros for Songo's funeral, entrusting Antonísi to buy and deliver 10 cases of Gandja (a fortified Spanish wine much appreciated by Saramaka women), 10 cases of rum, 16 cases of beer, 25 kilos of kidney beans, 25 kilos of salted pigs' tails, boxes and boxes of shotgun cartridges, 3 cases of black gunpowder, and a fine shotgun to hang in the house of mourning, which will later be hung by the new *gaamá* in his audience chamber; and he gave Antonísi another 3,500 euros to buy whatever he thought should be added. Now, complains Antonísi, some people are claiming behind his back that he took some of the money, and others that Pichet is going to reward him with 50 kilos of gold! (I do notice that he's got a massive new flat-screen TV.) Antonísi adds that Otjútju was improperly installed, because tradition has it that a *gaamá* must be enstooled in Dán-gogó, not in Asindóópo. So, Ozéni must be the real *gaamá*.

During the following days, rumors continue to fly. A supporter of Ozéni assures us that no one came to Otjútju's enstoolment except his brother and the *apínti* player—there were no captains or guests from elsewhere. It wasn't at all like a *gaamá*'s installation, he says. (But the photos we'd seen seem to give the lie to that.) A Dángogó supporter of Otjútju reports that all up and down the river the villages are for Otjútjú, that Dángogó is isolated in gen-erally supporting Ozéni. Otjútju is already sitting in his "office," receiving people and acting very much the *gaamá*.

The big news is that Gaama Gazón, the Ndyuka who is the most senior of all living Maroon chiefs, has sent a personal delegation to Saramaka to try to sort out the situation. They found Otjútju in his office and greeted him as *gaamá*, even offering him a "piece" of the Ndyuka god Gaán Tatá, as a gesture of friendship, to help him reign. When they visited Dángogó, Captain Amèèkán-óli (a.k.a. Aduéngi) threw them out! He said this wasn't a Ndyuka matter and they should get back to their own river. But the Ndyu-kas came ashore and walked right up to Gaán Tatá's house. (Since the early twentieth century, Dángogó has had a branch of Gaán Tatá that serves as the major village oracle. They brought it over from Ndyuka.) They asked Cap-tain Amèèkán-óli what that "thing" on the plank there was—the *sóói-gádu* of Mamá Ndyuka? Get outta here! they said. The Ndyuka captain pointed to his chest and said that the *sóói-gádu* of Mamá Ndyuka was there, and that what Dángogó had was worth nothing. The Ndyukas returned to Asindóópo, where they met with Otjútju and his councilors for three days. The Ndyukas said that Otjútju's name had been written in the whitefolks' book in the city for nearly a year already. He's sitting on the *gaamá*'s stool. Who's going to pull him off? No one knows the other man. If Amèèkán-óli enstooled him, he'll be the one to pay his salary and buy him a uniform, because the whitefolks never even heard of him.[6]

Tooy concludes that Otjútju will be the winner. "When Agbagó became *gaamá*, he sat on the stool with Todjê [his Wénti]. Songo did it all alone—and he did it badly. But Otjútju—he has the great avenging spirit of the Pikílío in his head! Who's about to take the *gaamá*-ship away from him? The person who tries—if they don't bury him in seven days, they'll bury him in fourteen days."

A Dángogó visitor reports that large numbers of people came for Otjútju's enstoolment—several planeloads of whitefolks and even some city policemen.

The Saramakas played Nanábulúku [a First-Time 'play' whose name derives from the Yorubaland cult of Nanã Burukú[7]], then Apúku, then Komantí! Otjútju has always worked with whitefolks/cityfolks. Even if only for that, they'll make him *gaamá*. You know that Pésé and Songo had agreed to open up a gold mine in the Pikílío, and the others knew if Otjútju won, he'd stop that, he wouldn't want some Frenchman to get all the profits. But if Ozéni won, the contract made by Songo would continue. Otjútju wants a new contract with the city. Nowadays, if you go more than 100 meters from the riverbank, whitefolks start telling you that it's not your river anymore. Otjútju will end all that! The city officials have summoned Otjútju to the city, but because of the national elections it's been postponed. Amèèkán-óli and Ozéni are really screwed! Saramakas had decided they'd make Ozéni a Headcaptain in compensation for him yielding to Otjútju, but now that Amèèkán-óli insulted the Ndyukas, he won't get a thing.

Tooy adds that when you take a knife away from a child, you give it a stick. But Amèèkán-óli ruined all hope of even that happening!

The latest news is that Otjútju has given a captaincy to Zabulón, who has Bêndêkôndè's great avenging spirit Ma Básukáma in his head—Lukéinsi's unborn daughter! Tooy says that between the two of them—Otjútju and Zabulón—no one will be able to defy them in any way and live to tell the tale. They're working with two great avenging spirits!

Meanwhile, the city government is at a standstill because of national elections on May 25—they will do nothing to sort out the dispute in Saramaka for weeks or months, until a president and a cabinet are in place.

Sensiló chimes in with some history, trying to put some perspective on present-day pretenders to the *gaamá*-ship. "Once, District Commissioner Junker summoned Gaamá Djankusó to a meeting. [Junker was trying hard to get the Saramaka *gaamá* under his thumb during the early years of the twentieth century, but Djankusó consistently outmaneuvered him.] Each one knew the other wouldn't kill him in public. So they arranged to meet on neutral ground, at the mouth of Gaánkiíki. The first thing Djankusó said to the whiteman was, 'Anacondas—I'm their boss. Jaguars—I'm their boss. Human beings—I'm their boss. Poisonous snakes—I'm their boss. Do you think you can fool with me? Let's live and work together.' That was a *gaamá*! Do you think we've seen another one lately?"

It's nine weeks after we leave Guyane on the final day of May 2005 that we get the news in a phone call from Tooy. Otjútju is the new *gaamá*.[8]

TOOY TEACHING I—
MOSTLY LUÁNGU
AND PÚMBU

Tooy's been thinking about the lackadaisical attitude of many youths toward learning and tells me two cautionary tales. "Once I went to an Apúku 'play' and heard a man sing, *Butá mayómbe na kwándikí, yengué sélélé*. And the man explained that it was with this song that the old people carried the gods in a square basket [*pakáa*]. I just sat there. Then I asked him, 'Where'd you hear that song?' 'That's what my elders said.' 'Was it your mother's brother, your older brother, or your grandfather who told you that?' He said, 'My mother's brother.' I said, 'Not true! He deceived you. Don't ever play that song again, you haven't got the head for it. Leave it alone. Never play that again!'" And Tooy explained to me, "It's not an evil or dangerous song, but he stole it. That song is only for Luángu 'plays.' In Luángu language, when they say *Butá mayómbe na kwándikí, yengué sélélé*, it means they're asking you to fill up this bottle with rum.[1] You see how they mess up the stories? This is not appropriate to an Apúku 'play,' it's a part of a 'play' for the dead! That man didn't know that Luángu is only played for the dead!"

Tooy then offers another example of his throwing someone out of an Apúku ceremony because he played a Luángu song, not realizing it was Luángu rather than Apúku. He explains that a man from some other clan might find himself on the coast with an older Lángu man and, say, they're in a canoe and the older man starts to sing and the other man neglects to ask him what he's singing and assumes it's Apúku. The song in question in this second example curses someone, saying, "You have chiggers, chiggers have got you, you walk around on your knees, you no longer walk like a person." "In Luángu," Tooy tells me, "you say it like this: *Kwímabo, wáka na pási tantúmbe, wimalúngu, wáka na pási tantúmbe, sípadúngu, wáka na pási tantúmbe, wédemalúngu, [ísikadúngu], wáka na pási tantúmbe, víe, tjátjá, hònhònhòn hòn-hònhòn* [the last two words are a sound made with the fingers tapping ones Adam's apple]."[2]

I press Tooy about Luángu—the language and the rites. Are they really only for the dead? "Luángu," he says, "is pure danger! When we're burying the dead in the morning, they play Papá all night. Then at dawn, they cover the *óbia* canoe and start playing Luángu. Nothing but *ógi-táki* [talk about evil, danger, bad things]. There are certain things to say at six in the morning, other things to say later on. That 'play,'" Tooy continues, "belongs to Bundjitapá [his village], since Wíi and his sister brought it over from Africa." I ask if it's still a lively tradition, if it's still well known by the descendants of Wíi and Antamá and Béti-Kadósu. He says, "You bet! Evil isn't hard to learn!"

Given its danger, it's not surprising that Tooy doesn't feel comfortable sharing this language. At the same time, I'm frustrated, realizing that if I were able to travel to Bundjitapá with Tooy and happen upon a funeral, I could fill pages and pages with Luángu songs and prayers. Absent that, here are a few fragments he's taught me. The common Saramaka—and African—proverb "Left hand washes right hand, right hand washes left hand" (Saramaccan *Toóto máu wási léti máu, léti máu wási toóto máu*) is expressed in Luángu as *Wási kagidí tjibaánga*. Another bit of proverbial advice, "Not everything that your eyes see or your ears hear should be spoken about by your mouth," is expressed in Luángu as *Paníka ní manyá folí*. And at a certain point in a Luángu "play," they say: *Lángu án yéi dúngu. Masángo fúlu na zó*, which means, "Go bring it back, cassava fills the house"—or "Go get the cassava from the house and bring it here." Tooy explains that in Luángu, *masángo* means "cassava" and *zó* means "house." This reminds him of another Luángu phrase, *Kitímba fúlú na zó*—"Tobacco [*kitímba*] fills [is in] the house."[3]

I'm equally interested in another esoteric language that I know is a specialty of the Lángu clan, the mysterious Púmbu that I began hearing about in the 1960s, when the erudite Gaamá Agbagó would occasionally throw out a Púmbu phrase, of which I understood nothing, during a major prayer to the ancestors. Whenever I ask Tooy, he's evasive, telling me that "those words are precious—if I speak them, the gods will start wondering what I'm up to and come to see." But he does tell me that Púmbu, unlike Luángu, was learned from the Indians. It's "forest talk"—Kaásipúmbu's Indian brother-in-law Piyái is its putative source. "Púmbu belongs to Béndiwáta, Kaási's village. That's the only place Púmbu is played! It's part of the Béndiwáta Mother. Piyái taught Kaási—Piyái's *apínti* name is *Sáki fíi búndu sódjodú anbupé!* He and his sister brought that language. The priests of that god are the ones who speak it. Púmbu is especially for major prayers, when a great drought or illness comes upon the land. That's when they whiten the jug, pour out water in libations, and speak Púmbu."

But, says Tooy, Púmbu also has things you can shoot the breeze about. And a couple of times, he shares fragments with me. One day he says, "When a baby is born, if it doesn't cry, it won't live. Púmbu says it this way: *Sébengé sabánga, lébengé sabánga, maabeengé sabánga* [with special emphasis on the penultimate word]. This is what the newborn says when it first cries, asking God that it be allowed to live!" And I've already mentioned that once, saying an emotional goodbye to us in the Dúnguláli shrine, Tooy spoke in Púmbu, saying, *nyam-nyam kuvánde, nyam-nyam vála* ("A long trip causes okra to dry on the branch")—see p. 215.

Once, when recounting how (during their migrations southward) his Lángu-clan ancestors went up the Saramacca River before coming over to see if they could settle on the Suriname River, Tooy told me some Púmbu fragments but stopped short of singing the climactic song, saying it was simply too dangerous. Now, when I press, he finally fills out the story and sings me the song.

> When Kaásipúmbu arrived at the mouth of Agámadjá Creek, he took his war club and knocked the tree known [in Púmbu] as *búgubúgu* three times, *púm, púm, púm*. The tree spoke with the bird called *kwáikwái*, who then called out to Kaásipúmbu, *Kolío, kolío, kolío, kolío, un sa líbi, un sa líbi, un sa líbi ku mi* [Come to the river . . . you can live . . . with me]. Then Kaási answered with this highly dangerous song in Púmbu: *Mángan mángan téebo-e, oló, we mi mása Zámbi-e* [well, my master Zámbi], *mi kó a yu náni-o* [I've come to your house] *akí akié* [to see if I can stay].

As he finished the song, Tooy took his right hand and tapped his fingers against his lips, uttering a falsetto *u-u-u-u-u-u-u-u-u-u-u* and explaining that this is the standard ending for dangerous songs in Púmbu, just as dangerous Luángo songs end with *vié tjátjá hònhònhònhònhòn* (the final sound being made by a jiggling of the Adam's apple with outstretched fingers).

Another time, I asked Tooy the meaning of a Púmbu phrase I'd heard in the 1970s, about the death of Antamá's brother Makambí. Tebíni had whispered to me *Saa baaba na wán tén fu gaán kindé, gaán kindé fu Makambí*. Tooy says, "What sadness! *Saa baaba* means, "Something terrible has happened," *gaán kindé* means, "It's a really big thing." I realize that it may have been with these very words that Antamá was told of his brother's death in battle!

Despite his sorrow over the impending loss of collective knowledge, Tooy still spends a lot of his time teaching kinsmen and almost anyone else who expresses interest. One day when I visit he is deep into a discussion with Mowêti, a younger man from Malobí whom he calls "brother."[1] Mowêti is hungry for knowledge about their collective early history, of which he is largely ignorant, and Tooy is happy to oblige.

As I sit down with them in the consulting room, where leaves and vines and barks are piled along the walls, Tooy remarks that their matrilineage didn't used to be "low," it used to have great men. And he adds that, in Papá language, a messed-up matrilineage is called *tíkití no vído,* while a matrilineage that's made something of itself is *tíkití didó.* An old man who doesn't know things is *Adòdì-í dòdò-ô. Kínde go na huntô* or *A hón tuntuú ya gavié da unún da úú-úún.*[2] "I'm not *a hón tuntuú yagazé! Da hunhun da o-o-o.* No, No No, No No! I have my reputation!" he insists, adding that if you want to say, "That matrilineage is forging ahead," you say, *Lawámaí didó. Lawáa mi kóo nodé.* "Papá!" he exclaims with glee, sharing precious bits of this esoteric language.

Mowêti asks him who their common ancestor Aségogó was, and Tooy tells the particularly "heavy" story of the origin of the avenging spirit shared by their two far-off lineage segments (though it affects Hwéte's progeny more fully). Hwéte, he begins, had a sister called Bánki and a brother called Aségogó, whose wife was Logoso-óbo. (Remember, Tooy is talking matter-of-factly about people who lived in the mid-eighteenth century!) That man loved dogs and had three that he particularly liked to hunt with. One day, the dogs surrounded something in a hole at the base of a giant *kwaháa* [a.k.a. *dónsedu*] tree that stood in the middle of a field of reeds, and they were barking their heads off when he and his wife arrived. He cut some wood and closed off the hole, thinking peccary were inside, and then set fire to the tree. Once it fell, he saw it was anacondas, not peccary! Logoso-óbo proclaimed, "The better part of all this will go to the descendants of Hwéte." The two

Wátawenú (anaconda) gods he burned that day were Bémba and Lonzái, the latter being the oldest active avenging spirit of Tooy's lineage.

Tooy tells us more about Lonzái, how he once watched while a priest from another lineage—it's always another lineage that directs the rites to appease a matrilineage's avenging spirit—went into the forest to gather everything he needed. He painted the god (who had possessed a person) with something yellow, but didn't say what he'd made the paint out of (though Tooy says he knows). "I learned that you never use soot to paint the black on a big avenging spirit—it would bring fire and destruction. And you don't use annatto for the red—it brings blood. Instead you use *totóbia* and *bemíndja uwíi* [two plants that provide those colors]. You can use these for Wátawenú avenging spirits or Vodú-gádu avenging spirits." He adds, "In Wátawenú language, *totóbia* is called *anúndeba* and *bemíndja uwíi* is *anúndedjême*! Before you anoint the avenging spirit with these leaves, paint them on yourself. Then, as you do it, you sing: *anúndeba, anúndedjême, gódogódobíi.*"

As Tooy continues instructing his downstream brother, Mowêti, and me, the brother dozes off and Tooy says to me in Papá, using a phrase he taught me the previous day: "It's *mokú felé moodán* for him! ['He doesn't appreciate his elders,' so the matrilineage loses what it once knew.] Let him sleep. I have one for you now!"

And then he sings me a hauntingly beautiful song in Papá that teaches that you are indeed your brother's keeper. (For this song, you need to know that hands of bananas grow in layers from the top of each stem to the bottom, with the hands opening, and eventually ripening—and rotting if they're not picked—one hand at a time, from top to bottom.)

Aládjio, Alágba Mêdo Keéno
Aládjio, Alágba Mêdo Keéno
Keéno góf'en a Zángodou, a góf'en a Kedé-ee, Dénua-ee, Alada ke, Aládjio ke, Alágba Mêdo Keéno
Keéno góf'en a Zángodou, a góf'en a Kedé-ee, Dénua-oo, o kióo Aládjiooo.

[*Aládjio, Alágba Mêdo Keéno* (four proper names), Keéno's [stink] went onto Zángodou (proper name), it went onto Kedé, Dénua, Alada (three proper names), Aládjio *ke*, Alágba Mêdo Keéno / Keéno's went onto Zángodou, it went onto Kedé, Dénua, oh young-guy Aládjio.]

"These are powerful words," he tells me,

about the kind of banana called *Bénteo-pú-bakúba* [or *Bénteo-pú-baana*]. It has twelve hands on each stem. So, the man cut a garden (I love talking with you!

I have so many things to give you, but you must give me some, too! So many
things you say fit what I know! And so many of the "lies" I tell you fit things
you've heard.) OK, the man cut the garden, then he burned the underbrush. He
worked it. He planted the bananas—the ones called *Bénteo-pú-baana*. Then he
left. The banana trees grew. They flowered. They grew their fruit. Till they got
ripe. The one banana stem had twelve hands. The upper hand said, "It's time to
split open." (Now, the way I'm speaking with you here, you must really absorb
what I'm saying.) So, when it split open, its juice began to drip down onto the
next one. The second brother thought to himself, "When the man who has
the garden comes and finds the stink of the juice from my big brother on me,
the death-liquid of my older brother, he'll think less of me—it's because my
big brother is punishing me." (Brother, when I look around at what my oldfolks gave me, then I wonder what I should pass on to the young ones.) Finally,
the last brother said, my older brother's dead, I'll play in his honor a whole half
hour. Because if I were the one who had died, it would have been my brother
who would have had to bear my stink. Because we both came out of the same
"sack." (That's the way this story goes. People may tell it to you some other way,
but they'd be lying. What I'm telling you here I heard from twelve Papá masters, and they all told it the same way.) When the first brother died, the second
one feared his stink. When the second one died, the third feared his stink. All
the way to the sixth brother. And finally, the littlest one said. . . . One brother
was Alágba, the others were Mêdo, Keéno, Zángodo, Kedé, Dénua, Aládjio. . . .
There were twelve brothers. The youngest one who said what he had to say
to the oldest, that's us here today. My own stink, that's what you must eat. I'd
want to eat your stink, but I don't really know the path to get to it. But if you
know the path to mine, then it's your responsibility to eat it, to take it on. Man,
you have to eat my stink! And I have to do my best to eat yours.

"Brother, that's Aladá [Papá] I'm teaching you!" He wipes away some tears.

Tooy begins ruminating about the dangers of Papá playing, how much
of what you say can kill you. One man, Adubóye, sent word in Papá to the
gaamá of the land of the dead that he was overstepping his mark, that there
were getting to be more people in his country than ours. "The land of the
dead is getting fat, the land of the living thin," he played on his drum. But,
says Tooy, the only time you can play that and get away with it is on the day
they're going to bury a corpse, just as dawn is breaking. Then you play (in
Papá) *Tjé hên kó dá mi-e* (normal Saramaccan for "bring him back to me").
*Un de ni todovi alobi alobi alobi alobi da u, tja tja u da o lólo kabódji, tje hên kó-e
keeto bóbiawata kó noínovi u mi. U tjé hên kó-o, todovi án sa kó noínovi, un tjé hên
kó dá mi e.* These are very heavy words! he whispers to me. They pray that
the big avenging spirit of the lineage shouldn't turn the person who's being
buried into another spirit to torment the lineage. Let the person come back

instead as a namesake for someone in the lineage and bring the lineage good things. He sings (in Papá), *Tódovi án sa kó noínovi*—someone else's lineage can't become your lineage, strangers can't become kinsmen. And the song that answers this is *Djáome dján-e, i músu djáome djan. Adúndiome, adúndiome, i músu djáome dján. Adúndiome, adúndiome, i músu djáome dján.* It's telling the dead person to leave. It should *djáome* go and then *djáome* come back, but as a namesake, not an avenging spirit. (*Djáome*, he says, means "carry" or "bring.") "What sadness these songs express!" he exclaims. "They're heartbreaking to sing and play! They really make you face your mortality. You're not yourself when you say these things. You're truly speaking with the dead."

Tooy has often expressed to me that his self-imposed exile from his Saramaka homeland has prolonged his life and happiness—that if he hadn't left, the envy of his peers would have long since finished him off. (I assure him I know whereof he speaks.) "If I'd stayed in my mother's village," he continues, "they'd have killed me long ago. There's nowhere in the world that people with knowledge are appreciated. They'd have killed me because of envy! My older brother Amiséti said to me once at Boonswéki, 'Don't continue learning. You know too much already!' I could tell you things from morning till night and on through tomorrow without repeating myself. But

Shooting the breeze, 2005.

I've left those things—it's been 'twelve years' since I really set out to learn. I've left that part of my life behind. But I still sure do love to shoot the breeze with you!"

*   *   *

As we shot the breeze during that first visit of 2005, Tooy several times ruminated about the alternate registers—the different languages—that knowledgeable Saramakas use to express identical ideas. "Komantí, Apúku, Vodúgádu, Wénti-gádu, Wátawenú-gádu, Apínti [drum language], and Anasi-tóli [folktales] all say the same things, but each in its own language." I encouraged him in these directions, and we spent many hours discussing esoteric language lore.

He tells me, for example, that

on the *apínti*, you play *Asanti bélen ku awándja, hên ku panga ngosí*. Which means, "The *pakúsi* fish [*Myleus rubripinnis*] loves the creek, he's the chief of the creek!" Because he used to live in the river, but when he went up the creek, he found a wife there and there was a big celebration. That's what the drum says: "He's headman of the creek." But Lángu-clan drummers play it differently—they play, *Yúnkuma a yú, a yú kantambilí*. It means the exact same thing!

Another time, I'm sitting in on a discussion between Tooy and a Dómbi-clan *apínti* master, where they are comparing notes. Both of them learned some of what they know from a man named Ayóo, whom Tooy called "mother's brother," and the Dómbi man called "grandfather." Tooy tells how one time at Boonswéki, they invited him to play for a death, an all-night "play." And at a certain point they requested that he play "bent-over tree and the owner of the garden." (He explains to me that in the garden there was an almost-dead tree with its head bent down who worried that the owner of the garden would come and chop it down. Meanwhile, the owner of the garden was afraid that the bent-over tree would fall on his head one day and kill him. Each, in other words, feared what the other would do.) "Lángu people play it, *Sese kái dúmba, sesembe sekái dúmba*." The Dómbi man tells how Ayóo taught it to him as *Goón mása, noa mása. Goón mása, noa mása. Noa mása lègèdè, lègèdè fu nóame*, which is the "standard" *apínti* version. Tooy says his own "father," Kulífubégi, told him that there are actually three ways of playing this! "But in general," he says, "as far as drumming goes, there's only one way Lángu people do it. In Púmbu there aren't two ways of saying the same thing. In Luángu there aren't two ways. In Yáka-ósu *óbia*, there aren't two ways. But in

Papá, Apínti, Anasi-tóli, or Adunké, every master does it differently." One thing seems clear: the Lángu clan, in some contexts at least, maintains its own parallel version of Apínti language.

From Tooy's perspective, folktales and esoteric languages also say "the same things." I once asked him whether he'd heard the tale about an old man named Gídigídi Zaabwóngolo, who lived off in the forest by himself and used to hold in his body all of the sicknesses of the world until Anasi, the spider man, inadvertently brought them back to where we all live.[3] He said he'd never heard the folktale but knew "the same story" in Félubéni (Papá).

A man and his wife made a garden-camp. One day, when they went off to work and returned, the food they'd left there in the morning was all gone. Another day the woman was at home alone and heard a big noise. The Evil One arrived. He said, "Woman, how're you doing?" She said, "Just fine." He said, "I want to ask you a favor—to carry Sickness for me." She said she couldn't do that for him—but if he ever learned her name, she supposed she'd have to do it. The Evil One departed. When the husband came home, she told him what had happened. Then one day the man went off to work and the Evil One arrived again. He grabbed the woman and put her in a deep hole, burying her alive with just a reed to breathe through. When the man came home, he searched for her everywhere. (If she screamed, you couldn't hear her.) The woman's name was Tóbodahuntján. The husband was Gáigán-fu-Adowé. The husband was beside himself and called out for his wife. [sings] *Tóbodahuntján-e-o ké, Tóbodahuntján de kó nyán-o, aínto tjêlele sída-o, Tóbodahuntján-o, Tóbodahuntján de kó nyán akí, aínto djêlele sídawá.* Then he called her name again. Three times. Finally she answered: [sings] *O-o-o, é-o-o, Wómi Gáigán-fu-adowé, de kó nyán aínto gbêlegede sídawa.*[4] She was saying, "I'm not dead, man, I'm still alive. Don't kill yourself over this." He sang his song again, and back and forth they sang to each other. "Woman, I went away and returned and no longer see you here. Where'd you go?" (*Aínto tjêlelé*, Tooy explains, means, "You're no longer here.") He looked around and saw where the earth had been moved around, and he dug there and pulled her out. Félubéni! [Papá]. Later thc Evil One, who'd now heard her name, came to the woman and gave her all the sicknesses in the world for people to have to bear.

Tooy added, "I once sang these songs at Boonswéki, where they were burying my mother's sister. I was singing and crying and drumming from midnight till morning! At one point twelve ghost-spirits were dancing right in front of me. Papá is so very sad!"

* * *

During that 2005 visit, understanding that I was hungry for lore about Papá—the quintessential esoteric language, which Saramakas had always been hesitant to discuss with me—Tooy generously shared fragments. Like other knowledgeable men I've talked with, he insists that Papá came late to Saramakas. "In the old days, Papá wasn't there—we buried the dead with Anasi-tóli [kóntu (folktales)], apínti [drumming], and Adunké [a First-Time secular song/dance]."[5] (When I ask, he says, "Yes, we already had Luángu and Púmbu.")

Three decades before, Kalusé's father, the Matjáu-clan Papá player Tandó, had told me how Papá came to Saramakas not from Africa but from a local incident that I can date to the mid-eighteenth century. And he explained why Abaísas and Matjáus have differential knowledge of Papá, Adugbá, and Adjú (the "plays" that follow one another in succession between midnight and full daylight on the morning before a Matjáu-clan burial, and for which Abaísas are said to have the edge for Papá and Matjáus for Adugbá and Adjú).[6] He said,

> Once, an Abaísa man married a Matjáu woman. A Matjáu man married an Abaísa woman. They went off, all four of them, to make a garden together. (It was on the site of an old cemetery, but they didn't know that.) In the evening, the two Matjáus fell asleep, but the Abaísas didn't. And the dead people began to play Papá, all night long until cock's crow. Then the Abaísas fell asleep, and the Matjáus awoke. The dead people began to play Adugbá. Until full dawn. Then they began the Adjú. The Abaísas slept right through the Adjú. Which is why each clan knows what it does.

And indeed, whenever Matjáu Papá players, such as the late Tandó, are invited as specialists to play at a funeral and are presented with the traditional baskets full of cloths, bottles of rum, and so on, they always transfer the baskets' contents as well as the rum to their own containers, brought for the purpose. But when the Abaísa Papá masters perform at a funeral, it is always their prerogative, and their practice, to go home with baskets, rum bottles, and all.

Then, one day when we were discussing esoteric languages, Tooy told me more about the Papá song that contains Tandó's story.

> An Abaísa named Ahúnsòalígbô had a Matjáu wife. There was a funeral in his wife's village, on the Upper Pikílío, in Baákawáta. He visited and went hunting but got lost in the forest. Around nightfall, he arrived in an abandoned cemetery. The headman of the cemetery asked what he thought he was doing

there, since it was far too late in the day for a living person to come there. He said he was lost. The headman said he'd hide him till morning, and he could listen to the way they played for a person who was going to be buried. He heard the Papá, which ended at dawn, and he asked if he could come back the next night and the man said yes, as long as he hid in the same place. So, he came a second night. The third night he brought along his brother-in-law, a Matjáu named Sámbo-gídjigídji, or Ahúmanyá-dekonú-tósida. Around midnight, the Abaísa fell asleep, since he'd been up two whole nights. But the Matjáu stayed awake and heard the Papá, and when they started Adjú before dawn and played until it was full morning, he heard it all. That's why Matjáus are the masters of Adjú and Abaísas of Papá. It's all in that Papá song!

And he added that the Matjáus were always trying to wrest further Papá knowledge from the Abaísas. For example,

When Ahúnsòalígbô was already dead (though Sámbo-gídjigídji was still alive), some Matjáus went to the Abaísas to learn more Papá. They really wanted to be the bosses of Papá. The first time they met at a "play" and played their praise names, the Abaísas won. The second time, they came out even. So they decided on a decisive competition, to meet at a "play" in the village named Gámatíen—I've never been able to get anyone to tell me exactly where on the river that village was! They played till it was really hot. And then the Abaísas played a song, *Mi avó gaán tía djómbo hên mi djómbo, hee-hee. I djómbo, hên mi djómbo. Hunsókedue di i djómbo, Sámbo-gídjigídji di i djómbo, Bákigáyo di i djómbo, Vitónokó di i djómbo, mi avó Avádja di i djómbo, Ma di i djómbo, hên mi djómbo, o hee-hee* [All in normal Saramaccan, "My grandmother Gaán Tía jumped, so I jumped. You jumped, so I jumped. When H jumped, when S jumped, when B jumped, when V jumped, when my grandmother A jumped, when you jumped—I jumped."] (The Old Woman named Gaán Tía had kept the "play" after the death of Ahúnsòalígbô—she was the one who taught it to the next generation. She's the one who taught Papá to Adjimúla. Once she was in the forest with a young boy, and they got to a large puddle and she jumped over it and the boy followed her. She asked him why he'd jumped, and he said because he'd seen her jump first. That's what the song commemorates.) When they played this, the Abaísa headman *sangáa* [the ritualized display of emotion involving rushing around almost madly, described on p. 64], *halahalahalahala* until he confronted the Matjáu headman. Three times this happened. Then the Matjáu—he had the kind of loincloth that's called . . . I can't say its name!—he grabbed his *ataká* [Komantí for "spear"] and stabbed him right through the heart, and the other Abaísas took off. The Matjáus really wanted that "play"! That song—you can't sing it in an Abaísa village! Even if no Abaísas are there to hear it, the ancestors will, and they'll kill you on the very spot. So, Abaísas were the first to have Papá, and the Matjáus took it from them. And the Matjáus gave the Abaísas Adjú. When Papá and Adjú came, it was after everyone had come down from Bákakúun [ca. 1750]. Komantí, Apúku, Luángu, and Púmbu were already there. But not Papá or Adjú.

Abaísas, Tooy reiterates, didn't used to have Adjú. Once they had buried someone, that was it—no "second funeral" many months later, culminating in the Adjú "play" that sends the ghost definitively to the land of the ancestors, the way all Saramakas do it today.[7]

> Abaísas didn't used to do that. Until one day Evil came to their village, and they didn't know how to get rid of it. So they went to the Matjáus and asked their help in cleaning up the village. The first time the Abaísas went to them, they saw Sámbo-gídjigídji, the man who'd learned Adjú in the land of the dead. A short little fellow. They asked him where the elders of the village were. He said they're not here, they're in their gardens. So they left a message. And the Matjáus sent back word, saying that the short little fellow who's sitting at the landing place making a basket is the very man you need. So, the Abaísas came back. And again he said he'd give the message to the others. After the Abaísas had left, Sámbo-gídjigídji had the town crier call everyone to a council meeting. So he told them about the request. They agreed to it, as long as once the Abaísas had chosen a day, they would offer libations the night before and clean the village path and boil a quantity of sugarcane juice. So, the day arrived and the Matjáus went downstream to the Abaísa village. They played Papá till midnight and then went into Adjú. Till dawn. Matjáus helped the Abaísas with the Adjú just as the Abaísas had helped the Matjáus with Papá. And once they brought the Adjú "play" outside [the house of death]—at daylight—then Sámbo-gídjigídji sang three songs. He sang, *Kwantiólu, wêbi káka zúme. Káuyómê, wêbi káka zúme. Aládan kenyánko weménu awánu, kényan, kényan ma fu adjú-e, adjú-e weménu, ma fu adjú kényan, kényan.* This isn't Papá, it's Adjú. (It's the same language, but this is only said when they're playing Adjú, not Papá.) So, they performed the Adjú until the Abaísa village was all clean. And then the Matjáus returned home.

This story reminds him of a time when the Abaísas had cleaned the world for Matjáus. (One of the protagonists, Sakóto, sometimes called Gúnkamê, is an immensely mysterious but historically important Matjáu who lived in the early eighteenth century. The Matjáus discovered Sakóto/Gúnkamê all alone in a watermelon field on the coast as they fled south from slavery. No one knew his origins—they say he fell from the sky. He was a giant of a man.)[8] All these stories, Tooy keeps reminding me with pleasure, are part of Papá lore.

Now, Tatá Sakóto (a Matjáu) had become *máti* [ritual friend] with Tatá Yágazé (an Abaísa). One day, Sakóto slept at Yágazé's place. (Yágazé isn't the same man as Adjimúla—they were two brothers, actually three: there was another called Tatá Boonskakéi, or Mákazúmu. This talk is Félubéni talk, Papá!) So, Sakóto told Yágazé, "*Máti*, when I die, the sun won't rise, the rains won't fall, fish won't come up to the surface to eat, cocks won't crow, no one will ever be hungry, and little children won't cry." Sakóto began to shake . . . till morning. He was gone. And the world became as he said. Yágazé got in his canoe, straight to Sakóto's village. He spoke with no one but went right ashore, carrying his paddle, and stuck it in the ground right in the great ancestor shrine there. He said, *Abudáma fu agudá. Abudáma fu agudá. Poóma fu ó.* Then Sakóto answered him so loud that he heard. He said he'd come down [to earth], but now he was going back. At which point, the earth became as it had been before. And this thing has stayed with us. When a *gaamá* dies, at three o'clock in the afternoon they shoot off a single gun salute, and it's like Sakóto's answer. It cleans the world. This isn't something you can just say. It's Sakóto's leave-taking. It's immensely sad! His final adieu! Papá. This is how Abaísas made the world clean for Matjáus. Later, Matjáus made the Abaísa village clean for them.

As I visited with him, Tooy shared other Papá lore, which encapsulated everything from remarkably precise information about eighteenth-century battles to the sexual foibles of particular ancestors.

Foló tutú agbáila. This is the first Papá song that belonged to the Lángu clan. No Papá mentions the Lángu clan before this! The man was Tatá Bákisipámbo. It happened at Bákakúun-Wéényé.[9] The whites walked along the path called Táimeenú [He explains that this is the path that led from Tuído, on the Saramacca River, to Bákakúun]. (The path from Bákakúun to the Gaánlío is called Zilámeenú—Flibánti is the expert on these secret names!) The whites arrived at the foot of the mountain. There were three platforms on that mountain, the lowest was called Mítjípai, the middle Dinomê, the top one Tèmèènú. They lived on the middle one. The battle wasn't with guns. There was a deep trench dug out by the rains before our people ever arrived. (It went down to Armadillo Creek, which leads into Kayana Creek.) Three tremendous tree roots—from an *awara* palm, a *maripa* palm, and a *giánti* tree—were poised at the head of the trench. The whites circled the mountain until they found the trench and started up. There was a certain "word" to say, but I can't speak it. The earth was already shaking with the sound of the whitemen's approaching footsteps. The *awara* tree was at the ready there—Komantí calls it Dókofáda. They said those "words," and the [magical] jug they had there began swirling around, still staying upright [he demonstrates with a bottle]. The first tree-root was launched. Then the second. Then the third. And then the three roots came back up, and the jug stood up straight! Well, Tatá Bákisipámbo arrived—he'd been out scouting around. He had the gun called Folú [Tooy sometimes says "Volú" or "Gulú" or "Foló"]. He grabbed it, loaded it, put in powder, and shot, and took off again. When he got to Kayana Creek, he saw the whitemen resting in a row on a log at the place called Zambí-a-wáta. He took one good shot and they all fell off. The people up on the mountain heard, and that's what this Papá song commemorates.[10]

And then Tooy adds, we Lángus sing *Foló tutú agbáila*. But Abaísas sing it [and he sings], *Kanivó, kanivó, kanivó nawa, kanivó nawa bélao, anáwaazúo, tutú gbezáan mafaadjó keedjé ímawan daudé, kanivó nawa bélao*. It's saying, when you go hunting and hear an animal in the underbrush, stand stock still and you'll manage to shoot it. Matjáus sing it, *Kédjé mani-e, mani kedjé manie, akatasú mandeu-u mándegbò-ò*. Another Saramaka who's listening with me says that he's seen that at funerals: when it's time to shoot the final gun salutes, when the coffin is about to be taken away to the cemetery, the Papá-men first play the Matjáu version, then the salutes are fired, and then they play *Foló tutú agbáila*, before ending with *Kanivó* . . . , the Abaísa version.

Papá, Tooy makes clear, also preserves incidents that are at least in part comic. The Nasí clan gave a young girl named Lomodjó to the much older Abaísa Tatá Gbosú to raise. When she became sexually ripe, he refused to give her away in marriage but kept her for himself. Try as he might, however, he couldn't get his cock to crow with her! Until finally one day he did, and made her pregnant. This Papá commemorates Gbosú finally getting it up for Lomodjó. Tooy sings, *Gbosú kili ke dili Lomodjánki, Alabáisa-o keli keli keli* ["He's already working away on top of her!" exclaims Tooy]. *Gboyón, líndomeyo-o, gboyón, líndome-o, kó nyánme-o, aladá kíi lomodjó-o.*

Other Papá songs Tooy sings for me resemble folktales in their "just-so story" character—they tell how Saramakas "found" some important aspect of their culture that wasn't present in the distant past. Many stories Tooy tells, for example, allude to the fact that in the early days Saramakas didn't bury people in coffins—they would wrap the corpse in cloths, lay it out on a banana leaf, and bury it like that in the cemetery. (Tooy's account of his ancestor Alúmba rising from the dead [p. 155], which we can date to the second half of the eighteenth century, anachronistically includes this feature, even though historical documents make clear that by that time Saramakas were routinely using coffins.) In any case, there seems to have been a time in the early eighteenth century when coffins were not yet in use.[11] Tooy tells of their "discovery" in the land of the forest spirits (Apúkus), which is preserved in Papá.

Abámpapá went hunting in the forest and got lost. As he wandered, he came to an Apúku village, where he heard them knocking something. They were making a coffin! They asked him who he was, and he told them he was lost. They brought him over to where they were working and told him he couldn't leave till the next day. So, he helped them make the coffin. The next day they sent him on his way and he arrived home, where he called a council meeting. He called to them in Papá: *Nayóo*. They answered, *Nyankí*. He said, *Abámpapá kimayónu, kifúngu kimayónu* [*Kimayónu*, Tooy explains, means "coffin" in Papá, *kifúngu* or *difúngu* means "death"]. And that's why Maroon coffins are gabled—they saw it in Apúku land—while whitefolks' coffins remain flat, like Noah's ship.

Tooy boasts to me of having learned Papá from a great Abaísa master who always said, "Here's how Abaísas play it" and then, "Here's how Matjáus play it." I marvel at the way each of these clans assiduously preserves not only its own version but that of its main rival down through the generations.[12]

TOOY TEACHING III—
KOMANTÍ, WÉNTI,
AND MORE

★ 04182005/05302005 ★

Often during that stay, understanding my keen interest, Tooy shared esoteric language lore in the course of daily activities. When Sally, who'd cooked lunch since Ma Yaai was off in her garden, came in to say it was ready, Tooy exclaimed, *Matjáu dê a gangáa, hôni dê a kiní* [The axe is at the throat, the bee is at the knee]. *Bi a kodiní, bi a kódi.* "Food's ready! That's the way the Old Ones said it. Apínti [drum] language!" He continues, "*Afítimoyon táki, Seímoyon táki. Hunhún da mi békese da hógogo.* The mother sends the child to go tell his father that food's ready. *Afítimoyontáki*, that's the mother. *Seímoyontáki*, that's the child. *Bêkese* [or *Mêkese*] means, 'Let's eat! Mother sent me to tell you'—Papá language!" It seems clear when I consider it that Tooy can't easily pull apart many of the Papá phrases he's learned by heart and that, in this case as in others, he knows the meaning of the phrase but not necessarily of its components.

On a day when Tooy got hungry early and Sally hadn't yet cooked, he suddenly sang out to us, *M'án bói-e, m'án bói yéti. A kête m'án bói tidé-o. Ké, m'án bói-o, m'án bói yéti. A kête m'án bói tidé-o* ("I haven't cooked, I haven't cooked yet. The pot hasn't cooked today"), explaining that "this is what the Wénti woman says to her husband when he returns from an absence and she doesn't have food cooked for him yet." And then he sang, *Kó mi-e, Gwakaká kó mi-e, Ké, Kómi-e, Kómi-e, Kená zámba kêntu-o* ("Come, *Gwakaká* come, [exclamation], Come, come, *Kená zámba kêntu-o*," adding that this is what the Wénti wife sings to call her husband to the table once the food is cooked. Sally took the hint and went to the kitchen.

Several times during that stay, when he got a hankering to snort tobacco,[1] Tooy sang an appropriate song; for example, this one in Apúku language: *I ta ganyá ganyá mi kuma zúngadému, zúngadému-o zipi-o. Ma lúku fa i ta ganyá mi kuma zúngadému, ma yú kasianáni* ("You are tricking me just like *zúngadému* [tobacco], *zúngadému-o zipi-o*. But look at how you're tricking me like *zúngadému*, but you're *kasianáni* [a clever one]," which refers to how tobacco's intoxication—Tooy uses the phrase "making you drunk"—sneaks

Tooy with his tobacco pot.

up on the user, who is paying attention only to the "sweetness" of snorting it. Another time, when he wanted tobacco, he sang, also in Apúku, *Zúnga-démbu-o, man dá mi zúnga. Zúngadémbu-o, man dá mi zúnga, ké kióo, bá mi lóngo i án yéi, no. Zúnga-e!* ("Tobacco-o, Man, give me tobacco. [repeat] Please, kid, give me some, you hear? Tobacco-e!") And a third time he spoke the following prayer, also in Apúku, the language of the forest spirits who are so enamored of tobacco: *Lukú maná luangí kimpô. Kimpô. Kimpô maléa* ("Look, kids, *luangí*, let's snort. Let's snort. Let's snort *maléa*."), and then in normal Saramaccan, *Bó hái!* ("Let's snort!")

Sometimes, a particular song (or set of phrases) takes on different meanings in different contexts with the change of only a word or two. Tooy was sharing some Apúku lore and told me that Mavúngu sings, *A bêni gó gó, a bêni yángi. A bêni gó gó gó, a bêni yángi-e, zalí mukóko tjêngewa-e.* "This," he explained, "is when someone knocks on your door (*gó gó gó* is the knocking)—you say, 'Come in!' and open the door—*zalí mukóko tjêngewa* is the door opening." But then he added, "Bási Gabói [an Apúku whom Tooy knew in possession] used to sing, *A bêni gó gó, mi na yángi. A bêni gó gó gó gó gó, mi na yángi, zalí mukóko téé n'en mamá gángi.* Whenever he lit up his pipe and smoke came out, then he'd sing this! *A bêni gó gó, a bêni yángi,* he'd already lit it up. *Zalí mukóko,* the smoke came out. *Téé n'en mamá gángi,* all the way to his mother's house." And then he sang it again.

Another day, out of the blue, Tooy exclaims, "I love the way you come and sit down with me!" "Do you know," he asks, "the names of Jaguar's teeth?" I say I don't. "The front one, the one he kills dogs with, is called *dámka kíí atjuá même háun.* Ndyukas call it *káfrika kabá u nú.* The big one in the back, that's *momokúmokúmokú a gwí, kuma kí.* This is Komantí, Brother!" I ask whether other animals' teeth are named. He thinks for a moment and then offers that, in their own language, Wéntis call Caiman's large front tooth *vindlío vikádja.*[2] Then, he treats me to a song by Anaconda. He sings, *Gêdje núnde-o, gêdje núnde-o, gêdje núnde, wán wómi sindó gèdje so, gêdje núnde-e, gêdje núnde wómi sindó gêdje-e, na mi ankónu-e,* adding, "That's the way you must sit and talk! There are so many words to learn!" And he sings it again and explains, "This is Wátawenú language! Once he's all coiled up in his place, he says, 'Come try to pull me outta here, and I'll teach you who's boss!' He's in his house, if you're a real man, try to get him to move from there! You'll see!" And then he tells me an insult or curse you can play in Wátawenú language: [singing] *Bedésidá bedésidá bedésidá bedésidá u dáome-eo-e, u dê na aladá viú kókolo, bedésidá, bedésidá u dáome.* He explains, "*Bedésidá* is what anacondas call water lilies [Saramaccan *tokóógbagba*]. The plant sings this song, boasting that it may not be able to touch the river bottom or the shore, but it sure can choke up the whole river! If you play this on the drums, you're cursing someone, saying, 'Get off my back, who do you think you are? You don't even touch the river bottom and you don't touch the banks, you're just adrift!'" And then he adds, "When they play Kitómbe for an anaconda god, the priest's canoe doesn't land prow first. It lands stern first. And the priest sings [in Wátawenú language], *Hokokó-o, lúku di bóto kumútu na Aladávi-kôndè ta kó. Tósida pikí mií ké un kóni-ee* [(Exclamation), look at the canoe that's arriving from Aladávi-Country. *Tósida* (anaconda god) children, (exclamation), be careful]. You must know the exact words to say during this ceremony. Otherwise you're finished!"

Often, as in an actual "play"—whether Papá, Apúku, or Komantí—Tooy lets one song or story lead to a similar one until there's a whole string of associations. (This is what allows "plays" to go on, uninterrupted, for hours at a time.) One day, Tooy's god Dúnuyángi, characteristically, was warning me about my tendency to trust people too much, citing the proverbs "A good greeting is a bad greeting"—always be on your guard—and (one of Tooy's favorites) "Anaconda says, 'The person who does something good for you, he's the one you must kill!'"

> Bat and Cock became formal friends. (They tell this in Komantí!) Bat asked Cock how he got so strong that he could carry fire on his head. Cock said, "Friend, this thing isn't really fire, it just looks like flames, come touch it." Bat touched it and said, "It's true, friend." In the evening, Bat returned, put Cock to sleep, and sucked out all his blood. When he awoke, he flapped his wings a single time and rolled over dead. Bat said to him [singing]: *Kétekétewéle kétewéli kétekétewéli kétewéli, kétekétewéle kétewéli kétekétewéli kétewéli, yémbu ta kói amímba, yémbu kói amímba, yémbu kói amímba, yémbu ta kói amímba, yémbu i kói mi amímba, yémbu kói amímba-e.*

"Now, when you're walking around in Guyane," Tooy's god continued, "look carefully at whoever asks you to eat at the same table with him. Otherwise, it could be the story of Bat and Cock. I'm giving you sound advice here!" And then the god tells me about how Possum became formal friends with Cock, a story also preserved in Komantí.

> Possum asked Cock, how did you get so "ripe" that you can carry fire on your head? Cock said, "Friend, come touch it. This thing isn't fire." So Possum touched it and saw it was cold. Well, once Cock went to sleep for the night, Possum came and grabbed him by the neck. Cock began to scream. Possum sang, "Don't cry out, it's your friend who's come to play with you." He sang, *Mi pelé kó a íni, bó pelé kó a íni, pèê pèê dóu pelé kó a íni, bó pelé, pelé kó a íni* ["I'm playing come inside, let's play come inside, play all the way play come inside, let's play, play come inside."][and then, spoken] "Friend, don't scream. Your friend has come to play with you."

The next day, Tooy says he'll teach me a Komantí song appropriate to sing to a "friend" who has deceived me. He sings, *Gêdegêdewéle gêdewéle gêde-gêdewéle gêdewéle. Gêdegêdewéle gêdewéle gêdegêdewéle gêdewéle yémbu mi kóima amímba, yémbu kói amímba yémbu, kói amímba, yémbu ta kói amímba yémbu, kói amímba-e. Yémbu, i kói mi amímba, yémbu*—except for the altered phonology (which is typical of the variation when Tooy sings songs on different occasions), it's the song of Bat and Cock! Tooy explains, "Bat wants to eat the person. But the person is awake, so how can he eat him? He must fool the person's 'soul' (*akáa*), which Komantís call *yémbu*. Bat is calling the person's *yémbu* to trick it. When you sing this song to someone, or even allude to it, you're saying to them, 'Don't live with me like Bat!'" (Cock has dropped out of this version of Tooy's story, but of course he's still there somewhere in the recesses of his mind . . .)

And then Tooy offers me a real gem, in that same series of ideas about deception and revenge, but this time in Papá. He sings, *Okódu vêlevêle, okódu vêlevêle, tatá taki alagbékúnu, f'en ku adjámadji kêlede avío, avío gwêsán, áye taína wei, okódo vêlevêle.* Old Woman, he tells me, had spread out some rice flour on a banana leaf to dry in the sun. When it looked like rain was coming, she asked her children to bring in the flour. She went to the river to get water and returned. The flour was gone. She asked the children if they'd taken it in for her, but they said they hadn't done it yet. "Who ate my rice flour?" she asked. Dog (*alágbeku* in Papá), the guilty party, said, "Don't worry, Mother. Just look for the person whose lips are moving, he's the one!" and pointed his nose toward Sheep (*adjámadji* in Papá), who's always moving his lips. Sheep said he would never forget the lie that Dog told about him, that he would be Dog's avenging spirit till the end of time. "So," concludes Tooy, "this is what you sing to someone who does something really bad against you. Because you won't forget it till the end of time ('till the earth is no more')." And he sings again, *Okódu vêlevêle, okódu vêlevêle, tatá taki alagbékúnu, f'en ku adjámadji kêlede avío, avío gwêsán, áye taína wei, okódo vêlevêle.*

★　★　★

One evening, as we're walking out the door of his waiting room together, Tooy and I catch our first glimpse of the new moon, low in the sky. He greets it, singing joyfully: *Mamá buánga, tatá buánga. Mi mamá buánga, mi tatá buánga, a Makwalá-e. U sí dóngo, hokóo. Ao-ye, mi mama buánga-e. Makwalá-e, tidé u sí dóngo, hokóo.* "If you kill big game, or a woman gives birth, or a man returns after a long stay in whitefolks' land, this is what you should sing!" When I ask him to tell me more about Tatá Makwalá, whom I'd already heard of as a great drummer in Apúku land, he divulges some complex Apúku lore. Tatá Bokó was the one who had taught Makwalá how to play the drum, saying that he should always begin the "play" with this rhythm: *Múku djélen djélen djélen djélen djélen djélen djélen djélen. Adánimínawa adánimínawa adánimínawa adánimínawa. Múku djélen djélen djélen djélen djélen. Adánimínawa adánimínawa. I sa gó a Dénawa, i sa gó a Dénawa. I sa gó a Tómezíla. Walénu, walénu tjá Tómezíla. Baákama méki lókpolókpo, gádu hangbónu.*[3] Makwalá became the greatest of drummers among Apúkus, no one could best him. But human beings—for reasons Tooy doesn't reveal—decided to do him in. (This story, emphasizes Tooy, is very dangerous!) They organized a "play" at the base of a *katu* tree (the sacred tree that Apúkus call *síkufuámba*), calling on twelve small black monkeys to help them. (As soon as one of the monkeys got tired, just as in various Saramaka folktales involving the Devil, another would replace it without anyone noticing, with the monkeys/humans thereby winning the contest of drummer versus dancer.) The humans also ritually prepared a centipede and stuck it inside the drum. Makwalá began drumming, the monkeys danced, until finally he was exhausted. When he put down the drum, the centipede crawled out and killed him. Then the humans flocked to the spot to celebrate as they sang, *Yu mamá buánga, yu tatá buánga, Makwalá-e-e-e. Tidé i si mamá Alímbodé-e. A-o, yu mamá buánga-e, Makwalá-e-e-e. Tidé i si mamá Alímbodé-e*, which means (in Apúku), "Your mother warned you, your father warned you, Makwalá. Today you see your mother, Alímbodé [in the land of the dead]." Tooy notes that this is the Lángu-clan version, but that downstream they substitute *Tidé man mi kísi dóngo-e* for *Tidé i si mamá Alímbodé*, and the song is sung to a different melody, which he then sings to me. In either case, he says, when they play this song, everyone must stand up. And finally, he teaches me the rhythm you need to play whenever you take up the Apúku drum in order to put the centipede to sleep so it can't harm you. When you begin the "play," you drum: *Gámbo, gámbo, gámbo kó, kó. kó,* [repeat all] *pákasa mitámbulábulá,* [repeat] *mulámutámbu,* [repeat] *sêsitamangáni tósitamangáni, támu fu léleko, kokiô kíki kokiômè, miêmîê miêmîê, tatá kupê, tatá kupê, tóombi, tómbi, tóombi vubémbo, tóombi, tómbi, tóombi vubémbo.* And then you can play all night long! So, a song of celebration at killing an (Apúku) enemy becomes a song of celebration when a baby is born, a man returns from a trip, or the new moon appears in the sky.

The next day, Tooy tells me why Apúkus no longer come to dance with human beings. (In other words, Apúkus "in the flesh" used to join humans at dances, but now appear only when they possess Saramakas who are dancing at a "play.") In those days, says Tooy, only Apúkus had the Apúku drum, which had been made by an Apúku man called Lôngo who had no hands, no feet, no eyes, and no mouth. Humans first saw an Apúku drum in his village. So, one day when Lôngo was absent, humans went to his village and invited the Apúkus to come to their own village for a dance contest. The humans won and took the drum as the prize. When Lôngo returned, the other Apúkus told him that humans now had his drum. He said, "What sort of *weyúu* [human] came and took my drum? This is bullshit. Go tell those people that now that I'm back, we'll have a real contest. The drum called *ngóma*, humans can't play it!" So, they arranged the contest. The humans were drumming, Lôngo kept on dancing, and the Apúkus won! (This is in a song, says Tooy.) And then, at the edge of the forest, where it meets the village, humans cursed Apúkus and Apúkus cursed the humans back. Back and forth they cursed each other! The humans called Apúkus *kúnangbáku* (roughly, "your mother's cunt"), singing *Lôngo, o mamuleké, ao-e mamuleké, mamuleké mamuleké-o, únu kúnangbáku-o!* And the Apúkus cursed them back, calling them *húlúlúpúmbu* (which means roughly the same thing), singing *Ao-aoo mamuleké, ao mamuléke mamuléke únu húlúlúpúmbu-e-o!* The Apúkus took the drum called *ngóma* back to Apúku land. And that was the last time that Apúkus and humans met face to face to dance together.

★ ★ ★

Akónomísi in her rice field, 1968.

A Wénti story that both Tooy and I see as somewhat bizarre nonetheless demonstrates something of the complexity of Saramakas' cosmological *imaginaire*. It began for me in 1967, when I met my very first Wénti, a boy named Sidó who appeared in the head of Akónomísi, a Lángu woman married to a man in the village of Dángogó, where we were then living. Akónomísi's husband, who was my friend, had already told me a little about the god—how it made trips to Wénti land, where it would take children and bring them back to place them in the wombs of infertile women. How throughout her pregnancy, the woman would wear a charm made by Sidó to protect her against the Wénti parents coming to try to take back their child. And how all of Sidó's babies bear a birthmark—a mole or other sign—that shows that they're a child of the water. Sidó, he told me, is actually Tonê and Wénti mixed: Akónomísi had a sister's son, Ganádji, who was on his way to the city with his grandfather when he drowned, killed by an avenging spirit. The men in the canoe had been trying to kill a tapir they'd encountered swimming across the river, near Domburg in the tidal zone, when their canoe sank. They buried the boy in a small coffin by the riverside, but the wake of the passing bauxite ships carried it downstream toward the city, where a Tonê woman named Bodiêê took him from the coffin and turned him into a Wénti with the new name of Sidó. When he arrived for the first time in Wénti land, he saw women at the landing place washing clothes and doing their dishes; they told him their names were Matilda, Syrop, and Akontumísimayéna. There was also a man there, Gòònsè, with his hunting dog.

My field notes dated 9/17/67 include:

> When I arrived in Akónomísi's house, Sidó was in her head, which was tied with a white kerchief, and over one shoulder and across her chest was a white tie with a bundle hanging in front. Sidó spoke pure Sranan-tongo [the language of coastal Suriname] but with a marked Kulí [East Indian] accent. Extremely realistic. Stunning. We all call Sidó "mati" [friend]. There are several clay pots with keéti wáta [kaolin water] in front and a ball of keéti the god gives out for people to crumble and rub on themselves. Sidó washes a child, then Pagai who's soon to leave for the coast, then another sick baby—all with keéti wáta. When I came in, the god said to me, "Fa Fa Fa, mang!" [How are you, man?] The god answers: "Turú!" to say "yes" to things. Sidó, after divining various things for people, looked straight at me and said our time to have a baby hadn't come yet but that it would soon. Sidó then shook hands all around and said he would wáka [walk, leave]. Then, a wild, loud, string of speech apparently in akulí tongo [Sranan Hindi, the language of East Indians] for 30 seconds, a sudden bending from waist, out-thrust of arms, and then silence. Akónomísi stays bent over on her stool, as if in pain. People smile and file out.

After a minute and a half she lifts her head and is herself. There'd been a dozen people present at one time or another. Note the great joy of talking with the god, the pleasure everyone felt.

Nearly forty years later, when we were chatting about Wéntis one day, Tooy filled me in on some of the more bizarre aspects of Sidó's story, reminding me that Akónomísi was from his own Lángu village of Bundjitapá and that he himself had been married to the woman who took care of Sidó's shrine after Akónomísi's death. He described how when Sidó had appeared in Akónomísi's head for the first time, he had told the story of how he'd become a Wénti and all the things he'd seen in Wénti land. Her kinsmen in the village of Debô, under the god's guidance, then made a shrine with an earthen statue of each of the gods he'd told them about, for example Gòònsè, whom they sculpted as a naked man. Then one day, a man named Amínidába from the village of Kayana stole into the shrine and began handling the statues, playing with Gòònsè's penis until it broke off! This happened during large rituals for an Apúku god called Petjúetjú-gbosô (sometimes, Wetjúwetjú-gbosô), and it was decreed that, for messing with the statue, Kayana would have to pay a fine of twelve bottles of sugarcane syrup, twelve bottles of beer, twelve lengths of cloth, three white kerchiefs, 5 liters of rum, twelve parrot feathers, twelve cowry shells, and twelve balls of keéti (kaolin). Kayana at first refused, saying that the statue was just a piece of earth, not a god. Then Sidó sang this song, which means, Tooy explains, that whatever is in a shrine and flecked with keéti is sacred—it might be as lowly as a lizard or a rat, but if you kill it, it's like killing a god. Tooy sings Gòònsè's song: Gòònsè-o, Gòònsè. Gòònsè, Gòònsè, mi yédo. Yédo, élola-ee. Wénti-e, zámbi nómò-e. Mi da sántroí sántroándi, hên da léventua lévemwádudú, mi da linzahúún línzamtómboyò, e-e Wénti dá wi nómo-e, after which Kayana immediately agreed to pay up.

★ ★ ★

Several times, Tooy alludes to a power I'd never before heard of, "Yáka-ósu," which he tells me is one of the "great óbias" of his natal village of Bundjitapá. When I press, he says that its drums and songs resemble the Eastern Maroon susa "play"[4]—indeed, he calls it a kind of "Apúku [forest spirit] súsa"—but he insists that its origin and significance are unique. At first, Tooy tells me that the óbia and its "play" were "found" by Lolói, an avenging spirit in the head of Bundjitapá Captain Diífóu "during the time of Gaamá Djankusó" (who died in 1932). But he later explains that the story is more complicated. There were three brothers who were avenging spirits for the lineage. The eldest was Bákabaáa—whenever he arrived in possession (and this is still true today), he sat with his back toward the people who called him for consultation. The second brother was Lolói, a mixed water-and-forest god (a Bumbá, a "water Apúku" who "walks" in a small caiman), and who came into possession in Tooy's house only last week, when his "master" was visiting. (Lolói likes to say, *Ná mi sanga yu. Kulú sanga yu. Tjái vinda kó*, which means, Tooy says, in the language of Bumbá gods, "I'm not the one who messed with you first. You went after me, which is why I've done what I've done. So get outta here!") It was Lolói (one day about a century ago) who "found" the third brother, Amaní, who was living on an island surrounded by water in the middle of the forest. Lolói tried to persuade his brother to come live with him and Bákabaáa, but Amaní insisted that he was just fine on his island with his wife, his mother, his father, his children, and his grandchildren. (Tooy says he heard all this from a god called Ma Agbaúnawí, who is "mixed" water and forest.) Later, when Lolói was speaking through Captain Diífóu one day, Amaní possessed him—one god possessing another (but "speaking through the same mouth," as Tooy says). And it was Amaní, speaking through Diífóu, who brought Yáka-ósu *óbia* to Tooy's village.

"Yáka-ósu," says Tooy, "is a very dangerous *óbia*, one of the great war *óbias* of this world—its strong name is Kwandjímun. Its 'leaves' are 'heavy,' heavier than those for Komantí! When they play Yáka-ósu, they sing *Kwinga kwé, kwinga kwí, nu ku yeló. Kwinga kwí, kwinga dobukaan, nu ku yeló. Kwinga kwé, kwinga kó, nu ku yeló. Kwinga kwé, hési kwinga dóu, nu ku yééé*, which means, 'Hurry! Grab your kids and get them into the house. Shut the doors! A jaguar is on the loose in the village and will eat them!' " And when they dance Yáka-ósu, when things really get hot, if you don't know how to do the footwork—when to lift your leg, when not to—you're dead! (Tooy tells me that Yáka-ósu dancing and drums resemble those for Pasiká, a god who lives in forest boulders, as well as those for Apúku, but they are distinct.)

In Yáka-ósu, there's a big prayer that commemorates what Amaní said to his brother avenging spirits, telling them that he's their pathfinder, the one who clears the path with his machete, the strongest of the three. Tooy sings it for me: *Adjíulalá lalá, Adjíulalá lalá, Naná kônde flambó, Naná nyankómpono, mi hélu ku adjéusúmani. Adjíulalá lalá, Naná kônde flambó, wemi yaú-ké, Naná nyankómpono, mí-i-ké adjeú sumaní-e.* (He explains that in Yáka-ósu, *adjíulalá* means "machete," *adjéusúmani* means "path," and *Naná kônde flambó* is the fire of Heaven—"You don't even think of playing with it.") He also tells me about a contest between Rum and Sugarcane Syrup to see who was the real man, a contest inscribed in a Yáka-ósu song: *Azúngunamitjé, manamitjé kaafu lalángmamí zúngunamitjé, botjéi kaafu lalángmamí zúngunamitjé, manamitjé*

kaafu lalángmamí zúngunamitjé. (In Yáka-ósu, Tooy explains, *zúngunamitjé*
means "rum" and *lalángmamí* "sugarcane syrup.") "One man drank a liter of
rum and had to sleep for three days before he could stand up. Another drank
a bottle of sugarcane syrup and was out cold for twelve whole days! That's
what the song says. Sugarcane Syrup won! By the time they play this song,
the Yáka-ósu priest on the drum is calling people to drink. After that, they
dance on fire!"

That's almost all I know about Yáka-ósu.[5] There must be literally hundreds of such village or lineage *óbias* in Saramaka, some very old, others
dating only from the twentieth century, each with its own drums, songs,
language, and lore.

DÚNUYÁNGI TAKES OVER

When Tooy is feeling drowsy, or bored with my questions, he sometimes tells me he doesn't really know much about Dúnguláli, Komantí, or Papá, but that when Tatá Dúnuyángi shows up, he certainly can give me the lowdown. And three or four times during our visit in early 2005, he did.

Thanks to Sally, we enjoy a delicious lunch, accompanied by a bottle of wine we brought. Then Tooy stands and leads us and Sensiló (who is visiting from Suriname) in a Wénti song that's appropriate after you've eaten well, to thank them and invite them to join you. We stand and hold our glasses (in the event, plastic and enamel cups) on high, waving them as we sing: *Keenidjó-yéi gaán lô gádu, mi keenidjó dá únu-e. Mi adjò, mi adjò. Mi keenidjò, mi keenidjò. Wêmêdjé fu ayónde, mi keenidjó dá únu-e. Mi adjò, mi adjò. Tjónugbé, gonobí olo matoo, hwémato, kínadu gadi mi hwénu kee, mi adjò, mi adjò, tjónugbé-o.*[1] Tooy, Sensiló, and I retire to the leaf room, where Tooy opens three beers from the six-pack that a client left earlier. He is feeling happy. And soon his god, Dúnuyángi, announces himself, reeling off some of his praise names:

> Me! I say that I'm Abún-dékpopo-yakpánu. I'm Ketjikí-dedomí-ma-wamái-di-domí-mawá-mi-koonu-dye! I didn't let my father down. Abún-dékpopo-yakpánu. He's the one who begins playing at twelve o'clock midnight and doesn't stop till daylight. He doesn't stop playing for anything. A real Lángu warrior! I'm Adúnuyángi. I'm Edjénamá-u-Musútu. I'm Dúnuyángi-fu-adjú. I'm Avungulá-dêbe. I'm Pakaká-fu-adjú. I'm Fulánkáma-vulá-bêmbú. I'm Dêmide-kalángu, Lazánkan-kalángu, Djididjí-kalángu. [to me] Man, come embrace me, Brother! [begins pouring a libation of beer:] Ma Yowentína, take some, Ma Dígbeónsu, take some. Ma Yemánzáa, take some. We're near the seaside. Near Afémaóla. We must live, we must grow old, we must enjoy our old age! You know how to bring us to the lake they call Simbámba [more usually he calls it "Kibámba"], let us bathe there and then come back. Let's drink together!

Sensiló teasingly asks me what I saw in the sea in Martinique one day, and Tooy's god encourages me to tell him about the Wénti ship moored below our house that I'd shown him a photo of at the hospital. After I describe it, Sensiló in mock reprimand says I shouldn't have taken that picture. "If there were women onboard, do you think they were *your* wives?" he asks. Tooy's god laughs loudly. Sensiló says he's only joking, that I did well. But I shouldn't forget that those Wénti women are his! He adds that the work I do really has its benefits—the ship that came, didn't Tooy get out of jail? Well, who do you think got him out of jail? It was those Wéntis on the ship!

Tooy's god tells me that the man over there—he points toward his brother—is very mischievous. If you're angry with him, you're angry with the earth and the forest. If you're angry with him, you're angry with the sea. . . . I realize that I'm in the presence of Flibánti as well as Dúnuyángi! So I ask this *óbia*, who knows so much about the way the world works, something I've been wondering for a long time. First excusing myself for my question—to which Dúnuyángi breaks in to say, "There's nothing evil about being curious!"—I explain that I come from America, but I don't know what country Tatá Dúnuyángi comes from. Sensiló's *óbia* says, "Friend, he hails from Olóni! [the great Wénti country in the middle of the sea]. That's where he was born. But he was raised on this earth and likes to hang around here on land. That's how you and he have gotten to be such buddies." He tells me, "Those people from Kínaazáu [another Wénti town], they sometimes have children with forest spirits here on earth." And he reminds me, boasting, "I'm the big man of the forest." He also informs me that "the person who owns the ship that was moored in front of your house is Mamá Dígbeónsu of Olóni! It's her grandchildren who are the crew."

Dúnuyángi interrupts to say, "Set your tape recorder, I want to tell you something. (Excuse me, 'taatá'—I call the *óbia* here 'taatá.' He owns the whole part of the earth we live in here!) [singing] 'If you seek me you will find me. [repeat] I'm Manídjíngmbe. I'm Sakíawángadjímbe as well! [falsetto] If you seek me you will find me.' I'm the headman of the water, I'm the headman of the forest. What could you do in the forest without my knowing about it? It's not by chance that Stupid-Head [Dúnguyángi's name for Tooy] and Skin [Dúnguyángi's name for Sensiló] love one another. When this man [Sensiló] comes to himself [comes out of possession], tell him that I'm Awámbadjíngmbe. I say, 'Skin! It's not because you and Stupid-Head have the same mother. There's a reason. Mother and child, father and child, they must love each other. Let's live like that.' Man, let me tell you something. If Stupid-Head were to forget about Skin or if Skin were to forget about Stupid-Head, it wouldn't be because they wanted that. It would be because someone put something between them. Let them stay together, however messed-up they are physically. If you try to kill them, you'll die before them. They're in the hands of God. The Sky God is the boss, the Earth God is the boss. . . . There's a prayer for every occasion. . . . " Tooy's god teases Sensiló's *óbia* for a while. Then Tooy's god gets on Sally's case—she's joined us after washing the dishes—saying that she really resembles a certain woman he knows, but he's not going to say her name. Finally, he says that it's the one who lives in the deep in front of our house in Martinique [Zoofayaónde]. "You should throw a bottle of beer out to her from time to time," he reminds me. Sensiló's *óbia* asks Sally if she's had children, and when she says yes he tells her to take good of them. He takes her hands: "The place you live by the sea, you know who sent you there?" He laughs . . . "They own that place, those Wéntis. Live there well, with those children of yours. . . . Take care of your husband. . . . Set a table there, make a little altar looking out at the sea, where the wind blows. That ship will come back again and dock there." Sensiló's *óbia* says his goodbyes. Tooy's god quietly departs as well.

Another afternoon, when Tooy and I are chatting alone, Dúnuyángi suddenly appears. "It's Bási Dúnuyángi talking to you here! That's Yêdjemaná-u-musútu. That's Adúnayángi-fu-adjú. I'm the singer/drummer for the whole world. Man, I really love to play! I'm Awángbadjíngmbe, I'm Kasi-fu-wámba! I'm Avúngula-bitjêbi. I'm Pákasa-fu-adjóbi-fu-ánkama fulá bêmbu!" Then he quickly tells me, "They say that the man called Stupid-Head loves 'plays,' that he loves to sing and drum. I say, 'Bullshit!' It's his head that's so stupid! He likes to think he's smart, but he's just a stupid-head. On the other hand, you and I have so much to talk about! When we sit down, we'll talk about Kwadjó [vulture Komantí], Apúku, Wátawenú, Mavúngu, and Yáu [river Komantí], before we talk about Djebí [jaguar Komantí]."[2] And he sings me a song in Komantí.

Yáoo, mi Yáo, mié mié mié mié mié mié mié mié mié. Adínka-e, mié mié, busikí mié mié ku adjú mié mié, mi óbia mi ka moomi odia poki mi sa fomaní mani o mi da awamba djebí-e, Yáoo. Brother, Giant Otter sang that to God. He'd been hunting underwater for twelve days and twelve nights without finding a single thing to eat. Finally he came to the surface and sang this to God. (What he said was dangerous—"If God wants him to kill, he'll eat, if God doesn't want him to kill, he'll still manage to find something to eat." You really should never say, "If God wants, you'll do something, and if God doesn't want, you'll still do it"—it's only if God wants that you'll do it. But that's what he said.) You should say these words only when you're really in need. As soon as Otter sang them, he dove under and caught a large *kumálu* [a tasty fish].

Dúnuyángi grabs Tooy's tape recorder and starts playing a tape of a Komantí "play" at his house. I notice that most songs are in normal Saramaccan, with a few Komantí words inserted. Dúnuyángi keeps telling me the circumstances in which to sing each song—you must prepare the clay pot of medicine leaves before you sing the one he's playing now, for example. Sometimes, he picks out pieces of a song to explain to me: the name of the ship that carried them from Africa was Dokofóankáma, the name of the captain of the ship was Abáan!

He turns off the tape and begins a story. "An old man and his wife, Abaníba—both blind—stayed home while everyone else in the village went out to hunt *kwimáta* [a heavily scaled swamp fish that can be caught when there are heavy rains and that Komantí calls *akántabúba*]. She had one fish but couldn't take off its scales because she couldn't see. So she cried, singing, *Ándo kó a kó pèê asánti vílivíli, djáifosó gwágwá kó pèê asánti vílivíli, Bási adínka gwagwá kó pèê asánti vílivíli, ma bandímba-e kiyóo un án yéi-o akántabúba, asánti baáa, u án yéi, lúku akántabúba.* And suddenly she could see! She cut the fish and cooked it. Komantí, Brother!" Which reminds him of another Komantí song, this one about Three-Fingered Sloth, whom Komantí calls *adínka*. The god sings, *Adínka, a ta yénde-o, woyo yénde-e, adínka hên ta yénde-e, bási adínka-e, medi a kái.* "The three-fingered sloth is small and ugly—but don't imagine you can bring him down from the tree with a single shot! He says, 'When you shoot me, twelve men will hear before I'm dead.' He says his praise name is 'Bási Adínka fu Umbádjini.' Or 'Dóble.' When he climbs up the *mombé* tree to seek food, he's so sweet to watch, good-looking guy!" And he sings again, *Adínka, a ta yénde-o, woyo yénde-e, adínka hên ta yênde-e, bási adínka-e, medi a kái.*

"You know what Three-Fingered Sloth says? 'If you mess with me, I'll mess with you! If you shoot at me, I'll get you!' In Komantí he sings, *Kwan, kwan, bó yéi, mi o pêpè yu, kwan, kwan.* And then the hunter says to him, [singing] *Kukube i míti mamima, a kukubele míti mamima.*" Dúnuyángi is getting excited and says, "Let's quit talking—there's too much to say!" and he begins dribbling some beer on the ground. "Bási Djesí, Bási Akoomí, Bási Yembuámba, Bási Sáka-Amáfu, Avó Adjó, Bási Ofilíbaní Mafuyewá, take this fine-looking liquid, let's drink." Then he sprays some to either side with his mouth and offers me the bottle.

"Let me teach you how to pray to the Gádu-a-Kamía, the 'god-of-the-place' that lives in each particular spot. You call it Kasiámba Naná Gwambísa, Kasiámba Naná Gadeénza. There's no place that doesn't have one! You say, 'My *djódjo*, my *saámba*, give me strength, Avó Kasiámba Naná Gwambísa, Avó Kasiámba Naná Gadeénza.'" And he explains, "*Saámba* is the soul [normal Saramaccan *akáa*], *djódjo* is the body of your namesake. Avó Kasiámba Gadeénza is the god on the west side, Naná Gwambísa is the one to the east. This is 'country' talk—not any other particular language." I try to confirm my understanding that there's an Earth Mother (a Mother-of-the-Earth) and then there are multiple "gods-of-the-place." Tooy's god says, "Yes, the Earth Mother is the boss and has various 'gods-of-the-place' who work for her. You should call her Malulú Matjángi." I ask which of these we prayed to at Roland's lumberyard in Martinique, the first time we met. "It wasn't the god-who-has-the place—it was the Earth Mother. What we said was, *Malulú Matjángi asákpáa asákpáa tjá kiníkiní kapêèkapêé kutjábíabía dumiyáyá mádesídagbó.* It's saying that the person who's trying to kill you there [Roland's enemy, in that case] has his thigh [Saramaccan *asákpáa*] above his knee [Saramaccan *kiní*]—that is, he's someone real—and that Malulú Matjángi should do the necessary to get him away from there. This is 'country talk.'

"Komantí men sing," Dúnuyángi continues, "*Téé mi yéi Afánti boóko mi o fiá! Téé mi yéi so mi sa fiá-e. Afántinêngè mi o fiá. Téé mi yéi so mi sa fiá-o!* [in normal Saramaccan, 'When I hear Afánti is defeated, I'll deny it; when I hear that, I'll deny it; Afánti people I'll argue; when I hear it, I'll argue']" "The country they call Afánti," he tells me, "no gun battle could defeat the Afánti people! If you're bullshitting me, you could tell me that Afanti's been defeated. If I'm bullshitting you, I could tell you that Afánti could be defeated. But if we're not bullshitting each other, there's no way Afánti could be defeated!"

GOODBYES

Our final day in Cayenne for a while. Tooy decides to offer me a gift—"This *óbia* is very special," he says. "For my closest friend, I'd charge 100 euros, but for anybody else it would be a thousand or more. Never, never make it for someone for less than 100 euros!" Not wanting to jack up the price of this book and not wanting the makers of Viagra or Cialis on my case, I record Tooy's recipe verbatim here—except that I leave out a single ingredient (as he sometimes does when making an *óbia*, when he's unsure whether he trusts the client), in this case to keep my part of the bargain.

> Take some *basilique gaán bwa* [Saramaccan *adóya*, a variety of *Ocimum basilicum*, "basil"]—it can be dried or fresh. Find a stand of sugarcane, pick out a stalk, and address it: "Sugarcane, I've come to you. You're filled with liquid, but you stand up straight! Make me stand up straight as well!" Leaving the cane standing, carefully remove the leaves and discard them. When the cane is stripped, slice it off at the bottom with a single stroke of the machete. Bring it home, cut it up and place in a mortar, with the basil on top, and pound them together. Then, place a small mound of salt in the center of a basin, and place little mounds of sugar around the salt in a triangle [Tooy said "like *makúku*"—the three earthenware hearthstones that define a woman's home]. Take three large peanuts and pray to them, open the shells, take the front nut from each, and throw the rear nuts behind you, saying that you're throwing away dirt and evil. Put the three good nuts right on top of the salt. With your hands, gently lift the mashed-up leaves from the mortar and place them on top of the basin. Add about a cup of cold water. Then, when you're ready to wash in the bath, add warm water. Do it every evening for seven days. It will keep you going for months!

As Tooy says his goodbyes to us in the Dúnguláli house, where we pray, drink the *óbia*'s liquid, and chat, he tells us that, according to Flibánti, Dúnguláli is the *gaán-óbia* of Wéntis—their "great *óbia*."

> Death doesn't come to Dúnguláli country, death doesn't come to Wénti country. The first man to have Dúnguláli was Moses—he used it in war, sending up

smoke from his pipe. With that smoke, he parted the sea and killed all those whitefolks! When he died, Moses became a Wénti. They call him Naosí—it's in Wénti songs.[1] He's the one who gave the *óbia* to Pupú, in the land of the dead. Dúnguláli isn't the *óbia's* real name, but you can only pronounce that name while you are making a sacrifice—perhaps on your next visit.

"Once," Tooy adds, "Naosí [Moses] divorced his wife. For a whole year she begged him to reconsider, sending captains and assistant captains to him to plead her cause. Finally, she went to him herself, stood before him, and dropped her clothes—she was stark naked! And she sang, *Naosí-e, Naosí, Naosí-elóo kióo ná máti, a tjalí, sô nôò sèmbè de f'en-e, Naosí. Naosí-elóo, kióo naá máti-e, baáa sô nôò sèmbè dê, Wénti-e* [Naosí, don't be angry kid, that's just the way people are, Wénti]. He looked at her hard and sang, *Wámilo wánwán, wámilo yú wánwán-o, M'án o dêdè f'i hédi, a tjalí-e, i án músu kèê fu mi, Wénti-e. Wámilo-e. Wámilo yú wánwán-o. M'án ta dêdè f'i hédi-o, ké. U án músu kèê fu mi, Wénti-e* [You're just a woman, I won't die over you, it's very sad, Wéntis please don't cry for me]. And Moses took her back!"[2] He comments, "Wénti songs are really heartbreaking."

"When you get on the airplane," he counsels us, "here's what to sing: 'Well, my mother Dígbeónsu. Come help, my mother. Well, my mother Dígbeónsu of Olóni, thank you thank you I pray to you. Mother, you see I'm up near the sun, come bring me back to the sea, Mother Dígbeónsu.'" He stops and says that these words make him feel too sad. "You're up in the sky, your feet can't reach the ground. What can you do?" (He sings the song again.) He urges Sally, "You and your husband, when you set that table [prepare that altar] in Martinique, call these [Wénti] people to come be with you!" Tooy is wiping away tears, his perennial enthusiasm now mixed with sorrow.

KNOCKING THE STONE

When we pull up the car behind the house, Tooy, shirtless, comes out singing, arms outstretched: *Ódo bái Anígo-o, ódo bái Anígo-o. Tjá, mênimi tjá. Ódo bái Anígo-o-yé, tjá Anígo tjái.* Embracing me, he says, "Greetings, Brother! That's how we greet Anagó óbia." Ushering us into his waiting room, he continues to sing, bursting with happiness: *Hangwé-e go na andúwe, hangwé-e go na andúwe,* [repeat] *andúwe go f'en na noíkadjá-e. Hangwé-e go na andúwe, hangwé-e go na andúwe, andúwe kísi noíkadjá, Wénti-e.* "This is about inseparable friends. Tortoise and Tick. You never catch a tortoise without finding a tick on the underside of its neck. Tick [in Wénti] is *hangwé*, Tortoise *andúwe*, and tortoise's shell *noíkadjá*, so the song says, 'Tick goes to Tortoise, Tortoise goes into his shell.' Friend with friend. You and me!"

I'd intended this trip as a near-final working visit to Cayenne, since this book was largely drafted, to check transcriptions of songs in esoteric languages. But Tooy decided that we should accomplish two things together.[1] He wanted us to pay a courtesy visit to the homeland of Dúngulái and the Wéntis, Kódji's village of Tampáki. And it was time, he said, to carry out the ultimate Dúngulái ceremony—knocking the stone.

Preparations for the ceremony begin almost immediately. Tooy pours libations at the ancestor shrine in front of his house, telling Kódji and Akoomí and some fifty others that in a week we will hold a "feast" (*nyanyá túe*) in their honor, and that we'll knock the stone a week after that. Tooy surprises me by praying, first, to "Master Yésus Kristus, our mother Santa María, Adam and Eve in Heaven," which has me imagining that his prayer might inscribe the conversion to Christianity of some of his Lángu ancestors in the Kingdom of Kongo two centuries before they arrived in Suriname. But my dream of this preserved trace of African Christianity in Saramaka is quickly shattered when Tooy tells me that his knowledge of these "Catholic" figures comes from his twentieth-century namesake Pobôsi, not from his more distant Lángu ancestors.[2]

Our first days in Cayenne are divided between my driving Tooy to sites near and far in search of the ingredients needed for knocking the stone, listening with him to recordings from previous visits to check the accuracy of transcriptions, and hanging out in his house as he receives clients, teaches younger Saramakas, and is occasionally possessed by his god, Dúnuyángi.

Mi ángbo tímbo, mi ángbo tímbo, he sings one noon when he feels hungry, teaching me the way Papá players ask for food. And eating lunch with Yaai and Sally, we have an animated discussion about whether a man and a woman can ever be "just friends"—he insists not. Dúnuyángi joins us and teaches some Papágádu language. And then Yontíni appears, and the two gods sing with each other for a good hour. It's much like opera, not in the melodies but in the alternation of voices and the universal themes: fear, betrayal, trust, and love. Then one of Tooy's old friends, Kayé from Bêndêkôndè, happens by and tells how Pésé, his boss at the St. Elie mine (where he pulls a wagon loaded with 700 kilos of supplies by hand, along rails that run through the forest for 33 kilometers from the riverside), has designs on Saramaka territory for his golden ambitions, but that Gaamá Otjútju will surely thwart him.

The forest trips bring me nostalgic pleasure—it's been many years since I've been in high forest. I'd forgotten the tremendous variety of tall trees, some corrugated, others smooth, others spiky, as well as the varieties of vines, thick and thin, white and pitch black, soft and stone hard. Tooy's a consummate guide, pointing out more plants and trees and vines (and their uses) than I could ever hope to remember. Each of our day trips is to a site he's visited many times, so he knows which ingredients he's likely to find. It's a bit like shopping in several giant supermarkets, walking the aisles and loading whatever you want into the baskets.

Once we drive for an hour and a half in the direction of Brazil, until he tells me to go slow and after a couple of kilometers says we've arrived. I pull onto the grassy shoulder, and then we walk through an abandoned banana grove before entering the forest. Our footsteps are muted by layers upon layers of moist brown leaves, and as I look upward, there are layers upon layers of branches and green leaves filtering the light. We soon cross a troop of little black monkeys leaping from branch to vine to branch. Tooy searches for the young shoots of a certain plant, but only finds three in fifteen minutes. He folds each one over on itself, wraps them in another kind of leaf, and using the stem of a third kind of leaf, which he splits with his machete, makes a string to tie the bundle. As we walk deeper, we come upon a *musánse* tree whose bark has clearly been harvested by several others before us. With his machete, Tooy slices off some chunks and puts them into the burlap sack I'm carrying. Over the next two hours, he harvests ten different barks from large trees, often from their impressive buttresses. The dozen or so vines he collects range from delicate creepers thinner than ivy to giant 4-inch-diameter vines that seem to fall from the sky. He often slices into a vine or even a tree with his machete and rejects it, either by mere sight of its flesh, by taking a bit and smelling it, or, in a few cases, by licking it for the taste. Sometimes he asks me, totally clueless, to taste it. As Tooy cuts bark, he occasionally addresses the tree, "Father, Oh father." We stock slabs of bark, branches, and lengths of vines by the path in piles, to pick up as we return. Our trajectory is downhill toward an unseen river, then back up, retrieving the piles we've left. The forest harbors active insect life, little flies, small wasps, mosquitoes, that bite us as we walk. Before emerging to the road, Tooy says a prayer to Tatá Dúnguláli and begins poking his machete into the path until he feels something more solid. He then clears a small area with his machete, digs out some earth, and exposes three horizontal roots, each about half an inch in diameter, which he cuts into foot-long pieces, wraps in a leaf, and ties with a thin vine. The trunk of our rental car is tightly packed with rainforest riches.

The forest trips multiply. Tooy keeps telling me how many leaves, barks, roots, and vines are still lacking. But a few days after the feast for the ancestors, he finally begins to feel ready. By now he's arranged his vines and barks in a 5-foot-tall tower held up against the wall of the leaf room by a giant sawfish beak. (The idea is to keep each variety of bark or vine separate so he can grind them up appropriately for each of the gods and óbias in the house.) And branches of leaves and piles of roots line the other walls outside the Dúnguláli chamber.

Tooy decides to take Sally and me and Yaai on a visit to his garden camp in the forest, forty-five minutes by car from the capital and then a quarter hour by outboard from the town of Roura, to find a few final ingredients. An Amerindian with a cell phone takes us upstream in an aluminum boat, promising to be back before nightfall for the return trip. The camp sits in a beautiful riverside stretch of forest, with a large clearing and three houses in disrepair. Tooy uses his machete and a broom made from forest plants to clean up two shrines where we pray and bathe, telling the local powers of the upcoming Dúnguláli rites. In an abandoned garden, amidst bamboo and other brush, we lift up some galvanized roofing to uncover an underground óbia pot—it's Dankuná, a fighting óbia that Tooy also keeps in a pot in his Dúnguláli chamber. He prays and sings to it here in the open air, and we are each obliged to wash our faces, hands, and ankles with the fetid

Tooy's gold-mining machine.

black liquid that he extracts with a calabash. (Later, he tells me that Pobôsi's god Sáka-Amáfu worked with this *óbia*, as did Akoomí, who learned it from Akeekúna, a woman in the land of the dead, in exchange for his own Kii-fú *óbia*.) Not far from this buried *óbia*, a giant mining machine looms out of the greenery. Tooy explains that ten years before, he and a partner ran a clandestine gold-mining operation here, employing nine Brazilians and, at another time, fifteen Saramakas, until the police closed them down. It was too expensive to move the machine out of the forest.

We also make a weekend trip to Tampáki, where Tooy says he wants to wet his head once more in Kódji's river. The visit is bittersweet. Another of the handful of knowledgeable old men who are left, Marcel, is dying. Others are aging fast. The younger folks who've arrived in the past few years, who came on a promise from the mayor of Saint-Georges that he would get them French papers, feel deceived—though it's not the mayor's fault but that of the far-off French Minister of the Interior, who for political purposes at home is cracking down on foreigners on French soil. On this visit, the old men treat me for the first time like a Saramaka rather than an outsider. I accompany them as Tooy prays and makes offerings at Kódji's ancestor shrine and the Wénti house, and visits the shrine of Mamá-Gádu and the ruins of the Dúnguláli shrine in the sacred grove behind the village.

As Tooy prays to Kódji and the other Tampáki ancestors, in the presence of other old men, I realize once again how special his knowledge is. In the course of the weekend, I hear him use esoteric phrases (often proverbs) from a variety of languages—Komantí, Papá, Apúku, Apínti, and Kôndè—and learn, from subsequent conversation with those present, that they had understood little of what he was saying when he addressed the ancestors in this way. I would estimate that few forty-year-old Saramakas would know even 20% of the phrases that Tooy likes to use in such circumstances and that only one in ten men in their sixties or seventies would know the meaning of half of them. Perhaps it's something like what the proverbial man on the street would "get" overhearing an exchange between Gayatri Spivak and Barbara Johnson on the finer points of Derridian deconstruction or between Einstein and Oppenheimer on quantum field theory. In any case, I realize that part of the specialness of Tooy's knowledge is its breadth. There are, in most large Saramaka villages, a couple of specialists in each of these esoteric languages. But it is rare to encounter a man who has more than a passing knowledge of so many.

★   ★   ★

Knocking the stone—even without the presence of Roland Legros, who ultimately chickened out—forms the logical culmination to this story. Tooy had first mentioned this ceremony the very night I met him in Martinique. (All *gaán-óbia* have such rites, designed to produce the mashed-up mix of leaves-roots-vines-barks-other ingredients to be ingested and bathed in by the adepts.) Yet no *bakáa*—outsider—had ever, to my knowledge, witnessed one. How, then, to write about a ceremony that is at once secret and intimate, without evoking the trope of the heroic anthropologist who goes where no whiteman has ever trod?

Let's fast-forward through the ceremony, stopping for a few details, as a way of getting an overview. (I have placed transcriptions of the Dúngulāli and Komantí songs that Tooy sang during the night, with his explanations, in the Coda to this book.)

FAST-FORWARD. Late afternoon, we join a couple dozen Saramaka men, women, and children clad, respectively, in towels, wrap skirts, and underpants, plus a couple of Creole clients in bathing suits, who follow Tooy out the back door, across the road, through some piles of garbage, and into a clearing cut in the brush for the Dúngulāli ceremony of "separation." The accumulated impurities of the year are to be left behind so that each participant will be ready for the New Year. Tooy's sister's son Frank lays a wood fire in a hole he's dug in the earth, places a parrot feather on top, and lights it. Tooy goes first. He spreads his legs over the blaze, which Frank extinguishes by pouring liquid over him with a calabash while Tooy prays that the year's "dirt" leave him. The plastic basin of leaves, roots, and vines is refreshed every few minutes with buckets of water brought by youngsters from the house. Tooy calls each person up to take his turn, handing each an egg to use as "soap," to wash away the "dirt" while praying out loud and straddling the hole, facing west. In the gathering darkness, Frank pours the liquid over each head. Intermittent rain. It's dark and muddy at the edge of the city as we huddle underneath a giant high-tension pylon. Frank washes each person a second time, using the egg on each body and pouring liquid over each head, turning them west, then east, before he breaks their egg into the hole. The bedraggled group troops back in the cold rain and darkness and stands shivering in Tooy's waiting room until all have changed clothes.

FAST-FORWARD. It's eight o'clock, and many of the bathers have gone home. In Dúnguláli's chamber, Tooy sits next to the altar with Yaai at his side. Eight men plus Sally and I are squeezed onto the benches along the sides of the tiny room, and a couple of others sit just outside the open door on chairs. Men take up seedpod rattles as Tooy launches into the first song. Frank tears up a red cloth, and each person ties a strip around his head—we look like pirates. As Tooy sings and the others chorus, he occasionally lights up Anánagóa and smokes a bit, and others take their turn at the pipe as they wish. Each of the thirty or so songs is followed by the Dúnguláli chant, spoken in unison: *Dúnguláli-é. Pási paatí óbia. Awíli. Awíli kándikándi. Dêde kôndè pási dúngu, líbi líbi kôndè pási límbo yéti* ("Dúnguláli-é. Path-splitting óbia. Awíli. Awíli kándikándi. The path to the land of the dead is dark, the path to the land of the living still light"). As they get into it, I realize that Tooy and his comrades are singing against Death, that Dúnguláli songs share the purpose of keeping Death at bay. Tooy sings: "Get out ghost, you get out! ([chorused:] Dúnguláli is smoking the place)" . . . "Dúnguláli, dangerous Indians are coming ([chorused:] *Hahhhhhhhhhh*), dangerous Indian story (*Hahhhhh*) . . . but the Pátakatjána are coming (*Hahhhhh*)." . . . "A deep grave, Dúnguláli, they're digging a large hole, but it's not for me!" . . . "*Lêgbelêgbe*, Death's left hand, Dúnguláli, Death's left hand has come. Chase it back to the land of the dead, Dúnguláli." As Tooy and his comrades sing on to the steady rhythm of their seedpods, it's easy to imagine Kódji a century before, with Akoomí in his head, teaching and leading the band of singers on the far-away Oyapock River.

FAST-FORWARD. It's ten o'clock, and the singers have moved into the waiting room, where it's cooler, to play Komantí. Tooy begins knocking the *dáulo* (a small hollow chunk of metal, beaten with a second piece of metal) in the five-stroke "time-line" rhythm that defines all Komantí music, and launches into the first song. The other men chorus and occasionally take over the lead for a song or two. Around midnight, the gong is laid aside and Tooy begins singing Apúku, which continues for another half hour. Sometime before 1:00 a.m., the "play" breaks up. A couple of men go into the leaf room, where under Tooy's direction they begin sorting and cutting up ingredients for knocking the stone. The others lie down on benches, beds, or the floor to catch a couple of hours' rest.

FAST-FORWARD. It's 3:00 a.m., and we're squeezed back into the Dúngulálí chamber. The altar has been removed to reveal a hole in the floor containing Dúngulálí's iron pot. And just inside the doorway, in a 2-foot-wide depression in the floor, there's a pile of the chopped-up leaves-barks-vines-roots that will be knocked with the stone. Tooy takes the first turn, sitting on the floor, spreading his legs around the depression, and picking up the large river stone with both hands to begin mashing the mixture, as he launches the first song. Each person present gets a turn at knocking the stone—usually about two songs' worth . . . By dawn, the mixture seems adequately mashed and Yontíni, who's come into Yaai's head, sings a song to indicate that this part of the ceremony is coming to an end. One of Tooy's assistants begins forming the mashed-up mixture into baseball-sized balls, which will dry hard. Tooy prays to Akoomí and then passes around a calabash of Dúngulálí liquid, straight from the pot, which we all sip, being careful to hold it with our left hand, palm down, Dúngulálí fashion.

FAST-FORWARD. It's 6:00 a.m. The fowl sacrifices begin, first a cock to Akoomí and then a hen to Tooy's ancestor Gisí (Kwasímukámba's son), whose *óbia* pot is also in the Dúngulálí chamber. Frank offers each chicken, in turn, a final sip of water and raises the first one by the back of the neck for Tooy to interrogate. "Did the ceremony not go well?" (Chicken doesn't move.) "Should we sacrifice to Gisí before you?" (Chicken doesn't move.) "Did we wait too long to do the ceremony?" (Chicken flaps its wings wildly.) So, knowing that the only problem is that the ceremony was done nearly a year later than Tooy had once planned it, he feels as if all is well, that he can simply pray to Dúngulálí for forgiveness on that one. As the song of sacrifice continues, the fowl expires and Frank lays him at the base of Akoomí's post. A knife is brought, the belly split, and the testicles examined. They're pure white, meaning all is well, and Frank places the tiny organs on top of the Dúngulálí pot, on a bed of *malêmbelêmbe* covered by that same leaf. (At Tooy's request, I do not describe here the songs or prayers or rites connected with the actual sacrifices.)

*　　*　　*

During the subsequent days, Tooy divides his time between preparing Dúnguláli bottles for those who participated in the rite, treating his usual clientele, and helping me understand the many hours of songs that I play back to him. One day three flirtatious Brasileiras visit and ask to be introduced to me. Tooy, feeling affectionate, tells them in Creole, "This man and I have the same father and mother—full brothers. It's just that he came out white and I black."

The day before our departure from Cayenne, Sally and I watch Tooy, in the leaf-room, preparing our own bottle, which he'd specified must be made of thick glass—a champagne bottle or Dutch *genever* jug, for example. (Even with a loose cork, an ordinary wine bottle would explode as the liquid ferments, he said.) Tooy stuffs the empty Veuve Cliquot bottle, which we'd recuperated from the trash bin of the *mairie*, with a vulture feather, vulture-bone shavings, barks, leaves, and a broken-up ball from knocking the stone which must contain twenty or thirty forest ingredients. He adds a liquid mixture of cane juice and the juice from a mashed-up banana tree before corking the bottle loosely. Then he wraps it tightly in a black cloth tied with a bright-red sash, and carries it into the Dúnguláli chamber.

Sitting down with us again, Tooy launches into one of his philosophical games: "Someday, you'll forget a person you love," he tells me, testing. I say it's not possible. But he insists that something could happen to come between us. "For example, I'm sure that if someone says something bad about me to you, you'll want to fight him. And if someone says something bad about you to me, I'll rip him apart. If someone comes to kill you with a gun, I'd say shoot me first. All that's clear. But something could still happen so that I would no longer want to take your bullet." I can guess where he's going. "It's called betrayal!" he says. "We could fight about something, but that wouldn't change the way we feel about each other. There's a god in [the village of] Kayana called Mitéénzu Banángoma. When it possesses someone, it says, 'Héé! I'm Magwénu from Ayówe. I'm Your-friend-who-deceives-you-till-you-find-evil!' If a true friend betrays you, do you think you'll ever cross his doorstep again?" Tooy pauses, then continues. "There are three kinds of false friends. There's the friend who loves you because of something you're doing that he wishes he could do, too. Or the friend who loves you because he wants your wife. Or the friend who loves you because you have lots of money. In each case, when he's finished getting what he wants, he's gone. But a true friend loves your breath, your sweat, the way you are. You know why I love you?" he asks. A bit embarrassed, I say I suppose it's because he is after my wife, which makes him laugh. "I love your sweat," he says, "your very blood. The way you sit down here, sweating." He waves us into the room adjoining the Dúngulálí chamber, where he has prepared an óbia canoe filled with leaves for us to bathe in. It's been a week since the leaves were left to soak, and the liquid is not only black but smells something awful. Tooy tells us cheerfully that he knows we can't bathe in it the next day: we're leaving, and we'd stink so much they wouldn't allow us onto the plane.

On our final evening, at Tooy's suggestion, we arrange for his lawyer Lamartine to join us for a long-postponed celebration of his liberation from prison, even though Yaai can't be present since she's off in her garden camp. We buy two bottles of champagne, and Lamartine, our journalist friend Adams, who'd testified at Tooy's trial, and Céline join us and Tooy in his dining room. Before long, Dúnuyángi makes his appearance, and the five of us are regaled with songs and stories from under the sea.

The warmth of that evening carries over into the morning, when Tooy takes us into the Dúngulálí chamber one last time to formally present our bottle, now ready for the voyage. *Mi kèê fu mafôndò, fu sa sí malóngo vitô,* he tells me, explaining that in Apúku language, *mafôndò* means "myself" and *malóngo vitô* "my best friend"—"I cry for myself, that I may see my best friend." He says he sometimes thinks of this when I'm far away. He also gives us each a waist-tie óbia that he's been making over the past couple of days and which, he says, will keep all manner of evil at bay. Together we drink some Dúngulálí liquid in a calabash. None of us likes goodbyes. He sings us out the door, *Aladjímèèdji-e, aladjímèèdji-o, téé na alosúgbe.* May our trip be safe.

REFLECTIONS FROM
THE VERANDAH

★ 01012007 ★

Batesú batesú—"Each person has his way of speaking," "Each country has
its wisdom," or "What Father taught you isn't what he taught me."
SARAMAKA PROVERB, in Komantí language

In his Nobel Lecture, *The Antilles: Fragments of Epic Memory*, Derek Walcott
spoke of what captive Africans brought to the New World:

> Deprived of their original language, the captured . . . tribes create their own,
> accreting and secreting fragments of an old, an epic vocabulary . . . from Af-
> rica, but to an ancestral, an ecstatic rhythm in the blood that cannot be sub-
> dued by slavery. . . . The original language dissolves from the exhaustion of
> distance like fog trying to cross an ocean. . . . The stripped man is driven back
> to that self-astonishing, elemental force, his mind. That is the basis of the An-
> tillean experience, this shipwreck of fragments, these echoes, these shards of a
> huge tribal vocabulary, these partially remembered customs, and they are not
> decayed but strong. They survived the Middle Passage.[1]

One day in 2005, quite spontaneously, Tooy gave me his own version: "When
the Old Ones came out from Africa, they couldn't bring their *óbia* pots and
stools—but they knew how to summon their gods and have them make new
ones on this side. They no longer had the original pots or stools, but they
carried the knowledge in their hearts."

Tooy's remark evokes both some of what was lost in the Middle Passage
and some of what his captive African ancestors successfully carried to the
Americas. Along with the rest of what he has taught me, it suggests as well
that it may be time to lay to rest the hoary academic debate between those
who stress African continuities in the Americas (including the ongoing importance of African "ethnicities") and those who stress the Africans' creation of institutions in the New World.[2]

For most scholars of the diaspora, the broadest historical question remains how—in each New World colony—enslaved Africans, coming from a
variety of nations and languages, became African Americans. To begin to explore these processes, across the many regions where Africans were landed
as captive laborers, we must first ask: How "ethnically" homogeneous (or
heterogeneous) were the Africans who arrived in a particular New World

locality—in other words, to what extent was there a clearly dominant group—and what were the cultural consequences? How quickly and in what ways did they and their African American offspring begin thinking and acting as members of new communities? In what ways did the African arrivants choose—and to what extent were they able—to continue particular ways of thinking and doing things that came from the Old World? What did "Africa" (or its subregions and peoples) mean at different times to African arrivants and their descendants? And how did the various demographic profiles and social conditions of particular New World settings encourage or inhibit these cultural processes? In short, what is it that made what Haitian anthropologist Michel-Rolph Trouillot calls "the miracle of creolization" possible, across the Americas, over and over again?[3]

The Saramaka world that Tooy inhabits provides rich grist for the historian's mill. In this final section of the book, I try to apply some of the lessons that this Saramaka experience offers up. It is my hope that Tooy's wisdom, and the generous ways he has allowed me to share parts of his life, may help us break the ideological logjam that continues to make it difficult for scholars to provide clear answers to the question of how Africans, drawing on "that self-astonishing, elemental force" and that "ancestral, . . . ecstatic rhythm in the blood," remade themselves in the Americas.

* * *

Tooy's religion is eminently practical.[4] He calls on gods and óbias and ancestors to help with life's problems. And these powers participate in their individual capacities in his social world, just as family members and other people do. The detailed stories that Tooy tells about the historical origins of these powers relate on the one hand to Africa, on the other to Suriname. Both form an integral part of his world.

Some of what Tooy identifies as African powers and practices, such as the apínti rhythms Wíi taught Antamá (who in turn taught Gadien, who taught others who eventually taught Tooy), or Gweyúnga's prowess as master of the rains, crossed the waters in the "hearts" of captives. Others came later, such as the four warrior gods (including Sáka-Amáfu) whom Tooy's Lángu ancestors summoned with a trumpet to come over from Africa near the end of the war in the mid-eighteenth century, or Dúnguláli-Óbia, which Akoomí, an "African-ghost-spirit" (Nêngèkôndè-Nêngè), taught Kódji in the early twentieth century. For Tooy, Africa and its remembered place-names—Komantí, Luángu, Dáome, and others—give each of the powers associated with them, whenever they made the Atlantic crossing, a special cachet of authenticity and strength.

But those powers that Tooy sees as originating in the New World are no less important to him or other Saramakas. From the whole cult of Papágádu (or Vodú) to that of Apúkus, many of the most esoteric, powerful, and dangerous aspects of Saramaka ritual are believed to have been "discovered" by their ancestors only after they established themselves in the rainforest. In the course of this book, Tooy has shared numerous detailed stories of discovery—from his ancestors finding the three great Apúku spirits Mavúngu, Malúndu, and Bayúngu in the Suriname forest to their discovering the whole complex of Papá (drums, songs, language) in an abandoned cemetery, and from Kaásipúmbu's inadvertent killing of Mênde while purifying the river (which began the process by which Saramakas learned about Wátawenú [anaconda] spirits) to the revelation of the whole gaán-óbia cult of Yáka-ósu by an avenging spirit in the head of the captain of Tooy's village in the early twentieth century.

What Tooy's ancestors were in most cases *not* able to bring with them on the ships seems clear enough: in addition to "óbia pots and stools" (and other material objects), what couldn't cross the ocean were most of the traditional African institutions themselves.[5] Members of kingdoms and villages of differing status came, but different status systems could not. Priests and priestesses arrived, but priesthoods and temples had to be left behind. Princes and princesses crossed the ocean, but courts and monarchies could not. Commanders and foot soldiers came, but armies could not.

Yet, as Tooy's teachings make clear, immense quantities of knowledge, information, and belief were transported in the hearts and minds of the captive Africans. Moreover, even though they came from many different ethnic and linguistic groups and were rarely in a position to carry on specific cultural traditions from their home societies, these people shared a number of cultural orientations that, from a broad comparative perspective, characterized most West and Central African societies. Despite the variety of sociocultural forms from one African society to the next, certain underlying principles and assumptions were widespread: ideas about the way the world functions phenomenologically (ideas about causality, how particular causes are revealed, the active role of the dead in the lives of the living, and the intimate relationship between social conflict and illness or misfortune);[6] ideas about social relations (what values motivate individuals, how one deals with others in social situations, the complementarity and relative independence of males and females, matters of interpersonal style); ideas about reciprocity and exchange (compensation for social offenses, the use of cloth as currency); and broad aesthetic ideas (an appreciation of call-and-response rhythms and sharp color contrasts, attitudes toward symmetry and syncopation). These common orientations to reality would have focused the attention of individuals from West and Central African societies upon similar *kinds* of events, even though the culturally prescribed ways of handling them might be quite diverse in terms of their specific form. To cite one example: historically, the Yoruba "deified" their twins at birth, enveloping their lives and deaths in complex rituals, while the neighboring Igbo summarily killed twins at birth—but both peoples might be seen to be responding to the same set of underlying principles having to do with the supernatural significance of unusual births, an idea widespread in West and Central Africa.

Some of these shared assumptions played pivotal roles both during initial creolization and in subsequent change. West and Central African logics of communion with the divine, for example, permitted spirit mediums to authorize a plethora of new institutions. And this process, as we have seen, continued through Kódji's time right up to the present. Indeed, the importance of spirit possession as a means for the transmission of historical as well as spiritual knowledge was something I only dimly understood before I met Tooy. As we have seen, for example, Sensiló's *óbia* Flibánti has taught Tooy (and me!) much about what goes on underneath the sea, but he was also an eyewitness to key eighteenth-century events, particularly those involving Kwasímukámba, and is in a privileged position to provide authorized versions of "what really happened." When I wrote *First-Time* and tried to lay out the various ways that Saramakas transmitted (and masked) history, the teachings of spirits in possession were not something I even mentioned.

Many of the captive African arrivants also shared a religious model that we might call additive or composite or agglomerative (in contrast to exclusivistic). African religion was always practical, and borrowing and incorporation were common. In Dahomey, to cite but one example, where practitioners themselves describe their religious ideas as "composite" in terms of their origin, "the importance of imported deities within the *vodun* corpus is complemented locally by the stress placed on foreign languages in *vodun* rituals and initiations. . . . Through the retention of these diverse languages, the unique histories of the *vodun* powers are at once recalled and promoted."[7] This type of agglomerative model, stressing esoteric languages and unique histories, provided an important framework for the development of the religious world that Tooy inhabits today.

★ ★ ★

The African origins of Suriname slaves, 1675–1725

	1675–1700	1701–1725	TOTAL
Windward Coast ("Mandingos")	4%	—	2%
Gold Coast ("Koromantees")	12%	13%	13%
Bight of Benin ("Papas")	41%	50%	45%
Bight of Biafra ("Calabaris")	3%	1%	2%
Loango/Angola ("Loangos" or "Kongos")	40%	36%	38%

For present purposes, "Windward Coast" corresponds to the coastal regions between modern Senegal and Côte d'Ivoire, Gold Coast is roughly coterminous with modern Ghana, Bight of Benin corresponds to the coastal regions of present-day Togo and Benin and the western coast of Nigeria, Bight of Biafra covers the region from the Niger Delta to the mouth of the Duala River, and Loango/Angola stretches from Cape Lopez south to the Orange River.

Where did the Africans who became Saramakas come from? The table above gives the latest figures from the *Transatlantic Slave Trade Database*[8] for the formative period of Saramaka society, whose outer limits we can place roughly between 1675 and 1725, and whose heart we can place between 1690 and 1712.[9]

Three broad African regions—the Bight of Benin, Loango/Angola, and in a far smaller proportion, the Gold Coast—were, then, the main ancestral homelands of Saramakas. What can we say about each during the relevant period?

The Bight of Benin (the "Slave Coast"), through which nearly half of the enslaved Africans who became Saramakas during the formative period of the society were shipped, was an area of many small states and kingdoms. Dominated by the kingdoms of Allada and Whydah until their conquest in the 1720s by the kingdom of Dahomey, it was inhabited mainly by speakers of what are today known as the Gbe languages (Ewè, Gèn, Ajá, Fòn).[10] Nonetheless, "Despite their distant-past linguistic connections, the . . . Gbè dialect cluster speakers never shared the same political allegiance or identity. In fact, the constituent political groups often warred against each other in ways quite profitable to the European slave traders on the coast. It was these European traders who first grouped the Gbè speakers together under a sequence of shared 'trade marks,' such as 'Rada' and 'Mina'"[11]—and, I would add, "Papa." Robin Law,[12] reviewing all available sources, concludes that the majority of slaves shipped through Slave Coast ports in these years were in fact prisoners of war and that "geographically, the slaves . . . were drawn from an extensive area" stretching far into the interior. One of his

late seventeenth-century sources asserts that twenty or thirty different na-
tionalities of slaves were sold at Whydah alone. And Law points out that "a
significant proportion of the slaves sold on the Slave Coast, in fact, came
not from the Gbe-speaking communities, but from their Yoruba-speaking
neighbors to the north and north-east," and, moreover, that during the late
seventeenth century, the area around Little Popo (a major slave-shipping
port) was largely made up of immigrants escaping the wars of the Gold
Coast. So, the Bight of Benin supplied Suriname not only with captive Gbe
speakers from a number of states at war with one another, but also Yoruba
speakers from the north and speakers of Gold Coast languages from the west.
At the moment they were forced onboard for the Middle Passage, these diverse people certainly did not share any common political or ethnic identity,
though they did bear whatever common label (Papa for the Dutch, Rada for
the French, Mina for the Portuguese . . .) the slave traders marked them with.
However, a goodly proportion of these people did share other things—for
example, "The diverse cultures occupying this region share[d] . . . a belief
in *vodun*, mysterious forces or powers that govern the world and the lives
of those who reside in it."[13] Such beliefs, and the linguistic, ritual, and cor-
poral practices that went with them—as well as the agglomerative model
already cited—were certainly part of what these "Papa" people were able to
"carry in their hearts" across the Atlantic to Suriname.

Loango/Angola was the African origin for more than one in three Saramaka ancestors. I have already quoted Joseph Miller on the geographic
origins of the slaves shipped through the West Central African ports of
the kingdom of Loango, much favored by the Dutch (see pp. 52–53, above).
To recapitulate briefly: forest peoples from modern southern Gabon were
prominent among the slaves whom the Dutch traders boarded, but after
1670, ever more distant parts of Central Africa were exploited, with the
BaVili traders assembling peoples of increasingly diverse origins to bring
to Loango; overall, the cargos brought by the BaVili to Loango in the early
years of the eighteenth century—when Tooy's remembered ancestors
arrived on that coast—were notable for "the extreme diversity of backgrounds they brought onto the ships." Nonetheless, there were undoubtedly various cultural assumptions shared by these diverse speakers of Bantu
languages that would have set them off from those shared by what Matory
playfully calls "the Voodoo Nation"[14] ("Papa," the peoples of the Bight of Benin) or the "Koromantin" peoples of the even more geographically distant
Akan states.

The Gold Coast provided about one in eight of Saramaka ancestors during the society's fifty-year formative period.[15] Slaves shipped through the

Dutch fort at Koromantin included Fanti, Ashanti, and a large number of other interior Gold Coast peoples, many of whom spoke a language of the family now called Akan. Loyalty or identity in the region was "likely to be to a village, or perhaps one of dozens of independent, often hostile states."[16] From 1670 on—the period that interests us here—larger, more powerful states emerged: "Denkyira, Akwamu, Axim, and Asante," which "fought frequently among themselves."[17] Many of the slaves who were shipped through Koromantin were prisoners of war. Many seem, as well, to have been soldiers. Like the people who came from each of the other two main shipment zones for captives bound for Suriname, despite their internal political and ethnic differences the people of this region tended to share more, culturally, with one another than they did with those from the other two regions.

The data of historical demography, then, tell us that the captives arriving in Suriname hailed primarily from three broad regions of Africa—the Bight of Benin, West Central Africa, and, to a lesser extent, the Gold Coast— that they spoke a large number of languages, and that they came from scores of different states and polities that were in many cases at war with one another. Yet despite their considerable internal cultural and political diversity, the peoples of each of the three regions shared more with one another than they did with those of the other two, owing to linguistic affinities, to trade and conquest, and to other kinds of intercourse over the centuries.[18]

*   *   *

My own research in the history of Suriname, and that of a number of other scholars, shows that once landed in the colony, each shipload of captive Africans was further dispersed by the planters, who chose their purchases with the specific intent to separate people who might have known each other or spoken the same language.[19] Combined with a firm policy not to separate slave families when plantations were sold—the slaves in Suriname were considered to belong to the soil—the primary identity of enslaved Africans rapidly shifted from their African origins to their plantation community, where they now had family and comrades, and where they had already begun to bury their dead. On the plantations (as among Saramakas today), the term for "best friend" was *máti*, which derived from "shipmate." And the Africans who lived together on a plantation soon began calling one another *síbi*, which had originated as a term of address for those who had shared passage on the same ship.

Within the earliest decades of the African presence in Suriname, the slaves had developed a new creole language (Sranan-tongo and, on the largely Jewish Suriname River plantations, the closely related Dju-tongo), the core of a new religion, and much else.[20] The striking "non-European-ness" of this early cultural synthesis, when compared to developments in other parts of the Americas, can be explained in part by the unusually high ratio of Africans to Europeans in the colony—more than 25:1 for much of the eighteenth century, with figures ranging up to 65:1 in the plantation districts.[21] On Suriname plantations, it was in large part recently arrived Africans (rather than Europeans) who effected the process of creolization. The central motor might best be termed "inter-African syncretism," for Suriname creolization was built on a diversity of African heritages, with far smaller inputs from European and Amerindian sources. What Walcott called "this shipwreck of fragments, these echoes, these shards of a huge tribal vocabulary, these partially remembered customs" became, for those African captives on early Suriname plantations, the building blocks of a new civilization. When the ancestors of the Saramakas escaped into the forest during the late seventeenth and early eighteenth centuries, they carried with them the seeds of a powerful cultural system.[22]

★   ★   ★

The great bulk of the people who, once in the forest, became known as Saramakas escaped from Suriname's plantations between 1690 and 1712. With very rare exceptions (such as Tooy's ancestor Antamá), they had been born in Africa. Most were men and most were young, still in their teens or twenties. Most had spent little time in slavery, more often months than years. By the time of their escapes, however, most spoke Dju-tongo (or the closely related Sranan-tongo), which they then very quickly developed into their own distinctive language, Saramaccan. As they faced the challenge of building institutions—political, family, religious—while waging war and trying to survive in an unfamiliar and hostile environment, they drew on the immense riches of their African pasts, though their relative youth meant that much of the esoteric and specialized knowledge of their home-lands was not available to them. Leadership drew authority not only from personal charisma and knowledge but also from divination, which encour-aged the communal negotiation of developing institutions. The runaways, fighting for their individual and collective survival, had strong incentives for rapid nation-building.

Among the initial African-born Saramakas, some of those who shared a broad regional origin—the "Komantís," "Papas," or "Loangos"—were undoubtedly the core who "invented" each "tradition" of playing particular drums and conducting particular rites together. How could it have been otherwise? But by the time their sons' and daughters' generation had taken over, those "African identities" (which had been created in Suriname through a complex process of ethnogenesis) had faded in salience, replaced by powerful new clan and village identities. The second generation of men had learned from their fathers, from their mothers' brothers, and from other elders. The cults of Papá, Komantí, and Luángu had already been effectively separated from their shared-African-region inventors to become part of a new system that included Apúku, Papágádu, Wátawenú, the cult of ancestors, and much more. Saramakas, with their love of expressive culture, celebrated using and sustaining the distinctive verbal and musical registers of each of these cults, saying, like Tooy, batesú batesú and "This is how you say it in Apúku, but here's how you say it in Papá."

As they confronted their new environment, these early Saramakas learned about local gods through a process of trial and error, drawing on a tightly interwoven complex of pan-sub-Saharan African ideas and practices regarding illness, divination, and causality. A misfortune (whether an illness or other affliction) automatically signaled the need for divination, which in turn revealed a cause. Often this cause turned out to be a local deity previously unknown to them (since they had never before lived in this particular environment). The idea that local deities could cause illness when they were offended (for example, when a field was cut too close to their abode in a large tree or boulder) was widespread in rural West and Central Africa. But the classification of local deities as well as the identities of individual deities in Africa varied significantly from one society to another.

These early Saramakas frequently engaged in communal divination, with people from a diversity of African origins asking questions together (through a spirit medium or other divinatory agent) of a god or ancestor in order to grasp the nature of the kinds of gods that now surrounded them. The detailed pictures that emerged of the personality, family connections, abode, whims, and foibles of each local deity permitted the codification by the nascent community of new religious institutions—classes of gods such as Vodús (boa constrictor deities) and their close cousins Wátawenús (anaconda deities) or Apúkus (forest spirits), each with a complex and distinctive cult, including shrines, drum/dance/song "plays," languages, and priests and priestesses. Indeed, such public divination, an arena for the communal creation of new cultural forms, worked as effectively as it did in part because of the widespread African preference for additivity over exclusivity in most religious contexts.

Linguistic and ritual evidence suggests that it was people born in those Bight of Benin cultures where snake gods were central who took the lead in developing the Saramaka Papágádu/Vodú complex, but that same evidence shows that there was significant participation also by Central Africans in this early syncretic process. Similarly, people from the Gold Coast seem to have taken the lead in developing warrior rites, but again Central African contributions are significant.[23] And, as people classified as "Papa" constituted nearly 50% of the initial Saramaka population, it makes sense that some of them would have drummed and sung together, and that within the developing ritual system, the Papá complex that they created (which, like Komantí, sang largely about New World, not African, events and people) would be passed on and learned by other men who felt an affinity with it.[24]

Saramaka accounts of the origin of their twin rituals provides one example of how they envision the process of discovery that they see as having so marked their early years in the forest. Here, the metaphor is not divination but a different kind of divine intervention. It nevertheless represents a precise Saramaka way of speaking about the process of legitimizing a newly created institution that took place nearly three centuries earlier. The story, as recounted in 1978 by my late Saramaka friend Peléki, runs as follows:

Ma Zoé was an early Wátambíi-clan runaway. Once in the forest, she gave birth to twins. One day she went to her garden, leaving the infants in a nearby open shed. But when she returned for them, she saw a large monkey sitting right next to them. So she hid to watch what would happen. She was afraid that if she startled the animal, it might grab the children and carry them into the trees. She was beside herself and didn't know what to do. So she just kept watch. She saw that the monkey had amassed a large pile of selected leaves. It was breaking them into pieces. Then it put them into an earthenware pot and placed it on the fire. When the leaves had boiled awhile, it removed them and poured the leaves into a calabash. With this it washed the child. Exactly the way a mother washes a child! Then it shook the water off the child and put it down. Then it did the same with the other child. Finally, it took the calabash of leaf water and gave some to each child to drink. The woman saw all this. Then, when it was finished, the monkey set out on the path. It didn't take the twins with it! And the mother came running to her children. She examined the leaves—which ones it had given them to drink, which had been used for washing. And those are the very leaves that remain with us today for the great Wátambíi twin óbia.[25]

Today, this Wátambíi cult services all twins born in Saramaka, involving their parents and siblings in a complex set of rituals that draw on ideas and practices from a variety of West and Central African societies (such as the widespread African association of twins with monkeys). From an anthropological perspective, Peléki, who was himself a twin and therefore a frequent witness to the Wátambíi rites, is describing—through this metaphorical historical fragment relating a Saramaka discovery—a particularly pure example of the process of inter-African syncretism.

⋆   ⋆   ⋆

Our first outsiders' view of what Saramaka religion looked like dates from the middle of the eighteenth century, thanks to the detailed diaries of the German Moravian missionaries who were sent out to live in Saramaka villages right after the 1762 peace treaty with the colonists.[26] What we learn is that Saramaka religion was already, in its main lines, remarkably similar to its present form, with frequent spirit possession and other forms of divination; a strong ancestor cult; and institutionalized cults for the Apúku and Vodú gods encountered in the forest, for the Tonê and Wátawenú gods who lived in the river, and for a variety of gods of war.

By the 1760s, Papá, Luángu, or Komantí rites and dances included people and ideas of quite varied (and mixed) African ancestry.[27] Very few African-born Saramakas were still alive, and Saramaka marriage had never been to any degree endogamous according to place of African ancestors' origin. Rather, each of several bundles of rites and drums/dances/songs/language associated with a particular African origin (Papá, Luángu, Komantí) was consciously being kept together by these eighteenth-century Saramakas (as they still are today). That is, a young Saramaka in 1760—who might well have been a fourth-generation Afro-Surinamer (as was Alabi, on his father's side), having, say, great-grandparents who hailed from as many as eight different African polities, would learn the bundle of Papá or Komantí or Luángu rites, not because he *was* a Dahomean or Gold Coaster or Kongo "by origin" or by "ethnic identity," but because of the particular meanings and uses these rites had taken on in contemporary Saramaka life.[28] A man learned Papá or Komantí or Luángu because he liked it and believed it could help him. He would later transmit his own knowledge to sons, sisters' sons, or younger friends for the same reason. *Batesú batesú.* All Saramakas, then as now, participated to some extent in such rites, but the responsibility for keeping each bundle discrete and alive fell on its chosen adepts. And these specialists never held a strongly preservationist ethic: gradual change and creativity has always been central to Saramaka ritual, so that the Papá drumming of one generation is expected to be modified (Saramakas would say "improved") by the experts of the next. Kalusé, who's not a bad Papá player, insisted on this point to me in the 1960s, when he demonstrated to me how his generation's way of playing compared with that of his father, Tandó, who was a well-known specialist.

By the mid-eighteenth century, a half century after most Saramakas' ancestors had made their escapes, the plethora of cults (rites/languages/songs/drums) that fell under the umbrella of Saramaka "religion" included some that were supposed to have been brought from Africa (e.g., Komantí, Luángu) and others that were supposed to have been discovered or learned in the Suriname forest (e.g., Papá, Púmbu, Apúku, Vodú/Papágádu, Wátawenú). Many of the *gaán-óbias*, whose ownership was vested in a clan, were said to have been brought by an ancestor from Africa, but others were considered new, discovered in Suriname. Likewise for lesser ritual complexes—*kangáa* (a kind of lie-detector ordeal) or *asêmpè* (a torture used to exact a confession out of an accused witch),[29] both believed to be from Africa, and the "twin" complex learned by Ma Zóe from a monkey in the forest. In other words, Saramakas envisioned various cults, with different origins and serving different purposes, as well as a constant accretion and growth of the whole religious repertoire.

From a historian's perspective, these cults already formed a system, whether or not they were thought of as "African" by Saramakas (and it seems clear that those which Saramakas considered "African" were neither more nor less so than those they considered New World discoveries). Each of the cults that comprised it were thought to have a unique origin along with other unique characteristics (language, drum rhythms, medicinal leaves, etc.). Adepts celebrated the history, language, and other wisdom and accomplishments of each cult as a joy and sacred duty. Individuals, like Tooy today, could become knowledgeable in as many of them as they wished. A half century after the initial Saramaka ancestors fled the plantations, Saramaka culture already represented an integrated, highly developed African-American synthesis whose main processual motor had been inter-African syncretism (which tended to be viewed in Saramaka logic as an ongoing process of discovery). There was ample evidence both of striking African continuities and immense New World creativity. African "ethnicities" had faded from the scene as meaningful markers of personal identity. The impure products of creolization had gone crazy.

Taking the long view, one might say that in 1690, Saramaka society and culture had not yet been born, but that by 1765, when the first window opened to the outside, it was already fully formed. The miracle of creolization, then, occurred over just several decades.

Bombarded by the recent explosion in cultural studies and postcolonial studies of "loose" uses of the creolization metaphor to cover all sorts of contemporary phenomena,[30] I would now opt for limiting its application to a strictly historicized process, one that took place in the earliest decades of each New World settlement. Although in exuberant moments I have occasionally described contemporary culture change in Caribbean societies as "continuous creolization, the ongoing invention and reinvention of unique Atlantic worlds,"[31] it now seems to me more prudent to conceptualize, for example, Saramakas' "discovery" of Wéntis and Dúngul'álí-Óbia (and so much else documented in this book) not as "continuing creolization" but rather as the subsequent unfolding of "creolization-like processes." This retains "creolization" as a strictly historicized set of processes. But it does not deny that societies born through creolization may have distinctive characteristics, especially in terms of cultural dynamism.[32] Indeed, one might even suggest that societies born of creolization—creole societies—are not, as some would have it, unusually poor but unusually rich in cultural resources, in their cultural "building blocks" and "grammar," and, especially, in the processes by which they play with, transform, and remodel these resources into something fresh. Thinking of Saramaka, one might say that from its intertwined African roots, the great tree grew and flourished.

* * *

The best recent studies of "classic" African American religions[33]—Brazilian Candomblé, Cuban Santería, and Haitian Vodou—teach us two lessons. First, the development of New World cults that claim a specific African origin (or have been identified by anthropologists as having one)—*anago, djedje,* and *angola* houses ("Yoruba," "Dahomean," and "Kongo," respectively) in Candomblé, *regla de ocha* and *palo monte* ("Yoruba" and "Kongo," respectively) in Santería, *rada* and *petro* ("Dahomean" and "Kongo") in Vodou—ultimately make sense to practitioners (and now to anthropologists) only as part of distinctive New World systems of oppositions, as part of a new system.[34] As Stephan Palmié writes for Cuba,

> We are dealing with an aggregate formation in which notions deriving from western Central African minkisi cults and Yoruba-derived forms of worship of divine beings known as òrìṣà were jointly conjugated through a single New World history of enslavement, abuse, and depersonalization. In the course of

this process, Yoruba-derived patterns of *oricha* worship and western Central African forms of manipulating minkisi objects, not only underwent parallel changes, but also became morally recalibrated in relation to each other.[35]

Palmié goes on to describe how in the course of the nineteenth century, with the arrival of large numbers of enslaved Yorubas in Cuba, a creolization-like process occurred in which "the two traditions [Yoruba and Central African] not only merged into a larger complex of partly overlapping conceptions and practices but came to offer functionally differentiated ritual idioms that spoke—and continue to speak—to fundamentally different forms of historical experience and contemporary sociality."[36] "Neither ocha nor palo," he continues, "could have evolved to their present phenomenology and moralized positions along a spectrum of differentiated ritual idioms without the presence of the other within the same social framework."[37]

The second lesson of these recent studies, which I will argue is of less relevance to the Saramaka case, is that these "classic" New World African religions—Santería, Candomblé, Vodou—developed and continue to develop in intense and ongoing dialogue with their roots and branches across the Atlantic world. As Matory argues for Candomblé, such religions are best understood as part of a centuries-old and ongoing participation in a circum-Atlantic movement of people, commodities, texts, recordings, photographs, and ideas, and, moreover, many of their central beliefs and practices—long considered "traditional" and "ancient"—in fact emerged only in the nineteenth (or even early twentieth) century.[38]

The first and second generation of Saramakas in the forest also conjugated their gods and other ritual powers, all origins combined, into a system. Komantí came to serve all villages for warfare, though each also possessed other *óbias*, including many for war, brought over from Africa by individual men. The cults of Apúku, Papágádu (Vodú), and Wátawenú became part of the repertoire of every village, and new gods of these types emerged to possess people in the normal course of garden clearing and burning, whenever spirits in trees or boulders, or snakes, were inadvertently disturbed. The use of the *apínti* (talking drum) and the now obsolete wooden trumpet (which also spoke messages) became generalized as well. Deities and practices that had a particular function in an African society were now being recalibrated against each other, changing their function and meaning in the process of nation-building. And by not long before the Peace of 1762, Papá and Adjú had also become the standard "plays" for all Saramaka funerals, joining folktales (*kóntu* or Anasi-tóli), which had become part of the system earlier. Particular villages, then as now, had their ritual specializations, some said to have been brought by an ancestor from Africa (e.g., the Biítu clan's Tonê cult, which Gweyúnga brought from Dahomey), others to have been found by an ancestor in the forest (e.g., the Dómbi clan's Mavúngu). These specializations, particularly the powers that a clan or village had found in the forest (rather than brought from Africa), gave it a unique solidarity and identity. This differentiation of social units according to the specialized ritual knowledge they possessed became an important part of the nation-building project. In other words, these various "more-or-less-creolized African" and "newly discovered" cults were formed into a new Saramaka religious system, in which the roles each played made sense in relationship to those played by the others. And that system permitted the addition of new beliefs and practices, of whatever origin, whenever they were discovered to be useful.

For the first generations of Saramakas, African ethnic identity quickly faded as nation-building progressed.[39] (Never, in several decades of detailed discussion with Saramaka experts about First-Time history—marriages, alliances, enmities—has there been the slightest indication that there was a preference for marriage partners based on a common African origin.) The identity of almost all the bands of runaways who fought their way southward in the early years was already based on a common plantation origin. So what became the matrilineal clans that form the major social units of the society are, in great majority, named for the plantation from which their initial ancestors fled: the Matjáu clan (whose runaway ancestors were owned by Imanuël Machado), Nasí (owned by the Nassy family), Dómbi (owned by the successors of Dominee ["Dómbi"] Basseliers), Biítu (owned by the Britto family), Papútu (owned by the widow Papot), Kasitú (owned by Joseph Castilho), Abaísa (owned by the Labadist ["Labadísa/Abaísa"] religious order), or Wátambíi ("Watermill"). The sole exception is Tooy's Lángu clan, at least part of which (the segment associated with Wíi and Antamá as apical ancestors, rather than that associated with Kaási) originated in a single shipload of Africans who arrived during an international war and quickly escaped together along with some abducted Amerindian women. During the early eighteenth century, as far as whitefolks were concerned, Saramaka villages/groups bore their current clan names, except for two: one group of villages the whites called Klaas-dorpen ("Kaási's villages," after the name of their Lángu leader) and another inhabited by the Abaísas, which they called Papa-dorpen, suggesting that the leadership of this village cluster maintained some sort of Papa identity, along with their Abaísa one.[40] In any case, the great bulk of initial Saramakas seem, from the time they escaped and began to have a common consciousness, to have conceptualized themselves in terms of their new communities (clans) rather than in terms of some sort of African "ethnicity." Anyone could now learn to play "Komantí," "Púmbu," or "Papá." And everyone, in the course of their daily lives, learned a good bit about Apúkus, Vodús, and other local spirits.[41]

That Saramakas consider Púmbu, Apúku, Vodú, or Papá (in contrast to Komantí, Luángu, or Tonê) to be New World discoveries tells us more about the way ideology works in nation-building than it does about the history of these languages and institutions. As in Candomblé, Santería, or Vodou, where "Africa" or Yoruba/Nago/Lukumi or Guiné are privileged ideological markers of continuity and authenticity but mask often-radical historical change, in Saramaka the ideological emphasis on local discovery can mask African continuities. Only long-term linguistic work, on both sides of the ocean and in many societies, will untangle the relationships that I present, in a very preliminary way, in the Coda to this book. Casually asking a graduate student from Accra or Lagos or Brazzaville to translate a Saramaka song, in the Herskovitsian manner, simply will not do. As Wyatt MacGaffey puts it, "In the search for trans-Atlantic parallels and connections, one cannot simply help oneself to traits as though Central African culture, or any other, were a sort of plumbers' supply store to which you can go in search of a widget like the one you have at home; enthusiasm may have to wait on patient labors of translation that recognize that each word, idea, or object is embedded in matrices of language, history, and ritual practice."[42] In other words, I suspect that Apúku may turn out to be as "African" (in this case, West Central African) as Komantí, but I also know how much both are products of (inter-African) creolization.

✳   ✳   ✳

Specialists in Candomblé and Santería have criticized the scholarly tendency to conflate "past" and "Africa" or the idea that "homelands [are] to diasporas as the past is to the present."[43] Matory asserts that "the political and demographic contexts shaping African-American cultures are *seldom* produced through a once-and-for-all departure from Africa and are *seldom* isolated from a broader circum-Atlantic context."[44] Studies by Palmié, Brown, Matory, and others now stress the ongoing dialogues between Africans in the New World and the Old, and the ongoing movements of people, commodities, and ideas around the Black Atlantic over the centuries. Yet these works, which have broken important new theoretical ground, have almost without exception failed to take into account the world of Maroons, whether in Suriname or, for example, in Jamaica[45]—presumably because the Maroon case, of which Saramakas are exemplary, doesn't fit their model. Maroons, from this perspective, exemplify Matory's "*seldom.*"

A more balanced judgment might posit two extremes in the development of African diasporic culture—on the one hand, the plantation/Maroon case, which was marked by early, rapid creolization; and, on the other hand, what occurred within the slave (and free black) sector of such cities as Havana and Salvador (Bahia), where creolization-like processes took hold much later, as new "African nations" came to dominate cultural life through a kind of ethnogenesis. In these urban contexts, the arrival of large numbers of enslaved Africans in the mid-nineteenth century meant that something resembling my "initial creolization" was ongoing as late as the second half of the nineteenth and the first half of the twentieth century, when Santería and Candomblé were largely developed and elaborated.

In any case, the ancestors of the Saramakas *did* pretty much leave Africa "once-and-for-all." Admittedly, during the first few decades of the society, they continued to welcome new recruits who were African born, but this had slowed to a trickle by the second half of the eighteenth century. And after that, many of their descendants of course interacted with people on the coast of Suriname and later in French Guiana, of whom a few would have been African born. But on the whole, the dialogues that truly marked Saramaka culture history were among the original African captives themselves, those people who, miraculously, built their new society and culture over a period of less than half a century. What was learned through subsequent dialogues—whether between Tooy's uncle and his three African friends in early twentieth-century Mana or between Tembái and the Brazilian immigrants in French Guiana who may have shaped his depiction of water spirits, or any number of other such encounters mentioned in this book—was icing on the cake.[46]

Social theory has recently been giving the study of "memory" and "continuities" something of a bad name. (The concept of "memory," of course, had played a signal role in the early twentieth-century debates between Herskovits and E. Franklin Frazier, who argued that Africa was, for African Americans, little but a "forgotten memory.") Matory argues that the agency of Africans has too often been ignored in narratives that stress "memory" and what he calls the "passive preservation" of "Africanisms."[47] David Scott, while recognizing that the kind of Afro-American anthropology pioneered by Herskovits and practiced by myself "manifests a deep, humanist inclination toward a story about continuities and embraces the earnest task of demonstrating the integrity and the intactness of the old in the new, and of the past in the present," nevertheless suggests that scholars must move beyond the (what he considers politically suspect) attempt "to place the 'culture' of the ex-African/ex-slave in relation to what we might call an authentic past, that is, an anthropologically identifiable, ethnologically recoverable, and textually representable past" and instead focus on "discourse."[48] Rosalind Shaw states the case more generally: "Given that disjuncture, rupture, and instability currently enjoy analytic privilege, a focus on memory as reproduction raises problematic issues of the historical continuity of social and cultural forms."[49]

I would suggest, however, that my own studies of Saramaka life and history, including the present work, place Saramaka agency and the politics of memory at their center. From the introduction to *First-Time*, which patiently lays out the importance of subject position and power in the Saramaka politics of knowledge (stressing the role of individual and clan interests, the ways that negotiation and strategic reshaping determine what is and is not passed on to the next generation), "memory" is analyzed as socially contingent, always subject to human agency.[50] I read Tooy's teachings as encouraging us, as scholars of the diaspora, to move beyond debates about "memory" and "forgetting" in order to explore the complex politics of self-representation and identity through time. We must remain focused on the historical conditions of cultural production. We must take account of conflict as well as consensus in representing culture and demonstrate its role in shaping and reshaping institutions. We must grant full agency to African Americans, recognizing them as the central actors in the construction of their cultures (as well as privileged spokesmen on their representation). We must remain focused on process and change, the ways certain continuities become privileged, the ways certain discontinuities become masked—the politics of culture through time. Where relevant (as in the case of Candomblé, Santería, or Vodou), we must explore dialogue between people in different class positions and in often distant places throughout the Americas and Africa. Historicization and contextualization remain a primary responsibility. And we must continue to do careful ethnography. For when all is said and done, all of our theories (whether about creolization, transnationalism, globalization, or whatever) depend on the adequacies of that ethnography—long-term immersion in diasporic sites and situations, command of the relevant languages, and, ultimately, earning the trust and respect of our interlocutors.[51]

It is also worth mentioning that in an oral culture such as that of the Saramakas, the mechanics and politics of memory—collective memory—are active subjects of Saramaka interest (not just that of anthropological theorists). Tooy has given us many examples of his deep concerns about learning and teaching, and the preservation and loss of knowledge. From the perspective of men like Asipéi and Tebíni and Gaamá Agbagó, whom I worked with in the 1960s and 1970s, it was men of their late uncles' or grandfathers' generations, like Pobôsi or Kódji, who "really knew things." For Tooy or Sensiló, it's men like Tebíni (who, Tooy once told me, was the first to teach him the story of how Kaási purified the river) or Sensiló's father's brother Asipéi who play this role of revered teachers now deceased. In our own society, anyone who really wants to learn about the past can become erudite in much the same way someone could have fifty years ago; in an oral society such as Saramaka, that is not true in the same way. Tooy was voicing a much-repeated complaint when he told me one day, "Saramakas have one fault. When an older kinsman tells you that you're the one to whom he's going to pass on a piece of knowledge, he'll always leave out three words, saving them for the day he's dying. But what if you're not there that day?" *First-Time* is peppered with further examples of this Saramaka anxiety. Indeed, the introduction to that book ends with an image that I intended as rather more than a nod to the anthropological trope of disappearing peoples:

> Some years ago, shortly before his death, the tribal chief's older "brother" Kositán addressed a large political gathering. Among his words, as remembered today, was a poignant image of the disappearance of First-Time knowledge. "The canoe of knowledge [*sábibóto*] of the Matjáu clan. . . . As it was about to 'go' forever, I caught a glimpse of it just as it passed that tree there [he indicated a tree downstream from the landing place]. Not a single other person still here [alive] even saw its wake. Only me." I often think of how much later it was when I caught my own glimpse of that canoe, which was even farther downstream, and ever increasing its rush toward the open sea.

For Saramaka men-of-knowledge like Tebíni, who taught me so much about First-Time in the 1970s, or Tooy, whom I met nearly thirty years later, the preservation of knowledge, the preservation of what they conceptualize as "memories," is a sacred duty, even as it is fraught with danger. There is nothing "passive" about their engagement with such knowledge—we are in the realm of the politics of memory. And as we have seen, the kind of knowledge that Tooy holds dearest is singularly circumscribed, restricted, and guarded. The opening paragraphs of *First-Time* explain why: "It is the fountainhead of collective identity; it contains the true root of what it means to be Saramaka."

*   *   *

In certain respects, Saramaka "religion" resembles the classic African American trio of Candomblé, Santería, and Vodou. Matory's initial sketch of Candomblé, for example, might make a reasonable beginning for Saramaka. Calling it a "religion of divination, sacrifice, healing, music, dance, and spirit possession," he adds that

> the only rival to its beauty is its complexity. . . . Believers attribute miraculous powers and exemplary flaws to gods. . . . The adventures, personalities, and kinship relations of these supernatural beings are described in an extensive mythology and body of oracular wisdom, which also serve to explain the personalities and fates of their human worshipers. . . . Through blood sacrifice and lavish ceremonies of spirit possession, the gods are persuaded to intervene beneficently in the lives of their worshipers and to keep the foes of those worshipers at bay.[52]

In the Saramaka case, one key feature that this leaves out is the major role that ancestors, and the dead in general, play in human affairs, and all the rites that this produces. Specific ancestors form the core of Saramaka spiritual concerns, far more than they do for adherents of these three other religions.

But there are other significant differences. For example, while the lavishly costumed deities of Candomblé are "all . . . represented as royals and nobles . . . arrayed in the crowns, swords, jewels, money, and sumptuous clothing associated with their aristocratic and cultured social class," Saramaka possession involves gods and *óbias* and ancestors who are normal people (or animals), not royals or nobles.[53] Saramaka possession also seems far more "raw" and less theatrical (it is not for an audience), far more family- and village-focused. It is closely tied to features of the local landscape: rocks, trees, streams, and other places that are intimate parts of village life.[54] Moreover, all three of the "classic" (and we might say more cosmopolitan) African American religions integrate all sorts of Western (Roman Catholic, Masonic, Spiritist) influences that are largely absent in the relatively isolated religion of Saramakas, which has stuck largely within its own inter-African logics of development, forged during initial creolization.

The spiritual life of Saramakas contrasts in another way with those of participants in the better-known trio. As I have mentioned, "religion" is not a separate or separable realm of life for Saramakas—it has no name—and undoubtedly, this has something to do with its relative analytical invisibility in scholarly and popular discussions of African American religions.[55]

But the single most important contrast between these other religions and the one that Tooy has shared with us throughout this book has to do with

the relationship of each to the larger society that surrounds it. Matory, focused on Candomblé, highlights what's at stake when he differentiates the
history of that religion from the process of creolization outlined by Mintz
and Price in the early 1970s.[56]

> If the term "creolization" is taken to imply that . . . each local African-Ameri-
> can religion quickly formed a bounded, internally integrated, and enduring
> "system" highly resistant to exogenous change, then a different term must be
> sought to describe the history of Candomblé [and we might add Santería and
> Vodou], where exogenous transformations have been as central as any quick-
> forming foundations.

And he adds a telling aside: "The local institutions of the racist American
republics have never been big enough to contain the communal imagina-
tions and aspirations of African-American peoples."[57]

Therein, perhaps, lies one key. In the case of Candomblé, Santería, or Vodou (where the Catholic Church and the State have periodically conducted
extermination campaigns even in the countryside), adherents have always
lived in "racist [or at least classist] American republics" and their religions
have provided various transnational bridges and escapes, however ephem-
eral. In the case of Saramakas, their religion (and their whole culture) was
forged after a radical and successful break with a racist colony, and its self-
conscious ideology has always been to maintain that separation. Saramaka
religion, then, was indeed "quickly formed" into "a bounded, internally
integrated, and enduring 'system' highly resistant to exogenous change," a
system that had the freedom to develop internally and with little interfer-
ence from racist republics. Which is why, in a sense, Herskovits was able
to view it as the most "African" of all Afro-American religions.[58] It is also
why Mintz and Price considered it the clearest exemplar of "creolization."
And it is why Tooy can conceptualize Komantís and Wéntis, Tonê gods and
Dúnguláli-Óbia as part of a seamless whole that guides his life, as it did that
of his ancestors.[59]

★　★　★

For readers who would like to celebrate or marvel at some of the strongest
African continuities in the Americas (and this in a society that—unlike, say,
urban Brazil or Cuba—has been largely cut off from its African roots for
three centuries), this book should provide a feast. For those readers who are
looking for evidence of creolization and creativity, there should be plenty to
savor as well. Looking at the whole of Saramaka life, including but not lim-

ited to esoteric ritual knowledge, it should be clear that, even in this "most African" of African American societies, direct formal continuities from Africa are more the exception than the rule; nor is some sort of African ideological purity an ideal in any realm of Saramaka life. The legacy of rapid, early creolization is everywhere, as is evidence of unbounded ongoing creativity. In the consciousness of the people who David Scott says have become, thanks to the work of Melville Herskovits and myself (and I'd add Frances and Sally), "a sort of anthropological metonym . . . providing the exemplary arena in which to argue out certain anthropological claims about a discursive domain called Afro-America,"[60] it seems fitting that such figures as "Africa," "slavery," "marronage," "warfare," and "peace"—and, ultimately, "discovery" or "creolization"—form such a seamless whole. The history of this remarkable people, as exemplified in Tooy's version, stands as a testament to the struggles of generations of captive Africans and their descendants who, against all odds, built lives of rare grace, beauty, and wisdom.

Walcott, in his Nobel Lecture, spoke about the concurrent joy, solemnity, and obligation of bearing witness to what we may call, with Trouillot, the miracle of creolization.

> There is a force of exultation, a celebration of luck, when a writer finds himself a witness to the early morning of a culture that is defining itself, branch by branch, leaf by leaf, in that self-defining dawn, which is why, especially at the edge of the sea, it is good to make a ritual of the sunrise. Then the noun the "Antilles" [but for me, it's "Saramaka"] ripples like brightening water, and the sounds of leaves, palm fronds, and birds are the sounds of a fresh dialect, the native tongue. The personal vocabulary, the individual melody whose metre is one's biography, joins in that sound, with any luck, and the body moves like a walking, a waking island.
>
> This is the benediction that is celebrated, a fresh language and a fresh people, and this is the frightening duty owed.[61]

It is this exultant joy and frightening duty that, with Tooy's help, I have tried however imperfectly to communicate in this text.

CODA: ESOTERIC LANGUAGE

⋆ TIP OF THE ICEBERG ⋆

Tip of the iceberg in four senses. First, only a small portion of what Saramakas once knew of esoteric language and lore remains today (that is, there has been genuine loss through the generations). Second, Tooy—though very well versed in these matters—like any Saramaka "expert," knows only a very tiny proportion of what Saramakas today collectively know. Third, I have heard and recorded only a sampling of what Tooy knows. And fourth, esoteric language is usually associated with music, drumming, and dance, so what I present here bears the same relationship to Saramaka realities as a screenplay to a film or a libretto to the performance of an opera.

For each esoteric language, I give a list of lexical items, followed by a list of phrases that are not in Saramaccan syntax and a list of phrases that consist of Saramaccan syntax and words with esoteric words inserted. An unknown proportion of the explanations (definitions) of esoteric words given by Tooy (or other Saramakas) falls into the class of folk etymologies (or, sometimes, guesses), particularly when given in response to my pressing for "breakdowns" of phrases whose use/meaning were learned as a unit. (Tooy has often memorized esoteric language phrases, along with appropriate context for their use, in this way.) I did not systematically elicit the lists of lexical items in the various esoteric languages, instead following Tooy's lead with what he chose to tell me in the course of our conversations and interactions.

The great bulk of the phrases and words reported here appear earlier in the book, and are referenced by page number to provide fuller context. In some cases, phrases or words are presented here for the first time, because I simply couldn't find a place to squeeze them into the narrative; these are indicated by an asterisk. And there are several cases of esoteric phrases I have published in some other book that I present here as supplementary examples (always identified as such).

In my translations, I use English equivalents for normal Saramaccan words and place the words in esoteric languages in italics. Note that in songs, diacritics (accents) often shift from their place in normal speech. Moreover, there is significant phonological variation in different performances (or utterances) of the same esoteric language song or spoken phrase.

· I have, with some ambivalence, provided possible African-language etymologies for lexical items whenever I (or, more often, helpful colleagues) could find them, placing them always between curly brackets. Because I spent the final two years of work on this book based in Martinique, away from university libraries, I have been unable to spend significant time with the relevant African-language dictionaries. In any case, I would imagine that, in terms of using these esoteric languages as markers of complex historical processes, their lexicons might be less revealing than their semantics, and their semantics less than their grammars and pragmatics.[1] Even with tracing lexical items (which include here only those that Tooy was able to gloss in Saramaccan), the methodological hazards are enormous—which dictionaries of African languages are available? From what eras (given the significant language change over the centuries since the ancestors of Saramakas left Africa)? How can dictionaries written for the most part by Christian missionaries reveal much about "native" religions (much of which might have been deliberately hidden from them)?[2] But more important, what does the lexicon of a language really tell us about the rest of a culture (what does the lexicon of Komantí tell us about the practices of Komantí-men)? The lexicon of standard (everyday) Saramaccan, for example, is something like 35% English-derived, 25% Portuguese-derived, 5% derived from Amerindian, Dutch, or French, and 35% derived from one or another African language, though a complete dictionary of Saramaccan (including esoteric languages) would raise the African contribution to 50%.[3] But those percentages would still wildly exaggerate the European input into Saramaka culture taken as a whole. Cultures do not consist of isolated traits any more than languages do of isolated words. That both Apúku and Papá have independent versions of Macaque's prayer to the thorny tree or that both Komantí and Luángu have independent versions of the proverb "Left hand washes right hand, right hand washes left hand" is far more interesting to me than word counts of one or another African origin. Fully exploring the history of Apúku, Komantí, Papá, Luángu, or Púmbu—not to mention standard Saramaccan—would require an enormous erudition about the languages and cultures of West and West Central Africa, as well as about Saramaccan and its esoteric languages. My hope is that this Coda may encourage such efforts over the long term.

A parable (but it really happened): In 1981, under the auspices of the National Endowment for the Humanities, I gave a series of identical lectures about Saramaka art and culture, accompanied by slides, at several U.S. universities. After each lecture, a different African professor came up to speak to me—first a man from Kumasi, then one from Kinshasa, then one from Cotonou. Each said the same thing: "These are my people—exactly the same clothes, the same shrines, the same way of doing things. They came from my town." In other words, when one looks at Saramaka culture (language, religion, art, cuisine . . .) from any single African perspective, much of it seems familiar. So, the devil is in the details. Figuring out "origins" requires knowledge of multiple African sites and extreme attentiveness to the complex ways that creolization operated both in the Old World and, especially, the New.

Finally, an ethical caveat. The publication of knowledge that gains its symbolic power in part by being secret risks diminishing its value and meaning. As I wrote in *First-Time* (which contains a much fuller consideration of these issues), "I would want to urge outsiders (whether they are Surinamers, Dutch, [French,] Americans, or whatever) who in the course of their work or leisure come in contact with Saramakas to respect the special 'unspeakable' status of this knowledge." I am well aware that Tooy's enthusiasms, or those of many of my teachers in *First-Time*, and their willingness for me to publish what they've taught me, in no way exonerates me of my own responsibility. My strong desire to celebrate the cultural achievements of Saramakas, and to permit others to share that appreciation, remains unavoidably balanced by a host of anxieties. But as Kenneth Bilby wrote recently, ruminating on similar dilemmas regarding the publication of Jamaican Maroon Kromanti knowledge, "In the final analysis, the pros of publication would seem to outweigh the cons," adding, "this seems to have been borne out by Price's *First-Time*, which has been received with much enthusiasm and appreciation by Saramakas themselves."[4] I fervently hope once again, with the understanding assistance of my readers, for such an outcome.

SOURCES FOR AFRICAN ETYMOLOGIES

My tentative African etymologies, and those of my generous colleagues, flow from the following sources, identified in the form of (for example) "Baker 1993" or "Bilby 2006," below.

Baker, Philip. 1993. "Assessing the African Contribution to French-based Creoles," In *Africanisms in Afro-American Language Varieties*, edited by Salikoko Mufwene pp. 123–55. Athens: University of Georgia Press.

Bentley, W. Holman. 1887. *Dictionary and Grammar of the Kongo Language, as Spoken at San Salvador, the Ancient Capital of the Old Kongo Empire, West Africa.* London: Baptist Missionary Society.

Berry, Jack. 1960. *English, Twi, Asante, Fante Dictionary.* Accra, Ghana: Presbyterian Book Depot.

Bilby, Kenneth. 2006. Personal communication.

Carterton, M. 1975. *Petite lexique Baoule-Français.* Côte d'Ivoire: Mission Catholique Bocanda.

Cassidy, F. G., and R. B. Le Page. 2002. *Dictionary of Jamaican English.* 2nd ed. Kingston: University of the West Indies Press. (Orig. pub. 1967.)

Christaller, J[ohann]. G[ottlieb]. 1886. *Vocabularies of the Niger and Gold Coast, West Africa.* London: Society for Promoting Christian Knowledge.

———. 1933. *Dictionary of the Asante and Fante Language Called Tshi.* Basel: Basel Evangelical Missionary Society. (Orig. pub. 1881.)

Delafosse, Maurice. 1894. *Manuel dahoméen.* Paris: E. Leroux.

Ellis, A[lfred]. B[urdon]. 1966. *Thsi-speaking Peoples of the Gold Coast of West Africa.* Oosterhout, The Netherlands: Anthropological Publications. (Orig. pub. 1887.)

Friederici, Georg. 1960. *Amerikanistisches Wörterbuch und Hilfswörterbuch für den Amerikanisten.* Hamburg: Cram, De Gruyter & Co.

Good, Jeff. 2006. Personal communication.

Huttar, George L. 1985. "Sources of Ndjuka African Vocabulary." *New West Indian Guide* 59:45–71.

———. 2006. Personal communication.

Kropp Dakubu, M[ary]. E[sther]. 1973. *West African Language Data Sheets.* Vol 1. Leiden, The Netherlands: West African Linguistic Society.

———. 1973. *Ga-English Dictionary.* Legon: Institute of African Studies, University of Ghana.

Laman, K[arl]. E[dvard]. 1964. *Dictionnaire kikongo-français.* Ridgewood, NJ: The Gregg Press. (Orig. pub. 1936.)

———. 1968. *The Kongo.* Vol. 4. Uppsala: Studia Ethnographica Upsaliensia.

Mohr, Adolphe Th., ed. 1909. *A Dictionary of English-Tshi (Asanti)* [by J. G. Christaller]. 2nd ed., revised and expanded. Basel: Evangelische Missionsgesellschaft in Basel.

Nketia, J. H. 1963. *Drumming in Akan Communities of Ghana.* London: Thomas Nelson and Sons.

Parkvall, Mikael. 1999. "Afrolex 1.15: Lexical Africanisms in Atlantic Creoles and Related Varieties." Unpublished manuscript kindly lent by the author, Stockholm University.

———. 2006. Personal communication.

Rattray, R. S. 1927. *Religion & Art in Ashanti.* Oxford: Oxford University Press.

Redden, James E., and Enoch N. Owusu. 1963. *Twi Basic Course.* Washington, DC: Foreign Service Institute, U.S. Department of State.

Schwegler, Armin. 2006. Personal communication.

Sebba, Mark. 1982. "A Note on Two Secret Languages of Surinam." *Amsterdam Creole Studies* 4:38–43.

Segurola, B. 1963. *Dictionnaire Fon-Français.* Cotonou, Benin: Procure de l'Archidiocèse.

Smith, Norval. 1983. "A Further Note on Two Secret Languages of Surinam." *Amsterdam Creole Studies* 5:47–51.

———. 1987. "A list of Kwa Words in Surinamese Creoles." Unpublished manuscript.

———. 2006. Personal communication.

Swartenbroeckx, Pierre. 1973. *Dictionnaire kikongo et kituba-français (vocabulaire comparé des langages kongo traditionnels et véhiculaires).* Bandundu, Zaire: Ceeba.

Van Wing, J., and C. Penders. 1928. *Le plus ancien dictionnaire bantu / Het oudste Bantu-Woordenboek.* Louvain, Belgium: Imprimerie J. Kuyl-Otto. (Orig. pub. mid-seventeenth century.)

Warner-Lewis, Maureen. 2003. *Central Africa in the Caribbean: Transcending Time, Transforming Cultures.* Kingston: University of the West Indies Press.

Warren, Dennis M. 1976. *Bibliography and Vocabulary of the Akan (Twi-Fante) Language of Ghana.* Indiana University Publications African Series, no. 6. Bloomington: University of Indiana.

Westermann, Diedrich. 1928. *Evefiala or Ewe-English Dictionary*. Berlin: Dietrich Reimer.

———. 1930. *Gbesela Yeye or English-Ewe Dictionary*. Berlin: Dietrich Reimer.

Wooding, Charles Johan. 1972. *Winti: Een Afroamerikaanse godsdienst in Suriname*. Meppel, The Netherlands: Krips Repro.

APÍNTI

The *apínti* is the "talking drum" used at major council meetings and rituals. At council meetings, its rhythms open the proceedings, summon and greet particular gods,
ancestors, and public officials, comment on current events, help set the tone of the
meeting through the imaginative use of proverbs, and dismiss people at the end.
Apínti language, also called Kobuá, is a verbalization of the rhythms played on the
drum. I have always assumed (on the basis of the drum's praise name and its name for
the Supreme God and the Earth, as well as what I have been able to learn about Akan
drumming) that the bulk of *apínti* messages are modified versions of Akan/Twi origi-
nals.[5] The existence of parallel (separate) Luángu versions of some of these rhythms
supports this hypothesis.

Lexical Items

[NB: "S." = standard (everyday) Saramaccan, provided for comparison]

avítjui = needle (S. *agúya*)
díafèba = rum (S. *daán*)
fala fala benkóa = do it fast! (S. *du hên hési!*)
kansái yawá = drinking glass (S. *gaási*)
Kediamá Kédiampon [or *Kedúamwá Kedíampô*] = The Supreme God and the Earth {in
    part from Twi *Twéaduàmpong*, "a byname of God . . . said to mean the Almighty"—
    Christaller 1933:551 via Bilby 2006}
kóonkóon = the bottle used to pour libations in an ancestor shrine (S. *djógo* or *báta*)
kotoko = an empty rum bottle
nákò = ancestor shrine (S. *faákapáu*)
Naná = The Supreme God {from Twi *naná*, "a title of respect or honour used in ad-
    dressing kings, great fetishes & c."—Christaller 1933:328 via Bilby 2006}
náwa = protective palm frond (S. *azáng páu*)

Phrases That Are Not in Saramaccan Syntax

Bandámbalá bandámba gákili bánda, bandámba gákili bánda, don don i dón, búnuyên. The
    rhythm that Anasi, the spider-man, uses in a folktale to call Tonê from the river
    and bring the god ashore to her shrine. See p. 61.

Asú muná fulú ben konú fulú. This means, "Your ancestors used to really know things, but now only 'children' are left and they have it all mixed up." (Tooy is unable to break down this phrase word by word.) See pp. 154–55.

Odú kwatakí bi de a bímba tála. This means, "Youngsters should live amidst elders, elders should live amidst youngsters," or, "You shouldn't forget your mother's and father's wisdom." (Tooy is unable to break down this phrase word by word.) See pp. 154–55.

Obímba de a bímba tála. This is the Ndyuka Maroon Apínti version of the previous message. (Tooy is unable to break down this phrase word by word.) See p. 154.

Sáki fíi búndu sódjodú anbupé. The drum name of Piyái, the Amerindian brother-in-law of the Lángu ancestor Kaásipúmbu. See p. 246.

Fúndi ofón, fúndi ofón, fúndi ofón, alákatáka fúndi ofón. "The Suriname River is without a headman. The ship has no steersman. The ship turns sideways and drifts dangerously." See pp. 240–41.

Séi kúnya, séi kúnya, séi kúnya, alábatáta séi kúnya. "The river has found a headman. The ship has found a steersman.'" This and the previous message were played at the installation of the new Saramaka *gaamá* in 2005. See p. 241.

Ma in tênè, ma in tênè búa. "When a leaf falls in the water, it's not the same day that it starts to rot," according to Gaamá Agbagó's drummer Peléki (see S. and R. Price, *Maroon Arts*, pp. 258–59). When I ask Tooy about this rhythm, he retells the story that he'd once used to express his joy at seeing me again. It's about a man far upstream who watched a leaf fall into the river and who met that same leaf many years later down in the tidal zone. He says that Gadien's drum played it this way: *Kotoko i kotoko tjim tjim, mam têne búa.* See p. 206.

Sese kái dúmba, sesembe sekái dúmba. This is in the Lángu dialect of Apínti and refers to "bent-over tree and the owner of the garden"—see below for the standard Apínti version. Tooy explained that in the garden there was an almost-dead tree with its head bent over who worried that the owner of the garden would come and chop it down. Meanwhile, the owner of the garden was afraid that the bent-over tree would fall on his head one day and kill him. It is appropriate to play in a situation where each party fears what the other might do. (Tooy is unable to break down these phrases word by word.) See p. 252.

Yúnkuma a yú, a yú kantambilí. This is in the Lángu dialect of Apínti and means, "The headman of the creek is the [fish called] *pakúsi*"—see below for the standard Apínti version. (Tooy is unable to break down these phrases word by word.) See p. 252. {Armin Schwegler (personal communication, 2006) suggests that Kikongo *nkúuma*, "poisson de l'espèce *mvulu*" (Laman 1964:733), might be the source of *Yúnkuma.*}

Adjá kankantí ágboní. The drum name of the planet Venus. See p. 403.

Udé udé bêle, bêle, bêle, bêle, bêle, udé udé bêle, bêle, bêle, bêle, udé udé, bêle, Kéduamwá Kéduampón.★ An old-time greeting, equivalent to the Saramaccan *Tío ódi, tángi tío* . . .

Sôdjowíangwi, Sôdjowíangwi, Sôdjosôdjowíangwi.★ The drum name for *gaamá.*

*Kílibentên tên tên tên tên. Kílibentên tên. Kílibentên tên odú asángbelé, má fu wan pandási.** The drum name for *kabitêni* (village/clan headman). (The final phrase means, in Saramaccan, "man from a plantation.")

*Opête bilidján, má fu wan pandási.** The drum name for *basiá* (assistant headman).

*Bombókásikaasi gêdegedê, bombókásikaasi gêdegedê. Bílibíli kóngo, kóngobílibíli.** The drum name for *muyêe basiá* (female assistant headman).

*Osóutu túbempónu, gidjí ankáma láli. Sánkamaósu mam tête djúa.** The drum name for a really good-looking woman.

*Kotokoí bomisán mámisan danvúla.** The drum name for "rum."

*Fala fala benkóa, kotokoí bomisán mámisan danvúla, fala fala benkóa.** "Fast, bring the rum here fast!"

*Díafêba, díafêba, fala benkóa.** "Rum, rum, bring it fast"

*Kotoko, fala fala benkóa.** "The empty rum bottle, bring it fast!"

*Kotokoí bomisán mámisan danvúla, kánkan túkutu, túkutu kánkan fala fala benkóa.** "Go fill the empty bottle with rum fast!"

*Kansái yawá bêlen djó.** "Bring a drinking glass!"

*Patagoosó dámasekié.** The drum name for stool.

*Kwa kwa mbáta kwa, ndúku ámêi.** The drum name for tobacco.

*Aví naná batá aví naná, ké día, avítjui naná batá aví naná, ké día.** Tooy glosses this proverb as "The humble needle [*avítjui*] manages to clothe the Gaamá's posterior" (S. *Sôsò apíkima, hên ta tapá gaamá gogó*). On another occasion, his Dómbi-clan *apínti*-playing friend told me, "If you were to come and live in my house, and I gave you food, a place to sleep, and so on, and then you became more important than I, I'd play on my drum: *avítjuí, bata fí naná, kilidí afíi*, which means, 'It doesn't bother me that you've become more important than I, because I know that I'm the one who helped you do it." These two versions of the drum rhythm seem closely related.{Recall that Twi *naná*, "a title of respect or honour used in addressing kings, great fetishes & c."—Christaller 1933:328 via Bilby 2006—is often found in drum rhythms relating to the *gaamá*; see also Gaamá Agbagó's *apínti* praise name, below.}

*Hándu ko a bilí, hándu ko a fo.** Tooy glosses this proverb as "Cow says, 'If you want to know the secrets of a man, ask his wife.'" I've heard Tooy say this in conversation, with listeners none the wiser until he explained that if you see a herd of cattle, all of whom are looking down except for one, and you want to know why this one is looking up, the best way to find out why is to ask his wife.

*Asantí kotoko bu a dú okáng, kobuá, o sá si watera dján de, djantanási.** Recital of the drum's praise name, including words for its parts (wooden body, pegs, ties, head), as taught to me by Peléki, the *gaamá's* drummer in the 1970s (see S. and R. Price, *Maroon Arts*, pp. 258–59.) {Twi *ɔkɔtɔkoro* means "drumstick"—Warren 1976:177 via Bilby 2006—and Twi *kɔtɔkɔ* means "brave companions, able teammates"—Redden and Owusu 1963:211 via Bilby 2006. NB: Asanti Kotoko is the name of one of Ghana's top football clubs, based in Kumasi.}

Asantí kotoko bu a dí, asánti kotoko bênte bénte bénte bóafo, asánti kotoko bóa fámelífa, pé miná djeí, pé miná dónkoso.* Tooy's version of the previous drum rhythm, with the last two phrases meaning, "I've sat down, I've sat down solidly."

Asánti kobuá, odún ankáma watera djánde, asánti kotoko tím tím.* These are the rhythms Tooy plays right after the drum tells its name and "sits down."

Kediamá Kédiampon, ódu a sáisi ódu a kêêmponu, sasi Naná bêtiè.* The name of the Supreme God and the Earth, according to Peléki (see S. and R. Price, *Maroon Arts*, pp. 258–59). Tooy also plays this rhythm as a matter of course but speaks the first two words as *Kedúamwá Kedíampô*, explaining that the first is the Great God Above and that Ampô is the Earth Mother. "*Bêtiè*," he adds, means "Stop it!," in this case that Naná (another name for "God Above") should stop any evil before it arrives.

Keí keí dí día, kêtekeí dí día.* "Good morning," as played by Peléki (see S. and R. Price, *Maroon Arts*, pp. 258–59). (*Dí día* means "the day" or "daylight" in normal Saramaccan.)

Téen téen di día, ketekéi di día, adjú apé di día, sánkamaónsu di día, di día te gbéle gbéle gbéle gbéle di día.* Tooy's version of "Good morning." He explains that the bird called *huntjêtje* says this to greet the dawn each day.

Kókoókokólo busikí, kókoókokólo kediámpa, dádiámpa, dádiámpa gwélegwéle, adjú apé di día, tánkamaónsu di día, di día téé di día, di día téé gbéle gbéle gbéle gbéle di día.* Tooy says that this is the way the bird called *huntjêtje* calls out by the riverside to wake up Busikí. Tooy likes to drum it after the previous wake-up.

Sekúinya ti sekúinya kata kái na tí sekúinya.* Peléki explained this as "However great the problem, the *gaamá* can find a solution" (see S. and R. Price, *Maroon Arts*, pp. 258–59). But Tooy plays the rhythm slightly differently, *Séikuinya, séikuinya, kata kái sékuinya, atjuába bilóngo*, explaining that this is simply the sound of the man poling the *gaamá*'s canoe (in other words, the canoe is coming—*séikuinya* is the sound of him pushing his pole).

Pátapáta kuma kukú saaná, pátapáta kuma kukú saaná, atjuá bambélu, pátapáta kuma kukú saaná, sékuinya, sékuinya, pátapáta kísi i kuinya, atjúa ba bilóngo.* This is what Tooy plays after the previous rhythm, as it also alludes to the *gaamá*'s arrival. *Pátapáta* is the sound of the flag waving on the back of the *gaamá*'s canoe.

Alíbête benté, bébetiêbenté a falí.* "The water lily floats downstream with the ebb tide, but the tide will bring it back up as well," according to Peléki (see S. and R. Price, *Maroon Arts*, pp. 258–59).

Sênsi a numá, bênsi a numá, a numá fu te manu tja nási betê.* When I ask Tooy about the previous rhythm (water lily), he says he plays it differently, as did his ancestors Antamá and Gadien. ("Only Lángu people know this one," he assures me.) Water Lily and Flood Tide challenged each other, Flood Tide boasting he'd sink Water Lily. This rhythm is the plant's reply, meaning, "Bullshit! No way you can sink me!" (Remember that Lángu people have a very special relationship with water lilies!)

Fébe tutú máfiakata bánta nási betê.* "When the mouth starts moving, hunger is afraid," according to Peléki (see S. and R. Price, *Maroon Arts*, pp. 258–59).

Sêmene tutú máfiakáta.* Tooy's version of the previous proverb. He adds that Ndyukas play it as *Sêmene tutú máfiakáta, máfiakáta zíngi zíngi.*

Dabikúku misí améusu.* "Smoke has no feet, but it makes its way to heaven," according to Peléki (see S. and R. Price, *Maroon Arts*, pp. 258–59). When I asked Tooy about this rhythm, he asked me, "Do you know the name of the man who made the fire? He was Okóontu. So I add on the drum, *Okóontu, ókóontu, dadí ameónsu.*" (*Ameónsu* is Komantí for "fire.")

Zokbo otjó, tjutjúadiyé. Vunkánda vunkánda. Tjútju kéike tjuké ku fênegi. Adjáso babaasié. Adjibála djibála djibála djibála djí.* Tooy told the Dómbi-clan *apínti* master, during the discussion I describe on pp. 252–53, that this is the biggest curse he knows how to play on the *apínti*—he uses it when he's really angry at someone. (He didn't break it down further.)

Atíatí bòòfi atí. Atíatí bòòfi akitaa.* Tooy teaches the Dómbi-clan *apínti* master this teasing, challenging insult, which means, "Your hunting sack has a hole and your flint [needed, before matches came in, to light fires] will fall out."

Atíaki bòòfi atí. Atíatí kêtêkêî, kêtêkêî i gángán.* This is the proper response to the previous challenge, Tooy tells the Dómbi-clan drummer: "My sack is solid, my flint won't fall out!" Tooy adds that he was taught this exchange by Sépi, the runaway slave spirit in his father's brother's head (see p. 227).

Atíatí bòòfi atí. Atíatí bòòfi atí.* Apropos the previous exchange, Tooy says that when Matawai Maroons play only these words (that is, without adding *atíatí bòòfi akitaa*), they are playing the common proverb "A darkened sky doesn't always mean rain" (S. *Fá tjúba baáka, ná sô a o kái*).

Agídigidígidí sósoasaí mutusí ataabiánga.* Tooy says, you've prayed for sun and gotten it, you've prayed for rain and gotten it. Now, which do you really want? This drum rhythm means, "I don't know what to do with you anymore."

Katú katú katú bílikatú, Katú katú katú katú bílikatú, vuláa vuláa vuláa mampêngene, vuláa vuláa vuláa mampêngene, koló koló píyen, koló koló píyen.* Tooy says this is how the hen calls its chicks (or how the drummer calls people to the gathering).

Kilibentênte, tíi a fe unkúma, Kéduamwa, Kéduampón, tíi a fe unkúma, ku kúdja kúbe mpónu, akí a fe unkúma, sausó akí sausó ánda, bobosú bosú bosú ánda, nenesú nesú nesú síeko kokoló gángan belí akó, azú kodó tangí, tangí, tangí, tangí.* Tooy once told me proudly that this is what you play to install a captain—a task he has done several times at the *gaamá*'s request.

Avún, avún, avún sakí kedjê, Avún, avún, avún sakí kedjê búa. Méiméimesí. Húnhún na mêkese, kumálu tjá tjelí, mi háun bélu.* Tooy explains that when divination finds that a captain is in danger, that he won't be able to live with the office, this is the rhythm you play to chase away the evil, the dog from the land of the dead whose name is Avún.

Kantámisángu, kántámisángu, kántámisángu, kálamisángu, djidjidjí kantámisángu, kwá!* Tooy explains that Woodpecker says, "This country is large. To fly across that river, I must show it some respect!" The final drumbeat, *kwa!*, is the sound of the bird alighting on a treetop on the other side of the river.

*Sánfo níni búa, sánfo níni búa, sánfo níni búa, sánfo níni búa, sánfo níni búa, kotoko íni búa, yáu tjíbilítjibitjí, yáu kobílabala, yáu zógidi, yáu zógidi gídi hía, tjibêmbe tjêtje.** Tooy says this is how the drummer asks for many things to be brought. "You're playing the rhythm of small black monkeys [S. *kusií*] here. There are so many of them that they just keep on bringing things!"

*Síkele bénten djumá, kwasí nanga antaamáni.** Tooy explains this parable as a plea for a little respect: "The towel says this. When a couple make love, they use the towel to wipe up, and put it aside till the next night. They don't give it a thought until they need it again. The towel complains with this rhythm, 'Only now do you pay attention to me?'"

Phrases That Are (at Least Partially) in Saramaccan Syntax/ Lexicon, with "Language" Words Inserted

Suun fu akí, suun fu andá. Suun fu akí, suun fu andá. Saanfo maíni, suun fu andá. "Suun from here, *suun* from there. *Saanfo maíni, suun* from there." Parrot says it has a tail, it has a body, and even if its body didn't go to a place, its tail has been there. Tooy explains, "Parrot says this when he's teasing a man about having slept with his wife or just to say he's sending along an offering but not showing up himself." See p. 83.

Avó Kêteke imisí a gángán, misí gangán hampê. "Grandmother *Kêteke imisí a gángán, misí gangán hampê.*" The *apínti* name of Paánza, founder of the Kasitú clan. (*Gángán* means "elder" or "ancestor" in Apúku.) See p. 118.

Naná-u-Kêlempé Kílintínboto-fu-Lámbote. "Naná-from-Kêlempé, Kílintínboto-from-Lámbote." The *apínti* name of Gaamá Agbagó. See p. 165. {Recall that Twi *naná* is "a title of respect or honour used in addressing kings, great fetishes & c."— Christaller 1933:328 via Bilby 2006}

Asanti bélen ku awándja, hên ku panga ngosí. "*Asanti bélen* with *awándja*, it and *panga ngosí.*" "The headman of the creek is the [fish called] *pakúsí*"—see above for the Lángu dialect version. See p. 252.

Goón mása, noa mása. Goón mása, noa mása. Noa mása lègèdè, légédè fu nóame. "Owner-of-the-garden, *noa* master. [repeat] *Noa* master lies, the lie of *nóame.*" This is the standard Apínti version of "bent-over tree and the owner of the garden"—see above for the Lángu dialect version. See p. 252.

Matjáu dê a gangáa, hôni dê a kiní. Bi a kodiní, bi a kódi. "The axe is at the throat, the bee is at the knee. *Bi a kodiní, bi a kódi.*" It means, "The food's ready to eat!" See p. 260.

*Kéduamá Kéduampón, sausó akí, sausó ánda, bobosú bosú bosú ánda nênesú nêsú nêsú síeko kókolo gángan bedé a ko.** "The Supreme God and the Earth, *sausó* here, *sausó* there, *bobosú bosú bosú* there, *nênesú nêsú nêsú síeko kókolo gángan bedé a ko.*" This is what Tortoise says when he is climbing a hill with his "house" on his back: "I may have short feet, but I'll get there little by little."

*Kóonkóon bi dê nákò, kóonkóon bi dê nákò, kóonkóon bi dê náwa.** "Kóonkóon [the bottle used to pour libations] was at the *nákò* [ancestor shrine], *kóonkóon* [the bottle used to pour libations] was at the *náwa* [protective palm frond]." This rhythm is played as libations begin at the ancestor shrine.

*Kokío kíki, kokío mên, má fu wan pandási.** "Kokío kíki, kokío mên, man from a plantation." The drum name of Hummingbird. The drum called him three times before he answered with the next rhythm.

*Mi dján ku amánde. Mi dánda mása kwáinya.** "I'm *dján ku amánde.* I'm *dánda* master of the *kwáina.*" Which means, says Tooy, "I'm so small that I didn't think anyone would be interested in what I had to say. But Hummingbird is master of the 'play!'"

Ngóm háin, ngóm háin, ngóm háin, ngóm háin, kaká a gogó [whole repeats], *aluwí gódjogódjo, mángi máu sabá, káfrika kabá unú, momomukúmokúmokú a gwí.** This is the way Jaguar roars his name in the forest, boasting how "baad" he is, saying (just before the repeat) that he has shit on his ass and, in the last two phrases, telling the name of his canine tooth (with which he kills dogs) and large back molar.

APÚKU

The forest sprits who speak this language are conceptualized by Saramakas as exclusively New World discoveries, beings from the surrounding forest who taught Saramakas everything they know about the relevant rites and language. Among Maroons, Saramakas are considered the real experts about Apúkus, and among Saramakas, the Lángu clan is considered the greatest specialist (though the Mavúngu priests of the Dómbi clan might dispute this). This cult is important among all Saramakas, and Apúku "plays" are, with the exception of funerals, perhaps the most frequent of all collective rites. (Certain less common gods, such as Akataási, who live in termite hills, and Bumbá [from Kikongo *mbúmba*, "evil water spirit"], who live in small caimans, come and dance at Apúku "plays" as well.) I have always assumed, on the basis of the phonology and lexicon, that Apúku was largely West Central African in origin. (Wooding, without citing any source, claims that "Apúku" derives from "Congo-Angola . . . *ampungu*."[6])

Lexical Items

agúngulámitêmbe = assistant headman (S. *basiá*)
ahuánwío = one of the three drums in Apúku "plays" (S. *tumáo*)
Akuínkan = the name of an important Apúku
aladé [or *aladí*] = maripa palm frond (S. *maipá azang*)
alándi = old people (S. *gaán sémbè*)
alúngu = children (S. *miíi*)
amánamána kutjímbe = a tree used in Apúku recipes (S. *musánse*)
anámusiásiá = toad (S. *bése*)

asákanamiké = rattle (S. *tjáka*)

asákanamikúlu = armadillo (S. *kapasí*)

asákpa núkpe (sometimes *asákpa núgbe*) = wind (S. *véntu*)

awóomakaa = old people (S. *gaán sèmbé*, but *awóo* = "old")

azankeémbu = main drum in Apúku "plays"

azô = a plant that Komantí calls *ahúsudadí djádésúmani*

baká a kú = bush hog (S. *píngo*)

Báku = female water spirit (S. *wáta mamá*)

Bakuí = forest spirit (S. *Apúku*)

bakêntu = rear crutch or walking stick (S. *kokotí u báka*)

bankámpanda = front crutch or walking stick (S. *kokotí u fési*)

bánzu = fire (S. *fáya*) {from Kikongo *mbazu*, "fire, heat"—Laman 1964:525 via Bilby 2006}

biyóngo = medicinal plants (S. *goón uwíi*) {from Kikongo *bilóngo*, "magical medicine"—Wooding 1972:168}

buánga = to warn (S. *bái*)

dénikbó = a kind of branch held under the arm by a dancing god

dóngo = death (S. *dêdè*)

gámbu = Apúku-drum pegs

gángán [sometimes *gangan motó* or *nêne gángan*] = old people, ancestors (S. *gaán sêmbe*) {possibly from Kikongo *nganga*, "a religious figure"—diviner, curer, priest—van Wing and Penders 1928:251—see also s.v. *kwanga*, below. *Gangan* = "grandfather," "grandmother," "old people" is found from Brazil to Jamaica—Parkvall 1999, s.v. *gangan*}

gángi [*gánge*] = house (S. *ósu*)

gidiónsu [*gedeonsu*] = the dwarf silkcotton tree

gúma = house (S. *ósu*)

gwetáno = we're in the middle of a "play" (S. *u dê a di pèê*)

húlúlúpúmbu = your mother's cunt (S. *mamá píma f'i*)

hungolamámba = bush hog (S. *píngo*)

húngu [= *púngu*] = "raise your ears," listen up! (S. *ópo yési!*)

kakíamba = evil (S. *ógi*)

kándikíla = a kind of cocoon (S. *bítju ósu* or *apúku biyóngo*)

kasianáni = smart or clever person (S. *kónima*)

kasi fu wámba = old person/people of Apúku land (S. *gaán sèmbè fu apúku kôndè*)

kibúnda [*kivúnda*] = ear(s) (S. *yési*)

kimúlele = dance (S. *baiyá*)

kimpó = snort tobacco (S. *hái tabáku*) {Armin Schwegler (personal communication, 2006) suggests this is from Kikongo *ki*, "he who," and *mpòla*, "tobacco," particularly associated with "inhaling through the nose"—Laman 1964:584}

kitête kitête pakasa or *luángo síi* ["Luango seeds"] = peanuts (S. *pindá*) {"There is a form *tete* meaning 'seed' found in zone L of the Bantu area, which is far inland from Loango. . . . I would say this etymology is tenuous. However, it seems worth looking into because, if it could be more firmly established, it could be construed as linguistic evidence for a slave trade network going far inland."—Good 2006}

kitímataangi = stool (S. *bángi*)

kívu-ndá = altar where Apúku images and pots are kept

kókiú kíki kopiúme = I'm not an older person (S. *mi ná gaánsémbè*)

kúnangbáku = your mother's cunt (S. *mamá píma f'i*)

kwamidjó = heart (S. *áti*)

kwanga = old person/people (S. *gaán sèmbè*) {from Kikongo *nkwá*, "someone who possesses knowledge," and *nga*, which has similar meaning—Laman 1964:737 via Schwegler 2006}

lóko = silkcotton tree (S. *kankantíi*)

lokpo = house (S. *ósu*)

lókpolókpo = a kind of black moss or muck, lichens (S. *bilolí*)

lóngu = half [or some] (S. *háfu*)

lontéi = hummingbird (S. *vúnvun*)

lúkutjáibiála = a tree whose bark is important in Apúku rites (S. *musánse*)

lukwándji = branches (S. *páu máu*)

lúngu = child, children (S. *miíi*) {Armin Schwegler (personal communication, 2006) suggests that this is "from Kikongo *ngu(ngu)* 'child' (see Laman 1964:695)," adding, "The Kikongo form is *ngungu*, but *lungu* is simply *lu* + the non-reduplicated *ngu*. The form is thus derived from a singular rather than plural 'base.'"}

malóngo vitô = best friend (S. *búnu máti*) {"The *longo* root looks like a form that in class 1 (which should be *mulongo* or some variant, not *malongo*) means 'brother' in the eastern Bantu area. (And in at least one language, Ila, the root appears to specifically mean 'friend.') Like *kitete*, the etymology is a bit of a long shot. But if it could be verified (perhaps by tracking down an etymology for *vitô*), one would have linguistic evidence for Eastern Bantu influence on Saramaccan."—Good 2006}

mafôndò = myself (S. *mi seéi*)

mamisêsi mamikólo = Mavúngu

mamuleké = the same to you! (S. *leki yú!*)

Mavúngu = an important Apúku {from Kikongo *ma-vúngu*, "*nkisi* [power object] for hunting"—Laman 1964:510 via Bilby 2006}

mavúngu maná = ancestors (S. *gaán sèmbè*)

mambá = river (S. *lío*) {from Kikongo *mamba*, "water"—Laman 1968 4:31 via Warner-Lewis 2003:22}

maná [sometimes *manewa*] = children (S. *miíi*) {"The root *-ana*, often with a prefix *mu-*, forming *mwana*, is the typical Bantu form for child."—Good 2006}

mayáa = tobacco (S. *tabáku*) {Armin Schwegler (personal communication, 2006) suggests that this is related to Kikongo *yáaya*, "burning tobacco."—Laman 1964:1121}

môle = small drying rack for food over hearth (S. *pikí suá*)

mukóko = smoke (S. *simóku*)

mutóalála = a lizard (S. *sapakáa*)

musínga = *pína* palm frond (S. *pína azang*) {from Kikongo *nsinga*, pl. *lusinga*, "palm fibers"—Laman 1964:768 via Schwegler 2006}

musútu = forest (S. *mátu*)

Naná Mampúngu Zamina Mpúngo = the Great God Above (S. *Mása Gaán Gádu*) {from Twi *naná*, "a title of respect or honour used in addressing kings, great fetishes & c."—Christaller 1933:328 via Bilby 2006—plus Kikongo *Nzambi mpungu*, "Supreme deity"—van Wing and Penders 1928:279}

nêne = child, kid (S. *miíi*)

ngóma = another name for the lead drum in Apúku rites {from Kikongo *ngoma* = drum—Bentley 1887:465, Laman 1964:895, both via Bilby 2006}

nukú tjêle tjêle = open your ears, listen up! (S. *ópo i yési*)

núndeomé = kaolin (S. *keéti*)

pákasa = elephant (S. *zaun*) {from various Bantu languages, where *pakasa* means "elephant" or "buffalo"}

pákasa f'a adjú = village headman (S. *kabiténi*)

púmbu [*púngu*] = large drying rack for food over hearth (S. *gaán suá*)

sêsemiosé kiingô = protective palm frond (S. *azang páu*)

sikángóma = another name for the lead drum in *apúku* rites {from Kikongo *sika ngoma*, "to play the drum" (*sika* = to play, *ngoma* = drum—Bentley 1887:465, Laman 1964:895, both via Bilby 2006}

sikángomakoló = macaque (S. *makáku*)

síkufuámba = a large sacred tree (S. *katu*)

sosoo = meat (S. *gwámba*)

sosoo gidigidi = bush hog (S. *píngo*)

susú = person (S. *sèmbè*)

tjáka-tjáka-benkwánzái = peccary (S. *pakía*)

tjêngewa = come in! (S. *i sa dóu*)

Tósida = anaconda god (S. *wáta gádu*)

tumbíaka = to twist something (S. *bía sondí*)

vángu = ear(s) (S. *yési*)

vula mutambu = listen up! (S. *haíka* or *ópo yési*)

vánda = sweep (S. *baí*)

vulá = rain (S. *tjúba*) {from Kikongo *mvúla*, "rain"—van Wing and Penders 1928:238}

vúlankáma vúlanbímbo = supreme chief (S. *gaamá*)

vúnda = bush hog (S. *píngo*)

wánda = water (S. *wáta*)

weyúu = human being (S. *líbi sèmbè*)

yanfaló = to pray (S. *bégi*)

yumbé = child (S. *miíi*)

yúnge = a small rat (S. *mafengé*)

zábiakóto = paddle (S. *páda*)

zóla = tobacco (S. *tabáku*) {possibly related to Kikongo *zóla*, "to long for" (desire)—Laman 1964:1170 via Schwegler 2006} *zúngadémbu* [or *zúnga* or *djúnga*] = tobacco (S. *tabáku*) {from Kikongo *nsunga*, "to-bacco"—Laman 1964:778 via Schwegler 2006}

Phrases That Are Not in Saramaccan Syntax

[sung] *Línga línga kólu, kólu tei, mangánu ta línga kólu-ee, kólu tei.* This is the song that Macaque sings to the Awara palm (which has long thorns all up and down its trunk, protecting its orange fruit), after which it simply drops its thorns so the monkey can climb up. It's a prayer you can use whenever things are really rough. For two different versions in Papá, see below. See p. 16.

[sung] *A bêni gó gó, a bêni yángi. A bêni gó gó gó, a bêni yángi-e, zalí mukóko tjêngewa-e.* Tooy says that this is a song that Mavúngu sings, and that the first two phrases are someone knocking (*gó gó gó* [or sometimes *kón kón kón*]) on the door; the final one, the person inside opening the door. On other occasions, Tooy has sung it differently, with the final phrase being substituted by *E kagaa gó gó gó e gangí* or *zalá mukóko-e gángi.* Once, he interrupted the song with a marvelous solo riff, before it was taken up again: *Alála máiduwee, Ba Keedu máiduwe. Un hái kó memwa-é. Alála máiduwe, e gádu u mi-e máiduwe, un hái kó memwa-é. Alála máiduwee, Ba Keedú-dú na me kwêle kwêle mudjimá kwele wánda ta i wánda, u alála-a máiduwe, un hái kó memwa-é. Alála máiduwee, alála máiduwee, un hái kó memwa-é. A bêni gó gó, a bêni yángi. A bêni gó gó, a bêni yángi. Daí gó gó gó tjêngewaa.* Tooy later told me that *Alála máiduwee, Ba Keedu máiduwe. Un hái kó memwa-é . . .* is calling the gods who are far away to come join the "play." See below, for yet another version. See pp. 261–62.

Gámbo, gámbo, gámbo kó, kó, kó [repeat all], *pákasa mitámbulábulá* [repeat], *mulámu-támbu* [repeat], *sêsitamangáni tósitamangáni, támu fu léleko, kokiô kíki kokiômè, miêmîè miêmîè, tatá kupê, tatá kupê, tóombi, tómbi, tóombi vubémbo, tóombi, tómbi, tóombi vubémbo.* This is the rhythm that Tooy drums to begin an Apúku "play" so that the centipede that killed Tatá Makwalá will stay asleep. See p. 265.

[sung] *Mónika bayé-é Mónika batí. Sáa-e-o. Anúma-e-o, Anúma bongó, Mónika bangísa wi-o, Sáa-e, Anúma-e-o.* This is the song that the famous Apúku Sáa sang when she first possessed Yáya. See p. 398.

Kái tjáfili tjámba [repeat]. *Sênsita gambáni, Tósida gambáni. Támu fu lêle góa.** This is what Tooy plays on the Apúku drum to summon the god of the creek mouth.

*Ma Otú kpasaká ku adjú búndjibúndji seó demán tokó bía búndjibúndji bía gámbu. Gámbu kó bía lúkusúlúkusú biá búndjibúndji biá Gámbu. Hé!** This is what Tooy plays on the Apúku drum when "washing" the gods. "If you don't tie a certain leaf into your kerchief before you play this, you die," he boasts.

Phrases That Are (at Least Partially) in Saramaccan Syntax/ Lexicon, with "Language" Words Inserted

[sung] *Déé neniángo sondí u mi-o-o, kêngivè-o. Un déé awó sondí u mi-o, kêngivèvè. Ma un déé ni awó sondí u malúngu loángo, kêngivè, un de heee, kêngivè-o.* [Tooy says to me,

"His wings have already opened!" and continues singing:] *Déé awó sondí u mi-o, biká malúngu mi mi mi mii. Un déé ni alándi gánga u mi-e, biká mi malúngu ózila-e.* "Those ancestral things of mine, *kêngivè-o*. You those ancient things of mine, *kêngivèvè*. But you those ancient things of mine from *malúngu* [faraway(?)] Loángo, *kêngivè*, you're high [important(?)], *kêngivè-o*. Those ancient things of mine, because *malúngu mi mi mi mii*. You those ancestors of mine, because my *malúngu ózila-e*." The song of the enslaved African "guide" in the ill-fated white soldiers' canoe, as he turned himself into a bird and flew home to Africa. See p. 109. Tooy also sang this, with many riffs, during the Apúku portion of the knocking-the-stone ritual in 2005. {Note that in Kikongo, *kwenda* [to go] *malongo* means "to voyage far away," with *malongo* [*malúngu*(?)] connoting great distance.—van Wing and Penders 1928:49, 111, 180}

[sung] *I ta ganyá ganyá mi kuma zúngadémbu, zúngadémbu-o zipi-o. Ma lúku fa i ta ganyá mi kuma zúngadémbu, ma yú kasianáni.* "You are tricking me just like *zúngadémbu* [tobacco], *zúngadémbu-o zipi-o*. But look at how you're tricking me like *zúngadémbu*, but you're *kasianáni* [a clever one]." This song refers to how tobacco's intoxication—Tooy uses the phrase "making you drunk"—sneaks up on the user who is paying attention only to the "sweetness" of snorting it. See p. 260.

[sung] *Zúngadémbu-o, man dá mi zúnga. Zúngadémbu-o, man dá mi zúnga, ké kióo, bá mi lóngo i án yéi, nô. Zúnga-e!* "*Zúngadémbu-o*, man, give me *zúnga*. *Zúngadémbu-o*, man, give me *zúnga*. Please, kid, give me some, you hear? *Zúnga-e!*" A song asking for tobacco, which Apúkus love to snort. See p. 261.

Lukú maná luangí kimpô. Kimpô. Kimpô maléa. "Look, kids, *luangí*, let's snort [tobacco]. *Kimpô* [Let's snort]. *Kimpô maléa* [Let's snort tobacco]." This spoken prayer was followed with the words in normal Saramaccan *Bó hái!* ("Let's snort"). See p. 261.

[sung] *A bêni gó gó, a bêni yángi. A bêni gó gó gó gó gó, a bêni yángi, zalí mukóko téé n'en mamá gángi.* When Bási Gabói (an Apúku) would smoke his pipe, he'd sing this, says Tooy. He'd sing, "*A bêni gó gó, a bêni yángi*," when he'd lit it. *Zalí mukóko* means "the smoke came out," and the rest, in normal Saramaccan except the final word, means "all the way to his mother's *gángi* [house]." Another time, Tooy sang Bási Gabói's version as follows, which shows how much phonological and performative variation there is in such songs: *A bêni gó gó gó, mi na yángi. A béndi gó gó gó, mi na yángi-e. Koo gagaa mi gó gó e gangí. A bêni gó gó, mi na yángi. A bêni gó gó, mi na yángi. Gagaa gó gó gó-e gangí.* See p. 262.

Mi kèê fu mafôndò, fu sa sí malóngo vitô. "I cry for *mafôndo* [myself], that I may see *malóngo vitô* [my best friend]." Tooy said he sometimes thinks of this when I'm far away. See p. 286.

Múku djélen djélen djélen djélen djélen djélen djélen djélen. Adánimínawa adánimínawa adánimínawa adánimínawa. Múku djélen djélen djélen djélen djélen. Adánimínawa adánimínawa. I sa gó a Dénawa, i sa gó a Dénawa. I sa gó a Tómezíla. Walénu, walénu tjá Tómezíla. Badkama méki lókpolókpo, gádu hangbónu. Apúku drum rhythms. The final five phrases are the only ones that are partially in Saramaccan: "You can go to Dénewa, you can go to Tómezila. *Walénu, walénu* brings *Tómezíla*. Black people make *lókpolókpo* [moss/lichens], god answers *hangbónu* [yes]." This is the rhythm that Tatá Bokó taught Tatá Makwalá to drum first, whenever he began an Apúku "play." See p. 264.

[sung] *Yu mamá buánga, yu tatá buánga, Makwalá-e-e-e. Tidé i si mamá Alímbodé-e. A-o, yu mamá buánga-e, Makwalá-e-e-e. Tidé i si mamá Alímbodé-e.* "Your mother warned you, your father warned you, Makwalá. Today you see your mother, Alímbodé, [in the land of the dead]." This is the "dangerous" part of the Makwalá story, the song humans used to celebrate his death. This Lángu-clan version is distinct from the one sung downstream, where they substitute *Tidé man mi kísi dóngo-e* ["Today, man, I died"] (or *Tidé u sí dóngo, hokóo* ["Today you saw death, hooray"]) for *Tidé i si mamá Alímbodé*, and the song is sung to a different melody. Tooy introduced me to this song when he used it joyfully to greet the new moon. See p. 265.

[sung] *Lôngo, o mamuleké, ao-e mamuleké, mamuleké mamuleké-o, únu kúnangbáku-o!* "Lôngo [the leader of the Apúks], o mamuleké [the same to you], ao-e mamuleké, mamuleké mamuleké-o, únu kúnangbáku-o [your mother's cunt]!" The song that human beings sang at the long-ago dance contest to curse the Apúkus. See pp. 265–66.

[sung] *Ao-aoo mamuleké, ao mamuléke mamuléke únu húlúlúpúmbu-e-o!* "Ao-aoo mamuleké [same to you], ao mamuléke mamuléke únu húlúlúpúmbu-e-o [your mother's cunt]!" The song that Apúks sang to curse the human beings. See pp. 265–66.

[sung] *Kái déé vúnda-o, kái déé vúnda-va, kái déé vúnda mooi wandá, kái déé vúnda dá mi. Un kái déé vúnda dá mi, un kái déé vúnda-o, kái déé vúnda mooi fo mi, kái déé vúnda mooi wandá, kái déé vúnda dá mi. Ma Gwandímbu, Ma Gwandímbu, nakimbódo, nakimbódo, malávu tjákutjáku, mafutalánkani, avúnvun balakú, Tjêntjeminatjêntje, Tjêntje Mamá Gumbá.* "Call those *vúnda* [bush hogs], call those *vúnda*, call those *vúnda mooi wandá* [bush hogs, which look so beautiful (*mooi* in Sranan-tongo and Ndyuka) running through the forest], call those *vúnda* for me. Ma Gwandímbu [the woman who owns all bush hogs], Ma Gwandímbu, nakimbódo [I'm very hungry], nakimbódo, malávu tjákutjáku [the meat that you have], mafutalánkani [let it go into my belly], avúnvun balakú [I've swallowed it!], Tjêntjeminatjêntje [the name of the savannah where Ma Gwandímbu lives], Tjêntje Mamá Gumbá [Ma Gwandímbu's savannah]." A beautiful hunting song.[7] {Note that *talankani* is, in Kikongo, an exclamation of satisfaction and congratulation—van Wing and Penders 1928:307—and *malávu tjákutjáku*, despite Tooy's gloss, might be from Kikongo *malavu* ("palm wine")—Laman 1964:486 via Bilby 2006—and *tjakutjaku*, which Bilby describes in Aluku as an ideophone expressive of the sound of drinking or lapping up water, like a dog, might derive from Kikongo *cáku, caku-caku* (*cháku, cháku-cháku*), "onomat. pour le claquement de la langue [en mangeant]."—Laman 1964:100 via Bilby 2006}

Avó Gwandímbo, mi avó Gwandímbo, nákimimbódo, nákimimbódo, malavú tjákutjáku, mafutálankani, avúnvún bálákú. "Grandmother Gwandímbo, my grandmother Gwandímbo, knock-my-belly [= I'm very hungry], knock-my-belly. The meat that you have, let it go into my belly, I've swallowed it!" Tooy once spoke these words as a hunting prayer, asking for the bush hogs to cross our path. Note that the accents (diacritics) differ from the sung version, just above.

[sung] *Di kálu u Ma Vulá, Vulá mi lúka, Vulá mi lúka, Vulá mi lúka.** "The corn of Ma Vulá, Vulá *mi lúka*, Vulá *mi lúka*, Vulá *mi lúka*." Tooy says that there was a woman in the land of the Apúkus called Ma Vulá, who planted her corn seeds, saying that the bad ones mustn't bear fruit. The song recalls this moment, saying, "Whatever evil you've said there, let it wither like the bad seeds of Ma Vulá before it even comes up through the ground, and let the good you've said flourish like her good corn seeds." "This song," says Tooy, "is normally for Apúkus and Wátawenús, but there's no god's doorway where if you sing it you'd be saying a bad thing."

*Túmbíaka kísi kakíamba.** An Apúku proverb. "*Túmbíaka* [twisting] brings *kakíamba* [evil, trouble]." Tooy explains that when you don't accept what is told to you and you change it ["twist it"], you'll get in trouble.

*Susú músu wátji hên gúma.** "*Susú* [person] must watch his *gúma* [house]." This is played on the Apúku drum when a hot moment of the "play" is coming. It means, "Watch out for your house, don't let it be damaged [by the wildness of the 'play']." Tooy says this can also be played for Watáwenú (anaconda) gods.

[sung] *Ná mi ta zénu, Awánu ta zénu. Mi Zabiakútu, lúku mi. Ná mi ta zénu-e. Awánu ta zénu. Mi Zabiakútu.** "I'm not the one who *zénu*. Awánu is *zénu*-ing. I'm Zabiakúta, look at me." Tooy says that this is what Tatá Mavúngu said when, leaving the sea and entering the Suriname River, his paddle fell from his hand into the water.

[sung] *Séki yu gángan! Séki yu gángan mutú! Sêsita mangáni, tositá mangáni, pamu fu léleko. Sêsemiosé kiingô. Búgulubutá, búgulugbángala.** "*Séki* [listen up(?)] you ancestors! *Séki* [listen up(?)] you ancestors! *Sêsita mangáni, tositá mangáni, pamu fu léleko*. Protective palm frond, *Búgulubutá, búgulugbángala*," all of which means, "Keep out the Evil!" according to Tooy.

[sung] *Gaán tangí f'únu, Pásikanúmba. Tangí de a musútu, tangí de a mambá.** "Great thanks to you, Pásikanúmba. Thanks to the *musútu* [forest], thanks to the *mambá* [river]." Yaai's god Bási Yontíni sang this at an Apúku "play" in 2005.

[sung] *I án músu pèê ku azô. I án músu pèê ku azô-e.** "You shouldn't mess with the plant called *azô*." Tooy sang this at an Apúku "play" in 2005.

*Asákpa núkpe músu waai fu Mavúngu músu sabô mayáa.** "*Asákpa núkpe* [the wind] must blow so Mavúngu can *sabô mayáa* [tobacco]." Tooy explains that Mavúngu prays that God Above will blow the wind so the tobacco seeds he's planted will have rain and grow.

*Pákanyan pákanyan púmbu. E púmbu kaí ku mboté, kébanzu kísi, vulá músu sa tapu bánzu. Kásikási ná músu lébi na bínga za kúlulú.** "*Pákanyan pákanyan púmbu. E púmbu* falls with *mboté*, *kébanzu* catches, *vulá* [rain] must put out *bánzu* [fire]. Bad talk should not come to replace *za kúlulú*." Tooy said this as part of a prayer in 2005, meaning, "When Fire is coming toward us, rain must fall to extinguish it. The things we're saying here must remain so."

[sung] *Tutú bái húún. Soviélo kêdje. Di ómi dê awá lamé.** "The trumpet blows *húún. Soviélo kêdje*. The man is across the sea." Tooy says this is a song for calling on the gods far away to come help with the "play."

[sung] *Pandamán fu Asikán-e, yu wè (ÓÓÓÓ* [cry of pain]). *Pandamán fu Asikán-e (ÓÓÓÓ). Téé i gó, nôò i táki dá Mamá Lúkumbí, báya heépi mi-e (ÓÓÓÓ). Pandamán fu Asikán i tjá di bóto-e (ÓÓÓÓ). Téé i kó, nôò i táki dá Ma Lúkumbí.** "Pandamán of Asikán-e, it's you. Pandamán of Asikán-e. When you go, be sure to tell Mother Lúkumbí, Brother help me. Pandamán of Asikán, you're piloting the canoe. When you come, tell Mother Lúkumbí." Tooy explains that a fish hook wounded a man who was tying his canoe way upriver at Sotígbo. Pandamán fu Asikán brought him downstream, trying in every village to get help. They were headed all the way to the city, where a woman named Lúkumbí was sure to be able to get the hook out. But as it turned out, the hook came out before they reached her. This is a song of encouragement, of prayer. (Tooy helpfully explains that the protagonists were not human beings but "water and forest, mixed—Wátawenú and Apúku.")

[sung] *Kwéle kwéle-o, zámbiapúnguma na kwéle kwéle dá mi-e, nómò. (Tósida mamá, un yéi, kwéle kwéle-o)* [spoken:] *Kwéle kwéle, Mamá Tósida. Kwéle kwéle, Kwéle kwéle, Mamá Tósida. Gambó misí gambó-la. Gambó misíki gambó-la.* [sung:] *Kwéle kwéle mamá, mi gádu. Kwéle kwéle mamá-e.** "*Kwéle kwéle-o, zámbiapúnguma na kwéle kwéle* give me forever. (Mother Tósida, do you hear? *kwéle kwéle-o*) [spoken:] *Kwéle kwéle,* Mother Tósida. *Kwéle kwéle, Kwéle kwéle,* Mother Tósida. *Gambó* I see *gambó-la. Gambó* I see *gambó-la.* [sung:] *Kwéle kwéle* mother, my god. *Kwéle kwéle* mother-e." Tooy says that the first *wétifóu* [white bird] to go up the Suriname River sang this to pray to the Mother of Waters (Mamá Tósida, the anaconda god). {Note that *zámbiapúnguma* suggests KiKongo *Nzambi mpungu*, "Supreme deity."—van Wing and Penders 1928:279}

[sung] *Sikángomakoló, tête nábuli nkándi-e. Sikángomakoló-e, ná séki mún na gánga, báya-yéi.** "*Sikángomakoló* [Macaque], *tête nábuli nkándi* [I'm resting]. Sikángomakoló-e, don't shake my whole trunk, Brother, y'hear?" Tooy explains that the tree called *zéntete* is telling Macaque that he doesn't mind that he's eating his fruit, but would he please be careful not to shake its top so that its leaves fall off.

[sung] *Gwánini táki Náwálawála, Kináwálawalantámbo kái Gombewóówówó. Gwánini táki Kináwálalantámbo. Kináwálalantámbo bási Gombewó. Gwánini táki Nánbókosa. Kinánbókosa kái Gombewó. Gámbu-e-o. Ma Gámbu-e. Gámbu-e-o (Gámbu-e, Gámbu-e).** "Eagle said Náwálawála, Kináwálawalantámbo called Gombewóó. Eagle said Kináwálalantámbo. Kináwálawalantámbo's boss is Gombewóó. Eagle said Nánbókosa. Kinánbókosa called Gombewó. *Gámbu* [Apúku drum pegs]." Tooy says that when you come from another country to live here, people must show you respect. You're not a nobody!

[sung] *Di mi gó a mi goón déndu dê, di mi gó a mi goón déndu. Mi kó si lukwándji dê-o. Lukwándji-oo-eee, kóni ku tênê koósu u mi e. Lukwándji-ee.** "When I was going to my garden, I saw some *lukwándji* [branches] there. Branches, please don't break my

cloth. Branches." Tooy explains that a woman was all alone with no one to look after her. She tied up the only rice she had in a cloth and set out for her garden to find some greens to cook with it. On the way she saw these sticking-out branches and she called on them not to poke a hole in her rice-cloth.

[sung] *Aladé ku núndeoméoméomé* [repeated, with riffs].* "*Aladé* [maipá palm] with *núndeomé* [kaolin]." Tooy says that the bird called *hótu*, who cries out "yúdu," is sitting on a termite nest and praying that the protective palm frond and ritual white clay will come help him pray.

[sung] *Anámusiásiá-e Anámusiásiá-o Anámusiásiá-e. Ná súku málungu. Ké, ku yu mamá-e-o.** "Anámusiásiá-e [Toad]. Don't go looking for *málungu* [trouble(?)]. Oh! with your own mother." Tooy explains that Toad—he uses the euphemism "jumping man" preferred by Komantí adepts—was bathing in a mud puddle with his mother and father. A man called out to him, "Watch out for that kind of muddy water. It can hide a snake. And it won't go after you, it will go after your mother!"

[sung] *Yúnge, yélu Pákasa, Yúnge, yélu Pákasa. Pákasa kái hen mamá. Yúnge-o, Pákasa-o. Pákasa mamá Yungé, yélu Pákasa dá mi-e.** "Yúnge [small rat], *yélu Pákasa* [Elephant], Rat, *yélu* Elephant. Elephant calls her 'mother.' Rat-o, Elephant-o. Elephant's mother is Rat, *yélu* Elephant for me." Tooy says that when someone insults you by saying you're a nobody, you can say this. You may be small, but you gave birth to Elephant!

*　*　*

NB: I recorded part of an Apúku "play" in Tooy's house on October 20, 2003, and later went over the songs with him. (Sally took the photos of Tooy drumming, on p. 160, during this "play.") I list here some of the songs played that night, in order. Each continues, with chorusing and often with solo riffs, for two or three minutes. These songs are not otherwise mentioned in the text.

[sung] *Déé pikí dê nyán fu gorón, kó bégi nyán fu gorón, Wanáisa.* "The children of the earth, let us pray for food from the earth, Wanáisa." Tooy says Apúku "plays" usually begin with this song, in modified Sranan-tongo, which comes from the Para region (near the city). Wanáisa is what Para people call the Earth Mother.

[sung] *Wayoo e, Wayoo e, Asinángo.* "Let's make pleasure, Asinángo." This is a song made up to honor the association called Asinángo (after a powerful Komantí vine) that Tooy founded in the early 1990s.

[sung] *Mi kó yanfaló, baáa, mi kó yanfaló-e, mi kó dê, Asinángo, yanfaló Asinángo-e.* "I've come to pray, Brother, I've come to pray, I've come there, Asinángo, to pray Asinángo-e."

Osánsan ofálan kókolo kánkán. Tooy plays this on the Apúku drum. It means, "Busikí, go bring me the machete!" (Komantís, he tells me, call Busikís *osánsan fálamaíni*, and Busikís call a machete *ofálan kókolo kánkán.*)

[sung] *Tatá Songi-o, kón gó yéi o, Tatá Songi-o, u dê a di bégi nómò.* "Father Songi [an Apúku], come listen, Father Songi, we're still praying here!"

[sung] *Mi yanvalú-e, Akuínkan-e, mi yanvalú, Zambí mi yanvalú-e.* "I'm praying, Akuínkan-e, I'm praying, Zambí I'm praying." Tooy says that Zambí is an important Apúku, as is Akuínkan, who lives in the tree Apúku calls *anagósúki.*

[sung] *Azankeémbu, kembú na yoyó, keémbuazán, azankeémbu-e, kembú na yoyó, mi mamá.* "Azankeémbu [Apúku drum], *kembú na yoyó, keémbuazán, azankeémbu-e, kembú na yoyó,* my mother." Three-Fingered Sloth sings this song, saying he's all messed up (that is, he's ugly and walks funny), but people shouldn't pay attention to that, he's come to play the drums. *Azankeémbu* is the lead drum in Apúku "plays," so in this song Sloth is simply riffing on its name and referring to it as his mother.

[sung] *Déé bòngò u mi dê a mambá-líba-o, bái héé-o, kó bó pèê-o!* "Those family members of mine who live in the *mambá* [river], call out hey, come to our 'play'!"

[sung] *Tatá Makwalá sikángoma vayayé, aoo ayee.* Father Makwalá is an Apúku who loves to "play." (See. p. 264.) *Sikángoma* is another name for the Apúku drum. So, it's calling on Father Makwalá to come play the drum with them.

[sung] *Asákanamiké, vungú yayángo yayángo.* "The rattle [*asákanamiké*] has shaken!" (So come dance with us!)

[sung] *Awóomakaa, kímuléle.* "Awóomakaa [old folks] kímuléle [dance]." Old folks, get up and dance!

[sung] *Sídawa-o. Mi ná sídawa-e. Fámu djêlele. Sídawa-o. Mi ná sídawa-e. Fámu djêlele.* Tooy explains this as "Look at me, I'm not a nobody, you're not a nobody. I'm not a witch, you're not a witch. The ceremony we're doing here should finish well, clean clean."

[sung] *Báya-e, fa i mêni. I mêni mi da musínga-o. Báya. Mi da musínga. Ú dénikbó, un nínga mi da musínga. Báya-o, báya-e.* "Brother, what were you thinking? You think I'm just a *musínga* [*pína* palm frond], Brother, that I'm a mere *pína* palm frond? You *dénikbó*, you think I'm just a *pína* palm frond. Brother-o, Brother-e." Tooy explains that this is an insult. The god-who-has-the-place sings this song to the man who, the day before, placed a *pína* palm frond on two sticks to ask the god whether he could cut a garden in that spot. When he returned the next day, the god sang him this song, refusing him, saying that even though he's only a mere *pína* palm frond, he does important work. (*Maipá* palm fronds are considered "heavier" and more important than *pina* palm fronds and are used, for example, to keep out Evil in front of shrine and village entrances.) The *Pína* palm frond is asking for a little respect.

[sung] *Pená-o pená-o yéi, o pená-e, pená-o pená-e, o we mi tatá-o. Asawína Naná Mampúngu Zamina Mpúngo dewa-e. Lúku fa mi pená-e.* "I'm in need, y'hear! [repeats] oh my father! *Asawína Naná Mampúngu Zamina Mpúngo* [Great God Above] *dewa-e.* Look at how I'm in need!" Tooy tells me that this prayer is so strong you shouldn't sing it except in great need, and never more than three times in one year.

[sung] *Bakulí nanga Bakú lóngo vílili. Akuínkan. Kó gó pèê-o.* "Bakulí [Apúku] with Bakú [Tonê] *lóngo vílili. Akuínkan* [an Apúku]. Let's play together." Tooy explains that the Apúku is on land and the water-mother in the river, but they both share the same landing place. So, let's all play together!

[sung] *Kaábu tjá yumbé-e, kaábu tjá paansú nómò-wè. Aoo, aoo, kaábu tjá paansú.* "Crab has its child, crab brings forth its offspring forever. Ah-o, ah-o, crab brings forth offspring." Tooy says that if your son takes something of yours and ruins it and you scold him, he could reply that he's the way he is because you made him that way.

[sung] *Un déé nêne gánga mútu fu mi-e, un vánda púmbu dá mi nôò, un kó vánda mi môle dá mi. Alándi gánga da fu mi-e, un vánda púmbu da mi nôò, un kó vánda mi môle dá mi-é.* "You those *nêne gánga mútu* [ancestors] of mine, *vánda púmbu* [sweep the large drying rack] for me, come *vánda môle* [sweep the small drying rack] for me. Those *alándi gánga* [old people] of mine, you must *vánda* [sweep] my *púmbu* [large drying rack] for me, come *vánda* [sweep] my *môle* [small drying rack] for me." This is one of Tooy's most frequently sung Apúku songs. It prays that the ancestors sweep out the dirt (evil), starting from the top of the house and ending at the bottom. (A sound clip of Tooy singing a version of this song, labeled "VandaPumbu-Apuku," can be found at http://www.press.uchicago.edu/books/price/ and http://www.richandsally.net.)

[sung] *Un ta búli mi. Báka ta áti mi, nêne.* "You're bugging me. My back hurts me, *nêne* [kid]!" Tooy explains that someone's insulting you, but once you really get going, there'll be no stopping you, you'll play till dawn.

[sung] *Déé mavúngu maná u mi-e, kiiá alúngu dá mi!* [repeated] "Those *mavúngu maná* [ancestors] of mine, bring up *alúngu* [children] for me!" This song is asking the ancestors to help bring up the children so they'll be strong and wise.

[sung] *Agadjí-e bi ábi lokpo. Agadjí ná ábi lokpo môò-e. Tidé un fiká sôsò gedeónsu naná, un án yéi?* "Agadjí had the *lokpo* [house]. Agadjí doesn't have the *lokpo* [house] any more. Today you're left just like *gedeónsu naná* [tiny children], you hear?" Tooy says that Agadjí was a big man in Apúku land, but they chased him away. Then, things really got bad for them. This is what he sang. (Had I known this song in the late 1980s, I might have sung it to certain colleagues.)

[sung] *Un déé nêne gángan fu mi-o, ké! Alánde biyóngo-e, Goyó biyóngo-e, Akwandé fu Ampê, un án yéi-o, déé gangán motó u mi.* "You those *nêne gángan* [ancestors] of mine, oh! Alánde's *biyóngo* [medicinal plants]. Goyó's *biyóngo* [medicinal plants], Akwandé of Ampê, do you hear? those *gangán motó* [ancestors] of mine." Tooy says that Alánde, Goyó, and Akwandé were Lángu ancestors who were specialists in Apúku plants. (Ampê is a post in a Komantí shrine, so, used as an epithet for Akwandé, it signals his ritual power.) This song calls on them to come help with the ceremony. Tooy and his friends play various versions.

[sung] *Mamisêsi mamikólo, agúngulámitêmbe, pákasá f'a adjú, vúlankáma vúlanbímbo, mi dê mi dê kalángo, zánzan kalángo, gigigí kalángo, zántan kalángo.* "Mamisêsi mamikólo [Mavúngu], agúngulámitêmbe [assistant headman], pákasá f'a adjú [headman],

vúlankáma vúlanbímbo [supreme chief], hello, hello *kalángo, zánzan kalángo, gigigí kalángo, zántan kalángo.*" This was one of Tooy's riffs during the previous song. It's the greeting that Parrot called out from the very top of the *kwátakáma* tree.

[sung] *Un déé nêne gánga fu mi-e, kó butá bakéntu dá mi, kó butá bankámpandá.* "You those *nêne gánga* [ancestors] of mine, come place the *bakéntu* [rear walking stick] for me, come place the *bankámpandá* [front walking stick]." This is one of Tooy's favorite Apúku songs, which he often alludes to in prayers. It asks the ancestors for support, which will hold you if you slip. (A sound clip of Tooy singing a version of this song, labeled "Bankampanda-Apuku," can be found at http://www .press.uchicago.edu/books/price/ and http://www.richandsally.net.)

[sung] *Tangí mi yéi, Tangí mi yéi, Manamutámbo-e. Kwangá mi yéi, kwangá mi yéi, gádu, Manamutámbo, ké!* "*Tangí* [a medicinal plant] I hear [repeat] Manamutámbo-e. *Kwangá* [a medicinal plant] I hear [repeat], god, Manamutámbo, oh!" Tooy says that *tangí* and *kwangá* are plants that work together. When you gather them in the forest, you sing this to them. Manamutámbo, he says, is an important man in Apúku land.

[sung] *Húngo-ye, húngo-ye, tidé mi húngo kándikíla-e. Bobókilibó mavúngu masênsi, tidé mi húngo kándikíla-e.* "*Húngo-ye* [listen up!], *húngo-ye*, today I *húngo* [pay attention to] *kándikíla-e. Bobókilibó mavúngu masênsi*, today I *húngo* [pay attention to] *kándikíla-e.*" This is the song in which a visiting Apúku priest asks the locals if they've put *kándikíla*—a kind of cocoon found in the forest, also known as *apúku biyóngo*—into the earthen pot of medicinal leaves.

[sung] *Nokú tjái biála. Hên amánamaná kutjímbe.* "*Nokú* brings *biála*. That's *amánamaná kutjímbe* [the tree called *musánse*]." As with the last song, the visiting priest will ask the locals if the bark of the *musánse* tree, important in Apúku rites, is in the pot.

DÚNGULÁLI

Dúnguláli-Óbia was revealed to Saramakas by the African-ghost-spirit Akoomí at the dawn of the twentieth century. Saramakas consider it related to Komantí, since Akoomí worked closely with a Komantí *óbia* called Afeemaónsu, and since there are numerous references to Komantí in its songs. Not surprisingly, there is a far higher proportion of normal Saramaccan in Dúnguláli songs than in those sung in, say, Komantí or Papá.

Lexical Items

Anánagóa = the name of Dúnguláli's pipe

aníniámba = work or ceremony (S. *woóko*)

bundi = ghost (S. *yoóka*)

djombí = ghost (S. *yoóka*) {from Kikongo *nzumbi*, "ghost"—Parkvall 1999 s.v. *dzómbi*; see also Jamaican *jumby* and Haitian *zonbi*} *gádjagádja* = unexpected [sudden] death (S. *ongóoku*)

gbádahún = earth or child of the earth (S. *goón* or *goónmiíi*)

gbígbíla = smoke (S. *simóku*)

hágbò = knock (S. *náki*)

Hédi asúmani kasámbile (sometimes *Hédi sumaní kasángelé*) = Akoomí's praise name {*Asúmani*, which is a Komantí ritual charm worn around the calf, seems to be from Twi *asuman*, "charm, amulet, talisman, worn as a remedy or preservative against evils or mischief, such as diseases and witchcraft, consisting or composed of various things, as feathers, hair, or teeth of various animals, beads, scraps of leather or paper inscribed with mystic characters & c. and tied round some limb or hung about the neck."—Christaller 1933:483 via Bilby 2006; see also *suman*, "fetish"—Rattray 1927:9–34}

lêgbalêgba = the left hand of Death (S. *dêdè tòôtòmáu*)

Pútukupútukunámitúzalípongólolo or *námitúza* = Dúnguláli's kaolin (S. *Dúnguláli keéti*), in fact the ashes of the wild papaya tree (S. *panpantíi*)

sêgbo = chase away [as in "Get out!"] (S. *yáka*)

tabá = sacrifical food

tjálala = a thorny plant (S. *makámaká*)

tóko no adú = be careful with it (S. *kóni ku hên*)

toodjí = I'm speaking with you (S. *mi ta fáán ku i*)

yámkoa = come! (S. *kó!*)

zánzan nyúma = machete (S. *ofángi*)

Phrases That Are (at Least Partially) in Saramaccan Syntax/Lexicon, with "Language" Words Inserted

[sung] *Aíng!, Aíng!, Aíng!, Kwaíng! Ma Íni kó a fin komani-e-o. Aíng!, Kwaíng!* This was Akoomí's lament when he came home and found his wife with the other man. (*Ma Íni* is the name of his mother.) See p. 214. After the knocking-the-stone ceremony in 2005, Tooy confided to me that he had deliberately not sung this song there, since there was a visiting (rival) Dúnguláli priest taking part, and he did not want to reveal all of what he knew.

* * *

I present here, in order, the songs sung in Tooy's Dúnguláli chamber in December 2005, the night/morning that included knocking the stone. Each song was repeated for a minute or two or three. Each song's chorus is indicated in parentheses. The Dúnguláli cheer or chant marked the ending of each and every song in the sequence [spoken in unison]: "*Dúnguláli-é. Pási paatí óbia. Awíli. Awíli kándikándi. Dêde kôndè pási dúngu, líbi líbi kôndè pási límbo yéti*" ("Dúngúláli-é. Path-splitting óbia. Awíli. Awíli kándikándi. The path to the land of the dead is dark, the path to the land of the living still light"—may the path to the land of the dead remain dark, may the path to the land of the living always be light.)

There were some thirty Dúngulali songs during the first part of the evening in the Dúngulali chamber before the "play" moved to Tooy's waiting room, where Komantí and some Apúku songs were sung till after midnight.

Ná dón-e, Dúngulali-Óbia, Ná dón-o, Dúngulali-Óbia (Ná dón, mi yákayáka) [cheer] "Don't be stupid, Dúngulali-Óbia, Don't be stupid, Dúngulali-Óbia (Don't be stupid, my chaser [of ghosts])." Tooy says this song always opens his Dúngulali ceremonies. It tells Dúngulali not to let anyone lord it over him.

Mi gólu boóko. Mi póto boóko. Fa mi sa dú téé mi nyán? (chorus is whole thing) [cheer] "My water gourd's broken, my cooking pot's broken. How am I going to be able to eat?" This is a prayer of distress.

Sêgbo-e, bundí un sêgbo. (Dúngulali ta gbígbíla ahúún.) [cheer] "Get out! *bundí* [ghost] you get out! (Dúngulali is *gbígbíla ahúún* [smoking the place].)" This is to chase evil, in the form of ghosts, by Dúngulali's purifying smoke, as we did in Roland's lumberyard in 2000.

A gódo mi gódo, a sí ên sí ên gáda-e. Ná mi óto didé. (A gódo mi gódo, a sí ên sí ên gáda-e) [cheer] "The hole, the hole, he sees it sees it open there. It's not my business, that." This grave is not for me!

A dêdè a wáta, ná mi kê (tjálala, nôò mi tjálala, Dúngulali-e, ma ná mi kê, tjálala nôò mi tjálala). A dêdè a mátu ná mi kê. (chorus) *A man dê dêdè ná mi kíí hên.* (chorus) [cheer] "He's dead in the water, I didn't wish it (tjálala [a thorny plant], oh my tjálala, Dúngulali, but I didn't wish it, tjálala, oh my tjálala). He's dead in the forest, I didn't wish it. (chorus) The man's dead, I didn't wish it." Tooy explains that the plant called *tjálala* chases Evil. The song is saying that if you happen upon a corpse in the forest, just pass by, Dúngulali (*tjálala*) will take care of it, if you happen upon a corpse in the river, the same. You're with Dúngulali, dead people aren't something you need to deal with. (A sound clip of Tooy singing a version of this song, labeled "Tjalala-Dungulali," can be found at http://www.press.uchicago.edu/ books/price/ and http://www.richandsally.net.)

Boó tú ganyá i, bundí ganyá i (agó waai-o, boó tú ganyá i) [cheer] "Toad cries out to trick you, *bundí* [the ghost] tricks you (protective ritual should blow it away, Toad is tricking you)." Tooy explains that you think that the cry you hear in the forest is that of *boó*, a toad, but it's really a ghost. This song asks Dúngulali for protection from such things.

Tjentjéndámu Dúngulali, Tjentjéndámu didé. (Kulé ku hên-e! Tjentjéndámu Dúngulali, Tjentjéndámu didé, Kulé ku hên-e!) [cheer] "Tjentjéndámu Dúngulali, Tjentjéndámu that's her! (Run with her/chase her off! Tjentjéndámu Dúngulali)." Tooy explains that there's a woman from the land of the dead called Tjenjéndámu, who sometimes calls to you on a forest path; and if you get involved with her, you're dead! This song asks Dúngulali to chase her away. {NB: in normal Saramaccan, *tjêntje* means "savannah" and is often a euphemism for "cemetery." *Dámu* is from French Creole *dame*, "woman." So, *Tjentjéndámu* is Cemetery Woman.} (A sound clip of Tooy singing a version of this song, labeled "Tjentjendamu-Dungulali," can be found at http://www.press.uchicago.edu/ books/price/ and http://www .richandsally.net.)

Ahúnsò fufúuma, Adjotó fufúuma (Dúngulâli-e, Ahúnsò fufúuma, Adjotó fufúuma, Dúngulâli-e) [cheer] "Ahúnsò's a thief, Adjotó's a thief." Tooy says that Ahúnsò is the avenging spirit who kills someone and steals his soul, and that Adjotó is the "strong name" for *thief* (it's used in a Papá song reported in Price, *First-Time*, p. 168). This song asks protection against the thief from the land of the dead.

Pípa-ye, pípa lóntu, pípa Anánagóa-e (pípa, pípa-o, pípa Anánagóa-e). "Pipe, pipe going around . . . Anánagóa." This song signals the lighting and passing around of Dúngulâli's pipe, Anánagóa. "With that pipe," says Tooy, "Akoomí would kill people who came to harm him!" See pp. 213, 283. (A sound clip of Tooy singing a version of this song, labeled "PipaAnanagoa-Dungulali," can be found at http://www .press.uchicago.edu/ books/price/ and http://www.richandsally.net.)

Avúnvun mi avún, Bási Dúngulâli. Avúnvun mi avún, Bási Dúngulâli. Avúnvun yéi, tóko no adú (avún-e avúnvun, avún-e avúnvun, avúnvun-e, avúnvun. Dúngulâli-e). [cheer] "Hummingbird my hummingbird, Boss Dúngulâli . . . Hummingbird listen, *tóko no adú* [be careful with it!]." Tooy says that when Hummingbird starts dancing, it's Evil that's dancing there. You're praying to Dúngulâli to protect you from Hummingbird. Tooy adds that you must smoke the Dúngulâli pipe before you sing this song (which he had in fact just done).

A gádji tó gádjagádja tó, a gádji tó, ná i! Ná mi óto Dúngulâli. (Dúngulâli, a gádji tó, Dúngulâli, a gádji tó) Síki a káma dêdè gádjagádja tó. A gádji tó a gádji tó, ná i óto. [cheer] "A gádji tó gádjagádja tó, a gádji tó [unexpected death], not you! It's not my business, Dúngulâli. Death in bed from sickness *gádjagádja tó* [unexpected death]. A *gádji tó gádjagádja, a gádji tó* [unexpected death], it's not your doing." Tooy says this song begs Dúngulâli to protect you from a tree falling on you in the forest, a car running you over in the city, or some other sudden, unexpected death. You're saying that you can accept dying after a long illness, but that Dúngulâli should protect you from other kinds of death.

Azang kó un kó, azang kó un kó. Mêmbè óbia dá mi, Kwádjo óbia dá mi óbia-e. Azang kó un kó, Azang kó un kó. Mêmbè óbia dá mi óbia. Busukí óbia dá mi tu. Azang-e kó, Azang kó un kó. (Azang un kó, azang un kó, manda óbia dá mi-o) [cheer] "Azang [protective palm frond] come you come. Remember the *óbia* for me. Vulture *óbia* bring me *óbia*. . . . Busukí *óbia* give me some, too." Tooy says we're calling on all the *óbias* whom we pray to with protective palm fronds to come help us.

A-eee, Kwándjímu-e, mamá kái i, Bási Kwándjímu-e (waa-e, waa-e, mi Kwándjímu-e, mmmmmmmm) [cheer] "A-eee, Kwándjímu-e, mother's calling you, Boss Kwándjímu-e (waa-e, waa-e, my Kwándjímu-e, mmmmmmmmm)." Tooy explains that this song can never be sung when not in the presence of Akoomí's *óbia* post in the Dúngulâli house. Kwándjímu is one of the *óbias* that Akoomí works with.

Seíseí Dúnguláli. Seíseí Dúnguláli (Ná gó Akwíbita. Kó gó Akwíbita. Seíseí Dúnguláli. Un sa sí mi kaa, un sa sí mi kaa) [cheer] "*Seíseí Dúnguláli.* (Don't go Akwíbita. Let's go Akwíbita. *Seíseí Dúnguláli.* You can see me already.)" Tooy explains that Akoomí is calling his wife, Djesú-akóbita, with this song. She's in the land of the dead, he in that of the living. He's teasing her, saying, "Don't go" and then "Let's go." But he really wants her to come.

Dúnguláli, zánzan nyúma hên kó pèê, a pèê f'en ku laú, ku laú (a dê a mi báka a laú). Ná mi óto didé, ná mi óto-e. Ná mi óto didé, didé ná mi óto. Zánzan nyúma hên kó pèê, a pèê f'en ku laú, ku laú (a dê a mi báka a laú) [cheer] "*Dúnguláli, zánzan nyúma* [machete] has come to play, play as if crazy (he's right behind me, he's nuts). It's not my business that, not my business. Not my business that, that's not my business." Tooy says, whoever is after you to kill you, you're asking that Dúnguláli take care of him for you.

Tokóógbagba-o, Dúnguláli, Tokóógbagba-e (sêlele bóto sêlele, tokóógbagba Dúnguláli tokóógbagba-e sêlele bóto sêlele-o). Tokóógbagba-e, sumáni kasámbile óbia, tokóógbagba-e [whole repeats, substituting "Akoomí" for "Dúnguláli" . . .] [cheer] "Water lilies, Dúnguláli, water lilies (the canoe is moving, water lilies Dúnguláli water lilies, the canoe is moving). Water lilies, *sumáni kasámbile óbia* [Akoomí's *óbia*], water lilies." Tooy explains that dangerous runaway slaves (Kótolíko-nênge) used to hide under the water lilies, waiting to grab your canoe and catch you to sacrifice to their *óbias*. So, this is a prayer to Dúnguláli to protect you from that fate.

A Dúnguláli-o, a Dúnguláli-Óbia, avúnvun-ma de kói-ma (a Dúnguláli-o, a Dúnguláli-Óbia, avúnvun-ma de kói). Avúnvun-ma de kói yu, wísima nángo kói yu nómo (a Dúnguláli-o, a Dúnguláli-Óbia, avúnvun-ma de kói). [cheer] "Dúnguláli, Hummingbird's a trickster (Dúnguláli, Hummingbird's a trickster). Hummingbird is tricking you, the witch man will surely trick you." Like the earlier version of the Hummingbird song, this one warns that he's out to get you and Dúnguláli must protect you.

Dúnguláli-e, táku íngi kó. ([on single note, sound of stereotypic Indians:] *Hahhhhhhhhh) Táku íngi tóli (Hahhhhhh), déé táku íngi kó. (Hahhhhh. Táku íngi tóli. Hahhhhhh) Ma di Awayáikulé taa Dúnguláli. (Hahhh. Táku íngi tóli. Haaah) Ma déé Pátakatjána kó. (Hahhh. Táku íngi tóli. Haaah) Ma di Awayáikulé taa. (Hahhhh) Un táki Dúnguláli táki táku íngi tóli. (Hahhhh) Ma di Awayáikulé taa Dúnguláli. (Hahhh. Táku íngi tóli. Hahhh) Ma da Kilibísi íngi. (Haaa. Táku íngi tóli. Hahhh) Ma déé Pátakatjána taa Dúnguláli. (Hahhhh. Táku íngi tóli. Hahhh) Déé taku íngi gó no. (Hahhh. Di táku íngi tóli. Hahhh) Ma di táku íngi tóón Dúnguláli. (Hahhh. Di táku íngi tóli. Hahhh)* [cheer] "Dúnguláli-e, dangerous Indians are coming. *(Hahhhhhhhhhh)* Dangerous Indian story *(Hahhhhhh)*, dangerous Indians are coming. *(Hahhhhh.* Dangerous Indian story. *Hahhhhhh)* But the Awayáikulé tell Dúnguláli. *(Hahhh.* Dangerous Indian story. *Haaah)* But the Pátakatjána are coming. *(Hahhh.* Dangerous Indian story. *Haaah). . . .* But the Kilibísi Indians. *(Haaa.* The dangerous Indian story. *Hahhh)* . . . The dangerous Indians finally go. *(Hahhh.* The dangerous Indian story. *Hahhh)* But the dangerous Indians become Dúnguláli. *(Hahhh.* The dangerous Indians story. *Hahhh)* [cheer]" Tooy tells me, with a smile and wink, that

Indians—he'd named Awayáikulé, Pátakatjána, and Kilibísi, but says he could also have mentioned Aluáka—are all cannibals! So, you're asking DúngulÁli to protect you. This song is sung almost in monotone and, accompanied by the usual seed-pod rattles, is intended to mime Amerindian music. (A sound clip of Tooy singing a version of this song, labeled "Taku Ingi-Dungulali," can be found at http://www.press.uchicago.edu/books/price/ and http://www.richandsally.net.)

Gaán baáku DúngulÁli, gaán baáku-e. (hókóó, déé biyóngo-o, gaán baáku-o, DúngulÁli-e, de ta díki gaán baáku-e, hókóó, déé biyóngo) Gaán baáku-e, DúngulÁli-e, de ta díki gaán baáku-e, ná mi óto! [riff: *Hédi asúmani kasámbile óbia, de ta díki gaán baáku-e.*] (chorus) [cheer] "A deep grave DúngulÁli, a large grave. (Oh, those protective powers, a deep grave, DúngulÁli, they're digging a large hole, those protective powers) A deep grave, DúngulÁli, they're digging a large hole, but it's not for me! [riff: *Hédi asúmani kasámbile (Akoomí's) óbia,* they're digging a deep grave.]" You're asking DúngulÁli to keep you very far from the grave that's being dug.

Awíli-e (Awíli kándikándi-o) Awíli awíli-e (Awíli kándikándi-o) DúngulÁli pásipaatí óbia. Awíli-e (Awíli kándikándi-o) DúngulÁli pásipaatí óbia. [repeated many times, then a new cheer, spoken:] *Awíli (awíli kándikándi) Awíli (awíli kándikándi)* [in unison] *dzindzíma de kó, dzindzíma de kó, tétete tétete kóliwá* [back to singing] *Awíli (Awíli kándikándi-o, DúngulÁli pásipaatí óbia) Awíli (Awíli kándikándi-o, DúngulÁli pásipaatí óbia)* [standard cheer] "Awíli awíli-e (Awíli kándikándi-o) DúngulÁli is the óbia that parts the paths. . . . [in unison] The insect called *dzindzím* is coming toward you, walking very slowly." Tooy explains that *dzindzím* bores holes, and you're calling on DúngulÁli to make sure the hole isn't for you. DúngulÁli's trademark as "the óbia that parts the paths" is based on the idea that one path leads to the land of the dead and the other to the land of the living. DúngulÁli keeps you on the right path.

De tòtò mi, mi tòtò de, fa de tòtò mi, mi tòtò de, da mi a páku djába, djení kó. ([repeat of whole]) [cheer] "They mess with me, I mess with them, the way they messed with me, I messed with them, *da mi a páku djába,* the master of the house has come back." Tooy says that Akoomí sang this song after he returned from the Country of Women to find his wife with another man, and killed the man, his wife, and his children. (See p. 214.)

DúngulÁli ná mi óto didé-e. Mbéi mwazála óto. A téki hên góni a téki hên ataká, a wáka f'en a gó na mawína se. (Ná mi tjáli hên, trá bási-o) A téki hên góni a téki hên ataká, DúngulÁli, a wáka f'en a gó na mawína se. (Ná mi tjáli hên, trá bási-o) [cheer] "DúngulÁli, it's not my affair, that one. I am not responsible. He took his gun he took his spear and went toward the Marowijne River. (I didn't lead him there, it was someone else.)" It's telling DúngulÁli that you're not involved in doing violence. Other people do that, not you.

Toodjí-o. Toodjí-e, toodjí-e. Toodjí-e, Yontíni-ké, únu mamá kái únu gbádahún. Toodjí-e, Toodjí-eo. (Toodjí-o. Toodjí-e, toodjí-e. Toodjí-e, únu mamá kái únu gbádahún. Toodjí-e, toodjí) Toodjí-e, mi Toodjí-o, hédi asúmani kasámbile óbia, Toodjí-e, avó lúku mi, Toodjí-e, DúngulÁli, yu mamá kái yu gbádahún, Toodjí-e, toodjí-e. [repeat whole] *Toodji-e, mi toodji-e, asúmani kasámbile óbia, djóngbó djóngbó djóngbó djóngbó djóngbó.*

(djóngbó djóngbó djóngbó djóngbó djóngbó, djóngbó djóngbó djóngbó djóngbó djóngbó)
Kasíkási kasíkási Kasíkási, kasíkási. Kasíkási kasíkási Kasíkási, kasíkási. Kasíkási ka-
síkási Kasíkási, kasíkásí. Todje-e, todje-e. Lúku fa mi toodjí-e, yu mamá kái únu gbá-
dahún-e. [cheer] *"Toodjí* [I'm speaking with you]... *Yontíni-oh!* [Yaai's god, merely
invoked here], your mother calls you *gbádahún* [earth or child of the earth]. . . .
asúmani kasámbile óbia [Akoomí's *óbia*], jump jump jump ... *kasikási kasikási ka-*
sikási [dance dance dance] ... " Tooy explains this song by saying, suppose you
arrive home after a very long absence and there's a man waiting inside with his
gun loaded, ready to shoot you. You say, "Father, don't you recognize me? I'm your
son." It means, "Listen to me, because I'm one of yours." You're asking Dúnguláli
to chase off the dancing, jumping ghost.

[chanted] *Ná díki ná díki. (Dúnguláli) Ná díki ná díki hên. (Dúnguláli)* [repeated many
times with variations such as] *ógima ná díki, wísima ná díki.* [cheer] "Don't dig,
don't dig. (Dúnguláli) Don't dig don't dig it. (Dúnguláli) [. . . evil person don't dig,
witchman don't dig]." This is a song against Death. "Don't dig me a grave."

[chanted] *Ná bólu ná bólu (Dúnguláli)* [repeat] *Dúnguláli-e (Pásipaatí óbia) Ná béi ná béi
(Dúnguláli)* [repeat] *Ná béi ná béi hên (D) Sikópo ná béi hên (D) ahó ná béi (D) ná béi ná
béi hên (D)* [repeat] *yoóka ná béi hên (D) wísima ná béi hên (D) ná béi ná béi hên* [cheer]
"Don't bore don't bore. (Dúnguláli) [repeat] Dúnguláli-e (path-splitting *óbia*) Don't
bury don't bury. (Dúnguláli) [repeat] Don't bury don't bury him. (D) Shovel, don't
bury him (D) Hoe, don't bury him (D) Don't bury don't bury him (D) [repeat] Ghost,
don't bury him (D) Witch man, don't bury him (D) don't bury don't bury him."
Another, similar, song against Death.

Tatá Faángu, ná ganyá mi. (Dúnguláli-o) Mi avó Sokotí-e, ná ganyá mi. (Dúnguláli-o) [re-
peated many times] [cheer] "Father Bofaángu, don't deceive me. (D) My grandfather Sokotí, don't deceive me." Tooy explains that the Abaísa *gaán-obia* called Bofaángu is Dúnguláli's older brother (see p. 18). Sokotí is the Bottom-of-Death's-Foot
óbia that Sáka-Amáfu had—it keeps the ghost of someone you've killed at bay (see
p. 116). In this song, you're invoking these two powers to help you.

Kó nyán kó nyán tabá. (Dúnguláli-e, Kó nyán kó nyán tabá) [repeated many times] [then,
spoken] *Dúnguláli-e! (Pásipaatí óbia) Yéngeyéngeyénge! (Dúnguláli-e) Yéngeyéngeyénge! (Dúnguláli-e) Awíli. (Awíli kándikándi) A paatí. (A paatí twálufu hóndo dúzu
pási búka! Líbilíbi kôndè pási limbo, dêdèkôndè pási dúngu.)* "Come eat come eat *tabá*
[the sacrifice] (Dúnguláli, come eat come eat *tabá* [the sacrifice]) Dúnguláli-e!
(path-spliting *óbia*) *Yéngeyéngeyénge!* (Dúnguláli-e) *Yéngeyéngeyénge!* (Dúnguláli-e)
Awíli. (Awíli kándikándi) It split! (It split twelve hundred thousand path entrances!
The path to the land of the living must stay light, the path to the land of the dead
dark.)" This song was sung again some hours later as the cock was being sacrificed
to Dúnguláli. Tooy says it must never be spoken, sung, or heard unless a sacrifice
is actually taking place—though, apparently, it was appropriate here, as the sacrifice was being prepared.

U lálang bá mi-e (Humm bá-e) [many repeats, with riffs] [cheer] "You *lálang* give me."
Tooy says this means, "Bring me something to drink." Yontíni, Yaai's god, led

this song, the first time during the ceremony that Tooy himself did not lead the singing.

A gódo a gódo-e a gódo séki (djámkamísa a gódo) ... *Alúa, Alúa, mi djógo (Alúalúa Alúalúa djógo) Alúalúa Alúalúa djógo (Alúalúa Alúalúa djógo)* [repeats a few times] [cheer] Tooy sang this Komantí song about Kwasímukámba's brother, Alúa, and his drinking calabash (see under Komantí, below), as he began passing around the calabash for all of us to drink Dúnguláli liquid.

Mamá bóbi dê, mi mamá bóbi dê (fálala fálala, mamá bóbi dê, Dúnguláli, mamá bóbi dê, fálala fálala fálala fálala), Mamá bóbi dê, Akoomí, mamá bobi dê. [cheer] "Mother's breast is there, my mother's breast is there. . . . "

Mi gó puu sèmbè, mi gó puu mi seéfi tu. (Dúnguláli-o. Mi gó puu sèmbè, mi gó puu mi seéfi tu) [repeat] *A dêdè a wáta, kulé ku hên. (Dúnguláli-o) Wísima dêdè dê, kulé ku hên (Dúnguláli-o), dêdèdêdè, kulé ku hên. (Dúnguláli-o)* [cheer] "I go save someone, I go save myself, too. (D) A death by drowning, chase it away (D), a witch is dead, chase him away (D), stone dead, chase him away."

[At this point in the evening, there was a switch to Komantí songs, which are in that section below.]

★ ★ ★

These are, in order, the songs sung in the Dúnguláli chamber beginning at 3 a.m. during the actual knocking-the-stone ceremony. Only eleven of the songs had not been sung in the earlier session that same evening.

Nokú-e, nokú ána. U séti kabá ku aníniámba. (chorus repeats whole thing) "*Nokú, nokú* with the ceremony. We're starting the work/ceremony." Tooy says this song begins the knocking-the-stone ceremony for every *gaán-óbia*, not just Dúnguláli. He sang it as he began knocking the stone.

Hágbò, Hágbò. Hágbò kélélé ná mi kélélé ná mi-e, Dúnguláli-e [repeated] (chorus is whole thing) [cheer] "*Hágbò* [knock], *Hágbò* [knock]. *Hágbò kélélé* [knock] *ná mi kélélé* [I'm not the one who's knocking], it's not me, *Dúnguláli-e*." Tooy says you should never speak these words if you're not at a knocking-the-stone ceremony, or all sorts of spirits will come to drink the *biyóngo* (the leaves, roots, and barks being mashed up); and if they don't find it, they'll take it out of your skin! Presumably, the denial of being the person who's "knocking" is equivalent to the way all men sitting around a coffin under construction knock on it with a piece of wood while one man is actually hammering the planks in place—all doing it is like no one doing it, collective responsibility, which is what happens at a knocking-the-stone ceremony as well.

Pútukupútukunámitúzalípongólolo, námitúza-e. (chorus is whole thing) [cheer] *Pútukupútukunámitúzalípongólolo* or *námitúza* is what Dúnguláli uses instead of kaolin. Tooy has burned some *panpantíi* (wild papaya) branches and put the ashes in a bucket, which he now blends into the mixture to be "knocked" with the stone as the song is sung. [Tooy gets up from the floor and Yaai replaces him.]

Hágbò, Hágbò. [cheer] As above. Yaai gets up from knocking the stone as the song ends.

Hágbò, Hágbò. [cheer] As above. Aduáli, one of Tooy's assistants, on Tooy's instructions, is now scraping bark off some sticks into the mixture as he knocks the stone.

Sêgbo-e, bundí un sêgbo.... [cheer] "Get out, ghost!" See earlier session for full song and explanation.

Uwíi kó téé, uwíi kó, Dúnguláli tatá, u án yéi. (chorus whole) [cheer] "Many leaves have come, leaves have come, Father Dúnguláli, y'hear?" Tooy says that there are leaves you haven't seen for years, and now they're back, ready for the ceremony.

Djombí, kulé! Pupú ku hên óbia ta kó! Pupú ku hên Dúnguláli ta kó! Kulé! (Pupú ku hên Dúnguláli ta kó!) [cheer] "*Djombí* [ghost], run! Pupú's come with his *óbia!* Pupú and his Dúnguláli are coming! Run!" Tooy tells me that this is the very song that Pupú sang that famous day in the land of the dead when he arrived to untie Akoomí from his ghostly captors, after which he taught him Dúnguláli-Óbia. See p. 19.

Pútukupútukunámitúzalípongólolo.... [cheer] This time Yaai's god Yontíni sings the "kaolin" song (see just above).

Vúngu maéla-o, vúnguu maéla-e (Dúnguláli-e, vúngu maéla-o, vúnguu maéla-e, Dúngu-láli-o) Dúnguláli-o, kóni ku vúngu maéla-o. [cheer] "*Vúngu maéla* [the shroud of the world], Dúngulái, be careful with the shroud of the world." Tooy says this song begs Dúnguláli to protect you from the great shroud, which would signal your death.

Dúnguláli ná mi óto didé-e.... [cheer] See earlier session for full song and explanation.

Ahúnsò fufúuma.... [cheer] See earlier session for full song and explanation.

Gakúun, Gakúun. Dêdèsèmbè lêgbelêgbe, Dúnguláli. Yoóka dóu, Dúnguláli-e. Lêgbelêgbe kó. Fa i sa kulé ku lêgbelêbe a dêdè kôndè, Dúnguláli-o. (chorus whole) [cheer] "*Gakúun, Gakúun* [sound of death rattle]. *Dêdèsèmbè lêgbelêgbe* [Death's left hand], Dúnguláli. The ghost has come, Dúnguláli-e. Death's left hand has come. See if you can chase Death's left hand to the land of the dead, Dúnguláli-o." Tooy warns that this dangerous song can only be sung in Dúnguláli's presence.

Hágbò, Hágbò. [cheer] As above.

Dúnguláli ná mi óto didé-e.... [cheer] See earlier session for full song and explanation. In the middle of this song, they did the alternative spoken cheer (see above): *Dzindzíma de kó, dzindzíma de kó, tétete tétete kóliwá.*

A dêdè a wáta, ná mi kê.... [cheer] See earlier session for full song and explanation.

A Dúnguláli-o, a Dúnguláli-Óbia, avúnvun-ma de kói-ma.... [cheer] See earlier session for full song and explanation.

De tòtò mi u tòtò i.... [cheer] See earlier session for full song and explanation. I begin knocking the stone.

Boó tú ganyá i.... [cheer] See earlier session for full song and explanation.

[chanted] *Ná díki ná díki....* [cheer] See earlier session for full song and explanation. I get up, another man takes over.

[chanted] *Ná bólu ná bólu.* . . . [cheer] See earlier session for full song and explanation.

Awíli-e (Awíli kándikándi-o).... [cheer] See earlier session for full song and explanation. Yontíni leads this song.

Azang kó un kó, azang kó un kó. . . . [cheer] See earlier session for full song and explanation.

A gádji tó gádjagádja.... [cheer] See earlier session for full song and explanation.

Gakúun, Gakúun.... [cheer] See this session, above, for full song and explanation.

Tjentjéndámu Dúnguláli.... [cheer] See earlier session for full song and explanation.

Dúnguláli ná mi óto didé-e.... [cheer] See earlier session for full song and explanation. Sally begins knocking the stone.

A téki hên góni a téki hên ataká, Dúnguláli, a wáka f'en gó na mawína se. (Ná mi tjáli hên, trá bási-o) [cheer] This part of a song from the earlier session here becomes a song in itself.

Seíseí Dúnguláli. Ná gó Akwíbita. . . . [cheer] See earlier session for full song and explanation. A visiting priest of Dúnguláli leads this song. Sally yields to the next person.

Tokóógbagba-o, Dúnguláli. . . . [cheer] See earlier session for full song and explanation.

A gódo mi gódo, a sí ên sí ên gáda-e a. Ná mi óto didé. (A gódo mi gódo, a sí ên sí ên gáda-e) [cheer] See earlier session for full song and explanation.

Déé ógi wáka djombó djombó djombó djombó djombó, ógi wáka (a djombó djombó).... *déé kúnu wáka djombó djombó (ógi wáka, djombó djombó), déé ógi wáka djombó djombó, kásikásika kásika, kásikásika kásika kásika, Dúnguláli.* [cheer] "Evil walks *djombó djombó djombó.* . . . The avenging spirits walk *djombó djombó, kásikásika kásika.*" Tooy says *djombó djombó djombó* means that Evil is walking very slowly, which is what you want. Same for *kásikásika kásika.*

Anyámani-o, taa a sa kíi febuági. Afebuági taa a sa kíi anyámini-e. Kamía kó a tán so-e, fu míti-e, a músu kó kakaaka-e. Anyámani-e, a o kíi febuági. Afebuági taa a sa kíi anyámini-o. Kamía kó a tán so-e, fu míti-e, a músu kó kakaaka-e. [cheer] "Anyámani [Gunpowder] said he would kill *febuági* [Fire]. Fire said he would kill Gunpowder. The way for them to meet should be very hard!" This song was sung by the visiting Dúnguláli priest. Tooy tells me it's not a Dúnguláli song but a Komantí song—*anyámini* and *febuági* are Komantí words! You can play this for any *gaánóbia,* he says. If someone swears he'll kill you and you swear you'll kill him, you shouldn't meet—that's what this means. Once, Gunpowder swore he'd kill Fire and vice versa. But as they approached each other for the big fight, God Above sent down massive rains, which ended it.

Hágbò, Hágbò. [cheer] As above.

A dêdè a wáta, ná mi kê. . . . [cheer] See earlier session for full song and explanation.

Mamá bóbi deê. . . . [cheer] See earlier session for full song and explanation.

Ná dón, Dúnguláli-Óbia, Ná dón. Sung by the visiting Dúnguláli priest. See earlier session for full song and explanation.

Mi gólu boóko. Mi póto boóko. Sung by the visiting Dúnguláli priest. See earlier session for full song and explanation.

Avúnvun mi avún, Bási Dúnguláli. Sung by the visiting Dúnguláli priest. See earlier session for full song and explanation.

Boó tú ganyá i. . . . [cheer] See earlier session for full song and explanation.

Lelembó, lelembá, náki hên tjótjótjó (tjótjótjó a náki tjótjótjó, náki lelembá, tjótjótjó). [cheer] "*Lelembó, lelembá,* knock it *tjótjótjó.*" This song, says Tooy, can be used for any *gaán-óbia* during a knocking-the-stone ceremony.

Pútukupútukunámitúzalípongólolo. . . . [cheer] The "kaolin" song, again.

A dêdè a wáta, ná mi kê. . . . [cheer] See just above.

Táki fara faro-o mêni mambá mi (U mêni hên, u mêni hên) [repeated a few times, then back and forth rhythmically between soloist and chorus, naming various gods/óbias] Agadjí *(u mêni hên)* Foóla *(u mêni hên)* Abámbáo *(u mêni hên).* . . . [cheer] "Saying far away remember my river (remember it, remember it)." This song is sung when the leaves-barks-roots-vines are at last properly mashed. Tooy says you're calling on these spirits to tell them the mixture is ready. Yontíni led this song.

A dêdè a wáta, ná mi kê. . . . [cheer] See just above.

[Tooy pours a libation to Dúnguláli at Akoomí's post and passes the calabash around to all of us. The songs that followed involve the fowl sacrifices, and Tooy did not want them reproduced.]

KOMANTÍ

Komantís are the ultimate Saramaka warrior and curing gods, the quintessence of the word *óbia*. (Unlike, say, Apúkus or Papágádus, they are not, in fact, referred to as *gádus* at all but always as *óbias*.) Saramakas believe that Ndyukas are perhaps even more expert about Komantís than they are. And this makes historical sense, insofar as *Komantí* is derived from Koromantijn, the Dutch fort on the Gold Coast through which an ever-increasing number of Fantis, Asantis, and members of other interior Gold Coast peoples were shipped out as slaves during the second quarter of the eighteenth century, when the Ndyuka people were in formation. As with Apínti, I would expect there to be a preponderant proportion of Komantí derived from the Akan languages.

Lexical Items

Abálawa = Earth Mother (S. *Mamá goón*)
adjá = medicinal plants (S. *goón uwíi*)

adjába = macaw (S. *alála*) {In normal Ndyuka, *dyábáa* refers to the same bird.—Huttar 2006}

Adjaíni = the jaguar spirit associated with Anía óbia {from Ewe *dzahíni*, "nickname of leopard"—Smith 1983:47—or Twi *a-gya-héne* (pl. of *gya-héne*), "the leopard; a species of leopard or panther, black and brown")—Christaller 1933:153, 435 via Bilby 2006}

adínka [or *adjínka* or *adínka fa umbádjèni*] = three-fingered sloth (S. *pikí siló*)

adowé = white person, foreigner (S. *bakáa*)

agálabúa = vulture (S. *opéte* {from Twi *o-pété*, "vulture, carrion-kite"—Christaller 1933:391 via Bilby 2006})

agódu = drinking calabash (S. *pikí kúya*) {probably from English *gourd*—Huttar 2006}

agonkíma = friend (S. *máti*)

ahuá = a medicinal plant (S. *tjêmbe-uwíi*)

ahúnsu djándiê súmani = a plant that Apúku calls *azô*

ákaónsu = Komantí broom (a.k.a. *aódja*) (S. *komantí basóo*)

akántabúba = a heavily scaled fish (S. *kwimáta*) {In normal Ndyuka and Sranan, *buba* means "skin."}

akatáasu = hunting sack (S. *sáku*)

akéma = drum (S. *doón*) {from Twi *okyerema*, "drummer"—Mohr 1909:68 via Bilby 2006}

akúnyama = a small drum beaten with sticks (S. *déindéin*)

aluámba = a vine made of two parallel attached strands (S. *gónilópo* or *tú búka góni*)

aluangête = the bark of the tree Komantí calls *odú fankáiya* (S. *wándji kakísa*)

ameónsu (or *ameósu*) = fire (S. *fáya*)

ampaní = trouble, loss (S. *toóbi*)

ampê = the post in a Komantí shrine, when made of iron. (See *bempêni*)

andjéle líba = Marowijne River (S. *mawína lío*)

ánimbláu = cemetery (S. *geébi*) {possibly from Anomabo, the Fanti homeland where the Dutch built a slave fort in 1630}

antamáni = wing (S. *hánsa*)

anumá = the bird called *adoboyé* in S.{from Twi *anomaá*, "bird, fowl"—Christaller 1933:351 via Bilby 2006}

anyámani = gunpowder (S. *poóba*) {Might this be related to Kikongo *yamini*, "to light a fire"?—van Wing and Penders 1928:353}

aódjá = ritual broom (S. *komantí basóo*)

asikán yogoyógo = money (S. *môni*) {from Twi *sika*, "money, gold"—Christaller 1933:456; or Ewe, *sika*, "gold, money"—Westermann 1928:215, both via Bilby 2006}

asamaká = skull of dead man (S. *hédi bónu*) {from Twi *a-sámáng, a-samangfó*, "departed spirit; skeleton of a man"—Christaller 1933:423 via Bilby 2006}

asiémi = macaw (S. *alála*)

asinángo (see *odú asinángo*)

asúmani = Komantí charm worn around the calf {from Twi *asuman*, "charm, amulet, talisman, worn as a remedy or preservative against evils or mischief, such as diseases and witchcraft, consisting or composed of various things, as feathers, hair, or teeth of various animals, beads, scraps of leather or paper inscribed with mystic characters & c. and tied round some limb or hung about the neck"—Christaller 1933:483 via Bilby 2006; see also *suman*, "fetish"—Rattray 1927:9–34}

ataká [or *otaká*] = spear (S. *lánza*)

atjuá = dog (S. *dágu*) {from Twi *ɔ-tweá* or Anyi *cjwùwá*—Smith 1983:49—or Twi *o-tweá*, "dog, bitch"; *atweaá*, "a small dog"—Christaller 1933:551 via Bilby 2006}

atjuá même háun = stray dog (S. *gánda dágu*)

azámadadí = firefly (S. *azonkínyênyê*) {from Kikongo *azima*, "to shine, light up" (?)—van Wing and Penders 1928:5}

balúa = death (S. *dêdè*)

beensúa = egg (S. *óbo*); see *okínsuá*

bempêni = the post in a Komantí shrine, when made of wood. (See *ampê*)

béniántjini = a blackish leaf (S. *dontuá*)

bóbo = child (S. *miñ*)

boofó = white person (S. *bakáa*) {from Fanti *boròfó*, Akuapem *a-boròfó* (pl. of *O-buroní*), "European, white man, mulatto")—Christaller 1933:41, 54 via Bilby 2006; Twi *borɔfó*, "in reference to a European language"; *aborɔfó* (pl. of *oburoní*), "in reference to a European"—Redden and Owusu 1963:204 via Bilby 2006}

boofóplási = Paramaribo (white peoples' place) (S. *foto* {from English "fort"}) {See s.v. *boofó* + English *place*}

bofóanúmu = a plant (S. *anadjénúmu*)

bubúsi = forest (S. *mátu*, Ndyuka *busi*)

busúu [or *bosóo*] = water or rain (S. *wáta* or *tjúba*) {from Twi *nsú*, "water"—Christaller 1933:478 via Bilby 2006—or Twi *nsúo*, *nsú*, "water, rain"—Redden and Owusu 1963:219 via Bilby 2006}

dabalá = cut off a head (S. *kóti hédi*)

dáma = hear (S. *yéi*)

dámaséke = chair (S. *situu*)

dámsófolobaní disádisá belêdjo = gun (S. *góni*)

dáulo = metal percussion instrument {from Twi *a-dáwúru*, "a kind of bell to be struck with a stick"—Christaller 1933:67 via Bilby 2006}

djádja = ocelot, associated with *djebí*

djámkamísa = cane juice (S. *tjéni wáta*)

djebí = jaguar (S. *pèndêmbéti*) {from Ga or Akan *dzebi*, "war god"—Wooding 1972:166}

dínta = daylight (S. *didía*)

dókofáda = the awara tree at Bákakúun (or any awara tree?) (S. *awáa*)

duámpo = canoe, boat (S. *bóto*)

dzámdzampeékò = Kwadjú, King of the Vultures

fankáiya (*odú fankáiya*) = a large tree (S. *wándji*), symbol of strength *febuági* = fire (S. *fáya*)

felémangáidjá = spear (S. *lánza*)

gídjimadjí afòòdjí = salt (S. *sátu*)

gweduánka = woodpecker (S. *tótómboti*)

golúmetaíni ahuá [or simply *ahuá*] = a medicinal plant (S. *tjêmbe-uwíi*)

hísi f'a adálue = machete (S. *ofángi*)

hóbotábêla (sometimes *obutábela*) = tobacco (S. *tabáku*)

húmba = to shoot (S. *súti*)

ínikóko = hen (S. *muyêè ganía*)

kantiánkáma [or *odú kwakwádabankáma kwakwá dadíafê*] = a tree (S. *gaán páu* or
    kwátakáma)

kítikoomá-daónsu = hawk (S. *gavián*) {possibly from Kikongo *nkíti-nkíti*, "foulque,
    morelle, oiseau échassier"—Huttar 1985:52 via Bilby 2006—and Twi *akoromá*,
    "bird of prey, hawk"—Christaller 1933:257 via Bilby 2006} If Bilby's etymology is
    correct, it is, as he suggests, another example of seamless fusion between Central
    African and Akan ideas in Komantí.

kólokwa = the dance of the Adátu [toad] spirit

konfó = Komantí priest or possessing spirit (S. *bási* or *óbia*) {from Twi *o-kómfo*, "fetish
    priest; a fetish-man, possessed with or prophesying by a festish; soothsayer,
    diviner, charmer, sorcerer"—Christaller 1933:248 via Bilby 2006}

kongoobusí = crooked scepter (S. *dobápáu*)

kótoko = dangerous name for "gun" (S. *góni*)—Tooy says if you call a gun that, it will
    fire {perhaps related to Twi *kotoko*, "brave companions, able teammates"—Red-
    den and Owusu 1963:211 via Bilby 2006}

kukubêe [or *kukubele*] = three-fingered sloth (S. *pikí siló*)

Kwáo = Jaguar (S. *pèndêmbéti*)

kwátakí = heart (S. *áti*) {from Twi *katakyí, kwatakyí*, "bravery, valor"—Christaller
    1933:231 via Bilby 2006}

kwenkwenkotjíba = large woodpecker (S. *tótómbotí*)

maíndjima = tobacco (S. *tabáku*)

masópima = ritual payment (S. *madjómina*—see p. 23)

mayándo = fire (S. *fáya*)

mêko = Jaguar's front teeth (S. *fési sê tánda u pèndê-mbéti*)

miiyán = war óbia (S. *gaán-óbia*), an óbia that has been in battle

Naná Nyanwé = what Busikís [a kind of Komantí] call the Great God Above (S. *mása
    gaán gádu*)

obólodiê = plantain (S. *baána*) {from Akyim *bodee*, "plantain"—Christaller 1933:34 via
    Bilby 2006—or Twi *o-b(o)rò-dé*, "plantain, *Musa paradisiaca*"—Christaller 1933:41
    via Bilby 2006}

odáni = house (S. *ósu*) {from Twi *o-dáng*, "house, native house; room, apartment"—
    Christaller 1933:64 via Bilby 2006}

odú = tree (S. *páu*), often said as an abbreviation of *odú fankáiya*, the strongest tree
    for Komantís

odú asinángo = a vine whose "head" bends downward and is much used in evil magic to bend someone's head down. If you've never had a wife die, you're not man enough to gather it in the forest. It signifies strength and was the name of the short-lived "association" formed in the 1990s by Tooy.

odú buánsikibuádji = a parasite (called in Saramaccan *pikífóukaká*) that grows in holes in the giant *kwátakáma* tree and whose leaves are much used in Komantí rites.

odú fankáiya = a large tree (S. *wándji*), symbol of strength {Twi *o-dóm*, "a kind of tree, the bark of which is used in performing an ordeal"—Christaller 1933:89 via Bilby 2006}

ofálan kókolo kánkán = what Busikís [a kind of Komantí] call a machete {first word from Ewe *aflá*, "ceremonial sword"—Sebba 1982:40}

ofaná [or *ofalá*] = machete (S. *ofángi*) {from Twi *afana*, "sword"—Mohr 1909:192 via Bilby 2006}

okínsuá = egg (S. *óbo*) {from Twi *kesuá*, "egg"—Sebba 1982:40—see also Baulé *klèn-zuá*—Smith 1983:48}

okókolo = cock (S. *wómi ganía*) {from Ewe *koklô*, "fowl, hen"; Twi *akóko*, "domestic fowl, hen, cock"; or any of a number of similar words in Yoruba, Edo, and other West African languages—via Bilby 2006}

okónturu = teeth (S. *tánda*)

Ogalabúa = Kwadjú, King of the Vultures

omámosán (sometimes *anámusán* or *mámusán*) = rum (S. *daán*) {possibly from Twi *nsá*, "strong drink, intoxicating liquor, palm wine"—Christaller 1933:417 via Bilby 2006}

ómbelekú = woman (S. *muyêè*)

osámpaní = wings (S. *hánsa*)

osánsan fálamaíni = male Wénti [a kind of Komantí] (S. *Busikí*)

otókoló mayándo = egg (S. *óbo*). Tooy says that this name for "egg," which recognizes that it has "fire" (*mayándo*)—a yolk—inside, is now obsolete.

otoló [or *otonú*] = gun (S. *góni*) {from Twi *o-túo*, "musket, gun"—Christaller 1933:543 via Bilby 2006}

oyéle = kaolin (white clay) (S. *keéti*) {from Twi *hyire*, "white clay" (?)—Rattray 1927:74}

patagoosú = stool (S. *bángi*)

pekipéki = respect (S. *lespéki*)

sántoofíanumá = the bird called *adoboyé* {from Twi *asánt(o)rofí*, "a species of night bird"—Christaller 1933:428 via Bilby 2006—and Twi *anomaá*, "bird, fowl"—Christaller 1933:351 via Bilby 2006}

sáwa = to wash (S. *wási*) {related to normal Saramaccan *sawá* = to rinse(?)}

séibidé dadí kamádadí híniba = a thorn bush (S. *mátunga*) that stays rigid once cut for *séibidé* (seven days)

sêminí (sometimes *osêminí*) = Komantí spirits (collectively)

sénsegòòsé = a small creek fish (S. *pèndê amáido*)

siisí mámba = great pleasure (S. *pizíi búnu*)

tandiátandíata = an ordeal played with cards in the country of Adátu (toad) spirits to determine who's telling the truth

Tándo = a Komantí god called over from Africa near the end of the eighteenth-century war {from *Tando*, Akan "thunder god," "war god"—Wooding 1972:164–65; and/or Twi *Tano*, "type of god that inhabits rivers; the river god of the King of Ashanti"—Nketia 1963:37, 95, 98 via Bilby 2006}

tjútjuapaata = to dance (S. *baiyá*)

umbádjêni = three-fingered sloth (S. *pikí siló*)

vulá = ears (S. *yési*)

vúngu = world (S. *múndu*)

Yáu [or *Yáo*] = river Komantí {from Yao, "war god of the Asante," "Asante blacksmith's god"—Wooding 1972:163}

yawalú = tongue (S. *tôngò*)

yembáfou = parrot (S. *papakái*) {S. *fóu* = bird}

yémbu = soul (S. *akáa*)—but see under the song of Bat and Cock, below

yímbu = great Komantí spirits

yímpenteú = horse (S. *hási*)

yôko = sickness (S. *síki*)

zanzumbúya = a water bird (S. *apiiti*)

zinkó = important ancestors

zawádja = the west side of a *kantiankáma* tree

Phrases That Are Not in Saramaccan Syntax

Dámka kíi atjuá même háun. The name of Jaguar's front tooth, the one he kills dogs with. See p. 262.

Káfrika kabá u nú. The Ndyuka name for Jaguar's front tooth. See p. 262.

Momokúmokúmokú a gwí, kuma kí. The name of Jaguar's large rear tooth. See p. 262.

Batesú batesú. Tooy explains this as "Each person has his way of speaking," "Each country has its knowledge," or "What Father taught you isn't what he taught me." This can also be played on the *apínti*. See p. 287.

*Atjúapetêmafú, udé awan mafú, mafúosúonú, mafúodankayêle.** The common Saramaka proverb "Left hand washes right hand, right hand washes left hand."

*Nákwa takí funán totó.** Tooy used this in a prayer in 2005 and says it means, "No one can stop your heart from beating (except God Above)."

[sung] *Ameósu, ameósu, búmkaiya!** "Ameósu [fire], búmkaiya [it's sat down, it's ready]." When Komantí men are about to dance on fire, this is the song that is played. "The fire's ready, whoever is man enough can try it out!" says Tooy, who drummed it at a "play" in 2003.

*Vúngu-o, vúngu-e, asinángo.** "Vúngu-o [world], vúngu-e, asinángo [the name of Tooy's association]." This is calling everyone in the world to join the association's "play." Tooy sang it at a "play" in 2003.

Phrases That Are (at Least Partially) in Saramaccan Syntax/ Lexicon, with "Language" Words Inserted

[sung] *Un déé kwéikwéi sèmbè, déé vándavánda sèmbè, tidé u bái kái sèmbè.* "You those crude people, those bullshitting people, today we're calling everyone." Tooy explains that all kinds of people—everyone—are being encouraged to come to the "play." "When folks get together," he says, "there will undoubtedly be liars among them and thieves among them, but whoever they are, let's all work together— this song summons them all!" It's a recent Komantí song, composed for Tooy's Asinángo Association in the early 1990s. See p. 15.

[sung] *Gingéé-o, gingéuwawa, góni dê f'en a kákikamba-e, zaun dê a nyán-e.* "Gingéé-o, *gingéuwawa* [a certain plant], the gun is cocked, the elephant is eating." Tooy explains, "The plant that the elephant likes to eat is ripe over there, the hunter sets his gun trap right on the path, yet the elephant manages to pass—the gun misfires—and the animal gets to eat his favorite food. That's how ritually strong *zaun* [elephant] is! This is a song to sing to the Komantís when you're hunting and need their help." See p. 15. Note that Saramakas have preserved memories of this animal, as well as the Kikongo word for it (*nzau*), for more than three hundred years.

[sung] *Hói mi kankan gweduánka-o-o, Ma Yímbo. Hói mi kankan gweduánka, Bási-o, ké Ma Yímbo.* "Hold me tight Gweduánka-o-o [Woodpecker], Ma Yímbo. Hold me tight Gweduánka-o-o [Woodpecker], My 'Boss' [exclamation] Ma Yímbo." This is Woodpecker's song, saying his beak is strong, his wings are strong, his feet are strong, but his tail is strongest of all. Tooy says that when you shoot him in a tree, his wings open wide and settle, his claws release their hold, but his tail holds him firm. See p. 15. (A sound clip of Tooy singing a version of this song, labeled "Gweduanka-Komanti," can be found at http://www.press.uchicago.edu/books/ price/ and http://www.richandsally.net.)

[sung] *Pelé kó a íni, i sa péle kó a íni, pèê ku pèndêmbéti bía ma ná pèê ku pusipúsi bía.* [repeated with riffs] "Play, come on in, you can play, come on in. Play with Jaguar's whiskers, but don't play with Pussycat's whiskers." This is the song that begins the cycle that includes the next eight songs. See pp. 30–31.

[sung] *Aaa-aa-ooo, Ooo-aaa-e o mi e mi hái-e aláli óbia-e, mi aoolí. Abaaya-oo, abaya-ooo, abaya-oo, ómi ooaa-e, aláli óbia, un yéi-e.* This is the song of Jaguar when he's famished, calling on his *óbias* to help him find food. See pp. 30–31.

[sung] *Sanfántaíni-o, Sankwánta-e. Míti míti-hun. Sanfántaíni-o, Sankwánta, kánkan. Ómi míti míti únu dá di kó f'i-e. Sanfántaíni-o. Míti míti-hun. Sanfántaíni-e, a dê f'en Sankwánta, kánkankan kan-e. Mi dê mi dê-hun.* "Sanfántaíni-o, Sankwánta-e [alternative names for Kwadjú]. *Míti míti-hun* [something's happened!(?)]. *Sanfántaíni-o, Sankwánta* [the names again], *kánkan* [the meat is tough!]. *Ómi míti míti únu dá di kó f'i-e* [Man, something's happened please come]. *Sanfántaíni-o* [name]. *Míti míti-hun* [something's happened]. *Sanfántaíni-e, a dê f'en Sankwánta* [name, he's there name], *kánkankan kan-e* [tough meat!]. *Mi dê mi dê-hun* [I'm here I'm here]."

After famished Jaguar has killed his prey with his left paw, he calls his older brother Vulture, complaining that the meat's too tough to eat. Vulture arrives, begins pecking at the anus, goes all the way along up till the nostrils, then back down again and then back up, pecking out both eyes. He tells Jaguar, "You see, it's all meat to eat!" See pp. 30–31.

[sung] *Naná-o, fá mi sa dú? Djádja-o, fá mi sa dú? Andadíki óbia, fá mi sa dú-e? Fá mi sa dú-e, naná kôndè sábima, fá mi sa dú, man, téé a tjámba-kôndè. Un f'á mi sa dú, naná kôndè sábima.* "Naná-o [Great God], what should I do? Djádja-o, what should I do? Andadíki óbia, what should I do? What should I do, wise man from God's country? What should I do, man, all the way from Tjámba-country. What should I do, wise man from God's country?" This is another song that Jaguar sang to call his older brother to come help him, after he'd killed the peccary with the wrong paw. See pp. 30–31.

[sung] *Ná mi máti kói yu, alúmba alúmba djêndje.* [repeated three times] "It's not my friend who tricked you, *alúmba alúmba djêndje.*" This is Kwadjú's song when he arrives and sees Jaguar moping about the meat. It means, "Your family is your family, your true friends are your kinsmen"—not Pussycat! See pp. 30–31.

[sung] *Mása dusa dê, naná kôndè sábima, mása dusa dê.* "Good God, what must I do to be able to eat that meat, wise man from God's country, what must I do?" This is Jaguar again asking his brother what to do. See pp. 30–31.

[sung] *Sábi-o-o-o, sábi sábi sábi aómo.* [repeat six times] "Knowledge-o, knowledge, knowledge, knowledge forever." Kwadjú tells Jaguar, "Go hunting, walk softly, you'll find game!" See pp. 30–31.

[sung] *Djindé, djindé, gínde, zúngadímba.* [repeated with riffs] Vulture continues to sing to his younger brother, "Walk through the forest, go up to the hilltops, you'll find meat." See pp. 30–31.

[sung] *Kwáo, náki búnu. Kwáo, náki hên búnu. Kwáo, wátji búnu. Kwáo, náki hên búnu.* "Kwáo [= Jaguar], strike well! Kwáo, strike him well! Kwáo, stalk well. Kwáo, strike him well!" Vulture continues giving advice to Jaguar, telling him not to miss, to strike well. See pp. 30–31.

[sung] *Zau tutú, zau djefelêbe. A kóti a kóti a baanabó, a kóti a kóti a kilínga, a nuwan geke búba, wán búba músu tán búba.* This is the way that the tree which Komantí calls *odú fankáiya* and whose bark it calls *aluangête* (the only tree a thunder axe cannot fell) boasts of the impenetrability of its skin. *A kóti* means, "It cuts"; *wán búba músu tán búba* means (in Saramaccan or Ndyuka), "A bark (or skin) must stay bark (stay whole)." See p. 80.

[sung] *Benko! Kaíndjima kaí kántamba-o, kaíndjima-e, mi óbia-e.* "Benko! [the sound of the sea crashing against the rock], *Kaíndjima* [the name of the rock] calls out *kántamba-o, kaíndjima-e,* my *óbia.*" Busikí sings this song about a great rock in the middle of the sea. When the sea comes crashing up against it, trying to break it, the rock says, "I was here when you arrived. I'm going to be here long after." And the sea recedes in a spray of froth. See p. 81. (A sound clip of Tooy singing a

version of this song, labeled "Benko-Komanti," can be found at http://www.press
.uchicago.edu/books/price/ and http://www.richandsally.net.)

[sung] *Djúa bête denaí-o-o, miam, djúa bête dendí, mi bási-o, bête dê a únu kámba-e. Djúa
bête denaí-o-o, ná fu toló ná fu taká ná fu ofalá, siisí mámba.* The phrase *bête dê a únu
kamba* is in normal Saramaccan (except for *bête*, which Saramaccan calls *gúdu*)
and means, "Wonderful things are in your room." Tooy explains: "The wonderful
things you have, my boss, give me some!" "I'm praying for good, I'm not asking
for a gun [K. *otoló*] or a club or a machete [K. *ofalá*] or a spear [K. *ataká*] but for great
pleasure [K. *siisí mámba*]." See p. 83.

[sung] *Djúa na bolóbi-o e i fankáiya, djúa téé a mi tatá bolóbi-e, djúa téé na bolóbi-e.* "Djúa
(= S. *djulá* [to swear(?)]) to Bolóbi, you *fankáiya* [strong tree], Djúa all the way to
my father Bolóbi, Djúa all the way to Bolóbi." Father Bolóbi's children (jaguars) all
went out, but they returned "between his legs" safely—this is their prayer that all
will go well. Tooy once told me that Abólobí (a word that appears in various forms
in Komantí songs) is another name for "Flibánti." See p. 83.

[sung] *Nêne nêne nêne nêne nêne kêlewa-e. Kêlewa-e. Nêne nêne nêne nêne nêne kêlewa-e. Akêlewa-
e-o. Akêlewa-o. Sábi dê a Nána-e-o.* "Nêne nêne nêne nêne nêne kêlewa-e. Kêlewa-e. Nêne
nêne nêne nêne kêlewa-e. Akêlewa-e-o. Akêlewa-o. God is wise." Though I remain uncertain, Tooy claims that *kêlewa* means, "I've come to live with you." In any case,
Pobôsi's Adátu (toad spirit) sang this song to persuade people to let him remain
with his master. See p. 118.

[sung] *Agódo, agódo séki-e, djámkamísa agódo.* "Agódo, agódo [small calabash drinking
bowl] shakes, *djámkamísa* [cane juice] *agódo.* (The chorus is, first, *djámkamísa
agódo* and later, *Alúa djógo,* which means "Alúa's jug.") Tooy says that it was with
this song that Kwasímukámba asked his brother Kwasí Alúa to pour him some
cane juice into the drinking calabash. See p. 215. This song was also part of Tooy's
knocking-the-stone ceremony in 2005.

[sung] *Mi pelé kó a íni, bó pelé kó a íni, pèè pèè dóu pelé kó a íni, bó pelé, pelé kó a íni.* [spo-
ken:] *Máti, ná bái. Di máti kó pelé ku i.* There are no specifically Komantí words
in this Komantí song about how Possum tricked Cock. Rather, the language is
(modified) Ndyuka or Aluku. Possum sings, as he is wringing Cock's neck, "I'm
playing come inside, let's play come inside, play all the way play come inside, let's
play, play come inside. Friend, don't cry out. Your friend has come to play with
you." See p. 263.

[sung] *Kétekétewéle kétewéli kétekétewéli kétewéli, kétekétewéle kétewéli kétekétewéli
kétewéli, yémbu ta kói amímba, yémbu kói amímba, yémbu kói amímba, yémbu ta
kói amímba, yémbu i kói mi amímba, yémbu kói amímba-e.* This is the song of Bat
when he's putting Cock to sleep so he can drink all his blood. *Yémbu,* says Tooy, is
Komantí for "soul," *kói* means "to fool" or "to trick" in normal Saramaccan, and
amímba means "a whoever person" (as in Spanish *fulano*). Bat is calling Cock's soul
to trick him so he can put him to sleep. *Yémbu ta kói amímba* = "Soul is tricking
amímba"; "*yémbu i kói mi amímba* = "Soul, you are tricking *amímba* for me." (For
a Papá version, see below.) See p. 263. (A sound clip of Tooy singing a version

of this song, labeled "Keteketewele-Komanti," can be found at http://www.press
.uchicago.edu/books/price/ and http://www.richandsally.net.) Kenneth Bilby (personal communication, 2006) persuasively suggests that *yémbu* in fact means not
"soul" but "vampire bat" (*djembu* means "vampire bat" in Aluku)—so Tooy seems
once again to be "guessing" when I press for a breakdown of a song whose meaning he's learned as a whole. Bilby derives this word from Kikongo *ngémbo*, "rous-
sette; sorte de grande chauve-souris" (Laman 1964:686) and *ngyémbo*, "flying fox;
bat" (Laman 1964:699).

[sung] *Yáoo, mi Yáo, mié mié mié mié mié mié mié mié mié. Adínka-e, mié mié, busikí mié
mié ku adjú mié mié, mi óbia mi ka moomi odia poki mi sa fomaní mani o mi da awamba
djebí-e, Yáoo.* This is the prayer of Giant Otter to the Great God, when he's been
hunting for twelve nights and twelve days and not found anything to eat. They are
words to be said when you are in need. They call on Yáu (river Komantí), Adínka
(Three-Fingered Sloth, who is a special Komantí animal), Busikí (water Komantí),
and Adjú, as well as others in the final phrase, which includes more Komantí language. See p. 273.

[sung] *Adínka, a ta yénde-o, woyo yénde-e, adínka hên ta yênde-e, bási adínka-e, medi a kai.*
"*Adínka* [Three-Fingered Sloth], [it + progressive] *yénde-o, woyo yénde-e, adínka hên
ta yênde-e* [boss/priest], *adínka-e, medi a kai.*" Song of admiration for how handsome Three-Fingered Sloth is when climbing. See p. 274.

[sung] *Kwan, kwan, bó yéi, mi o pêpè yu, kwan, kwan.* "*Kwan, kwan* [Three-Fingered
Sloth's cry], come listen, I will 'pepper' you, *kwan, kwan.*" The animal says this
when the hunter threatens to shoot him. It means, "If you mess with me, I'll mess
with you." See p. 274.

[sung] *Kukube i míti mamima, a kukubele míti mamima.* "*Kukube*, you've met up with
mamima, kuku belly has met up with *mamima.*" This is the boast of the hunter in
response to Sloth's boast. See p. 274.

[sung] *Ándo kó a kó pèê asánti vílivíli, Djáifosó Gwágwá kó pèê asánti vílivíli, Bási Adínka
gwagwá kó pèê asánti vílivíli, Ma Bandímba-e kiyóo un án yéi-o akántabúba, asánti
baáa, u án yéi, lúku akántabúba.* This is the prayer of the old blind woman Abaníba
that caused Great God to let her see once again. It invokes Ándo (Sáka-Amáfu),
Djaifosú Gwágwá, Three-Fingered Sloth, and Ma Badímba (or Ma Gwandimbu,
who owns the bush hogs—see under Apúku, above). *Lúku akántabúba* means,
"Look at the *kwimáta* fish." See p. 274.

[sung] *Anakaní-o, Balá Anakaní, di wán kódó biyóngo, biyóngo-e wómi agófuagó. Balá
Anakaní, Balá Anakaní-e, di wán biyóngo, biyóngo-e agófuagó.* "Anakaní-o, Brother
Anakaní [this is the name Komantís used for Captain Logofóu, Pobôsi's son], that
single power object, that power object, man, you must have the protective power
(*agó*). Balá Anakaní, Balá Anakaní-e, that single power object, you must have the
protective power." See p. 415.

[sung] *Djíndjo maniámba. Asantí dawáma. Djíndjo maniámba.* After I repeatedly
pressed him for it, Tooy sang me this dangerous song, related to a story he'd once

told me. After singing it, he offered a variant of the original story: Tatá Djíndjo had three sons, Kwadjú, Djebí, and Busukí. He made a garden near that of Tatá Maní (also known as Yáwadáda, though Tooy seems somewhat confused about the names) and asked him for some sugarcane for his children. Djíndjo warned his children never to go near Maní's garden by themselves, or he'd eat them. But they went and met up with him—at which point massive rains fell, thunder axes whizzed past, lightning flashed. Kwadjú called on their father with this song. See p. 428.

[sung] *Wáinso fu Ankáni-e, aódja wáinsó fu áti. Awáinso fu Ankaní. Aódja waínso fu áti. Wáinso Ankáni-e. Djebí waínso fu Ankani, waínso fu Ankani. Aódja waínso fu áti. Mamá kó táki nen yu-ké, ná mi a kête fu waimbó-ké. A tjalí naná kemponu naná gbêle gbêle gbêle gbêle gbêle gbêle.** "*Wáinso* from [or "of"] *Ankáni-e, aódja* [ritual broom] *wáinsó* from *áti*. *Awáinso* from *Ankaní*. *Aódja* [ritual broom] *waínso* from *áti*. *Wáinso Ankáni-e*. *Djebí* [Jaguar] *waínso* from *Ankani, waínso* from *Ankani. Aódja* [ritual broom] *waínso* from *áti*. Mother comes to say *nen yu-ké*, I'm not *a kête* from *waimbó-ké*. It's a shame Great God, *gbêle gbêle gbêle gbêle gbêle gbêle*." Tooy sang this to me after I'd repeatedly pressed him about the song relating the story of the three brothers (see previous song). He had told me, at various times, that you could sing it only if you were leaving the place you sang it in within a week—or you're dead. He finally sang it spontaneously in our little studio apartment in Cayenne the day before we left near the end of 2005, telling me this is (the expanded version of?) the very dangerous song that Kwadjú sang to beg his father's help as the lightning flashed. In the end, Kwadjú said there was no help for it and flew off into the sky, where he remains as King of the Vultures; Djebí turned into a stone and later became King of the Jaguars; Busikí dove into the river and became King of the Wéntis. "Once you sing this song, you must wait eight years before you return to where you sang it," said Tooy when he was finished. I later noticed that the song was also sung by Yaai's possession god, Basi Yontíni, with Tooy's god answering, on our last visit of 2005.

[sung] *Tj'ampaní, tj'ampaní-o. Bútji fupá-e, Anía, wímatjelê, wímatjelê. Andí án bi tjá ampaní-o, bítji fupá-e, wímatjelê, wímatjelê.** "It will bring *ampaní* [trouble, loss], it will bring *ampaní* [trouble, loss]. *Bútji fupá-e, Anía, wímatjelê, wímatjelê*. What didn't bring *ampaní* [trouble, loss], *bítji fupá-e, wímatjelê, wímatjelê*." Tooy says that Anía *óbia*, which works with Bayúngu to guard the Béndiwáta god, has this "talk," which means, "The thing you did, you didn't do it well, it will bring trouble." Another time, he tells me it means, "The thing you're doing, you're not the first one to do it, it was here before you came."

*Mi Káakabángukabángu. Mi tjíngi u mangói. Mi kaakabángukabángu. Mi Anía palulú. Mi gwangólugwangólu gidí. Mi guzálumutjá tjámpangó.** "I'm *Káakabángukabángu*. I'm *Tjíngi u mangói*. I'm *Kaakabángukabángu*. I'm *Anía*-wild banana tree. I'm *gwangólugwangólu gidí*. I'm *Guzálumutjá tjámpangó*." This is how Anía *óbia*, of Béndiwáta, says his praise name.

Mi Kwasí dántaká dánka adján. Mi Kwasí têntele medjiê. Mi uwíi a sêkie, uwíi embá. Na fósi kaosí na mambá. Na fósi kaosí nampô. Híni wán okókoló vesiá antánu kelêkelê bengúle. Kolúkolú mi sí djanuári. Adjú mêlem, mêlem mêlem nanga adjúa. "I'm Kwasí dántaká dánka adján. I'm Kwasí têntele medjiê. I'm the leaf *a sêkie*, the leaf *embá*. The first *kaosí* of the river. The first *kaosí* of the earth. Every cock *vesiá antánu kelêkelê bengúle. Kolúkolú mi sí djanuári. Adjú mêlem, mêlem mêlem nanga adjúa.*" According to Tooy, this is the way Kwadjú, King of the Kultures, King of the Skies, says his praise name.

Okónturu okónturu ufó yawalú, yawalú bi dê ufó okónturu.* "*Okónturu* [Teeth] *okónturu* [Teeth] before *yawalú* [Tongue], *yawalú* [Tongue] was there before *okónturu* [Teeth]." Tooy says that Teeth and Tongue were fighting. Teeth threatened Tongue, saying he could bite him anytime Mouth moved. Tongue replied that Teeth can fall out, Tongue is always there. Tongue was there before Teeth.

Papá meki dukú síki taanga.* Tooy says this Komantí fragment means, "I'm very hungry."

Okókolo meki okínsuá dátim.* "*Okókolo* [chicken] makes the *okínsuá* [egg]." The proverb "Chicken lays the egg, the egg makes the chicken again." I've also heard Tooy say it as: *okókolo méki kínsuá. Kínsuá méki okókolo báki*, with him explaining that *báki* is the way Komantí says [normal Saramaccan] *báka*, which means "back" or "again."

Téé okókolo náki osámpaní, téé okókolo dínta.* "When *okókolo* [cock] flaps his *osámpaní* [wings], it will be *dínta* [daylight]." I've heard Tooy use this expression to say, "Let's see what happens tomorrow."

Mi aluwé. Mi mangámbo. Mi lowémangámbo. Mi alowégódjgódjo. Mi mánimáusába.* "I'm aluwé. I'm mangámbo. I'm lowémangámbo. I'm alowégódjgódjo. I'm mánimáusába." Tooy says this is how Jaguar says his praise name.

Téé a kótoko húmba a músu toón bosóo.* "When the *kótoko* [gun] *húmba* [shoots], it must turn into *bosóo* [water]." Fragment of a prayer in 2005, meaning, "When the gun shoots, it [the bullets] must turn into water."

Téki pekipéki f'i sa nyán pikí donú pópu.* "Having *pekipéki* [respect] means you'll eat your child's shit." Tooy says that your child will piss and shit in your food, but you must have respect for him, since he's yours.

[sung] *San dê. San dê wán dê. U mbéi dê ku sán dê wán dê. Kadjá sán dê wán dê. Sán dê míkíli konfó. Adjaíni míkili konfó. Sán dê wán dê.** "What's there. What's there, something's there. We'll make do with what's there, something's there. *Kadjá* what's there, something's there. What's there *míkíli konfó. Adjaíni míkili konfó.* What's there, something's there." Tooy says this is what a person might say when he arrives and is hungry. If you have something to eat, you'd sing the next song to him.

[sung] *Ádja-e-e-e, mínimíni bó-nyán-o. Akópia-e-e, mínimíni bó-nyán. Mialé-e, mialé mi-o, mi nyonyo-o.** "*Ádja-e-e-e, mínimíni* let's eat. *Akópia-e-e, mínimíni* let's eat. *Mialé-e, mialé mi-o, mi nyonyo-o.*" See previous song.

[sung] *A Yáo-o, mi óbia-e. Komantí nêngè kó bó gí a Yáo béniántjini. Aya-e-e, mi óbia-o. Komantí nêngè kó bó gí a Yáo béniántjini. Námnámnám sálanúmagó sánuma. Námnám-*

nám sálanúmagó sánuma. Asánti kótoko yéi. Óbiama bái a nêngèkôndè, agó! Kó bó gí a
*Yáo wán béniántjini. A músu gó na píago. Yáo-o.** "A Yáo-o, my *óbia-e.* Komantí-men,
let's go give Yáo *béniántjini.* . . . *Námnámnám sálanúmagó sánuma. Asánti kótoko*
[dangerous name for "gun"] listen! *Óbia*-man calls out in Africa, be careful! . . .
It must go to *píago.* Yáo." There's a leaf called (in Saramaccan) *dantuá,* which is
black as gunpowder, and which Komantí calls *béniántjini.* Its praise name is *kum-*
fóayáwa. When you shoot it, it sings this song.

[sung] *A baiyó, yéi maíndjima-ye, matámbáo yéi maíndjima.** "A baiyó, listen *maíndjima-*
ye [tobacco], *matámbáo* listen *maíndjima* [tobacco]." This song calls for tobacco to
snort. Tooy made a point of telling me that the *maíndjima* of this song resembles
the *Kaíndjima* name of the rock-in-the-middle-of-the-sea (see an earlier Komantí
song), but that they have nothing to do with each other.

[sung] *Gó dê píi lúku Gonkíma, gó dê píi lúku Ayáwa. U dê píi lúku Agonkíma. Ma gó dê píi*
*lúku Ayáwa-ee, gó dê píi lúku Agonkíma-e.** "Go be still and wait for Gonkíma, go
be still and wait for Ayáwa." Tooy says that Gonkíma and Ayáwa are big men in
Komantí country. This song suggests the wisdom of waiting, not making a fuss,
and watching "what is coming and what is going."

[sung] *Asánti pútu pútu pútu pútu asánti bête asúmani. Asánti pútu pútu pútu pútu asánti*
*bête asúmani, Komantí. Lúku afánde kabá, téé a Mádjasí.** The chorus of the song is
"*anadjénúmu, bofóanúmu,*" the Saramaccan name for a medicinal plant followed
by its Komantí name. Tooy claims that *Asánti pútu pútu pútu pútu* means, "Man,
let's hurry up, everyone hurry up," with *Asánti* standing in for *man. Lúku afánde*
kabá, téé a Mádjasí, he says, is "You see the place '*faan*' [white and clear] already, all
the way to Mádjasí" (all in almost normal Saramaccan). Tooy adds that the sense
of this is, "We'll see which man is most manly and will get to Mádjasí first." Tooy
has told me that Mádjasí's strong name is Mádjawa and that she is "the mother
of us all." Tooy first told me that the song refers to which *bási* (boss, priest) will
get to the knowledge held by Mádjawa, who was living at the time among the late
runaways known as Kótolíko-nêngè, behind Plantation Groot-Chatillon. After
singing me the song, and explaining it, Tooy said we really shouldn't talk about
it further. A couple of years later, when I asked him about the song again, he gave
me a different explanation. It was first sung, he said, by Komantí men flying over
the ocean from Africa, competing to see who would arrive first at the mouth of
the Suriname River, where Mádjawa holds sway.

★ ★ ★

Here are the Komantí songs sung on the night of the knocking-the-stone ceremony
in 2005. Unless otherwise indicated, Tooy is the lead singer:

Mi dánsi-e Naná-o. Mi dánsi-e Naná-e. Naná kôndè mi dánsi tidé. Naná wénsi fu adjá.
Adjá mi dánsi. Golón mi yéi nawá. According to Tooy, "I'm dancing Great God,

I'm dancing Great God. God's Country I'm dancing today. God wishes for medicinal leaves. Medicinal leaves, I'm dancing. Earth, I hear *nawá*." This song, in mixed Saramaccan and Sranan-tongo (or Ndyuka/Aluku), often begins a Komantí "play." Kenneth Bilby (personal communication, 2006) suggests persuasively that the initial phrase does not refer to dancing but means, "I'm thanking God and the Earth," which is what Aluku Kumanti adepts told him in the 1980s. Alukus sing: *Midasi-oo, Nana-oo, yee . . .* , and in Aluku Kumanti language *midasi* means "thank you" (from Twi *da-ase*, "to thank"—Christaller 1933:66 via Bilby 2006). In this case, Tooy and his friends (or their forebears) have (lightly) changed the meaning of a word that's foreign to them to correspond to one that's familiar.

Mi dánsi o bóbo yéi (Mi dánsi o bóbo yéi). Tooy says: "I'm dancing, but I'm just a child." This song of humility often follows the previous one.

Anumá-o, mi wênsi anumá. Djádja-o, mi wênsi anumá-o. (Anumá-o, Anumá-e, mi wênsi anumá-o) We mi sántoofíanumá, konfó-o. Mi wênsi fu anumá-e, anumá-e. "Anumá, I'm making a wish for *anúma*." Tooy says that the bird called *adoboyé* is praying to the Great God Above for strength to finish what it has started. Its Komantí names are *sántoofíanumá* or *anumá. Djádja*, a kind of ocelot, is often invoked in Komantí songs.

Un kái-o, un kái sèmbè odún a yáo, un kái hên mbéi a kó. Djádja kó, a nêngèkôndè. "We're calling, we're calling people for the work we're doing here, we're calling on them to come. *Djádja* come, in Africa."

Un féndi pási, Adjaíni-e (un féni pási, Adjaíni) nêngèkôndè opéte, u féndi pási a Asanti-e. "You find the path, Jaguar spirit, African vulture, you find the path to Asanti!"

Íniwan, benkú a íniwan, kantánka íni (aaoo, íniwan, benkú a íniwan). Tooy says this means, "Everyone, every kind of person, come play."

Yáu, mi yáu, mié mié mié mié mié mié mié mié mié. Adínka-e, míe mié míe mié mié mié Busikí míe mié míe mié mié mié, ku Adjú mié míe mié míe mié mié, mi óbia-e. This is a version of the prayer of Giant Otter (see above). It's being used here, Tooy says, to greet various *óbias*: Yáu [river Komantí], Adínka [Three-Fingered Sloth], Busikí [male Wénti], Adjú [who chases the dead].

Gaánda ódio-o-e, gaánda ódio-o. (da yímbu, gaánda ódio-o-e, gaánda ódio-o) A yímbu na-o. Gaánda ódio-o-e, gaánda ódio-o. (da yímbu) A yímbu na. Da yímbu-e, dá-o mi yímbu. A yímuádda-o. "Old people, greetings (to the great Komantí spirits, greetings)." Another song of greeting.

Gingéé-o, gingéuwawa. . . . [etc.] The remarkable song about Elephant (see above).

Anúmu zénzenzen, anúmu zénzen, nêngekôndè falawé. "Anúmu zénzenzen, anúmu zénzen, Africa is faraway!" Tooy says, "The ceremony we're doing here resembles the original, but it can't really be what they did where it comes from, which is very far away. However, we do our best!"

Yámkoa-e, yámkoa, badá, azámadadí, yámkoa. [repeat] "Come here, come, Brother, *azámadadí* [Firefly], come here." Tooy says that a man went into the forest and got lost. Night was coming on. He sat down on a stump and called on Firefly, who came and lit his path all the way home. (In Tooy's scheme of things, fireflies are good, hummingbirds [see the Dúnguláli songs above] are evil.)

Otjóufo, yéi! Otjóufo Kofí Yobonkofí. Konsó yímbu-e, o Ánkama-e. Atuámba-yuun. Yobonkofí-e. Óbia Ánkama-e. "Otjóufo, listen! Otjóufo, it's Kofí Yobonkofí. *Konsó yímbu-e* [great Komantí spirits], *o Ánkama-e* [an *óbia*]. *Atuámba-yuun.* Yobonkofí-e. *Óbia* Ánkama-e." Tooy explains that this song commemorates an event in Africa. Two men, Otjóufo and Kofí Yobonkofí, went hunting and came to a fork in the path. They planted a stick in the ground, agreeing that whoever got back first would turn the stick as a signal that he'd already passed there. Somewhere down the path, Otjóufo was caught by Evil and buried alive in a deep hole. Yobonkofí returned and saw that the stick hadn't been turned, so he called to Otjóufo with this song. The third time, Otjóufo answered, and Yobonkofí eventually found the hole and dug him out, all covered with maggots, finally bringing him back to the land of the living. When you sing this song, says Tooy, you're asking someone to help you the way Yobonkofí helped Otjóufo in Africa.

San-o, ma san? O san san san o san-e. Agálabúa san, san du i so, o-ye-o, ma o san-o. "What what what? What what what? *Agálabúa* [Vulture] what? What's wrong with you, listen, but what?" Tooy says that the three brothers, Busikí [male Wénti], Djebí [Jaguar], and Kwadjú [Vulture], met at a "play." Kwadjú refused to join in, so Busikí sang this song, asking him what was wrong.

Adínka be ná be beebee kóti obélewa-e. "Three-fingered sloth blood and blood bloody-bloody's cut *obélewa.*" Tooy explains that Howler Monkey's wife dreamed that Hunter shot her husband. Though she warned him, he insisted on going out to find a medicinal plant the next afternoon. And he met up with Hunter! This is his cry after he was shot, still holding on to the branch with his tail, singing to tell his wife. Tooy says this is a very dangerous song, something to play in Gisí's house or the great *óbia* house at Dáome. It was sung here by Aduáli, one of Tooy's close friends.

Adínka, a ta yénde-o. . . . The song of praise about Three-Fingered-Sloth (see above).

Báya-ooo, báya-ooo-aaa-e, di agómaká sa nyán maká, agómaká o nyán maká-e, agómaká o nyán maká-o. [repeats] "Brother, thorns shall eat thorns!" Tooy explains that once, his brother Sensiló went hunting behind Kayana and arrived at a place that he didn't know was taboo to him. When he returned that night, he dreamed of a horseman with a lantern brighter than a car's headlights. This song is what the horseman sang him in the dream. It's saying, "You broke my horse, you broke my *djéndjekómaka* tree [the tree men make winnowing trays from]." Sensiló's *óbia* Flibánti possessed him and smashed up the house, saying that Sensiló had really met up with someone that day! (So, this is a relatively recent Komantí song, from several decades ago.)

Djánkoloví ku Amafú sélele. [repeated and chorused many times] Tooy says that Djánkoloví is Busikí's revered ancestor. Mafuéna or Mafúsélele plays the same role for the bird called *anumá* (*adoboyé*). They are people who should come help with the "play"!

Akúnyama bási. [repeated many times] "The *akúnyama* [*deíndéin* drum] is the boss!" Tooy also played this during a Komantí "play" in 2003. The *deíndéin* must beat a steady rhythm for the "play" to work.

[There followed here two songs involving Flibánti that are so dangerous that Tooy says not only to erase them from the recorder, but never even to mention them again, so I do not.]

Dí u bi dê a sabá, aódja waai. "When we lived in the savannah, *aódja* [the Komantí broom] swept away." Tooy explains that when we lived in the savannah, that is, in the old days, when the broom swept away it meant the wind had blown someone away—someone of yours had died. The song reminds us that living is better than dying. This song was led by Léo, one of Tooy's close relatives.

Sêkele bênte nya númu. Kandáma kó kandawé. Djifúma ta djufule. Yáo músu lúku ankáma biká i kó fu ankáma. This is the song of the *aódja*, the Komantí broom that possessed men carry along with a machete. It's saying that the house must be swept clean, that witches mustn't come there, that sorcerers mustn't come there.

Akúdayó. Fa mi dánsi, so seéi mi yéi noa. This song is sung by Voisin, another Dúnguláli priest who has come for the knocking-the-stone ritual. Tooy claims it's sung by a man named Akúdayó and says, "The way I'm dancing, that gives the play some real style!"

Djúa bête denaí-o-o.... As sung and explained above.

Djóbi-o, dabannkáma djóbi, djóbi djóbi, djóbi djóbi, dabankáma djóbi. Atjútjuabaní nêngè, dabannkáma djóbi. "Djóbi-o, I heard *djóbi*, *djóbi djóbi*, *djóbi djóbi*, I heard *djóbi*. People's footsteps, I heard *djóbi*." Tooy says that this is a heavy song, not to be sung or spoken except in special circumstances. It dates from the Battle of Bákakuún (in 1749; see Price, *First-Time*), when a woman went off to mash cassava on a large stone and heard the ground shaking: the whites were coming! So, she ran back to the mountaintop retreat where they lived and sang this song of warning.

[There followed a song that Tooy says not to reproduce, so I do not.]

Danga helú menu! Dánga, mi helú e-o. Fankáiya-nêngè dama mi helú, Abálawa-e. "Danger/ Witchcraft, I wash my hands of it. *Fankáiya-nêngè* [strong man] I wash my hands, Earth Mother." Tooy says that is the song of the protective palm frond at the doorstep of the *óbia* shrine. When it sees Evil, it dips down and stops it from entering, then rises back to its normal place. The song says it saw Evil and killed it!

Kokókolo bénza, djáni kensúa. Tooy explains that Cock (K. *okókolo*) owns no cloths and no bottles of rum. So, when his wife gives birth (K. *djáni kensúa* = lays an egg) he simply says cockadoodle-do, because that's the only way he knows to celebrate.

Bolóbi-o, sosolóbi. Téé i wáka a sonkompáni báka, no, i sa míti kónsomi. "Bolóbi-o, sosolóbi. If you walk behind [if you follow] *sonkompáni* [a person who doesn't know much] long enough, you'll still end up with some *kónsomi* [useful knowledge]." Tooy once sang this to me, saying, with self-deprecation, "That's what brought you to me!"

Nawí-o na wí. Nawí nawí nawá. "Just us, it's just us here!"

Bête fu ankáma. Unfá i o súku adjúa? Djáni bensúa. "Good things to *ankáma*. But how will you look for *adjúa*? The hen lays an egg." Tooy says, "Chicken says, 'you want the egg, but not the chicken shit.'" You go into the henhouse and take the eggs but leave the shit behind there.

Odú-we, odú-we. Odú dê na Ábasúmbu, odú dê Ábasúmbu, Gisí dê na Ábasúmbu, adínka dê na Ábasúmbu (odú-e, odú-e, odú dê na Ábasúmbu). "*Odú* [*fankáiya*, the Komantís' strongest tree], Odú is at Ábasúmbu, Gisí is at Ábasúmbu, Three-Fingered-Sloth is at Ábasúmbu" (in other words, some seriously powerful people are at Ábasúmbu!). Tooy explains that just after the Peace, there used to be a military post at Ábasúmbu (now Bookopondo) where they would check to see if you had a gun or other illegal property. Gisí was coming upriver and, when he arrived near the post, called down the rains with this song, so the soldiers wouldn't see him passing. (See the next two songs, too.)

Asúmani baya baya Asúmani. Asúmani baya baya Asúmani. Sama e pasá na mi na balá balá e e. "Asúmani, Brother. . . . Who is passing by me, Brother?" Tooy says that when Gisí got to the mouth of Sara Creek, he met "a real man like himself" who sang this to him.

Mi Afánti-o. Asúmani baya baya Asúmani. Sama e pasá na mi na balá balá e-o. Na mi Afánti-e (na mi Afánti-o) We, mi Afánti nênge, [spoken:] *víe víe víe víe, tjátjá, hònhònhòn hònhònhòn.* "I'm Afánti-o. Asúmani Brother. . . . I'm an Afánti-e. Well, I'm an Afánti person, *víe víe víe víe, tjátjá, hònhònhòn hònhònhòn.*" This is what Gisí sang back to the man at the creek mouth, to identify himself. (Note that the final spoken portion, including the final two words that are a sound made with the fingers tapping ones Adam's apple, is a speciality of Luángu speakers, used to end various of their songs—see below under Luángu.)

Kósokóso dê a mpêne líba. Djaíni-o i án yéi. Konfó Yáu (Djaíni-o i án yéi. Konfó Yáu). "*Kósokóso* is on top of *mpêne*. Djaíni [Jaguar spirit], do you hear? Konfó Yáu [river spirit]." Tooy says this is a song of warning. "Never mess with a coiled-up snake." Or, "Never walk around with a cocked gun."

Adínka bolóbio, hey-o, Bási Adínka-e. Bolóbio hey-o, Adínka bolóbio Abálawa-e, fankáiya-nêngé, bolóbio-e. "Adínka [Three-Fingered-Sloth] *bolóbio*, hey-o, Boss Adínka-e. Bolóbio hey-o, Adínka *bolóbio* Abálawa-e [Earth Mother], *fankáiya-nêngé* [powerful person], *bolóbio-e.*" Tooy often remarks (and I can certainly confirm this from experiences hunting in Saramaka) that you can't bring down a sloth with a single gunshot. This song, Tooy says, is Sloth boasting that when he dies, people back in the village will hear. There'll be "twelve" gunshots!

Efi i man, dan i kóngo! A andjéle líba de. Efi i man, dan i kóngo! A andjéle líba de. Efi i man, dan i kóngo! A Kawesína mámba. [in Ndyuka] "If you're man enough, let's go! To the Maroni River. . . . To the Kawesína River." I don't know the referent of the latter name—it may be the Cassewinica Creek. This song and two others in Ndyuka

Komanti that I don't transcribe here were sung by visitors, and Tooy couldn't help with their transcription.

Sanfántaíni-o, Sankwánta-e.... Jaguar calling on his older brother Vulture (see above for song and explanation).

Sán toóbi, sán toóbi-o baáa. Sán toóbi a nêngèkôndè, san toóbi-o baáa. San toóbi-o balá so. Sán toóbi, sán toóbi-o baáa-e. "What's the problem, what's the problem, Brother? What's the problem in Africa?" This song, begun by Frank and taken over by Tooy, is asking the spirits in Africa why they're not coming over to the "play"—is there some problem?

Benko! Kaíndjima.... The sea trying to break the rock (see above for song and explanation).

Gwémikankan gweduánka-o-o.... The song about Woodpecker's tail (see above for song and explanation).

Adínka bolóbi-o. The song of Three-Fingered-Sloth (see several songs above).

Odúmu óbia-o, yéi, Busiké, Odúmu óbia-o, Odúmuví mándze mándze kuun, Odúmuwe mándze mándze kóabelá, Adínka-a, no no Bási Odúmu. Odúmu bi kísi óbia-o, Odúmu-e. "Odúmu óbia-o, listen Busiké, Odúmu óbia-o, Odúmuví mándze mándze kuun, Odúmuwe *mándze mándze kóabelá* [tobacco], Adínka-a [Three-Fingered-Sloth], no no Bási Odúmu. Odúmu got the *óbia-o*, Odúmu-e." Tooy's god Dúnuyángi also sang this song in 2005 and explained to me and another man who was present that the eldest of three brothers, Kwadjú (Vulture), asked Djebí (Jaguar) and the youngest, Busikí, which of them had more of their father's powers. Busikí said he did. So they agreed that on a Friday, Busikí would try to pass by Djebí's landing place without his knowledge. Djebí placed a chicken there as watchman. When Busikí arose in the night to go bathe in the river, the chicken crowed, Djebí ran down to the river, and seeing no one, cut off the chicken's head, since it had betrayed him. On Friday, Busikí passed right by the landing place, which shows that he's ritually riper than Djebí. So, older brother Kwadjó, watching all this from above, sang this song. Now, at the knocking-the-stone ceremony, it's Tooy who sings it.

Odúmu án bi yéi-o. Tatá-e, tatá u dú môò mi-e. Odúmuví mándze mándze kuun, Odúmuwe mándze mándze kóablá. Koa táki ke osêmini. Osêmini osêmini abala-e, na wán gaán lívasio. Odúmuwi. Odúmuwi, kióo, ódiódio, Odúmuvie-o. "Odúmu didn't hear. Father, father, I've been had. *Odúmuví mándze mándze kuun, odúmuwe mándze mándze kóablá* [tobacco]. Koa says, oh, *osêmini* [Komantí spirits]. Komantí spirits, Brother, that's a big *lívasio. Odúmuwi. Odúmuwi,* kid, greetings, *Odúmuvie-o.*" Dúnuyángi continues his story, saying that Busikí then went to visit Djebí, who admitted that Busikí was the stronger, that he had taken after their father, and he sang this song.

Kólokwa djóndjo. [repeated many times] "We're at the *kólokwa* 'play!'" The Adátu (Komantí toad spirit) has the dance called *kólokwa.* Tooy says that you have to be careful while singing this song. If you slip, the Adátu will cut off your head! Tooy also sang this during a Komantí "play" in 2003.

Bête fu ankáma.... "Chicken says, you want the egg, but not the chicken shit" (see above for song and explanation).

Kétekétewéle kétewéli. . . . Bat tricking Cock (see above for song and explanation).

Bête fu ankáma. . . . See two songs above.

Gébenti, mi na aluámba nôò [repeat], *mi na aluámba-e.* "*Gébenti,* I'm *aluámba,* I'm *aluámba.*" Tooy says the vine that Komantí calls *aluámba* is boasting to its children that it's really strong ritually. *Gébenti,* Tooy claims, means "my children."

We gó, we kón. Ma u nái dóu a naná. "We go, we come, but we don't reach God." Tooy says this song, with its Ndyuka inflections, affirms that no one—not even a Komantí spirit—is man enough to see God's face. We just work with his messages.[8]

Akekelé-e dániamba. Yáu, pé a ma óbiama dê, akekelé-e daniámba. A Yáu diámba-o diámba, akekelé daniámba. "*Akekelé-e* [I'd like to see] *dániamba* [the man]. Yáu, where is the *óbia*-man? I'd like to see him." According to Tooy, this song is saying, "I'd like to see the man who could get to God Above."

Agó yoyóyo, agó nómo. Agó yóyo, agó yo. Vulá músu dáma. "Ritual protection *yoyóyo,* ritual protection forever! . . . *Vulá* [ears] must *dáma* [hear]." Tooy adds that ears must hear the footsteps that come *kángokángo, káfrikáfri,* as he sings in a riff.

M'án yéi, m'án yéi. Mi bási Dankuná-e. M'an yéi, seéi. A bígi a wáta m'án yéi. A bígi a údu, m'án yéi. M'án yéi. "I don't hear it. I don't hear it. My boss Dankuná. I don't hear a thing. It's big on the river, it's big in the forest, I don't hear it." This is a song for Dankuná *óbia,* which has an iron pot in Tooy's Dúnguláli chamber. It's begging Dankuná that, if a gun shoots somewhere, you won't hear it—it can't hurt you.

A paa wanyá! [with many riffs] "It splits open!" This song asks that if someone fires a gun at you, the barrel must split wide open.

[chanted] *A nuwan geke búba, a nuwan geke búba, a nuwan geke búba.* (*búba búba búba*) [riffs: *wómi búba búba, híni wán búba búba*] This is the song of the *fankáiya* tree, boasting of the strength of its bark (*búba*).

Sénsegòòsé, Sénsegòòsé. Sénsegòòsé kíi Angáta, Sénse. Hen go nyá nyá nyá. "*Sénsegòòsé* [a creek fish] killed Angáta. *Sénse.* He went *nyá nyá nyá* [dead]." Tooy says a spine of this small fish, called *pèndê amáido* in normal Saramaccan, poked a man named Angáta in Africa and killed him. So, Komantí men say, "Be careful with *sénsegòòsé!*"

Mi ku yú Kwánivo Djúabelé, Mi ku yú Kwánivo Djúabelé-e. Kwánivo, Djúabelé. (*Mi ku i Kwánivo*) *Mi ku yú Kwánivo Djúabelé-e. Kwánivo, Djúabelé. Mi ku i Kwánivo.* "Me and you Kwánivo Djúabelé. . . . " Tooy explains that a boy named Kwánivo was once walking around with his slingshot and came upon a corpse with its teeth showing and its fingers clawed up, so he exclaimed, "Whatever that is, it's sure ugly!" The third time he said it was ugly, the dead man—a certain Djúabelé—raised himself up, grabbed a machete blade, and began chasing the boy around the village, singing this song. When he couldn't catch him, he flung the machete blade at him, missing, but the blade stuck in the earth and brought forth a plant—a plant that can't be used by Komantí men without blood being shed somewhere, says Tooy. (He doesn't offer the name of the plant and I don't insist.)

Sankandaé-o, mandé kei i. Mi bási Sankandé-o, mandé kei i. Mandé kei i na fínga[?]*-e.* Tooy explains that this happened in the African country called Biián, where children never cried, people never laughed, dogs didn't bark, cocks never crowed. A man named Sakandaé visited there and said his praise name, thus breaking the country's taboo. Thenceforth, there was crying, laughter, cocks crowing, dogs barking. The headman of the country called Sakandaé and sang him this song to show him there were men in that country, too.

Mádjeni-e. [repeated many times] *Ma lúku yu sánsan kuma nyánmi ben kuma yáni. Mi sa penápená tjá e mi féni wán boóko boóko antamáni fu mi. Mi sí a dasíni, mi sí daóngo. A djáki hên naná-e, mi óbia (a-yaó, a-yaó).* "Mádjeni [a Komantí spirit]. But look how you *sánsan kuma nyánmi ben kuma yáni.* I can barely keep going with my messed-up wing. I see till *dasíni,* I see till *daóngo. A djáki hên naná-e,* my *óbia.*" Tooy explains that when Great Firefly decided to cross the sea "from west to east," this is what he sang in prayer—his wings must not tire so he falls in the sea and a big fish eats him. (Note that the phrase "I see till *dasíni*" recalls a simliar phrase in the Komantí song about *Kótolíko-nêngè,* above, calling into question Tooy's translation and explanation there.)

Mi lóbi Komantí-e, mi lóbi-e Komantí-e-o. Komantí mi lóbi, Komantí váva-e. "I love Komantí. . . . " Tooy says that this is what Jaguar sings when he's really hungry, trying to flatter his *óbia* to help him catch game.

Asánti bolóbio-e! Asánti-e. Bolóbie-o. Asánti bolóbio, a bái íyan íyan íyan íyan. "Asánti bolóbio-e! He calls out *íyan íyan íyan íyan.*" Jaguar continued along a creek and decided to cross it, first singing this song. His prey, hearing it, moved back to the other side of the creek. Tooy says that when you hear this song, it's time to move. You should sing it only near the end of a "play," when people are almost ready to get up.

Zinkó, mêmbe! Fu de án kó dabalá mi ándo. "Zinkó [strong ancestors], pay attention! That they don't come and *dabalá mi ándo* [cut off my head]." Tooy explains: "Let the great men protect me when I'm sleeping. Make sure no one comes and cuts off my head!" (In the days of war, Saramakas, like many warriors in Africa, routinely cut off the heads of slain enemies—see Price, *First-Time,* pp. 145–46.)

Sanfántaíni-o, Sankwánta-e. Jaguar calling his older brother Vulture, again. Frank sang this one. Part of the Pussycat cycle (see above for song and explanation).

Naná-o, fá mi sa dú? Djádja-o, fá mi sa dú? Jaguar, asking his older brother for help, again. Aduáli sang this one. Part of the Pussycat cycle (see above for song and explanation).

Naná-o, fá mi sa dú. Tooy sings another version of previous song.

Ná mi máti kói yu, alúmba alúmba djêndje. Vulture advising Jaguar. Part of the pussycat cycle (see above for song and explanation).

Kwáo, náki búnu. Further advice from Vulture to Jaguar. Part of the Pussycat cycle (see above for song and explanation).

Bái kái Ma Adjêni-o, kái Adjêni óbia. "Call out to Adjêni óbia." Tooy says this is calling on an important person in Komantí land.

Bayá yayá Ma Bóluwa-e. [repeat] *Komantí-nêngè kó tjá Bóluwa gó f 'en-e-o.* "*Bayá yayá* Ma Bóluwa. Komantí people came and took Bóluwa away. *A dowa-e.*" Tooy explains that this is how Lángu people "bought" their Komantí leaves and knowledge. One of their ancestors was lost in the forest and came to a large *fankáiya* tree, surrounded by more kinds of plants than he'd ever seen. Three men (Tooy says he can't say their names when he's not drumming the song) were there and asked him to sit down, saying he'd arrived in Adjá-Kôndè, where the Great God stores all his seeds: those for Komantís, those for Apúkus, those for Vodús, those for Wéntis. They asked him which he'd like to have. He said he'd like Komantí leaves. They said no problem and told him to go home and bring back a girl—but make sure it's on a Friday. He did as told and brought them his sister's daughter, Abóluwa, a young adolescent. They taught him the uses of the leaves, which ones were for "opening the mouth" of a new Komantí *óbia*, which were for washing it . . . and then they said to hand over the girl. They grabbed her, spun her around the great tree, and that was the end of her. They told him to go, but he asked where the girl was. They told him to get out, or else. ("They ate her!" says Tooy.) This song commemorates the event, which is why, says Tooy, women are the real "bosses" of Lángu Komantí. Underneath his *obia* canoe, just outside his Dúnguláli chamber, Tooy keeps a memorial to Ma Abóluwa, whose sacrifice made possible the Lángu clan's knowledge of Komantí.

Abayaa mhummm, Abayaa mhummm, dabaa feému, Abayaa mhummm, dabaa feému-e, a-a-uuu, kóni ku dabaa fému. "Brother, mhummm, *dabaa fému* [cutting off a head]. . . . be careful about cutting off a head." Leo sang this one, which Tooy says is another version of the head-cutting song above (where *dabaa* was *dabalá*).

Yímbo, Ma Yímbo, Yímbo, Ma Yímbo, Yímbo, Yímbo-e! Fu haíka Ma Yímbo. You're calling on Ma Yímbo—apparently another great Komantí spirit—to *haíka*, listen.

Atjuá bémbai. Di i kori mi a mambá, u sa míti a mêko. "*Atjuá* [Dog]. Since you tricked me by the river, we shall meet at *mêko* [My Front Teeth]." Yaai's god Yontíni sang this song, which Tooy explains with a story. Jaguar asked Dog for the *óbia* that allowed him to have so many women. Dog asked for fifty cents and said he'd need two weeks to find the ingredients. When Jaguar returned, he saw that Dog had spent the money and hadn't made the *óbia* for him. So Jaguar sang this song, saying, "Now we're in the village, but when you go into the forest, you're going to meet up with *mêko*," which Tooy says means Jaguar's front teeth. Dog and Jaguar have been enemies ever since.

Kòso kòso dê a bénde, yáo a bénde yáo. Tooy explains that "Chicken says, 'If you scratch around on the garbage heap long enough, you'll find your own mother's skull.'" Don't mess with me!

Míde huún. A tadjí táta kó. Ala mai sóboi tján. Yaai's god Yontíni sings this one, which Tooy explains is the song of Old Woman, who's cleaning the ground with a hoe and complaining about a weed that grows so fast it could even cover the small end of a coffin that's waiting to be buried.

[At this point in the evening, the metal Komantí gong was laid aside. People sang about twenty Apúku songs before taking a brief rest until the climactic knocking-the-stone ceremony in the Dúnguláli chamber.]

KÔNDÈ

Kôndè—"Country" language—is the way Saramakas as well as various other African Americans (e.g., Jamaican Maroons) refer to a generalized old-time language, the way the "older heads" used to talk in daily life. Fragments have been preserved through rituals, through the speech of ghost-spirits, and just for fun.

Lexical Items

afogán = cow (S. *káu*) {from Fon *afɔgãn*, "large foot"—Smith 1987:1 via Parkvall 1999, s.v. *afogán*}

agwití = agouti (S. *kokóni*) {from French or English *agouti*—Huttar 2006}

ahála = agouti (S. *kokóni*)—Tooy warns that if you call an agouti by this name and then eat it, you'll die.

Ahúngwadja = a greeting

Awesáánu = a greeting, answered by *Awesáánu*

Bakuí bangóni = a greeting, answered by *Batjêtje bangóni*, itself answered by *Bayáka bangóni*

Bangóni = person (S. *sèmbè* or *nêngè*)

Bótè = a greeting, answered by *Sikenai bótè*

étéla = I'm going (S. *mi nán-gó*)

Gbégbéde wédjamè = a greeting, answered by *Awandíkbóu*

gwínzu = man (S. *wómi*)

hú = woman (S. *muyêè*)

Kasiamba Naná Gwambísa = the god-who-has-the-place (S. *gádu-a-kamía*)

kási fu lélemba = old people, ancestors (S. *gaán sèmbè*)

káta-asú = hunting sack (S. *sáku*)

Lélembu = a greeting, answered by *Lélembu kizambíi*

Malulú matjángi = Earth Mother (S. *mamá goón*)

odóngo = belly, womb (S. *bêè*)

oníabò = river (S. *lío*)

oníabò baasuma akí = lower river (S. *básulío*)

oníabò líbama akí = upper river (S. *líbalío*)

paláka = God (S. *gádu*) {from Arabic *baraka*, "blessing"(?)}

paláka leméla = go with God

wáizaanga = open-sided house (S. *gangása*) {from Kikongo *sánga*, "hut (made from branches/leaves)"?—Huttar 1985:59}

Phrases That Are Not in Saramaccan Syntax

Bakuí bangóni, said Tatá Wíi. The woman replied, *Batjêtje bangóni*. And then he said, *Bayáka bangóni*. *Bangóni*, says Tooy, means "person." See p. 108.

Malulú matjángi asákpáa asákpáa tjákiníkiní kapêèkapêè kutjábíabía dumiyáyá máde-sídagbó. "*Malulú matjángi* [Earth Mother], *asákpáa asákpáa tjákiníkiní* [normal S. "thigh-thigh carries knee-knee" or "his thigh is above his knee"] *kapêèkapêè* [normal S. brushland-brushland] *kutjábíabía dumiyáyá mádesídagbó.*" Tooy says this is a prayer to the Earth Mother, Malulú matjángi, saying, "The person who wants to kill you there, his thigh is above his knee, Malulú matjángi, she must know about it! The evil that the person put there, let it follow him and stay with him!" See p. 275.

Bótè, to which one answers *Sikenai bótè,* and *Lélembu,* to which one answers *Lélembu Kizambíi.* Tebíni once told me these two "country" greetings, adding that "with these words, we came here." See. p. 410. {Commenting on my discussion of this greeting in *First-Time,* p. 26, Maureen Warner-Lewis notes that Kikongo *mbote* means "goodness," that *Sikenai bótè* might be a truncated form of Kikongo *ngi sikama na mbote*—"I walk/stand surely in health," and that *Lélembu Kizambíi* would mean, in Kikongo, "the peace of God" (*Central Africa in the Caribbean: Transcending Time, Transforming Cultures* [Kingston: University of the West Indies Press, 2003], p. 61). Armin Schwegler (personal communication, 2006) reports that *mbote* is "a common greeting in Kikongo, essentially meaning (literally) what one means in French when saying 'salut,'" and that in Kikongo, *mbote* also means "well-being," citing Laman 1964:537.}

The first man said, *Awesáánu.* The other replied, *Awesáánu.* The first said, *Gbégbéde wédjamè.* The other answered, *Awandíkbóu.* Captain Kala told me in 1978 about this greeting between two early runaways. See p. 410.

A fí a na kwonú, kwanákwa. Kwanákwa adjú, kwanákwa or *A fí a na kwonú, kwanákwa adjú, kwá kwá kwanákwa, kwanákwa adjú, kwanákwa.** This is a *nòngô,* a semantically compressed proverb, the meaning of which is not derivable (at least in the twentieth century) from the words themselves. Its meaning would be expressed in everyday Saramaccan as *disá ná a táki sábi sô*—"Not doing something can avoid 'I told you so'"; not commiting a rash act ensures that you will not later say, "If only I had known . . . " For context and the historical story as told by Tebíni, see Price, *First-Time,* pp. 96–97. In 2005, when I first told Tooy the proverb, which he'd never heard, he was keen on memorizing the words, which he practiced in my presence on at least ten different occasions. Not long after he'd mastered them, he mentioned to me, "Just the other day, I was sitting here with [my son] Jozef and said, 'The man called Lisati—if some kid thinks he can mess with him, he'd better watch his ass. That man there—there's not a thing about the Suriname River he doesn't know. Sitting until your bottom is tired, that's what learning is all about. And that's what he does.'"

Tútu samái ku samáika.* This refers to trying to wrest away something that belongs to someone else. Tooy says, for example, "I don't get involved in *tútu samái ku samáika*—what's yours is yours and mine mine."

Kátja kátja dúmbokú loúme. Dókoso púmbu luángo. Vié atjái. Dí na í atjái.* These are the words a man says, once he's set out the appropriate leaves to bathe in, for *muyêè* óbia, the widely known óbia that gets you the woman you desire, after you've pronounced her name. Although it certainly sounds like Luángu to me, Tooy insists it's known by all clans, making it Kôndè for him.

Zágba zágba mizáagba djeéhon dénákpò.* This is the way one of the hairs on Owl's head says his praise name. Tooy says it means, "When someone's nose is cut off, his face is ruined." It is a reminder that it's hard to bring up someone else's child, since if his nose is cut off, you won't want it anymore but neither will its mother. Or, more generally, there's a risk in taking on a big responsibility.

*   *   *

The following are two sets of children's finger-counting games, in which each finger is named. (I give three versions of the second set.) They were said to be very old; I collected the sets of words, which were always sung, from older people in the 1960s and 1970s. I do not have African proveniences. Tooy was not familiar with these lists.*

[palm up, beginning with the left thumb] Mínimínibô, batébo, teméziga, zikámbei, mbeigáa, [palm up, beginning with right thumb] gaaôngo, óngodidí, didíkabá, sobíankabá, mefèè.

[palm up, beginning with the left thumb; I'm uncertain where on the hands memory gave out for these three people] Boosú, tjolê, gbánunu, kwangámè [or kwanzmè], kwáame, talúme [or talówe], goómbi [or gúmbi]; boosú, tjolê, gwánunu, kwánzame, pákosa, tunênge, tunámi, talúme; boosú, tjolê, gbanúnu, paámbè, pakasa, kanángo, tunênge, mitalúme [or talúme], gúmbe.

Phrases That Are (at Least Partially) in Saramaccan Syntax/ Lexicon, with "Language" Words Inserted

Zuunzjé dê kwáyan, kwayán sa kó záádome. "Zuunzjé [súndju = "dirt" (?)] is kwáyan, kwayán can become záádome." This is what the main path said to the living person. "You come to ruin my name, and you've got shit sticking to your own body!" For context, see pp. 46–47.

Dí u bi dê a Puupangi, ná so u bi líbi. Dí u bi dê a Puupangi u bi líbi banáki so banáli móyon, avílijítjí bom tjélélé badjégba wínso avíuto kóoto kóbwe. "When we were at Puupangi, we didn't live as we do now. When we were at Puupangi, we lived banáki so banáli móyon, avílijítjí bom tjélélé badjégba wínso avíuto kóoto kóbwe." Tooy explains the "country" phrases: "We didn't live that badly—a single earthenware plate, a single earthenware pot, a single earthenware spoon. You'd go eat and then the next person would take his turn. When we were in slavery." See p. 403.

Ahúngwadja. Awángamádesúsu. Mi doro kó kadja.* "Ahúngwadja. Awángamádesúsu. I've arrived!" (The last phrase is in Sranan/Ndyuka.) Otjútju explained to me in 1978 that this is the way a new runaway greeted a Saramaka woman, telling her in the second word/phrase, "Old woman, put your chickens in their baskets." {NB: Note that "chicken" in Kikongo is *nsusu*—van Wing and Penders 1928:272.} See Price, *First-Time*, p. 59.

*Tjiví tavúnda, vundáma wáta.** "*Tjiví tavúnda, vundáma* water." This is what the mother peccary said to her child after he refused to bathe in the muddy water. Each day they had bathed there, and she had found him worms to eat. Now, when he refuses to bathe there, she no longer feeds him the worms. He asks why she no longer feeds him. This is her reply, which Tooy explains as "What you said to me, now you're seeing the results."

KÓNTU (ANASI-TÓLI)

The narratives of folktales (Anasi-tóli or *kóntu*) told at Saramaka wakes are frequently "interrupted" by songs, often in the esoteric language that is exclusively theirs. Because Sally Price and I have published a large book devoted to *kóntu*—*Two Evenings in Saramaka*—I do not list such song texts here, with the sole exception stemming from the only time that Tooy, spontaneously, told me a tale I'd never heard and sang the accompanying song. (As we indicate in the "translations" in that book, the meaning of much of this language—and the ability to break down the texts into their components—is often not known even to the performers. That language, like the others in this Coda, deserves further study.)

[sung] *Asínamai-o ku Asínafoló, Lágbakímbe, so mi dúngu akí Kwáadja, mi mádji Tólolo, dúngu akí Kwáadja.** "Asínamai-o with Asínafoló, Lágbakímbe, this is how I 'darken' [kill/blind] Kwáadja, I *mádji* Tólolo, kill/blind Kwáadja here." As Tooy tells it, Dog and his master were cutting a garden together—but it was right near where the devils lived! There they were, clearing the brush, cutting the trees. The devils got themselves ready to come eat them up. They arrived! The dog told his master to give him a needle. (In Saramaka folktales, a needle is the one thing that can kill a devil, when it's plunged through his fontanel.) Then he told him to bring out a drum. (In Saramaka folktales, devils can't resist dancing when they hear music.) The master began drumming and the devils circled around, dancing. The dog was sitting between his master's legs. Then Dog took over on the drum. *Kam kam, kam kam kam.* The dog told his master that when the devil came and kneeled before him, he should take the needle and spear his head. The dog played the drum and the first devil to approach was Asínamaí, the second was Asínafoló, the third was Lágbakímbe, the fourth was Kwáadja, the fifth was Gwémasi, the last was Tólolo. Dog kept playing the drum. [Tooy sings the song, with the devils' names.] Oh, they jumped up when they heard their names! They came over to the drummer and kneeled before him. First came the headman, Asínamai. The man speared him! [and so on, with each devil] The earth was freed!

LUÁNGU (LÁNGU)

Luángu—which Tooy usually refers to simply as "Lángu"—has, for as long as Tooy knows about, been used exclusively by the Lángu clan (and particularly that clan segment that lives in his natal village of Bundjitapá) as part of burying their dead. The people shipped through the port of Loango at the end of the seventeenth and beginning of the eighteenth centuries, when Tooy's ancestors arrived in Suriname, were an extremely diverse group of Central Africans, ranging from forest peoples who lived in what is present-day Gabon all the way to interior peoples sold at the great slave market at Mpumbu, far up the Congo River (see pp. 52–53). I would assume that Bantu languages form the origin for much of Saramaka Luángu speech.

Lexical Items

asumkáa = skull of dead man (see Komantí pronunciation, above) (S. *hédi bónu*) {from Twi *ɔ-sāmān*, "spirit, ghost"?—Smith 1983:48}

kibímbi = the land of the dead (S. *mísikôndè*) {possibly from Kikongo *simbi* (pl. *bimbi*), "spirit of a good person who is deceased; mischievous sea spirit; sacred place; dangerous mischievous spirit who frequents waters and precipices in the forest"— Laman 1964:899 via Schwegler 2006, who adds: for *ki-*, see Laman 1964:899}

kitímba [*kitâimba*] = tobacco (S. *tabáku*) {possibly from Kikongo *timmba*, "pipe"—Laman 1964:973 via Schwegler 2006—or from Kimbundu *quixima, kixima*, apparently "smoking with a pipe"—see Friederici 1960:111}

kitímatángi = stool (S. *bangi*)—Tooy contrasts this with the Apúku pronunciation, *kitímataangi*.

kwándikí = bottle (S. *báta* or, for an earthenware Dutch genever bottle, *kándiki*)

lobangáya = tongue (S. *tóngu*)

masángo = cassava (S. *kasába*) {from Kikongo *sángu* (pl. *ma-sangu*), "yam with thorny stem"—Laman 1964:876 via Schwegler 2006}

mayómbe = rum (S. *daán*)

Naná Mpúngu [+ *Zamina Mpúngu*] = Great God (S. *Mása Gaán Gádu*) {from Twi *naná*, "a title of respect or honour used in addressing kings, great fetishes & c."— Christaller 1933:328 via Bilby 2006; plus Kikongo *Nzambi mpungu*, "Supreme deity"—van Wing and Penders 1928:279}

sabanga = teeth (S. *tánda*)

vetú = ear(s) (S. *yési*) {"The root *tu* (with some variation) is a solid Proto-Bantu root for 'ear.'"—Good 2006}

zó = house (S. *ósu*) {from Kikongo *nzo*, "house"—van Wing and Penders 1928:281}

Phrases That Are Not in Saramaccan Syntax

Wási kagidí tjibaánga. "Left hand washes right hand, right hand washes left hand." Tooy is unable to break down this phrase word by word. *Wási* is normal Saramaccan for "to wash." See p. 246.

Paníka ní manyá folí. "Not everything that your eyes see or your ears hear should be spoken about by your mouth." Tooy is unable to break down this phrase word by word. See p. 246.

Phrases That Are (at Least Partially) in Saramaccan Syntax/ Lexicon, with "Language" Words Inserted

Lobangáya dyè a sabánga déndu. "*Lobangáya* [tongue] is inside *sabánga* [teeth]." See p. 92.

[sung] *Butá mayómbe na kwándikí, yengué sélélé, víe, tjátjá, hònhònhòn hònhònhòn'.* [The last two words are a sound made with the fingers tapping one's Adam's apple.] "Put the *mayómbe* [rum] into the *kwándikí* [bottle], *yengué sélélé* [exclamation of joy(?)], *víe, tjátjá, hònhònhòn hònhònhòn'.*" Tooy added the special Luángu ending when he sang it for my recorder in 2005. See p. 245.

Lángu án yéi dúngu. Masángo fúlu na zó. "*Lángu án yéi dúngu. Masángo* [cassava] fills up the *zó* [house]." Tooy claims the two phrases mean, "Go into the house and bring out the cassava." He is unable to break down the first phrase word by word. See p. 246.

Kitímba fúlú na zó. "*Kitímba* [tobacco] fills up the *zó* [house]" or "[There's a lot of] *Kitímba* [tobacco] in the *zó* [house]." See p. 246.

[sung] *Kwímabo, wáka na pási tantúmbe, wimalúngu, wáka na pási tantúmbe, sípadúngu, wáka na pási tantúmbe, wédemalúngu, [ísikadúngu], wáka na pási tantúmbe, víe, tjátjá, hònhònhòn hònhònhòn'.* [The last two words are a sound made with the fingers tapping one's Adam's apple.] "Chigger-foot man [Kwímabo, Wimalúngu, Sípadúngu, Wédemalúngu, Ísikadúngu—all insulting names for someone with chiggers], walk on the path *tantúmbe* ["on your knees" or "in crippled fashion"], *víe, tjátjá, hònhònhòn hònhònhòn'*" [with this last repeated sound being a special Luángu terminal phrase]. Tooy loosely translates the song as, "You have chiggers, chiggers have got you, you walk around on your knees, you no longer walk like a person." See p. 245.

[sung] *Sángono mi tóala! Mapána nénge tjá lówe kó! Sángono mi tóala! Bavíli Luángo tjá lowé-e. Sángono mi tóala, vié, tjátjá, hanhanhanhan.* [This last "word" is made by pushing on the Adam's apple with two fingers.] "*Sángono mi tóala! Mapána* people⁹ brought escape/Peace! *Sángono mi tóala!* Bavili Luángo people brought escape. *Sángono mi tóala, vié, tjátjá, hanhanhanhan.*" (Sometimes, Tooy substitutes *fií*—freedom—for *lowé*—escape.) This is Wíi's song of triumph, for having brought the Peace to Saramakas. See p. 107. (A sound clip of Tooy singing a version of this song, labeled "Sangono-Luangu," can be found at http://www.press .uchicago.edu/books/price/ and http://www.richandsally.net.)

PAPÁ

Saramakas refer to Papá and Aladá interchangeably (from the names of the major slave-shipping ports of Grand and Little Popo, in present-day Togo, and Allada/Ardra, the coastal kingdom of seventeenth-century Dahomey). This region provided nearly half of all slaves shipped to Suriname during the formative years of Saramaka society. I would expect the language to be heavily based on varieties of the Gbe dialect cluster (Ewè, Gèn, Ajá, Fòn). Saramakas affectionately call the language Félubéni, "bent iron," because its "play," used by all Saramakas to bury their dead, is marked by a prominent bent-iron percussion instrument (*gan*). Until the early twentieth century, it was common for Papá songs to be sung also at ancestor shrines.

Lexical Items

adjámadjí = sheep (S. *sikápu*)

agwígwí = owl (S. *ógi fóu*)

agítibóosu = tapir (in the Abaísa dialect) (S. *bófo*)

alágweku [alágbeku] = dog (S. *dágu*)

alógaan = blood (S. *buúu*)

aoyá = giant anteater (S. *tamanóa*)

azéimeku = house (S. *ósu*)

bála gádja gbáni síngbu = deer (S. *djángafútu*)

bekwá = parrot (S. *pápakái*)

dawédayón = the canoe of the dog in the land of the dead. (If that dog hunts someone/ something and puts him in the canoe, he's done for!)

difúngu (or *kifúngu*) = death (S. *dêdè*)

dokpóyankí = tapir (in the Abaísa dialect—see *agitibóosu*) (S. *bófo*)

dódo = evil (S. *ógi*)

gan = metal percussion instrument {from Fon *gã*, "métal, fer . . . cloche, cloch-ette, gong . . . c'est avec une clochette ou un gong qu'on rythmait le chant ou la danse"—Segurola 1963 s.v. *gã*, via Smith 2006}

gódomai = garden (S. *goón*)

gogó búka náni náni gogó maí saká bodjí = stool (S. *bángi*—NB: *Gogó* is Saramaccan for "buttocks.")

gulántjángo = a plant, the favorite food of tortoises (S. *logosofuúta*)

hwême = tortoise (S. *logoso*)—Tooy warns that if you call a tortoise by this name and then eat it, you'll die.

hwêméyol = we no longer have knowledge (S. *u án a sábi môò*)

kimayónu = coffin (S. *kési*)

kwêméyol = we are all messed up (S. *u fiká sòsò makisá*)

mooi sabalú = tapir (in the Matjáu dialect) (S. *bófo* but Ndyuka *mooi* = handsome)

muángolé = okra flowers (S. *asila* [or *lalú*] *foló*)

nayóo/nyankí = greeting between men

noínovi = your matrilineage, your close kinsmen (S. *di bêè f 'i*)

táagaló = man (S. *wómi*)

tódovi = others, strangers (S. *ná sèmbè f 'i*)

wátakailéun = caiman (S. *káima*)

yágba yágba = tapir (S. *bófo*)

yagaasé = old person, old people (S. *gaán sèmbè*)

zúme = forest (S. *mátu*)

zúme = howler monkey (S. *babúnu*)—homonymous with the word for "forest"

Phrases That Are Not in Saramaccan Syntax

Tíkití no vído. A matrilineage that's all messed up, that's been decimated. See p. 248.

Tíkití didó. Lawámaí didó. Lawáa mi kóo nodé. A matrilineage that's flourishing. See p. 248.

Mokú felé moodán. "The matrilineage has lost what it once knew." Tooy used this in the phrase, "It's '*mokú felé moodán*' for him!" to say, "He doesn't appreciate his elders," so the matrilineage will lose what it once knew. See p. 249.

Adòdì-í dòdò-ô. Kínde gó na huntô. "An old man who doesn't know things." See p. 248.

A hón tuntuú ya gavié da unún da úú-úún. Synonymous with the previous phrase. See p. 248.

[sung] *Kwantiólu, wêbi káka zúme. Káuyómê, wêbi káka zúme. Aládan kenyánko weménu awánu, kényan, kényan ma fu adjú-e, adjú-e weménu, ma fu adjú kényan, kényan.* When the Matjáus were asked by the Abaísas to come cleanse their village with the Adjú "play" (which follows Papá in the early morning), their leader Sámbo-gídjigídji sang three songs, of which this is one. See p. 256.

Abudáma fu agudá. Abudáma fu agudá. Poóma fu ó. These are the words said by the Abaísa Yágazé, in the ancestor shrine of the Matjáus, to report the death of the Matjáu Sakóto. See p. 257.

[sung] *Foló tutú agbáila.* "Foló shot the gun called Agbáila" is the explanation I received in the 1970s (see Price, *First-Time,* pp. 125–26). Tooy relates this phrase to a different historical incident involving his Lángu ancestors and "translates" it as "The gun called Foló shot and everyone [back in Bákakúun] heard." It would seem that different clans interpret the same words in Papá as referring to different incidents in their past, having in common a Saramaka man shooting a whole row of soldiers and the people back in the village hearing the sound of the gunshot. The phrase is played/sung today at the moment of shooting funeral salutes. See pp. 257–58.

[sung] *Kanivó, kanivó, kanivó nawa, kanivó nawa bélao, anáwaazú-o, tutú gbezdan mafa-adjó keedjé ímawan daudé, kanivó nawa bélao.* This is the version of *Foló tutú agbáila* in the Abaísa dialect of Papá. Tooy adds that it's saying, "When you go hunting and hear an animal in the underbrush, stand stock still, and you'll manage to shoot it." See p. 258. (A sound clip of Tooy singing a version of this song and the next one, labeled "KanivoandKedjemani-Papa," can be found at http://www.press.uchicago.edu/books/price/ and http://www.richandsally.net.)

[sung] *Kédjé mani-e, mani kedjé mani-e, akatasú mandeu-u mándegbò-ò.* This is the version of *Kanivó . . .* in the Matjáu dialect of Papá. In Saramaka funerals today, when

the coffin is about to be taken away to the cemetery, the Papá-men first play the Matjáu version, then the salutes are fired, and then they play *Foló tutú agbáila*, before ending with *Kanivó . . .*, the Abaísa version. See p. 258. (A sound clip of Tooy singing a version of this song and the previous one, labeled "Kanivoand-Kedjemani-Papa," can be found at http://www.press.uchicago.edu/books/price/ and http://www.richandsally.net.)

Abámpapá kimayónu, kifúngu kimayónu. This is what Abámpapá told his fellow villagers at a council meeting after he'd returned from Apúku land, where for the first time ever he saw a coffin. *Kimayónu*, Tooy explains, means "coffin" in Papá; *kifúngu* (or *difúngu*) means "death." See p. 259.

[sung] *Akónubábayétu makónubábayétume, mi ángbo tímbo. Mi ángbo tímbo, konóvalá djetómi, mi ángbo tímbo.* This is what the Papá players sing when they want food. Tooy says *mi ángbo tímbo* means, "I'm hungry." See p. 279.

Goyón-e alógan, yágase vísi alógan-e.* "You [your 'blood' (*alógan*)] will know when there's an elder [*yágase*] of yours far away who needs you." Tooy tells me this apropos Sensiló, who at the time was in Suriname and ill.

Aló mando gedjí, weménu sáiwa.* "For such a heavy load, what small ship could carry it?" This is the way the punt (a flat watercraft) says its praise name. Tooy tells how the heavy load was being slowly rowed upstream in the punt. A ship came along, and they asked it to take on the load. The ship nearly sank. They reloaded the punt, and all was well.

Mi kokólo yoobi, mi agwígwí yoobi. Alímandé mokómokó alímandé moyá.* Owl recites his praise name, saying, according to Tooy, that he can keep on playing till the cocks crow, till the owl hoots (till dawn). And when he's finished playing and he's hungry, he'll go eat.

[sung] *Kiyámbayámba, Kiyámbayámba. Kiyámbayámba.** Tooy explains that the bird called *adobóye* always looks as if its eyes are shut. With its three children, Konuvú, Aliá, and Anukú, it announces each new dawn. The Great God Above summoned a hawk called *kítikoomá-daónsu* (or *kíankían gavián*) to go ask that bird three times why it's always asleep. If it doesn't answer by the third time, he said, kill it, because it would mean I put it on the earth for no good reason. Hawk followed instructions, and this is the song he sang to the shut-eyed bird. On the third try, the *adobóye* answered, singing, "*Éya mónkomuwína*," which means, "I'm not asleep. Night comes and I'm *yaya fó*, daylight comes and I'm *yaya fó*, but I'm *kóikói* [tricking] *bênde*." In other words, says Tooy, when he closes his eyes, it's not to sleep but to see "everything that's coming in and everything that's going out in this world"—it's feigning sleep to see all. Tooy adds that there is a deeper Papá version of this song, but he can't sing it in his house. He also says you can say the words of *adobóye*, "*Éya mónkomuwína*," when someone asks you if you're asleep and you want to say, "No, my eyes are just shut."

[sung] *Bókudé bónukó un bezée tainawe, hokoko adjalú, bêzee tainawe.** This is the song of Bat as he's flying off after drinking a person's blood, thanking Great God for the feast. Tooy relates it to the Komantí song about Bat and Cock.

Phrases That Are (at Least Partially) in Saramaccan Syntax/ Lexicon, with "Language" Words Inserted

[sung] *Kónu gó na walá, walá mi yéi, walá mandekú tjénámewa.* Tooy explains that this song, in the Matjáu dialect of Papá, is what Macaque sings to the Awara palm (which has long thorns all up and down its trunk, protecting its orange fruit), after which it simply drops its thorns so the monkey can climb up. It's a prayer you can use whenever things are really rough. The context suggests that *Kónu* means "Macaque" and *walá* means "Awara palm": "*Kónu* goes to *walá, walá* I hear, *walá mandekú tjénámewa* [*wala* drops its thorns(?)]." See above for a version in Apúku. See also p. 16.

[sung] *A kónu misi waná, a kónu misi waná-o, wana mandekú mánde-o, a kónu misi waná, djáemade wána, wana mandekú mánde-o.* This is the version of *Kónu gó na walá* in the Abaísa dialect of Papá. Comparing it to the Matjáu version suggests that both are derived from a single protoversion which can no longer be broken down into meaningful segments. Put differently, the "resemblances" of words and syntax to Saramaccan may be purely perspectival—from a Saramaka perspective, *Kónu gó na walá/A kónu misi waná* might be read as "*Kónu* goes to *walá*" (Matjáu) or "*Kónu* slights *waná*" (Abaísa), but these may simply involve shaping original sounds that are meaningless in Saramaccan to come closer to familiar language, in part for mnemonic purposes. See p. 16.

[sung] *Alágba-o Aládjio Mêdo Keéno | Alágba-o Aládjio Mêdo Keéno | Keéno gó f'en a Zángodou, a gó na Kedé-ee, Dénua-ee, Alada-e, Alágio ke, Alágba Mêdo Keéno | Keéno gó f'en a Zángodou, a gó f'en a Kedé-ee, Dénua-e, o kióo Aládjioo.* "Alágba-o Aládjio Mêdo Keéno | Alágba-o Aládjio Mêdo Keéno | Keéno's [stink] went onto Zángodou, it went onto Kedé-ee, Dénua-ee, Alada-e, Aládjio *ke*, Alágba Mêdo Keéno | Keéno's went onto Zángodou, it went onto Kedé-ee, Dénua-oo, oh young-guy Aládjioo." As the banana stem with twelve hands of bananas began ripening, each of the named hands—twelve "brothers"—received, in turn, the sticky sap/juice from the one above it. Each complained of being ruined/soiled by the "dead" brother just above it. Except for the last brother, who accepted his responsibility, saying in effect that he was his brothers' keeper. See pp. 249–50. (A sound clip of Tooy singing a version of this song, labeled "Alagba-Papa," can be found at http://www .press.uchicago.edu/books/price/ and http://www.richandsally.net.)

[sung] *Tjé hên kó dá mi-e. Un de ni todovi alobi alobi alobi alobi da u, tja tja u da o lólo kabódji, tjé hên kó-e, keeto bóbiawata kó noínovi u mi. U tjé hên kó-o, todovi án sa kó noínovi, un tjé hên kó dá mi e.* "Bring him back to me. You *todovi* [strangers] *alobi alobi alobi alobi da u* [give us lots of love(?)], bring him back *lólo kabódji*, bring him back *keeto bóbiawata* to be my *noínovi* [in my matrilineage]. You bring him back, *todovi* [a stranger] can't become a *noínovi* [someone in my matrilineage], you bring him back to me." Tooy explains that these "very heavy words" pray that the great avenging spirit of the lineage won't turn the person who's being buried into an-other spirit to torment the lineage. Let the person come back instead as a name-

sake for someone in the lineage and bring the lineage good things. The song is sometimes abbreviated to *Tódovi án sa kó noínovi*—strangers can't become kinsmen. See p. 250.

[sung] *Djáome dján-e, i músu djáome djan. Adúndiome, Adúndiome, i músu djáome dján. Adúndiome, Adúndiome, i músu djáome dján.* "*Djáome dján-e*, you must *djáome djan*. Adúndiome, Adúndiome, you must *djáome dján*. Adúndiome, Adúndiome, you must *djáome dján*." This song follows the previous one. It's telling the dead person to leave. It should *djáome* (go) and then *djáome* (come back), but as a namesake, not as an avenging spirit. (*Djáome dján*, Tooy says, means "carry" or "bring" him back to me.) See p. 251.

[sung] *Tóbodahuntján-e-o ké, Tóbodahuntján de kó nyán-o, aínto tjêlele sída-o, Tóbodahuntján-o, Tóbodahuntján de kó nyán akí, aínto djêlele sídawá.* "Tóbodahuntján [the wife's name] exclamation. They've come to eat Tóbodahuntján, you're no longer here." This is Tooy's explanation of the husband's song calling his wife, who's been buried by the Evil One. See p. 253.

[sung] *O-o-o, é-o-o, Womi Gáigán-fu-Adowé, de kó nyán aínto gbêlegede sídawa.* "Oh, ay, Husband Gáigán-fu-Adowé. They've come to eat, *aínto gbêlegede sídawa* [a variant on the final phrase of the husband's song]. This is the wife's reply to the husband's song, saying, according to Tooy, "I'm not dead, man, I'm still alive. Don't kill yourself over this." See p. 253.

[sung] *Mi avó Gaán Tía djómbo hên mi djómbo, hee-hee. I djómbo, hên mi djómbo. Hunsókedue di i djómbo, Sámbo-gidjigidji di i djómbo, Bákigáyo di i djómbo, Vitónokó di i djómbo, mi avó Avádja di i djómbo, Ma di i djómbo, hên mi djómbo, o hee-hee.* "My grandmother Gaán Tía jumped, so I jumped. You jumped, so I jumped. When H jumped, When S jumped, when B jumped, when V jumped, when my grandmother A jumped, when you jumped—I jumped." (Except for the names of the people jumping, the words are all in normal Saramaccan.) This song was sung by the Abaísa-clan Papá specialists at a decisive competition with the Matjáu-clan specialists, leading to a murder. See p. 255.

[sung] *Gbosú kili ke dili Lomodjánki, Alabáisa-o keli keli keli. Gboyón, líndomeyo-o, gboyón, líndome-o, kó nyánme-o, Aladá kíi Lomodjó-o.* "Gbosú is fucking [*kili* < Sranan/Saramaccan *kili/kíi* = "to kill"] Lomodjánki, the Abaísa is fucking! *Gboyón, líndomeyo-o, gboyón, líndome-o*, come 'eat' some, Aladá is fucking Lomodjó." Tooy explains that the Nasí clan gave a young girl named Lomodjó to the much older Abaísa Tatá Gbosú to raise. When she became sexually ripe, he refused to give her away in marriage but kept her for himself. Try as he might, however, he couldn't get his cock to crow with her! Until finally one day he did and made her pregnant. This Papá commemorates Gbosú finally getting it up for Lomodjó. See p. 258.

Afítimoyon táki, Seímoyon táki. Hunhún dá mi békese dá hógogo. "*Afítimoyon* says, *Seímoyon* says. *Hunhún* give me *békese* give *hógogo*." According to Tooy, the mother sends the child to go tell his father that she's finished cooking, it's time to come eat. "*Afítimoyontáki*, that's the mother speaking. *Séemoyontáki*, that's the child. *Bêkese* [or *mêkese*] means, 'Let's eat!'" This seems to be a good example of how Tooy can't easily pull apart many of the Papá phrases he's learned by heart and that, in this case as in others, he knows the meaning of the phrase but not of its components. See p. 260.

Okódu vêlevêle, okódu vêlevêle, tatá táki alágbekúnu, f'en ku adjámadji kêlede avío, avío gwêsán, áye taína wei, okódo vêlevêle. "Okódu vêlevêle, okódu vêlevêle, father says *alágbekúnu* [dog], he and *adjámadji* [sheep] *kêlede avío, avío gwêsán, áye taína wei, okódo vêlevêle.*" The story of Dog's deception and Sheep's vengeance. See p. 264.

[sung] *I míti Sêgwenu-ee, i míti Sêgwenúawé. Ayò Asidamá i kó ayò, i kei yò, Sêgwenu-a, yesu Sêgwenúawé, i míti Asidamá sinko ayo.* "You've met up with Sêgwenu, you've met up with Sêgwenúawé. Ayò Asidamá, you've become *ayò*, you want to *yò*, Sêgwenu, *yesu* Sêgwenúawé, you've met up with Asidamá *sinko ayo.*" Tooy tells how Asidamá, a Saramaka man, was shooting fish with his bow at the front of the canoe while Ma Sêgbenu steered at the rear when the Evil Thing of the Riverbottom at Sotígbo, the Old Man called Sêgwenúawé, came up from the deep and pulled her under. Asidamá took off his clothes and dove after her to see what had pulled her under, and the creature sang this song to him. See p. 411.

[sung] *I míti dódo, i míti a mán dê . . . yesu adódoo, i míti a mándê-e.* "You've met with Evil, you've met with a real man . . . *yesu* Evil, you've met with a real man-e." This is the song of Howler Monkey, who saw the Evil Thing pull Ma Sêgbenu underwater at Sotígbo. The song brought the woman right back up to the surface, where the husband pulled her safely into the canoe. See p. 411.

Saka saká gó láme, kulé gó kulé kó. "*Saka saká gó láme*, run off, run back." The rhythm of the Adjú drum until it's time for the ghost of the deceased to depart definitively, at which point the drummer leaves off the last two words. See p. 426.

*Bése dê na azéimeku.** "Toad is in the *azéimeku* [house]." This means, "We're talking about personal/family/private things." Tooy uses the expression frequently.

*Di soní di i súku a taagaló, téé i féni hên na awángamaikónu, nôò téki hên na awángamaidéla.** "The thing you're trying to find out about *taagaló* [a man], once you find it in *awángamaikónu* [the land we live in here], well, take it to *awángamaidéla* [the land of the dead]." Tooy says this is what you might say in Papá when you're very angry at someone: "Leave me alone. The way you're trying to harm me, may Death kill you so you'll finally sit down."

[sung] *Bekwá nyán muángolé, nukú nyán muángolé, alólomí uazián.** "Bekwá [parrot] ate *muángolé* [okra flowers], *nukú* ate *muángolé* [okra flowers], *alólomí uazián*." Old Woman had a pet parrot and some okra plants. While she was washing dishes at the riverside, another woman saw the parrot eat her okra flowers, so she scolded the parrot and, when Old Woman returned, told her. This song is Old Woman's reply, saying that the parrot is hers, the okra is hers, and the other woman should mind her own business!

[sung] *Tindé sósó gwekí, mái bêtò. Tindé sósó gwekí, mái bêtò. Gwêsimahólu, gwêsimahólu volú fu yagazé-ze-ye.** "The bird called *tínde* may be *gweki*, but he's *bêtò*. [repeat] *Gwêsimahólu, gwêsimahólu* master of the elders." A small bird, *tínde*, stood on a

branch where a man had just cut and burned a garden and prayed to the god-who-owns-the-place to give the man strength to plant and weed the garden till the rice was ripe. Then, once the rice was ready, *tínde* stood on the branch again and prayed to the god to kill the man and let him become master of the garden. This song, explains Tooy, is his prayer. (Tooy says that in Papá, *volú fu yagazé* means "to play master.") The god said, "No way." He couldn't help him. The bird could share the rice, but it belonged to the man who'd cut the garden. Tooy spoke the words of the god in Papá: *Fítingolí a fítingolí yengolíbêe. Golí dê f'en a yaasónu, a gó na yaasónu, godúmai kázume, a gó a yaasónu, guúnkané de kái gódomái kázume. Gódomái* means "garden," *zúme* "forest," thus the final two words means "garden in the forest."

[sung] *Kolobí-e, kolobí. Kióo, muyêè a ósu gbógulo. A ósu gbógulo. Kolóbi-e, kolóbi-o. A ósu gbógulo.** "Come, love, come love. Kid, woman, to the house! To the house! Come, love, come, love. To the house." Tortoise, says Tooy, came upon the plant Papá calls *gulántjángo* and, with this song, invited his wife to come eat with him. (I'm sure there's much more to this story . . .)

[sings] *Wênsi-e, kóni ku Húmenosía. Húmenosía-e, Húmenosía-o. Wán de kái Kónu. Wán da Wênsi. Wan da Húmenosía. Húmenosía, kóni ku Huntô, Húmenosía.** "Wishful, be careful with Húmenosía. Húmenosía-e, Húmenosía-o. One was called King. One was Wishful. One was Húmenosía. Húmenosía, be careful with Huntô, Húmeno-sía." Tooy sang this twice in 2005, though it remains obscure to me. He explains that there were three brothers, Wishful, Put-It-Off, and King (or Clever-One). Wishful's village was broken. Put-It-Off's village was broken. And today we all live in the land of King.

*Yágba yágba. Agitibónsu. Dokpóyankê. Mi tjiká mi kôndè mátu ma m'án tjiká mi kôndè gandá.** "*Yágba yágba* [tapir]. *Agitibónsu* [tapir] *Dokpóyankê* [tapir]. I'm the big man of the forest but worth nothing in the village." This is how Tapir says his praise name. It means, says Tooy, that your home is your castle, that Tapir is king of the forest, but when they bring him (dead) to a village, he's finished. Tooy likes to exclaim, when he's feeling good, *Yágba yágba!*—"I'm king of the forest!"

*Mooi sabalú-e, mooi sabalú-e. Adjó, Adjó. Mooi sabalú-e, mooi sabalú-e. Adjó, Adjó. Mooi sabalú-e. Adjó. Awédánu-e. Mooi sabalú-e. Adjó.** "*Mooi sabalú-e* [tapir]. *Adjó* . . . *Awédánu-e.*" Tooy explains that this song commemorates a long-ago event that happened near the mouth of Matjáu Creek, where a Matjáu-clan woman, Awédánu, her husband, and their son-in-law Adjó were coming upriver after selling agricultural produce in Paramaribo, and Adjó killed a tapir swimming in the river. He butchered it, they sold it in the plantation area, and in some way that I don't yet understand, this became the origin of Matjáu wealth, according to Tooy.

*Novinoví kadjá. Kadjá kísi noví, hên noví kísi kádja. Mi Wátakailéun! Mi tasu demai we-bísu lémitji fu adámabolê. Heei, Mi Wátakaadjáku! Mi tasu demai webísu lémitji fu adámabolê, a taa fu ádjakba. Wátakaadjáku, mi tasu demai webísu, lémitiji fu adámabolê.** These phrases, which Tooy spoke rather than sang to me, are part of a Papá song that describes a wrestling match between Giant Otter (S. *awaapúya*) and Caiman (S. *káima*). Tooy tells how both animals used to have similar names; Otter was *Wátakaadjáku* and Caiman was *Wátakailéun*. So, they decided to meet on the riverbank on a Wednesday to have it out and see who would keep the name. They wrestled till they were spent. *Novinoví kadjá. Kadjá kísi noví, hên noví kísi kádja* [it sounds like *kádja* is Otter and *noví* is Caiman—"Kadjá grabs Noví, then Noví grabs Kadjá"]. They clinched. Then Otter threw Caiman in the air and said, "I'm *Wátakailéun!* I'm *tasu demai webísu lémitji fu adámabolê.*" Then Caiman threw Otter up in the air and said, "*Heei,* I'm *Wátakaadjáku!* I'm *tasu demai webísu lémitji fu adámabolê, a taa fu ádjakba.*" They kept wrestling. Then Caiman's "things" came upon him. And Caiman threw down Otter and bit him on the throat, saying, "I'm *Wátakailéun! Mi tasu demai webísu lémitji fu adámabolê!*" Tooy explains that when you say, *Wátakaadjáku, mi tasu demai webísu, lémitiji fu adámabolê,* you're the one who's lost. Otter lost. Caiman kept the name and is called *Wátakailéun* in Papá.

PAPÁGÁDU (OR VODÚ-GÁDU)

This is the language of boa constrictor gods, who play an important role in Saramaka life. The most common avenging spirits in any lineage because of the frequency with which they are inadvertently killed during the burning of garden sites prior to planting, they frequently come into their mediums' heads, and collective rites are held for them periodically. Tooy claims not to be expert in this language, which is played with the great *agidá* drum, straddled and beaten with one hand and one stick. (Nonethless, Tooy is proud that his father, Méliki, had in his head a Papágádu called Hondima-u-Búsi [Hunter of the Forest].) One would expect the language to be related to those of the "Slave Coast," a region where people speak one or another of the Gbe languages, and which is the home of *vodun* and the rainbow serpent Dangbe (or Da).

Lexical Items

Dagowé = the snake god (S. *Vodú*) {from Fon *dãgbe*, "serpent fétiche, python royal, divinité des Xueda"—Baker 1993:147 via Parkvall 1999, s.v. *dan*}
dámabódi = walking stick (S. *kokotí*)
djá = forest (S. *mátu*)
gwesíalíngi = the rising motion of the great Papágádu underground after sleeping for 150 days and then thumping down, causing earthquakes
gwíyu = beer (S. *bíi*)
wélu = water (S. *wáta*)
zúnukóko-fu-zúme = the praise name of the great Papágádu who causes earthquakes

Phrases That Are Not in Saramaccan Syntax

[sung] *Dánto misí a dánto, dánto misí kalágba.** This is what Howler Monkey says when he straddles the *agidá* (the great snake-god drum): "We're playing here! If a mother-

in-law bends over, pass by her anyway, if a father-in-law bends over, pass by him anyway. Once we finish playing, then we'll all go home and maintain proper respect once again." (Tooy is unable to break down these phrases word by word.)

[sung] *Dúwe, dúwe, dúwe. Dúwe, mi vólu yu.** [repeat] Tooy tells me that this is the way the *agidá* drum calls shy or reluctant people to get involved in the "play." (*Dúwe* means, "Do it!") "You sit down there," says Tooy. "You hide yourself, you say you're not a 'do man,' that you don't know how to do it. But come work together!" But another time, he tells me it's an "answer" to *Dánto misí a dánto* and means, "You're hiding yourself, but I see your arse" (because you're bending over).

*Mi Tumáayuwenú, mí Tjímaíbêêkèsè, mi Tjímaayúwenú, mi Tjímaíbêêkèsè, mi Gbám-lóko-gbám-tjèlé, mi Tjèèsím-tjèèsíe.** This is how the *agidá* of the Pikílío says its praise name.

*Tía waó-o, gwêkemaló-o, píawan. Píawan, gwêkemaló-o, píawan. Píawan bí-e mi toóbi-e, gwêkemaló-o, píawan, píawan bii akpúun fu Yagazé.** Tooy says he plays this on the *agidá* as part of the ritual of burying a boa constrictor god. It's saying that you don't know how to do it, but Tatá Yagazé can help.

*Tía waó-o, gwêkemaló-o, píawan-e. Tósutósu wêmilu, álabáta dê fu alêtemaónsu.** A variant of the previous *agidá* rhythm.

Phrases That Are (at Least Partially) in Saramaccan Syntax/ Lexicon, with "Language" Words Inserted

[sung] *Wánwan fu wan, nanga wánwan fu djawélu, wánwan fu wán, nanga wánwan fu djawélu, wánwan fu wán, asógáigái fu kôdomè, wánwan fu wán, asúgáigái fu kôdomè.* This is the way the drummer on the *agidá*—the great drum for the snake gods—challenges the gods during a "play," saying to them: You act like you're real men, but it's one big lie. I'll take you one by one (*wánwan fu wán*, in almost normal Saramaccan) and show you who's boss! The drum says, "If I go in the river [*wélu* = water in Papagádu language], I'll take you. If I go in the forest (*djá* in Papagádu language), I'll take you." Another time Tooy told me that Djáwelu is the name of the country he says he'll take you to, from which you'll never return. (Kenneth Bilby [personal communication, 2006] reports that among the Aluku, *kodome* or *tata kodome* means "*agidá*" in Papa Tongo.) See p. 84.

[spoken] *A sipán kobiáyeú, a dóu fu gelému.** "It's getting exciting *kobiáyeú*, it's time to *gelému*." Tooy says the evil Papágádu says this when he's been waiting for the deer to pass by and it finally does, and he gobbles him up! Tooy speaks it to mean, "The thing we've been speaking about, its time has come, let's do it!"

PÚMBU

Named for the Central African site near Malebo Pool far up the Congo River, where many people were sold into slavery, this language is adamantly claimed by Saramakas to have been learned from Amerindians after their ancestors' escape to the forest. Tooy insists that his great Lángu ancestor, Kaásipúmbu (Kaási from Púmbu)—whose carry-oracle, said to have been brought from Africa, still reigns as the ultimate arbiter for Saramaka society—learned the language from his Amerindian brother-in-law Piyái. Today, Púmbu is spoken only at rites for this oracle in the village of Béndiwáta, where Kaási's descendants live. I would assume it to be based on Bantu languages from the interior of the Congo.

Lexical Items

apatabúi = Kaási's magical basket
náni = house (S. *ósu*)
taí = eye (S. *wóyo*)
tumbú = mouth (S. *búka*)

Phrases That Are Not in Saramaccan Syntax

Sébengé sabánga, lébengé sabánga, maabeengé sabánga. [special emphasis on the penultimate word] This is what a newborn says when it first cries: "Great God, as we've already discussed, don't forget me, I'm still with you, grant me life!" Tooy told me that "one year there was a great drought. Everyone gathered to pray for rain. Then Ma Kotíi, in the head of a Kaapátu [Béndiwáta] person, said those very words. People didn't even get back to their houses carrying their stools before the floodgates opened!" So, these words themselves have great power. (Tooy is unable to break down these phrases word by word.) See p. 247.

Nyam-nyam kuvándi, nyam-nyam vála. Tooy translates as S. *Lánga pási mbéi asila dèê a páu* [distance ("long path") makes okra dry on the stem]. "You and I have known each other quite a while," he said. "Even when you're far away, you mustn't forget me," which is the meaning of the saying. See p. 215.

Phrases That Are (at Least Partially) in Saramaccan Syntax/ Lexicon, with "Language" Words Inserted

Kiingó ta gundámba. A bungu yó, i músu tjángini kó. Tjángini kó, tjángini kó, tjángini kó. "The drop-trap [progressive] *gundámba. A bungu yó,* you must *tjángini* come. *Tjángini* come, *tjángini* come, *tjángini* come." A prayer used in the village of Béndiwáta, saying, "You up above, let me pass, that's where I must pass!—Despite the danger, despite the *kiingó* [trap] poised to drop, I must get through, please let me pass through." See p. 211.

*Avúnvún gundámba, a salímútusaámba. A bungu yó, i músu tjángini kó. Salímútusaámba.** This is what the Béndiwáta Mamá says in response to Anía óbia saying his praise name (see under Komantí), giving approval, saying, "Yes, it's true," according to Tooy. (Compare to the previous prayer.)

[sung] *Mángan mángan téebo-e, oló, we mi mása Zámbi-e, mi kó a yu náni-o akí akié.* "*Mángan mángan téebo-e, oló,* well, my master Zámbi, I've come to your *náni* [house] *akí akié* [to see if I can stay]." This is the song of Kaásipúmbu telling the tree that the Lángu clan would move down to the Suriname River. As he finished this song, Tooy took his right hand and tapped his fingers against his lips, uttering a falsetto "*u-u-u-u-u-u-u-u-u-u*" and explaining that this is the standard ending for dangerous songs in Púmbu. See p. 247.

Saa baaba na wán tén fu gaán kindé, gaán kindé fu Makambí. "*Saa baaba* at the time of big *kindé,* big *kindé* for Makambí." Tooy says this expresses great sadness. *Saa baaba* means, "Something terrible has happened." *Gaán kindé* means, "It's a big thing." Makambí is the name of Antamá's brother who was killed in battle in 1753. I presume that this was the phrase used to announce Makambí's death to Antamá. See p. 247.

*Téé i taí, nôò i lúku tumbú, téé i tumbú, nôò i lúku taí.** "When you *taí* [see], wait for *tumbú* [mouth], when you *tumbú* [mouth], wait for *taí* [eye]." Tooy says this means, "When you see something, don't necessarily talk about it; when you hear about something, wait to see it." He uses it to mean, "Let's wait and see what happens."

TONÊ

River gods, apparently of Dahomean origin, speak this language. Tooy has a special relationship with them through his African-born ancestor Gweyúnga.

Phrases That Are Not in Saramaccan Syntax

[sung] *Kúte kúte kalákbo, kúte kúte kalákbo, kalékwé domó yogó domó asidá hóló gwêgede agáma líba hêngi-e.* The song sung by Chameleon (S. *agama*) to Tonê, praying to be able to reach the summit of the silkcotton tree. *Kúte kúte,* Tooy says, means he's climbing: *kalákbo,* that he's arrived. See p. 61.

[sung] *Bóluwé, bólué-wé-wé-wé-wé-wé-wé, gaán másu dendé, sêgbenu sêgbenu kaakbo kaakbo íni-we adánuwe bóluwe, agámasu dendé bóluwe-o, gánsa-e, adáni vêse yême.* The song sung by Chameleon once he arrived at the summit of the silkcotton tree. Tooy says that *sêgbenu sêgbenu kaakbo kaakbo íni* means, "Great God, I'm in"; that *Sêgbenu* means, "I'm praying [to Great God]"; and that *Sêgbenu mi ta kaakbo* [*kalákbo*] means, "Great God, I've arrived." It seems, then, that *Sêgbenu* means "Great God" in Tonê. See p. 61.

Mi yanvalú Nawé-o | So de adáni Sokoto | Tonê Gansa nivólo andáni Sokoto | Anáde miomío | Tonê nivôl, anadé de moyôto. "I pray to you Nawé [the Great Óbia of the village of Dáome] | as it was in Sokoto | Tonê Gansa [the Mother of Waters] *nivólo* in Sokoto | Anáde miomío | Tonê nivôl, anadé de moyôto." Tooy says this is a prayer to the Great God, saying that "the thing we were talking about, we're still talking about it. The work we were doing yesterday, we're still doing it today. The difficult thing we began, we pray that we can finish it." See p. 404.

WÁTAWENÚ

This is the language of anaconda gods. Tooy has a special relationship with them through Mênde, the god inadvertently killed by his Lángu ancestor Kaásipúmbu in the course of purifying the Suriname River, and through his namesake, Pobôsi, who had Mênde in his head. Only further study will show whether this language is related, as I suspect, both to those of the *vodun*-worshipping peoples of the Bight of Benin and to those of West Central Africans.

Lexical Items

adjalú = pleasure, celebration (S. *pizíi*)

aláda viú kokólo = the children (S. *déé miíi*) {Aláda is from Allada/Ardra, the coastal kingdom of seventeenth-century Dahomey, and *viú* is from Ewe *ví*, "child."—Westermann 1930:64 via Bilby 2006}

ankónu = stool (S. *bángi*)

anúndeba = a certain leaf [S. *totóbia*]

anúndedjême = a certain leaf [S. *bemíndjauwíi*]

bedésidá = water lily, water hyacinth [S. *tokóógbagba*]

huêne = child, kid (S. *miíi*)

Kitómbe = anaconda god [S. *Wátawenú*] {from Kikongo *ki-tombe*, "darkness"(?)—van Wing and Penders 1928:90}

odúngdúnggbó = large intestine

tósída = water [S. *wáta*]

vítje [or *vídji*] = come! (S. *kó!*)

Wátawenú = anaconda gods (S. *boma*; from Kikongo *mboma*, "kind of snake, python, dragon"—Van Wing and Penders 1928:187) {from English "water" plus Fon *wenu*, "god"—Wooding 1972:155–56}

Phrases That Are Not in Saramaccan Syntax

[sung] *Kwalo, nundeonê. Kó kolondeonê, nómò.* . . . This is the song that Mênde, the anaconda god who owned the Suriname River, sang to tell his children to come and snuggle under him, to warn them that danger was on the way—the day that Tooy's ancestor Kaásipúmbu "purified" the river with magical fish drugs. See p. 115.

[sung] *Anúndeba, anúndedjême, gódogódobíi.* [repeats] "Anúndeba [a leaf, S. *totóbia*], anúndedjême [a leaf, S. *bemindjauwíi*], gódogódobíi." This is a song used in rites for anaconda gods in Tooy's natal village of Bundjitapá. See p. 249.

*Odúndúnggbó.** Tooy explains that anaconda gods call the large intestine by this name. By citing the word, one alludes to the proverb "Small children should not know what goes in your belly"—which is why Anaconda eats only one time in six months.

Phrases That Are (at Least Partially) in Saramaccan Syntax/ Lexicon, with "Language" Words Inserted

[sung] *Wemee-e, mi na Tósida, Tósida bígi dá mi e.* . . . . "Wemee, I'm a *Tósida* [anaconda god], *Tósida* is what I like." Tooy's god once sang this to me. See p. 84.

[sung] *Gêdje núnde-o, gêdje núnde-o, gêdje núnde, wán wómi sindó gèdje so, gêdje núnde-e, gêdje núnde wómi sindó gêdje-e, na mi ankónu-e.* "*Gêdje núnde-o, gêdje núnde-o, gêdje núnde*, a man sits down solidly, *gêdje núnde-e, gêdje núnde* man sits down solidly, on my *ankónu-e*." Tooy says, "That's the way you must sit and talk! . . . Once the snake is all coiled up in its place, it says, 'Come try to pull me outta here and I'll teach you who's boss!' He's in his house; if you're a real man, try to get him to move from there! You'll see!" See p. 262.

[sung] *Bedésidá bedésidá bedésidá bedésidá u dáome-eo-e, u dê na alada viú kókolo, bedésidá, bedésidá u dáome.* "*Bedésidá* [water lilies] *bedésidá bedésidá bedésidá u dáome-eo-e* [water lilies of Dáume], we are at Alada, *viú kókolo, bedésidá, bedésidá u dáome* [water lilies of Dáume]." Tooy explains, "The plant sings this song, boasting that it may not be able to touch the river bottom or the shore, but it sure can choke up the whole river! If you play this on the drums, you're cursing someone, saying, 'Get off my back, who do you think you are? You don't even touch the river bottom and you don't touch the banks, you're just adrift!' " See p. 262.

[sung] *Hokokó-o, lúku di bóto kumútu na Aladávi-kôndè ta kó. Tósida pikí mií ké un kóni-ee. Hokokó-oo, ma un déé Tósida pikí, Tósida pikí un kóni-e. Oolό!* "[Exclamation], look at the canoe that's arriving from Aladávi country. *Tósida* [anaconda-god] children, [exclamation], be careful. [Exclamation], but you those *Tósida* children, *Tósida* children, be careful. Watch out!" This is what the priest coming to the *kitómbe* ceremony—the final part of the funeral rites for an anaconda—sings, after his canoe has landed stern first. It's a warning for mothers to get their children indoors! See p. 262. (A sound clip of Tooy's god Dúnuyángi singing a version of this song, labeled "Dunuyangi-Watawenu," can be found at http://www.press.uchicago.edu/books/price/ and http://www.richandsally.net.)

[sung] *Di kálu u Ma Vulá, Vulá mi lúka, Vulá mi lúka, Vulá mi lúka.** "The corn of Ma Vulá, *Vulá mi lúka, Vulá mi lúka, Vulá mi lúka*." See above, under Apúku, where Tooy says that this song is for both Apúkus and Wátawenús.

*Aladávi víl víl víl Ma Gandjé. Tósida pikí kióo vídjioo-ké, sombaa. Ma ná fu nê. Aladávi-e, Ma-e Gándje. Tósida pikí kióo vídjioo-é, sombaa. Ma ná fu nê.** "*Aladávi víl víl víl Ma Gandjé. Tósida* children *vídjioo* [come!] *ké* [exclamation], gods. But not for evil." Tooy says that you must be a real man to have the courage to play this on the drum—it's part of the Kitómbe ceremony. "We're at Mênde's thing here!" he exclaims with joy.

[sung] *Aladávi kái hên mamá-e. Aládavi kái hên mamá-o. Hên di mamá dê-o, Mamá Tósida.** "Aladávi calls his mother. Aladávi calls his mother. And the woman's OK, Mother Tósida [the Mother of Waters]." Tooy sang this during a spontaneous "play" for Apúkus and Wátawenús in 2005.

[sung] *Tósida, mi da huêmedji. Adanú, mi da huêmedji, wan kódó wóyo tofínoví. Tósida, mi da huêmedji.** "Anaconda god, I'm a *huêmedji*. Tonê, I'm a *huêmedji*, a single-eye *tofínoví*. Anaconda god, I'm a *huêmedji*." Tooy says that when an anaconda spirit comes into your matrilineage, he'll sing this to say he's come to take you as a friend, but you're not his family. He's come to live with you but remains an outsider, completely dependent on the way you treat him. Tooy says that "single-eye" alludes to the god's being alone.

[sung] *Adjalú. Yú ná huêne, mi ná huêne. Bó bái adjalú.** "Adjalú [celebration]. You're not a *huêne* [kid], I'm not a *huêne* [kid]. Let's call out *adjalú* [celebrate]." Yaai's god Yontíni sang this at a "play" in 2003.

WÉNTI

The language of Tooy's favorites, the sea gods he spends so much time singing to. They were unknown to Saramakas until the very end of the nineteenth century and have no known connections to Africa (though they partake of ideas about water spirits that are common from Sierra Leone to Kongo).

Lexical Items

adjú = father (S. *tatá*)

afémaóla = sea (S. *ze*), used in the expression *a di kánti fu afémaóla*, "at the seaside"

Akínawebí = a Wénti town

akuánulelé = evil or bad ("When you see a quick current in the river blown by the wind, *akuánulelé!* [S. *ógi*]")

alónu[g]bé [sometimes, "*alosúgbé*"] = sun [S. *sónu*]

andúwe = tortoise (S. *logoso*)

ayaúnde = the great gong under the sea, or any rocking motion, or the tides

dagwédayónu = rattle (S. *tjáka*)

djême = to lie (S. *lègèdè*)

Élola = Earth Mother (S. *Goón Mamá*)

Gaánlolo = a Wénti town

genú = child [S. *miíi*]

Godolyú-lúmadu-hwémado = the middle-of-the-sea place where the water is sucked up into the sky (see p. 62)

Gongongondóme = a Wénti town

hangwé = tick (S. *kaapátu*)

kédje-fu-ontó = Wéntis who live in rapids

kédje-tomé [or *kédje-tón*] = freshwater Wéntis (S. *súti-wáta Wénti*)

kêdji [or *kêdje*] = evil (S. *ógi*)

kéidjo = calabash rattle (S. *tjáka*)

kéénidju [*kénidjó*] = beer (S. *bíi*) {from S. *tjéni*, "cane" and French *jus*, "juice"(?)}

Kínazaan [or *Kínaazáu*] = a Wénti town

kwekwé = exclamation of surprise/danger (S. *oló*)

Laibení = a Wénti town

Loonza = a Wénti town

Luwézaan = a Wénti town

mavíolo = "interpersonal trouble" (S. *fiúfiú*) [in Wénti language, literally: "whirlpool"]

muádji = money barrel (S. *môni bali*)

niviélo = sea (S. *ze*)

noíkadjá = his house (or his shell[?]—said of a tortoise) (S. *ósu f'ên*)

Olóni = a Wénti town

sa bóbo = place it there (S. *sindó hên dê*)

senòò, senóó = greeting

Sináibo = a Wénti town

sobénu zogamê = roll them into the sun (S. *lolá de a sónu*)

tjòònúgbe = pour it into the glass (S. *kándi ên a gaásí dá mi*)

tósu-kédje-kédje = freshwater Wéntis (S. *súti-wáta Wénti*)

tósu-kpêke-kpêke = saltwater Wéntis (S. *sátu-wáta Wénti*)

tuusé = money (S. *môni*)

vindlío vikádja = caiman's front teeth (S. *fési-sê tánda u káima*)

wámilo = sea (S. *ze*) You can't say this word when your feet are in the water—it also means "woman's genitals."

Yedó = the Great God Above (S. *Mása Gaán Gádu*)

Phrases That Are Not in Saramaccan Syntax

*Vitokú denzáku, núsu tokú da keedjé, míomío fa alosó, alosó kó míomío.** This means, says Tooy, "We're talking about personal/family things." Tooy says, when I ask, that the first two words mean, "Man, let's sit down"; that the second phrase means, "Let's talk," with *keedjé* meaning "talk"; and that the final two phrases mean, "matrilineage with matrilineage (family member with family member)."

[sung] *Wêbigo, wêbigo-e. Djême-hun. Djême-o, kwínga-e, djême-o.** This, says Tooy, is what Ma Yowentína says to her father Adjéunsu, meaning, "We just talk bullshit (*djême*), we don't know what we're talking about."

Phrases That Are (at Least Partially) in Saramaccan Syntax/
Lexicon, with "Language" Words Inserted

[sung] *Tuun tuun tuun, tuun tuun. Tuun tuun, ma tuun tuun-o. O Zaaime-e! Akamí bái zanzáme, yeke djaíni. Hóvomí na yáifo, ke! Anáma folozán, ke! Yétezamé. Vúnvu mi na yáifo, pandá mafolozán, Yétezame.* "Tuun tuun tuun, tuun tuun ['Tuun tuun' is onomatopeia]. Tuun tuun, but tuun tuun. Oh, Zaaime-e! Trumpeter Bird called out zanzáme, yeke djaíni. Hóvomí na yáifo, ke! Anáma folozán, ke! Yétezamé. Vúnvu mi na

yáifo, pandá mafolozán, Yétezame." This is the song that the Wénti named Zaime once sang to stop a "war" between Papágádu (Boa Constrictor) and Akamí (Trumpeter Bird), who ever since have kept their distance from each other. Once, Tooy explained to me that it was really the Wénti called Mêtolan, who guards the entrance to the Mana River, who sang "*Tuun tuun*" to stop the fight, but that it was Zaime, in the head of Kositán, who told Saramakas about the incident. (Mêtolan, according to Tooy, never possessed anyone.) See p. 16.

[sung] *Den dóu-ye, den dóu-ya. Ya ya di bóto kó. Den dóu ya. Den dóu ya. Ya ya ya den bóto dóu a wi.* "They've arrived, they've arrived. Yes, yes, the ship's arrived. They've arrived. Yes, yes, the ship's come to us." The Wénti ship has finally landed in Tampáki. See p. 16.

[sung] *Naosí, Naosí. Naosí-e, mbéi máu. Foóu kó! Ópo kái Wénti-e. Naosí. Naosí-e, mbéi máu, baáa-o. Ópo kái.* "Naosí, Naosí. Naosí, all hands on deck. The tide's turned. Call the Wéntis [sailors]. Naosí. Naosí, hands on deck, Brother. Call everyone." The Wénti ship is loaded and ready to depart with the outgoing tide. The captain is calling Naosí and the other Wénti sailors on shore to come onboard. See p. 16.

[sung] *Tuusé, tuusé, a lólo muádji-oo, e-e-e* [sound of hard work], *a lólo muádji-oo, wómi, sobénu zogamê, a lólo muádji-oo, a lólo muádji, Wénti sobénu zogamê, sa bóbo, ádjita i gogó, a náki sobénu zogamê, sa bobó, e-e-e, Wénti a lólo muádji, a lólo muádji-oo, wómi, sobénu zogamê, sa bobó-o, tuusé, tuusé.* "*Tuusé, tuusé* [money, money], roll out the *muádji* [money barrels], *e-e-e* [sound of hard work], roll out the *muádji* [money barrels], man, *sobénu zogamê* [roll them into the sun], roll out the *muádji* [money barrels], roll out the *muádji* [money barrels], *Wénti sobénu zogamê* [Wéntis, roll them into the sun], *sa bóbo* [set them down there], *ádjita* your buttocks, it makes them *sobénu zogamê* [roll them into the sun], *sa bobó* [set them down there], *Wénti a lólo muádji* [Wéntis, roll them into the sun], roll out the *muádji* [money barrels], man, *sobénu zogamê* [roll them into the sun], *sa bobó-o* [set them down there], *tuusé, tuusé* [money, money]." See p. 16.

[sung] *Panyá mi akí. A lólo muádji-oo, wómi, sobénu zogamê....* "Grab me here. Roll out the *muádji* [money barrels], *sobénu zogamê* [roll them into the sun]...." A variation on the previous song. See p. 16.

[sung] *Aladjímèèdji-e, aladjímèèdji-o, téé na alosúgbe.* "*Aladjímèèdji-e, aladjímèèdji-o*, as far as *alosúgbe* [the sun]." Tooy explains that the water lily [or water hyacinth—*Eichhornia crassipes*] (S. *tokóógbagba*) has no paddle; the whole paddy of leaves is powerless to direct where it will go, it's completely adrift, at someone else's mercy. This song is its lament, the way it asks Mother Dígbeónsu to protect it. You can sing it when you've left one place and arrived in a new one and are asking the new one to receive you well, to give you a firm anchorage. See p. 16, 83, 286.

[sung] *Gòònsè-e, Gòònsè, Yedoo, ké mi Yedoo, Wénti-e.* "*Gòònsè-e, Gòònsè, Yedoo* [exclamation], my *Yedoo, Wénti-e.*" Interestingly, Tooy explains that this version of the "Gòònsè" song (see below for a different one) is a call to Ma Dígbeónsu for her to help you. He says, "Say that your ship is sinking, that you're going under. This

would be the way you call on Ma Dígbeónsu to help you." A song made for one purpose (see p. 268) thus becomes in other circumstances a song of Wénti sailors in distress at sea. See p. 17.

[sung] *Mi mánda ódio, mi mánda ódio. Tatá Yembu . . . Gonkíma-o. . . .* "I send greetings, I send greetings to Tatá Yembuámba, *agonkíma* ['friend' in Komantí]." Sung by Ma Yaai's Wénti. See p. 83.

[sung] *Tangí-o, davié, tangí dê a múndu-e. Tangí dê a mambá-o. Tangí dê a mambá.* "Thanks, blessings, thanks to the universe, thanks to the *mambá* ['river' in Apúku]." Sung by Ma Yaai's Wénti. See p. 83.

[sung] *Mamá Nyamútu, Tatá Nyumútu, wáta séki, sómba-we. . . .* "Mother Nyamútu, Father Nyumútu, the water is rough, gods. . . ." A song associated with the Wénti who lives at the mouth of Cassipora Creek, near Jews Savannah, in the tidal zone. See p. 84.

[sung] *Mamá, mi mamá Yemánzáa. Mi ta haíka i, yôôô. Yéi mi mamá yaaa.* "Mother, my mother Yemánzáa. I'm waiting for you-oh. Do you hear, my mother?" Another song Tooy dreamed in the hospital, in the wake of my having introduced the Brazilian sea goddess Iemanjá to him. See p. 89.

[sung] *Ma Yemá-e, Mamá Yemá, gaán tangí tangí mi ta bégi únu fu di súti ódi f'i, Ma Yamazala, mi ta mêni i-o, mi mamá, Mamá Yemá, mi ta bégi i yéti fu di súti ódi f'i yéi mamá-e, Ma Yemá . . . zaa!* "Mother Yemánzáa, I offer thanks for your sweet greetings, Mother Yemánzáa, I keep thinking of you, my mother, Mother Yemánzáa, I continue asking you for those sweet greetings of yours, mother, Mother Yemánzáa." The song Tooy sang us when we presented the statue of Yemánzáa to him in 2005. See p. 89.

[sung] *Ma Dígbeónsu-o, kó heépi, mi mamá! We mi mamá Dígbeónsu fu Olonu, gaán tángi-tángi mi ta bégi yu, mamá, i án si mi dê téé na alónugbe. Un tjá mi gó a niviélo namizamé. Ma Digbeónsu-e.* "Mother Dígbeónsu, come help me mother! Well my mother Dígbeónsu of Olonu, great thanks I pray to you, mother, don't you see I've come as far as *alónugbe* [the sun]. Please carry me back to *niviélo* [the sea] *namizamé.* Mother Digbeónsu-e." One of the songs/prayers Tooy dreamed in the hospital. See p. 96. (A sound clip of Tooy singing a version of this song, labeled "Digbeonsu-Wenti," can be found at http://www.press.uchicago.edu/books/price/ and http://www.richandsally.net.)

[sung] *M'án bói-e, m'án bói yéti. A kête m'án bói tidé-o, Ké, m'án bói-o, m'án bói yéti. A kête m'án bói tidé-o.* [in normal Saramaccan} "I haven't cooked, I haven't cooked yet. The pot hasn't cooked today. [Exclamation], I haven't cooked, I haven't cooked yet. The pot hasn't cooked today." This is what the Wénti woman says to her husband when he returns from an absence and she hasn't yet cooked for him. See p. 260.

[sung] *Kó mi-e, Gwakaká kó mi-e, Ké, Kómi-e, Kómi-e, Kená zámba kêntu-o.* "Come, *Gwakaká* come, [exclamation], come, come, *Kená zámba kêntu-o.*" This is what the Wénti wife sings to call her husband to the table once the food is cooked. (*Kêntu* is probably from Kikongo *nkènto* ["woman"].—Laman 1964:717 via Bilby 2006) See p. 260.

[sung] *Gòònsè-o, Gòònsè. Gòònsè, Gòònsè, mi Yédo. Yédo, Élola-ee. Wénti-e, Zámbi nómò-e. Mi da sántroí sántroándi, hên da léventua lévemwádudú, mi da linzahúún línzamtómboyò, e-e Wénti dá wi nómò-e.* "Gòònsè-o, Gòònsè. Gòònsè, Gòònsè, my *Yédo* [God Above]. *Yédo* [God Above], *Élola-ee* [Earth Mother]. *Wénti-e, Zámbi* [Great God(?)]] forever. I am *sántroí sántroándi,* that's the same as *léventua lévemwádudú,* I am *linzahúún línzamtómboyò,* e-e Wénti, keep giving it to us." The song of the Wénti Sidó, admonishing the people of Kayana to make good on their fine for one of their number having desecrated his shrine, which contained an image of Gòònsè. See p. 268. (A sound clip of Tooy singing a version of this song, labeled "Goonse-Wenti," can be found at http://www.press.uchicago.edu/books/price/ and http://www.richandsally.net.)

[sung] *Keenidjó-yei gaán lo gádu, mi keenidjó dá únu-e. Mi adjò, mi adjò. Mi keenidjò, mi keenidjò. Wêmêdjé fu ayónde, mi keenidjó dá únu-e. Mi adjò, mi adjò. Tjónugbé, gonobí olo matoo hwémato, kínadu gadi mi hwénu kee, mi adjò, mi adjò, tjónugbé-o.* "*Keenidjó* [beer], big-god of the clan, I give beer to you. *Mi adjò, mi adjò* [I pray, I pray]. *Mi keenidjò, mi keenidjò* [I offer beer, I offer beer]. *Wêmêdjé* from *ayónde* [the tides], I offer you beer. I pray, I pray. *Tjónugbé* [pour it in the glass], *gonobí olo matoo hwémato* [this sounds something like Godolyú-lúmadu-hwémado, the sacred place in the center of the sea], *kínadu gadi mi hwénu kee, mi adjò, mi adjò* [exclamation, I pray, I pray], *tjónugbé-o* [pour it in the glass]." Song of thanks, toasting the Wéntis after a fine meal. See p. 271.

[sung] *Naosí-e, Naosí, Naosí-elóo kióo ná máti, a tjalí, só no sèmbè dê f'en-e, Naosí. Naosí-elóo, kióo ná máti-e, baáa, só no sèmbè dê, Wénti-e.* "Naosí, Naosí, Naosí, don't be angry, kid, it's sad, that's just the way people are, Naosí. Naosí, don't be angry Brother, that's just the way people are, Wénti." The song of Moses's estranged Wénti wife, begging him to take her back. See p. 277.

[sung] *Wámilo wánwán, wámilo yú wánwán-o, M'án o dêdè f'i hédi, a tjalí-e, i án músu kèê fu mi, Wénti-e. Wámilo-e. Wámilo yu wánwán-o. M'án ta dêdè f'i hédi-o, ké. U án músu kèê fu mi, Wénti-e.* "You're just a woman, you're just a woman. I won't die over you, it's very sad, Wéntis please don't cry for me. [repeats]" Moses's reply to his wife's song, agreeing to take her back. See p. 277.

[sung] *Hangwé-e go na andúwe, hangwé-e go na andúwe* [repeat], *andúwe go f'en na noíkadjá-e. Hangwé-e go na andúwe, hangwé-e go na andúwe, andúwe kísi noíkadjá, Wénti-e.* "*Hangwé* [Tick] goes to *andúwe* [Tortoise], Tick goes to Tortoise, Tortoise goes into *noíkadjá* [his house/shell]. Tick goes to Tortoise, Tick goes to Tortoise, Tortoise goes into his shell. Wénti-e." This is about inseparable friends. Tooy says that you never catch a tortoise without finding a tick on the underside of its neck. See p. 278.

[sung] *Adjéunsu-oo, i míti kêdjè-ee, Adjéunsu. Adjéunsu baáa adjú, i míti kêdjê-ee kwêkwe, Dauté, ódio e mbáya-ee.* "Adjéunsu, there's been trouble, Adjéunsu. Brother Adjéunsu my father, there's been trouble [exclamation], Dauté, greetings my brother." The song that Gaamá Agbagó's Wénti Todjê sang as he brought Dauté ashore to place in Ma Booi's womb. See p. 398.

[sung] *Tangí-o, tangí nómò-e. Kiní a golón, u ta bégi tangí-e. Tangí-e, tangí nómò, Wámilo. Huêmedje fa Yaónde. Tangí nómò Kínazaan-e.** "Thanks, eternal thanks. Knees on the ground, we give thanks. Thanks, eternal thanks, Sea. Huêmedje of Yaónde. Eternal thanks to Kínazaan." This is a Wénti prayer that mentions a man named Huêmedje from the undersea town of Yaónde as well as another Wénti town called Kínazaan. Tooy sang it at a Wénti "play" in 2003.

[sung] *Dasó-e dasó nómò. Sèmbè fu mi e, mi kó mi na lóngi-e tidé. Mi kó lúku únu-e. Dáso-e, dáso-e.** "It is so, it is always so. My people/kinsmen, I'll come from afar today. I've come to visit you. It is so, it is so." You never forget your own kinsmen. You may be gone a very long time, but after a while, you'll come see them. Tooy sang it at a Wénti "play" in 2003.

[sung] *Wénti, u án fèêè, pèê dá mi-e. Kínazaan gádu. Téé mi yúu dóu mi sa kó lúku únu-e, Wénti u án fèêè, pèê dá mi-e.** "Wénti, fear not, play for me. God from Kínazaan. When the time comes, I'll come visit you, Wénti, fear not, play for me." Tooy sang it at a Wénti "play" in 2003.

[sung] *Naosí-e, Naosí-e. Naosí, Naosí nángo, Naosí ta kó, Naosí-e, mbéi máu dá wi-e, foóu o kó kaa, Wénti-e!* [after several repeats Tooy riffs:] *Naosí-o, Naosí aladjímèèdji gbóng-bogbo domêli kêdje légmaama, maama odjiêdjiêdji-o, u mbéi máu dá mi-e, baáa muyêê, foóu kó kaa-o-e, Wénti-e.** "Naósi-e, Naósi-e. Naósi is leaving, Naósi is coming, Naósi-e, get those hands busy for us, the tide's coming in already, Wénti-e!" This is one of the songs referring to the Wénti ship as it's waiting for the tide to turn and carry it into the river to Tampáki.

*Túma dê a djêkete fu sa ába wán bííon.** "Two men are a djêkete to get across a bíion." Tooy says two men need to get to the other side of the river but have no canoe. You can use it, says Tooy, like a prayer, to say, "We're at the seaside with our boats/canoes. The sea is getting rougher. We must have the strength to get across." Kenneth Bilby (personal communication, 2006) notes that "in normal Aluku, *djekete* means 'dead seriousness, in a deadly serious way.'"

[sung] *Bángi dôò yôyô, Bángi dôò yôyô. Sondí pikí miíi ta pèê f'en-téé, bángi dôò yôyô-e.* "*Bángi dôò yôyô, Bángi dôò yôyô.** The thing little kids play so much, *Bángi dôò yôyô-e.*" Tooy explains this as a song of humility, saying, "We're just playing around the way kids play in mud puddles. We don't know anything." *Bángi dôò yôyô* is a Saramaka nursery rhyme/game.

[sung] *Genu ye, Genu-o. Ma Genu ké! Ná wéi dá mi-o. Pèê dá wi-e, Genu-e, Wénti-e.** "*Genu* [children], *genu*, but *genu*! Don't get tired of me [praying to you]. [Come] play for us, *Genu*, Wénti." "Little children," says Tooy, "like to play in mud puddles. They drink the water. They don't know what they're doing. This song asks the Wéntis to clean out any dirt that's gone into the child's belly because it didn't know what it was doing. It asks them to protect all of us, even though we don't know what we're doing." And he adds, "The sadness Wénti songs give me! I love their 'play.' . . . If I was younger I'd get a Wénti to put in my head! We have to pray to the Wéntis repeatedly not to get tired of our praying to them, even though we do it all the time."

[sung] *Antína yauyau, Antína yauyau, Antína yauyau kiinga, nêngèkôndè kái mi Ándo, Antína yauyau yauyau. Bási Antína-o.** "Antína yauyau, Antína yauyau, Antína yauyau kiinga, Africa calls me Ándo, Antína yauyau yauyau. Boss Antína-o." Tooy sang this in 2005, saying that it was Busikí's song of seduction to a Wénti woman named Antína, whom he spotted once at a dance.

[sung] *Tatá Bokó náki hên bum bum bum bum bum bum dólame di gaándi. Tatá Bokó náki hên bum bum bum bum bum dólame. Ala de ké wí na wí-o, ké. M'an gó téé-o na unten, fu téé na unten, u sa kó míti a Bókodénawa.** "Old Man Bokó knocked it boom boom boom boom boom boom *dólame di gaandi.* Old Man Bokó knocked it boom boom boom boom boom *dólame.* All of them, it's just us. I won't go way far away, we'll meet yet in Bókodénawa." Tooy sang this at a Wénti "play" in 2003. He later explained that Old Man Bokó is knocking the drums to say that though he travels widely ("like you," Tooy said to me), he'll come back and see his family someday in the place called Bókodénawa.

[sung] *Déé Wénti fu Loonzá, déé Wénti fu Kínazaan, téé un gó, nôò, un ta kumútu a Kínazaan. Déé Wénti fu Loonzá, déé Wénti fu Kínazaan, téé un gó, nôò, un ta kumútu a Loonzá.** "The Wéntis from Loonzá, the Wéntis from Kínazaan, when you go, you'll be leaving Kínazaan. The Wéntis from Loonzá, the Wéntis from Kínazaan, when you go, you'll be leaving Loonzá." Tooy sang this at a Wénti "play" in 2003.

[sung] *Keidjó, keidjó, dagwédayónu, keidjó. Keidjó, keidjó, dagwédayónu, keidjó. Ngóli ngóli ngóli. Alêmitjé f'adjú. Keidjó, keidjó, dagwédayónu, keidjó.** Tooy says *keidjó* means, "We're at the meeting"; that *ngóli ngóli ngóli* is the sound made by the rattle (which Wéntis call *dagwédayónu*); and that Alêmitjé refers to Pobôsi's possession god.

[sung] *Mbéi u án sáa môò, un pèê dá wi-e.* [repeats three times] *Wè, téé di tén kísi, un sa kó a wi-o. Mbéi u án sáa môò un pèê dá wi.** "Let's not be sad any longer, come 'play' for [with] us. . . . Well, when the time is right, you can come to us." This song was often sung by Kódji when possessed by his Wénti, Wánanzái. Tebíni first sang it to me in the 1970s—see Price, *First-Time,* p. 177, for a musical transcription.

YÁKA-ÓSU

This is the language used by a particular *gaán-óbia* in the village of Bundjitapá. I include a few fragments here as a reminder that every village has one or several such powers and that each has its own special language, rites, songs, drum rhythms, dances, and taboos. There must be scores of similar powers, and minilanguages, in Saramaka.

Lexical Items

adjeú = path (S. *pási*)
adjíulalá = machete (S. *ofángi*)
flambó = fire (S. *fáya*) {from French Creole *flambo,* "torch")

lalángmamí = sugarcane syrup (S. *súti sópi*)
zúngunamitjé = rum (S. *daán*)

Phrases That Are Not in Saramaccan Syntax

[sung] *Azúngunamitjé, manamitjé kaafu lalángmamí zúngunamitjé, botjéi kaafu lalángmamí zúngunamitjé, manamitjé kaafu lalángmamí zúngunamitjé.* The song commemorating the contest between Rum and Sugarcane Syrup to see which was stronger. See pp. 269–70.

Phrases That Are (at Least Partially) in Saramaccan Syntax/ Lexicon, with "Language" Words Inserted

[sung] *Adjíulalá lalá, Adjíulalá lalá, Naná kôndè flambó, Naná Nyankómpono, mi hélu ku adjéusúmani. Adjíulalá lalá, Naná kôndè flambó, wemi yaú-ké, Naná Nyankómpono, mí-i-ké adjeúsumaní-e.* "*Adjíulalá lalá* [machete], *Adjíulalá lalá* [machete], *Naná kôndè flambó* [the fire of heaven], *Naná Nyankómpono* [God Above], *mi hélu ku adjéusúmani* [I praise the path]. *Adjíulalá lalá* [machete], *Naná kôndè flambó* [the fire of heaven], *wemi yaú-ké, Naná Nyankómpono* [God Above], *mí-i-ké adjeúsumaní-e.*" This prayer commemorates what Amaní said to his brother avenging spirits, telling them that he's their pathfinder, the one who clears the path with his machete, the strongest of the three. See p. 269. (A sound clip of Tooy singing a version of this song, labeled "YakaOsu," can be found at http://www.press.uchicago.edu/books/price/ and http://www.richandsally.net.)

[sung] *Kwinga kwé, kwinga kwí, nu ku yeló. Kwinga kwi, kwinga dobukaan, nu ku yeló. Kwinga kwé, kwinga kó, nu ku yeló. Kwinga kwé, hési kwinga dóu, nu ku yééé.* "*Kwinga kwé, kwinga kwí, nu ku yeló. Kwinga kwi, kwinga dobukaan, nu ku yeló. Kwinga kwé, kwinga* comes, *nu ku yeló. Kwinga kwé,* hurry *kwinga* is arriving, *nu ku yééé.*" Tooy glosses this as "Hurry! Grab your kids and get them into the house. Shut the doors! A jaguar is on the loose in the village and will eat them!" It's the warning that they are going to play Yáka-ósu. (From the context, it would seem that Kwinga is synonyomous with the *óbia* itself, with the penultimate phrase of the song saying, "Hurry *kwinga* arrives.") See p. 269.

MISCELLANEOUS

Selebóbo selefála, anatá djóbidjóobi, bêtele djóbidjóobi, abeyé beyówa. The Anagó (Yoruba) phrase that the African immigrants in Mana taught Tooy's uncle in the early twentieth century. Tooy's god Dúnuyángi told me it means, "If you're looking to kill me, you'll kill yourself!" Another time Tooy said the phrase as part of a prayer at the ancestor shrine in his house, explaining to me that it meant, "If you wish Evil for me, may Evil come to you!" See. p. 169.

[sung] *Ódo bái Anígo-o, ódo bái Anígo-ye. Tjá, mênimi tjá. Ódo bái Anígo-o-yé, tjá Anígo tjái.* "I call out greetings to Anagó. Bring, think of me bring. I call out greetings to Anagó, bring Anagó bring." In 2005, Tooy greeted Sally and me with this Anagó song, saying it was the greeting used when Anagó *óbia* arrives. When I asked for details, he confirmed that the Nasí clan are the bosses of that *óbia*, and said he knew nothing more about it. See p. 278.

DRAMATIS PERSONAE

Adjéunsu. Master of the Sea, the Wénti who is married to Ma **Dígbeónsu.**

Afaata. Daughter of **Gweyúnga** and **Hwéte,** who founded Tooy's matrilineage in the village of Bundjitapá, ca. 1755.

Afeemaónsu. A Komantí spirit who worked closely with **Akoomí.**

Agbagó Abóikóni. Highly respected Saramaka *gaamá* (paramount chief) from 1951 to 1989.

Akoomí. The African-ghost-spirit who taught **Dúngul
áli-Óbia** to **Kódji** in the early twentieth century.

Aniké Awági. Octogenarian Headcaptain of the Saramakas in Suriname, who was raised in Tampáki.

Annette. Tooy's "Amerindian" ex-wife, whose sister accused him of rape.

Antamá. Tooy's favorite First-Time ancestor, who was a renowned eighteenth-century *óbia*-man and political leader.

Asipéi. A Saramaka man, now deceased, who taught me a great deal during the 1960s and 1970s.

Atjúa-Gbéung. A late eighteenth- or early nineteenth-century man who was considered the embodiment of the forest spirit **Mavúngu.** In the late nineteenth century he became the "namesake" of **Sansimé.**

Baala. The sister's son of **Pobôsi,** who inherited most of his *óbias* and presented Tooy with his first loincloth.

Babiá (Jozef). Tooy's mother's brother who served as his host in Saint-Laurent during the 1950s and 1960s.

Ben (Moesoela Amiemba). Born 1970 in the Saramaka village of Kambalóa, he is president of the Association of Young Active Saramakas of Guyane (AJASG) and a close friend of Tooy's.

Béndiwáta Mother (or Béndiwáta goddess or Béndiwáta *sóói-gádu*). The most important Saramaka oracle, brought over from Africa by **Kaásipúmbu,** ever since a possession of the Kaapátu segment of the Lángu clan in the village of Béndiwáta.

Béti-Kadósu. African-born sister of **Wíi,** wife of **Gweyúnga.**

Brigitte. The woman who accused Tooy of rape.

Céline. Tooy's wife of a dozen years, born in Guadeloupe.

Dígbeónsu (of Olóni—"a name to be very careful with, she *is* the sea"). The Wénti married to **Adjéunsu;** her daughters include **Yowentína,** Korantína, and Amantína.

Djakái. Liberated from the coast as a "replacement" for **Antamá**'s brother **Makambí** (killed in battle), he later slept with **Antamá**'s wife and was given **Afaata,** with whom he had children, including **Gadien.**

Djankusó. Revered Saramaka *gaamá* (paramount chief) from 1898 to 1932.

Djesu-akóbita. The wife of **Akoomí,** who moved with him between the land of the dead and the world of the living on the early twentieth-century Oyapock River.

Djéunsu-Etéunsu. The Wénti who posseses **Tembái,** who maintains a lavish shrine and celebrates the Wénti's annual fête.

Dúnguláli-Óbia. The power that protects against Death, taught to **Kódji** by **Akoomí** on the early twentieth-century Oyapock, and now presided over by Tooy.

Dúnuyángi. Tooy's possession god, affiliated with both the forest and the sea.

Flibánti. The *óbia* that **Kwasímukámba** taught **Antamá** and is now in the head of Tooy's brother **Sensiló.**

Frenchwoman. A powerful avenging spirit, created by **Sansimé**'s kinsmen in the mid-twentieth century, that haunts Tooy.

Gaán Tatá. The powerful Ndyuka carry-oracle that exists in several Saramaka villages, including Dángogó.

Gadien. Heir to many of his (mother's brother) **Antamá**'s *óbias* and master of the *apínti* drum, he is credited by Tooy as the source for his knowledge of drum language and much else.

Gisí. The son of **Kwasímukámba** and **Hwéte,** he lived out his life with Tooy's matrilineal ancestors. Tooy keeps an iron pot with his *óbia* in his **Dúnguláli** shrine.

Gweyúnga. Tooy's African-born ancestor who was priest of Tonê, master of the rains.

Herskovits (Melville and Frances). American anthropologists who carried out fieldwork in Suriname during the summers of 1928 and 1929.

Hwéte. Wife of **Gweyúnga** (and lover of **Kwasímukámba**), who with her daughter **Afaata** founded Tooy's lineage in the village of Bundjitapá after **Antamá** rescued her from execution, ca. 1755.

Kaásipúmbu. Born in Africa, Kaási served as First-Time war leader and priest of the Lángu clan.

Kalusé (Ronald Pansa). Our friend since we met in the 1960s in his father's Saramaka village, he has lived in Cayenne since around that time. He introduced us to Tooy.

Kiinza. Daughter and spiritual heir of **Antamá** (and still known by Komantís as "Woman-like-a-Man"), she was **Pobôsi**'s "namesake," and Tooy feels very close to her.

Kódji. A man of many gods, he discovered Wéntis, **Dúnguláli-Óbia,** and **Máma-Gádu** at the turn of the twentieth century and served as captain of Tampáki until his death in 1923.

Kositán. Brother of Gaamá **Agbagó** who accompanied him to the Oyapock in the early twentieth century and returned to Dángogó around 1920 with **Mamá-Gádu** and **Dúnguláli-Óbia.**

Kuset Albina. The Saramaka soldier who survived the Nazi stalags thanks to ritual protections, including the one Tooy wears around his neck, which he also offered to **Roland** in Martinique.

Kwasímukámba. The African-born double agent who first befriended Saramakas and then brought a colonial army against them in the 1750s. Father of **Gisí** and original source of **Sensiló's Flibánti-***óbia.*

Léon (Mathurin). With a Saramaka father and a mother whose parents were Saint-Lucian, he grew up in Saint-Georges but became a pillar of the Tampáki community and, with his wife Julie, our generous host on the Oyapock.

Lógofóu. Son of **Pobôsi** who inherited many of his powers.

Lonzhé. The Wátawenú (anaconda) god of Miséi **Tembái.**

Makambí. The brother of **Antamá** who was killed in battle in 1753.

Mamá-Gádu. The carry-oracle discovered by **Kódji** that became the arbiter of life in Tampáki (as well as in Dángogó, where we lived in the 1960s).

Mamá Nyamútu. A Wénti who guards the rapids near Jews Savannah in the coastal floodplain.

Mása Heépiman (a.k.a. Mása Líbiman, or Jesus, or Jesus-Maria). The possession god of **Pobôsi** that helped him build his idiosyncratic church, but which many Saramakas believed to be the avenging spirit of the Dutch explorer J. G. W. J. Eilerts de Haan.

Mavúngu. The Apúku (forest-spirit) *gaán-óbia* for which the Dómbi clan are masters. It finds people lost in the forest and cleanses the forest after deaths have taken place within.

Méliki. Tooy's father, called by whitefolks Alexander Merki.

Mênde. The giant Wátawenú (anaconda god) which owns the Suriname River. He was killed when **Kaásipúmbu** purified the river so Saramakas could live along it, and he was in the head of Tooy's "namesake" **Pobôsi.**

Morssink (Father Franciscus). The Redemptorist priest who missionized the Lángu region of Saramaka in the early twentieth century, playing an important role in the life of **Pobôsi.**

Naai. Elder sister of Gaamá **Agbagó** and our closest neighbor in Dángogó during the 1960s.

Otjútju (a.k.a. Belfon Abóikóni). Selected as *gaamá* (paramount chief) of the Saramakas in 2005.

Ozéni. A Dángogó man who was **Otjútju's** main rival for the position of *gaamá.*

Pobôsi. A man of many gods. The greatest Saramaka *óbia*-man of the early twentieth century, he is Tooy's beloved "namesake."

Roland Legros. Martiniquan who asked me to contact a Saramaka curer to come and cure his business, which is how I met Tooy.

Sáka-Amáfu. An important Komantí *óbia*, called over from Africa near the end of the wars, that has been in the heads of **Antamá, Kiinza,** and **Pobôsi.**

Sansimé. The Apúku man who played the central role in the creation of the **French-woman** avenging spirit.

Sensiló. Tooy's (now-blind) older brother who has **Antamá**'s (and **Kwasímukám-ba**'s) *óbia* **Flibánti** in his head.

Sibên. A major avenging spirit in the village of Béndiwáta, who was in **Pobôsi**'s head.

Sidó. A Wénti whom I knew when it possessed Akónomísi in Dángogo in the 1960s and which is in Tooy's lineage.

Tebíni. A Saramaka elder, now deceased, who was, in the 1970s, considered the most knowledgeable man alive regarding First-Time history.

Tembái (Miséi Tembái Mayóko). Founder and captain of the village of La Flêche near Iracoubo (Guyane), who has both the Wátawenú **Lonzhé** and the Wénti **Djéunsu-Etéunsu** in his head.

Todjê. The Wénti that possessed future *gaamá* **Agbagó** in Tampáki soon after 1900 and helped him rule Saramaka during much of the second half of the twentieth century.

Wánanzái. The Wénti of **Kódji**, the first ever to possess a Saramaka.

Wíi. Tooy's African-born ancestor who is credited with "bringing the Peace" in 1762 and founding the village where Tooy was born.

Yaai. Tooy's Nduyka Maroon wife of some forty years.

Yayunn. Kalusé's ex-wife, who has a Saramaka father and Saint-Georges-de-l'Oyapock mother.

Yemánzáa. Tooy's Wénti whom he learned about from us and who is his transformation of the Brazilian sea goddess Iemanjá.

Yembuámba. The powerful Wénti (Busikí) that possessed **Pobôsi**.

Yontíni. The Wénti (Busikí) that possesses **Yaai,** and whose mother is **Yowentína** and father is **Flibánti.**

Yowentína. One of Tooy's favorite Wéntis, daughter of **Adjéunsu** and **Digbeónsu** and mother of **Yontíni.**

Zaime. The Wénti that possessed **Kositán.**

NOTES

PRELUDE

1. Clifford Geertz, *Available Light: Anthropological Reflections on Philosophical Topics* (Princeton, NJ: Princeton University Press, 2000), p. 64.

2. The others are the Ndyukas (about the same in number as Saramakas), and the much smaller Paramaka, Aluku, Matawai, and Kwinti peoples.

3. In general, *creolization* refers to the process by which people, flora and fauna, ideas, and institutions with roots in the Old World are born, develop, and reproduce themselves in the New. In this book, the term refers to the ways that enslaved and self-liberated Africans in the Americas, coming from a diversity of Old World societies, drew on their knowledge of homeland institutions (from languages to religions to legal systems) to create new ones that they could call their own and pass on to their children, who further elaborated them.

4. Courting several audiences complicates my writing task. A single example may illustrate. Most Western historians expect or require oral sources to be complemented and verified by written ones—and in general, I do my best to satisfy them. (Saramakas, too—particularly younger ones—have often encouraged me to find "paper" proofs that their orally transmitted histories are "true.") So, when I recount, using oral sources, how a Saramaka in French Guiana joined the army in 1939, fought on the German front, was captured and interned in a Nazi stalag, and escaped all the way to England, I provide numerous citations from military archives; and when documentary proofs of some of his apparently extravagant claims are lacking (e.g., because certain written records were destroyed by fire during the war), I document the exploits of another soldier from that stalag who successfully escaped to England. But for readers who are postcolonial scholars, including many younger anthropologists, such a use of archives may smack of "verificationism," a sin I have sometimes been accused of. Why should a Saramaka account of the past require verification from a Western archive? such critics might ask. And when I do utilize archives, why isn't there the same close attention to the politics of metropolitan (or colonial) memory as there is with Saramakas? I would answer, first, that *Travels with Tooy* is primarily about the production and transmission of Saramaka knowledge, the politics of Saramaka knowledge—not about the ways that Western archives, in their own different ways, are eminently political projects, having their own equally complex histories. Other books I have written, for example *Alabi's World* (1990) and *The Con-*

vict and the Colonel (1998, 2006), treat oral and archival materials more evenhandedly, exploring the politics of memory in both. Here, in part because of considerations of length, I limit myself mainly to Saramaka history-making, to representing (what is from a Western perspective) another, unfamiliar but immensely rich reality, largely through Tooy's experiences. (As Marshall Sahlins has put it, "To transcend critically our native categories in order to understand how other peoples have historically constructed their modes of existence—even now, in the era of globalization—is the great challenge of contemporary anthropology"—catalog copy for *Culture in Practice: Selected Essays* [New York: Zone Books, 2000].) In any case, my occasional use of archives—whether written and curated by German Moravians, French military and colonial administrators, or Dutch and Surinamese government officials—is always grounded in the knowledge that these written documents have histories that involve radical processes of selection (choice and suppression), politics of transmission, arcane codes for distribution, and all the rest. *Silencing the Past: Power and the Production of History* (Boston: Beacon Press, 1995), the excellent *leçon* written by Michel-Rolph Trouillot on this subject, is a useful starting point; although many historians might claim, "We already knew all that from our first-year classes in method," they'd be wrong. I would stress that the strategic use of archival materials to complement Saramaka narratives need not be naive or politically retrograde. For me, and many of my Saramaka friends, it can be a decisive and progressive political act, one intended in part to foster social justice (see Richard Price, "On the Miracle of Creolization," in *Afro-Atlantic Dialogues: Anthropology in the Diaspora,* ed. Kevin A. Yelvington [Santa Fe, NM: SAR Press, 2006], pp. 113–45).

5. For Saramakas and other Maroons, *óbia* means "medicine" or "helpful supernatural power." The malevolent associations of "obeah" that exist today in much of the Anglophone Caribbean are absent among Maroons and seem very much part of the colonial legacy (see Kenneth M. Bilby and Jerome S. Handler, "Obeah: Healing and Protection in West Indian Slave Life," *Journal of Caribbean History* 38 [2004]: 153–83).

6. Referring to two earlier books of mine, Trouillot writes that I have

systematically undertaken to record the Saramaka Maroons' voices and narratives from and about the past and present them to an academic audience. Price excels at inventing intellectual quotation marks, new ways of marking on the published page both the boundaries and the dialogs between voices; but he keeps prudently away from epistemological issues. . . . Yet it may be worth asking which philosophy of knowledge we should use to evaluate native historical or sociological discourse or, for that matter, that of any participant. How do we handle the overlaps and incompatibilities of participants' judgments with Euroamerican scholarship? . . . Anthropology has yet to reach a consensus on both the epistemological status and semiotic relevance of native discourse anywhere. Is native discourse a citation, an indirect quote, or a paraphrase? Whose voice is it, once it enters the discursive field dominated by the logic of academe? Is its value referential, indexical, phatic, or poetic? ("The Caribbean Region: An Open Frontier in Anthropological Theory," *Annual Review of Anthropology* 21 [1992]: 19–42; citation on pp. 24–25)

7. Derek Walcott, *Another Life* (Boulder, CO: Lynne Rienner, 2004 [orig. pub. New York: Farrar, Straus and Giroux, 1973]), p. 147.

MARTINIQUE

1. A recent study of "dealings with the devil" suggests that in the Martiniquan imagination, there are three "countries" where sorcery and other magico-religious powers reign supreme: Haiti, Africa, and French Guiana (Guyane)—with the latter representing the veritable center of non-Christian, animist practices (Franck Degoul, *Le commerce diabolique: Une exploration de l'imaginaire du pacte maléfique en Martinique* [Petit Bourg, Guadeloupe: Ibis Rouge Editions, 2000], pp. 45–47). Many Martiniquan men are familiar with the fame of Saramaka "sorcerers" and healers from having done their compulsory military service in Guyane.

THE SOLDIER'S CHARM

1. According to one Antillean specialist, such tiny squares of red cloth with a prayer inside, often sewn into underpants or bra since they need to be in contact with the skin, are also common in Martinique, where they're called *kabilistik* (Geneviève Leti, *L'Univers magico-religieux antillais: ABC des croyances et superstitions d'hier et d'aujourd'hui* [Paris: L'Harmattan, 2000], p. 35).

SEA GODS

1. For readers who would like to hear Tooy's voice, I have posted several sound clips of Tooy singing at http://www.press.uchicago.edu/books/price/ and http://www.richandsally.net.

2. To a Saramaka, these place-names all sound strange, intriguingly "other," roughly the way the place-names in Narnia mark that land as clearly in another realm for English speakers today.

3. In French Guiana and Suriname, *Creole* refers to a person of African descent who is not a Maroon. (In Martinique and French Guiana, the same word refers to the mother tongue of most of the population, sometimes called French Creole.) The mother tongue of Surinamese Creoles is a different (English-based) creole language called Sranan-tongo ["Suriname language"] or simply Sranan.

4. Tooy's elder brother Sensiló told me recently, with the greatest tone of wonder, of having worked for a time near the mouth of the Coppename River where Wánanzái had first appeared to Kódji. One day, seeking palm nuts in the forest, he happened to wander into the god's realm and found himself in a veritable Garden of Eden: forest pools overflowing with fish, a stream running through where you could sit down in

the rapids on flat, white stones that were like tables, beautiful varieties of pineapples and other fruits that no one had ever seen elsewhere, and other miraculous proofs of the powers of Wéntis.

5. Below Mamádan, the Saramaka villages were largely Christian, not considered fully Saramaka by the men of the Upper River. We saw Mamádan for the first and last time in 1966, just before the waters of a massive artificial lake, built as part of Alcoa's hydroelectric project to make cheap aluminum, covered it over forever—along with some 43 villages where 6,000 people lived. (The count of inundated villages varies between 28 and 43, depending on whether smaller settlements are counted.)

6. As Tooy tells it, Mamá Booi (a.k.a. Wilhelmina), one of Gaamá Abóikóni's wives, was bearing sons but no daughters. So he made an *óbia* to cause her to bear daughters (to assure that her lineage and clan would grow). But it backfired and ended her fertility. She was incensed, accusing him of witchcraft and saying she would much rather bear sons than no children at all. His Wénti, Todjê, then took over, and Booi once again began to menstruate. At dawn on the day she was to emerge from menstrual seclusion for the first time, Todjê appeared and told the villagers of Santigoon to come to the landing place, where he would bring ashore a son named Dauté, whom he had brought from the undersea Wénti village of Olóni, to place in Booi's belly. He sang, *Adjéunsu-oo, i míti kêdjè-ee, Adjéunsu. Adjéunsu baáa adjú, i míti kêdjê-ee kwêkwe, Dauté, ódio-e mbáya-ee* ("Adjéunsu, there's been trouble, Adjéunsu. Brother Adjéunsu my father, there's been trouble, [exclamation], Dauté, greetings my brother"). And some months later Dauté was born and then spent most of his life on the coast, nearer to his relatives in Olóni.

7. Derek Walcott, "Reflections on *Omeros*," *The South Atlantic Quarterly* 96 (1997): 229–46; citation is on p. 235. I am not suggesting that Tooy and Walcott fully share a sense of the Caribbean sublime, only that there are certain shared elements. Clearly, Tooy is not privy to Walcott's Aegean-Caribbean interconnections, nor is Walcott (until he reads this book) to Tooy's relations with Wéntis. And what I share with Walcott when I look out from the verandah—he lives by the sea on the neighboring island in the archipelago, St. Lucia, which we can make out from the hills near our home—is vastly expanded by what Tooy has taught me about the undersea world in front of our house (for our conversations with Walcott, see Sally and Richard Price, *Romare Bearden: The Caribbean Dimension* [Philadelphia: University of Pennsylvania Press, 2006]).

DÚNGULÁLI-ÓBIA

1. On my exchanges with Tebíni and other Saramaka historians, see Richard Price, *First-Time: The Historical Vision of an African American People*, 2nd ed. (Chicago: University of Chicago Press, 2002).

2. One day while hunting on the Upper Pikílío, Gbagidí (who would be designated *gaamá* in 1821) discovered a mysterious swamp surrounded by tempting bananas, wild rice, and various other crops. After cutting samples and setting out for home, he was horrified to see his favorite hunting dog being swallowed up by the swamp's

quicksand. So he called out to the god of that locality (whose identity he did not know) that he would give it anything it desired if it would only spare the dog. The animal emerged immediately, unscathed. Then, as Gbagidí, paddling downstream, neared his village, he heard shouts and commotion. His sister Yáya had just been violently possessed by a previously unknown Apúku (forest spirit). As Gbagidí arrived, the god (speaking through Yáya) proclaimed, "My name is Kokobandámama or Sáa," and it recounted in detail how Gbagidí had taken its bananas, rice, and other crops and how he had promised obedience; it then demanded that Gbagidí wash it immediately with an entire demijohn of rum. This done, the god demanded Gbagidí's gun and broke it. In the course of a few minutes, the god had summoned to it all of Gbagidí's possessions and had destroyed them all. Sáa then instructed Gbagidí to construct a canoe and go to the city. In Paramaribo, Gbagidí was miraculously given a whole boatload of every kind of whitefolks' goods by city merchants. With Gbagidí's triumphant arrival back in Saramaka, the extraordinary powers of Yáya's god, Sáa, were confirmed. "Here's the song that Sáa sang when she came," said Tooy, singing: *Mónika bayé-é Mónika batí. Sáa-e-o. Anúma-e-o, Anúma bongó, Mónika bangísa wi-o, Sáa-e, Anúma-e-o.* All those years in Saramaka, and I'd never before heard Sáa's song!

3. The large-scale communal events that Saramakas call *pêè* ("plays") combine complex, intense, and stylized performances. Often lasting till dawn and bringing together festively dressed people from a number of villages to participate in multimedia performances of song, dance, and drumming, "plays" are organized on a variety of occasions and serve also as the primary public opportunity to meet potential lovers and spouses. They form the high point of each of the several stages of funeral rites. They accompany the installation of chiefs, headmen, and other officials. And they are used to honor particular gods and ancestors. Whether a gathering in honor of a forest spirit or the climactic rite of a funeral, each "play" calls for a specialized set of dances, drum rhythms, and kinds of singing.

4. For Saramakas, these two clans are the masters of Papá language, and they compete actively in this arena. Several stories recounted in Price, *First-Time*, pp. 148–49, help explain why.

5. In the 1960s, my Dángogó (Matjáu-clan) friends often told me Apúku stories they'd heard from Lángu men. For example, a man hunting on the Oyapock became lost in the forest but eventually came upon a village where he was welcomed and offered a meal, a house, and a beautiful young-adolescent girl to sleep with. She insisted on sleeping in her own hammock, no matter how many nights he begged her to join him, explaining that in this place men could have but one woman, and that once he'd had her he could never again sleep with another. Finally, he agreed, and they stayed together for a time. Then he returned to Tampáki. What a celebration—salutes were fired, dances performed! And he slept with his old wife. One day, when he was urinating at the edge of the forest, he saw his Apúku wife beckoning to him. Soon after, he got leprosy and died.

6. I tell Tooy and Kalusé about my understanding of currents (part of which comes from my earlier ethnographic work with Martiniquan fishermen), they tell me about

Wéntis. Such knowledge exchanges, occurring throughout the book (and my life or Tooy's), highlight how much of his knowledge (and óbia magic)—however different from mine—relies on the West and how much my own (anthropological magic) relies on people like Tooy. In July 2006, having a drink in the Café de Flor (Paris) with Édouard Glissant—one of the icons of postcolonial thought—I asked him for the meaning of the title of his latest book, La Cohée du Lamentin: Poétique V, which is never explained in the text, and he replied with another tale of what lurks below the surface of the Caribbean Sea. In the Bay of Lamentin, where he used to swim as a youth, there's a cove known as "la Cohée du Lamentin." In it lived a toothless shark one hundred years old, which the boys could see down below. In earlier days, the beast would wait at the end of the wharf where the barrels of sugar were loaded onto the ships, and whenever a barrel fell into the water, the animal would gobble it up, eventually losing all its teeth. Whenever he tells the story, said Édouard, listeners doubt its veracity. "But it's true, you know," he assured me.

7. Alónugbe or alosúgbe is the Wénti word for "sun," so the last phrase means "as far as the sun."

8. Wéntis seem largely unrelated, both to me and to Saramakas, to coastal Suriname Creole water spirits, who are usually represented as Amerindian women (see, for example, Alex van Stipriaan, Creolisering: Vragen van een basketbalplein, antwoorden van een watergodin [Rotterdam: Inaugurele Rede Erasmus Universiteit, 2000]). Although they show numerous similarities—whiteness, bringers of wealth, merchandise, and children, and much else—to various water spirits in West and West Central Africa, I have been unable to find any direct connections—see, for example, from West to East/South, Rosalind Shaw, Memories of the Slave Trade: Ritual and the Historical Imagination in Sierra Leone (Chicago: University of Chicago Press, 2002); Luis Nicolau Parés, "Transformation of the Sea and Thunder Voduns in the Gbe-Speaking Area and in the Bahian Jeje Community," in Africa in the Americas: Interconnections during the Slave Trade, ed. José C. Curto and Renée Soulodre-La France (Trenton, NJ: Africa World Press, 2005), pp. 69–93; Henry John Drewal, "Celebrating Water Spirits: Influence, Confluence, and Difference in Ijebu-Yoruba and Delta Masquerades," in Ways of the Rivers: Arts and Environment of the Niger Delta, ed. Martha G. Anderson and Philip M. Peek (Los Angeles: UCLA Fowler Museum of Cultural History, 2002), pp. 193–215; and Robert W. Slenes, "The Great Porpoise-Skull Strike," in Central Africans and Cultural Transformations in the American Diaspora, ed. Linda M. Heywood (Cambridge, Cambridge University Press, 2002), pp. 183–208.

9. Among Maroons, sangaáfu (Costus spp.) is one of the most important óbia plants. Kenneth Bilby (personal communication, 2006), citing Wyatt MacGaffey, "The Eyes of Understanding: Kongo Minkisi," in Astonishment and Power, by Davis C. Driskell, Wyatt MacGaffey, and Sylvia H. Williams (Washington, DC: Smithsonian Institution Press, 1993), p. 96, suggests that its name and uses derive from Kikongo nsanga-lavu—"Costus sp. . . . a juicy and luxuriant plant . . . one of the most significant medicines used in the composition of minkisi."

10. I can only speculate about the reasons for Tooy's quick generosity. It was probably some combination of stories he had heard about me (my inflated reputation as a repository of Saramaka knowledge), our physical distance from Saramaka territory and its complex and rigorous modes of social control about esoteric knowledge, and the personal affinity that was already developing between us.

11. In the old days, I am told, Saramaka canoemen heading upstream with a load of merchandise for the gold miners would always leave a protective iron or brass biceps ring on one of the stones in the great savannah there and then, on their way down weeks later, recover it all fixed up ritually by the gods and spirits who had the place. On an island not far downstream from Dadíafê, says Tooy, there was once a battle royale between Akoomí and some other Komantí spirits over a woman, causing the island to sink. When you pass there on the river today, you can still hear cocks crowing underwater.

12. The priest who presided over our rites was Asêni, Gasitón's brother's son. The "mother" shrine of Dúnguláli remains at Tampáki, on the Oyapock, though it has recently fallen into disuse. The most important subsidiary is at Haarlem, on the Saramacca River, where Kódji's son brought it before he died; it was to this latter shrine that Chief Agbagó repaired briefly, just before leaving the hospital and Paramaribo to go back to his village in the interior to die in 1989, at the age of 102. Besides the lesser shrine in Dángogó, there has for some years been an important Dúnguláli shrine in Cayenne, where the priest, none other than Tooy himself, who is something like Kódji's classificatory sister's daughter's daughter's son (he sometimes claims a more complicated genealogical connection), learned the rites from his cousin, the Dúnguláli priest in Haarlem.

13. E. E. Evans-Pritchard, *Witchcraft, Oracles and Magic among the Azande* (Oxford: Clarendon Press, 1937), a classic work of British social anthropology.

THE BEACH AT COCK'S CROW

1. Kenneth Bilby (personal communication, 2006), citing K. E. Laman, *Dictionnaire kikongo-français* (Ridgewood, NJ: Gregg Press, 1964 [orig. pub. 1936]), pp. 1171, 1197, has proposed the following etymology for *Madjómina*—from Kikongo *ma-zoomina* ("honoraires de médecins" [doctors' payments])—and for *Ká*—from Kikongo *káa, e kaa* ("interj.: oui [à appel]"), *ye káa* ("mais oui, eh bien").

2. Tooy later boasts to me that when a chicken is sacrificed to Dúnguláli, you don't kill it, the *óbia* does, right there at the sacrificial stone.

NIGHT OF THE CATS

1. Cited in Pierre Verger, *Notes sur le culte des Orisa et Vodun à Bahia, la Baie de tous les Saints, au Brésil et à l'ancienne Côte des Esclaves en Afrique* (Dakar, Senegal: IFAN, 1957), p. 54.

2. This song cycle is documented in the Coda, pp. 347–48.

END OF THE ROAD

1. Richard and Sally Price, *Equatoria* (New York: Routledge, 1992), pp. 39–40. Guyane (officially part of Europe) is today a land of immigrants, with more than half its population foreign born. The average per-capita income is roughly five times that in Brazil, ten times that in Suriname, sixteen times that in Guyana, and thirty-seven times that in Haiti (*L'Express*, no. 2839, 1/7 [December 2005], p. 110).

2. Saramakas and other Maroons usually refer to Tooy by his normal Saramaka name, Asipéimáu. Creoles, Haitians, Brazilians, and others tend to call him Alexandre, the French version of his *bakáa-nê* ("whitefolks' name"), Alexander, which was also the whitefolks' name of his father. His "family name," Tooy, was the Saramaka name of his mother's mother's mother's mother—it's the name on his mailbox and on official documents. His wives call him Alexandre or Alêke.

3. I've also heard Tooy call this powerful Komantí spirit Ofilibaní Makondewa or Bási Oflíbaní Mafuyéwa, adding that this god's father refers to him as Kuyé kwatakí fu hándugbáu.

TOOY POSSESSED

1. Another time he says it as *"hungolamámba"*—and *gídigídji* is sometimes *gídigídi*.

MOTHER AFRICA

1. Joseph C. Miller, *Way of Death: Merchant Capitalism and the Angolan Slave Trade, 1730-1830* (Madison: University of Wisconsin Press, 1988), p. 35.

2. Joseph C. Miller, "Central Africa during the Era of the Slave Trade, c. 1490s–1850s," in Heywood, *Central Africans,* pp. 21–69; citation is on pp. 42–43. Elsewhere, Miller emphasizes that "'Congo' meant one thing in sixteenth-century Lima or São Tomé, something else in Cartagena early in the 1600s, quite another in the late eighteenth century in Rio or Saint Domingue, something else again in New Orleans early in the nineteenth century, and something still different by 1850 or so in Cuba" ("Retention, Reinvention, and Remembering: Restoring Identities through Enslavement and under Slavery in Brazil," in *Enslaving Connections: Changing Cultures of Africa and Brazil during the Era of Slavery,* ed. José C. Curto and Paul E. Lovejoy [Amherst, MA: Humanity Books, 2004], 81–121; citation is on p. 87.)

3. Miller, "Central Africa," p. 56.

4. Ibid., p 62. The timing is right for Tooy's Lángu ancestors to have included refugees (captives) from the Antonian movement and the civil wars that accompanied its demise in the Kongo, but I have not found any specific traces of that religious orientation (see John K. Thornton, *The Kongolese Saint Anthony: Dona Beatriz Kimpa Vita and the Antonian Movement, 1684-1706* [Cambridge: Cambridge University Press, 1998]).

5. Other Komantí "countries" that Tooy has told me about include Agubaa and Boókosáni. "The most dangerous one," Tooy confides, "was Sánfaíni, where the

bones of human beings formed the sand you walked on—that's how much fighting went on there. If you went to a 'play' in one of those places, you had to be sure not to slip, or they'd cut off your head! There was a place there called Nyanibláu, whose people weren't friendly—if you met up with them, they'd kill you. Yet another place was called Ánimbláu, but that was a cemetery. Today, Komantí men call all cemeteries *animbláu*." I wonder whether this latter might not be a transformation of Anomabo, the Fanti homeland where the Dutch built a slave fort in 1630. Animbaw was also the name of the late eighteenth-century village of the Ndyuka *gaama*, where the Ndyukas suffered a humiliating defeat at the hands of the Alukus (see, for example, Wim Hoogbergen, *De Boni-oorlogen, 1757–1860: Marronage en guerilla in Oost-Suriname* [Utrecht, The Netherlands: Centrum voor Caraïbische Studies, 1985], pp. 339–48).

6. See Price, *First-Time*, p. 77.

7. Tooy has told me that when Akoomí came into Kódji's head and recounted his praise name, he'd say he was "the man from Sanfómaíni," as if this was an African place-name. Variations of the word appear in several Komantí songs.

NEW WORLD BEGINNINGS

1. Price, *First-Time*, p. 81.

2. Tooy preserves a memory fragment of his people's brief stay at Puupangi, three hundred years ago. He once told me, using impenetrably esoteric "country" language, "When we were at Puupangi, we lived *banáki so banáli móyon, avílijítjí bom tjélélé badjégba wínso avíuto kóoto kóbwe*. It wasn't so bad. A single earthenware plate, a single earthenware pot, a single earthenware spoon. You'd go eat and then the next person would take his turn. That's what this says."

3. Captain Diífóu ("Disiforo"), speaking to government official Junker ca. 1918; quoted in L. Junker, "Eenige mededeelingen over de Saramakkaner-Boschnegers," *De West-Indische Gids* 4 (1922/23): 449–80; citation is on pp. 461–62.

4. Tooy has told me that the name for "Venus," "the star that brings the day," is played on the *apínti* drum as *Adjá kankantí ágboní*.

5. See Price, *First-Time*, pp. 81–82 passim.

GWEYÚNGA, THE RAIN PRIEST

1. Melville J. and Frances S. Herskovits, *Rebel Destiny: Among the Bush Negroes of Dutch Guiana* (New York: McGraw-Hill, 1934), p. 353.

2. The stories are reported in Price, *First-Time*, pp. 122–24.

3. A Dutch soldier's journal entry recording the incident reports laconically, "Although we saw the tracks of the runaways and heard the drums they use in their celebrations, the heavy rains did not permit us to advance to discover whence they came" (Archieven van de Sociëteit van Suriname, Algemeen Rijksarchief, Eerst Afdeling, The Hague, 199, February 2, 1743).

4. Price, *First-Time*, pp. 66–68.

5. In former times, such Tonê children were simply laid to rest at birth in the riverbank, for the waters to take away (see also Chris de Beet and Miriam Sterman, *People in Between: The Matawai Maroons of Suriname* [Meppel, The Netherlands: Krips Repro, 1981], pp. 248, 497. NB: Until their fission in 1767, the Matawais and Saramakas formed a single people). Similarly, among Gweyúnga's descendants in the village of Malobí, Tonê priests were not buried in the cemetery but in a coffin that was released into the river, where the Tonê spirits would take the person out of the coffin and carry him to their country. This was done until Tooy's own lifetime, though such priests are now buried in the cemetery.

6. I have a recording of Tooy singing a version of this Tonê song/prayer: *Mi yanvalú nawé-o / So de adáni Sokoto / Tonê Gansa nivólo andáni Sokoto / Anáde miomío / Tonê nivôl, anadé de moyôto.*

7. In another version, Tooy told me that if you managed to climb to the top of the tree, you could eat there "until your belly was full."

8. In another folktale, Anasi calls Tonê from the river with a song (see Richard and Sally Price, *Two Evenings in Saramaka* [Chicago, University of Chicago Press, 1991], p. 98).

9. "Gbeyò[n]gbo," in Melville J. and Frances S. Herskovits, *An Outline of Dahomean Religious Belief* (Menasha, WI: Memoirs of the American Anthropological Association 41, 1933), pp. 19–20; "Gbeyongo," in Melville J. Herskovits, *Dahomey: An Ancient African Kingdom* (New York: J. J. Augustin, 1938), 2:152ff.). Note that in Saramaccan, \gb\ and \gw\ are allophones, in free variation, so *Gbeyongo* and *Gweyongo* would be identical.

10. M. and F. Herskovits, *Outline*, pp. 29–30.

11. Might *Tòxòsu* be the etymon of *Tósuósu*, the great Wénti village that lies under the Oyapock across from Tampáki, where a hand reaches up to take offerings of bottled beer? (In standard Saramaccan, *Tósuósu* would translate as "House of Tósu," but neither Tooy nor other Saramakas know what or who Tósu might be.)

12. M. and F. Herskovits, *Outline*, p. 30; and *Rebel Destiny*, p. 353. It may be worth noting that, according to Wyatt MacGaffey, a similar relationship between abnormal births (twins, albinos, the handicapped) and water spirits exists in Central Africa, where "all abnormal bodies . . . should be buried not in the clan cemetery but at a crossroads or in water" ("Twins, Simbi Spirits, and Lwas in Kongo and Haiti," in Heywood, *Central Africans*, pp. 211–26; citation is on p. 214.)

13. On Ndyuka *Tone*, see W. F. van Lier, "Aanteekeningen over het geestelijk leven en de samenleving der Djoeka's (Aukaner Boschnegers) in Suriname," *Bijdragen tot de Taal-, Land- en Volkenkunde van Nederlandschindië* 99, no. 2 (1940): 131–294; see in particular pp. 188–89.

ANTAMÁ AT WAR

1. Djógilési speaking on tape to future *gaamá* Otjútju, 1977 or 1978; cited in Price, *First-Time*, p. 83. Tooy once told me that, once Kaási had escaped with his people,

he summoned his older brother Bákisi, who had remained in Africa, with a wooden trumpet, to come join them in the forest.

2. Frank Dragenstein documents this battle at Victoria in January 1753—one colonial eyewitness claimed that the Saramakas lost thirty men, though not a single body was found by the whites (Frank Dragenstein, *"De Ondraaglijke Stoutheid der Wegloopers": Marronage en koloniaal belied in Suriname, 1667-1768* [Utrecht, The Netherlands: Bronnen voor de Studie van Suriname 22, 2002], p. 150).

3. See Price, *First-Time*, pp. 107, 117–19. In that book, I suggested that Makambí's death took place somewhat earlier, though I had no solid temporal anchors.

4. Johannes King, cited in Richard Price, *Alabi's World* (Baltimore: Johns Hopkins University Press, 1990), pp. 324–25.

5. T. J. Desch-Obi, "Combat and the Crossing of the *Kalunga*," in Heywood, *Central Africans*, pp. 353–70; citation is on p. 359.

THE SOLDIER'S TALE

1. I've heard rival versions of Kuset's departure from Saramaka and arrival in Guyane, all from people who had heard it from someone else: that Kuset's mother effectively banished him from Saramaka after he'd gotten a close relative pregnant; that when he arrived on French soil the gendarmes said, "We need two more" (because they already had 250 Guyanese volunteers), so Kuset and another Saramaka, neither of whom knew a word of French, stepped up; and so forth. These versions, from members of other (rival) Saramaka clans, seem designed to denigrate Kuset's heroism and depict him as the unwitting victim of circumstance.

2. I acknowledge here the generous assistance of Françoise Lemaire, directrice des archives départementales de la Guyane; Dominique Taffin, directrice des archives départementales de la Martinique; le lieutenant-colonel Christian Bru, directeur du bureau central d'archives administratives militaires (Pau); and le colonel J-J Senant, chef du service historique de l'armée de terre (Vincennes).

3. A one-page document ("Certificat de Position Militaire," dated February 4, 1946), in the Archives départementales de la Guyane, uses the exact same language, except that it lists the date of Kuset's enlistment as September 8, 1939.

4. "Rapport du Lieut. de réserve Larrive, Georges, de la 5e Cie du 23 RIC," n.d. [fall] 1940, Archives du Service Historique de l'Armée de Terre, Vincennes.

5. Discussion of the role of the Twenty-Third RIC during the Battle of the Meuse, in *Les grandes unités Françaises: Historiques Succincts* (Paris: Ministère des Armées, Service Historique, 1967). See, for an account of the "violent bombardments in an extremely exposed position" suffered by the regiment during two days in mid-May, "Rapport du Capitain Souriac, 10e compagnie, 23 RIC, daté 23 septembre 1940" (Archives du Service Historique de l'Armée de Terre, Vincennes).

6. "Rapport du Lieut. de réserve Larrive, Georges."

7. In the archives at Vincennes, I saw a report by a certain Lieutenant Jacques Bous-

sard of the Sixth [Kuset's] Company, stating that he (and apparently some others) had not been captured by the Germans until June 13.

8. Julian Jackson, *The Fall of France: The Nazi Invasion of 1940* (Oxford: Oxford University Press, 2003), p. 179.

9. Ibid., pp. 178–79.

10. Tony Judt, "The Way We Live Now," *New York Review of Books*, March 27, 2003, pp. 6–10; citation is on p. 9. These figures are on the high end of historians' current estimates.

11. Jackson, *The Fall*, p. 180.

12. Some of my information about Nazi policies toward black troops comes from a ninety-minute TV special directed by Marie-Jo Alie, aired on RFO in Martinique, January 27, 2005, to commemorate the liberation of Auschwitz.

13. Robert W. Kestling, "Forgotten Victims: Blacks in the Holocaust," *Journal of Negro History* 77, no. 1 (1992): 30–36; citation is on pp. 31–32; Serge Bilé, *Noirs dans les camps nazis* (Monaco: Editions du Rocher, 2005), p. 46. See also Robert W. Kestling, "Blacks under the Swastika: A Research Note," *Journal of Negro History* 83, no. 1 (1998): 84–99.

14. Bilé, *Noirs*, p. 48.

15. Testimony of Edouard Ouédraogo, originally from Haute-Volta (Burkina Faso); cited in Charles Onana, *La France et ses tirailleurs: Enquête sur les combattants de la République 1939-2003* (Paris: Duboiris, 2003), pp. 130–35.

16. Richard Price, *The Convict and the Colonel* (Boston: Beacon Press, 1998), p. 98.

17. Bilé, *Noirs*, p. 51; Kestling, "Forgotten Victims," p. 32.

18. A *mutête* is an openwork Saramaka backpack for carrying game, woven from a liana (*Heteropsis jenmanii Oliv.*) using techniques learned from Amazonian Indians (though its name derives from Kikongo). Kuset's son, Nokó, told me that the iron cage was secured by a large padlock in front.

19. Though some of the details of this part of Kuset's story may be shaky, the idea of escaping from Stalag IV-B all the way to England is not absurd. Eddie James, an English prisoner, escaped from this stalag three times and the last time made it all the way to England, according to his daughter (see http://www.pegasus-one.org/pow/pSt_4B.htm). And while Stalag IV-B was bereft of four-story buildings, other stalags, for example Stalag VI-A, had them, and quite imposing they were (see the photo at http://www.hemer.de/STALAG_IVa/sta114.htm). I have not found information on the height of the buildings in Stalag IV-D, where Kuset was also incarcerated.

20. Lieutenant-Colonel Bru, director of the central bureau of administrative military archives, apologized to me in a letter for the incompleteness of Kuset's service records, noting that many of the relevant archives "were burned in a fire on 6 May 1944."

21. Although Kuset may never have seen a streetcar or the inside of a schoolhouse, Walter Benjamin's remarks seem apt: "Was it not noticeable at the end of the war that men returned from the battlefield grown silent—not richer, but poorer in communicable experience? . . . A generation that had gone to school on a horse-drawn

streetcar now stood under the open sky in a countryside in which nothing remained unchanged but the clouds, and beneath these clouds, in a field of force of destructive torrents and explosions, was the tiny, fragile human body" (Walter Benjamin, "The Storyteller," in *Illuminations*, ed. Hannah Arendt [New York: Schocken, 1969], p. 84).

SIDEBAR, THE SOLDIER'S TALE

1. Jackson, *The Fall*, p. 165.

2. Jackson, *The Fall*, p. 169. Paul-Andre Lesort, *Quelques jours de mai-juin 40: Mémoire, témoignage, histoire* (Paris: Seuil, 1992), pp. 159-60.

3. Jackson, *The Fall*, p. 171. Gustave Folcher, *Les carnets de guerre de Gustave Folcher, paysan languedocien, 1939-1945* (Paris: La Découverte/Poche, 2000), pp. 68-69.

4. Howard W. "Mutt" McCord, from Sheffield, Alabama. http://scmilitary. homestead.com/files/Camp_Croft/people/mccord.html

5. Stanley J. Lambert, from Ewing, Nebraska. http://www.trailblazersww2.org/ stalag_ivb.htm

THUNDER AXES

1. MJH diary, July 21, 1928 (Schomburg Center for Research in Black Culture, New York Public Library, Melville J. and Frances S. Herskovits Papers). He would have been thinking, one imagines, of the Yoruba's well-known Shango, god of thunder and thunderstones. Had Herskovits read the available literature on Suriname, he'd already have been familiar with these thunderstones and local beliefs about them—see, for example, H. D. Benjamins and Joh. F. Snelleman, eds., *Encyclopaedie van Nederlandsch West-Indië* (The Hague, Netherlands: Martinus Nijhoff, 1914-17), s.v. "Dondersteenen," "Amuletten," and "Oudheden I."

2. Not, he explains, because the wood of this tree—which in normal Saramaccan is called *wándji*—is particularly hard. A thunder axe simply can't cut it.

3. More generally, Tooy distinguishes between saltwater and freshwater Busikís. For him, there are Wéntis from the sea who divide into female (Wénti) and male (Busikí). These latter are also Komantí, but a special kind of Komantí. For example, such Busikí-*óbias* don't wash in leaves, as other Komantís do, for a full week but rather for three days only (so the leaves don't ferment and get dark-colored or bad-smelling), because all Wéntis like bright, white, clean things; these Busikí walk in shrimps and resemble naval officers. Then there are river Wéntis, who divide into female (Wénti), who live near to but are not identical to Wátawenús (anaconda gods), and male (Busikí), who are also Komantí, and walk in stingrays. These are not to be confused with Tonés, who live in rivers, but not too deep, and whose sacred leaves are found in the forest rather than the river, and who can also walk in stingrays. Nor with Búmbas, small caimans, who are the gods of landing places. Nor with Yáus, who are the little brothers of (river) Busikís (and like them a kind of Komantí), and who live only in the deeps of rivers.

MASTER OF THE HOUSE

1. I have corrected some of the esoteric-language (song) transcriptions according to later conversations. I give glosses of the esoteric words in square brackets whenever I know their meaning.

2. Tooy later explained to me that this is the way the drummer on the *agidá*—the great drum for the snake gods—challenges the gods during a "play," saying to them: You act like you're real men, but it's one big lie. I'll take you one by one and show you who's boss! The drum says, "If I go in the river, I'll take you. If I go in the forest, I'll take you." The Vodú gods really go crazy when they hear you play that!

3. Schomburg Center for Research in Black Culture, New York Public Library, Melville J. and Frances S. Herskovits Papers, Box 27, Folder 175. Herskovits should have written "wátawenú"—meaning an anaconda god—not "wata wentu," which is meaningless. "Sweet Sopi" is in Saramaccan "súti sópi" (sugarcane syrup), used for libations to Wéntis. And these gods, as Herskovits noted, characteristically bring children to (often-infertile) women.

4. See Richard and Sally Price, "Widerstand, Rebellion und Freiheit: Maroon Societies in Amerika und ihre Kunst," in *Afrika in Amerika*, ed. Corinna Raddatz (Hamburg: Hamburgisches Museum für Völkerkunde, 1992), pp. 157–73, which describes and illustrates pieces from this important collection, including some for which only a photograph remains.

5. Aniké Awági once told me that in fact there are *three* kinds of Wéntis: those who live in rapids, who are called Kedjè-fu-ontó, those who live in the floodplain, who are called Yakedáu, and those in the sea, like Wánanzái from Loizá. Such distinctions are common elsewhere in the black Atlantic: the Brazilian sea goddess and goddess of motherhood, Iemanjá, is in Yorubaland a river goddess called Yemoja (J. Lorand Matory, *Black Atlantic Religion: Tradition, Transnationalism and Matriarchy in the Afro-Brazilian Candomblé* (Princeton, NJ: Princeton University Press, 2005), pp. 22, 247.

6. Diane Vernon, *Money Magic in a Modernizing Maroon Society*, Caribbean Study Series, no. 2 (Tokyo: Institute for the Study of Languages and Cultures of Africa and Asia, 1985).

7. The figure is 14 inches high, dated 1998, and signed by Mimo.

STORM CLOUDS

1. Cary Fraser, "Guyana's Political Breakdown," *Trinidad and Tobago Review* 23, nos. 5–6 (June–July 2001): 8, 11, 15; citation is on p. 8. Just when I'd almost given up on confirming my forty-year-old memory of Sparrow's lyrics, John Rickford (born and raised in Guyana) came to the rescue, e-mailing Ian Robertson (also a Guyanese linguist) in Trinidad, who says the calypso is called "B. G. War" and provided verses from memory. And just before I received page proofs for this book, my friend Adiante Franszoon managed, miraculously, to find a copy of the original record. Here are Sparrow's opening words: "Well they drop a hydrogen bomb in BG / Lord have mercy. (Repeat

the first two lines) Riot in town mamma / I hear de whole place on fire. / From Kitty to de waterfront all that / Bun down flat, flat, flat. (Chorus:) I en care if all a BG bun down. / I en care if de whole a Bookers bun down. / But they'd be putting me out me way / If they tackle Tiger Bay / An bun dung me hotel whey all dem wabeen [easy women] does stay." Rickford and Robertson both report that they know the *óbia* Tooy referred to, but where they come from it's called "fire-bun" ("fire-burn") rather than "firebomb."

SEX, MAGIC, AND MURDER

1. See Price, *First-Time*, pp. 153–59.

2. Mètisên's account is recorded in Price, *Alabi's World*, pp. 245–47. Tooy tells me that Mètisên erred in one detail—whenever he has heard this version of Gweyúnga's death, the dish Hwéte prepared for him was *pindá batáta* (peanuts and sweet potato), not *pindá bakúba* (peanuts and plantains).

3. Afaata (and her matrilineal offspring, like Tooy) were in effect adopted into the Langu clan. As one of "Alabi's wife's people," a group of several women who were abducted from a plantation and harbored by the Awaná clan, Afaata did not have a relevant clan association of her own (see Price, *Alabi's World*, pp. 139, 315–16). Such clan adoptions were common during the formative period of the society in the eighteenth century, as isolated newcomers or small new groups joined larger established Saramaka clans (see, for example, ibid., p. 357).

4. Tooy's several accounts of Kwasímukámba teaching Antamá to fly are inconsistent as to exactly when and where it happened. This does not bother him and needn't bother us. The fragments are, after all, what Flibánti told him, on different occasions and for different purposes.

FRICTION

1. Anna Lowenhaupt Tsing, *Friction: An Ethnography of Global Connection* (Princeton, NJ: Princeton University Press, 2004), p. xi.

2. Michael Taussig, *Shamanism, Colonialism, and the Wild Man: A Study in Terror and Healing* (Chicago: University of Chicago Press, 1987), p. 218.

3. From this perspective, Saramaka Wéntis might be seen as a sort of anti- or inverse *bakúlu*, a kind of god who brings you wealth and children but asks nothing in return except prayer and bubbly, sugary offerings—a pure-white, anti-evil tutelary spirit.

4. Leti, *L'Univers magico-religieux antillais*; Ary Ebroïn, *Quimbois: Magie noire et sorcellerie aux Antilles* (Paris: Jacques Grancher, 1977), p. 72.

SÁNGONO MI TÓALA!

1. Tooy's version of Wíi's song and the story of how he brought the Peace may be compared to those reported in Price, *First-Time*, pp. 167–71.

2. Tooy explained to me that Wíi had the banana *óbia*. You eat the bananas but leave the peels on the stem. The next day, they're full with new bananas again.

3. Relating a famous greeting that would have occurred a half century before Wíi's, Captain Kala described in 1975 how one man said, "*Awesáánu*," and the other replied "*Awesáánu*," to which the first said, "*Gbégbéde wédjamè*," and the second replied, "*Akwandíkbóu*" (Price, *First-Time*, p. 58). And Tebíni once told me about an experience he had while in Lagos, Nigeria (on his first visit to Africa as part of a 1977 Suriname delegation to FESTAC—the Second World Black and African Festival of Arts and Culture). Tebíni had long been proud of preserving the memory of two of the "original African" styles of greeting brought by his ancestors (which are no longer used or analyzable in Saramaccån): "*Bótè*," to which one answers "*Sikenai bótè*," and "*Lélembu*," to which one answers "*Lélembu Kizambíi*." "With these words," he liked to say, "we came here." And he told me, "I tried them out on an old African [in Nigeria]. But he just stood there. I said them again. He just stared. I said to him [scolding, in Saramaccan], 'You've learned English, so you no longer know our own language!'" (ibid., p. 26).

4. Tooy's taking responsibility (by saying that his Lángu ancestor Bákisipámbo was the perpetrator) for the shooting at Gaándan Falls, one of the most contested and guarded and secret of all First-Time events, bears comparison with the versions in ibid., pp. 140–43; see also Richard Price, *To Slay the Hydra: Dutch Colonial Perspectives on the Saramaka Wars* (Ann Arbor, MI: Karoma, 1983), pp. 21–26, 43–84.

5. Archieven van de Sociëteit van Suriname, Algemeen Rijksarchief, Eerst Afdeling, The Hague, 154, May 4, 1762 (March 8, 1762).

6. Archieven van de Sociëteit van Suriname 154, February 16, 1762 (February 5, 1762).

7. Neither does the Matjáu clan, which revels in disputing with the Lángus "who brought the Peace," differ on the order of the events themselves. It's rather their interpretation that's in dispute, with the Matjáus stressing that if it were not for their having rightfully chased Wíi from Saramaka, he would never have "happened upon" the Peace. One Matjáu told me with considerable passion: "Wíi didn't go to Ndyuka because he wanted to! He went there because he had gotten in trouble [with the Matjáus]." Any credit or positive motivation is relentlessly denied him by Matjáus, whose counterclaims and deprecations are sometimes backed up with further elaborations upon the story itself. Otjútju, who would become Saramaka *gaamá* in 2005, once explained: "When Dabí prepared the musket ball ritually, he told his sister [Wíi's wife] what he had done. He said he was going to shoot Wíi. But she [surreptitiously] removed the ball from the gun, leaving only the [other] *óbia* ingredients with which he had loaded it. Dabí did not know the ball had been removed, and when he shot at Wíi, that is why only his finger fell off. Otherwise it would have killed him [for his witchcraft]."

8. Wíi was murdered by Ndyukas in their territory in 1763, nearly provoking a Saramaka-Ndyuka war. For details, see Price, *First-Time*, p. 174; *Alabi's World*, p. 45; and *To Slay the Hydra*, pp. 179–91.

THE NAMESAKE

1. Pobôsi drew on all his knowledge to keep the white man both happy and in the dark. Besides steering him clear of the remnants of battles against the whites,

and former villages and cemeteries with all their memories, he guided the expedition past countless sacred spots. Tooy has told me, for example, about a particularly dangerous deep at a place called Sotígbo, five days by paddle up the Gaánlío from the last village. The story is maintained in the esoteric language of Papá, sung at funerals. "At the mouth of the Pikílío, three Matjáu-clan men [he names them] saw five Indian women and one man. They killed the man. The women were Mokolimô, Sêgbenu, and Agwé, and they were with two of their daughters, Agúngun and Ayôô." Those are the names, he tells me, that you must invoke whenever there is a really large ceremony for the ancestors. After describing where they had their gardens and other details, he says they were so "wild" that Saramakas weren't sure they should keep them as wives. "Asidamá, a Saramaka man, was shooting fish with his bow at the front of the canoe while Ma Sêgbenu steered at the rear when the Evil Thing of the Riverbottom at Sotígbo, the Old Man called Sêgwenúawé, came up from the deep and pulled her under. Asidamá pulled off his clothes and dove after her to see what had pulled her under, and the creature sang to him, *I míti Sêgwenu-ee, i míti Sêgwenúawé. Ayò Asidamá i kó ayò, i kéi yò, Sêgwenú-a, yesu Sêgwenúawé, i míti Asidamá sinko ayo* ["You've met up with Sêgwenu. . . . "]. Then a howler monkey which saw all this from a tree next to the river sang out: *I míti dódo, i míti a mán dê . . . yesu adódoo, i míti a mándê-e.* Howler Monkey's song brought the woman right back up to the surface! The husband took her and put her in the canoe, and all was well! This story remains in Félubéni [bent-iron, the nickname for 'Papá']." Gaamá Djankusó trusted Pobôsi to know all such dangers and to make sure the whitefolks gave them a wide berth.

2. J. G. W. J. Eilerts de Haan, "Verslag van de expeditie naar de Suriname-Rivier," *Tijdschrift van het Koninklijk Nederlandisch Aardrijkskundig Genootschap* 27 (1910): 403-68, 641-701. The report calls Pobôsi "Bosk"—in Saramaccan, the name is pronounced "po-BAW-si."

3. Ibid., p. 663.

4. Several versions of the story are presented in Price, *First-Time*, pp. 98-99.

5. Tooy says Sáka-Amáfu was one of five *óbias* summoned that day by the horn of A-nyán, the *gaán-óbia* of Bundjitapá, including Abátaába of Béndiwáta, Abaitú, and two others he doesn't name. One of these did a terrible thing. He had a wife (a living woman) who would continue to cook for him when she had her period. People warned her over and over, but she continued. One day the woman took her dishes to wash at the creek just below Béndiwáta. The *óbia* (in a man's head) was sitting there, sharpening his machete. She greeted him, and he cut her into tiny little pieces! The *óbia* disappeared and never came back. (I'm sure there's much more to this story, which Tooy casually mentioned one day; I never followed up.)

6. I derive Pobôsi's death date by triangulation between his last mention in archival documents (1930) and the transfer of one of his gods, Sáka-Amáfu, to its next medium, which other documents report in early 1932.

7. Th. Müller, "Uit het Jaarverslag van 1921 over Suriname," *Berichten uit de Heiden-Wereld* no. 4 (July-August 1922): 71.

8. M. Schelts, "De reis naar Pobosi en de Sentea Kreek." Zeister Zendingsgenoot-schap 319, Rijksarchief Utrecht, 1922.

9. Father Morssink's account is contained in his unpublished book-length manu-script, "Boschnegeriana (misschien beter: Silvae-nigritiana?): Enige gegevens om-trent geschiedenis en missioneeringe onzer Surinaamsche Boschnegers" [Bosch-negeriana (Perhaps Better: Silvae-nigritiana?): Some Materials about History and Missionizing among Our Suriname Bush Negroes"], a copy of which was in the bish-opric in Paramaribo in the 1960s.

10. Male Wéntis are Busikí, which is a kind of water Komantí, so Morssink was not wrong, just incomplete, in his characterization.

11. MJH diary, July 24, 1928 (Schomburg Center for Research in Black Culture, New York Public Library, Melville J. and Frances S. Herskovits Papers). Comparing Morssink's "Boschnegeriana" to the Herskovitses' contemporaneous writings, it seems clear that Morssink (who spent considerably more time "in the field") under-stood many aspects of Saramaka politics and history better than the anthropologists. Indeed, his ventures into Maroon clan and village history constitute the best work in these domains before the coming of anthropologists André Köbben, Bonno and In-eke Thoden van Velzen, and ourselves in the 1960s. Nonetheless, Morssink's colonial (and personal) assumptions that Saramakas behaved like children and could be easily manipulated—he frequently pretends to be angry to get his way; for example, in 1928 he gave his Saramaka hosts in Ligólio "the silent treatment" for several days—or his practice (shared with other Catholic missionaries of the day) of referring to the Lángu villagers as "my little black ones" or "my darkies" (mijn zwartjes) must be taken fully into account in trying to understand the materials he gathered.

12. Morssink adds details about this trip and the photos in a letter dated December 26, 1928, published in Petrus Donders 9, no. 4 (March 1929): 88.

13. In 1967, I interviewed Msgr. St. Kuypers, C.SS.R., bishop of Paramaribo, who said that Morssink once told him how, before the official ceremony, Pobôsi had taken his wives aside to tell them that he would marry only the oldest in front of the white man, but that he promised to take care of them all.

14. M. and F. Herskovits, Rebel Destiny, pp. 188, 263.

15. On Sáka-Amáfu in Ndyuka, beginning with Wensi's first possession in 1932, see H. U. E. Thoden van Velzen and W. van Wetering, In the Shadow of the Oracle: Religion as Politics in a Suriname Maroon Society (Long Grove, IL: Waveland, 2004), pp. 177-88, 193-94.

FRENCHWOMAN'S REVENGE

1. I also learned from reading shortly thereafter that the Ndyukas have a cult with similar goals and rites that is called Mayombe (A. J. F. Köbben, "Unity and Dis-unity: Cottica Djuka Society as a Kinship System," Bijdragen tot de Taal-, Land- en Volkenkunde 123 [1967]: 10–52, in particular p. 17.) See also Richard Price, "KiKoongo

and Saramaccan: A Reappraisal," *Bijdragen tot de Taal-, Land- en Volkenkunde* 131 (1975): 461–78, in particular p. 473.

2. Much later, Tooy told me that Malúndu and Mavúngu have a younger brother called Bayúngu, who guards the Béndiwáta Mother—the most important carry-oracle in Saramaka—from danger. While Mavúngu is pure "forest," and Malúndu works with both "forest" and "water" (being associated with the great Wátawenú Mênde), Bayúngu is a stone god and works with the *óbia* called Anía. "When they play Bayúngu at Béndiwáta, if you need to urinate, you must ask permission, and they'll send men to accompany you—or else you'd be facing the forest, peeing, and the Anía jaguar (called Adjaíni) would appear right in front of you!" Bayúngu told the priests at Béndiwáta that as long as he stood watch, the legacy of Kaásipúmbu, the Béndiwáta Mamá, was safe.

3. This paragraph summarizes information from Moesoela Amiemba, "De aan-komst van de Baikutubuka bêê bij de Nasi-lô" (typescript, 2003), which compiles in-formation from various Nasí elders.

4. See Price, *First-Time*, pp. 162–65.

5. Government official L. Junker provides another confirming testimony. In 1920, he was present at a celebration in honor of Mavúngu, and he asked the Dómbis whether the god had come with their ancestors from Africa. "They denied this and told me that their ancestors had found this god . . . in the forest on the Upper River" (Junker, "Eenige mededeelingen," p. 461).

6. Rachel E. Harding, *A Refuge in Thunder: Candomblé and Alternative Spaces of Blackness* (Bloomington: Indiana University Press, 2000).

7. Tooy specifies that the version of Mavúngu that Sansimé used to settle the Frenchwoman's god was Malóko, an *óbia* that his mother's brother Anatól and San-simé had made together after finding it in the forest. Malóko, which has its shrine in Tooy's natal village of Bundjitapá, has its own drums and songs. "That god," Tooy says of Malóko, "doesn't get along with Flibánti or any other strong men. It prefers women. It doesn't want rivals."

TAMPÁKI

1. Tampáki, and its sister sites of Saramaka settlement in Guyane, also allowed Saramaka to be (re)constructed from afar via this new diaspora—the nation in dia-logue with its diaspora through time. Wéntis, Dúnguláli, Mamá-Gádu, and *palepú* fruits are all icons of this shifting identity. As are the new names returning men brought home to give their children born in Saramaka: Kenkiná (Quinquina—a French apéritif wine), Kataýé (Justin Cataýé was a Guyanais politician who died in a plane crash), Labié (Creole for "beer"), and of course Tampáki itself.

2. Jonas Marçal de Queiroz, "História, Mito e Memória: O Cunani e Outras Re-públicas," in *Nas Terras do Cabo Norte: Fronteiras, colonização e escravidão na Guiana Brasileira nos séculos XVIII/XIX*, ed. Flávio dos Santos Gomes (Belém, Brazil: Editora

Universitária/UFPA, 1999), pp. 319–47; citation is on p. 323. Coudreau, who gained some fame as an explorer of the interior of Guyane (and Amapá), is characterized by the modern French geographer Jean Hurault as having "not only a complete lack of objectivity but a psychotic paranoia . . . a wild and confused mind, obsessed by fixed ideas, observing little and badly" (Hurault, *Français et Indiens en Guyane, 1604-1972* [Paris: Union Générale d'Editions, 1972], p. 191).

3. Marçal de Queiroz, "Historia," pp. 319, 320.

4. Marie-José Jolivet, *La question créole: Essai de sociologie sur la Guyane française* (Paris: ORSTOM, 1982), p. 121. See also Serge Mam-Lam-Fouck, *Histoire de la société guyanaise; Les années cruciales: 1848-1946* (Paris: Editions Caribéennes, 1987), pp. 110–11.

5. Emilio A. Goeldi, "Exposição sumária da viagem realisada ao Territorio contestado" (1895), cited in Flávio dos Santos Gomes, Jonas Marçal de Queiroz, and Mauro Cézar Coelho (eds.), *Relatos de Fronteiras: Fontes para a História Amazônia séculos XVIII e XIX* (Belém, Brazil: Editora Universitária/UFPA, 1999), pp. 99–105; citation is on pp. 104–5.

6. Michel Lohier, *Les grands étapes de l'histoire de la Guyane française: Aperçu chronologique, 1498-1968* (Clamecy, France: Imprimerie Laballery, 1969), p. 117.

7. "Note pour M. Souvent, Chef de cabinet de Mr le gouverneur du territoire de l'Inini" (Cayenne, 6 mars 1934), Archives départementales de Guyane (Dossier Saramacca).

8. Aniké would have been my last direct link between Saramakas still alive and the Carsewene gold fields of the 1890s. In 2001, he told me that his mother's mother's brother, Amónika Gayó, the man who brought him up as a child, had been on the Carsewene with many other Saramakas before they came back to "open up" the Oyapock. To my regret, I did not press him for details.

9. Saramakas are proud that the official map of Guyane holds a memory trace of Tuálo, designating a group of islands on the upper Oyapock "Ilets Toïlopiké."

10. For a discussion of these events, see de Beet and Sterman, *People in Between,* pp. 177–233, and H. U. E. Thoden van Velzen and W. van Wetering, *The Great Father and the Danger: Religious Cults, Material Forces, and Collective Fantasies in the World of the Suriname Maroons* (Dordrecht, The Netherlands: Foris, 1988), and *In the Shadow of the Oracle.* Fear of witches has, since the beginning, been a feature of both Ndyuka and Saramaka life. In the eighteenth century, Saramakas periodically identified witches using various forms of divination and, after forced confessions, executed them by burning (see, for numerous examples, Price, *Alabi's World*), but these practices ceased at some point during the nineteenth. Numerous Ndyuka witch burnings are documented for the nineteenth century but seem to have ended before the turn of the twentieth (see Thoden van Velzen and van Wetering, *The Great Father*). Today, Ndyukas continue to try to identify witches—as this book goes to press, there is a new witch-hunting movement active on the Tapanahoni—and the occasional lynching (hanging) of witches has continued into the present decade. Saramakas, meanwhile, have long since decided to live with the witches presumed to be in their midst and

not risk trying to identify them before or after death, in part out of fear that a false accusation could lead to the creation of a fierce avenging spirit. For Saramakas such as Tooy, fear of witchcraft remains an everyday reality.

11. An archival document ("Note pour M. Souvent, 1934") dates Kódji's arrival in Tampáki to 1901, when there were still fewer than twenty Saramakas living there (Archives départementales de Guyane [Dossier Saramacca]).

12. With the help of his gods, Kódji continued to discover other gods and *óbias* including Anúnu, a carry-oracle he used in Tampáki for curing and which Tooy says he knows and almost made for his house in Cayenne. Kódji had learned it from Akoomí (or his tutelary Komantí spirit Afeemaónsu). Its particularity is that only small boys may carry it for divination, and Tooy ultimately decided it would be more trouble than it was worth.

13. Jean-Claude Michelot, *La guillotine sèche: Histoire du bagne de Cayenne* (Paris: Fayard, 1981), pp. 192–93.

14. For various cannibalism stories regarding escapees from the *bagne*, see ibid., pp. 154-59.

15. For stories of encounters between Saramakas and escaped prisoners, see ibid., pp. 153–59, 193; Michel Pierre, *La terre de la grande punition: Histoire des bagnes de Guyane* (Paris: Ramsay, 1982), pp. 223, 235; Price, *The Convict and the Colonel*, p. 107. There is much to ponder in the ways that Saramakas—France's primitives—engaged with *bagnards*—France's criminals—at the margins of empire.

16. A list made in 1926 shows that 28% of these prisoners—several hundred men— had succeeded in escaping (Alexandre Samis, *Clevelândia: Anarquismo, sindicalismo e repressão política no Brasil* [São Paulo: Imaginário, 2002], pp. 175–76).

17. Tooy adds that Komantís call Lógofóu "Anakaní" and used to sing to him, saying, *Anakaní-o, Balá Anakaní, di wán kódó biyóngo, biyóngo-e wómi agófuagó. Balá Anakaní, Balá Anakaní-e, di wán biyóngo, biyóngo-e agófuagó*. After the incident with the Brazilians, he made a canoe he named Peevú ("to dare") that he paddled all the way from Tampáki, by sea, to his home village in Lángu. During the Saramakas' ordeal in the Brazilian forest, it is said that Pobôsi, back home in Suriname, was unable to eat for twenty-four days.

18. The mayor's mother, married to a Creole, speaks Saramaccan. Her father was a Saramaka immigrant; her mother (who also speaks Saramaccan) is herself the daughter of a Saramaka immigrant. This pattern of Saramaka men marrying the daughters of a Saramaka man and a Creole (often half-Saramaka) woman was common throughout the twentieth century in Saint-Georges and Tampáki. Think of Yayunn, Kalusé's ex-wife.

19. Héikúun obtained rights to Dúnguláli when Adêso of Héikúun, who considered Kódji like a father and used to leave his wife to take care of the old man when he went off to work, found out that the two had slept together. Kódji offered to give him a piece of the *óbia* in compensation. It was Adêso's descendants who came and took the pot from Tampáki.

PALIMPSESTS

1. Samvel Pvrchas, *Haklvytvs posthumus; or, Pvrchas his Pilgrimes* (London: Imprinted for H. Fetherston, 1625), p. 1263.

2. Frédéric Bouyer, *La Guyane française: Notes et souvenirs d'un voyage exécuté en 1862–1863* (Paris: Hachette, 1867), pp. 244–47.

3. These incidents are described in Tristan Bellardie, "Les relations entre Français et Bonis en Guyane française, 1836–1893," Mémoire de Maîtrise, Université Toulouse-Le Mirail, 1994, pp. 40–49.

4. Jules Crevaux, "Exploration de l'Oyapock et du Parou (1878–1879)," reprinted in J. Crevaux, *Le mendiant de l'Eldorado* (Paris: Editions Phébus, 1987), pp. 170–348; citation is on p. 186. For more on "the faithful Apatou," see Kenneth Bilby, "The Explorer as Hero: Le Fidèle Apatou in the French Wilderness," *New West Indian Guide* 78 (2004): 197–227.

ANTAMÁ THE ÓBIA-MAN

1. "Whitefolks can write it down as much as they like, but I'm telling you, Antamá didn't stand there at the Treaty-Signing. The man you see in Sensiló's head [Flibánti]—he was with Antamá that day. He told me that Tatá Wíi chased Antamá away from the ceremony, saying, 'Get outta here with all that óbia stuff!'"

2. F. Staehelin, *Die Mission der Brüdergemeine in Suriname und Berbice im achtzehnten Jahrhundert* (Herrnhut, Germany: Vereins für Brüdergeschichte in Kommission der Unitätsbuchhandlung in Gnadau, 1913–19), vol. 3, pt. 1, pp. 144–46.

3. Anon., *Periodical Accounts relating to the Missions of the Church of the United Brethren Established among the Heathen* (London, 1790–1834), vol. 2, p. 97.

4. Staehelin, *Die Mission*, vol. 3, pt. 1, pp. 147–48.

5. Ibid., p. 143.

6. Price, *Alabi's World*, pp. 124ff.

7. Though Flibánti, like other African-ghost-spirits and Komantí-type gods, "works with" iron and weapons, visitors may never bring them near his (or their) shrine—or war will break out. At the time I wrote *Alabi's World*, I was ignorant of the existence of Flibánti and much other relevant Lángu lore.

8. Another time, Tooy tells me that the forest between Regina and Saint-Georges may be the most dangerous place on earth. All kinds of evil walk there! Once he went there with some friends to gather leaves and met up with a giant poisonous snake which bit one of his companions before Tooy was able to kill it and cut it in four pieces with his machete in a dramatic battle—merely shooting it would have killed his friend, who eventually survived.

9. The references in this paragraph come from Archieven van de Sociëteit van Suriname, 331, 28 March 1767 [9 January 1767]; Archieven van het Hof van Politie en Crimineele Justitie, Algemeen Rijksarchief, Eerst Afdeling, The Hague, 79, 17 December 1768; Archieven van het Hof, 87, 4 March 1773; Archieven van het Hof, 87, 26 February 1773 [8 May 1772].

10. Staehelin, *Die Mission*, vol. 3, pt. 3, p. 59.

11. Ibid., pp. 45–46; see also vol. 3, pt. 3, p. 21.

12. This proverb means, "The person who did you harm this time won't be the one who does it next time." Like other *óbia*-men, Tooy cannot say, or hear, the normal word for "toad."

13. "The Bobo [in Mali] have no traditional theatre as we, or the Bambara, know it, so that when I broach the subject of theatrical performance the day before Nazu's story about another world, Chief Séé replies with a proverb: 'If someone asks you to make a rope out of sand, you had better ask to see the old one first.'"—from http://www.comminit.com/papers/p_0037.html

14. Staehelin, *Die Mission*, vol. 3, pt. 1, pp. 147–48; see also Archieven van het Hof, 84, 25 October 1771.

15. Archieven van het Hof van Politie, 90, 5 August 1774.

16. Antamá was Afaata's half brother, and Gadien called him (as well as Afaata's other half brother Gisí) *tío*—"mother's brother," which assimilates him, from Tooy's perspective, into his matriline.

17. Historical memory is strategically selective. Tooy would have 256 direct ancestors (great-great-great-great-great-great-grandparents) in Hwéte and Gweyúnga's generation.

CHRONOLOGY

1. Léon-Gontran Damas, *Retour de Guyane* (Paris: José Corti, 1938), p. 45.

2. Alexander Miles, *Devil's Island: Colony of the Damned* (Berkeley, CA: Ten Speed Press, 1988), p. 2.

3. Albert Londres, *Au bagne* (Paris: Albin Michel, 1923), pp. 89-90, 95-96.

4. Marius Larique, cited in Pierre, *La terre de la grande punition*, p. 110.

5. The archives permit us to date these beginnings to the 1860s—see Mam-Lam-Fouck, *Histoire*, pp. 88–96; Dossier benoeming Akrosoe, Landsarchief, Paramaribo.

6. See Richard Price and Sally Price, *Les Marrons* (Châteauneuf-le-Rouge, France: Vents d'ailleurs, 2003), p. 58.

7. The farthest placers were 350 kilometers upstream, through innumerable rapids, and took some sixty days to reach.

8. The first telephone lines were established in Suriname in 1888, and it's a good bet that Teefón came into Agáduhánsu's head only a few years later.

9. Since the 1880s, Saramakas had enjoyed a special status in Guyane, remaining throughout their stays under the legal authority of the Saramaka Paramount Chief in Suriname. A later colonial governor explained that formal agreements of 1883 and 1892 gave Saramakas the right of entry without official papers, entry without a deposit against repatriation, residence without registration, and exemption from all levies and taxes, all designed to facilitate transport on the rivers. By the first two decades of the twentieth century, there were already so many Saramaka men in Mana that France and The Netherlands held numerous discussions about establishing a Dutch subcon-

sulate in that tiny town. In 1947, shortly before Tooy's arrival, there were still twenty to twenty-five Saramaka canoes working between the town of Mana and the upstream gold fields. (See, for references, R. and S. Price, *Les Marrons*, pp. 56–59, 122.)

10. Tooy has twice told me other, much longer versions of these events, including complex mystical relations, e.g. the spirit of his own father was in the head of one of the women he slept with on this occasion.

11. Sometime in the 1980s, after he'd moved to Cayenne, Tooy's house in Saint-Laurent was torn down, and he was offered a replacement in the new public housing project of La Charbonnière, which is where Yaai now lives when she decides to go off on her own.

12. My field notes from the 1960s make clear that Saramakas in French Guiana were already consulting diviners who used tarot cards by the end of the nineteenth century. A man who often did so at Mana in the 1920s told me: "You'd tell him that things weren't going well. He'd ask if you had a wife. You'd lie. 'Is your mother alive?' Lie again. 'Is your father alive?' Again you'd lie. He'd lay out his cards, speak in tongues, and then say, 'I'm not someone to fool around with like that. Everything you told me was a lie!'—at which point you could start working with him with confidence."

13. In the world of the gods, this kind of "mixed" marriage or parentage is not unique. One of the most famous early Wéntis in Tampáki, Zaime, had an Apúku father. As Tooy tells it, "Níango, the king of the Apúkus, once came upon Zaime's mother, a Wénti. He said, 'Ho! This is one beautiful woman! I love you, baby!' She just walked off. But she became pregnant! Just from his words! When the girl was born, she had a name stamped on her back—'Zaime of Níango.' Gaamá Níango, the king of the Apúkus!"

14. Matory, *Black Atlantic Religion*. See "Reflections from the Verandah" in the present text for further thoughts on this.

15. I haven't felt right about searching through his envelopes of papers—old bills and so forth—to figure it out precisely.

MY FIRST-TIME MUSEUM

1. Jan Jacob Hartsinck, *Beschrijving van Guyana of de Wilde Kust in Zuid-America* (Amsterdam: Gerrit Tielenburg, 1770), p. 763.

2. SvS 132, 14 December 1730; Hartsinck, *Beschrijving*, pp. 764–65.

3. Price, *To Slay the Hydra*, p. 212.

4. *Nouná* alludes to a cautionary tale—at the very center of the Saramaka moral universe—that teaches never to reveal all of what you know (Price, *First-Time*, pp. 13–14).

5. See R. and S. Price, *Two Evenings in Saramaka*, p. 126–38.

6. See Richard Price, "Executing Ethnicity: The Killings in Suriname," *Cultural Anthropology* 10 (1995): 437–71.

7. Adiante Franszoon, "Crisis in the Backlands," *Hemisphere* 1, no. 2 (1989): 36–38; citation is on p. 36.

8. Ibid., pp. 37–38.

9. It is worth noting that anthropological evidence, based on long-term ethnographic fieldwork of the sort that this book represents, proved decisive in both the Atjóni and Moiwana cases before the tribunal in Costa Rica, where I (in the first) and my former student Kenneth Bilby (in the second) served as expert witnesses. During the May 2007 hearings on the Saramaka land-rights case, I again served in that capacity. What I have learned from Tooy and other Saramakas about Saramaka history making, the production of knowledge, and the meaning of the past in the present constituted the core of this testimony, which may have far-reaching consequences for indigenous peoples and Maroons throughout the Americas.

THE TRIAL

1. Inevitably, my friendship with Tooy and my role here as advocate colors the account. And given the circumstances, I have been unable to discuss the case with Tooy's accusers and cannot present their perspectives on the case, as I otherwise would have wished. For a sensitive ethnographic analysis of a rape case which, like this one, poses challenges to easy moral judgments, see Donna M. Goldstein, *Laughter Out of Place: Race, Class, Violence, and Sexuality in a Rio Shantytown* (Berkeley and Los Angeles: University of California Press, 2003), particularly chapters 6 and 7.

2. See Sally Price, *Co-Wives and Calabashes* (Ann Arbor: University of Michigan Press, 1984, 1993).

3. R. and S. Price, *Les Marrons*.

4. I am unable to assess the overall prevalence of rape, but there is a widespread perception, among all classes, that it is very much on the rise. It is my impression, from media accounts and discussions with friends, that two categories of rape cases are especially frequent in contemporary Guyane: abuse by a man of his wife's daughter, which seems as common a plague as it is in Martinique; and interethnic (often statutory) rape. The latter situation often involves, as in the Old South, a woman from a higher ethnic/racial status accusing a man in a lower one. In a neocolony whose legal system and official norms are French but whose political (dominant) class is also black, discourses of purity and racial boundary policing become complex. Cultural markers of difference (the languages and other ethnic markers that define *ingi*, Saramaka, and so forth) take on heightened importance. While in the courthouse one day, I came upon a monolingual Ndyuka couple who explained, when I asked, that their sixteen-year-old son had been accused of raping a fourteen-year-old Haitian with whom he, in fact, had been having consensual relations for months; but when the girl's mother found out, the girl decided to tell her it was rape. Reading the local newspaper, I get the impression that it is common for Creoles to accuse Haitians or Brazilians, and for Haitians to accuse Maroons of rape.

5. Another document in the dossier states that the man received a sentence of seven years. The lawyer for Agnès in this case was the same woman who defended Brigitte in her divorce case and later in her case against Tooy.

6. Lest the reader forget: the official psychiatrist's report states, "The only language spoken by Tooy Alexander is TAKI-TAKI." But as the Coda to this book makes clear, besides his native Saramaccan and the Creole he speaks on a daily basis in Cayenne (plus Ndyuka, which he speaks well), Tooy sings, drums, and prays in more than a dozen other languages. France's language ideology (including its views of those who do not speak its language) and Tooy's could hardly be more at odds.

7. Traditionally Saramakas, like many nonliterate peoples, knew their relative age (sibling orders, who is older or younger than whom) with great accuracy but did not keep track of years as Westerners do. As Sensilo's óbia Flibánti once told me, "I don't know my age in years, but I can tell you I was here before Noah."

8. Michel Foucault's 1975 lecture series, *Les Anormaux*, "begins with a long quotation from a psychiatrist offering expert testimony at a murder trial: a bizarre checklist of personality failings . . . followed by the conclusion that the prisoner was entirely capable of the offenses he was accused of, and fully responsible for them. . . . Its style is so flatfooted that it gives an impression not of solemn majesty but of grotesque comedy: not so much Sigmund Freud as King Ubu. But manifest foolishness has never been a hindrance to ritualistic power; and in the case of forensic psychiatry, according to Foucault, it simply demonstrates the overwhelming potency of the modern compulsion to psychologize crime—to match up every objective offence defined by the law with a subjective character defect defined by medical science" (Jonathan Rée, "No good reason," *TLS* [August 13, 2004], p. 27).

9. It goes almost without saying that Sally's arguments fly in the face of certain fundamental ideas of the French nation (e.g. about gender relations, including polygyny), ideas that came to the fore during the political debates engendered by the Parisian riots of fall 2005 and the immigration law of 2006 championed by minister of the interior (and presidential candidate) Nicolas Sarkozy—see for discussion Sally Price, *Paris Primitive: Jacques Chirac's Museum on the Quai Branly* (Chicago: University of Chicago Press, 2007).

10. The fifth character witness, Kalusé, was unable to get out of his construction job for the day and didn't show up.

11. Two years later, talking about how hard it is to really understand a foreign culture, Tooy reminisced about his testimony. "Those people asked me if what had been said was true, and I replied that I really didn't know. How could I really know what they'd said? And what part of it was true? A piece of timber, when it's cut and put in the river, doesn't sink. But it doesn't have a paddle, so it just floats wherever the current wants to take it, wherever the wind blows it, that's where it goes. I had no way of knowing whether I was saying the right thing or the wrong thing. Whatever they said was what I had to go along with."

12. A Creole woman on the jury who knew Tooy's wife Céline later told her that Tooy's lack of contrition—his refusal to admit guilt—had weighed heavily against him when the jury debated the appropriate sentence.

GROUNDS FOR APPEAL?

1. Rape crystallizes issues of race, class, and gender, of sexuality, violence, and power, as perhaps no other crime. The history of French laws about rape—the role of virginity, age of consent, appropriate compensation (and to whom), spousal rape, and all the rest—would require a volume in itself. And a French Guiana jury's common sense about all of these might well be at some distance from current constructions of enlightened, cosmopolitan ideas. Brigitte's education in schools, the military, and the university may have awakened her to ideas about patriarchy as well as the financial benefits that such an awakening can bring in the modern world. Or, this education may have simply given her the toolkit necessary to deal in a modern, French way with the unequal gender relations she had experienced. Without being able to speak with her and her family, I cannot know.

2. Véronique Brocard, "En Guyane, Rocard veut mettre de l'ordre aux frontières," *Libération*, April 9, 1990.

3. Xavier Ternisien, "L'outre-mer s'alarme de l'afflux d'immigrés clandestins," *Le Monde*, November 21, 2006.

4. Kenneth M. Bilby, "The Remaking of the Aluku: Culture, Politics, and Maroon Ethnicity in French South America" (Ph.D. diss., Johns Hopkins University, 1990), p. 456.

5. Jolivet, *La question créole*, p. 404.

6. Hurault, *Français et Indiens*, p. 300.

7. Bilby, "The Remaking of the Aluku," pp. 439–40.

8. Ibid., pp. 440–45.

9. For details, see Isabelle Léglise and Bettina Migge, "Language Naming Practices, Ideologies, and Linguistic Practices: Toward a Comprehensive Description of Language Varieties," *Language in Society* 35 (2006), pp. 313–39, especially pp. 327–28.

10. Kalusé told us that at this same meeting at Kourou, an Amerindian leader said his people categorically refused to pay any rent at all for the new houses. They were willing to pay for electricity, which was supplied by the French, but not for the land. The land had been theirs long before the French came along, and God (not the French) put it there for them to build houses.

11. During World War II, Papon served as General Secretary for the Prefecture of Gironde, the right-hand man of the prefect charged with "police and Jewish matters" for the occupied region that included Bordeaux. In this capacity, he signed orders leading to the deportation of more than 1,500 Jews, almost all of whom died in Auschwitz. After the war, he reinvented himself, was decorated by de Gaulle, became Prefet de Police of Paris, where he presided over the massacre of some 200 Algerian demonstrators in 1961, and from 1978 to 1981 served France as Minister of the Budget. Protected for a time by François Mitterrand, he was finally brought to justice and convicted in 1998 of "complicity in crimes against humanity" and imprisoned, after the longest trial in the history of France. Suffering from severe cardiac illness, he was

released in September 2002, under the new law stating that prisoners should be freed if two court-appointed doctors agree that their health is endangered by remaining behind bars. He died in early 2007.

THE PRISON

1. "He was sent to the Cayenne of French museums" is a way of speaking about a curator who has been demoted and exiled to a bottom-ranked institution in Paris (Emmanuel de Roux, "Les musées meurent aussi," *Le Monde*, October 10, 1990, p. 1). My thanks to Sally Price for this citation.

2. Swiss anthropologist Alfred Métraux, an experienced traveler, described his own introduction to the town in 1947: "The passengers in the van confirm everything I've heard about the destitution and decadence of Cayenne. The descriptions of the city that have been told to me were so unfavorable that I expected the worst, but in fact, Cayenne is even more down-and-out than it was possible for me to foresee. The Place des Palmistes is a wasteland. . . . The houses, mostly of a yellowish or brown tone, are terribly dilapidated. Vultures roam the streets. . . . Talked with a blind convict. A beggar with twisted limbs cries out 'God is crazy!'" (*Itinéraires 1 [1935–1953]: Carnets de notes et journaux de voyage* (Paris: Payot, 1978), pp. 191-92 [diary entries for May 28–30, 1947]).

3. Lafcadio Hearn, *Two Years in the French West Indies* (New York: Harper & Bros., 1923 [orig. pub. 1890]), pp. 64-65.

4. Louis Rousseau, *Un médecin au bagne* (Paris: Armand Fleury, 1930), cited in Pierre, *La terre de la grande punition*, p. 141, without page reference.

5. Pierre, *La terre de la grande punition*, pp. 101, 103–5.

6. Blair Niles, *Condemned to Devil's Island: The Biography of an Unknown Convict* (New York: Grosset & Dunlap, 1928), pp. 43–44.

7. See, for references, Price, *The Convict and the Colonel*; Peter Redfield, *Space in the Tropics: From Convicts to Rockets in French Guiana* (Berkeley and Los Angeles: University of California Press, 2000).

8. Our 1992 field notes say, "There are really no words to describe the obscenity of the new lycée-en-construction. It is more than dehumanizing, it écrasé-s humanity. First, it is gigantesque, it goes on forever. It's filled with little prison-like windows. There's absolutely no 'play' in it; it's a no-nonsense prison-factory. One gazes at it and wonders how a human being could have designed it, imagined its use as a school, imagined children inside. It's a totalizing building, it absolutely dwarfs, in every sense, any human being." Kalusé, and the Saramaka illegals he brought along at the contractor's request, worked for months on this project.

9. Anon., *Destination Guyane: Guide pratique* (Cayenne, French Guiana: Outre-Mer Editions, n.d. [1991?]), pp. 86–88.

10. Since that contract ran out, Ben's been unemployed but taking special training to be a cultural mediator at the hospital. In 2004, he became a citizen of France. During 2006, he was once again hired at the prison, but only on a part-time basis.

11. Tooy had been president of another Saramaka association, Asinángo (named for a powerful forest vine), founded around 1990, but its aims were largely cultural, focusing on such things as men getting together in Cayenne to play Komantí. The association collapsed a few years later when its treasurer, a Creole, emptied the bank account of the several thousand dollars' worth of francs given the group by the town of Cayenne.

THE WETLANDS AT KAW

1. Saramakas mine *keéti* from stream-bank deposits and use it ritually on their bodies, on ritual implements, and in making *óbias*. Tooy tells me that before the Peace, Saramakas didn't use white *keéti* but only *gúndji keéti*, which is reddish. When you see a *gaán-óbia* being made with regular *keéti*, it dates from after the Peace, says Tooy. For an *óbia* from the days of war, it depends on whether it ever *nyán fáya* (was actually in a firefight)—if it was, you'd use blood rather than *keéti*; if it wasn't, you'd use the reddish variety of *keéti* plus (red) annatto. Dúngulále-Óbia, Tooy reminds me, doesn't work much with *keéti* at all, using the ashes of the wild papaya in its place.

2. *Kiingó* is a kind of drop trap used in hunting, a log set to drop from a height when a vine is tripped by an animal. Tooy once told me about an exchange between Armadillo and *kiingó*: Armadillo, taunting *kiingó*, greeted him, "*Pená-u-sósó, ódi!*" (You-who-took-the-trouble-for-nothing, Greetings—i.e. I see that you're there waiting for me, so no problem, you won't catch me). *Kiingó* then replied to Armadillo, "*Tangí, fêkête na gaán soni*" (Thank you, but forgetting is the key—i.e. someday you'll forget and I'll have you!) Kenneth Bilby (personal communication, 2006), citing Laman, *Dictionnaire*, p. 269, proposes that *kiingó* derives from Kikongo *kíngu* ("ratière" [rat trap]).

3. In Saramaccan, this "First-Time" variety is called *toto*. Note that the Yombe (West Central African) word for banana is *thoóto*.

4. My learning from Tooy about the existence of more than one spy named Kwasí, preserved by Saramakas in Komantí songs, parallels my learning that the archival evidence about Kwasí is more complex than I once thought, involving not only Quassie van Nieuw Timotibo but Quassie van Pareyra, and perhaps another one as well (see Jean Jacques Vrij, "Review of Frank Dragenstein, '*Trouw aan de blanken*': *Quassie van Nieuw Timotibo, twist en strijd in de 18de eeuw in Suriname*," Oso 24 [2005]: 190–94).

TEMBÁI'S VILLAGE

1. This is Djéunsu's main shrine. Lonzhé's main shrine, dating from the time of Miséi's namesake, is in Gódo, where Djéunsu has nothing more than a tiny room and a little canoe devoted to him.

2. During 2005 and 2006, Sally was working on a project of her own in Guyane, a NEH- and Wenner-Gren Foundation–supported study of contemporary Maroon arts and artists. We divided our fieldwork time between our respective work schedules. See Sally Price, "Into the Mainstream: Shifting Authenticities in Art," *American Ethnologist* 34 (4) (2007).

FLEEING TRUMPS STANDING

1. Tooy is casual in his claims of being able to cure AIDS. "That sickness has been around a long time but really took off after the civil war [1986–92]. It's a 'ghost sickness'—the sort of thing Dúngulálí handles. It's caused by a dead husband coming back to sleep with the widow and ejaculating in her. That fluid is the AIDS. And if you sleep with her (and ejaculate), you'll get it, too." He says that since he cured Nélia five years ago, the several children she's had have been free of HIV.

2. The reflections in this paragraph are directly inspired by comments that Peter Redfield made after reading about the case.

POLITICS

1. Sally and Richard Price, *Les arts des Marrons* (La Roque d'Anthéron, France: Vents d'ailleurs, 2005).

2. A Ndyuka acquaintance of Gaamá Agbagó's claims that the chief told him of this preference as early as the 1970s (André R. M. Pakosie, "Een analyse van het huidige conflict om het gaamanschap bij de Saamaka," *Siboga* 15, no. 1 [2005]: 17–27).

3. See Price, *First-Time*, pp. 45, 160, passim.

4. In August 2005, both Cambior (based in Montreal) and Golden Star (based in Denver)—which owns another concession nearby—announced with considerable fanfare that their holdings in the area included even greater gold reserves than they had previously believed (Fenny Zandgrond, "Goudreserves Gross Rosebel overtreft verwachting," *De Ware Tijd*, August 6, 2005, and "Golden Star ontdekt meer goud in Saramacca-concessie," *De Ware Tijd*, August 12, 2005).

5. Rochambeau Airport, Guyane's international airport, was named by the Americans who built it during World War II to honor the French general who fought alongside George Washington in the American Revolution. But that general's son, who had accompanied his father in fighting the British, became a notoriously brutal slave owner in Saint-Domingue and served as leader of Napoleon's expeditionary force from 1802 until its defeat in 1803 by Haitian freedom fighters. In the Caribbean, he remains infamous for having imported bloodhounds from Cuba to use against the Haitians, for his massive use of torture, and for his unrelenting hatred of blacks. That the name remains, largely uncontested, speaks volumes about the neocolonial status of Guyane.

6. In an e-mail of July 2006, anthropologist Bonno Thoden van Velzen reports that, according to Ndyuka friends, the five men who made up the delegation returned home feeling unappreciated and "abused" by the Saramakas, who paid them little heed and did not treat them with due respect.

7. Matory calls Nanã Burukú "the goddess of death" (*Black Atlantic Religion*, p. 98), while Pierre Verger characterizes her as a "very ancient goddess" who shows people "how to act with calm, benevolence, dignity and gentleness" (*Orixás: Deuses Iorubás na África e no Novo Mundo* [Salvador: Corrupio, 1981], pp. 236–41; see also his *Notes sur le culte des Orisa*, pp. 271–90).

8. An article in *De Ware Tijd* on August 2, 2005, described how in a "great council meeting" held the previous day at Brokopondo, the Saramaka officials from all clans met with the Suriname government Minister for Regional Development and declared Otjútju (Belfon Abóikóni) to be the new *gaamá*. The minister said that he would be officially recognized by the national government without delay. A follow-up article on August 3 reported that the leaders of Dángogó were still not accepting this decision, saying that Otjútju might be *gaamá* as far as cityfolk were concerned, but not for "real Saramakas." However, it seemed clear that Otjútju had won at last. And then on October 29, *De Ware Tijd* reported that Otjútju would be received that day in the presidential palace and officially recognized by President Ronald Venetiaan as Saramaka *gaamá*. On October 31, the newspaper published his photo wearing his new *gaamá*'s uniform, presented by the president.

TOOY TEACHING I—MOSTLY LUÁNGU AND PÚMBU

1. In normal Saramaccan, with Luángu words inserted: "Put the *mayómbe* [rum] in the *kwándiki* [bottle], *yengué sélélé*," with the final two words apparently stylistic ideophones.

2. Again, in normal Saramaccan with Luángu words inserted, it means: "Chigger-foot-man [Kwímabo, Wimalúngu, Sípadúngu, Wédemalúngu, Ísikadúngu—all insulting names in Luángu for someone with chiggers], walk on the path *tantúmbe* ["on your knees" or "in crippled fashion"], *víe, tjátjá, hònhònhòn hònhònhòn*" [with this last a special Luángu terminal phrase].

3. In Sranan-tongo, the Creole of coastal Suriname, "X furu na Y" means "There's lots of X in Y," so in this case, two Luángu words are substituted into a Sranan sentence.

TOOY TEACHING II—MOSTLY PAPÁ

1. Remarkably, the descendants of Hwéte in Bundjitapá, Tooy's birthplace and the southernmost village on the river, and those of Hwéte's younger sister Bánki in Malobí, on the middle river, have maintained their kinship reckoning over 250 years of physical separation, ever since Hwéte was spirited away from Malobí to Bundjitapá in the aftermath of Gweyúnga's death, at which time Bánki sided with those who accused Hwéte of witchcraft (see p. 98). Each still knows whether to call the other (classificatory) "mother's brother," "brother," "grandfather," and so on. Tooy and Mowêti know that their mothers called each other "sister," so they call each other "brother."

2. Another time he says it as *A hón tuntuú yagazé da unún da oo-oo.*

3. The tale is recorded in R. and S. Price, *Two Evenings in Saramaka*, pp. 174–75.

4. Another time, Tooy sang this song with the final word replaced by *díki táta ma di día yabí.*

5. Tooy continued: "Anasi-tóli used to be told on the night before burial, when we play Papá now. Anasi-tóli is a great heavy thing! Papá, Komantí, Anasi-tóli, and

Apínti all say the same heavy things." (Today, folktales are told on the night[s] after burial.)

6. See Price, *First-Time*, p. 149. Adugbá, according to Tooy, is closely associ-ated with a major avenging spirit, Ma Básukáma, of Bêndêkôndè—his father's vil-lage—but at the same time, that play "belongs to" Dángogó. Lukéinsi (the daughter of Adjágbò [Matjáu] and Paánza [Kasitú-Bêndêkôndè]), who served as the late eigh-teenth-century medium for the forest spirit Wámba, had a husband from Dángogó [Matjáu]. She died while pregnant, but the unborn child became a major avenging spirit who taught the Adugbá "play" to Dángogó, whose men play it for her. (Her current medium, Zabulón, appointed Headcaptain by Gaamá Otjútju in 2005, lives in Cayenne.)

7. Tooy once mentioned to me that the Adjú drum plays *Saka saká gó láme, kulé gó kulé kó* (with the last phrase meaning, "run off, run back") until it's time for the ghost of the deceased to depart definitively, at which point the drummer leaves off the last two words.

8. His son held one of the original 1762 captain's staffs; his daughter's son was Gbagidí, who was named *gaamá* in 1820; his daughter's daughter's son Wétiwóyo was named *gaamá* in 1835; and his direct descendant ruled Saramaka during the whole first third of the twentieth century as Gaamá Djankusó. For more on Sakóto/Gúnkamê, see Price, *First-Time*, pp. 63–64, 172–74.

9. For lore about this great mountain redoubt, where Saramakas fought a decisive battle against the whites in 1749, see ibid., pp. 135–37.

10. In the 1970s, I heard completely different explanations for this Papá song, though one—which I dismissed at the time—seems identical to Tooy's. It would seem that different clans interpret the same words in Papá as referring to different incidents in their past, having in common a Saramaka man shooting a whole row of soldiers and the people back in the village hearing the sound of the gunshot. See ibid., pp. 125–26.

11. Tooy enjoys telling me about how various common features of Saramaka life weren't present at first: "Runaway people didn't have *agbán* [clay pots for rituals], so they would dam up a little stream, make a place that filled with water, put their medicinal leaves in there, and wash in them." Or again, "When the runaways went into the forest, the first liquid they used for libations was from the *palulú* [wild ba-nana] tree—you'd cut the tree and catch its 'water'—that was those people's rum! After that, they used the water of the *malêmbelêmbe* plant. After that, the water of the *sangaáfu* plant. And after that sugarcane juice. After sugarcane juice came rum, and after rum, beer. We kept the final three to use in libations."

12. An extract from my field notes of 1967, at a time when I was only ambivalently welcome to approach the Papá players in action (see Price, *First-Time*), evokes the am-bience of Papá performance in situ:

> The Papá drum points directly out of the *kèê ósu* [house of death]. The two main singers sit farthest into the house, facing the door. Much rum and

apínkusu [fermented sugarcane juice] is consumed. By dawn, the singers seem high, arguing a lot, very loud. The Papá singing is high-spirited, persuasive, almost like a pep rally. Songs sung with real feeling. Often a soloist stands dancing in place as he sings, moving his arms, fists clenched. Two punches forward with one hand, then the same with other. All heads are tied [with kerchiefs]. The first soloist in a song is often replaced after the chorus by another, then another, before he takes it up again. Soloist acts almost like a cheerleader.

TOOY TEACHING III-KOMANTÍ, WÉNTI, AND MORE

1. Tooy, like other Saramaka addicts, keeps a wad of leaf tobacco and some ashes in a small tin can (or plastic jar), sometimes with wintergreen added for flavor, and after squeezing out the juice with a thumb and pouring it out into a cupped palm, brings the palm to his nose and inhales the juice strongly through one nostril (closing off the other) and then the other.

2. In a popular Saramaka folktale, a "devil" pulls out one of his teeth, flings it into the river, and dries up all the water—that tooth is called *Azángana mi kolóbi, azángana mi koló* (R. and S. Price, *Two Evenings in Saramaka*, p. 238).

3. The final five phrases are the only ones that are partially in Saramaccan: *I sa gó a Dénawa* [You can go to Dénewa]. *I sa gó a Tómezíla* [You can go to Tómezila]. *Walénu, walénu tjá Tómezíla* [*Walénu, walénu* brings *Tómezíla*]. *Baákama méki lókpolókpo* [Black people make moss/lichens], *gádu hangbónu* [god says yes].

4. *Susa*, which consists of two men "dancing" at each other using intricate steps that mime combat (and with one man "killing" the other in the game), is part of a family of African/African American martial arts/dances that includes Brazilian *capoeira* and Martiniquan *damier*. It was described among slaves on Suriname plantations and is common among eastern Maroons, but not Upper River Saramakas—see Jan Voorhoeve and Ursy M. Lichtveld, *Creole Drum: An Anthology of Creole Literature in Suriname* (New Haven, CT: Yale University Press, 1975), pp. 54, 62–65. Kenneth Bilby (personal communication, 2006, which credits prior conversations on the origins of *susa* with Robert Farris Thompson), citing Laman 1964:526, 779–80, derives the dance and name from Kikongo *nsúusa* ("le jeu mbele ['un jeu avec battements de main']" and *nsúnsa* ("danser en avance les pieds joints à peu près comme dans le jeu mbeele").

5. Tooy gave me several intriguing indications that Yáka-ósu may be distantly related to the cult of *bakúlus* (or *bakuu*) that arose around the turn of the twentieth century, particularly in Ndyuka (see, for example, Vernon, *Money Magic*). Tooy used to exorcize *bakúlus* for clients but quit when he decided it was too dangerous. In any case, he says, *bakúlus* are less effective than in the past, because of the prominence of paper money. They used to go into a bank for you and swallow all the coins, then come home and shit them out for you. But with paper money, that doesn't work.

DÚNUYÁNGI TAKES OVER

1. When I asked Tooy for an explanation, he said, "Open the beer, pour it in the glass!" and he sang: *Mi kénidjó, mi gádu mi gádu mi kénidjó dá únu-e, mi adjoo, mi adjoo, tjòònúgbe,* adding that *tjòònúgbe* means, "pour it in the glass" and *kéénidjú* [or *kénidjó*] means "beer" (though it sure sounds like it came from "cane juice").

2. Tooy himself once told me a dangerous story about some of these powers, preserved in a Komantí song. A man named Yáwadáda had three sons: Kwadjó, the eldest, Djebí, the middle one, and Busikí, the youngest. A man named Djíndjo had a garden camp, but Yawadáda came along and made a new one right next to his and also began cutting Djíndjo's sugarcane. Yawadáda told his sons never to set foot in Djíndjo's camp, but they went anyway. Three times the children snuck into the forbidden garden camp, and three times their father scolded them. The next time they went, Djíndjo saw them and fought with them. Kwadjó said to his younger brothers, "We've been beaten," and flew off into the sky—he became a vulture. Djebí turned into a stone in the forest. Busikí went into the sea.

GOODBYES

1. I had long known that one of the Wéntis in Tampáki was called Naosí. (He'd been in the head of a man named Lindí.) But I hadn't realized, until Tooy casually mentioned it, that Naosí is the Wénti name for Moses, and that Moses must have told these stories about his life when he appeared in possession.

2. I have no way of knowing to what extent the story of the return of Naosí's wife draws on the biblical story of the return of Moses's first (Ethiopian) wife after many years of separation.

KNOCKING THE STONE

1. Tooy has never displayed the slightest curiosity about this book (though he cares deeply about teaching, and exchanging knowledge with, and pleasing me). I expect my presentation of a copy upon publication to be largely a nonevent to him, though Céline and Yaai will be interested in the pictures. In contrast, I expect Ben and many of his agemates (as well as Gaamá Otjútju, once a copy reaches him) to consider it a treasure trove, a shortcut to (and authorization of) certain important fragments of Saramaka knowledge, as well as something to argue about for years to come. As I've learned from similar experiences over the years, there's no way I can successfully predict the effects the book may have on Tooy's life (or my own), on Saramakas more generally, or on others mentioned herein. The lesson of Goethe's sorcerer's apprentice (*Der Zauberlehrling,* 1797) remains apt.

2. I later confirmed that Lángu elders who are not connected to Pobôsi don't invoke these Roman Catholic figures. (I have known a few Saramakas such as Gaamá Ag-

bagó Abóikóni who, having been baptized by Roman Catholic priests in their youth, occasionally referred to such figures in prayers, but they were not from the Lángu clan.)

1. The full text of the 1992 lecture (unpaginated) can be found on the Internet at http://nobelprize.org/literature/laureates/1992/walcott-lecture.html. It was also published by Farrar, Straus and Giroux under the title *The Antilles: Fragments of Epic Memory; The Nobel Lecture* in 1992—also unpaginated.

2. An adequate history of how the terms of this debate came to matter so much in the twentieth-century U.S. academy, and why they continue to resonate so strongly today, remains to be written.

3. Michel-Rolph Trouillot, "Culture on the Edges: Creolization in the Plantation Context," *Plantation Society in the Americas* 5 (1998): 8–28.

4. Astute readers may note that this is my first use of the word *religion* in regard to Saramakas in this book (nor did I use it other than very sparingly in *First-Time* or *Alabi's World*). For Saramakas, religion is not a separate or separable realm of life, and unlike, say, Candomblé or Vodou or Santería, it has no name. Nor is religion—that which gives Saramaka life much of its meaning—a domain that is easily separable for the analyst. Religion cannot be described by saying that practitioners believe this or that, but can only be understood by describing and analyzing the connections between events, experience, and social relationships, and the ways people represent these to themselves. In the comparative context of this chapter, I use it as a convenient label or shorthand.

5. Much of this paragraph and the next echoes Sidney W. Mintz and Richard Price, *The Birth of African-American Culture* (Boston: Beacon Press, 1992).

6. A useful attempt to specify "six foundational characteristics of continental African religions" describes "(1) a communotheistic (as opposed to a monotheistic or polytheistic) understanding of the Divine, which corresponds with a community of venerated deities and invisible beings; (2) ancestral veneration; (3) possession trance and mediumship; (4) food offerings and animal sacrifice; (5) divination and herbalism; and (6) an entrenched belief in neutral mystical power" (Dianne M. Stewart, *Three Eyes for the Journey: African Dimensions of the Jamaican Religious Experience* [New York: Oxford University Press, 2005], p. 24).

7. Suzanne Preston Blier, "Vodun: West African Roots of Vodou," in *Sacred Arts of Haitian Vodou*, ed. Donald J. Cosentino (Los Angeles: UCLA Fowler Museum of Cultural History, 1995), pp. 61–87; citation is on p. 75.

8. Unpublished figures from the second edition of the *Database* were kindly provided by David Eltis in January 2006.

9. *First-Time* and *Alabi's World* present detailed evidence about the dates of marronage of Saramakas' ancestors. Although the initial clans continued to receive

occasional new recruits into the 1760s, their numbers pale before those who ma-
rooned between 1690 and the second decade of the eighteenth century.

10. Blier mentions as well speakers of Mahi, Hueda, Hwla, Ouatchi, Wemenu, and
Mina—"Vodun," p. 61.

11. Matory, *Black Atlantic Religion*, p. 79.

12. Robin Law, *The Slave Coast of West Africa 1550-1750: The Impact of the Atlantic
Slave Trade on an African Society* (Oxford Clarendon Press, 1991), pp. 185–89.

13. Blier, "Vodun," p. 61.

14. Matory, *Black Atlantic Religion*, p. 76.

15. In contrast, the Gold Coast provided nearly *half* of the people who became
Ndyukas and Alukus—Maroon nations that formed a generation after that of Saramakas—according to the figures from the second edition of the *Database*. This fits
well with Saramakas' belief that Ndyukas and Alukus are the greatest specialists of
Komantí.

16. John Thornton, *Africa and Africans in the Making of the Atlantic World, 1400-1800*
(Cambridge: Cambridge University Press, 1998), p. 322.

17. John K. Thornton, *Warfare in Atlantic Africa, 1500-1800* (London: UCL Press,
1999), p. 57.

18. It is impossible to specify degrees of cultural similarity or diversity in general terms. Between John Thornton's bold claim that "there were only three different
cultures ['Upper Guinea,' 'Lower Guinea,' and 'the Angolan coast'] that contributed
to the New World, and among them only seven distinct subcultures" (*Africa and
Africans*, p. 187), and views that insist on the cultural diversity of even tiny regions of
West Africa (and significant shifts through time in identities and practices), the issue
is always one of levels of abstraction.

19. References supporting the next three paragraphs may be found in Richard
Price, *The Guiana Maroons: A Historical and Bibliographical Introduction* (Baltimore:
Johns Hopkins University Press, 1976), pp. 16–22.

20. On the importance of Gbe grammatical structures in the formation of the Suriname creole languages, see Bettina Migge, ed., "Substrate Influence in the Creoles
of Surinam," special issue of *Journal of Pidgin and Creole Languages* 22 (1), 2007. Saramaccan is notable for the variety of the African languages that contributed to its
vocabulary.

21. Compare this to Jamaica's ratio of 10:1 in 1780, "the highest in the British West
Indies," and to those of "4:1 for Barbados, parity for Bermuda, Virginia, and Georgia, and a white predominance of 15:1 for the American Middle Colonies" (Michael
Craton, "Jamaican Slavery," in *Race and Slavery in the Western Hemisphere: Quantitative Studies*, ed. S. L. Engerman and E. D. Genovese [Princeton, NJ: Princeton University Press, 1975], pp. 249–84; citation is on p. 254). All this in the context of David
Brion Davis's timely reminder that "by 1820 . . . at least ten million African slaves
had arrived in the New World, as opposed to a grand total of two million Europeans" (*Challenging the Boundaries of Slavery* [Cambridge, MA: Harvard University Press,
2003], p. 17).

22. One line of evidence is provided by the numerous similarities between Saramaka religion and that of the Creoles of the Para region (the most culturally conservative of coastal Afro-Surinamers), which cannot be explained simply on the basis of subsequent contact (see, for example, Charles J. Wooding, *Winti: Een Afroamerikaanse godsdienst in Suriname* [Meppel, The Netherlands: Krips Repro, 1972]). Today, Para religion retains the idea that its adherents speak several ritual languages—Luangu, Papa (or Vodu), Kromanti, and "Amerindian"—but by the twentieth century these "languages" seem to have consisted of normal Sranan-tongo sentences with an occasional esoteric word plugged in. Researchers have not documented more than a handful of such words in any of these special languages (see, in addition to *Winti*, Melville J. Herskovits and Frances S. Herskovits, *Suriname Folk-Lore* [New York: Columbia University Press, 1936], and Jan Voorhoeve, "Church Creole and Pagan Cult Languages," in *Pidginization and Creolization of Languages*, ed. Dell Hymes [Cambridge: Cambridge University Press, 1971], pp. 305–15).

23. On reading a draft of this manuscript, Kenneth Bilby (personal communication, 2006) wrote with a supportive example from the Aluku Maroons, concerning *sangáa* (see p. 64):

In Aluku, the cognate, "sanga," means something quite different from what it does in Saramaka, but clearly related—it's a particular genre of music and dance that goes with a rite that is supposed to be held for any Aluku who kills another human being, a way of honoring the killer for his fierceness (said originally to have been a kind of celebration of the heroic slaying of one of the enemy during the First-Time days of war) but required in more recent times even for more ignominious killers, since one of its purposes is also to protect the killer from being troubled by the victim's spirit. (Both the Saramaka and Aluku terms seem very clearly to be derived from Kikongo.) What's wonderful about the cultural complex denoted by the Aluku term is that it's another example of how complex cultural transmission and recombination were among Suriname Maroons—the name and some of the associated concepts have Kongo origins, but the whole complex is identified by Alukus as being in the Kumanti domain; and sanga music and dance are seen as being variants of Kumanti music and dance (and they are in fact very similar). So among the Aluku, Kongo-derived (and other Central African) elements and concepts related to war and military organization are now seamlessly interwoven with Kumanti ideology and practice (often thought by scholars to be derived exclusively from Akan speaking peoples).

24. We have seen earlier, p. 254, that twentieth-century Saramakas envision the Papá complex as having been discovered in the mid-eighteenth century on the site of an abandoned cemetery.

25. Price, *First-Time*, pp. 60–61.

26. Much of *Alabi's World* is devoted to the missionaries' testimony about Saramaka religion.

27. The following four paragraphs summarize materials in *Alabi's World*.

28. At the same historical moment on the plantations of coastal Suriname, where some 70% of slaves were still African born (and where half of the slaves had arrived in the New World only during the previous decade), lively rituals and "plays" associated with Loango, Papa, Nago, and other African "nations" were commonly performed (see, for example, Richard and Sally Price, eds., *John Gabriel Stedman's Narrative of a Five Years Expedition against the Revolted Negroes of Surinam* [Baltimore: Johns Hopkins University Press, 1988 (1790)], 292, 646–47). But the similarly named rites among the post-treaty Saramaka, with hardly any African-born personnel, had long since become fully creolized and were not tied to individuals' parentage or some sort of putative "ethnicity." (For discussion of the extensive creolization of even these coastal "plays," see Alex van Stipriaan, "'Een verre verwijderd trommelen . . .' Ontwikkeling van Afro-Surinaamse muziek en dans in de slavernij," in *De Kunstwereld: Produktie, distributie en receptie in de wereld van kunst en cultuur,* ed. Ton Bevers, Antoon Van den Braembussche, and Berend Jan Langenberg [Hilversum, The Netherlands: Verloren, 1993], pp. 143-73.)

29. The Saramaka ordeal of *kangáa*, described by missionaries soon after the peace treaty, provides a fine example of an African ritual complex that was sufficiently self-contained and compact—and sufficiently meaningful to people from diverse African societies—to be transported largely intact in the "heart" of an Abaísa ancestor and integrated into his clan's repertoire. It consisted of thrusting a medicated feather through the subject's tongue to see if it swelled up (or alternately, applying a red-hot machete to the subject's calf to see if it blistered). This rite can be traced directly to the eighteenth-century Kingdom of Benin (for references and details, see Price, *Alabi's World*, pp. 162, 373–74). A missionary dictionary from 1778 describes *asêmpè* ("asempreh") as "A kind of torture; a knotted rope is tied around the head and very strongly tightened, to wring a confession out of the criminal." In 1967, I overheard a Saramaka who had a bad headache saying, "They're doing *asêmpè* to my head," showing that memories of this long-obsolete ordeal are collectively preserved in everyday speech. And in 1978, future *gaamá* Otjútju—after ritually spraying a mouthful of rum to the ancestors—revealed knowledge of more specific esoteric details when he told me that *asêmpè* was the personal *óbia* of his Matjáu forebear Musumba Kokoko. "You know what 'Father' Musumba used to do when someone refused to confess? He would tie their heads with a band made from the *kwatíi* tree. Then he'd place the drum pegs [wedged between the person's head and the band]. Then he'd hammer them down! That's *asêmpè*. Now, when he knocked one *gán!* [intensifier], the person would say, 'óóó, AAíííí! This is what I did . . .' until the interrogation was over. Nothing more to it. The person would just keel over. Some died from it, some lived."

30. Mimi Sheller points to some examples in *Consuming the Caribbean: From Arawaks to Zombies* (London: Routledge, 2003), especially pp. 174–203.

31. See, for example, Richard Price, "Afterword/Echoes," in *Religion, Diaspora and Cultural Identity*, ed. John W. Pulis (Amsterdam: Gordon & Breach, 1999), pp. 403–11; citation is on p. 405.

32. I am in sympathy with the arguments of linguists who insist that creole languages, despite their unusual and recent origins, are not different (read: deficient), grammatically or otherwise, from noncreole (read: normal) languages—see, for example, Michel DeGraff, "Morphology in Creole Genesis: Linguistics and Ideology," in *Ken Hale: A Life in Language,* ed. Michael Kenstowicz (Cambridge, MA: MIT Press, 2001), pp. 53–121; DeGraff, "On the Origin of Creoles: A Cartesian Critique of Neo-Darwinian Linguistics," *Linguistic Typology* 5 (2001): 213–310. But it does not necessarily follow that societies born of creolization do not share certain kinds of strong cultural dynamism.

33. For example, Matory, *Black Atlantic Religion;* Stephan Palmié, *Wizards and Scientists: Explorations in Afro-Cuban Modernity and Tradition* (Durham, NC: Duke University Press, 2002); David H. Brown, *Santeria Enthroned: Art, Ritual, and Innovation in an Afro-Cuban Religion* (Chicago: University of Chicago Press, 2003); Donald J. Cosentino, *Sacred Arts of Haitian Vodou* (Los Angeles: UCLA Fowler Museum of Cultural History, 1995); and Karen E. Richman, *Migration and Vodou* (Gainesville: University Press of Florida, 2005).

34. Kenneth Bilby (personal communication, 2006) suggests that a similar argument could be made for Jamaica, where Kromanti, practiced by the Windward Maroons and derived largely from Akan practices, and Kumina, practiced by members of the "Bongo nation" (non-Maroons) and derived largely from Central African practices brought by post-emancipation contract laborers, have since the mid-nineteenth century "developed in relation to one another, and today are part of a larger system or logic that depends on the existence of both." See also Kenneth Bilby, *True-Born Maroons* (Gainesville: University Press of Florida, 2005), pp. 110–19.

35. Palmié, *Wizards and Scientists,* p. 26.

36. Ibid., p. 27. See Richman, *Migration and Vodou,* pp. 150–83, for an analysis of the radical recalibration of "Guinea" and "Magic" (*rada* and *petro*) in Haiti, based not on ideas and practices brought by new African migrants but by changing local relations to international capitalism.

37. Palmié, *Wizards and Scientists,* p. 193. These studies also make clear the extent to which ideology, including the stories practitioners tell about the relationship of their religion to Africa, is contingent and socially transformed—see, for example, Brown, *Santeria Enthroned,* p. 90; Palmié, "Santería Grand Slam: Afro-Cuban Religious Studies and the Study of Afro-Cuban Religion," *New West Indian Guide* 79 (2005): 281–300; Richman, *Migration and Vodou,* pp. 116–49; and Matory, *Black Atlantic Religion.*

38. Matory, *Black Atlantic Religion.* See also Brown, *Santeria Enthroned,* and Richman, *Migration and Vodou.*

39. It may be worth noting that of the sixteen named ancestors who Saramakas have told me made the Middle Passage and about whom a good deal is remembered, only three (Wíi, Béti-Kadósu, and Kaásipúmbu) are associated with a specific African provenience ("Lángu"). And Tooy told me that these three also came from "Dahomey."

40. During the 1740s, the whites also referred to the village Saramakas called Tuído, where Kaási and his people lived, as "Loangodorp" (see Price, *First-Time,* p. 83).

434 * NOTES TO PAGES 302–306

41. For a sampling of the critiques I have written of what I consider the overemphasis on essentialized African ethnic categories in the recent historiography of the diaspora, see "On the Miracle of Creolization," in *Afro-Atlantic Dialogues: Anthropology in the Diaspora*, ed. Kevin A. Yelvington (Santa Fe: SAR Press, 2006), pp. 113–45; and "The Concept of Creolization," in *World History of Slavery*, ed. David Eltis and Stanley L. Engerman (Cambridge: Cambridge University Press, 2007).

42. MacGaffey, "Twins, Simbi Spirits, and Lwas in Kongo and Haiti," p. 211.

43. Matory, *Black Atlantic Religion*, pp. 281, 38.

44. Ibid., pp. 281.

45. Kenneth Bilby's *True-Born Maroons* constitutes a superb analysis of the meaning of memory and history among the Maroons of Jamaica.

46. There is a haunting Komantí song, *Asánti pútu pútu*, that may testify to the desire of early nineteenth-century (or possibly late eighteenth-century) Saramaka Komantí men to find a specific piece of *óbia* knowledge among a very late group of runaways, who presumably would have been closer in time to the African source— see the Coda. Haunting, even touching, but still icing on the cake.

47. Matory, *Black Atlantic Religion*, pp. 35, 70, 277, passim. Meanwhile, books stressing memory in a neo-Herskovitsian vein continue to appear regularly—see, for example, Maureen Warner-Lewis, *Central Africa in the Caribbean: Transcending Time, Transforming Cultures* (Kingston, Jamaica: University of the West Indies Press, 2003), and Jesús Fuentes Guerra and Armin Schwegler, *Lengua y ritos del Palo Monte Mayombe: Dioses cubanos y sus fuentes africanas* (Madrid: Iberoamericana, 2005).

48. David Scott, "That Event, This Memory: Notes on the Anthropology of African Diasporas in the New World," *Diaspora* 1 (1991): 261–84; citation is on pp. 262–63. I have engaged Scott's critique at length in "On the Miracle of Creolization."

49. Shaw, *Memories of the Slave Trade*, p. 9, cited in Bilby, *True-Born Maroons*, p. 412.

50. For a detailed, actor-centered account of the history of Ndyuka Maroon religion, see Thoden van Velzen and van Wetering, *In the Shadow of the Oracle*.

51. As Clifford Geertz writes, "It seems likely that whatever use ethnographic texts will have in the future, if in fact they will have any, it will involve enabling conversation across societal lines. . . . The next necessary thing . . . is to enlarge the possibility of intelligible discourse between people quite different from one another in interest, outlook, wealth, and power, and yet contained in a world where, tumbled as they are into endless connection, it is increasingly difficult to get out of each other's way" (*Works and Lives: The Anthropologist as Author* [Stanford, CA: Stanford University Press, 1988], p. 147).

52. Matory, *Black Atlantic Religion*, p. 1.

53. Ibid., p. 31. Likewise, the relationship between sexuality and possession, as described by Matory for Candomblé (his chapters 5 and 6), is distinctly foreign to Saramaka ways of thinking and acting, and may well be less widespread outside Bahia than he implies.

54. Of these other religions, the rural version of Haitian Vodou probably comes closest to that practiced by Saramakas in the ways it fits into everyday life. Saramaka remains quite distant in feeling and organization from the urban Vodou described by, say, Alfred Métraux or Cosentino (who derives aspects of Vodou's theatricality from eighteenth-century *commedia dell'arte*)—for Métraux's "classic" description, see *Le Vaudou haïtien* (Paris: Gallimard, 1958); for Cosentino's discussion, his "Imagine Heaven," in *Sacred Arts,* ed. Cosentino, pp. 25–55. Richman, *Migration and Vodou,* is particularly persuasive in demonstrating the atypicalness of this urban style and the complex forces that have radically transformed both rural and urban Haitian religion during the twentieth century.

55. In this regard, it is probably no coincidence that while Candomblé and Santería have recently been the subject of penetrating historical analyses, the historical study of Vodou remains less developed. For Vodou comes closest of the three to resembling Saramaka religion in the way it infuses all aspects of daily life, the way it resists becoming a separate object of study. The three historical chapters in Cosentino's *Sacred Arts of Haitian Vodou*—Suzanne Preston Blier on Dahomean continuities, Robert Farris Thompson on Kongoisms, and Sidney W. Mintz and Michel-Rolph Trouillot on the social history of the religion (plus Cosentino's own remarks on the creation of "hybridity")—all seem to catch aspects of a complex whole. Read together, they begin to trace a general picture. But, as Mintz and Trouillot insist, the history of Vodou remains "murky . . . a comprehensive picture is elusive" ("The Social History of Haitian Vodou," p. 124). A full history of Vodou could only be a truly ethnographic history, a task that remains for future scholars. Richman's *Migration and Vodou,* despite its modest scope, constitutes an excellent beginning in this direction. Like other ethnographers of rural Haiti, Richman insists that the people she lived with do not speak of "vodou" as a religion, as something they "practice" or "believe in," and that this cosmopolitan usage remains "foreign to many in the countryside" (p. 22).

56. See Mintz and Price, *The Birth of African-American Culture.*

57. Matory, *Black Atlantic Religion,* p. 268.

58. Melville Herskovits, "The Negro in the New World: The Statement of a Problem," *American Anthropologist* 32 (1930): 145–55.

59. Another significant divergence between Saramaka religion and Santería, Candomblé, and Vodou is the active advisory role that middle-class (sometimes foreign) scholars/patrons often played in the local temples of these latter three religions during a good part of the twentieth century. From Fernando Ortíz and Lydia Cabrera in Havana to Raimundo Nina Rodrigues and Pierre Verger in Bahia to Odette Mennesson-Rigaud and Alfred Métraux in Port-au-Prince, a large number of such "respectable" people wielded influence on practitioners' ideology/discourse, including that regarding relationships with putative African roots, and on ritual practice itself. See Brown, *Santería Enthroned,* Matory, *Black Atlantic Religion,* Palmié, *Wizards and Scientists,* and Richman, *Vodou and Migration* for the complex relations between practitioners of these more cosmopolitan religions and scholarly patrons, and their varied ef-

fects. (In comparison, Melville and Frances Herskovits in 1920s Saramaka, trying to teach the people they met the "African" origins of their institutions, left no mark at all—see Richard and Sally Price, *The Root of Roots; or, How Afro-American Anthropology Got Its Start* [Chicago: Prickly Paradigm Press, 2003].)

60. Scott, "That Event, This Memory," p. 269.

61. Walcott, *The Antilles* (unpaginated).

CODA: ESOTERIC LANGUAGE

1. For an analysis of the dangers of traditional etymological archaeology in the diaspora, see Kristina Wirtz, "Divining the Past: The Linguistic Reconstruction of 'African' Roots in Diasporic Ritual Registers and Songs," *Journal of Religion in Africa* 37, no. 2 (2007).

2. Just one example: the several-thousand-word online Saramaccan-English dictionary compiled by the Summer Institute of Linguistics, the fruit of a nearly twenty-year-long residence by two linguists in Asindóópo (the *gaamá*'s village), defines *Paasitónu* as "a rapids and a large flat rock on the Gran Rio." They were apparently unaware that Paasitónu, less than a kilometer by canoe from Asindóópo, is the name of the cemetery in which all people from that village and surrounding ones are buried.

3. All available dictionaries understate African contributions because of the concentration of these words in domains (from sex to religion to the natural world) that dictionary compilers consistently underexplore. More than three decades ago, I wrote that "Saramaccan is very probably the most lexically African of all New World Creoles" and suggested that "a dictionary which included *all* of the words in Saramaccan would show a proportion of African-derived words closer to 50%" (Price, "KiKoongo and Saramaccan," pp. 461–62). Today, after some thirty years of subsequent research, that estimate seems solid. Kenneth Bilby, who is in the process of finishing a large etymological dictionary of the closely related Aluku language—he has to date found etymons for over 5,300 items—suggests that words of African origin constitute *at least* 43% of the total lexicon of that language (Bilby, "Reevaluating the African Lexical Component of the Surinamese Maroon Creoles: The Aluku Case," paper presented at the Thirty-First Annual Conference on African Linguistics, Boston University, March 3, 2000).

4. Bilby, *True-Born Maroons*, p. 14. Bilby has worked for several years in French Guiana as well as Jamaica, and has had ample time to observe and consider the reception of *First-Time*, which was translated into French with the local readership in mind.

5. The origins of the form of the *apínti*, once simply presumed to be Akan, now appear to be more complex. Recent work on the subject suggests that in the seventeenth and eighteenth centuries, peoples of both the "Slave Coast" and the "Gold Coast" had drums of this general type—Ewe *kagan*, Yoruba *apínti*, and Akan *apentemma*. For pictures, see Price, *First-Time*, title page; and Sally and Richard Price, *Maroon Arts: Cultural Vitality in the African Disapora* (Boston: Beacon Press, 1999), pp. 255–57.

6. Wooding, *Winti*, p. 190.

7. This song provides a telling example of my difficulties in transcribing and deciphering esoteric language. In April 2005, Tooy sang me a song, which I carefully transcribed from the recording. Before singing it, he told me, "This a prayer to Ma Gumbá, Old Woman of the Apúkus, who's the mother of all the bush hogs in the world and who lives in a great savannah called Tjíntjiminatjíntji. Her bush-hog children come to her from time to time to ask to be let out so they can go to the river for water. Now, if you call out, 'Tjíntjiminatjíntji, tjíntji Mamá Gumbá,' she'll let out a certain number of her children whom she knows will go out and be killed, but she warns the others that they should just return to the savannah. When you go hunting, you can pray to her." And then he sings the very sweet song/prayer that I transcribe as *Kái déé vúnda-o, kái déé vúnda-va, kái déé vúnda mooi wandá, kái déé vúnda dá mi. Un kaai déé vúnda dá mi, un kaai de vúnda-o, kái déé vúnda mooi fo mi, kái déé vúnda mooi wandá, kái déé vúnda da mi. Ma Bandíngbo, Ma Bandíngbo, nakímbóto, nakímbóto. Gó ála vútjavútja kó. Ma Futjálamkáni. Avó Búmbalálo. Tjêntjeminatjêntje, tjêntje Mamá Gumbá.* Later, when I asked, he explained that in Apúku language, *vúnda* means bush hog, and *kái de vúnda mooi wandá* means, "Call those bush hogs, which look so beautiful running through the forest."

But a couple of days later, when I asked him about *Ma Bandíngbo, nakímbóto, go ála vútjavútja ko, Ma Futjálamkáni,* and *Avó Búmbalálo*—those words/phrases I still didn't understand fully—he told me that *Ma Gwandímbu* is another name for Ma Gumbá; that *nakimbódo* means (S.) *náki bêê* (= I'm very hungry), that *gó ála vútjavútja kó* should be *malávu tjákutjáku*, meaning "the meat that you have"; that *Ma Futjálamkáni* is not a person as I thought, but should be transcribed *mafutalánkáni* and means, "Let it go into my belly"; and *avó Búmbalálo* is in fact *avúnvun balakú*, which means, "I've swallowed it!" My corrected transcription of the second half of the song is then: *Ma Gwandímbu, Ma Gwandímbu, nakimbódo, nakimbódo, malávu tjákutjáku, mafutalánkáni, avúnvun balakú, Tjêntjeminatjêntje, tjêntje Mamá Gumbá.*

8. Flibánti has told Tooy that even he has never gotten close enough to see God's face, but he has gotten to Adjákôndè [Adjá land] (sometimes Adjápási [Adjá path]), where you can hear his voice. According to Komantís, Adjá country is where all the seeds in the world for all the medicinal plants come from. It's where God goes to get the seeds that he then blows down to earth.

9. "Mapána people" was a standard eighteenth-century Saramaka term for the Ndyukas—see Price, *To Slay the Hydra*, p. 235. But it is just possible that Wíi's boast links him to a 1717 Maroon village on the Commewijne, in the area of Mapana Creek, reported to have been under the leadership of a certain "Will"—J. A. Schiltkamp and Th. de Smidt, *Plakaten, ordonnantiën en andere wetten, uitgevaardigd in Suriname I (1667-1761)* (Amsterdam: S. Emmering, 1973), p. 312, though no supporting oral evidence is known to me.

BIBLIOGRAPHY

Amiemba, Moesoela. 2003. "De aankomst van de Baikutubuka bêê bij de Nasi-lô." Typescript, Cayenne, French Guiana.

Anonymous. n.d. [1991?] *Destination Guyane: Guide pratique*. Cayenne, French Guiana: Outre-Mer Editions.

Anonymous. 1790–1834. *Periodical Accounts relating to the Missions of the Church of the United Brethren Established among the Heathen*. London.

Beet, Chris de, and Miriam Sterman. 1981. *People in Between: The Matawai Maroons of Suriname*. Meppel, The Netherlands: Krips Repro.

Bellardie, Tristan. 1994. "Les relations entre Français et Bonis en Guyane française, 1836–1893." Mémoire de Maîtrise, Université Toulouse-Le Mirail.

Benjamin, Walter. 1969. "The Storyteller." In *Illuminations*, edited by Hannah Arendt, pp. 83–109. New York: Schocken.

Benjamins, H. D., and Joh. F. Snelleman, eds. 1914–17. *Encyclopaedie van Nederlandsch West-Indië*. The Hague: Martinus Nijhoff.

Bilby, Kenneth M. 1990. "The Remaking of the Aluku: Culture, Politics, and Maroon Ethnicity in French South America." Ph.D. diss., Johns Hopkins University.

———. 2000. "Reevaluating the African Lexical Component of the Surinamese Maroon Creoles: The Aluku Case." Paper presented at the Thirty-First Annual Conference on African Linguistics, Boston University, March 3.

———. 2004. "The Explorer as Hero: *Le Fidèle Apatou* in the French Wilderness." *New West Indian Guide* 78:197–227.

———. 2005. *True-Born Maroons*. Gainesville: University Press of Florida.

Bilby, Kenneth M., and Jerome S. Handler. 2004. "Obeah: Healing and Protection in West Indian Slave Life." *Journal of Caribbean History* 38:153–83.

Bilé, Serge. 2005. *Noirs dans les camps nazis*. Monaco: Editions du Rocher.

Blier, Suzanne Preston. 1995. "Vodun: West African Roots of Vodou." In *Sacred Arts of Haitian Vodou*, edited by Donald J. Cosentino, pp. 61–87. Los Angeles: UCLA Fowler Museum of Cultural History.

Bouyer, Frédéric. 1867. *La Guyane française: Notes et souvenirs d'un voyage exécuté en 1862–1863*. Paris: Hachette.

Brocard, Véronique. 1990. "En Guyane, Rocard veut mettre de l'ordre aux frontières." *Libération*, April 9.

Brown, David H. 2003. *Santeria Enthroned: Art, Ritual, and Innovation in an Afro-Cuban Religion*. Chicago: University of Chicago Press.

Cosentino, Donald J. 1995. "Imagine Heaven." In *Sacred Arts of Haitian Vodou*, edited by Donald J. Cosentino, pp. 25–55. Los Angeles: UCLA Fowler Museum of Cultural History.

———, ed. 1995. *Sacred Arts of Haitian Vodou*. Los Angeles: UCLA Fowler Museum of Cultural History.

Craton, Michael. 1975. "Jamaican Slavery." In *Race and Slavery in the Western Hemisphere: Quantitative Studies*, ed. S. L. Engerman and E. D. Genovese, pp. 249–84. Princeton, NJ: Princeton University Press.

Crevaux, Jules. 1987. "Exploration de l'Oyapock et du Parou (1878–1879)." In *Le mendiant de l'Eldorado*, pp. 170–348. Paris: Editions Phébus. (Orig. pub. 1881.)

Dalzel, Archibald. 1793. *History of Dahomey*. London.

Damas, Léon-Gontran. 1938. *Retour de Guyane*. Paris: José Corti.

Davis, David Brion. 2003. *Challenging the Boundaries of Slavery*. Cambridge, MA: Harvard University Press.

Degoul, Franck. 2000. *Le commerce diabolique: Une exploration de l'imaginaire du pacte maléfique en Martinique*. Petit Bourg, Guadeloupe: Ibis Rouge Editions.

DeGraff, Michel. 2001. "Morphology in Creole Genesis: Linguistics and Ideology." In *Ken Hale: A Life in Language*, edited by Michael Kenstowicz, pp. 53–121. Cambridge, MA: MIT Press.

———. 2001. "On the Origin of Creoles: A Cartesian Critique of Neo-Darwinian Linguistics." *Linguistic Typology* 5:213–310.

Desch-Obi, T. J. 2002. "Combat and the Crossing of the *Kalunga*." In *Central Africans and Cultural Transformations in the American Diaspora*, edited by Linda M. Heywood, pp. 353–70. Cambridge: Cambridge University Press.

Dragenstein, Frank. 2002. *"De Ondraaglijke Stoutheid der Wegloopers": Marronage en koloniaal belied in Suriname, 1667–1768*. Utrecht, The Netherlands: Bronnen voor de Studie van Suriname 22.

Drewal, Henry John. 2002. "Celebrating Water Spirits: Influence, Confluence, and Difference in Ijebu-Yoruba and Delta Masquerades." In *Ways of the Rivers: Arts and Environment of the Niger Delta*, edited by Martha G. Anderson and Philip M. Peek, pp. 193–215. Los Angeles: UCLA Fowler Museum of Cultural History.

Ebroïn, Ary. 1977. *Quimbois: Magie noire et sorcellerie aux Antilles*. Paris: Jacques Grancher.

Eilerts de Haan, J. G. W. J. 1910. "Verslag van de expeditie naar de Suriname-Rivier." *Tijdschrift van het Koninklijk Nederlandisch Aardrijkskundig Genootschap* 27:403-68, 641-701.

Evans-Pritchard, E. E. 1937. *Witchcraft, Oracles and Magic among the Azande*. Oxford: Clarendon Press.

Folcher, Gustave. 2000. *Les carnets de guerre de Gustave Folcher, paysan languedocien, 1939-1945*. Paris: La Découverte/Poche.

Franszoon, Adiante. 1989. "Crisis in the Backlands." *Hemisphere* 1, no. 2:36–38.

Fraser, Cary. 2001. "Guyana's Political Breakdown." *Trinidad and Tobago Review* 23, nos. 5–6 (June–July): 8, 11, 15.

Fuentes Guerra, Jesús, and Armin Schwegler. 2005. *Lengua y ritos del Palo Monte Mayombe: Dioses cubanos y sus fuentes africanas*. Madrid: Iberoamericana.

Geertz, Clifford. 1988. *Works and Lives: The Anthropologist as Author*. Stanford, CA: Stanford University Press.

———. 2000. *Available Light: Anthropological Reflections on Philosophical Topics*. Princeton, NJ: Princeton University Press.

Goldstein, Donna M. 2003. *Laughter Out of Place: Race, Class, Violence, and Sexuality in a Rio Shantytown*. Berkeley and Los Angeles: University of California Press.

Gomes, Flávio dos Santos, Jonas Marçal de Queiroz, and Mauro Cézar Coelho, eds. 1999. *Relatos de Fronteiras: Fontes para a História da Amazônia séculos XVIII e XIX*. Belém, Brazil: Editora Universitária/UFPA.

Harding, Rachel E. 2000. *A Refuge in Thunder: Candomblé and Alternative Spaces of Blackness*. Bloomington: Indiana University Press.

Hartsinck, Jan Jacob. 1770. *Beschrijving van Guyana of de Wilde Kust in Zuid-America*. Amsterdam: Gerrit Tielenburg.

Hearn, Lafcadio. 1923. *Two Years in the French West Indies*. New York: Harper & Bros. (Orig. pub. 1890.)

Herskovits, Melville J. 1930. "The Negro in the New World: The Statement of a Problem." *American Anthropologist* 32:145–55.

———. 1938. *Dahomey: An Ancient African Kingdom*. New York: J. J. Augustin.

Herskovits, Melville J., and Frances S. Herskovits. 1933. *An Outline of Dahomean Religious Belief*. Menasha, WI: Memoirs of the American Anthropological Association 41.

———. 1934. *Rebel Destiny: Among the Bush Negroes of Dutch Guiana*. New York: McGraw-Hill.

———. 1936. *Suriname Folk-Lore*. New York: Columbia University Press.

Hoogbergen, Wim. 1985. *De Boni-oorlogen, 1757–1860: Marronage en guerilla in Oost-Suriname*. Utrecht, The Netherlands: Centrum voor Caraïbische Studies.

Hurault, Jean. 1972. *Français et Indiens en Guyane, 1604–1972*. Paris: Union Générale d'Editions.

Jackson, Julian. 2003. *The Fall of France: The Nazi Invasion of 1940*. Oxford: Oxford University Press.

Jolivet, Marie-José. 1982. *La question créole: Essai de sociologie sur la Guyane française*. Paris: ORSTOM.

Judt, Tony. 2003. "The Way We Live Now." *New York Review of Books*, March 27, pp. 6–10.

Junker, L. 1922/23. "Eenige mededeelingen over de Saramakkaner-Boschnegers." *De West-Indische Gids* 4:449–80.

Kestling, Robert W. 1992. "Forgotten Victims: Blacks in the Holocaust." *Journal of Negro History* 77 (1): 30–36.

———. 1998. "Blacks under the Swastika: A Research Note." *Journal of Negro History* 83 (1): 84–99.

Köbben, A. J. F. 1967. "Unity and Disunity: Cottica Djuka Society as a Kinship System." *Bijdragen tot de Taal-, Land- en Volkenkunde* 123:10–52.

Laman, K[arl]. E[dvard]. 1964. *Dictionnaire kikongo-français*. Ridgewood, NJ: Gregg Press. (Orig. pub. 1936.)

Law, Robin. 1991. *The Slave Coast of West Africa 1550–1750: The Impact of the Atlantic Slave Trade on an African Society*. Oxford: Clarendon Press.

Léglise, Isabelle, and Bettina Migge. 2006. "Language Naming Practices, Ideologies, and Linguistic Practices: Toward a Comprehensive Description of Language Varieties." *Language in Society* 35:313–39.

Lesort, Paul-André. 1992. *Quelques jours de mai–juin 40: Mémoire, témoignage, histoire*. Paris: Seuil.

Leti, Geneviève. 2000. *L'Univers magico-religieux antillais: ABC des croyances et superstitions d'hier et d'aujourd'hui*. Paris: L'Harmattan.

Lier, W. F. van. 1940. "Aanteekeningen over het geestelijk leven en de samenleving der Djoeka's (Aukaner Boschnegers) in Suriname." *Bijdragen tot de Taal-, Land- en Volkenkunde van Nederlandschindië* 99 (2): 131–294.

Lohier, Michel. 1969. *Les grands étapes de l'histoire de la Guyane française: Aperçu chronologique, 1498–1968*. Clamecy, France: Imprimerie Laballery.

Londres, Albert. 1923. *Au bagne*. Paris: Albin Michel.

MacGaffey, Wyatt. 1993. "The Eyes of Understanding: Kongo Minkisi." In *Astonishment and Power*, by Davis C. Driskell, Wyatt MacGaffey, and Sylvia H. Williams, pp. 18–103. Washington, DC: Smithsonian Institution Press.

———. 2002. "Twins, Simbi Spirits, and Lwas in Kongo and Haiti." In *Central Africans and Cultural Transformations in the American Diaspora*, edited by Linda M. Heywood, pp. 211–26. Cambridge: Cambridge University Press.

Mam-Lam-Fouck, Serge. 1987. *Histoire de la société guyanaise; Les années cruciales: 1848–1946*. Paris: Editions Caribéennes.

Marçal de Queiroz, Jonas. 1999. "História, Mito e Memória: O Cunani e Outras Repúblicas." In *Nas Terras do Cabo Norte: Fronteiras, colonização e escravidão na Guiana Brasileira nos séculos XVIII/XIX*, edited by Flávio dos Santos Gomes, pp. 319–47. Belém, Brazil: Editora Universitária/UFPA.

Matory, J. Lorand. 2005. *Black Atlantic Religion: Tradition, Transnationalism and Matriarchy in the Afro-Brazilian Candomblé*. Princeton, NJ: Princeton University Press.

Métraux, Alfred. 1958. *Le Vaudou haïtien*. Paris: Gallimard.

———. 1978. *Itinéraires 1 (1935–1953): Carnets de notes et journaux de voyage*. Paris: Payot.

Michelot, Jean-Claude. 1981. *La guillotine sèche: Histoire du bagne de Cayenne*. Paris: Fayard.

Migge, Bettina, ed. 2007. "Substrate Influence in the Creoles of Surinam." Special issue, *Journal of Pidgin and Creole Languages* 22, no. 1.

Miles, Alexander. 1988. *Devil's Island: Colony of the Damned*. Berkeley, CA: Ten Speed Press.

Miller, Joseph C. 1998. *Way of Death: Merchant Capitalism and the Angolan Slave Trade, 1730–1830*. Madison: University of Wisconsin Press.

———. 2002. "Central Africa during the Era of the Slave Trade, c. 1490s–1850s." In *Central Africans and Cultural Transformations in the American Diaspora*, ed. Linda M. Heywood, pp. 21–69. Cambridge: Cambridge University Press.

———. 2004. "Retention, Reinvention, and Remembering: Restoring Identities through Enslavement and under Slavery in Brazil." In *Enslaving Connections: Changing Cultures of Africa and Brazil during the Era of Slavery*, edited by José C. Curto and Paul E. Lovejoy, pp. 81–121. Amherst, MA: Humanity Books.

Mintz, Sidney W., and Richard Price. 1992. *The Birth of African-American Culture.* Boston: Beacon Press. (Orig. 1973.)

Mintz, Sidney W., and Michel-Rolph Trouillot. 1995. "The Social History of Haitian Vodou." In *Sacred Arts of Haitian Vodou*, edited by Donald Cosentino, pp. 123–47. Los Angeles: UCLA Fowler Museum of Cultural History.

Morssink, F. n.d. [1934?] "Boschnegeriana (misschien beter: Silvae-nigritiana?): Enige gegevens omtrent geschiedenis en missioneering onzer Surinaamsche Boschnegers." Manuscript (seen in 1960s in RC Bishopric, Paramaribo, Suriname).

Müller, Th. 1922. "Uit het Jaarverslag van 1921 over Suriname." *Berichten uit de Heiden-Wereld* no. 4 (July–August): 71.

Niles, Blair. 1928. *Condemned to Devil's Island: The Biography of an Unknown Convict.* New York: Grosset & Dunlap.

Onana, Charles. 2003. *La France et ses tirailleurs: Enquête sur les combattants de la République 1939-2003.* Paris: Duboiris.

Pakosie, André R. M. 2005. "Een analyse van het huidige conflict om het gaamanschap bij de Saamaka." *Siboga* 15 (1): 17–27.

Palmié, Stephan. 2002. *Wizards and Scientists: Explorations in Afro-Cuban Modernity and Tradition.* Durham, NC: Duke University Press.

———. 2005. "Santería Grand Slam: Afro-Cuban Religious Studies and the Study of Afro-Cuban Religion." *New West Indian Guide* 79:281–300.

Parés, Luis Nicolau. 2005. "Transformation of the Sea and Thunder Voduns in the Gbe-Speaking Area and in the Bahian Jeje Community." In *Africa in the Americas: Interconnections during the Slave Trade*, edited by José C. Curto and Renée Soulodre-La France, pp. 69–93. Trenton, NJ: Africa World Press.

Pierre, Michel. 1982. *La terre de la grande punition: Histoire des bagnes de Guyane.* Paris: Ramsay.

Price, Richard. 1975. "KiKoongo and Saramaccan: A Reappraisal." *Bijdragen tot de Taal-, Land- en Volkenkunde* 131:461–78.

———. 1976. *The Guiana Maroons: A Historical and Bibliographical Introduction.* Baltimore: Johns Hopkins University Press.

———. 1983. *First-Time: The Historical Vision of an Afro-American People.* Baltimore: Johns Hopkins University Press. (2nd ed., Chicago: University of Chicago Press, 2002.)

———. 1983. *To Slay the Hydra: Dutch Colonial Perspectives on the Saramaka Wars.* Ann Arbor, MI: Karoma.

———. 1990. *Alabi's World.* Baltimore: Johns Hopkins University Press.

———. 1995. "Executing Ethnicity: The Killings in Suriname." *Cultural Anthropology* 10:437–71.

———. 1998. *The Convict and the Colonel*. Boston: Beacon Press. (2nd ed., Durham, NC: Duke University Press, 2006.)

———. 1999. "Afterword/Echoes." In *Religion, Diaspora and Cultural Identity*, edited by John W. Pulis, pp. 403–11. Amsterdam: Gordon & Breach.

———. 2006. "On the Miracle of Creolization." In *Afro-Atlantic Dialogues: Anthropology in the Diaspora*, edited by Kevin A. Yelvington, pp. 113–45. Santa Fe, NM: SAR Press.

———. 2007. "The Concept of Creolization." In *World History of Slavery*, edited by David Eltis and Stanley L. Engerman. Cambridge: Cambridge University Press.

Price, Richard, and Sally Price, eds. 1988. *John Gabriel Stedman's Narrative of a Five Years Expedition against the Revolted Negroes of Surinam*. Baltimore: Johns Hopkins University Press. (Orig. 1790.)

———. 1991. *Two Evenings in Saramaka*. Chicago: University of Chicago Press.

———. 1992. *Equatoria*. New York: Routledge.

———. 1992. "Widerstand, Rebellion und Freiheit: Maroon Societies in Amerika und ihre Kunst." In *Afrika in Amerika*, edited by Corinna Raddatz, pp. 157–73. Hamburg: Hamburgisches Museum für Völkerkunde.

———. 2003. *Les Marrons*. Châteauneuf-le-Rouge, France: Vents d'ailleurs.

———. 2003. *The Root of Roots; or, How Afro-American Anthropology Got Its Start*. Chicago: Prickly Paradigm Press.

Price, Sally. 1984. *Co-Wives and Calabashes*. Ann Arbor: University of Michigan Press. (2nd ed., 1993.)

———. 2007. "Into the Mainstream: Shifting Authenticities in Art." *American Ethnologist* 34 (4).

———. 2007. *Paris Primitive: Jacques Chirac's Museum on the Quai Branly*. Chicago: University of Chicago Press.

Price, Sally, and Richard Price. 1999. *Maroon Arts: Cultural Vitality in the African Diaspora*. Boston: Beacon Press.

———. 2005. *Les arts des Marrons*. La Roque d'Anthéron, France: Vents d'ailleurs.

———. 2006. *Romare Bearden: The Caribbean Dimension*. Philadelphia: University of Pennsylvania Press.

Purchas, Samuel. 1625. *Haklvytvs posthumus; or, Pvrchas his Pilgrimes. Contayning a history of the world, in sea voyages, & lande-trauells, by Englishmen and others . . . Some left written by Mr. Hakluyt at his death, more since added, his also perused, & perfected. All examined, abreuiated, illustrates w[i]th notes, enlarged w[i]th discourses, adorned w[i]th pictures, and expressed in mapps. In fower parts, each containing fiue bookes.* [Compiled] by Samuel Purchas. London: Imprinted for H. Fetherston.

Redfield, Peter. 2000. *Space in the Tropics: From Convicts to Rockets in French Guiana*. Berkeley and Los Angeles: University of California Press.

Rée, Jonathan. 2004. "No good reason." *TLS* (August 13), p. 27.

Richman, Karen E. 2005. *Migration and Vodou*. Gainesville: University Press of Florida.

Rousseau, Louis. 1930. *Un médecin au bagne*. Paris: Armand Fleury.

Roux, Emmanuel de. 1990. "Les musées meurent aussi." *Le Monde*, October 10, p. 1.

Sahlins, Marshall. 2000. *Culture in Practice: Selected Essays*. New York: Zone Books.

Samis, Alexandre. 2002. *Clevelândia: Anarquismo, sindicalismo e repressão política no Brasil*. São Paulo: Imaginário.

Schelts, M. 1922. "De reis naar Pobosi en de Sentea Kreek." Zeister Zendingsgenootschap 319, Rijksarchief Utrecht.

Schiltkamp, J. A., and Th. de Smidt. 1973. *Plakaten, ordonnantiën en andere wetten, uitgevaardigd in Suriname I [1667–1761]*. Amsterdam: S. Emmering.

Scott, David. 1991. "That Event, This Memory: Notes on the Anthropology of African Diasporas in the New World." *Diaspora* 1:261–84.

Shaw, Rosalind. 2002. *Memories of the Slave Trade: Ritual and the Historical Imagination in Sierra Leone*. Chicago: University of Chicago Press.

Sheller, Mimi. 2003. *Consuming the Caribbean: From Arawaks to Zombies*. London: Routledge.

Slenes, Robert W. 2002. "The Great Porpoise-Skull Strike." In *Central Africans and Cultural Transformations in the American Diaspora*, edited by Linda M. Heywood, pp. 183–208. Cambridge: Cambridge University Press.

Staehelin, F. 1913–19. *Die Mission der Brüdergemeine in Suriname und Berbice im achtzehnten Jahrhundert*. Herrnhut, Germany: Vereins für Brüdergeschichte in Kommission der Unitätsbuchhandlung in Gnadau.

Stewart, Dianne M. 2005. *Three Eyes for the Journey: African Dimensions of the Jamaican Religious Experience*. New York: Oxford University Press.

Stipriaan, Alex van. 1993. "'Een verre verwijderd trommelen . . .' Ontwikkeling van Afro-Surinaamse muziek en dans in de slavernij." In *De Kunstwereld: Produktie, distributie en receptie in de wereld van kunst en cultuur*, edited by Ton Bevers, Antoon Van den Braembussche, and Berend Jan Langenberg, pp. 143–73. Hilversum: Verloren.

———. 2000. *Creolisering: Vragen van een basketbalplein, antwoorden van een watergodin*. Rotterdam: Inaugurele Rede Erasmus Universiteit.

Taussig, Michael. 1987. *Shamanism, Colonialism, and the Wild Man: A Study in Terror and Healing*. Chicago: University of Chicago Press.

Ternisien, Xavier. 2006. "L'outre-mer s'alarme de l'afflux d'immigrés clandestins." *Le Monde*, November 21.

Thoden van Velzen, H. U. E., and W. van Wetering. 1988. *The Great Father and the Danger: Religious Cults, Material Forces, and Collective Fantasies in the World of the Suriname Maroons*. Dordrecht, The Netherlands: Foris.

———. 2004. *In the Shadow of the Oracle: Religion as Politics in a Suriname Maroon Society*. Long Grove, IL: Waveland.

Thornton, John K. 1998. *Africa and Africans in the Making of the Atlantic World, 1400–1800*. Cambridge: Cambridge University Press.

———. 1998. *The Kongolese Saint Anthony: Dona Beatriz Kimpa Vita and the Antonian Movement, 1684–1706*. Cambridge: Cambridge University Press.

———. 1999. *Warfare in Atlantic Africa, 1500–1800*. London: UCL Press.

Trouillot, Michel-Rolph. 1992. "The Caribbean Region: An Open Frontier in Anthropological Theory." *Annual Review of Anthropology* 21:19–42.

———. 1995. *Silencing the Past: Power and the Production of History*. Boston: Beacon Press.

———. 1998. "Culture on the Edges: Creolization in the Plantation Context." *Plantation Society in the Americas* 5:8–28.

Tsing, Anna Lowenhaupt. 2004. *Friction: An Ethnography of Global Connection*. Princeton, NJ: Princeton University Press.

Verger, Pierre Fatumbi. 1957. *Notes sur le culte des Orisa et Vodun à Bahia, la Baie de tous les Saints, au Brésil et à l'ancienne Côte des Esclaves en Afrique*. Dakar, Senegal: IFAN.

———. 1981. *Orixás: Deuses Iorubás na África e no Novo Mundo*. Salvador: Corrupio.

Vernon, Diane. 1985. *Money Magic in a Modernizing Maroon Society*. Caribbean Study Series, no. 2. Tokyo: Institute for the Study of Languages and Cultures of Africa and Asia.

Voorhoeve, Jan. 1971. "Church Creole and Pagan Cult Languages." In *Pidginization and Creolization of Languages*, edited by Dell Hymes, pp. 305–15. Cambridge: Cambridge University Press.

Voorhoeve, Jan, and Ursy M. Lichtveld. 1975. *Creole Drum: An Anthology of Creole Literature in Suriname*. New Haven, CT: Yale University Press.

Vrij, Jean Jacques. 2005. "Review of Frank Dragenstein, 'Trouw aan de blanken': Quassie van Nieuw Timotibo, twist en strijd in de 18de eeuw in Suriname." *Oso* 24:190–94.

Walcott, Derek. 1992. *The Antilles: Fragments of Epic Memory; The Nobel Lecture*. New York: Farrar, Straus and Giroux.

———. 1973. *Another Life*. New York: Farrar, Straus and Giroux.

———. 1997. "Reflections on *Omeros*." *The South Atlantic Quarterly* 96:229–46.

Warner-Lewis, Maureen. 2003. *Central Africa in the Caribbean: Transcending Time, Transforming Cultures*. Kingston, Jamaica: University of the West Indies Press.

Wirtz, Kristina. 2007. "Divining the Past: The Linguistic Reconstruction of 'African' Roots in Diasporic Ritual Registers and Songs." *Journal of Religion in Africa* 37, no. 2.

Wooding, Charles J. 1972. *Winti: Een Afroamerikaanse godsdienst in Suriname*. Meppel, The Netherlands: Krips Repro.

Facing page: Back wall of Tooy's consulting room, with basin of *tokóógbagba* (water lilies or water hyacinths), so important to Lángu history.

ACKNOWLEDGMENTS

For a project that, in a sense, began in the 1960s and continues apace, it is nearly impossible to separate out particular people to thank. Even restricting myself to the years since meeting Tooy in 2000, the number of people from different walks of life who have helped me—from the hundreds of Saramakas who shared in one or another aspect of this adventure all the way to the various (to me) faceless InterLibrary-Loan employees at the College of William and Mary who provided scans of obscure articles—makes adequate recognition impossible. Nonetheless, I'd like at the least to record here my thanks to Tooy, Yaai, Céline, and the rest of Tooy's extended family for their generous hospitality and unswerving friendship. For their assistance as this project unfolded, I would also like to thank Moesoela Amiemba (Ben), Adams Kwateh, Ronald Pansa (Kalusé), Patrick Lacaisse, Roland Legros, Danielle Quist, Saramaka Headcaptain Aniké Awági, and Saramaka captains Antonisi (Saint-Laurent), Miséi Tembái (La Flêche), and Adaisso (Kourou). For their hospitality in Cayenne, thanks to Pedro Ureña and Claude Charlery Ureña, and in Saint-Georges/Tampáki, Léon and Julie Mathurin. My heartfelt thanks to Raphaël Constant for his legal assistance *à distance* and to Anne Kayanakis and Robert Robeiri for theirs closer to the scene.

I am grateful to a number of people and institutions for providing the images used in this book: Jodi Amiel, Moesoela Amiemba, les Archives départementales de Guyane, the E.B.G. Archif-Herrnhut, Pedro Ureña Rib, Baj Strobel, Miséi Tembái, the Trustees of the Imperial War Museum, and especially Sally Price. For help in securing photos, I thank Mark Hickman (whose Web site provided many of the World War II images), Stephan Augustin (for serving as intermediary with the E.B.G. Archif), and Joop Vernooij (for sending the Morssink photos from *Petrus Donders*). See the Photo Credits for further information.

In the Netherlands, Bonno Thoden van Velzen and Rosemarijn Hoefte helped me put my hands on some hard-to-find materials. I am also grateful to Meredith Holaday for drawing the sketch maps and genealogies (after my own messy drafts). At William and Mary, Carol Roe and Mark Kostro facilitated my access to materials while I was in Martinique. David Eltis kindly provided unpublished materials from the second edition (in preparation) of the *Transatlantic Slave Trade Database*.

I have tried out parts of the text on classes at William and Mary and in a lecture series at the École Pratique des Hautes Études (Paris), where colleagues and students made helpful comments.

I would like to thank Stuart Plattner for helping make possible a grant from the National Science Foundation that came late in the project but was much appreciated, and which supported my fieldwork in 2005 and 2006 and permitted me the time to finish this book. As stipulated by the NSF, I hereby affirm that "this material is based upon work supported by the National Science Foundation under Grant No. BCS-0450170," and further that "any opinions, findings, and conclusions or recommendations expressed in this material are those of the author and do not necessarily reflect the views of the National Science Foundation." Robert Kinser's generosity, based on his long-standing fascination with Tooy's story, helped support the publication.

I owe a singular, daunting yet joyful debt to those friends and colleagues who took the time to seriously engage drafts of this book and offer far more criticisms than I have been able to incorporate. The book is much improved because of their often-Herculean efforts (including one twenty-seven-page-long critique). So, my most heartfelt thanks to Ken Bilby, John Collins, Jeff Good, George Huttar, Mark Kostro, Phil Morgan, Stephan Palmié, Mikael Parkvall, Peter Redfield, Raquel Romberg, Armin Schwegler, and Norval Smith. And then there are my three toughest critics: Leah Price (Professor of English at Harvard), Niko Price (Latin America Editor for the AP), and Sally Price, who has shared everything with me from the beginning and took time from her own latest book project (*Paris Primitive*) to help me finish my own. All three continue to try to teach me to write better (in part by their own example), and I try, however inadequately, to follow at least the spirit of their suggestions.

Finally, I'd like to thank David Brent, Elizabeth Branch Dyson, Sandy Hazel, and the rest of the editorial and production team at the University of Chicago Press for their grace in helping me transform Tooy's story into a handsome physical object.

To everyone named on these two pages (as Saramakas say), a very special *gaán tangí tangí f'únu!*

ILLUSTRATION CREDITS

Jodi Amiel: p. 49. **Archives Départementales de Guyane**: p. 135. **Moravian Archives, Herrnhut, Germany** (LBS 05302): p. 121 (The photo seems to have been taken on 12 February 1926, when Dr. Stahel's expedition briefly visited.) **Sally Price**: title page and pp. x (2 images), 14, 36, 37, 38 (2 images), 46, 79, 89, 95, 134, 160 (4 images), 208, 210, 217, 218 (2 images), 219 (3 images), 220 (2 images), 221 (2 images), 222 (top), 229, 233, 251, 261, 266, 281, 447. **Richard Price**: pp. 62 (two images), 85, 144, 452. **Baj Strobel**: p. 142. **The Trustees of the Imperial War Museum, London** (negative number GER 18): p. 72. **Pedro Ureña Rib:** p. 203.

FROM BOOKS, JOURNALS, AND THE INTERNET

p. 11: from O. J. R. Jozefzoon, *De Saramaccaanse wereld* (Paramaribo, Suriname: Varekamp, 1959), p. 28.

p. 78: Art Renewal Center, http://www.artrenewal.org.

p. 76: from http://www.pegasus-one.org/pow/S4B/PicSt_4B_Aerial.htm. (My attempts to find the photo's origin, via generous help from Webmaster Mark Hickman, have failed.)

p. 76: from http://www.pegasus-one.org/pow/S4B/PicSt_4B_Gate2.jpg. (Copyright Barry Seddon. My attempts to contact Barry Seddon, via Webmaster Mark Hickman, have failed.)

p. 76: from http://www.pegasus-one.org/pow/S4B/PicSt_4B_Shower.jpg. (Photo by N. Uchtmann, a Dutch prisoner; the image was later made into a postcard. My attempts to find the owner of the postcard, via Webmaster Mark Hickman, have failed.)

p. 76: from http://www.pegasus-one.org/pow/S4B/PicSt_4B_GoonTower1.jpg. (Photo by N. Uchtmann, a Dutch prisoner; the image was later made into a postcard. My attempts to find the owner of the postcard, via Webmaster Mark Hickman, have failed.)

p. 114: from J. G. W. J. Eilerts de Haan, "Verslag van de expeditie naar de Suriname-Rivier," *Tijdschrift van het Koninklijk Nederlandisch Aardrijkskundig Genootschap* 27 (1910): 403–68, 641–701—photo facing p. 666.

p. 123: from *Petrus Donders* 9 (4), March 1929, facing p. 81.

p. 124: from *Petrus Donders* 9 (4), March 1929, facing p. 88.

p. 137: from Henri Coudreau, *Chez nos Indiens, quatre années dans la Guyane française (1887–1891)* (Paris, Hachette, 1893), p. 57.

p. 148 (top and bottom): from Frédéric Bouyer, *La Guyane française: Notes et souvenirs d'un voyage exécuté en 1862–1863* (Paris: Hachette, 1867), pp. 245, 247.

p. 173: from John Gabriel Stedman, *Narrative of a Five Years Expedition against the Revolted Negroes of Surinam*, edited with an introduction and notes by Richard Price and Sally Price (Baltimore, Johns Hopkins University Press, 1988 [1790]), p. 105.

PHOTOGRAPHER UNKNOWN

p. 222 (2 images, bottom) and p. 223: prints courtesy Miséi Tembái.

p. 240: print courtesy Moesoela Amiemba.

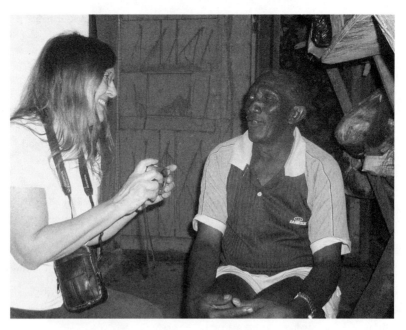

Sally, who took most of the photos for this book, with Tooy, 2005.